S0-BAW-641

Essential Papers on Israel and the Ancient Near East

ESSENTIAL PAPERS ON JEWISH STUDIES
General Editor: Robert M. Seltzer

Essential Papers on Judaism and Christianity in Conflict: From Late Antiquity to the Reformation
Edited by Jeremy Cohen

Essential Papers on Hasidism: Origins to Present
Edited by Gershon David Hundert

Essential Papers on Jewish-Christian Relations: Imagery and Reality
Edited by Naomi W. Cohen

Essential Papers on Israel and the Ancient Near East
Edited by Frederick E. Greenspahn

ESSENTIAL PAPERS ON ISRAEL AND THE ANCIENT NEAR EAST

Edited by
Frederick E. Greenspahn

New York University Press
New York and London

BS
1184
.E77
1991

Copyright © 1991 by New York University
All rights reserved
Manufactured in the United States of America

Library of Congress Cataloging-in-Publication Data
Essential papers on Israel and the ancient Near East / edited by
Frederick E. Greenspahn.
p. cm. — (Essential papers on Jewish studies)
Includes bibliographical references and index.
ISBN 0-8147-3037-X (acid-free paper) — ISBN
0-8147-3038-8 (pbk. : acid-free paper)
1. Middle Eastern literature—Relation to the Old Testament.
2. Bible. O.T.—Criticism, interpretation, etc. 3. Middle East—
Civilization—To 622. 4. Bible. O.T.—Comparative studies.
I. Greenspahn, Frederick E., 1946– . II. Series.
BS1184.E77 1991
221.6—dc20 90-49289
CIP

New York University Press books are printed on acid-free paper,
and their binding materials are chosen for strength and durability.

Contents

III Common Themes and Motifs

IV "Foreign" Elements in Ancient Israel

V Biblical Differences from the Ancient Near East

VI The Importance of Context

Abbreviations

A		accession number for tablets in the Louvre
AASOR		Annual of the American Schools of Oriental Research
Ab. Z.	*	*ʿAvodah Zarah*
ADD		*Assyrian Deeds and Documents,* ed. C. H. W. Johns
AfK		*Archiv für Keilschriftforschung*
AfO (AFO)		*Archiv für Orientforschung*
AHw		*Akkadisches Handwörterbuch,* by Wolfram von Soden
AJSL		*American Journal of Semitic Languages and Literatures*
Akk.		Akkadian
AnBib		Analecta Biblica
ANET		*Ancient Near Eastern Texts Relating to the Old Testament,* ed. James Pritchard
Ant		*Antiquities* by Josephus
AOAT		Alter Orient und Altes Testament
AOS		American Oriental Series
AOTS		*Archaeology and Old Testament Study,* ed. D. Winton Thomas
Aq.		Aqhat (see *ANET* pp. 149–55)
Aram.		Aramaic
ARM(T)		Archives Royales de Mari (texts in transliteration and translation)

* biblical and rabbinic texts

ArOr	*Archiv Orientâlni*
ARu	*Assyrische Rechtsurkunden,* by J. Kohler and A. Ungnad
AS	Assyriological Studies
AT	*The Alalakh Tablets,* ed. D. J. Wiseman
A.T.	= OT
ATD	Das Alte Testament Deutsch
ATT	excavation number of tablets found at Alalakh
AV	Authorized Version of the Bible
b.	* Babylonian Talmud
BA	*Biblical Archaeologist*
Baba B.	* *Baba Batra*
BAR	*Biblical Archaeology Review*
BASOR	*Bulletin of the American Schools of Oriental Research*
BBSt	*Babylonian Boundary Stones,* by L. W. King
Ber.	* *Berakhot*
Ber. R.	* *Gen. R.*
BH	*Biblical Hebraica*
Bib	*Biblica*
BIES	*Bulletin of the Israel Exploration Society*
Bik.	* *Bikkurim*
BIN	Babylonian Inscriptions in the Collection of J. B. Nies
BiOr	*Bibliotheca Orientalis*
BK	Biblischer Kommentar
BKAT	Biblischer Kommentar: Altes Testament
BL	*The Babylonian Laws,* by G. R. Driver and John Miles
BO	= *BiOr*
BWANT	Beiträge zur Wissenschaft vom Alten und Neuen Testament
BZ	*Biblische Zeitschrift*
BZAW	Beihefte zur Zeitschrift für die altestamentliche Wissenschaft

c(a).	circa
CAD	*The Assyrian Dictionary of the Oriental Institute of the University of Chicago*
CAH	*Cambridge Ancient History*
Cant	* Song of Solomon
CBQ	*Catholic Biblical Quarterly*
CCD	Confraternity of Christian Doctrine
CH	Code of Hammurabi (see *ANET* pp. 163–80)
Chr	* Chronicles
CIS	Corpus Inscriptionum Semiticarum
col.	column
Corp.Inscr.Himyar.	*Corpus Inscriptionum Himyariticarum*
CRAIBL	*Comptes Rendus de l'Académie des Inscriptions et Belles-Lettres*
CT	Cuneiform Texts from Babylonian Tablets
CTA	*Corpus des tablettes en cunéiformes alphabétiques,* ed. A. Herdner
Dan	* Daniel
Deut	* Deuteronomy
DP	*Documents présargoniques,* ed. M. Allotte de la Fuÿe
Dt. R.	* *Deut. R.*
EA	*Die El-Amarna Tafeln,* ed. J. A. Knudtzon
Eccl	* Ecclesiastes
EI	*Eretz Israel*
Esth	* Esther
Eth.	Ethiopic
Ev. Pr.	*De Evangelica Praeperatione,* by Eusebius
Ex. R.	* *Exod. R.*
Exod	* Exodus
ExpT	*Expository Times*
Ezek	* Ezekiel
GAG	*Grundriss der akkadischen Grammatik,* by Wolfram von Soden

Gen	* Genesis
Gen. R.	* *Genesis Rabbah*
GN	geographical name
Hab	* Habakkuk
Hag	* Haggai
HAT	Handbuch zum AT
HK(AT)	Handkommentar zum AT
HL	Hittite Laws (see *ANET* pp. 188–97)
Hos	* Hosea
HR	*History of Religions*
HSM	Harvard Semitic Monographs
HSS	Harvard Semitic Series
HTR	*Harvard Theological Review*
HUCA	*Hebrew Union College Annual*
HzAT	HAT
ICC	International Critical Commentary
IDB	*Interpreter's Dictionary of the Bible*
IEJ	*Israel Exploration Journal*
Isa	* Isaiah
IV R	*The Cuneiform Inscriptions of Western Asia*, ed. Henry C. Rawlinson, vol. 4 (2d ed.) ed. T. G. Pinches
j.	* Jerusalem (Palestinian) Talmud
JA	*Journal Asiatique*
JANES(CU)	*Journal of the Ancient Near Eastern Society of Columbia University*
JAOS	*Journal of the American Oriental Society*
JBL	*Journal of Biblical Literature*
JCS	*Journal of Cuneiform Studies*
JEA	*Journal of Egyptian Archaeology*
JEN	Joint Expedition with the Iraq Museum at Nuzi
Jer	* Jeremiah
JESHO	*Journal of the Economic and Social History of the Orient*
JNES	*Journal of Near Eastern Studies*

Jon	* Jonah
Josh	* Joshua
JQR	*Jewish Quarterly Review*
JR	*Journal of Religion*
JRAS	*Journal of the Royal Asiatic Society of Great Britain and Ireland*
JSOT	*Journal for the Study of the Old Testament*
JSS	*Journal of Semitic Studies*
JTS	*Journal of Theological Studies*
Jub	* Jubilees
Judg	* Judges
KAI	*Kanaanäische und aramäische Inschriften,* ed. H. Donner and W. Röllig
KAR	Keilschrifttexte aus Assur religiösen Inhalts
KAT	Kommentar zum AT
KAV	Keilschrifttexte aus Assur verschiedenen Inhalts
KB	Keilschriftliche Bibliothek
KBo	Keilschrifttexte aus Boghazköi
Kgs	* Kings
Ḳidd.	* *Qiddushin*
Koh. R.	* *Eccl. R.*
KUB	Keilschrifturkunden aus Boghazköi
l.	line
Lam	* Lamentations
l.c.	loc. cit.
LE	Laws of Eshnunna (see *ANET* pp. 161–63)
Lev	* Leviticus
LSS	*Leipziger semitistische Studien*
LXX	Septuagint
Macc	* Maccabees
Mal	* Malachi
MAL	Middle Assyrian Laws (see *ANET* pp. 180–88)
Mand.	Mandaic
M.A.R.I.	*Mari, Annales de Recherches Interdisciplinaires*
MDOG	*Mitteilungen der Deutschen Orientgesellschaft*

MDP	*Mémoires de la Délégation en Perse*
Meg.	* Megillah
Men.	* *Menaḥot*
MGWJ	*Monatschrift für Geschichte und Wissenschaft des Judentums*
Mic	* Micah
Mid(r).	*Midrash*
MIO(F)	*Mitteilungen des Instituts für Orientforschung*
Moed Kat.	* *Moed Katan*
MSL	Materialien zum sumerischen Lexikon
MT	Masoretic Text
MVA(e)G	*Mitteilungen der Vorderasiatisch(-Ägyptisch)en Gessellschaft*
n.	note
Nah	* Nahum
NBC	tablets in the Nies Babylonian Collection of Yale University
NEB	New English Bible
Ned.	* *Nedarim*
Neh	* Nehemiah
NF	neue Folge (new series)
Nik.	*Dokumenty Khoziaistvennoi otchetnosti drevneišei epochi Chaldei iz sobraniia N. P. Likhacheva*, ed. Michail Vasilevich Nikolskii
Nr	number
NS	new series
NT	New Testament
Num	* Numbers
Obad	* Obadiah
obv.	obverse
OIP	Oriental Institute Publications
OLZ	*Orientalische Literaturzeitung*
Or	*Orientalia*
OSP	*Old Sumerian and Old Akkadian Texts in Philadelphia Chiefly from Nippur*, ed. A. Westenholz

OT	Old Testament
OTS	*Oudtestamentische Studien*
Pal. Tg.	* Palestinian Targum
Pes. Rab.	* *Pesikta Rabbati*
PG	*Patrologia Graeca,* ed. J. Migne
Pl.	plate
PL	*Patrologia Latina,* ed. J. Migne
PN	personal name
Prov	* Proverbs
PRU	Le Palais Royal d'Ugarit
Ps	* Psalms
Qoh	* Ecclesiastes
R.	*Rabbah*
RA	*Revue d'Assyriologie et d'Archéologie orientale*
RAI	*Rencontre assyriologique internationale*
RB	*Revue biblique*
REJ	*Revue des Etudes Juives*
RES	*Revue des Etudes Sémitiques*
Rev.	reverse
RHA	*Revue Hittite et Asianique*
RHR	*Revue de l'Histoire des Religions*
RLA	*Reallexikon der Assyriologie,* ed. E. Ebeling et al.
Rm	Rassam tablets in British Museum collection
Rosh Hash.	* *Rosh Hashanah*
RS	Ras Shamra tablets
RSO	*Rivista degli Studi Orientali*
RSV	Revised Standard Version of the Bible
S.	Sura
SAKI	*Die sumerischen und akkadischen Königsinschriften,* ed. F. Thureau-Dangin (VAB 1)
Sam	* Samuel
Sanh	* *Sanhedrin*
SBL	Society of Biblical Literature
SBT	Studien zu den Boğazköy-Texten

SD	*Studia et Documenta ad Iura Orientus Antiqui pertinentia*
Sept.	Septuagint
Shabb	* *Shabbat*
SL	*Sumerisches Lexikon,* by A. Deimel
SLB	Studia ad tabulas cuneiformes a F.M. Th. de Liagre Böhl pertinentia
SS	"The Gracious and Beautiful Gods" (*CTA* 23)
StudOr	Studia Orientalia
STVC	*Sumerian Texts of Varied Contents,* ed. E. Chiera
S(upp)VT	Supplements to *VT*
Syr.	Syriac translation of the Bible (Peshiṭta)
Tanh.	* *Tanhuma*
Targ.	* *Targum*
TCL	Textes cunéiformes du Louvre
Tg. Y.	* *Jerusalem Targum*
ThZ	*Theologische Zeitschrift*
TLB	Tabulae Cuneiformes a F.M. Th. de Liagre Böhl collectae
TMH	Texte und Materialien der Frau Professor Hilprecht Collection . . . in Jena
Tos.	* *Tosefta*
UF	*Ugaritische Forschungen*
v.	verse (plural vv.)
VAB	Vorderasiatische Bibliothek
VAT	tablets in Vorderasiatischen Abteilung der Berliner Museen
VL	Vetus Latina
VS	Vorderasiatische Schriftdenkmäler der königlichen Museen zu Berlin
vs.	verso
VT	*Vetus Testamentum*
V.T.	=OT
VTSup	=SVT

W	field number of tablets from Warka
WM(z)ANT	Wissenschaftliche Monographien zum Alten und Neuen Testament
WO	*Die Welt des Orients*
WZKM	*Wiener Zeitschrift für die Kunde des Morgenlandes*
y.	* Jerusalem (Palestinian) Talmud
Yalk.	* Yalkut Shimoni
YBC	tablets in Babylonian Collection of Yale University
Yeb.	* *Yebamot*
Yer.	* Jerusalem (Palestinian) Talmud
YNER	*Yale Near Eastern Researches*
YOS	Yale Oriental Series, Babylonian Texts
ZA	*Zeitschrift für Assyriologie*
ZAW	*Zeitschrift für die Alttestamentliche Wissenschaft*
ZDMG	*Zeitschrift der Deutschen Morgenländischen Gesellschaft*
ZDPV	*Zeitschrift des Deutschen Palästina-Vereins*
Zech	* Zechariah
Zeph	* Zephaniah

Troy
Cappadocia
Kultepe
Hatti
Dan
Hazor
Sea of Chinnereth
Megiddo
Dor
Beth-Shean
Samaria
Shechem
Jordan
Tel Qasileh
Joppa/Jaffa
Shiloh
Bethel
Gilgal
Gezer
Gibeon
Ashdod
Jerusalem
Ashkelon
Dead Sea
Gaza
Hebron
Beer-Sheba
Arad
MEDITERRANEAN SEA
Karatepe
Tarsus
Carchemish
Aleppo
Alalakh
Ras-Shamra (Ugarit)
Sefire
Ebla
Balikh
Cyprus
Orontes
Byblos
Sidon
Damascus
Tyre
Ammon
Moab
Edom
Heliopolis
Sinai
Midian
Egypt
Tel el-Amarna
Nile
Karnak
Elephantine
RED SEA

Urartu
Mitanni
Nineveh
Mesopotamia
Assyria
Asshur
Nuzi
Mari
Tigris
Euphrates
Akkad
Sippar
Babylon
Nippur
Susa
Elam
Babylonia
Lagash
Uruk
Larsa
Eridu
Ur
Sumer
Arabia
PERSIAN
GULF
The Ancient Near East
Scale
Miles
0
125
250
Kilometers
0
125
250
N

Introduction

Frederick E. Greenspahn

The Bible is a familiar book. Year in, year out more copies are sold than of any other published work. It is found in almost every hotel room throughout the United States. Children hear its stories before they go to bed, and preachers and politicians invoke its authority with great regularity. Yet despite its comfortable familiarity, the Bible is in some respects surprisingly distant. The people and places it mentions are far removed from our direct experience. There are no Philistines or Assyrians in the United Nations, nor even on our maps. The gods it mentions, such as Baal, Dagon, and Asherah, are worshiped by no one that we know. We do not practice its customs, placing our hands on someone's thigh to take an oath (Gen 24:9) or removing a shoe in order to confirm a commercial transaction (Ruth 4:7). The product of a culture far removed from our own, the Bible differs from other ancient works only because it has been preserved in synagogues and churches rather than beneath the sands of the Middle East.

Biblical authors themselves sometimes seem aware of the gulf separating potential readers from the events they sought to describe. In *those* days, they explain, *nephilim* were on the earth (Gen 6:4), but no king (yet) in Israel (Judg 17:6, 18:1, 19:1, 21:25). The ark was still in Bethel (Judg 20:27), and divine visions were rare (1 Sam 3:1). Elsewhere, we are told that what is "today" called a prophet had once been called a seer (1 Sam 9:9), that only until the exile was the tribe of Dan's worship led by descendants of Moses (Judg 18:30), and that priestly use of the Urim and Thummim was apparently part of the past (Ezra 2:63, Neh 7:65).

More than chronological changes separate biblical narratives from their readers. Cultural differences can also be sensed in the authors' felt need to explain the use of bricks and bitumen for Mesopotamian construction rather than the more familiar stone and mortar (Gen 11:3) or the absence of metalsmiths in ancient Israel (1 Sam 13:19; see also Judg 1:19).

We moderns scarcely need such reminders of the chronological and cultural gaps separating us from the biblical world. Geography alone makes that apparent. The events the Bible describes are centered in a small country on the eastern edge of the Mediterranean and reflect its relationships with a variety of neighboring nations—the Philistines and Arameans, Edom and Moab, as well as Egypt, Assyria, and Babylonia, the superpowers of that day. Many of the places it mentions no longer even exist. Their locations can be determined only from archeological excavations or references in other ancient texts. Just a little more knowledge is needed to recognize that the Bible is written in an ancient Semitic dialect. Because its words are frequently obscure, one must not only master a second language to understand it, but also bring scholarly expertise to bear on the evidence provided by other exotic ancient languages and literatures in order to make sense of its frequently difficult text.

It is no wonder, therefore, that the results of the past century's archeological explorations have been greeted with an air of expectant eagerness on the part of biblical students, anticipating their potential for providing a wealth of resources which will revolutionize our understanding of the Bible. Much of what has been found has illumined the meaning of individual words. For example, 2 Kings 4:42 describes a man who brought some produce to the prophet Elisha. Included in his offering was grain that the Bible describes as having been *beṣiqlono,* a word which occurs no where else in the biblical text and has usually been understood as a noun preceded by the prepositional prefix *be-*, meaning "in." A *ṣiqalon* would, therefore, appear to be something in which grain might be carried—a basket or a garment of some type. However, in the early decades of this century poetic texts were found at what had been a prominent port near the northeastern corner of the Mediterranean, known as Ugarit. These poems, which were written without vowels in a language closely related to biblical Hebrew, include the word *bṣql,* which apparently refers to part of a plant.[1] Since *-on* is a standard suffix for many Hebrew nouns, the Ugaritic evidence suggests that the initial *b* may be an actual part of the word, which would then designate a plant or part of a plant, a meaning well suited to the context of 2 Kings.

Needless to say, this is only one of many biblical passages to have been illuminated by the evidence of various documents in a wide variety of ancient Semitic languages. Nor has the contribution of such texts been limited to linguistic problems. A host of stylistic features familiar from the Bible have also been discovered in ancient works. These include stereotypical phrases, such as "lift up one's eyes and see," and various literary patterns. One interesting example has to do with the system of semantic parallelism which characterizes much of biblical poetry. In such passages, an initial statement is typically repeated in words that are similar to or even synonymous with the original assertion. Biblical poets reveal a marked propensity for using the same synonyms over and over again, as if drawing from an ancient equivalent of our own rhyming dictionaries. The fact that Ugaritic texts, which have a similar poetic style, often use the same word pairs as biblical Hebrew makes it reasonable to suspect that Israelite poets were, in fact, adhering to the conventions of a larger, Northwest Semitic tradition.[2] This inference has been confirmed time and again, as in the use of numbers, which pose an interesting problem for this technique since they so rarely have synonyms. To deal with that, biblical poetry follows the Canaanite practice of juxtaposing such terms with the next higher number, as happens repeatedly in Amos's opening speech: "For Damascus's three transgressions, yea for four . . . ," etc.

Modern research has shown that biblical authors not only followed the stylistic canons of their time, but sometimes borrowed from and even incorporated other ancient Near Eastern works into their own. A particularly striking example is found in the book of Proverbs, where an entire section (22:17–23:22) appears to have been based on an Egyptian document known as "the Teaching of Amen-em-opet."[3] In addition to the numerous parallels between individual sections of these two works, an obscure phrase in Proverbs 22:20 seems to allude to "thirty sayings," which calls the thirty sections comprising the Egyptian work to mind. Because neither text can be dated with complete certainty, their exact relationship is difficult to prove; however, it is generally considered more likely that the biblical work followed an Egyptian model than the other way around. Confronted with such cases, scholars have suggested that other biblical passages with manifest similarities to ancient Near Eastern culture may also have had foreign prototypes. An intriguing example is Psalm 29, which refers to a number of places located north of Israel and includes several linguistic and stylistic features now known from Ugaritic texts. It has consequently been proposed that this psalm was adapted from a Canaanite hymn.[4]

Even where direct borrowing cannot be shown, there is ample indication of more general cultural influence. The Code of Hammurabi, with its numerous similarities to biblical laws, is one example. The plausibility of such links has been strengthened by subsequent discoveries of several other ancient law codes. Likewise, Fensham's essay in this volume (chapter 8) demonstrates that the biblical interest in "the stranger, the widow, and the orphan" draws on a widespread Near Eastern motif, and Spiegel has found a biblical allusion to the heroic Dan'el, who is also known elsewhere in subsequent Jewish tradition (see chapter 9). Biblical ideas have also been compared with those of other cultures. For example, the essays by Weinfeld and Moran explore the impact of ancient treaty language on the biblical concept of Israel's covenant with God (chapters 3 and 4).

Broader influence has been detected in biblical literature's conformity to a variety of ancient genres. Analogs to both prophecy and the wisdom teachings found in Proverbs, Job, and Ecclesiastes are described by Malamat and Würthwein (chapters 7 and 6), while Gwaltney connects the book of Lamentations with a well-known genre from ancient Mesopotamia (chapter 10). A similar proposal has been made for the love poetry found in the Song of Songs, which seems so out of place in the biblical canon. In this case, the analogs have come from ancient Sumer, one of the earliest-known human civilizations, which originated near the Persian Gulf in the third pre-Christian millennium. There scholars have found liturgies celebrating the sacred marriage between a god and a goddess, which was presumably connected with some sort of fertility ritual. Similar texts from Israel or Canaan, it is claimed, may have found their way into the Bible.[5]

Although one can hardly assume that the Bible's view of things was shared by all ancient Israelites—the frequent critiques of popular practice in both prophetic and narrative texts point in the opposite direction—it does provide some evidence of foreign influence on Israel as a whole. For example, its description of David and Solomon's royal administration bears remarkable similarities to what we know of nearby Egypt.[6] Given that Israel had no prior experience with a centralized government, it would hardly be surprising for her to have drawn on foreign analogs. In a similar vein, Volkmar Fritz explores the possibility that the Temple built under Solomon was also based on foreign models (see chapter 5), as the Bible itself implies in acknowledging foreign involvement, particularly as associated with the Phoenician city of Tyre, in its construction.[7]

Such connections have sometimes been ascribed to the absorption of outsiders into ancient Israel. In an earlier generation, various biblical ideas and practices were widely attributed to Moses's Kenite in-laws or to the Jebusite population of pre-Israelite Jerusalem. Other scholars have suggested that the early Israelites may have included the "Habiru," a class of social outcasts mentioned in various Near Eastern texts, whose name is suggestive of the word "Hebrew" (see Cazelles, chapter 11). Of the same type is the intriguing suggestion of a genetic link between Israel and the Greeks, discussed here in the essay of Yigael Yadin (chapter 12). However, the most famous example of this approach involves the Egyptian pharaoh Akhenaton, who instigated a "monotheistic" reform during the fourteenth pre-Christian century. In a theory popularized by Sigmund Freud, that reform was proposed as the source for Israelite monotheism associated with Moses, who led the exodus from Egypt which is widely believed to have taken place over a century after the reign of that eccentric Egyptian.[8] There are, however, several problems with this theory. For example, Akhenaton's reform did not last beyond that one reign. On the contrary, his teachings were quickly reversed by one of his successors, the famous Tutankhamon.[9] Whether Akhenaton's teachings can even be characterized as monotheistic is problematic, since it was only in the royal court that worship was limited to Aton, while the "masses" were apparently expected to continue the long-standing Egyptian tradition of worshiping the Pharaoh along with the sun disk whose theology he espoused.[10] More importantly, Akhenaton's "monotheism" bears little resemblance to the religion of Israel, with its emphasis on God's benevolent acts toward the Hebrew people, whether in the promises made to the patriarchs or the divine intervention to extricate them from Egyptian slavery. Nor is it entirely clear that Israel's religion was truly monotheistic at this point in her history. That innovation has most commonly been ascribed to the latter chapters of Isaiah, which were probably written during the sixth-century Babylonian exile, many hundreds of years after Akhenaton.[11] Even those who consider monotheism to have developed earlier in Israel are often skeptical about identifying it as Mosaic.

The widespread interest in finding connections between the Bible and other ancient Near Eastern cultures has bred its own reaction in the warning raised by several scholars against exaggerating the importance of such similarities, a practice baptized with the name "parallelomania."[12] Of particular concern has been the often tacit assumption that such parallels can be construed as evidence for a genetic connection between the cultures that share them, which in turn might lead to a variety of historical conclusions. It is concerning this that Jacob Finkelstein and Shemaryahu Talmon warn, emphasizing that proposed similarities be carefully scrutinized in order to determine how similar the individual elements actually are and whether they play similar roles within their respective cultures (chapters 15 and 16).

Despite such warnings, the pendulum of biblical studies has continued to swing back and forth with remarkable regularity over the generations, as initial archeological discoveries have led to enthusiastic claims of similarities with various biblical practices and the implied, if not always stated, conclusion that these constitute *the* source for the biblical practice in question. Only in the afterglow of more careful inspection has the questionable nature of these parallels become apparent.

Changing views about the biblical patriarchs, Abraham, Isaac, and Jacob, provide a vivid example of this process. Differences between their practices and those described elsewhere in the Bible have long raised questions in the minds of those seeking to understand the historical background of these accounts. Since later generations are unlikely to have ascribed deviant behavior to such venerated figures, one would expect these anomalies to be evidence of the traditions' antiquity. But there are indications pointing in a different direction, particularly the presence of various phenomena that do not fit the Middle Bronze Age period implied by biblical chronologies. These include references to domesticated camels, Philistines, and Chaldeans, all of which seem not to have been present in ancient Palestine until at least the time of the exodus, if not later. The paucity of references to the patriarchs outside of Genesis and the fact that so much of what the Bible does tell us about them is theologically oriented merely compounds these problems, since

God's repeated promise to them is clearly intended to justify later circumstances.

Ancient sources are unlikely to mention a small group of nomads whom the Bible describes as having lived almost forty centuries ago. The search for the patriarchs' historical setting has, therefore, centered on seeking corroboration for the cultural background reflected in Genesis. Discoveries from sixteenth-century B.C.E. Nuzi, located north of the Tigris River, seemed to have vindicated this quest. Legal documents found there were interpreted as including evidence for many of the idiosyncratic practices ascribed to the patriarchs, such as inheritance of an estate by a family servant (Gen 15:2–3) and the sale of privileged inheritance rights (Gen 25:29–34).[13] The fact that these practices had been found in northern Mesopotamia, precisely where the patriarchs are said to have originated before their arrival in Canaan (see Gen 12:31), lent further credence to the biblical account.

On closer scrutiny, however, almost every aspect of these arguments was discovered to have been flawed.[14] Many of the supposed parallels turned out not to be parallel at all. Often Israelite practices had been read into the cuneiform texts rather than legitimately found there. What valid parallels did exist turned out to have been widely practiced, often over a long period of time, rather than limited to any particular epoch, much less the early second millennium.

Such dead ends have not weakened the impulse to find and explore similarities between the biblical account and what is known to have been practiced elsewhere in antiquity. Indeed, that has persisted through a succession of permutations, revitalized by every archeological discovery, whether from Egypt and Babylonia or, more recently, Ugarit and Ebla. Sometimes evidence has come from even farther afield. Most recently, biblical scholarship has extended its reach to incorporate the fruits of sociological and anthropological research.

In fact, both the presentation of these arguments and the responses they evoke conceal a broader agenda. At least one author has charged that the search to find extra-Israelite origins for what is conventionally regarded as unique or at least valuable in the Hebrew Bible is but a modern variation of the long-standing religious effort to deny Israel any innovation.[15] The credibility of this charge is supported by the career of an early seeker after parallels, Friedrich Delitzsch, a prominent German Assyriologist. In a series of lectures entitled "Babel und Bibel," delivered at the German Oriental Society in the early years of this century, Delitzsch sought to demonstrate that biblical teachings were comparable to those of the ancient Babylonians, which were becoming increasingly familiar from the archeological discoveries of his day.[16] (Coincidentally, the famous Code of Hammurabi was uncovered during the years that Delitzsch was delivering these lectures.) As the series developed, however, it became clear that the lecturer's motives were not entirely pure. His interest was to minimize the value of Old Testament teaching so that it could be contrasted with that of the New, particularly as embodied in the words of Jesus, whom Delitzsch regarded as a Galilean and therefore possibly not of Semitic stock at all.[17]

If much of the impetus for seeking parallels between biblical and ancient Near Eastern cultures is not entirely objective, the response that its practioners are trying to minimize the Bible's Jewish value also echoes a long-standing Jewish perception of Christian interest in the Bible.[18] Nor are those who cite such parallels as evidence of Israelite superiority without interests of their own. A famous example of this kind of logic draws on the biblical story of a great flood, which has counterparts in a large number of traditions. Several Mesopotamian accounts are particularly similar to that of the Bible. Among these, the version embedded near the end of the Babylonian Epic of Gilgamesh stands out.[19] It, too, depicts a divinely mandated, world-engulfing flood as leading to the destruction of virtually all human beings, and much else as well, with the exception of a single survivor. Some of the vocabulary with which this story is told is cognate to that found in Genesis, and several minor details, such as the release of a dove and a raven or the ship's coming to rest on top of a mountain, are the same. Both stories also culminate in their heroes' offering a sacrifice in return for which he receives a divine blessing.

Yet few readers familiar with these texts would argue that they are in every way equivalent. From a purely stylistic perspective, Gilgamesh is a poetic epic, while the story of Noah is in narrative prose. These stylistic variations are accompanied by differences of spirit. For example, the biblical account is governed by the presence of God, who mandates the flood in response to human evil and maintains complete control of it throughout. This moral dimension is completely lacking in the Mesopotamian tradition, where the flood functions, at least in some versions, as a device for the gods to reduce human noise, after which they find themselves overwhelmed by its apparently uncontrollable consequences. It is no wonder that in addition to providing evidence that biblical authors relied on ancient Near Eastern traditions (a fourteenth-century B.C.E. fragment of the Gilgamesh Epic was even found in the Canaanite city of Megiddo),[20] this story is also frequently cited as evidence for the significant ways in which Israelite culture differed from its surroundings.

The contrast between Israelite culture and that of her environment, apparent also in Moshe Greenberg's study of the Bible's criminal law (chapter 14), is supported by the large number of biblical texts which mock the religions of Israel's neighbors. Sometimes this is explicit, as in the Bible's various satires on idolatry, its account of what happened in the Temple of Dagon when the ark was stored there by the Philistines, or its report of Elijah's confrontation with the prophets of Baal and Asherah on Mount Carmel which manages to make their beliefs and practices look ridiculous.[21] Other passages are more subtle in their treatment of Near Eastern traditions. For example, the Bible's opening story of creation and its account of the Tower of Babel are both constructed in such a way as to counteract major assertions of the Babylonian Enuma Elish.[22]

These observations place us in a better position to appreciate a debate which emerged in biblical studies earlier this century. On one side, Yehezkel Kaufmann had argued that the Bible's presentation of these polemics demonstrates Israel's fundamental ignorance of the religions that surrounded her. To make this point, he emphasized how little knowledge biblical authors reveal of the religions they choose to condemn, treating foreign deities as lifeless statues and showing no familiarity with the extensive Canaanite mythology which has become increasingly familiar from the Ugaritic texts. Not so, replied John McKenzie, citing allusions such as those mentioned above to prove that the biblical authors were very much aware of the traditions they rejected.[23]

Whichever side one finds more convincing, the fact remains that the Bible's relationship to the other cultures of its time and place has been an animating force in contemporary scholarship. On one side are those such as H. W. F. Saggs and Morton Smith, who see its ideas as typical of the ancient Near East (chapters 1 and 2); others have adopted what William Hallo characterizes as a "contrastive approach," using the striking parallels as a backdrop against which to demonstrate how much biblical concepts differ from those of their time (chapter 13), an approach explicitly evident in the title of G. Ernest Wright's book *The Old Testament against Its Environment.*[24]

This latter position—that the Bible's values are unique—is no less polemical than the reverse. Indeed, much of its fundamental impetus derives from the Bible itself, which, as demonstrated by Peter Machinist (chapter 17), is unabashed in contrasting its views with those of surrounding cultures.[25] It is this which accounts for the repeated emphasis on Israel's avoiding contact with foreigners, whether through marriage (Lev 18:3, Deut 7:1–4, Ezra 10, Neh 13:23–27) or diet (Dan 1:8). This view even pervades biblical language, which describes foreign deities as "other" gods *('elohim aḥerim),* refers to foreign practices as abominations *(to'avot),*[26] and reserves distinctive terminology for Israelite priests *(kohen)* in contrast to their foreign counterparts *(komer).*

Whether couched in religious, philosophical, or even social scientific terms, therefore, the issues discussed in the essays collected here are not simply academic, in the unfortunately pejorative sense that term has acquired. As we have seen, the vested interests of both Christians and Jews are at stake in many of the esoteric arguments on these seemingly pedantic points. Nor are their authors entirely disinterested parties, even if the debates are sometimes cloaked in the rhetoric of archeology or linguistics and defended on the basis of supposedly objective, "external" evidence.

These essays have been chosen to illustrate the various dimensions of this ongoing discussion.[27] Several criteria have been used to select them from the far larger number which might have been included. In general, an effort has been made to find presentations which are competent, typical of the methods they employ and, to the extent possible, sufficiently in dialogue with other views to include a history of the issue with which they are concerned and a description of the positions with which they both concur and disagree. It was also obviously desirable that a variety of methods and topics be represented, along with evidence pertaining to as many of the major sites from which our knowledge of Israel's world derives and as many sections of the Bible as possible. A final criterion is a function of this book's intended audience, who have been presumed intelligent but not expert in these matters. Concretely, that has meant that the selections had to be available in English and be clearly written in a way that makes their argument reasonably comprehensible to competent nonspecialists.[28]

In achieving these goals, the guidance and assistance of several friends and colleagues, including Tanya Haynes, Paul Kobelski, Peter Machinist, David Petersen, Kent Richards, and David Wright, have been immensely valuable, along with the support and assistance of Jason Renker, Despina Gimbel, and Robert Seltzer, whose idea this volume originally was. Where balance has been lost in the process of making the final selections, the editor accepts full responsibility, pleading only that simultaneously meeting all these guidelines has sometimes proven rather daunting.

Although the stated criteria were the only ones applied during the initial stages of selection, the abundance of Jews among the authors of these essays (approximately half) is appropriate for a volume intended as part of a series devoted to the academic study of Jewish history. Nor is this entirely accidental. Whatever the distribution's statistical validity, the subject itself reflects the interests of both the editor and the larger, contemporary culture which has made these issues a distinctive, if hardly exclusive, concern of modern Jewish biblical scholars, much as Christian efforts have often shared a more theological orientation.

It is scarcely likely that these issues, which have engaged biblical scholarship for over a hundred years now, will be solved in these pages. In light of what has been said above, it may be reasonable to expect that they will never be solved, since the seeds of this debate lie so deeply within the biblical text itself. As Machinist observes, every culture, like every individual, is unique, even while all inevitably share certain features both with those in their immediate environment as well as with many that came before. What sets us apart, both as individuals and as groups, is not, therefore, any one characteristic so much as the configuration of all our features—our face as a whole rather than our eyes or our nose or complexion. In consequence, it is probably unrealistic to expect that one could find any single element of Israelite culture which occurs nowhere else, just as it would obviously be foolish to think that any culture could be identical with it, regardless of the period in which one looks. Whether Israel is superior or inferior to the others is a different matter, a value judgment not susceptible to objective evaluation. Nor is any of this relevant to the theological debate about the Bible's validity or divine origin, both of which necessarily rest on commitments outside of the Bible itself.

In the end, the material gathered here is intended to help explore an issue which has animated much of modern biblical scholarship over the past century, albeit in several different ways. Whether one chooses to stress the similarities or the differences, it is to be hoped that the discussion itself can help illuminate the biblical text as well as those who have chosen to study it. Should the reader be enticed into exploring these issues more deeply, this effort would have been a significant success.

NOTES

1. This passage is translated in *ANET*, p. 153, where the word *bṣql* is found on lines ii.62ff. of what is there identified as tablet AQHT C.
2. The evidence for this assertion is fully developed by Umberto Cassuto, "Biblical and Canaanite Literature" in his *Biblical and Oriental Studies* (Jerusalem: Magnes Press, 1975), vol. 2, pp. 16–59.
3. Selections from the Egyptian work can be found in *ANET*, pp. 421–24, where the parallels are listed in note 46.
4. E.g., H. L. Ginsberg, "A Phoenician Hymn in the Psalter," *Atti del XIX Congresso Internazionale degli Orientalisti* (Rome: Tipografia del Senato, 1938), pp. 472–76.
5. See Samuel N. Kramer, *The Sacred Marriage Rite, Aspects of Faith, Myth, and Ritual in Ancient Sumer* (Bloomington: Indiana University Press, 1969), pp. 85–106.
6. See Roland de Vaux, *Ancient Israel*, (New York: McGraw-Hill, 1961), pp. 129–32.
7. See 1 Kgs 4:21–32 (English versions 5:7–18) and 7:13–14.
8. Sigmund Freud, *Moses and Monotheism*, trans. Katherine Jones (New York: Vintage Books, 1939), pp. 21–32.
9. Cf. Alan Gradiner, *Egypt of the Pharaohs* (London: Oxford University Press, 1961), p. 236.
10. Ibid., pp. 227–29.
11. E.g., Isa 44:6. See Bernhard W. Anderson, "God, OT Views of" in *IDB* vol. 2, pp. 427–28.
12. Samuel Sandmel, "Parallelomania," *JBL* 81 (1962) 1.
13. E.g., Cyrus H. Gordon, "Biblical Customs and the Nuzu Tablets," *BA* 3 (1940) 1–12 (reprinted in the *Biblical Archaeologist Reader*, ed. G. Ernest Wright and David Noel Freedman [Graden City, N.Y.: Doubleday, 1961], vol. 2, pp. 21–33). This approach underlies much of E. A. Speiser's commentary on *Genesis* (Anchor Bible, vol. 1; Garden City, N.Y.: Doubleday, 1964).
14. The issues are summarized by Roland de Vaux, *The Early History of Israel* (Philadelphia: Westminster Press, 1978), pp. 241–56.
15. B. Z. Luria, *"Meḥqar ha-Miqra' bi-levay Sin'at Yisra'el,"* *Beth Mikra* 23

(1977–78) 508–18 and *"He'arot 'al Darkhei Meḥqar ha-Miqra',"* *Beth Mikra* 24 (1978–79) 426–36.

16. A translation of these lectures was published under the English title *Babylon and the Bible* (Chicago: Open Court, 1906).
17. See Herbert B. Huffmon, "Babel und Bibel: The Encounter between Babylon and the Bible," in *Backgrounds for the Bible,* ed. Michael Patrick O'Connor and David Noel Freedman (Winona Lake: Eisenbrauns, 1983), pp. 125–36. For the background to this treatment of Jesus, see Alan T. Davies, "The Aryan Christ: A Motif in Christian Anti-Semitism," *Journal of Ecumenical Studies* 12 (1975) 569–79.
18. Cf. *Midrash Tanḥuma* (Buber) *Vayera* §6 (p. 88) and *Ki Tissa* §17 (pp. 116–17). Christian interest in co-opting the Jewish Bible is supported by such statements as that of Justin Martyr, who tells the Jew Trypho that "your Scriptures [are] not yours, but ours. For we believe and obey them, whereas you, though you read them, do not grasp their spirit" (trans. Thomas B. Falls in *The Fathers of the Church* [New York: Christian Heritage, 1948], vol. 6, chapter 29, p. 191).
19. For the story, see *ANET,* pp. 93–97.
20. A. Goetze and S. Levy, "Fragment of the Gilgamesh Epic from Megiddo, *ʿAtiqot* 2 (1959) 121–28.
21. Isa 44:9–20, Ps 115, 1 Sam 6 and 1 Kgs 18. For full discussion of this aspect of biblical literature, see Horst Dietrich Preuss, *Verspottung fremder Religionen im alten Testament* (Stuttgart: W. Kohlhammer, 1971), who compares ridicule in other cultures on pp. 35–41.
22. Cf. Nahum M. Sarna, *Understanding Genesis: The Heritage of Biblical Israel* (New York: Schocken Books, 1970), pp. 1–23 and 63–77. The Enuma Elish is translated in *ANET,* pp. 60–72.
23. McKenzie's "The Hebrew Attitude toward Mythological Polytheism" was initially published in *CBQ* 14 (1952) 323–35 and reprinted in his volume *Myths and Realities: Studies in Biblical Theology* (London: Geoffrey Chapman, 1963). Kaufmann's essay, "The Bible and Mythological Polytheism," which was published in *JBL* 70 (1951) 179–97, grows out of a much larger work which has been abridged and translated as *The Religion of Israel from its Beginnings to the Babylonian Exile* (Chicago: University of Chicago, 1960).
24. London: SCM Press, 1950.
25. How much biblical theology has been informed by this desire to contrast itself with neighboring traditions is explored by Jon D. Levenson, "Is There a Counterpart in the Hebrew Bible to New Testament Antisemitism?" *Journal of Ecumenical Studies* 22 (1985) 242–60.
26. The same language is used in Gen 46:34 for a practice which was unacceptable to the Egyptians.
27. Part titles indicate the perspective each essay was selected to illustrate; however, their positions are carefully nuanced, so that there are few which

could not have been put in several different parts. As a result, they might be read in a variety of different sequences. For example, one could use them to illustrate issues pertaining to the specific sections of the Bible to which they refer, reading Finkelstein and Weinfeld in conjunction with Genesis, Greenberg with the legal sections of Exodus, and so forth.

28. The essays have, for the most part, been reprinted in their original form, but with minor, stylistic changes to accommodate this setting. Thus footnotes in articles which used more than one numerical sequence (Fritz, Weinfeld, and Spiegel) have been renumbered and foreign scripts transliterated, with post-biblical Hebrew following the guidelines of the Association for Jewish Studies (see *AJSreview* 6 [1981] 209–10) while Greek and biblical Hebrew follow those of the Society of Biblical Literature (see *JBL* 107 [1988] 582–83).

I

SIMILARITIES BETWEEN ISRAEL AND THE ANCIENT NEAR EAST

1

The Divine in History

H. W. F. Saggs

There have been repeated attempts to identify the difference between Israelite religion and the religions of other parts of the ancient Near East in terms of a different way of looking at history. The basic premiss is that the Israelites saw their God as active within history in an immediate and direct manner not found in the thought of other ancient Near Eastern peoples.

This view has been developed in several different directions. In one direction it has had considerable influence in the modern presentation of Old Testament theology. In many works on Old Testament theology, or on Old Testament history or religion written from a theological approach, there is repeated mention of "salvation history" or "saving acts" or "saving institutions" in relation to ancient Israel. These saving acts or institutions are supposed to be related to divine interventions in Israelite history. Such concepts are treated as central to the Old Testament, sometimes to the obscuration of other aspects of the religion of Israel. Thus von Rad writes:

> It has been shown that practically the entire literature of the Old Testament is attached, in the form of larger or smaller accumulations of tradition, to a few saving institutions ordained by God; and this means that Israel was incessantly at work upon making her God's saving acts and institutions actual.[1]

In the following pages some criticisms are made not only of the concepts but also of the terminology associated with the "salvation

Reprinted by permission of the Athlone Press from H. W. F. Saggs, *The Encounter with the Divine in Mesopotamia and Israel* (London: Athlone Press, 1978), 64–91. © H. W. F. Saggs 1978.

history" interpretation of Israelite religion. In the case of criticisms of the terminology, the arguments are (unless otherwise stated) in relation to the English terms translating von Rad's German. It should not be overlooked that the English terms have in most cases a different semantic spread, different overtones, and a different religious cultural context from the German, so that some criticisms valid for the English terminology used by British followers of the traditio-historical school may not be equally applicable to the German terminology originally employed by von Rad.

What one fails to find in works in English referring to "salvation history" or "saving acts" or "saving institutions" is a satisfactory explanation of what is meant by "salvation" or "saving" in such contexts.[2] These heavily loaded, emotive, and sometimes ambiguous, terms seem to be left undefined to allow them the better to serve as a lubrication by which to slide imperceptibly from concepts of the Old Testament to concepts of Christian theology. "Salvation" in English usage does not connote a static situation but rather something dynamic—the saving of some individual or group either from something or for something or both. In Christian theology the sense of "salvation" is clear enough: it is the saving of the individual soul from destruction or damnation by sin, for eternal life. But clearly, when Old Testament theologians of von Rad's school speak of "salvation history" or "saving acts," they are not using the terms in that sense; they apply them not to individuals but to some entity referred to as "Israel," without any overt definition of the sense being attached to that term. There are various senses in which the term "Israel" may be used. There was an historical religio-ethnic entity bearing that name. It consisted of a group of men, women and children who had, or at least claimed, common ancestry, and who practised a common pattern of social and religious behaviour. Like their neighbours, they passed their time in such activities as ploughing, gathering the olive harvest, cooking, weaving, making love with their own or other people's spouses, stealing, participating in festivals, complaining about taxation, recounting old myths and folk-tales, and keeping the children in order. But there is no indication that it is this flesh-and-blood Israel of which the Salvation History theologians are thinking. Von Rad's Israel seems to be a purely theological abstraction that does such things as being "incessantly at work upon making her God's saving acts and institutions actual,"[3] learning "to look at herself from outside,"[4] having "the assurance of being able at all times to reach [Yahweh's] heart,"[5] working "for a long time on the Decalogue before it became . . . capable of standing for an adequate outline of the whole will of Yahweh,"[6] recognizing "the Decalogue [not] as an absolute moral law prescribing ethic [but] . . . as a revelation vouchsafed to her at a particular moment in her history, through which she was offered the saving gift of life."[7] Looking at that final phrase, one may fairly ask: who received this so-called "saving gift of life," and what was it? Above all, what was Israel (whether the abstraction or the historical entity) being saved from, or saved for? An explicit answer, other than in terms of Christian theology, does not appear to be offered by the Salvation History school; but it would seem that the fate from which Israel secured escape by means of the so-called "salvation" was, when one blows off the froth of theological sophistry, simply its extinction as a religio-ethnic entity. That is, God repeatedly intervened in history to preserve a particular ethnic stock. This is certainly the implication of von Rad's taking Deut 26:5–9 as the central Credo of Israelite religion.[8] This passage summarizes Jacob's descent into Egypt, the rapid increase of his descendants, the Egyptian bondage, the Exodus and the Settlement; and on it von Rad comments:

these words are . . . out and out a confession of faith. They recapitulate the main events in the saving history from the time of the patriarchs . . . down to the Conquest, and they do this with close concentration on the objective historical facts . . . there is no reference at all to promulgated revelations, promises, or teaching . . .[9]

If this represents what is understood by "saving history," then "saving history" basically means no more than that God maintained a particular religio-ethnic group in existence, when the operation of normal political and social factors might have been expected to result in its extinction.[10] That is, whilst Israel was historically only one of a number of ethnic groups, amongst them Egyptians, Greeks and Persians, which continued to exist as recognizable social entities throughout the first millennium B.C., despite numerous political and social pressures, the survival of Israel is taken as a special case involving "salvation," the unique factor being a special divine intervention in history. It is not always made clear, in writings on "salvation history," whether the special divine intervention is accepted as an objective reality, or whether it is only thought of as a subjective element in the Israelite interpretation of its own history.[11]

What is certainly postulated on the "salvation history" approach to the Old Testament material is that whether or not actual divine interventions occurred in Israelite history, the Israelites not only believed there were such interventions, but also held that belief in such a form and with such emphasis, and drew such theological conclusions from it, that this belief was not just an aspect of, but was the very heart of, the assumed distinction between Israelite religion and all others.

Von Rad's approach is open to another criticism in his use of the concept "faith" in relation to Iraelite religion. He thinks of Israelite religion in terms of acceptance or rejection of "the message" of "the living word of Yahweh coming on and on to Israel for ever,"[12] that is, in terms of (a word specifically used in the English translation of his writings) a "faith." In this approach von Rad is making the fundamental methodological error of imposing upon ancient religion the approach and attitudes of modern German Protestantism. Faith implies a system of belief voluntarily adopted from more than one possibility (including non-belief as a possibility). But this is a modern concept, not an ancient one. An ancient religion was not a faith in that sense but a way of regarding and reacting to the cosmos which was an inescapable part of the society as a whole. There was no question of the devotee deciding that he would believe one complex of propositions after consideration of various alternatives: the religious ideas of the ancient Israelite or Mesopotamian involved not things that he believed (in the sense of accepting by conscious decision) but things that he thought he knew. Thus Job says "I know [not "I believe"] that my vindicator lives" (19:25), the point about the distinction between supposed knowledge and belief being independent of the exact sense of the verse. The Israelite was born into a culture in which a certain view of the world was held. Because it was not a completely closed culture, there were certain tensions, with the opportunity of inclining to one or other alternative explanations of phenomena and answers to related theological problems—such as the problem of who gave fertility, or who was creator—but the opportunity for alternative views was restricted within quite close limits.

In the religions of the modern world, a person identifies himself with a particular religion by subscribing to a certain Credo, and can dissociate himself by refusing to subscribe. But to think of something definitive called "Israel's faith," to which (by implication) an individual Israelite, or Israelites collectively, might subscribe by confessing a Credo, or from which an Israelite might withdraw by refusing to utter a Credo, is imposing upon the Old Testament evidence categories which do not derive from the Old Testament. There exist specific statements of the manner in which a non-Israelite might become a member of the Israelite community, and also of the manner in which an Israelite might be cut off from the community, and in neither case is a Credo involved.[13] By imposing the concepts of "faith" and "Credo" upon the Old Testament data, von Rad is attempting to force the evidence into a Christian straitjacket.[14]

A theologian is entitled to use his own categories for analysing and synthesizing the evidence from the religion he is studying, and in the course of this may legitimately utilize categories which do not derive from his sources. What is not legitimate is to read back into the sources categories which come not from the sources themselves but from the theologian's methodology, and then to base arguments upon the falsely postulated presence of those categories within the source material. "Israel's faith," in the sense in which that term is used by von Rad, is a concept deriving from his own abstraction from the sources rather than from the actualities of Israelite religion. To base arguments, as von Rad does, upon the existence in Israel of something called "Israel's faith," taking this to mean not the sum of religious beliefs but a conscious decision upon and definition of beliefs in the modern Protestant manner, is methodologically invalid.

Whether or not divine intervention occurred at particular points in history is a matter of modern faith and not a problem susceptible to investigation. It is, however, possible to discuss whether or not Israel was distinguished from other religio-ethnic groups of the ancient Near East by the view that God constantly intervened in history on her behalf, to preserve the nation's existence, or, to use the more impressive-sounding terminology of von Rad, to give it "the saving gift of life."

A number of other scholars, who would not subscribe to the Salvation History interpretation of Israelite religion in the form presented by the school of von Rad, nonetheless argue for a distinctive Israelite way of looking at history. This view is stated in its baldest form by Mowinckel: "While the other peoples experienced the deity in the eternal cyclic process of nature, the Israelites experienced God in History."[15] Fohrer, although he does not accept the view in question, gives a useful representation of it in the following terms:

That Yahwism is definable as a theology of history, that all the basic confessional statements of the O[ld] T[estament] refer to history as the locus of Yahweh's actions, and that his revelation or activity takes place in or through history seems to be the characteristic principle for the so-called historical books of the O[ld] T[estament] and for prophecy. In this linkage with history we seem to see the true difference between Yahwism and other religions, with their timeless or non-historical basis, and thus the revelatory nature of Yahwism.[16]

This interpretation of the difference between Israelite and other ancient Near Eastern religions has been challenged by B. Albrektson in his monograph *History and the Gods.*[17] Albrektson, whilst modestly calling himself no more than "an amateur in Assyriology,"[18] has made a valuable comparative study of a number of Sumerian and Akkadian texts which specifically speak of actual or potential interventions of gods in human affairs, not in mythic time but in historical time. His general conclusion may be summed up in what he concludes from one particular text; that is, that the Mesopotamian texts bear

testimony to the belief that historical events are in one way or another caused by supernatural agents, that the gods create history. The idea that their main sphere of activity is nature does not even begin to emerge: here they are all concerned with what happens in the relations of states and men.[19]

Examining the Old Testament data, Albrektson claims to show that it

does not speak so much of a divine "plan" in a proper sense as is commonly assumed, and that the ideas of the deity's purposeful control of history and of the belief in the course of events as a realization of divine intentions are common to the ancient Near East.[20]

By this approach, Albrektson challenged some of the most cherished ideas of the theological establishment, and the reviews reflect the considerable interest aroused.[21] In some reviews, there was a tendency to overlook that Albrektson was neither attempting to deny the uniqueness commonly claimed for Israelite religion nor purporting to give a definitive statement of the relationship between Israelite religion and the religions of neighbouring peoples, but merely clearing away "too facile definitions of [the] distinctiveness"[22] of Israelite religion as a preliminary to a more correct description. It is thus hardly a relevant criticism of

Albrektson's work that he "had merely selected similar aspects as between the Hebrews and other nations, and not investigated the differences;"[23] he selected similar aspects because the predominant view of Israelite religion assumed the absence of such similarities.

W. G. Lambert has, in response to Albrektson's monograph, offered an interesting restatement of the basic differences between the Israelite and the ancient Mesopotamian attitudes to the activity of God in history.[24] This important, even though brief, study of one aspect of the subject merits some attention.

Professor Lambert begins from the premiss that "Israel was distinctive in her ancient Near Eastern context,"[25] and then proceeds to examine, as one aspect of this claimed distinctiveness, the differences between "the Hebrew and the ancient Mesopotamian ideas of destiny and divine intervention in human affairs."[26] It is clear from the context that when Professor Lambert speaks of the distinctiveness of Israel, he is not thinking merely of ways in which Israelite thought differed from that of ancient Mesopotamia: he is thinking of ways in which Israelite thought was distinguished from that of all other ancient Near Eastern cultures. It is therefore proper to point out that differences which one may succeed in establishing between Israel and ancient Mesopotamia do not necessarily establish the distinctiveness of Israel in the absolute sense: there is the possibility that the mode of thought in ancient Mesopotamia might have stood on one side, over against a mode of thought on the other which not only belonged to Israel but also was shared by some of her neighbours, so that it could have been the mode of thought of ancient Mesopotamia, not of Israel, which was distinctive in the sense of being unique —if, indeed, there did exist a conceptual chasm between the two sides.

Professor Lambert offers a summary of the characteristics of ancient Mesopotamian modes of thought. According to him, the Sumerians, Babylonians and Assyrians saw a world subject to various disasters, such as plague and flood, which were, however, never total. What held the force of disaster in check was something called n a m . t a r in Sumerian and *šimtu* in Akkadian; these terms are conventionally translated "destiny" in English.[27] Another term, m e in Sumerian and *parṣu* in Akkadian, often rendered "decree," falls in the same semantic area.[28] Lists of the things denoted by the latter term occur in some texts;[29] they include such functions or concepts as godship, the throne of kingship, shepherdship (as a royal function), the royal insignia, various priestly offices, truth, sexual intercourse, prostitution, music, falsehood, various crafts, various kinds of religious awe or dread,[30] judgement and decision.[31] Professor Lambert, following Landsberger,[32] shows that these terms refer to the essential function in society or nature which an object, class of persons or institution was primevally invested with by the gods; the existence of such permanent functions was a basic concept in Mesopotamian civilization. He summarizes his conclusions by saying that

> in the ancient Mesopotamian view every aspect of human society was decreed by the gods. Nothing was left to be chosen by the human race as suitable and convenient for it at a particular stage of development and in a particular geographical location.[33]

It may be useful to add two qualifications to this statement. Firstly, gods were not restricted to primeval time for decreeing fates. Thus, in a poem on the Sumerian city Kesh, it is repeatedly stated that the god An decreed its fate (apparently favourable for the future) after its destruction,[34] that is, in historical time. Secondly, divine decrees were not unalterable. Thus, it is stated in connection with the death of the Sumerian king Ur-Nammu:

> An altered his holy word . . . ;
> Enlil . . . changed his decree of fate.[35]

Though Professor Lambert's statement of the situation in Mesopotamian thought is substantially acceptable, it is possible to question the correlated suggestion that the Mesopotamian view on the divine decreeing of the framework of human life and society was conceptually wholly distinct from the situation in Israelite thought. Professor Lambert says: "The Hebrews lacked of course any idea of a series of impersonal regulations governing the whole universe. Yahweh laid down rules and could change them."[36] The validity of this statement, as the basis of a distinction between the Israelite and Mesopotamian situation, may be questioned. It is difficult to understand why in the Mesopotamian context the destinies or decrees governing the universe are regarded as necessarily impersonal. In a number of cases—for example, in the myth *Enki and the World Order*—it is specifically stated that a named god bestowed the particular qualities, or "destiny," upon the thing, place, group, or institution. Thus the decreeing of the destiny of the city of Ur is stated in the following terms:

He went to the shrine of Ur,
Enki, the lord of the *apsu,* decreed (its) destiny:
'City, possessing all that is appropriate, cleansed by water, firm-standing ox,
Dais of abundance that extends over the highland, green like a mountain,
Hashur-forest with wide-spreading shade, self-confident,
May your perfected decrees operate aright.
The great mountain, Enlil, has pronounced your great name in heaven and earth;
City, whose destiny Enki has decreed,
Shrine Ur, may you raise your neck to heaven.[37]

A destiny decreed by a named god in a polytheism is no more impersonal than, say, such a decree as that of the sequence night and day in the setting of Israelite monotheism.

A further point must be made on the comparison of Mesopotamian and Israelite data in relation to divine decrees. In this comparison, it is necessary to distinguish between the existence of concepts and the existence of categorization of concepts. It would have been possible for the idea to be held that there had existed from primeval times something called kingship, and something called marriage and something called music, and so on, without the superimposed concept that there was a general category to which each and all of these concepts belonged. There is evidence suggesting that though Israelites did not achieve the categorization of the concepts regarded as divine decrees, the concepts themselves existed.

Thus, although it is certainly true that there are no terms in Hebrew serving as near equivalents of the Sumerian n a m . t a r and m e , it is possible to challenge the assertion of Professor Lambert that in Israel "there is no . . . divine will manifested in the precise forms of human social life and the arts of civilization."[38] One might argue that human marriage is a very clear example of something decreed by God as a permanent institution in Israel no less than in Mesopotamia. However, Professor Lambert attempts to forestall this argument by suggesting that a crucial difference existed between the Israelite and the Mesopotamian situations. He says:

Marriage . . . was to the Hebrews a divinely appointed institution, but there is no evidence that the precise details of the marriage rites were held to have been laid down once for all by God, and were as such immutable. No doubt traditional forms of the wedding ceremony were clung to tenaciously amongst the Hebrews as elsewhere, but this was not an article of faith. In contrast the

Babylonians of one period were enjoined to observe a celebration of nine days' duration because the mother goddess had so decreed at the creation of man.[39]

What is proved by the data adduced is that in Israel marriage as a social institution had been laid down by God in primeval times, and in Mesopotamia the details of weddings had been laid down by a deity in primeval times. It is difficult to follow the argument that, because there was in Israel no fixed length for a wedding, or if there was a fixed length we do not know it, the concept behind the divine appointment of the institution of marriage in Israel was totally different from that in Mesopotamia.

There are other instances which can be adduced of God in Israel having determined destinies in primeval times, in the sense (already accepted as found in Mesopotamia) of decreeing particular aspects of nature or of human society.

One clear example is represented by the words of God in Gen 3:19: "to dust you shall return." In our terms this merely aetiologically explains an observed phenomenon, but then so does the determining of destinies for the various aspects of nature or society in Mesopotamia. Clearly, from the Israelite point of view, the disintegration of a dead body is represented as a divine decision in primeval times, and God could equally well have determined that the dead body should remain without corruption or should turn to ashes or be exposed to wild beasts and vultures, or it might have been decreed that men should—as Tertullian alleged was the case with the people of Pontus—"carve up their fathers' corpses along with mutton, to gulp down at banquets."[40]

A second example of God in Israel decreeing a destiny in the sense established for Mesopotamia is found in Gen 8:22:

> While the earth lasts
> seedtime and harvest, cold and heat,
> summer and winter, day and night,
> shall never cease.

This is a divine decree relating both to nature and to human society, inasmuch as the mention of seedtime and harvest is meaningless without reference to human agricultural activities. Similarly, the preceding example, of the return of the body to dust—rather than being cremated, mummified, eaten cannibalistically or exposed to creatures of the wild—unquestionably presupposes the human institution of burial.

A clear example of a primeval divine decree fixing the framework of human life occurs in Gen 6:3, recording God's decision that man "shall live for a hundred and twenty years." God did, indeed, later change his mind and reduce the period to seventy years, but this is no different in principle from the gods' treatment of some of their decrees in Mesopotamia. Kingship, for example, though a m e or "decree," could be withdrawn from earth and taken back to heaven, as it was at the time of the Flood.[41]

Another passage, Gen 9:6, without question makes God decree the institution of the blood feud:

> He that sheds the blood of a man,
> for that man his blood shall be shed.

The seventh-day Sabbath, as an aspect of human society decreed by God in primeval times, comes into the same category, at least in the late Priestly source (Gen 2:3), though here there is the possibility that the concept of fixing the exact details of an institution in primeval times might have been directly influenced by Mesopotamian thought. Such influence is hardly possible, however, in the J story of God decreeing labour pains in primeval times as a permanent aspect of human life (Gen 3:16).

Another instance, showing a clear parallel between Mesopotamian and Israelite modes of thought about the permanent nature of certain aspects of society, is seen in two references to the campaign season. Sargon II of Assyria refers to a certain month as being one which the Lord of Wisdom, Ninshiku, had prescribed in an ancient tablet for mustering the army.[42] One may set this alongside the statement in 2 Sam 11:1 that King David started a campaign "at the turn of the year, when kings take the field." Granted, the biblical passage does not say that it was Yahweh who had decided that kings should follow this practice; but it was clearly thought of as a part of the scheme of society, fixed—whether personally by Yahweh or by some impersonal power—in ancient times. Both in Assyria and in Israel the campaign season was a fixed institution, anciently pre-ordained as a facet of human society, not a matter upon which particular kings might decide for themselves.

In the light of such data, it seems difficult to accept that there was absent from Israelite religion the concept of divinely ordained and permanent regulations, decreed in primeval times, governing both the universe and human institutions. It is therefore not valid to find an antithesis between Mesopotamian and Israelite thought which might be summed up by saying (as Professor Lambert asserts) that in Mesopotamia "the contrast was not, as among the Hebrews, between morally right and wrong, but between order and disorder."[43] In all the Israelite examples given above, the fulfillment of the divine plan is a question of order or disorder, not of morally right or wrong. There was, for example, surely nothing morally wrong in a woman in childbirth in Israel not suffering labour pains; the fact was simply that this was part of human life as God had decreed it. This idea is, indeed, so strongly emphasized in the Genesis story, that the passage concerned could still be adduced in the nineteenth century A.D. for the argument that it would be impious, and a frustration of the divine intention, to employ anaesthetic methods in childbirth.

Thus it is as difficult to concur with the view that there was a total absence from Israelite thought of the concept of "destiny" (in the sense earlier defined) as to accept the earlier suggestion that the gods were not, in Mesopotamian thought, believed to intervene directly in history. Both ideas are present in both cultures, and the supposed absence of one idea from one side or the other cannot be used to explain the distinctiveness of one side or the other. One may certainly feel that there is a greater emphasis upon direct intervention in history in Israel and upon destiny in Mesopotamia, but this impression can hardly be quantified, and, even if it is factually based, represents differences of degree, not of principle.

Some scholars have gone beyond Albrektson's demonstration that in Mesopotamia as in Israel the gods were accepted as intervening in history, to see parallels not only in principle but also in detail. Thus, a number of writers have used terminology suggesting the presence in Mesopotamia of that particular view of divine intervention in history known by Old Testament scholars as the Deuteronomic theory of history, which predominates in the Bible in the books from Deuteronomy to Kings. This Deuteronomic view of history has two elements: it sees history as cyclic, and it sees the fortunes of a nation or a dynasty as directly linked to observance or disregard of the will of Yahweh. In the Bible both elements together are seen most clearly demonstrated in the Book of Judges, where this particular interpretation of history is set out in paradigm form. Thus, we find the following typical example:

> The Israelites did what was wrong in the eyes of Yahweh; they forgot Yahweh their God and worshipped the Baalim and the Asheroth. Yahweh was angry with Israel and he sold them to Cushan-rishathaim . . . , who kept them in subjection for eight years. Then the Israelites cried to Yahweh for help and he raised up a man to deliver them, Othniel . . . , and he set them free. The spirit of Yahweh came upon him and he became judge over Israel. He took the field, and Yahweh delivered Cushan-rishathaim . . . into his hands. . . . Thus the land was at peace for forty years until Othniel . . . died. Once again the Israelites did what was wrong in the eyes of Yahweh. (Judg 3:7–12)

The view of the cyclic nature of historical events is very clearly seen. Adversity led people to call to Yahweh, Yahweh raised up a deliverer, the deliverer gave security, security led to religious laxity, religious laxity brought down adversity upon the people. In the Books of Kings the retributive element remains very clearly seen, but the cyclic element is much less marked, although still present, being shown for example in weal under Hezekiah following his penitence (2 Kgs 20:6), succeeded by disaster consequent upon the evil-doing in the time of Manasseh (2 Kgs 21:9–12).

Some scholars have applied the terminology of the Deuteronomic theory of history to what is called the Tummal inscription, a Sumerian composition from the beginning of the second millennium. Tummal was a district in the city Nippur containing a shrine of the goddess Ninlil, spouse of the national god Enlil, and the inscription gives a schematic history of the fortunes of this shrine from its foundation to the time of the text's composition. It takes the following pattern:

> For the second [third, fourth, etc.] time, the Tummal fell into ruins.
> X built a building in the complex of Enlil's temple.
> Y, son of X,
> brought Ninlil to the Tummal.
> For the third [fourth, fifth, etc.] time, the Tummal fell into ruins.[44]

This certainly expresses a cyclic view of history, but whether it is proper to regard it as presenting a Deuteronomic view seems less assured. It is certainly the case that, except at the end of the text, the falling into ruins of the Tummal is mentioned immediately before a ruler of a new dynasty exercising the kingship in Sumer. There is, however, no positive indication that the change in dynasty was thought of as a consequence of the Tummal's falling into ruins, and the absence of a specific statement that the Tummal fell into ruins immediately before the rise of the final dynast mentioned is against this view. The purpose of the text could equally well have been to promote the interests of the Tummal shrine, by demonstrating that all the greatest rulers made a point of restoring it. Oppenheim might be right by intuition in saying that the Tummal inscription serves "to illustrate [the] belief that pious rulers received divine favors and those who did not respect the temple fell by divine interference,"[45] but evidence to prove such an interpretation does not appear to be at present available.

Another Mesopotamian text for which an attempt has been made to establish the presence of a Deuteronomic view of history is the Weidner Chronicle.[46] This badly damaged text comprises a summary narrative of rulers of third-millennium dynasties. The piety of some, and the impiety of others, is mentioned, and related to the favour or disfavour of the gods towards the particular ruler. But whilst the retributive element is plain, it is difficult to see here a cyclic element, in the sense in which that is demonstrable in the biblical Deuteronomic history or in the Tummal inscription. The picture is not, as in Israel, of the fortunes of the state rising and falling in consequence of the piety or impiety of the ruler or of the people, but of the shifting of the power centre in accordance with the actions of particular rulers or dynasties, without any mention of the fortunes of the state itself. Certainly this shows, if further proof were needed, that the divine powers were thought in Mesopotamia to intervene in history to reward pious and to punish impious rulers, just as in Israel, but the case does not appear to have been made out for this intervention to have constituted a regular cyclic pattern of disobedience, disaster, repentance, divine support.[47]

This raises the wider point of whether, under a common acceptance in Israel and Mesopotamia of the possibility of divine intervention in history, there may have been quite different theological assumptions. Professor W. G. Lambert takes the view that there was such a difference. His argument is that in Israel the understanding of the events related to Abraham and his descendants implied "a concept of history as including the working out of a plan,"[48] and that this notion of a dynamic divine plan in the working out of history was not found in the Mesopotamian cultural area.

This is a very significant point, which deserves examination. In comparing the two civilizations in relation to this matter, it is particularly important to ensure that we are comparing like with like. Ideally, what we need to be able to compare is the concept of history held by contemporaries of similar social groups in the two cultural areas, for example, the kings Sargon II and Sennacherib in Assyria and Hezekiah in Judah. A difficulty is that although we have documents bearing on the matter from both sides, not only is there no reason to suppose that the two groups of documents were drawn up for the same purpose, but also the Old Testament documents, unlike the Assyrian documents in the main, are not in the raw state; they have been edited through many stages, and by the time of the final recension there had been abundant opportunities for introducing reflections upon Israelite history from a much later period, and with these reflections, concepts which were not those of the Israelite contemporaries of Sargon and Sennacherib. Source criticism reduces this difficulty, but does not eliminate it entirely; to appreciate the possible non-conclusiveness of source criticism, one has only to think of the areas of doubt still remaining about what may be accepted as originating from the eponyms themselves in the books of the three major prophets.

We may first examine the concept of the working out of a divine plan as attested in Israel in the pre-exilic period. In view of the fact that Yahwism was the religion associated with two distinct political entities, it might be productive to examine the concept comparatively between the two kingdoms of Israel and Judah. Since part of the divine plan as understood in Judah was specifically related to the Davidic monarchy, and as there was no comparable permanent dynasty in the political kingdom Israel, there must certainly have been some differences of concept in this area, though not necessarily major ones.[49] However, this itself would require a substantial monograph for adequate treatment, and for the present purpose discussion will be limited to the overall picture presented by the Old Testament, based mainly on evidence relating to Judah.

Eliminating any demonstrably post-exilic developments, and disregarding the superstructure built on the evidence by some modern theologians, we may recognize in the Old Testament, during the Monarchy period, two lines of thought about a divine plan in history. One saw a covenant of Yahweh with Abraham and his descendants, the other a covenant with David and his dynastic descendants. In terms of belief in a divine plan in history, the meaning of the so-called "covenants" (or, better, "treaties," to use a term without tendentious theological overtones) was that God had promised continued existence to the Israelite ethnic group, and to the line of David. Although it is true that some prophets actually questioned the popular understanding of the divine promises in such categorical terms,[50] this serves only to confirm that the predominant pre-exilic concept of a divine plan was centred on nothing other than the absolute belief in God's intention to preserve both the ethnic group and the dynasty. It is not denied that exilic and post-exilic reflection upon the catastrophic end of the Judaean kingdom produced developments and modifications of these beliefs, but these are not relevant to the point at issue, which concerns the general pre-exilic Israelite view of history, not theological extrapolations from it engendered by a particular trauma.

In Mesopotamia, as in the Israelite cultural area, there is the possibility, and indeed the strong likelihood, that different views of history were held in the two kingdoms. This is indicated by the fact that royal inscriptions of the Annals type, characteristic of later Assyria, never developed in Babylonia. It is in later Assyria that belief in a divine plan in history is most clearly discernible. To establish an Assyrian belief in a divine plan in history, it is not necessary to prove in the Assyrian sources indications of a view precisely analogous with that in Israel, containing the concept of a covenant between God and man—though one scholar has indeed gone so far as to use "covenant" terminology of one aspect of Assyrian religion.[51] What is needed to prove the presence of the concept of plan is to establish that the activities of the gods were thought of as directed to some more remote objective than the achievement of the immediate event, and that they were thought of as operating a continuing intervention in history to that end.

Now it is precisely the claim of some of the Assyrian kings that their elevation to the kingship is directed towards fulfilment of a divine plan. Thus Sargon II ascribes his succession to the favour of Ashur, and says of him that

> (in order) to renew the cultus of the temple, to make the ritual perfect, to make the cult-centre splendid, he steadfastly gazed on me amongst all the black-headed (people) and promoted me. He fully made over the land of Assyria into my hands for administration and direction; he made my weapons bitter over the four (world) regions.[52]

Here it is indisputable that Sargon II claimed that Ashur was using him as the instrument by which to prosecute a plan, with both cultic and political implications. This is comparable with the claims made for Yahweh's use of Judaean rulers. The same Assyrian text gives further indications of a divine plan, not in the sense of something established by divine decree in primeval times and unchangeable, but of something which the god had decided should be effected within history. The text speaks of the city Ashur as "the exalted cult-centre which (the god) Ashur its lord had chosen for the (world) region (as) the central base of kingship,"[53] and then states that Sargon's predecessor had "brought his hand to that city for evil."[54] In consequence "the Enlil of the gods in the anger of his heart overthrew his reign,"[55] and, as Sargon put it, "me, Sargon, the legitimate king, he promoted; he made me grasp sceptre, throne (and) crown."[56] It is difficult to see how the overthrow of an Assyrian king by the god Ashur because of offences against his cult-city can be regarded as differing in principle from, for example, the overthrow by Jehu, at Yahweh's direction, of the dynasty of Ahab for cultic offenses, or indeed, from the threat of death (subsequently modified) made against Hezekiah in 2 Kgs 20:1–19. In all cases—Israelite and Assyrian—the change or threatened change is related to the prosecution of a supposed divine plan.

That it was the intention of the gods that the ruling Assyrian dynasty should endure, just as it was assumed to be part of Yahweh's plan that the Davidic dynasty should endure, is shown in numerous passages. Thus Tiglath-Pileser I, a century before King David, already claimed that the gods had given his dynasty a promise of eternal rule. Addressing the gods, and speaking of himself in the third person, he says:

> You have given to him his lordly destiny for power, and said that his high-priestly seed should stand for ever in the temple Ehursagkurkurra [the temple of the national god Ashur].[57]

This is no less definite, as marking a divine plan, than the covenant of Yahweh with the house of David. One sees the same belief, in the concern of the Assyrian gods for the dynasty, some four centuries later under Esarhaddon. Esarhaddon's father and predecessor Sennacherib had been murdered, and there was rivalry over the succession. Esarhaddon records:

In the matter of exercising the kingship of my father's house I clapped my hands. To Ashur, Sin, Shamash, Bel, Nabu and Nergal, Ishtar of Nineveh and Ishtar of Arbela, I raised my hands (in prayer) and they responded favourably to my utterance.[58]

Here it is unquestioningly assumed that it was the plan of the gods that the kingship should remain with the particular dynasty. The only question was which of the sons should succeed, and this problem was not different at all from that which arose at the death of David in Israel. There the eternal kingship as already assured by the divine will to David's house, but there was room for dispute as to which of David's sons was the destined heir. To settle this dispute in his own favour, the steps which Solomon took, which involved obtaining formal divine approval for his own claim and besmirching and then murdering possible rivals, were similar to those Esarhaddon took later.

There are other passages in Esarhaddon's inscriptions which reinforce the view that the gods of Assyria had a plan in history, effected through the continuance of one particular dynasty. Esarhaddon, makes the specific claim of a continuing dynasty of Assyrian kings caring for the temple of Ashur, from Ushpia, the original builder, through named rulers of the second millennium, down to himself.[59] His own restoration of the temple was more than a matter of ensuring the proper continuance of the cult: he specifically stated that for the purpose of rebuilding he employed captives from other lands, so that other peoples might observe the might of the god Ashur, to which end he ensured that they saw him himself (Esarhaddon) carrying the building-hod on his head.[60] He specifically claimed "[the gods] commissioned me myself against (any) land that sinned against Ashur," and added "Ashur, father of the gods, filled my hand (with power) to disrupt and to settle, to make broad the boundary of the land of Assyria."[61] Clearly, to preserve the royal dynasty, to lead the Assyrian armies victoriously into foreign lands, to punish rebellion against Ashur, to extend the Assyrian boundaries, and to show the might of Ashur to all mankind, both by the god's conquests and by his splendour in the Assyrian capital, were all aspects of the divine plan, in the view of Esarhaddon. The divine plan for the continuation of the dynasty, for the purpose of exalting the might of Ashur, is frequently alluded to elsewhere in Esarhaddon's inscriptions. Thus he refers to himself, with his genealogy given through his immediate predecessors, as of "the eternal seed of kingship of Bel-bani son of Adasi, founder of the kingship of the land Assyria,"[62] and this is in the context both of restoration of temples and of the gods bringing all lands into submission under his feet. Sennacherib equally thought in terms of the gods willing the continuation of the dynasty for ever, subject to due piety to the gods. He set up a stele which should say to Ashur: "May his sons and grandsons abide . . . for ever,"[63] with the exhortation to dynastic successors to restore the temple if it fell into ruins and to anoint the stele; the inscription contained further the threat that any successor who failed in this duty would be met with the divine curse and the overthrow of his kingship.[64]

The very epithets applied to Ashur as national god of the military state of Assyria reflect his divine plan, which was to ensure the dominion of Assyria and to quell those who sought to disturb the *pax Assyriaca.* He is the one "who overthrows all the disobedient," "who scatters the wicked," "who acts against him who does not fear his work,"[65] the one "from whose net the evil-doer cannot flee";[66] the one who "as to him who does not fear his word, who trusts in his own strength and, forgetting the might of his divinity, speaks arrogance, rushes against him furiously in the clash of battle and shatters his weapons."[67] The various instances of evil mentioned in these phrases refer to particular offences against the god Ashur in the form of opposition to the military might of Assyria, which clearly supports the view that Ashur had a plan in history for Assyrian imperialism, and that any opposition to Assyria was an impiety against him. W. von Soden speaks in connection with Assyrian imperial expansion of "a kind of theology of holy war,"[68] in which the dominant theme was that the god Ashur had made the claim to rule over all men. The idea that Assyrian military activity was in prosecution of a plan of the god can be exemplified again and again. Thus we find Sargon II using phrases such as "At the command of Ashur I defeated them," "I mustered the mighty hosts of Ashur," "I raised my hand to Ashur that the Mannaean land might be avenged."[69] Evidence of this kind, which could be much multiplied, shows that the gods, in particular Ashur, were promoting Assyrian imperialism, not in terms of a destiny decreed in primeval times, but as an activity within history relating to extending the might of the nation Assyria and perpetuating the dynasty. Whilst it is true that we do not find covenant terminology used for these concepts, it is difficult to see how the situation differs in principle from that relating to the divine plan for the continuance of the nation deriving from Abraham and the line founded by David in Israel. Such differences as there are between Israel and Assyria in this respect must be looked for in terms of relative emphasis, not of basic principle.

There is one piece of evidence, not relating specifically to the Assyrians, that could be adduced as an explicit, and possibly native, statement of a wholly static view of society in Mesopotamia, contradicting the idea of a continuing dynamic plan. This comes in a fragment attributed to the third-century B.C. Babylonian priest Berossos, as quoted by Alexander Polyhistor. The passage in question refers to the appearance of the divine being Oannes to the people of Mesopotamia in primeval times, and reads:

> (Oannes) [the god of Wisdom] gave men acquaintance with letters and skills and crafts of every kind. (He taught them) to build cities, to found temples, and to frame laws. . . . He showed them seeds and how to harvest the fruits; all in all, he bestowed on men everything tending to make life comfortable. From that time, nothing further has been discovered.[70]

This might appear to be conclusive as a representation of Mesopotamian attitudes, since the earlier part of the quotation is a substantially accurate reflection of traditions and attitudes found in original cuneiform sources. Yet one may fairly ask whether the conclusion to the section—"from that time, nothing further has been discovered"—really does represent an encapsulation of a traditional Babylonian view, or whether it might not be a later deduction from the earlier traditions under the influence of Hellenistic thought. It should be remembered that a Jewish contemporary of Berossos expressed very much the same view as that just quoted:

> What has been is what will be,
> and what has been done is what will be done;
> and there is nothing new under the sun.
> Is there a thing of which it is said,
> "See, this is new"?
> It has been already,
> in the ages before us. (Eccl 1:9–10 [RSV])

It would be grossly misleading to take this as representing the characteristic Israelite view during the monarchy, and we must therefore be chary of accepting the view ascribed, at the end of the previous quotation, to Berossos, as typical of earlier Babylonians and Assyrians.

It is, in fact, easy to demonstrate that the Assyrians of the first millennium did not think in terms of details of life primevally fixed, to which nothing new could be added or in which nothing could be altered. We know of many instances in Assyria in which humans recognized that they had made new technological advances. In some cases they piously said that the gods had revealed the new discovery to them, but even so that revelation, and the new process or material or architectural form, came in their own lifetime, not in primeval mythic time. Sennacherib, for example, recorded a number of changes from what had been done in older times. He re-designed Nineveh, and although he did indeed refer to its plan as having been "designed from of old," he then went on to say that the site of the palace there had become too small, and that no previous ruler had thought "to lay out the streets of the city, to widen the squares, to dig a canal, to plant trees."[71] Despite the theoretical primeval plan, Sennacherib held that it was according to the will of the gods that he should make considerable alterations quite out of keeping with the earlier scheme of things. This included altering the channel of one of the tributaries of the Tigris.[72] The gods also showed him various sources of minerals which had not been discovered before.[73] As a result of the clever understanding which the god Ninshiku had given him, Sennacherib pondered over the problem of casting large objects in bronze and worked out a technique which no one had ever used before.[74] There was nothing about this piece of technology having always existed hidden in the womb of time; Sennacherib was quite specific about having thought it out for himself. He claimed:

> Through the clever understanding which the noble Ninshiku had given me, in my own wisdom I pondered deeply the matter of carrying out that task. Following the guidance of my head and the prompting of my heart, I fashioned a work of bronze and skilfully achieved it.

Other kings introduced architectural innovations;[75] it is true that these were borrowed from Syria rather than invented from scratch, but even allowing that the Mesopotamian gods had "decreed the destiny" of particular types of building in Syria (and this is nowhere claimed or even hinted at), it has to be accepted that those gods had left it to human initiative to discover the appropriateness of such buildings for Mesopotamia.

The foregoing evidence has been adduced against the suggestion that the people of ancient Mesopotamia saw their gods as having decreed everything in primeval times, with no place left for divine intervention and the development of a divine plan within history. The other side of the claim that Israelite religious thought was distinctive in that it alone saw God as acting in history is that the people of ancient Mesopotamia saw the divine in the cyclic process of nature and that in this they differed significantly from the Israelites. Yet there are very clear indications that in some quarters and periods in Israel Yahweh was also recognized as operating in and through nature. It is, indeed, not always possible to make a sharp distinction between intervention in history and operation in the realm of nature, as one may be an aspect of, or the mechanism of, the other; obvious cases are famine, flood, or the giving or withholding of rain and fertility.

It must be conceded, however, that the activity of Yahweh in and through nature was sometimes questioned. Yet it is significant that this questioning came not primarily from Yahwists concerned to preserve the distinction between Yahweh and gods representing aspects of nature; on the contrary, it originally came from polytheistic quarters, in which it was claimed that some other deity, and not Yahweh, controlled particular aspects of nature. The latter situation was clearly operative when Hosea found it necessary to insist that it was Yahweh, not Baal, who granted fertility. He represented Yahweh as saying: "[Israel] does not know that it is I who gave her corn, new wine, and oil" (2:8). Furthermore, the question of the control over nature appears to have been one aspect of the contest between Elijah and the prophets of Baal at Carmel; this is certainly suggested by the coming of rain, to break the long drought, which immediately followed upon the vindication of Yahweh in the contest (1 Kgs 18:41).[76]

Such evidence, which has been amply discussed in the standard works on Israelite religion,[77] makes it clear that, whatever the precise form of the link between Yahweh and nature, Yahweh was certainly thought to act in nature, not only in the primeval creation but also within history. J. L. Crenshaw, one of the scholars to touch upon this problem most recently, is certainly justified in concluding that both Yahweh and the Mesopotamian gods were regarded as controlling both history and nature.[78]

Yet even though the operation of both Yahweh and the Mesopotamian gods could be recognized in the cyclic process of nature, there remains the possibility of a significant difference in the mechanism. One possibility which requires examination is the suggestion that, albeit he controlled nature equally with the Mesopotamian gods, Yahweh stood outside nature in a way the Mesopotamian gods did not.

T. Jacobsen (not, it may be noted, writing in the context of a direct comparison between Israel and Mesopotamia) states the Sumerian situation for the relationship of the gods to natural phenomena in these terms:

> Utu is the numinous power that comes into being as the sun, the sun-god, and the visible form which that power takes is the flaming sun disk; the language allows no distinction between the two.[79]

It is, however, doubtful if the claimed lack of possibility of differentiation can be maintained in the rigid terms in which Jacobsen states it. One does in fact find passages where a distinction is made between the Sun-god and the physical sun. Thus, in the myth *Enki and the World Order* we read:

> The valiant Utu [the Sun-god], the firm-standing bull . . . ,
> The father of the great city, the place where rises the sun, the great herald of holy Anu.[80]

Here undoubtedly the god and the physical sun are distinguished, the latter not being marked with the god determinative. Yet it has to be added that two lines later the distinction becomes blurred, for the text continues:

> The judge, . . .
> The one wearing a beard of lapis lazuli, who rises from the horizon to the pure heaven.[81]

Here the epithets clearly refer to the Sun-god, not merely to the sun, and it is the Sun-god himself who moves across the sky. The situation as to the phenomenon and the numen might therefore be re-stated in the following terms. The Mesopotamian was consciously aware that the phenomenon was not the actual divine being. Yet he felt so vividly the numinous power behind the visible object that the latter immediately made real for him the presence of the god himself. That is, there was a very strong sense of the immanence of the divine in the natural world, although this stopped short of pantheism.

Jacobsen elsewhere adduces a text which offers a striking example to substantiate both this sense of the immanence of the divine in nature, and at the same time the clear recognition of the distinction between the divine being and nature. The text, commenting on the death of the god Dumuzi, reads (in Jacobsen's translation):

> You who are not the cream were poured out with the cream,
> You who are not the milk were drunk with the milk.[82]

Unmistakably this test on the one hand makes a positive distinction between the god and the milk, and on the other sees the numinous power of the god as present in the milk.

Other examples of the immediate relationship between the numinous power and the divine being may be adduced. Thus, just as it is possible to say that Utu represented both the Sun-god and the sun-disk, so Ishkur represented both the Sumerian Weather-god and the south wind. But this statement again requires some refinement. We have a hymn which contains the following lines:

> When Father Ishkur goes out of his house, he is a roaring stormwind,
> When he goes out of his house, out of his city, he is a young wild ox;
> When he roars from the storm to heaven, he is a booming stormwind.[83]

This might appear to be conclusive for the identification "Ishkur equals stormwind." But it is not quite so simple. That this straightforward identification did not fully cover the concept is clear from what is said elsewhere in the hymn. In one group of lines the god is praised as "Father Ishkur, who rides on a stormwind," and in another place in the same composition he is told by Enlil:

> My son, I have given you the stormwinds, I have harnessed the stormwinds for you, . . .
> I have harnessed the seven winds for you like a team, I have harnessed the stormwinds for you.[84]

Here the stormwinds are something distinct from and controlled by Ishkur. The Sumerian was conscious that the stormwinds were not Ishkur. None the less, they had a numinous quality which for the Sumerian meant that Ishkur was indeed immanent in the stormwinds.

When we turn to the Old Testament we find that some of the things quoted as said about Utu the Sun-god or Ishkur the Weather-god could in Israel be said about Yahweh. Thus he might ride on the clouds or the wings of the wind.[85] But, contrary to the situation in Mesopotamian religion, he could never be directly equated with the physical sun or with the wind.

That last categorical statement requires to be justified, in the face of evidence which some would say exists for sun-worship in Israel.[86] There is a passage in Job which bears directly on this:

> If I ever looked on the sun in splendour
> or the moon moving in her glory,
> and was led astray in my secret heart
> and raised my hand in homage;
> this would have been an offence before the law,
> for I should have been unfaithful to God [El] on high. (31:26–28)

Also, astral worship is specifically forbidden in Deut 4:19 and 17:3, implying knowledge of it in Israel. Some have also taken Ps 19 to contain lines borrowed from a hymn to the sun, but even if one accepts this improbable suggestion, it is irrelevant to the discussion of Israelite religion, since, as Ringgren points out, this Psalm "never equates Yahweh with the sun; instead, Yahweh (or El) is the creator of the sun."[87]

The passages from Job and Deuteronomy, on the other hand, certainly envisage the possibility of sun-worship in Israel. However, they clearly regard such a thing as apostasy from Yahweh. This, therefore, reinforces the idea that the sun could not be thought of as simply an aspect of Yahweh; if one worshipped the sun one was not worshipping Yahweh in another manifestation, one was worshipping something other than Yahweh. The sun is merely a part of Yahweh's creation, and wholly distinct from him. Yahweh is never regarded as being immanent in the sun.

A corresponding situation applied for the stormwind. Indeed, to emphasize this, we have the story of the theophany to Elijah at Horeb. Yahweh was passing by, and there was first a hurricane, then an earthquake, and then fire. Yahweh was present in none of these, but in what came finally—not "a still small voice" as conventionally rendered, but rather "a numinous silence."[88] Yahweh controlled all the forces of nature, but was immanent in none of them.

This suggests a new direction in which to look in seeking a principle to which to attach the differences ascertainable between Israelites and Mesopotamian religion. The usual procedure has been to look for something positive in Israelite religion which is not found elsewhere, such as particular view of history or a particular view of the nature of man.

Here, however, in the Israelite view of God in history and nature, we find close parallels between the Israelite and Mesopotamian concepts right up to the final question of the being of God himself. At this point comes a marked divergence; the sense of Israelite religious thought is given by a negative—not by what God is but by what he is not. He is not immanent in the heavenly bodies or the wind, and—by another negative in another context—God is not representable in human form or animal form, and—by yet another negative—the divine has not a multiplicity of forms. Furthermore, as we shall see later, he is not approachable by certain techniques. It might well be productive to re-examine the whole of Israelite religious thought not in terms of positives but in terms of negatives, to identify not new concepts added by Israel but common ancient Near Eastern concepts rejected. If indeed Israelite religion was unique, it is possible that the essence of that uniqueness lay in the recognition of what God was not.

NOTES

1. Gerhard von Rad, *Old Testament Theology* (Edinburgh: Oliver and Boyd, 1962–65) vol. 2, 368. On the unbalance of such a view see J. Barr, *Old and New in Interpretation* (London: SCM Press, 1966) chapters 1 and 3. See also N. W. Porteous, "Magnalia Dei," in H. W. Wolff (ed.), *Probleme biblischer Theologie, Gerhard von Rad zum 70. Gerburtstag.* (Munich: Chr. Kaiser Verlag, 1971), 417–27. Von Rad's "Salvation History" views in relation to the prophets have been examined, on a literary-critical basis and strictly inside the Israelite context, by J. Vollmer, *Geschichtliche Rückblicke und Motive in der Prophetie des Amos, Hosea und Jesaja* (=BZAW 119; Berlin: de Gruyter, 1971). Vollmer rejects von Rad's view that the prophets looked on past Israelite history as an unfolding of a divine plan of salvation. Rather the prophets referred to history to point out the past guilt of the Israelites and the penalty this entailed in terms of divine judgement.
2. S. G. F. Brandon, "The Ritual Technique of Salvation in the Ancient Near East," in S. G. F. Brandon (ed.), *The Savior God* (Manchester: Manchester University Press, 1963), 17–18, offers a definition of the concept of salvation: "Even if kept within the context of religion, its application ranges from the idea of safety from disease and misfortune, engendered by demoniac agency to that of deliverance from some form of eternal damnation." On the translation "salvation history" for the German *Heilsgeschichte,* see Translator's Preface in Oscar Cullmann, *Salvation in History* (London:

SCM Press, 1967). 17. On the difficulty of arriving at the precise meaning of "Heilgeschichte" for von Rad, see D. G. Spriggs, *Two Old Testament Theologies* (London: SCM Press, 1974), 34–8; Spriggs concludes (38): "we are left with the uncomfortable feeling that *[Heilsgeschichte* in von Rad's *Theology]* does not have any clear or uniform meaning." Some scholars (not von Rad) have attempted to define "salvation" in the OT context by reference to the semantic spread of the root *yšᶜ*, but the inappropriateness of this is sufficiently made evident by the nonsense which results; e.g., "David gained salvation when he reduced the surrounding peoples to obedience (2 Sam 8:14) (F. J. Taylor, in A. Richardson [ed.], *A Theological Word Book of the Bible* [London: SCM, 1950], 219. For *tĕšûᶜâ,* often translated "salvation," as denoting "victory," see A. R. Johnson, *The Cultic Prophet in Ancient Israel* (2d ed., Cardiff: University of Wales Press, 1962) 40, n. 1. R. J. Sklba, "The Redeemer of Israel," *CBQ* 34 (1972) 1–18, makes (see especially 13–17) an attempt to explain what he understands by salvation concepts.

3. Von Rad, *Old Testament Theology,* vol. 2, 368.
4. Ibid., vol. 1, 178.
5. Ibid., vol. 1, 183.
6. Ibid., vol. 1, 191.
7. Ibid., vol. 1, 193–94.
8. J. Muilenburg, "A Liturgy on the Triumphs of Yahweh," in W. C. van Unnik and A. S. van der Woude (eds.), *Studia Biblica et Semitica Theodoro Christiano Vriezen . . . Dedicata* (Wageningen: H. Veenman & Zonen N.V., 1966), 233, regards Exod 15:1–18 "the most primitive of the old credos (Deut 26:8; 6:21–23; Josh 24:6–7; 1 Sam 12:6)." On Deut 26:5–10, note also that literary analysis leaves only the beginning of v. 5 and v. 10 as primitive (see R. de Vaux, *Histoire ancienne d'Israël, des origines à l'installation en Canaan* [Paris: Gabalda, 1971], 161, and references in n. 12).
9. Von Rad, *Old Testament Theology,* vol. 1, 122.
10. It might be argued that God preserved Israel in order to transmit a particular revelation of him (a view which—as a theological judgement—the present writer would accept). If so, there are two possibilities for the nature of the transmitted revelation (which could overlap). The postulated revelation could relate to the nature of God and man, or it could be teaching about what God had done in history. If, as von Rad implies, it was overwhelmingly the latter, then one reaches the conclusion that in the Israelite view it was not to ensure the continuance of Israel as a religio-ethnic unit that God intervened in history, but rather, in order to provide striking deeds, the records of which Israel might transmit. If this was the case, God was in effect thought of as undertaking spectacular interventions in history for no better ultimate end than publicity. This would be not Salvation History but Advertisement History. Fohrer is certainly correct in saying (*History of Israelite Religion* [Nashville: Abingdon Press, 1972], 182) that "the view

that Yahweh acts in or through history is one-sided, and comprehends only a single aspect of the totality and fullness of Yahwism."

11. It is to be noted that Amos met, and rejected, the idea that Yahweh made interventions in history affecting Israel of a different kind from those affecting other nations; see Amos 9:7. Doubts as to the originality of the verse have no more substantial basis than *a priori* assumptions as to the kind of ideas appropriate to Amos.
12. Von Rad, *Old Testament Theology,* vol. 1, 112.
13. The Gibeonites were alleged to have entered the Israelite community (albeit as second-class members) by political treaty, without reference by either party to religious belief; Josh 9:3–23. For cutting off from the community (in some cases by death, in others perhaps only by excommunication, but in all cases for wrong actions and not for false beliefs) see Exod 12:15,19; 30:33,38; 31:14; Lev 7:20,21,25,27; 17:4,9–10; etc.
14. Von Rad's importations of the Christian concept of Credo into his treatment of the Old Testament data is made explicit in his further comment on Deut 26:5–9. "As in the Apostles' Creed, there is no reference at all to promulgated revelations, promises, or teaching, and still less any consideration of the attitude which Israel on her side took towards this history with God" (*Old Testament Theology,* vol. 1, 122). The conclusions von Rad appears to wish to draw from this comparison are invalidated by the circumstance that the statement about the Apostles' Creed is factually inaccurate. It does contain "reference . . . to promulgated revelations, promises, [and] teaching": what else than this is the epithet "Maker of heaven and earth" applied to God the Father, or the statement "from thence he shall come to judge the quick and the dead" applied to God the Son, or the specific mention of the doctrines of the forgiveness of sins and the resurrection? The Apostles' Creed cannot, moreover, be compared with the Deuteronomy passage on form-critical grounds; its *Sitz im Leben* is quite different. On von Rad's argument, the Deuteronomy Credo is a very early document, standing near the beginning of the Israelite religious tradition. But the Apostles' Creed is, within the Christian tradition, a relatively late compilation, having been formulated in the eighth century as a definitive statement of Christian belief, to which a man must consciously subscribe if he wishes to be regarded as a Christian. It was not a formative element in Christian faith, but rather a summary of Christian faith, arrived at after the great controversies on the Trinity, the Incarnation, and the Atonement. Thus the Apostles' Creed cannot be invoked in aid of arguments concerning the Deuteronomy Credo; the one stood at the end of a period of intense theological discussion; the other was itself a starting point.
15. Quoted from Albrektson, *History and the Gods* (Gleerup: Lund, 1967), 11. The original work was not available to the present writer.
16. Fohrer, *History of Israelite Religion,* 182.
17. See note 15.

18. Albrektson, *History and the Gods,* 8.
19. Ibid., 27.
20. Ibid., 96.
21. For references to reviews see *Keilschriftbibliographie* 30 (*Or* NS 38 [1969]), 59*, no. 635; 31 (*Or* NS 39 [1970]), 64*, nos. 736, 747; 32 (*Or* NS 40 [1971]), 68*, no. 945; 33 (*Or* NS 41 [1972]), 57*, no. 828.
22. Albrektson, *History and the Gods,* 7.
23. W. G. Lambert, "Destiny and Divine Intervention in Babylon and Israel," *OTS* 17 (1972), 65.
24. Ibid., pp. 65–72.
25. Ibid., 65.
26. Ibid.
27. Ibid., 66.
28. On m e see G. Farber-Flügge, *Der Mythos "Inanna und Enki" unter besonderer Berücksichtigung der Liste der* m e (Rome: Pontifical Biblical Institute Press, 1973), 116–26.
29. See S. N. Kramer, *The Sumerians, Their History, Culture, and Character* (Chicago: University of Chicago Press, 1963), 116, and Farber-Flügge, *Inanna und Enki,* 97–115.
30. Farber-Flügge, op. cit., 113, nos. (79)–(81), and 58, lines II vi 4–6.
31. This is not a complete list. It may be noted that extant complete lists do not include some of the essential bases of Sumerian civilization, such as irrigation. The origin of the latter is, however, reflected in a myth; see C. J. Gadd in *Cambridge Ancient History* (3d ed., Cambridge: Cambridge University Press, 1971), vol. I, part 2, 125.
32. B. Landsberger, "Die Eigenbegrifflichkeit der babylonischen Welt," *Islamica* 2 (1926), 369.
33. Lambert, op. cit., 67.
34. S. N. Kramer, "Keš and its fate; laments, blessings, omens," *Gratz College Anniversary Volume* (Philadelphia: Gratz College, 1971), 165–75.
35. S. N. Kramer, "The death of Ur-Nammu and his Descent to the Netherworld," *JCS* 21 (1967), 112, lines 8–9.
36. Lambert, op. cit., 69.
37. Carlos Benito, *"Enki and Ninmah" and "Enki and the World Order" (Sumerian and Akkadian texts with English Translations and Notes)* (Ph.D. dissertation, University of Pennsylvania, 1974), 97, lines 210–18. The translation is slightly modified from that given in, op. cit., 124–5.
38. Lambert, op. cit., 70.
39. Ibid.
40. E. Evans (ed.), *Tertullian adversus Marcionem* (Oxford: Clarendon Press, 1972), book I, 3: "Parentum cadavera cum pecudibus caesa convivio convorant."
41. Thorkild Jacobsen, *Sumerian King List* (Chicago: University of Chicago Press, 1939), 76, lines 40–41.

42. F. Thureau-Dangin, *Une relation de la huitième compagne de Sargon (714 av. J.-C.)* (Paris: Geuthner, 1912), 2, lines 6–7.
43. Lambert, op. cit., 67.
44. See Kramer, *Sumerians,* 46–49, and E. Sollberger, "The Tummal Inscription," *JCS* 16 (1962), 40–47.
45. A. Leo Oppenheim, *Ancient Mesopotamia, Portrait of a Dead Civilization* (Chicago: University of Chicago Press, 1964), 150.
46. For edition of the text, see H.-G. Güterbock, "Die historische Tradition und ihre literarische Gestaltung bei Babylonian und Hethitern bis 1200," *ZA* 42 (1934), 47–57. For the attempt to establish a Deuteronomic view of history therein, see E. Osswald, "Altorientalische Parallelen zur deuteronomistischen Geschichtsbetrachtung," *MIOF* 15 (1969), 286–96.
47. For a reference to an article by B. Albrektson ("Ve och väl. Till frågen om det s.k. främreorientaliska växlingsschemat," *Svensk Teologisk Kvartalskrift* 47 [1971], 28–36, not available to the present writer) taking "the Oriental cyclic view of woe and prosperity [as] unproved," see *Keilschriftbibliographie* 33 (*Or* NS 41 [1972]), 58*, no. 829.
48. Lambert, op. cit., 72.
49. T. C. G. Thornton, "Charismatic Kingship in Israel and Judah," *JTS* 14 (1963), 1–11, denies (against Alt) the existence of any distinctive type of "charismatic" ideal of kingship in northern Israel that was not present in Judah.
50. E.g., Amos 9:7.
51. A. L. Oppenheim, "Analysis of an Assyrian ritual (KAR 139)," *HR* 5 (1966), 255.
52. H. W. F. Saggs, *Iraq* 37 (1975), 14, lines 13–15.
53. Ibid., line 30.
54. Ibid., lines 31–32.
55. Ibid., line 34.
56. Ibid., lines 34–35.
57. E. A. W. Budge and L. W. King, *Annals of the Kings of Assyria* (London: British Museum, 1902), 31, lines 24–27.
58. R. Borger, *Die Inschriften Asarhaddons Königs von Assyrien* (Graz: Archiv für Orientforschung, 1956; new impression Osnabrück, 1967) p. 43, lines 58–60.
59. Ibid., 3–5, lines III 16 to V 40.
60. Ibid., 4, lines 33–40.
61. Ibid., 46, lines 29–31.
62. Ibid., 97, lines Rs. 16–17.
63. OIP, II, 139, lines 59–60.
64. Ibid., lines 60–72.
65. For these epithets, see K. Tallqvist, *Akkadische Götterepitheta mit einem Götterverzeichnis und einer Liste der prädikativen Elemente der sumerischen Götternamen* (Helsinki: Societas Orientalis Fennica, 1938), 267, "Aššur als Krieger und Kriegsherr," and alphabetically in pp. 1–244.

66. Thureau Dangin, *Une relation,* 20, line 118.
67. Ibid., lines 119–20.
68. W. von Soden, "Aufstieg und Untergang der Grossreiche des Zweistromgebietes (Sumerer, Babylonier, Assyrer)," in W. F. Mueller (ed.), *Aufstieg und Untergang der Grossreiche des Altertums* (Stuttgart: Kohlhammer, 1958), 53.
69. P. E. Botta and E. Flandin, *Monument de Ninive découvert et décrit par M. P.-E. Botta, mesuré et dessiné par M. E. Flandin* (Paris, 1849–50) IV, pl. 71, lines 2, 10; pl. 73, lines 3–4.
70. P. Schnabel, *Berossos,* 253, III. De Oanne, lines 27–37.
71. OIP, II, 94–95, lines 64, 68, 69.
72. Ibid., 99, lines 46–49.
73. Ibid., 108, lines 57–64. New sources of massive timber were also discovered; see ibid., 107, lines 49–53. Ashur opened new springs in historical times for an Assyrian king of the early second millennium; see E. Ebeling, B. Meissner, and E. F. Weidner, *Die Inschriften der altassyrischen Könige* (Leipzig: Quelle and Meyer, 1926), 6–8, IV, no. 2, col. 1, lines 27–30 (for *a-ga-am* read *a-bi-iḫ* = Mt. Epih).
74. OIP, II, 109, lines VI 89 to VII 19. The succeeding translation is from ibid., lines VII 1–8.
75. E.g., the *bīt ḫilāni;* for references, see *CAD,* Ḫ, 184b–185a. See also A. L. Oppenheim, "On Royal Gardens in Mesopotamia," *JNES* 24 (1965), 328–33.
76. For other Yahwistic claims that Yahweh was active in the sphere of nature, see Amos 4:7–13; Hos 10:12; Isa 5:6; Jer 14:22.
77. See, e.g., Fohrer, *History of Israelite Religion,* 176ff.
78. J. L. Crenshaw, *Prophetic Conflict: Its Effects upon Israelite Religion* (Berlin: de Gruyter, 1971), 81–82.
79. Thorkild Jacobsen, *Towards the Image of Tammuz and Other Essays in Mesopotamian History and Culture,* ed. W. L. Moran (Cambridge, Mass.: Harvard University Press, 1970), 3.
80. Benito, *Enki,* 107, lines 374–75; and I. Bernhardt and S. N. Kramer, "Enki und die Weltordnung," *Wissenschaftliche Zeitschrift der Friedrich-Schiller-Universität Jena* 9 (1959/60), 238, lines 373–74.
81. Benito, *Enki,* 107, lines 376–77; Bernhardt and Kramer, op. cit., 238, lines 375–76.
82. *Tammuz,* 337, n. 16. Jacobsen mentions a differing older version of the text, published in *RA* 8, a volume to which the present writer has not had access.
83. A. Falkenstein and W. von Soden, *Sumerische und Akkadische Hymnen und Gebete* (Zurich and Stuttgart: Artemis-Verlag, 1953), 82–83.
84. Ibid., 82.
85. Ps 104:3.
86. H, Ringgren, *Israelite Religion* (London: S.P.C.K., 1969, 2d impression, corrected), pp. 97–98.

87. Ibid., 63.
88. 1 Kgs 19:11–12. *qôl,* qualified by *dĕmāmāh* "silent," is taken as related to Akkadian *qūlu,* on which see *AHw* 927b. See also Farber-Flügge, *Inanna und Enki,* 119, adducing A. Falkenstein, *ZA* 57 (1966), 87 for nì . me . gar = *qūlu* "ehrfurchtsvolle Scheu" (reverential awe).

2

The Common Theology of the Ancient Near East

Morton Smith

I.

We have recently heard much about the importance of archaeology for the study of the Old Testament. Just because this importance is great, it should be described accurately.

The need for this caution is shown by the recent exaggeration of the importance of the material from Ras Shamra. That material is admittedly of great importance for the history of the Near East in the second millennium B.C., but for the understanding of the bulk of the OT, which dates from about the middle of the first millennium, it is somewhat less relevant than would be the material preserved in mediaeval French mystery plays for the understanding of the English deists of the early eighteenth century. Linguistically, the two groups are about equally distant,[1] but the fifteenth-century mysteries are much closer in time to the deists than Ugaritic literature is even to Isaiah, let alone Jeremiah or Deuteronomy.[2] From the mysteries to the deists there is a continuous development of a single culture, whereas between the Ugaritica and the OT lies the complete destruction of the former culture by barbarian invasions.[3] However much the religion of the deists differed from that of the authors of the mysteries, it yet preserved the same dramatis personae and the same sacred literature, whereas the striking thing about the religion of the Ugaritica is its almost total lack of any direct relationship

Reprinted by permission of Scholars Press from the *Journal of Biblical Literature* 71 (1952):135–47.

to that of the OT. The weakness of the evidence which has been alleged as proving direct relationship is actually the best evidence against it. A few traces of Ugaritic mythology are found in OT poetry—but the striking fact is the rarity of such references, and when they do occur they are pieces of poetic imagery, probably of no religious significance.[4] A good deal of poetic jargon also found in Ugaritic is preserved in the OT, but much of it is the common jargon of most ancient Semitic poetry, and to be explained by the common linguistic and cultural background of that poetry.[5] At any rate, it does not prove the direct relationship of the religions: *Paradise Lost* is full of the poetic jargon of Homer. As for the evidence supposedly furnished by the preservation of proper names: Nothing can be clearer from the entire known course of Israelitic and Jewish history than the fact that, like most other peoples, the Israelites and the Jews preserved place names and adopted foreign names often without any knowledge of the original meaning, and often, when they did happen to know it, without any concern for it.[6] In sum: Ugaritic literature is of great importance for many aspects of ancient history, but its importance for the study of the OT is at best indirect and incidental, and the recent exaggeration of this importance is symptomatic: Had there been much that was really near, less would have been made of what was really remote.

All this being granted, however, the fact remains that to see the OT against a remote background is better (for historical purposes) than to see it against no background at all. Fortunately, many important fragments of such background as we have are now collected in the magnificent volume produced by Princeton,[7] and it seems therefore worthwhile to try to state in outline just how the theological material in that collection *is* relevant to the theological material in the OT.

By "theological material" I mean that which describes a god (or gods) and his (or their) actions.

Now the striking thing about the theological material of the great majority of these ancient Near Eastern texts is that, despite superficial differences, it shows one overall[8] pattern, which is the following:

II.

Prayer and praise are usually directed to one god at a time,[9] and peoples and persons are often represented as, or appear to have been, particularly devoted to the worship of a single god.[10] The mythology tells of many gods, of course—you can't have much mythology about a solitary being—and it accounts for many of the practices of worship[11]—no doubt because it was invented to do so. But the mythology seems rather a literary than a religious product. And just as it, for its own purposes, exploited polytheism, so prayer and praise, no doubt because of their own nature, are usually directed to one god at a time. This fact is characteristic of the rest of the theological pattern.

The god being worshiped is regularly flattered—that is to say, exalted. Though he may occupy a minor position in the preserved mythological works, yet in the worship addressed to him he is regularly represented as greater than all other gods.[12] It is often said that he created not only the world, but also the other gods.[13] He is the only true god; sometimes, even when worshiped in close connection with other deities, the only god.[14] This does not mean, of course, that he is actually thought to be the only god; the expression is usually no more than a form of flattery; only in a few special cases does it come to be taken literally. As a form of flattery it is often an expression of local patriotism,[15] which achieved it by a chain of exaggeration something like this: Our god is the greatest of all gods, there is none other like him, there is none other.[16]

Such exaltation of the god being worshiped is motivated also by the worshiper's desire to convince himself that this god can grant his requests. Therefore this god has all power necessary to do what his worshipers ask (and this is the important thing; this granted, whether or not he has *all* power is an academic question sure to be answered in the affirmative sooner or later by the natural development of flattery.) His activity is by no means limited to his own land;[17] he regularly discomfits foreign enemies in their own territories, makes over foreign lands to his own worshipers,[18] or gives other lands (or even the lands of his own worshipers) into the hands of foreign rulers.[19] Having created the order of nature, he not unnaturally maintains it (makes the crops grow, and so on),[20] but he can also change it by miracles. He maintains by rewards and punishments the moral order,[21] but he is independent of it and can pardon sin at will.[22]

He is regularly described by comparisons with the most conspicuous or the most powerful objects known to the culture, for instance, the sun,[23] the father,[24] the king[25] and the bull.[26] His minor attributes are usually those of the objects to which he is compared: As bull he is noisy, violent and fertile. As the sun he is glorious, perfect in beauty, the source of light and knowledge, the enemy of darkness, ignorance and falsity, the witness and judge of all that is done on earth. He is the father and king of his people,[27] his child,[28] whom he especially favors. The human king is his son,[29] servant,[30] or favorite,[31] whom he especially protects. But he also protects ordinary men, cures diseases and grants other material favors,[32] cleanses sin,[33] and comforts the afflicted.[34] In short, the god described by prayer is everywhere the god who will do the things which are most prayed for by the people who have most cause to pray.

But as father and king, the god of worship is just[35] as well as merciful,[36] an object—not to say an objectification—of fear as well as love.[37] His justice has accordingly expressed itself in the law, both the law of his cult[38] and the law of the land,[39] which he has given or caused to be given. The law of his cult provides that his worship shall be conducted, frequently under the supervision of a special priesthood, by sacrifices which are often strikingly similar from one country to another,[40] and with the observation of tabus which vary from place to place but show a general similarity of attitude toward the divine.[41] The similarities of ancient codes of civil law are too well known to need description, and their practical independence is well recognized.[42] But it should be noticed that everywhere the civil law, like the cult law, is the god's law, and an offender against either is an offender against the god.[43]

Now—since the gods were like men—it was expected everywhere that a god would punish men who offended him and would reward those who did what he wanted;[44] this, moreover, was what he was for. And since he was everywhere thought to want sacrifices,[45] it was also by sacrifices that men sought to placate him when they thought they had offended him or to secure his good will when they wanted special favors. The *do ut abeas* and *do ut des* relationships are found in all countries of the ancient Near East. But since everywhere the major deities demanded other things beside sacrifice, it was natural that the different ways of pleasing them should sometimes be contrasted, and that there should be some individuals who decided that it was better not to sin in the first place than to sin and offer sacrifice, or who maintained that the sacrifice of a wicked man was less pleasing to god than the prayer of a righteous one.[46] Moreover, since religious observance, whether of moral or of ritual requirements, naturally lends itself to abuse by the temperamentally scrupulous (in psychological jargon the "compulsives"), it is not surprising that everywhere there were some who came to advocate a righteousness greater than that required by law.[47] Naturally, such individuals were rare, and there was no such economic interest to preserve their works as that which preserved works embodying the priesthood's doctrine of atonement by sacrifice; consequently there is no reason to believe that the earliest preserved instances of their opinions are the earliest which actually occurred. Individual perfectionists, like individuals with other psychological abnormalities, are regularly produced and neglected by every large society.

As against such eccentrics, most people were probably content to believe that rewards and punishments were given, whether to individuals or to the whole people, according as men obeyed or disobeyed the usual social and religious codes of the society. The relation between people and god was therefore always essentially a contractual one, and the question as to when it was first given dramatic expression in a formal contract is one for the history rather of rhetoric than of theology.

Because of their contractual relationship with the gods, people gave attention to the prophets who everywhere[48] claimed to know by revelation the country's state of obedience or disobedience and the rewards or punishments soon to be allotted. (All the major prophets—i.e., those whose works have been preserved in quantity—prophesy change. Why? In the first place, because change is "news"; the prophet was the newspaper editor of his day, and if he had no news he got no audience. In the second place, because change always comes, and those prophets who foretold a continuation of the old order were sooner or later discredited. Of course, given the common theological structure outlined above, change, if for the better, was conceived as divine reward, if for the worse, as punishment.) Now the punishment of a society has to be effected by drought or flood, famine, pestilence, internal discord, or defeat by an enemy.[49] Therefore the prophets everywhere ring the changes on these five themes,[50] supplement them by threats of miracles—usually earthquakes and eclipses—and sometimes even foretell that if the people continue in their wickedness their god will utterly destroy them.[51] Likewise, the good things they prophesy are merely the reverse of these, except that, in place of the earthquakes and eclipses, they often foretell, as something no less miraculous, the coming of a good king who will save his people.[52]

III.

Such was the common theology of the ancient Near East—and not only of the ancient Near East, but of most periods and countries where polytheism has been the religion of civilized peoples. In describing it I have discussed only its appearance in the ancient Near East, because that alone is usually referred to in the study of the OT, and I have tried to suggest how, for psychological, social and rhetorical reasons, it might have developed independently in any ancient Near Eastern country. That it did develop independently in each is strongly suggested, I think, by the uniformity of the results, which can be explained better by postulating relatively uniform causes, that is, social, psychological and rhetorical patterns, rather than accidents of historical transmission. The interaction of these patterns produced a single "pattern for major deity" to which every deity who in that area and time became major had more or less to conform, whatever the historical or mythological accidents of his ancestry.

Consequently, parallels between theological material in the OT and in "Ancient Near Eastern Texts" cannot be taken off hand as indicating any literary dependence, common source, or cultural borrowing. The number of instances in which the OT has hitherto been supposed to depend on foreign sources—small though that number is—is probably too large. It is only when the texts are parallel in some peculiar, accidental detail, something which *cannot* be explained as a probable product of natural development, that the parallelism can be taken as *proving* literary connection.

The knowledge of this general pattern should serve as a guide and a caution in OT studies. It should serve as a guide by making clear the peculiarities of the OT, the points which need special explanation—for instance, Yahweh's abnormal jealousy and the almost complete neglect of the underworld. It should serve as a caution, not only to those who would discover foreign influences everywhere, but also to those who think it possible to reconstruct the history of theological thought in Israel and then detect and date interpolations by the stage of theological development which they show. In the first place, this procedure depends on arguments from silence, and the OT probably contains so small a selection of the literature of ancient Israel that arguments from silence are utterly untrustworthy. In the second place, it is possible that there never was any major theological development in Israel, that there were only shifts of emphasis and occasional working out of corollaries. The system outlined above is essentially that of Philo as outlined by Wolfson,[53] but it is quite primitive enough to have been held by a tribe of nomads, and there is no good proof that the Israelites in their nomadic period did not hold it. To suppose that Yahweh's control of foreign nations began with Amos[54] is to neglect the deliverance from Egypt and the conquest of Palestine. To suppose that Yahweh's concern for morality began with Nathan[55] is to neglect the divine backing of the law, which is characteristic of such primitive legislation as that from which the present legal documents of the OT must have developed. As for the famous "discovery of monotheism" by second Isaiah, that was probably not a discovery of monotheism, but an exaggeration of patriotism. Two things, at least, are certain: It has patriotic precedents and it was used for patriotic purposes. No sooner was the God of Israel declared to be the only God than he promised Israel the hegemony of the world. If this be philosophy it is puzzling, but if it be patriotism it may be primitive. In that event the fact that God's rule of the whole world had never before been *so much emphasized* could be explained on practical grounds: As to power, the attribute of the god of Israel was merely that of the major god of any ancient Near Eastern people, viz., to be greater than the gods of their neighbors. Thus when he gave them Canaan he was greater than the gods of the hill cities, when they fought the Philistines he was greater than Dagon, when they were established as a kingdom he was greater than the gods of the adjacent kingdoms, and when they were scattered in a diaspora from one end of the known world to the other, what was left for him but monotheism?

NOTES

1. C. H. Gordon, *Ugaritic Handbook*, Rome, 1947 (*Analecta Orientalia*, 25) nos. 14.3–9 repudiates as unproved his former classification of Ugaritic with Hebrew as belonging "to the same subdivision (often called Canaanite) of the Northwest branch of the Semitic languages." He concludes that because of our ignorance of the exact relationship of the Semitic languages generally, it is impossible to determine the proper place of Ugaritic, which "has been grouped with everything from Heb. to South Arabic" and had best be treated "as a separate Semitic language."

2. W. F. Albright, *The Archaeology of Palestine* (Harmondsworth, 1949), p. 187, says "all the datable texts from Ugarit belong to the first third of the fourteenth century." In that event, the poems contained in these texts can hardly be later than the fifteenth century B.C. This would put Ugaritic poetry about as far from Isaiah (late 8th cent.) as Isaiah was from Meleager of Gadara (1st cent. B.C.).
3. W. F. Albright, *The Present State of Syro-Palestinian Archaeology,* in *The Haverford Symposium on Archaeology and the Bible* (New Haven, 1938) p. 23: "At the threshold of the Iron Age we enter a new historical world, in which the great nations of the Bronze Age seem incapable of making a constructive cultural effort, and in which Israel and Hellas play an increasingly important part." So also T. J. Meek, *Hebrew Origins* (revised ed., New York, 1950) p. 74, "Excavations in Palestine . . . show a definite break between Canaanite (Late Bronze) and Hebrew (Early Iron) cultures, with a number of differences between them."
4. Albright, *The Archaeology of Palestine,* p. 233, notes this lack of religious significance. See also p. 235. It is also noted by H. L. Ginsberg, *Ugaritic Studies and the Bible,* in *Biblical Archaeologist* 8 (1965) 54, whence I have taken the comparison to the unimportance of classical mythology in English poetry. Contrast the theories of Dussaud.
5. This is the opinion of Gordon, *op. cit.,* 17.4–13. What is true of poetic jargon is equally true of the forms of the poems, which have also been used as evidence of close relationship. Cf. Gordon, *ibid.* 13.98.
6. For ignorance in the early period see the false etymologies in Genesis; for indifference in the late, the history of the name Isidore.
7. *Ancient Near Eastern Texts Relating to the Old Testament,* ed. J. B. Pritchard (Princeton, 1950). Hereafter cited merely by page and column, e.g., 389a means *ANET,* p. 389, col. a.
8. Particular exceptions can be found to every one of the following points, but are not relevant to the argument, which is concerned only to describe the common pattern. This pattern is clearest in the Egyptian and neo-Babylonian material, it is least clear in the Hittite (as might be expected, since the Hittites, in race, language, social structure and environment stand rather apart from the majority of ancient Near Eastern peoples, and it is here suggested that this pattern was largely a product of those causes. The Hittite pantheon, like Hittite society, seems to have been more feudal than those of the city states and centralized empires.) But it is contended that the pattern here described gives on the whole a correct account of the structure of belief expressed by the actual devotions to any one of the major deities, including the Hittite—so far as the preserved material enables that structure to be determined. (In some instances, of course, notably in Ugaritic, very little devotional—as opposed to mythological—material has been preserved, but if any arguments are to be made from silence, they should be rather for than against the common pattern.)

Two specifications in the above claim require special notice: one is *structure of belief,* the other, *major deity.*

Any great religion, considered in detail, presents such a bewildering mass of particular practices and convictions as to seem to defy classification, but classification is none the less possible. A comparison with anthropology may be useful here: The average man who lives among and is constantly concerned with the members of one racial group, will be the first to deny that they all look alike, and will be able to prove his point by reference to innumerable particular differences as well as by appeal to his own undoubtedly expert opinion; but the anthropologist will none the less maintain that certain structures are typical of this racial group. This paper, then, is concerned with the underlying structure of belief, not with the accidents of expression.

The structure of belief reaches full development only in the cults of the major deities. No doubt much of the popular devotion was to minor deities, either of unimportant localities (e.g. Meres-ger, 381a–b) or specialists (e. g. Thoth, 379a, 476a). These, of course, were not usually exalted further than was necessary for the purpose for the worshiper. If the deity was by definition "He who does x," then, in calling on him to do x, one had only to remind him of his well-known power. But it should be noticed that within their own limits, these minor deities remain true to the general theological pattern, e. g. Meres-ger (see above) punishes her servant when he transgresses, shows her power, and then, on his repentance, shows her mercy and heals him. Notice, too, that her servant is devoted to her and addresses her and addresses her alone. So, for the scribe, Thoth is "my god" and "a shield about me," 676a.

9. All of the Egyptian hymns and prayers (365a to 381b) are concerned with single deities (the Pharaoh, of course, is a god), so are all but one of the Sumero-Akkadian hymns and prayers (383a to 392b). (The composition entitled "Prayer to Every God" should have been entitled "Prayer to Any God"—it is not addressed "to all gods in general" (p. 391a), but to that *one* god or goddess whom the petitioner supposes to be punishing him or her, and it is significant that the petitioner takes it for granted that this unknown deity is singular.) Even when two deities are worshiped simultaneously, as Bel and Beltiya in the Akkadian ritual, the prayers and praises are directed most often to one or the other *singly,* 332a–334a; contrast the magical formula 333b–334a. So in the Hittite rituals (346a–361b) though 9 of the 13 involve sacrifice or prayer to several gods *successively,* yet there are only 3 in which prayer is directed to several gods at *once.* So, too, of the Hittite prayers (393ff.) only 3 (section b of the plague prayers of Mursilis, the "Prayer to be Spoken in an Emergency" and the "Prayer of Arnuwandas") are really directed to many deities. The others, though several of them contain incidental references to a number of gods, are primarily directed, each one, to one single divine being. So, too, most of the prayers put in the

mouths of mythological characters or found in the mythological material: The Hittite ritual in the Telepinus myth (126b–128b), such prayers as there are in the Gilgamesh epic, the prayers in the Etana story, the prayers in the story of the two brothers, etc.

10. "King Apophia . . . made him Seth as lord, and he would not serve any god who was in the land except Seth." King Seqnen-Re, on the other hand, "relies upon no god who is in the entire land except Amon-Re, King of the Gods" (231b). The story is not historical, of course; what is historical is the fact that the author should consider such a procedure perfectly natural and use it as a point of departure for his story. Historical evidence of such behavior in Egypt is provided by the case of Akh-en-Aton. That his policy merely carried to an extreme a common tendency is suggested by many details, e.g., the practical absence, from the records of Thut-mose III (234b ff.) of reference to any god save Amon (and, of course, Thut-mose III himself.) Montu, the god of war, is occasionally mentioned, evidently by literary convention, but the actual direction of the war is wholly Amon's and there are dozens of references to him for every one to any other deity. Contrast the frequent appearances of Montu in the material of the next Pharaoh, Amen-hotep II. Outside Egypt, Mesha of Moab is almost exclusively devoted to Chemosh, Atrahasis has Ea as "his god" and "his lord" (106a–b) etc. (see the refs. above, ends of notes 8 and 9). Other instances of cities or individuals especially devoted to the worship of a particular god are numerous, e. g.: Mesopotamian: Esarhaddon to Ashur 290a ff.; Babylon to Bel 331a; a priest to Bel 333a; the poet to Ishtar (cf. the psalmist to Yahweh) 384b f. Egyptian: Hermopolis to Thot 379b, Heliopolis to Re 379b; Karnak to Amon 380a; Thebes to Amon, *ibid.* Hittite: Puduhepas to the sun goddess of Arinna 393a; Kantuzilis to the sun god 400b, a patient to Uliliyassis 350a (and see below end of n. 15).

11. Myths explain rites or practices: 8b–9a, 10b, 11a–b, etc.

12. Mythologically secondary or derivative deities who are declared greatest of the gods or ruler of the gods: Ashur 298a; Bel Marduk 62a, 332a f.; Enlil 337b; Ishtar 383a ff.; Isis 14a; Nanna-Sin 311a ff.; 386a f.; Ptah 5a; Shamash 387a; the sun goddess of Arinna 393b; Telepinus 397a. These passages illustrate, but by no means exhaust, the common practice. Even commoner is the representation of a mythologically minor deity as greater in some particular than one of his mythological superiors. More attention should be given the passages in which a foreign deity is referred to as greatest of, or ruler of, the gods: Anath (in Beisan, but by an Egyptian) 249b, Qedesh and Rashap (in Egypt) 250b, Marduk (in an Assyrian document) 299b, Marduk (for Cyrus) 315b. In most of these instances it is clear that the author has adopted the conventional rhetoric of the god's professional servants, which was evidently very much the same all over the ancient Near East. Theology, in these expressions, is a by-product of politeness. Just so, when the eloquent peasant appealed to the chief steward, he called him "greatest of the great" and attributed to him omnipotence, 408b.

13. El is the "creator of creatures" (132a ff.) but it is not certain that "creatures" here include the other gods. The Akkadian creation epic has at least five universal creators: Apsu (61a), Mummu-Tiamat (*ibid.*), Mother Hubur (62b), Ea (64a) and Marduk-Marukka (69b) (cf. Marduk-Aranunna "creator of the gods, his fathers" and Marduk-Shugurim, 71a–b). Elsewhere in the same literary tradition Anu and Mammi give birth to all the gods (111a ff.). Yet again it is Nanna who did so, 385a; again, Enlil, 50b. I doubt that for the purpose of this paper it is worthwhile to distinguish between a "father" of the gods and a "creator" of them. The Hittite Kumbarbis is "the father of all gods" 121b ff. Atun of Heliopolis is either father or creator of all other deities, 3a ff.; Ptah of Memphis created all other deities, 5a–b; Re created all things, including the gods, 6a ff., etc. Notice that Re himself has a father, Nun, 6b, 11a, 13a. Here one sees clearly the conflict between mythology (to which Re is only one figure in a genealogy) and local patriotism (which made him the supreme god and origin of godhead). Note 4 of p. 13 a recognizes this conflict but does not grasp its significance. (cf. the attribute of Marduk-Aranunna, above.)
14. Bel is sole lord, 333a; Nanna is unique, 386a; Amon is unique in nature, 365a, sole one, 366b ff.; Aton is sole god, 370b. Cf. the later Greek expression *heis Theos*—, which means approximately "—is a great god," *not* "—is the only god."
15. So H. Ranke, in his note on a Ptah inscription, *Altorientalische Texte zum Alten Testament,* ed. H. Gressmann, (Berlin, 1926), sec. 1, no. 4: "This is a typical example of local theology in ancient Egypt. In similar fashion the local divinity at Heliopolis and at certain of the other great temples of the country was set above all other divine beings and credited with their creation." The same process is visibly at work in Sumero-Akkadian hymns, but has not there achieved such full expression. Evidences of local loyalties, however, are numerous, e. g. Babylon's for Bel (331a ff.), Nippur's for Enlil (455b), etc. (see 53b ff. and n. 27 below). The intimate relation of Yahweh to a people rather than a place is paralleled most closely by the relation of Ashur to the Assyrians. The reader will, I trust, pardon the application of the term "local patriotism" to such tribal loyalties as well as to strictly local ones.
16. Examples of this line of thought in various stages of development: 365a–b (Amon-Re), 383a (Ishtar), 386a (Nanna), 71b f. (Marduk), Exod 15:11 and Ps 50:1 (Yahweh). The final step in the process is to dispose of the other gods. This may be done by reducing them to parts or names or activities of the great god (as in Egypt, 4a ff.), by reducing them to demons (as the Persians did, 317a), or by denying their existence altogether (as did II Isaiah). The choice of method was probably determined less by theology, or even by superstition, than by economic considerations. The various gods were sanctions of financial concentrations (esp. local temples) of which the beneficiaries were not inclined to deny their existence. It was probably the annihilation of such vested interests in Judea by the Babylonian conquest

(they seem to have survived the attacks of Josiah) which cleared the way for II Isaiah's theological centralization. That, however, was too much for Jewish common sense, which might abuse the concepts of divinity formed by men of other traditions, but would not wholly deny their correspondence to some objective fact. Therefore in this point, as in others, Hellenistic Judaism did not follow II Isaiah consistently, but adopted various explanations of the pagan gods, e. g. it followed the Persians and was itself followed by Christianity in explaining that they were demons. The rhetoric of II Isaiah was preserved as a literary exercise but, even by the Rabbis, was transferred from the deities to the idols, see S. Lieberman, *Hellenism in Jewish Palestine* (New York, 1950), p. 126, n. 60.

17. Gods who are worshiped or said to exercise power outside their own lands (those starred rule the whole world, or all mankind): *Amon-Re 6a ff. (All-Lord), 27b, 237a, 263a, 366b ff, etc.; *Ashur 275a, 281b ff.; Anath, Astarte, Baal 250a–b; *Aton 370a ff.; *Bel-Marduk 72b, 164a, 309a, 331a ff.; *Enlil 50b, 159b, 337b, 455b, 481b; The Hattian storm god 395a; *Ishtar 383ff.; Khonsu of Thebes 30b; *Nanna 385b; Ningirsu 269a; Qedesh and Rashap 250a–b; *Shamash 116b, 387b ff.; The storm god of Nerik 400a; *The sun goddess of Arinna 392a–b; *Telepinus 397a. This list has no pretention to completeness.

18. Amon-Re to various pharaohs 23b, 248a f., 251a, 263b. Enlil to Sargon 267b. The Assyrian rulers regularly claim to be "king of the world . . . king of all the four rims of the earth" 274b ff., and their kingship is ordained by the gods, esp. by Ashur, who also specifically orders their foreign conquests 275a ff., and helps them in the conquering 275b ff. The Assyrian formulae were taken over by the neo-Babylonians (vestiges in 307a and—applied by Cyrus to Nabonidus?—in 315b) and by the Persians (316a) who at first claimed to hold them from Marduk (*ibid.*), later from Ahuramazda (316b).

19. Amon gives Egypt to the kings of Cush, 448a. El is the god of Udum, but gives it to be harassed by Keret, 144a. The Hattian storm god "brought people of Kurustama to the country of Egypt," 395a. "Marduk . . . beheld with pleasure his (Cyrus') good deeds . . . and therefore ordered him to march against his (Marduk's) city Babylon . . . going at his side like a real friend." 315b. See also n. 49 below.

20. Gods who maintain the order of nature: Amon 366b ff.; Aton 370a ff.; Bel-Marduk 71a, 332b f.; Nanna 386a; Shamash 389b; Telepinus 397b.

21. Gods who back up the moral order by rewards and punishments: Amon 380a–b; Ashur 300a; Bel-Marduk 70b f., 316a; "The god" of Amen-em-opet 421ff.; "God" in Ahikar 429a–b; Hittite gods generally 355a; Shamash 388b f.; Telepinus 397a. for other refs. see below notes 35, 39, 43, 44.

22. Gods who pardon sin: Amon-Re 379b f.; Bel-Marduk 310a, 390a–b, 436b; the Hattian storm god 395b; Ishtar 385a; Sin 386b. It is necessary to

emphasize again that these lists are intended to be exemplary, not exhaustive, and that considerations of economy have necessitated their reduction to a minimum. Note also that they are derived from a small (but representative, or so the editors claim—pp. xiv ff.) selection of the total material. One should not, therefore, on the basis of these, exaggerate the difference between, say, Ishtar who pardons sin and Shamash who punishes it. As a matter of fact Shamash also pardons sin (117b) and Ishtar punishes it (385a) but, in the list above, only the most typical passages were cited. This note is intended to forestall any attempt to refute the argument of this paper by splitting up the major divine functions among various specialists. As a matter of fact, most of the major deities have most of the major functions. Consequently I have tried to give full illustration only of attributes frequently denied to the original Yahweh.

23. Gods identified with or compared to the sun: Amon 365a ff.; Aton 370a ff.; Bel-Marduk 331a ff.; Ishtar 384a–b; Shamash 387a–b; Sin 386b; Telepinus 397a.
24. Gods as fathers: Amon 365a ff.; Anu 390a; El 143a ff.; Enlil 72b, 390a, etc.; the Hattian storm god 357a–b; the Hattian sun god 401b; Nanna 385b; Telepinus 397a.
25. Gods as kings/queens: Amon 15a ff., 365a–b; Anu 101b; Ashur 281b; Ea 108a; El 133a; the Hittite gods 120a–b; Ishtar 383b f.; Marduk 307a, 332a; Nanna 385b.
26. Bulls: Amon 16a, 365a; El 129b ff.; Enlil 455b; the Hattian storm god 398b, Horus 244b f.; Ishtar (!) 384b; Nanna 385b.
27. His/her land/city/people: 365a ff., Egypt, of Amon; of Aton 370b; 369a Heliopolis, Thebes, Memphis; 347b, 398a Hatti land, of the storm god; 393b Hatti land, of the sun goddess; 390b Nippur etc., of Bel-Marduk. See also above, n. 15.
28. Egypt is the only daughter of Re 377a.
29. Sons: Adapa 101b; the Hittite king 357a–b, Keret 143a ff.; the Pharaoh (of Amon-Re) 4b, 23b, etc. (Ramses II claimed to be the son of Montu 256a, and Seth 257a, as well as Re, 257a. In such instances the purely conventional—i. e., rhetorical—nature of the relationship is clear.)
30. Servants: The Assyrian kings regularly execute the order of Ashur 275a ff.; Hammurabi, of Anum and Enlil, 164a, of Marduk 165b; Kantuzilis, of the sun god, 400b; Keret, of El, 144b; Mesha, of Chemosh, 320b; Mursilis, of the storm god, 394b ff., of Telepinus, 396b; Nabonidus, of Marduk, 310b; Nebuchadnezaar, of Marduk, 307a; Sargon, of Ishtar, 267b.
31. Favorites: Cyrus 316a, Esarhaddon 289a, Hammurabi 270b, Mursilis 203b, Nabonidus 313a, Ramses II 199a, Thut-mose III 235b.
32. Gods who cure diseases or do other material favors: Amon-Re 369b, Bel-Marduk 70b, the Hittite gods generally 352b, Ishtar 384a, the sun goddess of Arinna 393b; Tarpatassis 348b, Telepinus 397a.
33. See above n. 22.

34. Gods who comfort the afflicted or help the poor and oppressed: Amon 366a, Ishtar 383a, Marduk 436b, Shamash 391a, Telepinus 397a.
35. This is true not only of gods who are singled out as judges, e. g., Osiris 34a, Shamash 178a, Yamm 130a; but also of the major gods generally, e. g., Amon is the source of truth 372a, and requires truth 381a; slander and false accusation are "disliked by the gods" of Assyria 289a, baseness is an abomination to Ashur and Marduk *(ibid.);* further: Bel 70b, the Egyptian gods generally 410a, Sin 386b, Telepinus 397a. The justice of the gods appears especially in the actions of those who serve them. (E. g. the gods made Hammurabi king that he might establish justice, 704a; and the messiah, as servant of the Egyptian gods, will establish justice, 446a.) Also, in the claims of those who seek their favor. (E. g. the Egyptian "Protestation of Guiltlessness," 34a–36b, concludes, "I have done that which men said and that with which gods are content. I have satisfied a god with that which he desires. I have given bread to the hungry, water to the thirsty, clothing to the naked . . . I have effected justice for the Lord of Justice.") See further the evidence cited above, n. 21, and cross refs. there.
36. See above nn. 22 and 24.
37. Fear: Amon 11a, Anum and Enlil 164a, Ashur 285a, Hittite gods generally 394b, Ishtar 384a, Marduk 69b.
    Love: Amon 366a, Bel-Marduk 332b f., the Hattian sun god 400a f., Ishtar 383a, Shamash 388a.
38. Gods who establish cults or cult laws: The Akkadian gods generally 43b; Ea 68b; Marduk 69a f., 311a, 316b; Nanna 385b; Ptah 5b; Telepinus 397a.
39. Sumero-Akkadian kingship is of divine institution 43b, 265b; Egyptian likewise 4b f., 17a. Gods as givers of civil law or legal decisions: Bel 331a; Ishtar 384a; Shamash 388a ff.; Shamash, Sin, Adad and Ishtar 391a. Egyptian law is inadequately represented in *ANET,* as in the remains, but the Pharaoh appears elsewhere as the establisher of the laws given by the gods, e. g., H. I. Bell, *Egypt* (Oxford, 1948) p. 57 (Philometor I, where the title is a dynastic hand-me-down). The goddess Maat ("Truth" or "Justice") will not rest unless the king's decrees be enforced, 213a and n. 2 *ibid.* "The good ruler, performing benefactions for his father (Amon) and all the gods," is one who sets up justice, 251b. For Queen Hat-shepsut's statement that the Asiatics "ruled without Re, and he did not act by divine command down to the reign of my majesty" (231a) the translator (*ibid.* n. 4) proposes Gardiner's explanation that the Pharaoh "ascribed all his official acts to obedience to orders given him by the deity." This is what would be expected, given the practice elsewhere in the ancient Near East. All the law codes of ancient Near Eastern origin to which we have coherent preambles state in them the divine authorization of the law. Lipit-Ishtar "established justice in Sumer and Akkad in accordance with the word of Enlil," 160b; Enlil called him "to the princeship of the land in order to establish justice in the land" *(ibid.).* The bas-relief at the top of the Hammurabi stela shows Shamash

giving either the law or the order to write it. The prologue says, "Anum and Enlil named me . . . Hammurabi, . . . to cause justice to prevail in the land, to destroy the wicked and the evil, that the strong might not oppress the weak," 164a. The conclusion says, "By the order of Shamash, the great judge of heaven and earth, may my justice prevail in the land; by the word of Marduk, my lord, may my statutes have no one to scorn them," 178a.

40. Egyptian bread offerings 416a, oblations 417b, incense 420a, animal sacrifice 36b, 327a, 417b, 447a. El commands the sacrifice of sheep, goats and turtle doves, and libations of wine and honey, 143b. Hittite sacrifices involve the same general materials, though the rites seem to have been peculiar, 348a ff. The similarities of the sacrificial cult of Uruk to that described in the P material of the OT are clear, 343a ff. Even of later times, when the Jews were self-consciously insisting on their difference from the heathen, Lieberman can remark (*op. cit.*, p. 130), "There was a general pattern in the ancient world of temples and sacrifices . . . which the Jews shared."

41. The pig an abomination to the Egyptians, 10b; Sumero-Akkadian tabus 117a (eating abominations), 344b (materials tabu in the service of particular deities). Hittite tabus 207b ff., 400b. Later parallels, Lieberman, *op. cit.*, 164 ff., esp. 169.

42. T. J. Meek, *Hebrew Origins*, p. 74, finds Hebrew law closest to Canaanite (doubtless because so little is known of the latter) and the relation even between these one of gradual and indirect adaptation. It may be questioned whether even this be not an overstatement of the importance of the connection, for the details in which Meek finds clearest evidence of the influence (pp. 70–73, e. g. the law of the goring ox, with its recognition of the special case of the ox known to be dangerous and its substitution of a fine for a death penalty) easily admit of explanation by common cultural background and by the generally consistent pattern of cultural change from primitive societies, in which death is primarily an occasion of expiation and purification, to more advanced ones, which are more concerned with the financial loss it occasions.

43. The "Protestation of Guiltlessness," 34a ff., contains both civil (B 2, 4, 5) and ritual (A 21, 34) offences. Evildoers, whatever the evil, violate the law of Re, 8a. Those who neglect to punish the wicked will themselves be punished by the god (Shamash) 117a. The law of Hammurabi is the law of Shamash, 178b. See above, n. 39.

44. Gods punish offenders: Ashur 300a, the Egyptian gods generally 251b f., Enlil 95a, the Hattian sun god 400b, Hittite gods generally 208a, Marduk 266b, 315b. For the general presupposition, see esp. the prayer to any god or goddess, 391a ff. (cf. above n. 9).

Gods reward their worshipers: Ahuramazda 317a, Egyptian gods (even non-Egyptian rulers) 27b, Hittite deities 396a, Marduk 315b.

See also above, n. 21.

45. Gods want sacrifices: Akkadian 117a, Egyptian 36a, Hittite 124a.

46. "The Instruction for King Meri-ka-Re" 417b.
47. "The Instruction of Amen-em-Opet," the *locus classicus* of this "higher morality" has every appearance of having been produced by long accretion. The same tradition has also furnished most of the items in the "Protestation of Guiltlessness" 34a ff. For similar developments in the Mesopotamian tradition cf. 426b (recompense evil with good) and 430b (resist not evil and Shamash will reward you).
48. Oracles of Bel 331a, prophets in Egypt 30b and n. 19 *ibid.*, but the presence there of prophets in the ordinary sense of the word is known from references to prophecies (416a) and from the prophecies themselves (441 a ff.). Prophets of Baal and Astarte in Egypt 250a, n. 13; Assyrian kings act on oracles of Ashur 275a ff. Prophets (ecstatics) in the Gilgamesh epic 87a; Hittite prophets 396a; oracles of Shamash 388a; of Sin 386b.
49. The Egyptian gods punish Egypt by military defeat 251b; "God Enlil . . . gave the accumulated possessions (of his city) to the enemy" 337b; Marduk punished his land by subjecting it to Assyria 309a, he subjects it to Cyrus 315b; the Hittite gods leave their land to its enemies 396b; Omri "humbled Moab many years . . . for Chemosh was angry at his land" 320b. The other punishments are too common to illustrate, see the following note.
50. See the oracles and prophecies collected on pp. 441 ff. *passim.*
51. Enlil 481a, the coming destruction of Babylon, *Cuneiform Texts,* 13:49. Egypt is to be destroyed so thoroughly that Re must found it anew, 445a.
52. Hat-shepsut claims to be the fulfilment of a messianic prophecy, 231a. Several examples of such prophecies, 445b–452 b. It is hard to decide whether the customs at the accession of a new ruler imitate these prophecies more than the prophecies imitate the customs, or vice versa. For the customs —or, at least, the court rhetoric—in Egypt see 378b f., parallel Assyro-Babylonian material in R. F. Harper, *Assyrian and Babylon Letters,* vol. 1, (Chicago, 1892), no. 2.
53. H. A. Wolfson, *Philo* (Cambridge, 1947). By "system" I refer, of course, to Philo's foregone conclusions, not to the philosophy with which he justified them.
54. This supposition is made by R. H. Pfeiffer, *Introduction to the Old Testament* (New York, N. D. [1948]), p. 580, "Like other religions of antiquity, the religion of Israel before Amos was national in its appeal. Jehovah was the God of Israel, his jurisdiction limited to the land of Israel." Amos, because he extended Jehovah's jurisdiction over all nations, "marks the beginning of a new era in the history of religions" (*ibid.,* cf. notes 18–20 above.)
55. Pfeiffer, *op. cit.,* p. 359, thinks the teaching, put in the mouth of Nathan (2 Sam 12), "that Jehovah would not tolerate criminal actions and that his worship involved moral conduct" . . . "was truly revolutionary in the time of Solomon, when Jehovah was merely champion of Israel and still approved of bloody deeds as treacherous as those of Ehud (Judg 3:20f.) and

Jael (Judg 5:25f), and even later, through Elijah and Elisha, sanctioned the assassination of kings (I Kgs 19:15–17; II Kings 9)." To suppose a god indifferent to morality because he approves the murder of national enemies or of the patrons of his competitors (or because of his personal peccadilloes as recorded in mythology) is to misunderstand not only ancient, but a good deal of modern religion.

II

ISRAEL DRAWS ON ITS ENVIRONMENT

3

The Covenant of Grant in the Old Testament and in the Ancient Near East

Moshe Weinfeld

Two types of covenants are found in the Old Testament: the obligatory type reflected in the covenant of God with Israel and the promissory type reflected in the Abrahamic and Davidic covenants.[1] The nature of the covenant of God with Israel has been thoroughly investigated and recently clarified by a comparison with the treaty formulations in the ancient Near East.[2] The nature of the Abrahamic-Davidic covenant however is still vague and needs clarification. The present study suggests a new way of understanding the character of the Abrahamic-Davidic covenants and this by means of a typological and functional comparison with the grant formulae in the ancient Near East.[3]

Two types of official judicial documents had been diffused in the Mesopotamian cultural sphere from the middle of the second millennium onwards: the political treaty which is well know to us from the Hittite empire[4] and the royal grant, the classical form of which is found in the Babylonian *kudurru* documents (boundary stones)[5] but which occurs as such also among the Hittites[6] in the Syro-Palestine area,[7] and in the neo-Assyrian period.[8] The structure of both types of these documents is similar. Both preserve the same elements: historical introduction, border delineations, stipulations, witnesses, blessings and curses.[9] Functionally, however, there is a vast difference between these two types of documents. While the "treaty" constitutes an obligation of the vassal

Reprinted by permission from the *Journal of the American Oriental Society* 90 (1970):184–203.

to his master, the suzerain, the "grant" constitutes an obligation of the master to his servant. In the "grant" the curse is directed towards the one who will violate the rights of the king's vassal,[10] while in the treaty the curse is directed towards the vassal who will violate the rights of his king. In other words, the "grant" serves mainly to protect the rights of the *servant,* while the treaty comes to protect the rights of the *master.* What is more, while the grant is a reward for loyalty and good deeds already performed, the treaty is an inducement for future loyalty.

The covenant with Abraham, and so the covenant with David, indeed belong to the grant type and not to the vassal type. Like the royal grants in the ancient Near East, so also the covenants with Abraham and David are gifts bestowed upon individuals who excelled in loyally serving their masters. Abraham is promised the land because he obeyed God and followed his mandate (Gen 26:5; cf. 22:16, 18) and similarly David was given the grace of dynasty because he served God with truth, righteousness and loyalty (I Kgs 3: 6; cf. 9:4; 11:4, 6; 14:8, 15:3). The terminology used in this context is indeed very close to that used in the Assyrian grants. Thus in the grant of Ashurbanipal to his servant Bulta[11] we read: "Baltya . . . whose heart is devoted (lit. is whole) to his master, served me (lit. stood before me) with truthfulness, acted perfectly (lit. walked in perfection) in my palace, grew up with a good name[12] and kept the charge of my kingship." Similar formulations are to be found in connection with the promises to Abraham and David. Thus we read in Gen 26:4–5: "I will give to your descendants all these lands . . . inasmuch as Abraham obeyed me (*šâmaᶜ bĕqōlî*)[13] and kept my charge (*wayyišmōr mišmartî*), my commandments, my rules and my teachings,"[14] a verse preserving verbally the notion of keeping guard or charge (*iṣṣur maṣṣarti*) found in the Assyrian text. The notion of "serving perfectly" found in the Assyrian grants is also verbally paralleled in the patriarchal and the Davidic traditions. Thus, the faithfulness of the patriarchs is expressed by "walk(ed) before me" (*hithallēk lĕpānay;* Gen 24:40, 48:15 = JE; 17:1 = P) which is equivalent to the expression: *ina maḫriya ittalak/izziz* in the Assyrian grant. The P source adds to *hithallēk lĕpānay* the phrase *wĕhĕyēh tāmîm* (17:1) which conveys the idea of perfect or loyal service expressed in the Assyrian document by *(ittalak) šalmiš.*[15] According to P not only Abraham but also Noah was rewarded by God (Gen 9:1–17) for his loyalty which is expressed by the very phrases used of Abraham's devotion: *tāmîm hāyâ, hithallēk ʾet hāʾĕlōhîm* (6:9).[16]

David's loyalty to God is couched in phrases which are closer to the Neo-Assyrian grant terminology. Thus, the terms: "who walked before you in truth, loyalty[17] and uprightness of heart" (*hālak lĕpāneykâ beʾĕmet ûbiṣĕdāqâ ûbĕyišrat lēbāb;* 1 Kgs 3:6), "walked after me with all his heart" (*hālak ʾaḥăray bĕkŏl-lĕbābô;* 14:8), "a whole heart (like the heart of David)" (*lēb šālēm ([kilbab dāwid];* 15:31),[18] are the counterparts of the Assyrian terms: "with his whole heart" *(libbašu gummuru);* "stood before me in truth" *(ina maḫriya ina kināti izizuma);*[19] "walked with loyalty (perfection)" *(ittalaku šalmiš),* which come to describe the loyal service as a reward for which the gift was bestowed.[20]

In the grants from Ugarit the loyalty of the donee is expressed by terms like: "he exerts himself very, very much for the king his lord."[21] Similarly, in a gift deed from Susa of a husband to his wife we read: "it is given her as a gift because she took care of him and worked hard for him."[22] The same motivation occurs in a deed from Elephantine which reads: "I have turned my thoughts to you *(ʿštt lky)* during my lifetime and have given you part of my house. . . . I Anani have given it to Yehojišma my daughter in affection since she took care of me (supported me) *(lqbl zy sbltny)* when I was old in years and unable to take care of myself."[23] The verb *anāḫu* expressing the exertion of the vassal to his lord and the wife to her husband actually means to toil, to suffer, but in our context they denote exertion and devotion. The notion of exertion is sometimes completed by the verb *marāṣu* "to be sick" as, for instance, in a letter from El-Amarna where the vassal says: "Behold I exerted myself to guard the land of the king *(etanḫu ana nāṣar māt šarri)* and I am very sick" *(marṣaku danniš).*[24] In fact the verb *marāṣu* in Akkadian has also the meaning of "to care for" and so has the Hebrew *ḥlh*.[25] Held pointed out recently the correspondence of Hebrew *sbl* to the Ugaritic *zbl* "to be sick";[26] the same correspondence actually exists between *anāḫu* and *marāṣu* on the figurative level of these expressions.

In the light of all this we may properly understand Ps 132:1: *zĕkôr lĕdāwid ʾēt kŏl-ʿunnôtô,* which the Septuagint and the Syriac misunderstood by reading *ʿanwātŏ* ("his humility"), which does not fit the context. In line with what we have said above, it has to be understood as "his submissiveness[27] or devotion." To introduce God's promise to David the Psalmist depicts the devotion of David to God which found expression in his deep concern for the ark and this is what is meant by the opening prayer: "Remember to David all his submissiveness."[28] *Zĕkŏr lě-* here is the semantic equivalent of *ʿšt lě-* in the quoted Aramaic gift deed, which means "to take favorable thought."[29] The Akkadian *ḫasāsu,* the equivalent of Hebrew *zkr,*[30] likewise means "to think about" or to "consider"[31] and, in fact, occurs in this sense in the Neo-Assyrian grant quoted above. After describing the loyalty of his servant upon whom he bestows the grant, the Assyrian emperor says: *īna attašu aḫsusma ukîn ši-ri-[ik]-šu*[32] = "I raised my eyes thereunto, considered him (favorably) and established his gi[ft]." The establishing of God's grant to the Patriarchs is expressed by *hāqîm* which is the semantic equivalent of *ukîn* in the Assyrian grant.[33]

David's exertion for which he was granted dynasty is expressed then in Ps 132 by *ʿnh* which somehow corresponds to the discussed *anāḫu, marāṣu* and *ʿml.*[34]

In the deuteronomic historiography, however, David's devotion is expressed, as in the Neo-Assyrian grants,[35] in a more abstract way: "walking in truth," "acting with whole-heartedness and integrity," etc. The phraseological correspondence between the deuteronomic literature and the Neo-Assyrian documents is very salient in the description of the benevolence of God towards the Patriarchs and towards David. Thus, the Assyrian king before announcing the grant says: "I am the king . . . who returns kindness to the one who serves in obedience (lit. to the reverential) and (to the one who) guards the royal command."[36] This phrase is close to the Biblical phrase: "the God . . . who keeps his gracious promise *(habběrît wěhaḥesed)* to those who are loyal to him (lit. who love him) and guard his commandments" (Deut 7:9–12) which appears in connection with the fulfillment of God's promise to the Patriarchs. A similar phrase occurs in the context of the promise of dynasty to David: "who keeps his gracious promise *(habběrît wěhaḥesed)* to your servants who serve you wholeheartedly" (*hahōlěkîm lěpaneyka bēkōl-libbam,* I Kgs 8:23,cf. 3:6). The grant par excellence is an act of royal benevolence arising from the king's desire to reward his loyal servant.[37] It is no wonder, then, that the gift of the Land to Abraham and the assurance of dynasty to David were formulated in the style of grants to outstanding servants.

The grant and the treaty alike are named *běrît,* a word which conveys the general idea of an obligation concerning two parties, similar to *riksu* in Akkadian and *išḫiul* in Hittite. However, in the more developed and therefore more reflective sources like P and D one can find a certain distinction between the term for grant and the term for treaty.

As we have already seen, the deuteronomic sources refer to the Abrahamic and Davidic covenants as *habbĕrît wehaḥesed.* ("the gracious covenant") in contradistinction to the covenants of Sinai and the Plains of Moab which are referred to as *bĕrît* only. On the other hand, P reserved the term *bĕrît* for the grant whereas the treaty is referred to as *ʿēdût.*[38] This becomes especially clear when one compares the terms used for the tablets of the covenant in D and in P. D always uses the term *lûḥōt habbĕrît* while P uses in a very consistent manner the term *lūḥōt hā ʿēdût.* It is true, the word *bĕrît* is used in P also in connection with the Exodus (cf. Lev 26:45); what is, however, meant here is not the obligation of the people but the promise of God[39] to establish relations with the people by releasing them from Egyptian bondage.[40] One should admit that not fulfilling the commandments of God is considered violation of the covenant also by the Priestly author (Lev 26:15, 25), but the covenant in this case is not the sworn obligation of the vassal, which is never alluded to in P, but the solemn promise of God to establish a steadfast relationship with the people. Disobedience constitutes of course a violation of this relationship.

THE UNCONDITIONAL GIFT

Although the grant to Abraham and David is close in its formulation to the Neo-Assyrian grants and therefore might be late, the promises themselves are much older and reflect the Hittite pattern of the grant. "Land" and "house" (= dynasty), the objects of the Abrahamic and Davidic covenants respectively, are indeed the most prominent gifts of the suzerain in the Hittite and Syro-Palestinian political reality, and like the Hittite grants so also the grant of land to Abraham and the grant of "house" to David are unconditional. Thus we read in the treaty[41] of Hattušiliš III (or Tudḫaliyaš IV) with Ulmi-Tešup of Datašа:[42] "After you, your son and grandson will possess it, nobody will take it away from them. If one of your descendants sins (*u̯aštai-*) the king will prosecute him at his court. Then when he is found guilty . . . if he deserves death he will die. But nobody will take away from the descendant of Ulmi-Tešup *either his house or his land* in order to give it to a descendant of somebody else."[43] In a similar manner Muršiliš II reinforces the right of Kupanta-Kal to the "house and the land in spite of his father's sins."[44] A similar wording occurs in the royal decree of Tudḫaliyaš IV and Puduḫepa for the descendants of Šaḫurunuwas, a Hittite high official. There we read:[45] "Nobody in the future shall take away[46] this house from ᵈU-manava (or Tesup-manava), her children, her grandchildren and her offspring. When anyone of the descendants of ᵈU-manava provokes the anger of the kings . . . whether he is to be forgiven[47] or whether he is to be killed, one will treat him according to the wish of his master but his house they will not take away and they will not give it to somebody else."[48]

A striking parallel to these documents is found in a will of Nuzi[49] where it says: "Tablet of Zigi . . . in favor of his wife and his sons. . . . All my lands . . . to my wife Zilipkiashe have been given . . . and Zilipkiashe shall be made parent of the sons.[50] As long as Zilipkiashe is alive the sons of Zigi shall serve/respect her *(ipallaḫšunuti)*.[51] When Zilipkiashe dies the sons of Zigi shall receive their inheritance portions, each according to his allotment.[52] Whoever among my sons will not obey Zilipkiashe, Zilipkiashe shall put him in the house of de[tention],[53] their mark (on the head) shall be affixed and (they) will be put in (their) fetters,[54] but (their) right shall not be annulled[55] . . . and Zilipkiashe shall not give away anything to strangers."[56] The same conception lies behind the promise of the house to David and his descendants in 2 Sam 7:8–16 where we read: "I will establish the throne of his kingdom forever, I will be his father and he shall be my son, when he sins I will chastise him with the rod of men and with human afflictions but my grace will not be removed . . . your house and your kingdom will be steadfast before me forever, your throne shall be established forever."

The phrase "I will be his father and he shall be my son" is an adoption formula[57] and actually serves as the judicial basis for the gift of the eternal dynasty. This comes to the fore in Psalm 2 where we read: "he (=God) said to me: you are my son, this day[58] have I begotten you. Ask me and I will give you nations for your patrimony and the ends of the earth for your possession" (vv. 7–8).

Similarly we read in Psalm 89:[59] "I have found David my servant . . . with whom my hand shall be established, my arm shall hold him *ʾăšer yādî tikkôn ʿimmô ʾap-zĕrôʿî tĕʾammeṣĕnnû;*[60] . . . I will smash his adversaries before him and will defeat his enemies . . . he will call me 'you are my father[61] my god . . . and I will make him as my first born, the highest of the earthly kings. I will keep my grace forever and my covenant shall endure for him. Should his children forsake my law and will not follow my decrees . . . I will punish their rebellion with the rod and their sin with afflictions. But I will never annul my grace with him and shall not betray my pact[62] (with him). I will not profane my covenant and alter what came out of my lips."

"House" (= dynasty), land and peoples are then given to David as a fief and as it was the rule in the second millennium this could be legitimized only by adoption.[63] That this is really the case here may be learned from the treaty between Šupilluliumaš and Mattiwaza.[64] Mattiwaza, in describing how he established relations with Šuppiluliumaš, says: "(The great king) grasped me with [his ha]nd . . . and said: when I will conquer the land of Mittanni I shall not reject you, I shall make you my son,[65] I will stand by (to help in war) and will make you sit on the throne of your father . . . the word which comes out of his mouth will not turn back."[66] A similar adoption imagery is to be found in the bilingual of Ḫattušiliš I.[67] In this document, which actually constitutes a testament, we read:[68] "Behold, I declared for you the young Labarna: He shall sit on the throne, I, the king, called him my son,"[69] "he is for you the offspring of my Sun" (= he is for you the offspring of his majesty).[70] On the other hand, when he speaks of his rejected daughter he says: "she did not call me father I did not call her 'my daughter' "[71] which reminds us of Ps 89:27.

Ḫattušiliš I himself is similarly described as adopted and legitimized by the sun goddess of Arinna: "She put him into her bosom, grasped his hand and ran (in battle) before him."[72] According to Psalm 89, David is also grasped and held by God's hand as a result of which he succeeds in the battles with his enemies (vv. 22–26).[73] If the emendation of Ps 2:7[74] is correct, then the idea of the heir placed into the bosom of his adoptant also occurs in connection with David.[75] It is also not without significance that the promise of Šuppiluliumaš to Mattiwaza as well as God's promise to David (v. 35) are accompanied by the declaration that the suzerain will not alter his word. Ps 132:12 also says that "the Lord swore to David in truth from which he will not turn away."

The notion of sonship within the promise of dynasty comes then to legitimize the grant of dynasty. It has nothing to do with mythology; it is a purely forensic metaphor. The metaphor is taken from the familial sphere[76] as may be seen from the quoted Nuzi will. In this document the father decrees that in case of disorder the rebellious son might be chained and confined but his inheritance rights will not be cancelled. The same concept is reflected in 2 Sam. 17, where the phrase *hōkiaḥ bĕšēbeṭ* ("chastening with the rod") is used, which in other places occurs in a didactic context (cf., e.g., Prov 13:24, 23:14). Furthermore, on the basis of the comparison with the familial documents from Nuzi, the phrase rod of men *(ʾănāšîm)* and afflictions of the sons of man *(bĕnê ʾādām)* may be now properly understood. In the so-called *ṭuppi šīmti* documents from Nuzi published recently[77] and analyzed by Speiser[78] we find often, in connection with the provisions about obedience to the adoptive father,[79] phrases like: "if PN (the adopted child) fails to show respect for PN_2 (the adoptive father) then just as a man treats his son so too shall PN_2 treat PN."[80] In another document it says that "just as one treats the citizen of Arrapḫa, so should PN treat PN_2: he shall put fetters upon his feet, place a mark on his hand, and put him in the house of detention."[81] The intention is clear: the son given into adoption has the duties of a son (= respecting his parents) but has also the privileges of a son: he has to be treated like the son of a free citizen and not like a slave. This is implied in another document of this collection where the father says that the adoptive parent "may act as though she were I."[82] This kind of privilege for the adopted can be traced back to the Old Babylonian period. In a document of adoption by manumission the master of the manumitted slave says: "If Zugagu will say to his father Sinabušu 'you are not my father' they will impose upon him the punishment of the free born,"[83] i.e., he will not be enslaved but disciplined as the son of a free citizen.[84]

What is then meant in 2 Sam 7:14 is that when David's descendants sin they will be disciplined like rebellious sons by their father[85] but they will not be alienated. One must say that this lenient approach towards rebellious sons was not the rule in familial relationships in the ancient Near East. On the contrary, in most of the cases rebelliousness brought about the dissolution of sonship, be it a real son or an adopted.[86] In the quoted adoption documents from Nuzi we find that the adoptive parent may chastise the disobedient son and also disinherit him, if he wants.[87] Similarly we find that the Hittite suzerain did not always grant land unconditionally. In a land grant of Muršiliš II to Abiraddaš, the Hittite suzerain guarantees the rights of DU-Tešup, Abimardaš' son, to throne, house and land, only on condition that DU-Tešup will not sin *(uaštai-)* against his father.[88] The unconditional promise is therefore a special privilege and apparently given for extraordinary loyal service.

This privilege in connection with David is also reflected in the fact that David is given the right of the first born. As is now known to us from Nuzi, Alalaḫ, Ugarit and Palestine,[89] the father had the right to select a "first born" as well as making all his heirs share alike,[90] and was not bound by the law of primogeniture.[91] Needless to say that the selection of the first born elevated the chosen son to a privileged position in the family and thus entitled him to a double share in the inheritance. Indeed, the phrase *běkôr ʾetnēhû* means I will *appoint* him or make him first born, which speaks for a given right and not one acquired by nature.

In fact not only David is named the first born to God but also Israel is called by God "my son the first-born Israel" (Exod 4:22; cf. Jer 31:8) and as the adoption of David is aimed to legitimize the inheritance of nations, i.e. the Davidic empire, so is the adoption of Israel by God aimed to validate the gift of land. Though this is not expressed explicitly in the Pentateuch it is clearly indicated in a prophetic text (Jer 3:19) where we read: "I said I will surely[92] put you among the sons (= I will adopt you as a son) and give you a pleasant land, the goodliest heritage of the host of nations, and I said you shall call me my father[93] and you will not turn away from me." The phrase *ʾăšîtēk babbanîm.* ("I will put you among the sons") undoubtedly alludes to adoption as Ehrlich indicated[94] and as such anticipates the inheritance of the *land.*[95]

The use of familial metaphors in order to express relationships belonging to the royal-national sphere should not surprise us, since the whole diplomatic vocabulary of the second millennium[96] is rooted in the familial sphere. So, for instance, the relationship between the states is defined as *abbūtu* = fathership (suzerainty); *mārūtu* = sonship (vassalship); *aḫḫūtu* = brotherhood (parity relationship). The phrase: *itti nakrīya lū nakrata itti sālmīya lū salmata* = "with my enemy be an enemy, with my friend be a friend," which is so common in the Hittite-Ugaritic treaties[97] and is already found in the Elamite treaty of the third millenium B.C.,[98] is known to us from an Old Babylonina marriage contract in which we read: *zenî sa PN PN$_2$ izenni salāmiša isallim* = "PN$_2$ (the second wife) will be angry with whom PN (the first wife) will be angry, she will be on good terms with whom PN will be on good terms."[99] Similarly we read in a Mari adoption document: *damāqišunu idammiq* *lemēnišunu ilemmin* = "their joy will be his joy, their sorrow will be his sorrow."[100] The close relationship of familial and political alliances has also been seen long ago by N. Glueck[101] who says: "Allies had the same rights and obligations as those who were blood relatives."

The gift of land to Abraham and the gift of kingship to David are then formulated in the way Hittite grants used to be formulated and especially those bestowed upon privileged vassals. Contrary to the prevalent law in the Hittite kingdom,[102] in Ugarit[103] and in Alalaḫ,[104] according to which the property of the condemned is to be confiscated, in the cited documents the property of the condemned cannot be taken away.

It was the Deuteronomist, the redactor of the Book of Kings, who put the promise of David under condition (I Kgs 2:4, 8:25, 9:4f.) and so did Deuteronomy with the promise to the patriarchs.[105] The exile of Northern Israel and the destruction of Jerusalem and disrupting of the dynasty refuted, of course, the claim of the eternity of the Abrahamic and Davidic covenants and therefore a reinterpretation of the covenants was necessary which was done by putting in the condition, i.e., the covenant is eternal only if the donee keeps his loyalty to the donor. It is true, even in the pre-deuteronomic documents the loyalty of David's sons and the sons of the patriarchs is somehow presupposed[106] but it is never formulated as the condition for national existence as it occurs in the deuteronomic literature. In the JE source Israel is never threatened with destruction for violating the Law. The non-observance of the covenant will certainly bring punishment (Exod 23:33, 34:12) but no annihilation. Even the parenetic section of Exodus 19, which sounds like a condition, is in fact a promise and not a threat: "if you will obey me faithfully and keep my covenant you shall be my treasured possession.[107] Indeed all the earth is mine but you shall be to me a kingdom of priests and a holy nation."[108] The observance of loyalty in this passage is not a condition for the fulfillment of God's grace as in Deuteronomy (cf. 7:12f, 11:13f) but a prerequisite for high and extraordinary status.

The priestly Code also, in spite of the curses in Leviticus 26 and the threat of exile there, does not end with the breach of the covenant but on the contrary it has God saying: "Even when they are in the land of their enemies I will not reject them or spurn them so as to destroy them, violating my covenant with them *(lĕhāpēr bĕrîtî 'ittām)*. I will remember in their favor[109] the covenant with the ancients *(wĕzākartî lāhem bĕrît riʾšōnîm,*" Lev 26:44–45). Deuteronomy however concludes chap. 28 with the threat that the people will be sent to Egypt and no allusion to the grace of the covenant is made.[110]

In regard to the Davidic covenant, it should be admitted that the conception of conditionality is implied in Psalm 132 (v. 12) which seems to be an ancient Psalm. It is indeed possible that alongside the conception of unconditional promise of the dynasty there was also in existence the concept of a conditional promise.[111] The conception of conditionality might have especially developed after the division of the kingdom. However, this ambiguous approach could not have been maintained after the fall of Judah. The Deuteronomist who was active at the time of the destruction and Exile therefore turned the conditionality into a dogma and built his ideology around it. As with most of the other motifs and ideas in the deuteronomic work so also with this idea there is nothing new in the very idea of conditionality. What is characteristic of the deuteronomic work is the transformation of this concept of conditionality into the dominant factor in the history of the monarchy. What is also characteristic of the Deuteronomist is the linking of the conditionality not only to *bĕrît* and *ʿēdût* as in Ps 132:12 which have the meaning of obligation in general[112] but especially to "the law of *Moses*" (*tôrat mōšeh,* cf. 1 Kgs 2:4; 2 Kgs 21:7–8).

THE COVENANT WITH ABRAHAM IN GENESIS 15

In the light of our analysis we may properly understand the nature of the covenant in Genesis 15. In this covenant it is God as the suzerain who commits himself and swears, as it were, to keep the promise.[113] It is he accompanied by a smoking oven and a blazing torch *(tannûr ʿāšān wĕlappîd ʾēš.)*[114] who passes between the parts as though he were invoking the curse upon himself. Though the torch and the oven are usually held to be related to the theophany[115] it seems that in this particular context they have a different meaning. In the *Šurpu* documents[116] we read about an oath taken by holding a torch[117] or about the oath of furnace, stove etc.[118] In the same series we find the oath of the slaughtered sheep and the touching of its wound.[119] It therefore stands to reason that like the cutting of the animals so also the torch and the oven are part of the procedure of taking the oath.

A similar oath occurs in the Abba-El—Yarimlim deed where Abba-

El, the donor, takes the oath by cutting the neck of a lamb (*kišād 1 immeru iṭbuḫ*) saying: "(May I be cursed) if I take back what I gave you."[120] In another document which completes the data of this gift we read: "On that day Abba-El in exchange for Irridi gave the city . . . On that day Yarimlim delivered (or brought up) to Ištar . . ."[121] which seems to reflect a situation similar to that of the covenant in Genesis 15, i.e., that the inferior party delivers the animals while the superior swears the oath.

In Alalaḫ as well as in Genesis 15 the animals slaughtered at the scene of the covenant are considered as sacrificial offerings.[122] That the act of cutting the neck of the animal is of sacrificial nature may be learned from another covenantal description in Alalaḫ where we read: "the neck of a sacrificial lamb was cut in the presence of PN the general."[123] A later Alalaḫian covenantal text[124] tells us about an offering[125] and a brazier[126] in connection with the oath that the parties had taken which reminds us of the offerings and the oven and torch in Genesis 15.[127] The ancient covenant in Exodus 24 is wholly based upon sacrifices and the secular patriarchal covenants are also ratified by sacrifices (Gen 21:27,[128] 31:54). From Mari we learn about different traditions of sacrifices.[129] The provincial tribes seem to prefer a goat[130] and a puppy for the ceremony while the king of Mari insists on killing an ass.[131]

In fact this tradition of covenantal sacrifices goes back to the third millennium B.C. Thus in the treaty between Naram-Sin and the Elamites (2300–2250 B.C.)[132] we find sacrifices offered and statutes erected at the Elamite sanctuary. In the treaty between Lagash and Umma, recorded on the stele of the vultures, we hear about sacrificing a bull[133] and two doves.[134] The doves remind us of the pigeon and the turtledove in Genesis 15 whereas the NINDÁ + GUD (= fattened bull) which equals Akkadian *bīru* is in many cases three years old[135] and may therefore be paralleled with Gen 15:9.[136]

It is true, in the ceremony of Genesis 15 the passing between the parts symbolizes the self-curse, similar to the act of seizing the throat,[137] but this does not nullify the sacrificial nature of the ceremony. On the contrary, the ritual adds solemnity to the oath. It is only in the covenantal ceremonies of the first millennium that the sacrificial element gradually disappears and gives way to the dramatic act. Thus, the Assyrian treaty and similarly the deuteronomic covenant become binding and valid not by virtue of the treaty ritual but by the oath-imprecation (the *māmītu*)[138] that accompanies the ceremony. The ritual itself—if it was performed—served only a symbolic and dramatic end: to tangibly impress upon the vassal the inevitable consequences that would follow from his infringement of the covenant. The treaty between Ashurnirari V and Matiʿilu of Bit-Agusi[139] even states explicitly that the ram is brought forward in the treaty ceremony not for sacrificial purposes, but to serve as a palpable example of the punishment awaiting the transgressor of the treaty (= Drohritus): "This ram was not taken from its flock for sacrifice (UDU.SISKUR) . . . if Matiʿilu (shall violate) the covenant and oath to the gods, then, as this ram, which was taken from its flock and to its flock will not return, and at the head of its flock shall not stand, so Matiʿilu with his sons, (ministers), the men of his city, shall be taken from their city, and to his city he shall not return, and at the head of his city he shall not stand . . . if he who is specified by name shall violate this covenant . . . as the head of this ram shall be struck off so shall his head be struck off."[140]

Like Saul, who cut a yoke of oxen into pieces and proclaimed; "Whoever does not come after Saul and Samuel, so shall it be done to his oxen" (I Sam 11:7),[141] so Bir Gaʾyah declared in his treaty with Matiʾilu: "(As) this calf is cut into two so may Matîʿel be cut into two."[142] Zedekiah's covenant with the people on the manumission of the slaves (Jer 34:8–22) is to be understood in an analogous manner. Hence, those passing between the two parts of the calf (v. 18) must have accepted the consequences ensuing from a violation of the oath-imprecation in this manner: "so may it befall me if I shall not observe the words of the covenant."[143] Dramatic acts of this sort were not, however, only performed with animals. In the Sefire treaty,[144] in the vassal treaties of Esarhaddon,[145] and in Hittite military oath-taking ceremonies[146] similar acts were performed with wax images and other objects.[147] Generally speaking, however, it appears that this act was not a requisite part of the ceremony. Many Hittite and Assyrian treaties make no mention of such acts and neither does the book of Deuteronomy. Apparently the oath-imprecation, which was recorded in the treaty document, was believed to be enough to deter the treaty party from violating the stipulations of the treaty.

Distinction should therefore be made between the covenant in Genesis 15 which similarly to the covenants of Alalaḫ and Mari preserves the sacrificial element alongside the symbolic one and between the covenant in Jeremiah 34 in which the ceremony, although performed before God, seems to be nothing more than a self-curse dramatized by a symbolic act. Another difference betwen Genesis 15 and Jeremiah 34 should also be mentioned and that is: while in Genesis 15 and similarly in the Abba-El deed it is the superior party who places himself under oath, in Jeremiah 34 and similarly in the treaty of Ashurnirari V it is the inferior who does it. As we already indicated, this difference stems from the fact that the Abba-El deed and Genesis 15 constitute a covenant of grant which binds the suzerain whereas Jeremiah 34 and similarly the treaty of Ashurnirari V are none other than commitments of the vassals to their masters.

THE LEGAL FORMULAE IN THE COVENANT WITH ABRAHAM

It has already been indicated that the legal formulae expressing the gift of land to Abraham are identical with the legal formulae of conveyance of property in the ancient Near East.[148] Especially instructive in this case are the formulations of conveyance in perpetuity. So, for example, the formulae: "for your descendants forever" (*lĕzarʿăkā ʾad ʿolām,* Gen 15:15), "for your descendants after you throughout their generations"[149] (*lĕzarʿăkā ʾaḥăreykā lĕdōrōtām,* Gen 15:7–8) are identical with the conveyance and donation formulae from Susa,[150] Alalaḫ,[151] Ugarit,[152] and Elephantine.[153] In Assyria and Babylonia proper we meet with different clichés in this context such as: *ana arkāt ūmē*[154] or *ana ṣāt ūmē*[155] which although not as close to *ʿad ʿolām* or *lĕdōrōtām* as the expressions of the peripheral documents (*adi dāriš*[156] etc.) nevertheless render the same idea of perpetuity.

The proclamation of the gift of land in Genesis 15 is also styled according to the prevalent judicial pattern. In the gift-deed of Abba-El to Yarimlim we read: "On that day (*ina ūmišu*) Abba-El gave the city . . ." Similarly we read in Genesis 15:18: "On that day (*bayyôm hahûʾ*) Yahweh concluded a covenant with Abraham saying: "To your offspring I give this land." The phrase "on that day" in these instances has certainly legal implications.[157] The delineation of the borders and the specification of the granted territories in vv. 18–21 indeed constitute an important part of the documents of grant in the ancient Near East.[158]

The formulation of the priestly covenant with Abraham, "to be unto you a God" (*liheyôt lĕkā leʾlōhîm,* Gen 17:7, 8) and the priestly formulation of the covenant with Israel, "I will be your God and you shall be my people" (*wĕhāyîtî lākem lēʾlōhîm wĕʾattam tihĕyû-lî lĕʿām* Lev 26:12, Exod 6:7; cf. Deut 29:12), is taken from the sphere of marriage/adoption legal terminology[159] like its Davidic counterpart in 2 Sam 7:14.

The Covenant with Abraham and the Covenant with David are indeed based on a common pattern and their literary formulation may have the same historical and literary antecedents.[160] The promise of the land to Abraham is preceded by the promise of progeny (Gen 15:4–5) and the latter is formulated in the way the promise of the dynasty is phrased in 2 Sam 7:12: *ʾăšer yēṣēʾ mimmeyka.*[161] Similarly the promise of a great name to Abraham (*waʾagaddĕlâ šĕmekā*, Gen 12:2) sounds like 2 Sam 7:9: "David will have a name like the name of the great ones of the earth" *(kĕšēm haggĕdōlîm ʾăšer bāʾāreṣ).*[162] As I have shown elsewhere,[163] the greatness of the name has political significance,[164] a thing which also finds expression in the Genesis traditions, which apparently had been crystallized under the impact of the united monarchy.[165]

The priestly source in Genesis goes even further and combines the promise of land with the promise of dynasty. To the promise of progeny he adds that "Kings shall come out from you" (17:6, 16, 35:11), which sounds like a promise of dynasty.

THE GRANT OF HEBRON TO CALEB

On the basis of the grant typology, discussed here, we may properly understand the nature of some other promises and bestowals in the Old Testament. Thus, the accounts of the conquest inform us about the gift of Hebron to Caleb (Josh 14:13–14, Judg. 1:20; cf. Num 14:24, Deut 1:36).[166] The reason for the gift was the faithfulness of Caleb during his mission with the spies: "because he filled up after the Lord" (*yaʿan kî millēʾ ʾaḥărê yhwh ʾĕlōhê yiśrāʾēl*, Josh 14:14; cf. vv. 8, 9 and Num 14:24, 32:11–12, Deut 1:36), a phrase which is semantically equivalent to *heyēh tāmîm* (= be perfect i.e., wholly devoted) of the Abrahamic covenant and *hāyāh šālēm* of the Davidic covenant. Furthermore as in the Abrahamic-Davidic covenants and in the grants of the ancient Near East so also in the Caleb gift we find the conventional formulae of conveyance in perpetuity: "to you and your descendants forever" (*lĕkā . . . ûlĕbāneyka ʿad-ʿôlām*, Josh 14:9).

Granting a city or a territory to the one who excelled in the king's expedition is indeed very common in the *kudurru* documents[167] and the case of Caleb has therefore to be considered as a grant although we don't know whether the grant reflects an authentic historical fact of the times of the conquest or is rather a back projection of later times.

Clements[168] suggested that Hebron was the birth place of the traditions of the Abrahamic and Davidic covenants. The tradition about the grant to Caleb is certainly rooted in Hebron. It therefore seems plausible that the tradition of the grant of Hebron to Caleb had been transmitted by the same circle which transmitted the tradition of the Abrahamic-Davidic covenants.

THE GRANT OF PRIESTHOOD AND PRIESTLY REVENUES

The documents of grant in the ancient Near East also include grants of status: *maryannu*-ship,[169] priesthood,[170] etc. The priesthood of Aaron in Israel had also been conceived as an eternal grant. Thus we read in Num 25:12–13: "Phinehas, son of Eleazar son of Aaron the priest, has turned back my wrath from the Israelites by displaying among them his passion for me . . . say, therefore, I grant him my pact of friendship *bĕrît šālôm*. It shall be for him and his descendants after him a pact of priesthood forever (*bĕrît kĕhunnat ʿôlām*)." As in other grants so also here the grant is given for showing one's zeal and devotion for his master; and like the other grants so also the gift of priesthood is given in perpetuity.[171] In other biblical texts which do not follow the rigid distinction (of the priestly code) between priests and Levites, but rather adopt the deuteronomic attitude of priests and Levites as one group, the grant applies to the whole tribe of Levi. Thus, we read in Malachi 2:4f: "that my covenant might be with Levi . . . my covenant was with him of life and well being *(haḥayyîm wĕhaššālôm)*." In the continuation an indication is also found about the loyalty and devotion of Levi which is similar in its phraseology to the descriptions of the loyalty of Abraham and David:[172] "he walked with me (= he served me) with integrity and equity" (*bĕšālôm ûbĕmîšôr hālak ʾittî,* v. 6).[173] The eternal covenant with Levi is also mentioned alongside the covenant with David in Jer 33:17ff.

Priestly revenues in the ancient Near East were also subject to grants and royal bestowals. This is indeed also reflected in Israel. The holy donations assigned to the Aaronide priesthood are formulated in the manner of royal grants: "All the sacred donations of the Israelites, I grant them to you and to your sons as a perquisite,[174] a due for all time" (*lĕkŏl-qôdĕšê bĕnê yiśrāʾēl lĕkā nĕtattîm lĕmŏšḥâ ûlĕbāneykâ lĕḥŏq-ʿôlām,* Num 18:8, cf. Lev 7:34ff.) and in a slightly different formulation: "all the sacred gifts that the Israelites set aside for the Lord I give to you, to your sons . . . as a due forever, it shall be an everlasting salt covenant . . . for you and your offspring as well (v. 19)."

Similarly the tithe which, according to Num 18:21f., belongs to the Levites, was also given to them as a grant for their service: "And to the children of Levi I grant all the tithe in Israel for an inheritance in return for the services that they perform" (*ḥēlep ʿăbōdātām ʾăšer-hēm ʿōbĕdîm).* Grants of the tithe of a city to royal servants are actually known to us from Ugarit, as we read for instance in the grant of Ammistamru II.[175] "Ammistamru granted everything whatsoever (that belongs to the city) to PN . . . forever for his grandsons: his grain, and his wine of its tithe."

The connection of the Aaronites and the Levites to Hebron has been recently pointed out[176] and we may suppose therefore that the "Sitz im Leben" of the grant to Aaron and the Levites is rooted in Hebron like the other grant traditions discussed.

As we have shown, the grants to Abraham, Caleb, David, Aaron and the Levites have much in common with the grants from Alalaḫ, Nuzi, the Hittites, Ugarit, and Middle-Babylonian *kudurru's,* i.e., mainly in documents from the second half of the second millennium B.C. This fact and the possible link of the mentioned Israelite grants to Hebron, the first capital of David's kingdom, may lead us to the contention that it was Davidic scribes who stood behind the formulation of the covenant of grant in Israel.

APPENDIX: THE ABRAHAMIC COVENANT IN THE PRIESTLY SOURCE

Clements[177] argues justifiably for the dependence of the Abrahamic covenant in P upon the Davidic covenant. Following the Wellhausenian view about the lateness of P, however, he explains this dependency as a post-exilic reinterpretation of the Abrahamic covenant. This can hardly be maintained. First, the Davidic royal tradition is already reflected in the JE Abrahamic covenant, as Clements admits. Why then can we not simply say that P follows this tradition, to which it is literally attached?

Secondly, as Y. Muffs has shown,[178] D's covenant formula in Deut

26:17f. is actually a reworking of P's covenant formula ("I shall be your God and you shall be my people"), the difference being only this, that in P the covenant relationship is one-sided, i.e., the initiative is God's: it is God who adopts the people,[179] whereas in Deuteronomy Israel takes an active part in establishing the relationship with God: Israel affirms that Yahweh is its Lord (26:17).

Thirdly, what could have prompted an exilic or post-exilic author to create an ideal of "kings coming forth from Abraham" or of Abraham as "father of the host of nations" which we find in the priestly source (Gen 17:5–6, 16, 35:11, 28:3, 48:4)? As a matter of fact, these ideas go hand in hand with the concept of dominion over the nations expressed in the Yahwistic source (Gen. 27:29).

As evidence for the contention that the Abrahamic covenant was formulated in the Davidic court circle, Clements rightly refers to the old Jerusalemite Psalm 47, in which we hear about "the chiefs of the peoples assembling together, the people[180] of the God of Abraham" (v. 10). He overlooks, however, the fact that this idea has been preserved not in the JE tradition, but in the priestly tradition where Abraham is called "Father of the host of nations" and where he is promised "that Kings shall stem from him." The phrase "the God of Abraham" is found elsewhere only in a Patriarchal context and its appearance in this psalm can be explained only on the basis of its reference to Genesis 17. The rulers of the nations gather in Jerusalem for the celebration of God's kingship by virtue of their belonging to the God of Abraham who was the father of a host of nations. This psalm undoubtedly reflects the political situation of the Davidic Empire when Ammonites, Moabites, Edomites, Ishmaelites and Midianites were vassals of Israel,[181] a fact indicated by verse 4. Here God is depicted as subduing peoples and nations under Israel *(yadbēr ʿammîm taḥtênû ûlĕʾummîm taḥat raglênû)*, an idea found in Isaac's blessing of Jacob: "let peoples serve you and nations bow to you" (Gen 27:29) which is reminiscent of the language of David's victory psalm (Ps 18:44, 48; cf. 2 Sam 22:44, 48).

The argument that the sign of the Abrahamic covenant in P, the circumcision, reflects the period of exile when circumcision assumed a new importance in Jewish life can hardly be maintained.[182] Circumcision has to be observed, according to P, also by the Ishmaelites. The question then to be posed is who would be interested in the time of the exile, when circumcision became the badge of Jewish distinctiveness, to share this very symbol of distinctiveness with the Ishmaelites? Wouldn't it be more reasonable to say: the priestly scribes who based their theology on "signs of covenant" used in the covenant with Abraham, "the father of a host of nations," a sign which absolutely marked these nations? As is well known, in contradistinction to the Philistines, Hittites, Mesopotamians, etc. who were not circumcised, the ethnic groups which belong to the family of the Hebrews like the Ishmaelites, Midianites, Edomites, Ammonites and Moabites were circumcised[183] and thus could be considered as forming the family of Abraham. As may be learned from Genesis 34, circumcision had been considered also in old Israel as a prerequisite for joining the people of Israel. No wonder, then, that the circumcised peoples were looked upon as having a common ethnic-cultural background and stemming from Abraham "the father of a host of nations."

NOTES

1. See, e.g., most recently R. E. Clements, *Abraham and David* (Studies in Biblical Theology, Second Series No. 5, 1967). Cf. also N. Lohfink, *Die Landverheissung als Eid* (Stuttgarter Bibelstudien 28, 1967); F. C. Fensham, "Covenant, Promise and Expectation in the Bible," *ThZ* 23 (1967) 305–22.
2. Cf. G. Mendenhall, "Covenant Forms in Israelite Tradition," *BA* 17 (1954) 50ff.; K. Baltzer, *Das Bundesformular* (WMANT 4, 2d ed., 1964); D. J. McCarthy, *Treaty and Covenant* (AnBib 21, 1963); M. Weinfeld, *Deuteronomy and the Deuteronomic School* (1972).
3. A. Poebel, *Das appositionell bestimmte Pronomen der 1. Pers. Sing. in den Westsemitischen Inschriften und im A.T.* (AS 3; 1932) already suggested that the promise to the Patriarchs bears the character of an oral "Belehnungsurkunde." His suggestion was based on the syntactical function of the phrase "I am the Lord" preceding the promise of the Land. According to his view, the phrase "I am the Lord" is a typical opening phrase of royal documents in the ancient Near East which has to be connected with the following and to be understood as: "I am the one who did so and so, etc." and not "I am the Lord" as an independent phrase of self-introduction. This assumption, which seems to be correct, is not sufficient to bear out the thesis about the identity of the Abrahamic-Davidic covenant with the grant. We must, however, give credit to Poebel for his penetrating glance into the nature of the covenant in Israel which, although expressed in one sentence, antedated Mendenhall (see note 2) by 22 years. Cf. his summation of the syntactical discussion: "Wir sahen auch, dass in jedem einzelnen Fall die

Anwendung der dem Herrscher und Urkundenstil entlehnten Formell durchaus der Situation angemessen war, weil die Verheissung, den Nachkommen der Erzväter das Land Kanaan zu verleihen, gewissermassen eine mündliche Belehnungsurkunde ist und auch die Bundesschliessung Gottes mit Israel nach der Absicht der Erzähler ähnlich wie der Abschluss eines Bündnisses zwischen politischen Staaten oder Herrschern unter dem Gesichtspunkt eines rechtlichen Staatsaktes betrachtet werden soll" (p. 72).

4. Cf. E. Weidner, *Politische Dokumente aus Kleinasien: Die Staatsverträge in akkadischer Sprache aus dem Archiv von Boghazköi* (Boghazköi Studien vol. 8, 1923); J. Friedrich, *Staatsverträge des Hatti Reiches in hethitischer Sprache* (*MVAG* 31 [1926], 34 [1930]).
5. L. W. King, *Babylonian Boundary Stones* (1912). Cf. also F. X. Steinmetzer, *Die Babylonischen Kudurru (Grenzsteine) als Urkundenform* (Studien zur Geschichte und Kultur des Altertums, vol. 11, 1922).
6. Cf. H. Gueterbock, *Siegel aus Bogazköy* (AfO Beiheft 5, 1940), especially pp. 47–55 dealing with the "Landschenkungsurkunden."
7. Cf. the gift-deed of Abba-El to Yarimlim (D. J. Wiseman, *AT* no. 1*, complemented by the tablet ATT/39/84 published by Wiseman in *JCS* 12 [1958] 124ff., for which see also: A. Draffkorn, *JCS* 13 [1959] 94ff.) and the Ugaritic donation texts in PRU II and III.
8. Cf. *ARu* nos. 1–30.
9. For the structure of the Hittite treaties, cf. V. Korošec, *Hethitische Staatsverträge* (1931) and for the structure of the *kudurru* documents cf. F. X. Steinmetzer, *Die Babylonischen Kudurru.*
10. Cf. the *kudurru* inscriptions in L. W. King, *Babylonian Boundary Stones* and the Neo-Assyrian grants in *ARu* nos. 1–30. A peculiar threat occurs in an Old Babylonian grant from Hana: *bāqir ibaqqaru . . . kupram amman qaqqassu ikkappar* = "whoever challenges the gift, his head will be covered with hot pitch," M. Schorr, *Urkunden des altbabylonischen Zivil- und Prozessrechts* (VAB 5; 1913) no. 219:17–24. At times the donor takes upon himself a conditional self-curse as for instance in the grant of Abba-El where Abba-El takes the following oath: *šumma ša addinukummi eleqqû* = "(May I be cursed) if I take back what I gave you" (Wiseman, *AT* 1*:16–20). For the conditional oath sentences, see W. von Soden, *GAG,* 185 g, i.
11. *Baltya . . . (ša) libbašu gummuru ana bêlijšu, ina maḫriya ina kināti izi[zūma], ittalaku šalmiš qirib ekallija, ina šumi damqi irbûma, iṣṣarti šarrūtiya, ARu* 15:13–17, cf. 16:13–17, 18:16–20.
12. Translation of this phrase according to Y. Muffs, *Studies in Aramaic Legal Papyri from Elephantine* (SD 8, 1969) pp. 134, 203, who joins *qirib ekalliya* with *ittalaku šalmiš* and not as the *CAD* (vol. 3 [D] p. 69) reads: *qirib ekalliya ina šumi damqi irbûma* = "he grew with a good name in my palace." A support for Muffs' reading may be found in Ps 101:2, where *hithallēk bĕtōm lēbab* (walk with integrity) joins *bĕqereb bêtî* (within my house/palace).

13. Cf. in the Amarna letters: *amur arda ša išmē ana šarri bêlišu,* "behold, the servant who obeys the king, his Lord" (*EA* 147:48f.).
14. There is nothing deuteronomic in this verse. *Šāmaᶜ bĕqôl,* along with other terms expressing obedience, is very frequent in the deuteronomic literature which stresses loyalty to the covenant, but this does not mean that the terms as such were coined by the deuteronomic school. The combination of *ḥûqqîm wĕtôrôt,* "laws and teachings," is never found in the deuteronomic literature. Deuteronomy always uses Torah in the singular and usually with the definite article: *hattôrâ,* "the Law." On the other hand, this combination is attested in JE (Exod 18:16,20). The origin of *šāmar mišmeret* is not deuteronomic; see Weinfeld, *Deuteronomy and the Deuteronomic School,* Appendix A.
15. Cf. Mal 2:6: *bĕšālôm ûbĕmîšôr hālak ᵓittî,* which means "he served me with integrity and equity"; see Y. Muffs, *Studies,* pp. 203–4 (following H. L. Ginsberg). This phrase occurs in connection with the grant of priesthood to Levi (see below). For the interpretation of *ittalaku šalmiš* as "served with integrity" and not as Koehler-Ungnad translate, "in good or peaceful condition (wohlbehalten)," see Y. Muffs, ibid., p. 203. *Alāku/atalluku šalmiš* is equivalent to *hôlek battōm,* "walk with integrity" (Prov 10:9), and to *hithallēk bĕtōm lēbab,* which in Ps 101:2 is connected with *bĕqereb bêtî* (within my house/palace) as in *ARu* 15:13–17; see note 11.
16. However, in contradistinction to the JE source where the loyalty of the Patriarchs is a matter of the past, in the priestly source it is anticipated.
17. *Ṣĕdāqâ* here has the meaning of loyalty and faithfulness as does *ṣdq* in a similar context in the Panamuwa inscriptions (*KAI* 215:19, 216:4–7, 218:4) where *bṣdq ᵓby wbṣdqy hwšbny mrᵓy . . . ᶜl krsᵓ ᵓby* has to be understood: "because of my father's and my own loyalty, the king has established me on the throne of my father"; cf. H. Donner, *MIO* 3 (1955) 96ff. Virtually the same idea is expressed in 1 Kgs 3:6: "You have done grace with your servant David my father as he walked before you in truth, loyalty and uprightness of heart and you kept your grace (=promise) and gave him a son to sit upon his throne as at present."
18. Cf. also 2 Kgs 20:3.
19. As in Hebrew so also in Akkadian *hithallēk/hālak lipnê, ina pāni alāku/atalluku* is similar in connotation to *ᶜāmad lipnê, ina pāni uzzuzu,* but the latter seems to have a more concrete meaning: praying, interceding, worshiping and serving whereas the former is more abstract. Cf. Jer 18:20. For discussion of these terms, cf. F. Noetscher, *'Das Angesicht Gottes schauen,' nach biblischer und babylonischer Auffassung* (1924) pp. 83ff., 112f.
20. The close affinities to the Neo-Assyrian phraseology in these verses may be understood in the light of an identical chronological and cultural background. All of these verses appear in a deuteronomic context which means that they were styled in the seventh century, a period in which the abovementioned documents were written. On the affinities of the deuteronomic

literature to the Neo-Assyrian literary tradition, see Weinfeld, *Deuteronomy and the Deuteronomic School.*

21. *Ana šarri bêlišu aniḫ danniš dannišma,* PRU III, 140:27–30; cf. *ana šarri aniḫ/ītanaḫ,* PRU III, 84:24, 141:29, 108:16, 110:7. Cf. the Barrakib inscription: *wbyt ʾby [ʿ]ml mn kl*= "and my father's house exerted itself more than anybody else" (*KAI* 216:7–8), which occurs in a passage expressing the loyalty of Barrakib to Tiglath-Pileser (see above, note 17). Two different interpretations have been given to the phrase *wbyt ʾby [ʿ]ml mn kl,* but neither of these is satisfactory. F. Rosenthal (*ANET*[2] p. 501) following H. L. Ginsberg (*Studies in Koheleth,* 1950, p. 3, note 2a) translates: "the house of my father has profited more than anybody else," but this does not fit the immediate context which is concerned with loyalty to Tiglath-Pileser. The same argument applies to B. Landsberger's translation which is diametrically opposed to Rosenthal's translation: "the house of my father was more miserable than anybody else" (*Samʾal, Studien zur Entdeckung der Ruinenstätte Karatepe,* 1948, p. 71). Besides, the latter translation is contradicted by the Panamuwa inscription (*KAI* 214:9), a fact which Landsberger was not unaware of (ibid., note 187). Donner's translation, which we have adopted, is the most satisfactory and is now supported by the Akkadian parallels. It seems that *ʿml* is the semantic equivalent of *anāḫu.* Similarly *mānaḫātu* is "results of toil" as is also the Hebrew noun *ʿml;* for Hebrew *ʿml* in this sense, cf. H. L. Ginsberg, *Qohelet* (Tel Aviv—Jerusalem, 1961, in Hebrew), pp. 13–15.
22. *Aššum ittišu īnaḫu dulla ill[iku] nadišši qīš[ti], MDP* 24, 379:7f.; for an analysis of this document see J. Klíma, *ArOr* 28 (1960) 39.
23. E. Kraeling, *The Brooklyn Museum Aramaic Papyri* (1953) 9:16–17.
24. *EA* 306:19–21.
25. Cf. especially 1 Sam 22:8: *wĕʾên-ḥōleh mikkem ʿālay,* "and nobody cares about me," in the context of loyalty to the king. Cf. also Amos 6:6, *wĕlōʾ neḥlû ʿal-šēber yôsēp* ("they do not care about the breach of Joseph") and Jer 12:13, *zārĕʿû ḥiṭṭîm wĕqōṣîm qāṣārû neḥlû lōʾ yôʿîlû* ("they have sown wheat and have reaped thorns, they exerted themselves but did not profit").
26. M. Held, "The root ZBL/SBL in Akkadian, Ugaritic and Biblical Hebrew," (Speiser Memorial Volume) *JAOS* 88 (1967) 93.
27. Cf. *wʿn ʾnk ʾrṣt ʿzt*= "I subjugated mighty countries" in the Azittawada inscription (*KAI* 26:18); cf. Mesha inscription l. 5 and Exod 10:3: *ʿad-mātay mēʾantā lēʿānōt mippānāy,* which has to be rendered: "how long will you refuse to surrender before me." Cf. also Gen 15:13, Num 24:24, 2 Sam 7:10, 1 Kgs 11:39, Nah 1:12.
28. The notion that the promise of dynasty to David is to be seen as a reward for his devotion seems to lie behind the juxtaposition of chapters 6 and 7 in the second book of Samuel.
29. Cf. H. L. Ginsberg, "Lexicographical Notes," *Hebräische Wortforschung* (Festschrift W. Baumgartner, VTSup 15, 1967) pp. 81–82.

30. See, e.g., *EA* 228:18–19: *liḫsusmi* glossed by *yazkurmi;* cf. M. Held, AS 16 (B. Landsberger Festschrift, 1965) p. 399. On the root *zkr* cf. P. A. H. de Boer, *Gedanken und Gedächtnis in der Welt des A.T.* (1962); B. S. Childs, *Memory and Tradition in Israel* (1962); W. Schottroff, *'Gedenken' im Alten Orient und im Alten Testament*[2] (1967).
31. See Y. Muffs, *Studies.*
32. *ARu* 15:19; 16:19; 18:22. For the text, see Johns, *ADD* 647:19 and Peiser KB II, 583 (seventh line). Peiser (ibid., p. 566) and Koehler-Ungnad read after *ukin: ar-x-šu,* and Peiser even restores: *ar-[ḫu]-šu.* The context, however, demands something like "his gift" and therefore I suggest the reading *ši-ri* instead of *ar* and the restoration to: *ši-ri-[ik]-šu.*
33. Compare the Latin *foedus firmare*="to establish a pact"; cf. J. J. Rabinowitz, *Jewish Law* (1956) pp. 1–2.
34. See note 21. For the correspondance of *ʿml* to *ʿnh,* cf. Gen 41:51–52, Deut 26:7, etc.
35. See above note 20.
36. *Ana pāliḫi nāṣir amat šarrūtišu utirru gimilli dumqi* (*ARu* 15:6–7; 16:6–7; 18:9–10).
37. Cf. F. Thureau-Dangin, "Un acte de donation," *RA* 16 (1919) 118: "Ces titres de propriété sont généralement des actes royaux de donation dont le bénéficiare est, soit un enfant de roi, soit un prêtre temple, soit quelque serviteur que le roi veut récompenser."
38. For the term *ʿedūt,* cf. most recently B. Volkwein, *BZ* 13 (1969) 18–40.
39. The priestly conception of a promissory oath given by God at the time of the Exodus is also reflected in Ezek 20:6, cf. A. Jepsen, "Berith. Ein Beitrag zur Theologie der Exilszeit," *Verbannung und Heimkehr* (Festschrift W. Rudolph, 1961) p. 168; N. Lohfink, *Die Landverheissung,* p. 111.
40. See below.
41. In fact this document can also be considered as a grant and according to V. Korošec ("Einige juristische Bemerkungen zur Šaḫurunuva-Urkunde," *Münchener Beiträge zur Papyrusforschung und antiken Rechtsgeschichte* 35 [1945] 221, note 5) is something between a grant and a treaty.
42. KBo IV, 10, obv. 8–14; for translation see E. Cavaignac, *RHA* 10 (1933) 65–76 and cf. E. Laroche, *RHA* 48 (1948) 40–48 for a discussion of the date of this treaty. The connection between this treaty and the Davidic covenant has been seen by R. de Vaux, "Le roi d'Israel, vassal de Yahve," *Mélanges E. Tisserant I* (1964) pp. 119–33.
43. Cf. KBo IV, 10, rev. 21ff.: "Now as for what I, the Sun, have given to Ulmi-Tešup . . . I have engraved on an iron tablet and in future no one shall take it away from any descendant of Ulmi-Tešup, nor shall any one litigate with him about it; the king shall not take it, but [it shall belong] to his son. To another man's descendant they shall not give it." It seems that this iron tablet was the original gift-deed.
44. J. Friedrich, *MVAeG* 31 (1926), treaty no. 3 §7–8 (pp. 112–15), §21–22 (pp. 134–37).

45. KUB XXVI, 43 and 52. Cf. V. Korošec, "Einige juristische Bemerkungen" for analysis of this document.
46. *Ziladuu̯a arḫa lē kuiški dāi;* cf. the same formula in KBo IV, 10, vs. 11. Cf. *urram šērram mamman lā ileqqe ištu qāti* X in the grants from Ugarit written in Akkadian (PRU III passim) and *šḫr. ʿlmt bnš bnšm* (or: *mnk mnkm* "whoever you are") *l . yqḥnn . bd* PN in the Ugaritic version of the grants. Compare the conveyance formula from Elephantine: *mḥr ʾw ywm ʾḥrn lʾ ʾhnṣl mnky lmntn lʾḥrnn* = "on a future day I will not take it away from you in order to give it to others" (A. Cowley, *Aramaic Papyri of the Fifth Century B.C.* [1932] 8:18–19). On the correspondence between *urram šērram* and *mḥr ʾw ywm ʾḥr* see J. J. Rabinowitz, *Jewish Law,* p. 161. Hebrew *mḥr* and so *ywm ʾḥrwn* have also the meaning of future, cf. Gen 30:33, Exod 13:14, Deut 6:20, Josh 4:6,21, 22:24,27 for *mḥr* and Isa 30:8 for *ywm ʾḥrwn.* Cf. also the Neo-Assyrian formula: *ina šērtu ina lidiš* = "some time in the future"; see Y. Muffs, *Studies,* pp. 206–7.
47. *Duddunu* = "to forgive"; cf. recently A. Goetze, *JCS* 18 (1964) 93.
48. *Nat damēdani lē piu̯anzi;* cf. the Abba-El deed from Alalaḫ: *ana šanîm ul inaddin* = "he shall not give it to anyone else" (D. J. Wiseman, *JCS* 12 [1957] p. 128, l.63), and the Nuzi deed quoted below: *mimma ana awēli nakari la inandin* = "she shall not give anything (from the inheritance) to stranger" (HSS V, 73:27–28). Compare the deed from Elephantine quoted above (note 46): *lmntn lʾḥrnn,* "to give it to others."
49. *Excavations at Nuzi I,* HSS V, 73:1–28; cf. E. A. Speiser, *New Kirkuk Documents Relating to Family Laws AASOR* 10 (1930), no. 20 (pp. 51–52).
50. Read: *a-na a-bu-ti ša marê iteppuš* (11.10–11) with P. Koschaker, *OLZ* 35 (1932) 399f.
51. *Ipallaḫšunuti* has to be translated, "she shall respect them," but as Speiser pointed out (see, e.g., *Introd. to Hurrian,* pp. 206f.) this grammatical confusion is characteristic of the Hurrian scribes (cf. also recently Speiser, *JCS* 17 [1963] 66 to lines 21f.).
52. *U mārū ša Zigi attamannu kī emūqišu zitta ileqqū* = lit. "and the sons of Zigi, *whoever you are,* shall receive his inheritance portion according to his allotment." *Attamannu* here is the equivalent of the Ugaritic *mnk* (mn + ka) quoted above note 46. Cf. the Canaanite and Aramaic inscriptions *KAI* 13:3 *(my ʾt),* 225:5 *(mn ʾt),* 259:2 *(wmn zy ʾt)* and Zech. 4:7: *mî-ʾattâ har-haggādôl lipnê zĕrubbābel lĕmîšōr* = "whoever you are big mountain before Zerubabel, you will become a plain."
53. *Ina bīt nu-[pa-ri] inandin,* cf. E. Cassin, *RA* 57 (1963) 116 and *AASOR* 16 (1936) 3:40: *ina (bīt) nupari ittadanni;* 12:12: *bīt nupari* (on *neparu* in Mari and other Old Babylonian documents cf. A. Leo Oppenheim, *JNES* 11 [1952] 133–34). Compare HSS XIX, 19:29–30: *ina bīt kīli inandin* in a similar context, cf. also HSS XIX 39:23 and see below.
54. *Abbutašunu umaššaršu u in kurṣišunu* (GÌR-šu-nu, the determinative GIŠ before GÌR has been omitted, similarly È before *nupari* in *AASOR* 16, 3:40)

inandinu; cf. HSS XIX 19:28–30, 23:12–13, 32:9–10, 37:37–38, 39:21–23 *(abbutam šakānu).* On the meaning of *abbutu* in this context, see E. Cassin, *RA* 57 (1963) 116; E. A. Speiser, *JCS* 17 (1963) 65ff.

55. *Kirbāna lā iḫeppē* = lit. "lump (clod) of earth (symbolizing tablet of rights) will not be broken"; cf. E. Cassin, *JESHO* 5 (1962) 133.
56. See note 48 above.
57. Cf. C. Kuhl, "Neue Dokumente zum Verständnis von Hos. 2, 4–15," *ZAW* 52 (1934) 102ff.
58. *Hayyôm* "this day" indicates the formal initiation of a legal contract; cf. Ruth 4:9–10,14, Gen 25:33; see most recently G. M. Tucker, *CBQ* 28 (1966) 42–45. Compare S. E. Loewenstamm, *Tarbiz* 32 (1963) 313–16 for the formula *išu ūmi annīm* (= from today) in the Akkadian documents from Alalaḫ and Ugarit.
59. On the relationship of this Psalm to Nathan's oracle, see N. M. Sarna, "Psalm 89, A Study in Inner Biblical Exegesis," *Biblical and Other Studies* ed. A. Altmann (Philip W. Lown Institute of Advanced Judaic Studies, Brandeis University, 1963) pp. 29–46.
60. *Ḥzq* and *ʾmṣ*, verbs connoting strength (cf. *ḥăzaq weʾĕmāṣ*), when intensified by *hiphʿil* or *piʿel* express the concept of keeping and holding, cf. Ps 80:18: *tĕhî yadĕkā ʿal ʾîš yĕmînekā ʿal-ben-ʾādām ʾimmaṣtā lāk* ("May your hand be on the man at your right, upon the man you held with you"); cf. also Isa 41:10: *ʾimmaṣtîkā ʾap-ʿăzartîkā ʾap-tĕmaktîkā bîmîn ṣidqî* ("I have taken hold of you and helped you, I kept you with my victorious right hand"). For the understanding of *ʾmṣ* in Ps 80:18 and in Isa 41:10 I am indebted to Prof. H. L. Ginsberg.
61. Cf. Jer 3:4,19 and see below.
62. Cf. Sefire III:7, *šqrtm bʿdyʾ ʾln*, "You will have been false to this treaty"; see W. Moran, *Bib* 42 (1961) 239. *ʾĔmûnâ* here and in v. 50 has the same meaning as *ʾămānâ* in Neh 10:1 (cf. J. Greenfield, *Acta Orientalia* 29 [1965] 8). *ʾĔmunâ* in 2 Kgs 13:16 and in 22:7 has also, in my opinion, the meaning of "pact" or "contract" and the reason for not calling to account the people in charge of the work was that they were bound by the oath to deal honestly. On the loyalty oath of craftsmen, see D. B. Weisberg, *Guild Structure and Political Allegiance in Early Achaemenid Mesopotamia* (1967).
63. Cf., e.g., Yarimlim of Alalaḫ who is named son of Abba-El (see Wiseman, *AT* *444a, seal impression) but actually was the son of Hammurabi (*AT* *1:9, cf. *444b). According to Alt (*WO* 3:1–2 [1964] 14ff.), Abba-El adopted Yarimlim in order to create the legal basis for installing him as king of Haleb.
64. E. Weidner, *Politische Dokumente,* no. 2, ll. 24ff. (pp. 40–41).
65. *Ana mārūtija ēppuškami . ana mārūti ĕpēšu* means "to adopt as a son"; cf. E. A. Speiser, "New Kirkuk Documents Relating to Family Laws," *AASOR* 10 (1930) pp. 7ff. Cf. also below.
66. *Amātu ša ina pīšu uṣṣu ana kutallišu ul itār.*
67. F. Sommer-A. Falkenstein, *Die hethitisch-akkadische Bilingue des Hattušili*

I (Labarna II) (Abhandlungen der Bayerischen Akademie der Wissenschaf-ter, Phil.-hist. Abt. N.F. 16, 1938).

68. *ù a-nu-um-ma* TUR-*am la-ba-ar-na [aq-b]i-a-ak-ku-nu-ši-im šu-u li-it-ta-ša-ab-mi* LUGAL-*ru [al]-si-šu-ma* DUMU(?)-*am* = in Hittite: *[nu-uš-ma-aš* TUR-*la-an] la-ba-ar-na-an te-nu-un [a-pa-a-aš-u̯a-aš-ša-an e-ša-ru* LUGAL-*ša-an-za]* DUMU-*la-ma-an ḫal-zi-iḫ-ḫu-um* (I/II; 2–4). Akkadian *qabû* = Hittite *te-* which equals Hebrew *ʾāmar* have in this context the same connotation as *ʾāmar ʾēlay* in Ps 2:7: "proclaim" or "declare." The newly appointed king is not the real son of Hattušiliš but the son of his sister who is being adopted.
69. Compare I/II:37: "Behold, Muršiliš is now my son."
70. II:44: NUMUN [d]UTU[ši].KU.NU.
71. III:24–25.
72. *Ana sūnišu iškunšu u qāssu iṣbatsu, ina pānišu irtup alākam,* KBo X, 1 vs. 13–14 (cf. H. Otten, *MDOG* 91 [1958] 79 and A. Goetze, *JCS* 16 [1962] 125). For the corresponding Hittite restoration (KBo X,2 vs. I: 28–30), see H. A. Hoffner, *JNES* 27 (1968) 201, note 27.
73. According to H. L. Ginsberg (private communication), Isa 41:9ff., also dealing with grasping the hand and helping against enemies, refers to the election of Abraham (cf. end of v. 8), which supports our view about the common typology of the Davidic and Abrahamic covenants. On "grasping the hand" in Deutero-Isaiah and the corresponding Neo-Babylonian royal imagery, see S. Paul, *JAOS* 88 (1968) 182, note 19.
74. *ʾOsipô ʾel ḥêqî, ʾōmar ʾēlāyw* ("I will gather him to my bosom, I will say to him") instead of *ʾăsappĕrâ ʾel ḥoq, yhwh ʾāmar ʾēlay* ("I will recite the law, the Lord said to me"). Cf. H. Gunkel, *Psalmen* (HKAT) ad loc., who follows Torczyner.
75. Cf. Ruth 4:16 and see Hoffner, loc. cit. We must admit, however, that putting into the bosom as such does not necessarily indicate adoption, it may just as well signify care and protection. T. Jacobsen (*JNES* 2 [1943] 120) denies that nourishing by the goddess or placing on her knee in Sumero-Akkadian literature implies adoption. Similarly giving birth on one's knees in the Old Testament (Gen 16:20, 30:3, 50:23) does not necessarily imply adoption; see J. Tigay, "Adoption," in the forthcoming volume of *Encyclopedia Judaica.*
76. Cf. G. Cooke, *ZAW* 73 (1961) 202–25.
77. E. R. Lachemann, *Excavations at Nuzi VIII:* Family Law Documents, HSS XIX (1962).
78. E. A. Speiser, "A Significant New Will from Nuzi," *JCS* 17 (1963) 65–71; cf. also E. Cassin, "Nouvelles données sur les relations familiales à Nuzi," *RA* 57 (1963) 113–19.
79. This means of course anybody who assumes parenthood of the children *(ana abbūti)* as for instance the wife or the daughter of the one who draws the will.
80. *Šumma* PN PN_2 *la [ipal]laḫšu u kīmē awēlu māršu ḫuddumumma ippuš*

kinannama ḫuddumumma ippuš, JEN 572:26–31. Cf. the analysis of this passage by E. A. Speiser, "A Significant New Will," pp. 68–69. *Ḫuddumumma epēšu* means, according to Speiser, "to discipline." E. Cassin ("Nouvelles données", p. 116) translates it as "enfermer."

81. *Kīmē māršu ša awīl Arrapḫe ippušu, kinannama* PN PN_2 *ippussuma, kurṣa ina šēpešu išakkan, abbuta ina qaqqadišu išakkan, ina bīt kīli inandin,* HSS XIX, 39:16–23; cf. E. A. Speiser, "A Significant New Will," p. 69.

82. *K[ima] yaši eteppuš,* HSS XIX, 19:31–32; cf. E. A. Speiser, "A Significant New Will," p. 70 and note 22 for the grammatical problem involved.

83. PN *ana* PN *abišu ula abi atta iqabbīma, aran mārū awīlē immidušu,* M. Schorr, *Urkunden* (1913) 23:23–27 (p. 46).

84. Contrary to M. Schorr (ibid.) who understands it as deprivation of freedom, i.e., enslavement.

85. B. Jacob (*ZAW* 22 [1902] 91–92) interprets *bĕšēbeṭ ʾănāšîm ûbĕnigʿê bĕnê ʾādām,* "Schläge wie sie die Kinder vom Vater erhalten d. h. aus Liebe und daher mit Maassen" which generally fits our understanding of the phrase. However his interpretation of *ʾādām* and *ʾănāšîm* as parents literally (on the basis of Palestinian Syriac *ʾnašutaʾ*) is not warranted. It might as well be understood as "human" (cf. Hos 11:4: *bĕḥablê ʾādām ʾemšĕkēm baʿăbōtôt ʾahăbâ* = "I drew them with human cords, with bands of love").

86. Cf., e.g., CH §168–69 and the discussion in G. R. Driver and J. C. Miles, *Babyl. Laws* (1952) vol. I, pp. 348–49, 395–405. These laws apply to the real son as well as to the adopted. That this is so may be learned from a Nuzi document (HSS V,7) where it is stated that the adopted son might be disinherited following repetitive trials (ll. 25ff.), which is similar in attitude to CH §168–69, according to which the son is to be disinherited only after he had been brought up before the judges for the second time. Compare Deut 21:18–21 where the rebellious son is to be condemned to death only after being chastised before. For dissolution of sonship as a result of disobedience, cf. also RS 8.145, *Syria* 18 (1937) 249–50.

87. PN *kurṣi inandinšu, abbuta umaššaršu, ina bīt kīli inandin, šumma ḫašiḫšu kirba[na] iḫeppē u ukaššasu k[ima] yaši eteppuš* = "PN may put fetters upon him, apply the slave mark to him, put him in the house of detention or, if it pleases her, break the clump of clay to disinherit him *(kuššudu)*, she may act as though she were I" (HSS XIX, 19:28–32).

88. F. Hrozny, *Boghazköi Studien* 3 (1919) 142–44, vs. II:10–18; cf. J. Friedrich, *Der Alte Orient* 24:3 (1925) p. 20, 11.10–18; cf. also E. Cavaignac, *RHA* 6 (Jan. 1932) 196.

89. Cf. I. Mendelsohn, "On the Preferential Status of the Eldest Son," *BASOR* 156 (Dec. 1959) 38–40 and the references there.

90. Cf., e.g.: *ina libbišunu ša mārīya rabi yānu* = "there is none among them who shall be the oldest," HSS XIX, 23:5–6; cf. 17:12–13; see E. A. Speiser, *JCS* 17 (1963) 66 and the discussion on p. 70.

91. This is prohibited by the Deuteronomic Code (21:15–17). The Deuteronomic Law stands in clear contradiction to Gen 48:13–20 where Joseph,

the son of the "loved" woman Rachel, is given the double share while Reuben, the son of the "unloved" Leah (cf. Gen 29:33: *śĕnûʾâ*), is repudiated as the first born.

92. Read *ʾak* instead of *ʾêk;* cf. A. Ehrlich, *Randglossen zur hebr. Bibel* (1908), *ad loc.*

93. Cf. above pp. 74–76.

94. Ibid. Cf. in the Azitawadda inscription: *wʾp bʾbt pʿln kl mlk,* "and every king made me his father (=his suzerain)"; see N. H. Tur-Sinai (Torczyner), *The Language and the Book* II[2] (1964) p. 76 (Hebrew). In Greek *poieisthai=pʿl, epēš* or *thesthai=śym, šyt* are the verbs used for adoption. *Wayyāśîmû bānîm* in Ezra 10:44 implies adoption (cf. S. Feigin, *JBL* 50 [1931] 196f., though we do not accept his restoration).

95. Inheritance of land in connection with divine sonship occurs in Deut 32:8 (LXX and Qumran). Compare the cone of Entemena of Lagash: "Enlil, the king of all the lands, the father of all the gods, marked off the boundary for Ningirsu and Shara by his steadfast word" (Cone A, 1–7); cf. F. Thureau-Dangin, *SAKI,* p. 36; G. Barton, *Royal Inscriptions of Sumer and Akkad* (1929) p. 56.

96. Cf. J. Munn-Rankin, "Diplomacy in Western Asia in the Early Second Millennium B.C.," *Iraq* 18 (1956) 68ff.

97. Cf. PRU IV, pp. 36, 49.

98. Cf. W. Hinz, *ZA* 24 (1967) 66ff. See also the text in *Baghdader Mitteilungen* 2 (1963) 54 (W 19900, 147) which according to Kraus (*BiOr* 22 [1965] 289) is part of a treaty, where we read: *[lu a-n]a-ki-ir [is-l]i-mu lu-ú a-sa-li-im.*

99. M. Schorr, *Urkunden des altbabylon. Zivil- und Prozessrechts* (1913) 4:21–23; cf. 5:7–8; Schorr's translation is wrong and Ungnad's is correct; see p. 11 there. Cf. *CAD* v. 21 (Z) *zenû* b.

100. ARM VIII, 1:4–5. After completing this article I saw that R. Yaron, *Journal of Juristic Papyrology* 15 (1965) 173–75, discussed this text in the context of some of the above-mentioned texts and reached similar conclusions.

101. *Ḥesed in the Bible* (1967), p. 46.

102. Cf., e.g., J. Friedrich, *Staatsverträge,* no. 3, 7C:13–17 (pp. 112ff.); V. Korošec, "Juristische Bemerkungen," pp. 218ff., although the different attitudes toward the condemned should not reflect a historical development, as Korošec puts it, but might be explained as a double standard: to the privileged on the one hand and to the unprivileged on the other.

103. PRU III, 16.249:22–29 (pp. 97–98); 16.145 (p. 169, *bêl arni*).

104. *AT* no. 17 (p. 40: *bêl māšikti*).

105. It is not without significance that in spite of frequent references to the promise of the Patriarchs, Deuteronomy never mentions the eternity of this promise *(bĕrît ʿôlām, lĕdôrôtām, ʿad ʿôlām)* in contradistinction to JE and P (see below).

106. Cf. Gen. 18:19. This is an expectation and not a condition.

107. For the meaning of *sĕgullâ* and its Akkadian equivalent *sikiltum*, see M. Greenberg, *JAOS* 71 (1951) 172ff. Cf. now PRU V, 60 (18.38), 11.7–12 (p. 84) where the Ugaritic vassal is called the *sglt* of his suzerain, which is rendered by C. Virolleaud as "propriété." The *sglt* in the Ugaritic text now elucidates the *sĕgullâ* in the Pentateuch. It seems that *sglt* and *sĕgullâ* belong to the treaty and covenant terminology and that they are employed to distinguish a special relationship of the suzerain to one of his vassals. On the basis of Ugaritic, biblical and also Alalaḫian evidence (cf. the seal impression in D. J. Wiseman, *AT*, pl. III, where the king Abba-El is said to be the *sikiltum* of the goddess), we may safely say that the basic meaning of the root *sakālu* is to set aside a thing or certain property either with good intention (as Israel is set aside from other nations) or with an evil purpose as in CH §141 and in other Babylonian sources. Cf. the discussion of M. Held in *JCS* 15 (1961) 11–12. For the Ugaritic text cf. also H. B. Huffmon, *BASOR* 184 (1966) 36f.

108. As a reward for her loyalty, Israel will in turn be God's most precious possession: she will be God's priesthood. A similar idea is indeed expressed in the consolation prophecy in Isa 61:6: "And you shall be called the priests of Yahweh. You will be named servants of our God, you shall eat the wealth of the nations and in their splendour you shall excel," cf. R. B. Y. Scott, *OTS* 8 (1950) 213–15. For a recent thorough discussion of this passage see: W. L. Moran, "A Kingdom of Priests," *The Bible in Current Catholic Thought,* ed. J. McKenzie (1962) pp. 7–20.

109. Cf. above.

110. Deut 30:1–10 is a later addition and revolved around the deuteronomic doctrine of return to God, cf. H. W. Wolff, "Das Kerygma des deuteronomistischen Geschichtswerks," *ZAW* 73 (1961) 180ff.

111. Cf. M. Tsevat, "Studies in Samuel III," *HUCA* 34 (1963) 75f., though I cannot accept his opinion of 2 Sam 7:13b–16 being a gloss.

112. Compare the corresponding Akkadian terms: *riksu/riksāte* and *adê*.

113. On the covenant with Abraham in Genesis 15 as representing an oath, cf. N. Lohfink, *Die Landhverheissung*, pp. 11–23.

114. Cf. D. J. McCarthy, "Three Covenants in Genesis," *CBQ* 26 (1964) 179ff.

115. Cf., e.g., Isa 31:9. The Akkadian divine epithets: *tinūru lā anīḫu* = "the incessant oven" (Dilbat); *išātum napiḫtum* = "the blazing fire" (Ištar), (cf. K. Tallqvist, *Akkadische Götterepitheta* [1938], pp. 33–34) and *dipār šamê u erṣeti* = "the torch of heaven and earth" (Ištar) (cf. E. Ebeling, *Die akkadische Gebetserie "Handerhebung"* etc. [1953], p. 130:34–37) are attributed solely to the astral deities and cannot therefore be considered as parallels to our case.

116. E. Reiner, *Šurpu* (AfO Beiheft 11, 1958).

117. *Māmīt dipāru našû šum ili zakāru,* "curse caused by holding a torch and taking an oath" (*Šurpu* III:93).

118. Cf., e.g., KI *ma-mit* UDUN *la-ap-ti ti-nu-ri* KI.NE (= kinūnu) KI.UD.BA *u nap-pa-ḫa-tú* = "together with the oath of furnace, grill, kiln, stove, brazier

or bellows" (*Šurpu* VIII:75); *ma-mit* [d]IZI.GAR u KI.NE = "the oath of lamp and stove" (*Šurpu* III:145). On ovens in Mesopotamia, see A. Salonen, "Die Öfen der alten Mesopotamier," *Baghdader Mitteilungen* 3 (1964) 100ff.

119. *Šurpu* III:35: *māmīt immeru ṭabāḫu nikissu lapātu* = "an oath sworn by slaughtering a sheep and touching the wound."

120. D. J. Wiseman, "Abban and Alalaḫ," *JCS* 12 (1958) 126:39–42; cf. above note 10. In the continuation Abba-El states that if Yarimlim betrays him he will forfeit his territory, which then makes the gift conditional. We must, however, keep in mind that the deed of Abba-El to Yarimlim is not a deed of grant but rather a deed of exchange. Alalaḫ was given to Yarimlim in place of the destroyed Irridi. The gift of Alalaḫ is therefore not a reward for loyal service as is the case in grants, but is a part of a political arrangement between two parties.

121. *Ina ūmišu Yarimlim . . . [ana* [d]*]Ištar ušêli,* reading with *CAD* vol. 4 (E), p. 130a. According to N. Lohfink (*Landverheissung,* pp. 93f.) the tradition of Gen 15:7ff. reflects an incubation dream in a sanctuary (Hebron or Shechem). If true this might be an additional parallel feature to the Alalaḫ covenant.

122. For the sacrificial nature of the offerings brought at the ceremony in Genesis 15, see S. E. Loewenstamm, "Zur Traditionsgeschichte des Bundes zwischen den Stücken," *VT* 18 (1968) 500ff. However, in view of the evidence presented here, we cannot accept his opinion that the sacrifice is a late element in the tradition of Genesis 15.

123. *AT** 54:16–18: GÚ SILÁ *a-sa-ki* IGI PN UGULA UKU.UŠ *ṭa-bi-iḫ* (cf. A. Draffkorn, *JCS* 13 [1959] 95, n. 11). The presence of the general at this transaction may be paralleled with Gen 21:22f. and the Yahwistic counterpart in 26:25ff. where the covenant between Abimelech and Abraham and Isaac respectively is made in the presence of Phicol the general (for this parallel I am indebted to Dr. Y. Muffs of the Jewish Theological Seminary).

124. S. Smith, *The Statue of Idrimi* (1949); cf. the review by A. Goetze, *JCS* 4 (1950) 226–31.

125. Read in line 55 with Goetze (ibid., p. 228) SISKUR instead of GAZ; compare line 89 the same sign (SISKUR) with *ni-iq-qi* ḪI.A.

126. *Kinūnu* in line 55.

127. Cf. note 118 above.

128. We are also told there that Abraham gave seven lambs to Abimelech as a "witness" *(ʿēdâ)* or as E. A. Speiser (*Genesis,* Anchor Bible, ad loc.) translates a "proof" for his rights on the well. A similar procedure is found in an Old Babylonian act of partition where one of the partners gives to the other two lambs as a proof of the agreement: E. Szlechter, *JCS* 7 (1953) p. 92, 5:16–17. Compare also A. Goetze, *JCS* 4 (1950) 228, n. 20.

129. ARM II, 37.

130. *Ḫazzum* (cf. *ḫanzum* and *enzum*) is Hebrew *ʿēz* (see *AHw*).

131. *Ḫayarum qatālum,* ARM II, 37:6,11.

132. Cf. W. Hinz, "Elams Vertrag mit Naram-Sin von Akkade," *ZA* 24 (1967) 66–96.

133. Rev I:37–40: [d]*Utu lugal ni-sig$_{10}$-ga-ra larsam*[ki] *é-babbar* NINDÁ + GUD-*šè an-kú* which is translated by E. Sollberger (*Le système verbal dans les inscriptions "royales" présargoniques de Lagaš* [1952] example 161): à Utu, le roi étincelant, à Larsa dans l'Ebabbar, j'y ai fait le sacrifice (alimentaire).

134. "Two doves on whose eyes he had put spices (and) on whose heads he had strewn cedar(?) he caused to be eaten for Enlil at Nippur (with the plea): 'As long as days exist . . . if the Ummaite . . . breaks his word . . .' " (translation according to S. N. Kramer, *The Sumerians* [1964] p. 311). An offering of a similar kind although in a different context is to be found in Lev 14:4,49 where two birds are taken together with cedar wood, crimson stuff and hyssop. The word translated by Kramer "spices" is *šim/šimbi* (Akkadian *guḫlu*, Hebrew *kḥl*), full form *šim-bi-zi-da*, which is actually antimony.

135. Cf. *CAD* vol. 2 (B) p. 266. The three-year-old bull in 1 Sam 1:24 (LXX and Qumran) and the three-year-old animals in Genesis 15 do not therefore reflect precisely a Shilonite tradition as Loewenstamm contends ("Zur Traditionsgeschichte"). It seems that the three-year animal was considered of good quality in general; cf. e.g.: 1 *immeru ša šullušītu damqu* = "one three-year old sheep of good quality" (*RA* 23 [1926] 154, 47.15); *šullušīta enza* = "a three-year old she-goat" in connection with a feast (*Anatolian Studies* 6 [1956] 152:44); 1 *alpu šuluššū ešrū ša* . . . PN *ana Ebabbara iddinu* = "the three-year old ox, the tithe which PN has given to Ebabbara" (J. N. Strassmaier, *Inschriften von Nabonidus* 1071:1). For cattle and sheep and their ages in Mesopotamia, cf. MSL VIII, 1 and especially p. 47 there. For the age adjective *šuluššū*, compare also *ʿeglat šĕlišiyyâ* (Isa 15:5, Jer 48:34) and see *m. Parah* 1:1 *(šĕlāšiyyit)*.

136. The vultures (*hāʿayiṭ* and *haṣṣipōr* are collective nouns) coming down upon the carcasses might visualize the fate of the one who will violate the oath (compare the threat in Jer 34:20 and the conventional curses of the betrayer being eaten by animals and birds; cf. D. R. Hillers, *Treaty Curses* [1964] pp. 68–69). This is actually the function of the scene of vultures eating the carcasses on the stele of Eannatum.

137. Cf. ARM II, 62:9′; 77, passim; I, 37:20, cf. Enuma Elish VI:98.

138. Cf. I. Gelb., *BiOr* 19 (1962) 159–62.

139. Cf. E. Weidner, *AfO* 8 (1932–33) 16ff.

140. Ibid., col. I:10ff.

141. Compare the Mari letter (ARM II,48) where it is proposed to cut off the head of a culprit and circulate it among the cities of Ḫana so that the troops may fear and quickly assemble.

142. Cf. J. A. Fitzmyer, *The Aramaic Inscriptions of Sefire* (Biblica et Orientalia 19, 1967) I A:39–40.

143. See W. Rudolph, *Jeremia*[2] (HAT, 1958) p. 205.

144. I A:35–42.
145. D. J. Wiseman, *Iraq* 20 (1958) 11. 608–11.
146. J. Friedrich, "Der hethitische Soldateneid," *ZA* 35 (1924) 163, I:41–45, II:1–3.
147. This type of symbolism was also employed in Babylonian magic; see E. Reiner, *Šurpu,* III:60–112.
148. Cf. J. J. Rabinowitz, *Jewish Law* (1956) pp. 130–31; idem, "The Susa Tablets," *VT* 11 (1961) 55ff.
149. *Dôr*=*dūru* with the pronominal suffix is also attested in Old Babylonian documents pertaining to conveyance in perpetuity. Cf. e.g., *eqlam ana dūrišu idna*="give the field as his permanent property" (*TCL* VII, 16:13; cf. F. R. Kraus, *Altbabylonische Briefe* [1964]) to which one might compare Lev 25:30="that house shall be established forever to him that bought it throughout *his generations*" (i.e. for his permanent property).
150. Cf. *ana dūr u pala ana šêršêri . . . kima abu ana māri išāmu,* PN *ana dārāti išām* (*MDP* XXII, 45:10–21)="forever and for all times, for the offspring . . . like a father, who bequeathes to his son, so shall PN bequeath forever."
151. *Mārmārišu ana dāria marianni:* "his descendants will have the status of *mariannu* forever," *AT* 15:8–9; cf. S. Smith, *The Antiquaries Journal* 19 (1939) 43.
152. Cf., e.g., PRU III, p. 160, 16.132:27–38: *u ittadinšu ana* [m]*Adalšeni [u] ana mārēšu adi dārīti*="and gives it to Adalšeni and his sons forever"; cf. 16.248:14 (p. 48: *ana dāri dūri*), 16.182+199:9 (p. 148: *ana dārīti ana dāri dūri*), 16.146:10–12 (p. 146: *eqlatu ṣāmid ana dārīti*). The formula in Ugaritic is *wlbnh ʿd ʿlm* (PRU II, 16.382: 20–21).
153. Cf. A. Cowley, *Aramaic Papyri* (1932) 8:9 (p. 22): *ʾnty šlyṭh bh mnywmʾ znh wʿd ʿlm wbnyky ʾḥryky*="you have rights over it from this day forever and your children after you"; cf. 25:9 (p. 85). On preservation of ancient legalistic formulae in the Elephantine Papyri, see recently Y. Muffs, *Studies in Aramaic Legal Papyri from Elephantine* (1969), pp. 179ff.
154. F. Steinmetzer, "Die Bestallungsurkunde Königs Šamas-šum-ukīn von Babylon," *ArOr* 7 (1935) pp. 314–18, II:9.
155. *Ana ṣāti irenšu*="he granted to him in perpetuity," *BBSt* 8, I:13; cf. also 34:6.
156. Cf. *CAD* vol. 3 (D) p. 198.
157. Cf. above note 58.
158. Cf. *BBSt* (passim) and also A. Cowley, *Aramaic Papyri,* 8:3ff.; 13:13f.; 25:4f. See on this point M. Weinfeld, *Deuteronomy and the Deuteronomic School.*
159. Cf. Y. Muffs, "Studies in Biblical Law IV (The Antiquity of P)," Lectures at the Jewish Theological Seminary, 1965. On the prophetic vs. Pentateuchal imagery of the covenantal relationship between God and the people, see M. Weinfeld, *Deuteronomy and the Deuteronomic School.*
160. The tradition of the covenant with Abraham is very ancient and reflects the covenant customs in Mari and Alalaḫ but the literary formulation of

this covenant is later and seems to be from the time of the United Monarchy; cf. R. E. Clements, *Abraham and David* (Studies in Biblical Theology, sec. series 5, 1967).

161. Cf. R. A. Carlson, *David the Chosen King* (1965) p. 122.

162. Ibid., pp. 114–15.

163. "Holy People and Great Nation," *Molad* 21 (1963) 662–65 (Hebrew). Cf. also *ʿOz le-David* (Ben-Gurion Festschrift, 1964) pp. 399f.

164. Cf. *šumam rabēm* in connection with military victories in ARM I, 69:14′–16′.

165. The extent of the promised land in Gen 15:19–21, and especially the Kenites, Kenizzites and Kadmonites mentioned there, also point to a Davidic background; cf. B. Mazar, "Historical Background of the Book of Genesis," *JNES* 28 (1969) 79f.

166. Joshua is secondary in this tradition (cf. Num 14:24, Deut 1:36). The promise of land to Joshua was incorporated later when the conquest was nationalized and the original account of spying out the south (till Hebron and the valley of Eshkol, Num 13:22–23) was expanded by an alleged excursion to the northern part of the country (till Rehob at Lebo-Hammath, v. 21). See commentaries and recently J. Liver, article "Caleb," *Encyclopedia Miqraʾit* (Hebrew).

167. Cf., e.g., L. W. King, *BBSt*, pp. 31ff, 43ff, 96ff.

168. R. E. Clements, *Abraham and David.*

169. Cf. S. Smith, *The Antiquaries Journal* 19 (1939) ATT/8/49 (p. 43): *mār mārēšu ana dāria marianni u šangī ša Enlil* = "his grandsons in perpetuity are (will be) *mariannu* and priests of Enlil."

170. Cf., e.g., M. Schorr, *Urkunden*, VAB 5, no. 220; F. Thureau-Dangin, *RA* 16 (1919) 141ff. and the Alalaḫ text in the previous note.

171. Cf. above.

172. Cf. above.

173. See note 15 above.

174. Following the translation of *The Torah* (Jewish Publication Society of America, 1962).

175. GN *qadu gabbi mimmi šumšiša iddin ana* PN . . . *ana dāriš ana mārē mārēšu: šêšu, šikarsu ša maʾšariša*, PRU III 16.153:4–11 (pp. 146–47). As in Ugarit so in Israel the tithe is taken from grain and wine (and also oil), whereas in Mesopotamia tithe is mostly taken from barley and dates; cf. BIN I, 109:2; YOS VII, 188:4.

176. Cf. the unpublished dissertation by M. D. Rehm, "Studies in the History of the Pre-Exilic Levites," announced in the *HTR* 61 (1968) 648–49. Cf. also B. Mazar, "Cities of Priests and Levites," VTSup 7 (1959) 197ff.

177. *Abraham and David*, pp. 70ff.

178. "Readings in the History of Biblical Thought, Covenant Traditions in Deuteronomy," Lectures at the Jewish Theological Seminary, 1965.

179. It is Muffs' opinion (ibid.) that the pattern of P's covenant is one of adoption by manumission (= redemption from slavery, i.e. Exodus). This

seems to be supported by the fact that in describing the election of the people (cf. e.g., Exod 6:56f.) P uses the verb *g'l* which is the terminus technicus in P for redemption and release.

180. The LXX and the Syriac read *ʿim ʾĕlōhê ʾabrāhām,* "*with* the people of the God of Abraham," but this seems to be a tendentious reading prompted by the wish to avoid the identification of the nations with "the people of the God of Abraham" itself.

181. On the interrelationship between these nations at the end of the second millennium B.C., see O. Eissfeldt, *JBL* 87 (1968) 383ff. Cf. also B. Mazar, "Historical Background of the Book of Genesis," *JNES* 28 (1969) 79–80.

182. On Sabbath and circumcision in P, see also my article in *Tarbiz* 37 (1968) 105ff. (Hebrew with English summary).

183. Cf. Jer 9:25 and read: *kî kŏl-haggôyim hāʾēleh wĕkŏl-bêt yiśrāʾēl ʿarlê-lēb* (cf. W. Rudolph, *Jeremia*², HAT, ad loc.). On the whole problem, see M. Haran, "The Religion of the Patriarchs," *Annual of the Swedish Theological Institute* 4 (1965) 42–43.

4

The Ancient Near Eastern Background of the Love of God in Deuteronomy

William L. Moran

Probably no subject in the book of Deuteronomy, "le document biblique par excellence de l'*agapân*,"[1] has been so thoroughly studied as its teaching on love: Yahweh's love for Israel, and the imperative necessity of Israel's love for Yahweh in return.[2] Study of the theme has resulted in a certain consensus of opinion. It is generally agreed that the deuteronomic teaching has distinctive features, that it is not lacking in originality; it is also, though less commonly, agreed that for the conception of God and people bound by a mutual love, Deuteronomy is indebted to the prophet Hosea.[3] We propose here to broaden the basis for the discussion both of deuteronomic originality and dependence.

The point of departure for our inquiry is suggested by certain fundamental differences between Hosea's preaching on love and the doctrine of Deuteronomy. Hosea speaks of Yahweh's love *(ʾāhēb, ʾahăbâ)* for Israel, but never of Israel's "love" for Yahweh—neither as a fact (Israel's love is invariably presented as the love of other gods), nor as a present duty, nor as an ideal to be realized in the future restoration. This can hardly be explained except as a conscious, intentional avoidance of the term. In Deuteronomy, on the other hand, *ʾāhēb* is commonly predicated of Israel in relation to Yahweh; indeed, it epitomizes the book's central preoccupation, namely, observance of the Law. Secondly, in Hosea God's love for Israel is either that of a husband for his wife (3:1)

Reprinted by permission of the author from the *Catholic Biblical Quarterly* 25 (1963):77–87.

or of a father for his son (11:1). In Deuteronomy we find the father-son relationship (8:5; 14:1, etc.), but never in connection with love,[4] and of the marriage-analogy there is not a trace. This absence of all allusion to marriage is the more striking in that *ʾāhēb* is the verb most apt to express conjugal love.[5]

It is evident that, if Deuteronomy does depend on Hosea, it has transformed the prophet's teaching into a notably different view of love. Can this be accounted for simply by appeal to Deuteronomy's "originality?"[6] It is doubtless better accounted for if no radical transformation need be supposed—that is, if the distinctive deuteronomic view, which nowhere draws on the image of parental or conjugal love, was guided by the analogy of another and different love-relationship.

The nature of this relationship we may hypothetically reconstruct, *mutatis mutandis,* from the distinctive features of the love Deuteronomy proposes. Love in Deuteronomy is a love that can be commanded.[7] It is also a love intimately related to fear and reverence.[8] Above all, it is a love which must be expressed in loyalty, in service, and in unqualified obedience to the demands of the Law.[9] For to love God is, in answer to a unique claim (6:4), to be loyal to him (11:1,22; 30:20),[10] to walk in his ways (10:12; 11:22; 19:9; 30:16), to keep his commandments (10:12; 11:1,22; 19:9), to do them (11:22; 19:9), to heed them or his voice (11:13; 30:16), to serve him (10:12; 11:1,13). It is, in brief, a love defined by and pledged in the covenant—a covenantal love.

The problem, therefore, is: (1) is there evidence elsewhere in our sources for the existence of a comparable covenantal love; (2) if there is, is there also evidence which suggests that Deuteronomy knew of such a love and therefore may have been influenced by this knowledge?

Beginning outside the Old Testament, we may point to texts from the eighteenth to the seventh centuries B.C., in which we find the term love used to describe the loyalty and friendship joining independent kings, sovereign and vassal, king and subject.[11] In a letter to Yasmaʿ-Addu, the king of Mari, one writer declares himself the king's servant and "friend" (*rāʾimka,* literally, "the one who loves you").[12] Here, however, we must be cautious. This is an isolated example in this period, while the contents of the letter and the otherwise unknown identity of the writer do not allow us to determine the implications of this friendship. But the sequence of servant and friend, especially in the light of later texts, is noteworthy.

When we come to the Amarna period we no longer need hesitate, for then, as Korošec has briefly remarked, "love" unquestionably belongs to the terminology of international relations.[13] In the correspondence between Tušratta of Mitanni and the Egyptian court it is the principal topic, and denotes the friendship between the rulers, who are independent and equals ("brothers").[14] Like *ṭābūtu,*[15] with which it is virtually synonymous, this friendship is the object of agreement and established by treaty.[16]

However, a similar love also binds sovereign and vassal. The Pharaoh is expected to love his vassal.[17] The nature of the latter's obligations is seen in the following text: "My lord, just as I love the king my lord, so (do) the king of Nuḫašše, the king of Niʾi . . .—all these kings are servants of my lord."[18] The vassal must love the Pharaoh; this is only another way of stating his basic relationship to the latter, that of servant. Rib-Adda implies the same thing when in noting the defection of still another governor (vassal), he asks: "Who will love, should I die?"[19] To love the Pharaoh is to serve him and to remain faithful to the status of vassal. And again, in describing the rebellion which closed to him the gates of his own city Byblos, the same king defines loyalty to the Pharaoh, which he assumes to be the same as loyalty to himself, in terms of "love": "Behold the city! Half of it loves the sons of ʿAbd-Ašir-ta [who fostered the rebellion], half of it (loves) my lord."[20]

Finally, subjects must love their king. Rib-Adda's loyal subjects are "those who love me," and they are opposed to the treacherous and rebellious.[21] Analogously, the Amorites "do not love ʿAbd-aširta," for in general they serve the strong, and at the moment ʿAbd-aširta is weak.[22]

Coming down to the first millennium, we find this terminology still in use. A vassal must still love his sovereign. The vassals convoked by Esarhaddon to insure loyalty to his successor Assurbanipal are told: "You will love as yourselves Assurbanipal."[23] In another text we find a similar declaration under oath: ". . . the king of Assyria, our lord, we will love."[24]

In the Old Testament one passage at least clearly belongs to the same juridical vocabulary. It is 1 Kgs 5:15, where Hiram of Tyre is called David's "friend" *(ʾōhēb).* The entire section, vv. 15–26, "presents an early picture of correct historical similitude, reporting diplomatic and commercial relations between two states of Syro-Palestine—actually in its extent a fairly unique report."[25] It begins by telling of Hiram's embassy to Solomon when he heard of the latter's being anointed king, "for Hiram had always been a friend to David." It ends by informing us that Hiram and Solomon concluded a treaty. The interpretation of the designation "friend" must be guided not only by the result of the embassy, namely, a treaty, but by two other facts: (1) as follows from 2 Sam 5:11, Hiram and David were united by treaty[26] and (2) on the death of the treaty partner and the enthronement of his successor, the other party was expected to send an embassy. Thus David sends one to Hanun of Ammon,[27] and the king of Cyprus is represented in Egypt when a new Pharaoh takes the throne.[28] The importance attached to such embassies is clear from Hattusili III's letter to Rameses II, in which with some bitterness he complains that this practice had not been observed on the occasion of his own enthronement.[29] In brief, "friend" in 1 Kgs 5:15 must be understood as a reference to the treaty relationship which existed between Hiram and David, and is now renewed with David's successor.

This is the only instance in which *ʾāhēb* refers to international relations.[30] But at least two other passages are strongly reminiscent of some Amarna texts. In 2 Sam 19:6–7 Joab protests bitterly to David for grieving at the death of a rebellious son while showing no concern for those who had remained loyal. He charges David with "loving those who hate you and hating those who love you *(ʾōhăbêkā)*."[31] "Those who love you" have already been identified as "your servants" (v. 6). This recalls of course Rib-Adda's way of designating those loyal to him, as well as *EA* 53:40–44, where loving and being a servant were equated.

In view too of what we have seen one may perhaps appreciate more fully the significance of the statement in 1 Sam 18:16: "But all Israel and Judah loved *(ʾōhēb)* David, for he went out and came in before them." It is clear that the writer sees this as another important step in David's way to the throne; the north as well as the south is attached to him.[32] However, if we see in this attachment, as the Amarna and the Assyrian evidence encourages us to do, an essential requirement of the king-subject relationship, then the writer implies that the people at the point were already giving David a *de facto* recognition and allegiance, which his actual leadership and success in a sense justified.

In answer therefore to the first part of our problem, we may affirm, on the basis of biblical and extra-biblical evidence, the existence of a conception of a profane love analogous to the love of God in Deuteronomy. This profane love is also one that can be commanded, and it is a love too that may be defined in terms of loyalty, service and obedience. It is, like the love of God in Deuteronomy, a covenantal love.[33]

In a sense we have also answered the second half of our problem, namely, whether Deuteronomy knew of such a love and therefore may have been influenced by this knowledge. The biblical passages alone which we have adduced show that we may assume it did know of this profane covenantal love, and the fact that the love required of Israel is, *mutatis mutandis* (of course!), so similar argues strongly in favor of assuming the influence of analogy.

Other considerations support this conclusion. It should be remarked first of all that, if Deuteronomy is the biblical document *par excellence* of love, it is also the biblical document *par excellence* of the covenant. No book of the Old Testament is so penetrated in every stage of its formation by the literary form which we now know goes back as far as the vassal treaties of the second millennium.[34] If therefore there is any book of the Old Testament in which a love analogous to that required of a vassal is likely to be found, it is in the book of Deuteronomy.

We must also take into account the juridical vocabulary in which the commandment of love is embedded. The dominance of legal language in Deuteronomy is evident and needs no proof. Moreover, many of the expressions have close parallels in the treaties of the first and second millennium.[35] Once therefore we realize that love has its place in this vocabulary, it is only sound to conclude that this explains its presence in Deuteronomy.

Even if in its use of the term love Deuteronomy should represent an innovation in Israel's covenant tradition, this would not diminish the probability of the interpretation we give the term. As we have seen, in the first millennium love still remains a duty of the vassal towards his sovereign. Influence from this direction on Deuteronomy is quite possible, for there is other evidence for very close contact with Assyrian treaty practices and expressions.

We may point first to the very long list of curses in Deuteronomy. Such length is unknown in treaties of the second millennium, but it does appear in the Esarhaddon text cited above.

More important is the presence in this same text of a curse which is substantially repeated in Deut 28:23. The Assyrian curse reads: "May they make your ground (hard) like *iron* so that none of you may flourish.

Just as rain does not fall from a *brazen* heaven, so may rain and dew not come upon your fields . . . ."[36] In Deut 28:23: "The sky over your heads will become like *bronze* and the earth under your feet like *iron*." So similar are these curses that Borger writes: "Der Deuteronomist muss doch irgendwie dieses ebenso gesuchte, wie einprägsame Bild einer assyrischen Quelle entnommen haben. Kam es vielleicht auch vor in einem Vertrag zwischen den Assyrern und den Judäern?" ["The Deuteronomist must have derived this somehow, taking it over as an impressive image from an Assyrian source. Did it perhaps occur in a treaty between the Assyrians and the Judeans?"—F. G.][37]

One more example, in fact one of the most striking parallels the writer knows between cuneiform and biblical literatures in any period. In a passage of his annals which describes an Arab revolt, Assurbanipal states that the curses written in the treaties were brought down upon the rebels by the gods of Assyria. The text goes on: "The people of Arubu asked one and other again and again, 'Why has such an evil thing as this overtaken Arubu?' (and) they say, 'Because we have not kept the mighty oaths of the god Assur, we have sinned against the favor shown us by Assurbanipal, the king beloved of Enlil.'"[38] In Deut 29:23ff. we read: "They and all the nations will say, 'Why has the Lord dealt thus with this land? Why this fierce outburst of wrath?' And they will say, 'Because they forsook the covenant which the Lord, the God of their fathers, had made with them . . . and they went and served other gods . . .'"[39] Identical contexts (the curses of the treaty/covenant), identical literary form. The biblical passage shows only insignificant differences: the question is asked and answered by future generations, not by those suffering from the curses; the biblical answer, though basically identical with the Assyrian, is considerably expanded and of course is a statement of deuteronomic theology.[40]

In view of such parallels between Assyrian treaties and Deuteronomy,[41] we may be virtually certain that deuteronomic circles were familiar with the Assyrian practice of demanding an oath of allegiance from their vassals expressed in terms of love. In line with Borger's proposal above, we may even assume that they knew of such oaths by Israelite kings.[42]

But is the term love an innovation in the Israelite covenant tradition? We think not, at least it is no innovation made by the author of Deut

6:5, which is generally considered the earliest reference to the love of God in Deuteronomy.

First, Judg 5:31: "May all your enemies perish thus, O Lord! but your friends[43] be as the sun rising in its might!" It has often been debated whether this verse, so unlike the rest of the Song of Deborah and so reminiscent of the Psalms, belongs to the original poem. The question will undoubtedly remain *sub judice,* but Weiser's cultic interpretation of the entire Song is persuasively argued, and if correct, would prove the antiquity of v. 31.[44] Certainly the conclusion has an archaic ring, and the reference to the Israelites as Yahweh's "friends" becomes perfectly intelligible in the light of our remarks on the covenant background of the term love. The Israelites are those bound to Yahweh in covenant, and therefore naturally opposed to his enemies; the war and victory described in the Song are those of the people of God. It is probable therefore that the term love goes back to a very early period in the Israelite covenant tradition.

Certainly the use of the term is earlier than its appearance in Deut 6:5. We make this assertion on the ground that Deut 6:4–18[45] is by way of commentary a series of citations and allusions to the beginning of the Decalogue. "And thou shalt love the Lord, thy God, . . ." in 6:5 presupposes therefore "those who love me" in 5:10 (Exod 20:6).

The citations and allusions to the Decalogue in 6:10–15 are clear.[46] 6:12 ("the Lord, who brought you out of the land of Egypt, that place of slavery") cites the beginning of the Decalogue. 6:14 ("You shall not follow other gods") is a restatement of the first commandment in typically deuteronomic terminology. 6:15 ("for the Lord, your God, who is in your midst, is a jealous God") repeats the motive clause, with the addition of "in your midst," of 5:9 (Exod. 20:5).

Framing, so to speak, the concrete application of the Decalogue to the period of the settlement in Palestine are the allusions to the Decalogue in 6:5 and 6:17, which refer to 5:10 (Exod 20:6): *wĕʾāhabtā = lĕʾōhăbai, šāmôr tišmĕrûn ʾet miṣwōt YHWH ʾĕlōhêkem = ulĕšōmĕrê miṣwōtai.*[47] This seems evident from a number of considerations:

(1) In the context of 6:10–15, which is one of allusion to and citation of the Decalogue, the injunction to love Yahweh and keep his commandments is most likely also an allusion to the Decalogue.

(2) The sequence of *miṣwōt-ʿēdōt-ḥuqqîm,* though found elsewhere (1 Chr 29:19; 2 Chr 34:31; cf. 2 Kgs 23:3), never occurs in Deuteronomy. This points to a special reason guiding the author's choice among the many expressions for law, commandments, etc. An adequate explanation would be the desire to allude to the Decalogue.

(3) The superscription of 4:45 has the sequence *ʿēdōt-ḥuqqîm-mišpāṭîm,* which is repeated in 6:20. Since 6:17 is the only other passage in Deuteronomy where *ʿēdōt* is used, one would expect the sequence of 4:45 and 6:20. The initial position of *miṣwōt* and its replacing *mišpāṭîm* may again be explained by the influence of the Decalogue.[48]

(4) The phrase *ʾăšer ṣiwwāk* looks back to Horeb, not to the present time in Moab. In the relevant passages,[49] the general rule is that, where Yahweh is said to have commanded, and the speaker is Moses at the time of the promulgation of the deuteronomic laws,[50] then the perfect *ṣiwwâ* refers either to laws given the people at Horeb,[51] or to the command given Moses at Horeb to remain with Yahweh and learn the laws he was to communicate in Moab.[52] For this reason one never finds ". . . which Yahweh has commanded TODAY," or "just as Yahweh has commanded TODAY." The TODAY of Deuteronomy is confined to the participle *mĕṣawwe.*

Thus in 4:13 Moses speaks of the Decalogue as *ʾăšer ṣiwwâ ʾetkem,* and continues in 4:14, "but me he commanded *(ṣiwwâ)* at that time . . . ." Similarly in 5:32–6:2: in vv. 32–33 (*ṣiwwâ* twice) we have a brief parenesis on the observance of the Decalogue, recalled in 5:6–21; in 6:1 *ṣiwwâ* refers to the personal revelation to Moses at Horeb; in 6:2, however, we shift to the participle, *mĕṣawwekā,* because the laws revealed to Moses at Horeb are now being promulgated.

Most of the exceptions to this rule are apparent rather than real. In 13:6[53] and 17:3 the subject is the worship of other gods, and therefore based on the first commandment of the Decalogue. 20:17 is concerned with the destruction of the Canaanites, which was also commanded at Horeb.[54] 24:8 speaks of commands given the priests and Levites; it is difficult to say what commands are referred to, but they are not to be found in Deuteronomy.[55] 12:21 does refer to a law in Deuteronomy, namely 12:15, and 28:45 speaks of the entire law in Deuteronomy as having been commanded by Yahweh, which is quite without parallel (cf. 28:1,13,14,15). It should be observed, however, that 12:21 and 28:45 regard laws already announced to the people.

If, however, 6:5 and 6:17 allude to the Decalogue, then it is clear that *lĕʾōhăbai ulĕšōmĕrê miṣwōtai* was in the Decalogue at the time of the composition of 6:4ff.[56] No one would suggest that it was added by the author of 6:4ff. so that it could be subsequently alluded to. For this author the Decalogue in its present form represented the old normative tradition, the basis of Israelite existence, elements of which he singled out, commented upon, and applied to the Israel of his own time.

To sum up: our ancient Near Eastern sources suggest a quite new approach to the problem of the origins of the deuteronomic doctrine on the love of God. In their light it seems highly questionable whether Hosea's preaching is at all relevant, except perhaps in the sense that Hosea's highly personal vision was grounded in the older covenant tradition we find in Deuteronomy. It is of course possible that the emphasis placed on love in the deuteronomic tradition is to be partially explained by the prophet's influence. But the deuteronomic love of service is older, probably as old or almost as old as the covenant itself. If so, and if the old sovereign-vassal terminology of love is as relevant as we think it is, then what a history lies behind the Christian test of true *agape*—"If you love me, keep my commandments"!

NOTES

1. C. Spicq, O.P., *Agapè, Prolégomènes à une étude de théologie néo-testamentaire* (Studia Hellenistica 10; Louvain: E. Nauwelaerts—Leiden: E. J. Brill, 1955) 89.
2. More recent studies: Spicq, *op. cit.*, 71–119; V. Warnach, *Agape, Die Liebe als Grundmotiv der neutestamentlichen Theologie* (Düsseldorf: Patmos-Verlag, 1951) 54–88; C. Wiéner, *Recherches sur l'amour pour Dieu dans l'Ancien Testament* (Paris: Letouzey et Ané, 1957) especially 38–46. See also W. Eichrodt, *Theologie des Alten Testaments* (4th ed.; Stuttgart: E. Klotz—Göttingen: Vandenhoeck u. Ruprecht, 1961) 200–207; G. von Rad, *Theologie des Alten Testaments* (München: Chr. Kaiser, 1958) 222–223.
3. Cf. A. Alt, *Kleine Schriften zur Geschichte des Volkes Israel* (München: C. H. Beck, 1953) II, 272; H. Breit, *Die Predigt des Deuteronomium* (München: Chr. Kaiser, 1933) 158; Eichrodt, *op. cit.*, 203; G. von Rad, *Das Gottesvolk im Deuteronomium* (*BWANT* 47; Stuttgart: W. Kohlhammer, 1929) 81; A. C. Welch, *ExpT* 41 (1929–30) 550; cf. also H. W. Wolff, *Dodekapropheton* (BK 14; Neukirchen: Neukirchener Verlag, 1957) 76.
4. Against von Rad, *Theologie des A.T.*, I, 223.
5. On the meaning of *ʾāhēb*, see most recently Wolff, *op. cit.*, 42.

6. Alt, *op. cit.*, 272–73, sees the necessity of allowing for others besides the prophet who prepared the ground for the deuteronomic call to the love of God. Cf. also von Rad, *Theologie des A.T.*, I, 223.
7. Wiéner, *op. cit.*, 43.
8. Eichrodt, *op. cit.*, 206; Spicq, *op. cit.*, 92, n. 2.
9. Eichrodt, *op. cit.*, 205; Wiéner, *op. cit.*, 41. The Deuteronomist substitutes *ʿăbādîm* for *ʾōhăbîm* in 1 Kgs 8:23; cf. Deut 7:9.
10. We so translate *dābēq* in view of 2 Sam 20:2.
11. For a similar semantic development cf. *amicitia (amo)* and *philia (phileō)* for the friendship between nations established by treaty.
12. Georges Dossin, *Correspondence de Iasmaḫ-Addu* (Archives royales de Mari V; Paris: Imprimerie nationale, 1952) 76:4.
13. V. Korošec, *Mednarodni odnošaji po klinopisnih poročilih iz el-amarnskega in hetitskega državnega arhiva [International Relations according to Cuneiform Reports from the Tell el-Amarna and Hittite State Archives]* (Ljubljana: Državna založba Slovenije, 1950) 340 (English summary, 393). Elsewhere in the legal language of the Akkadian sources *râmu* denotes the free choice of a person; P. Koschaker, *JCS* 5 (1951) 108, n. 14.
14. For references see the Glossary in J. A. Knudtzon, *Die El-Amarna-Tafeln* (=*EA*, Leipzig: J. C. Hinrich, 1915) II, 1493–1494, under *raʾāmu* and *raʾamūtu*. Note especially "friendship and brotherhood," *ibid.*, I, 29:166.
15. Cf. *EA* 8:8–12. In *JNES* 22(1963)173–76 the writer attempts to show that *ṭābūtu* and related forms occur in Assyrian texts and in the Sefîre inscriptions *(ṭbtʾ)* with reference to the friendship established by treaties.
16. *EA* 27:72–73.
17. *EA* 121:61; 123:23; 158:6. Also E. F. Weidner, *Politische Dokumente aus Kleinasien* (Boghazköi-Studien 8; Leipzig: J. C. Hinrich, 1923) 56:59–62.
18. *EA* 53:40–44.
19. *EA* 114:68. For the reading and syntax of the line see the writer's remarks in *Orientalia* 29 (1960) 14.
20. *EA* 138:71–73.
21. *EA* 83:51; 137:47.
22. *EA* 73:15–19.
23. D. J. Wiseman, *Iraq* 20 (1958) 49 col. iv 266–68; cf. also 43 col. iii 207. For variant readings, see R. Borger, *ZA* 54 (1961) 181–82.
24. L. Waterman, *Royal Correspondence of the Assyrian Empire* (Ann Arbor: University of Michigan Press, 1930) 266, 1105:32. This document contains the oath imposed by Assurbanipal on his vassals and high officials to insure loyalty to himself in the imminent war with Šamaš-šum-ukin, his brother, in Babylon.
25. Montgomery-Gehman, *The Books of Kings* (ICC; Edinburgh: Clark, 1951) 132.
26. John Bright, *A History of Israel* (London: SCM Press, 1960) 183.
27. 2 Sam 10.
28. *EA* 33–34.

29. Cf. V. Korošec, *Hethitische Staatsverträge* (Leipziger rechtswissenschaftliche Studien 60; Leipzig: Theodor Weicher, 1931) 47,48. For reasons, however, to doubt that this practice fell under *parṣu ša šarrāni,* "(divine) regulation for kings," as Korošec asserts, see A. Goetze, *Kleinasien* (2d ed., Handbuch der Altertumswissenschaft, III.1.3.3.1; München: C. H. Beck, 1957) 98, n. 5.
30. It should be remarked that "friendship" was never a narrowly defined term, applicable only to one type of relationship, e.g., among equals. Cf. again *amicitia* and the observations of D. Timpe, *Hermes* 90 (1962) 336ff., especially 338 on the wide variety of power relations covered by metaphorical terms like *amicitia* and *patrocinium.*
31. Cf. *EA* 286:18–20: "Why do you love the ʿApiru and hate the (loyal) governors?"
32. H. W. Hertzberg, *Die Samuelbücher* (ATD 10; Göttingen: Vandenhoeck u. Ruprecht, 1960) 126.
33. Cf. the covenant between David and Jonathan, which seals their love for each other (1 Sam 18:1, 3; 20:17; cf. Spicq, *op. cit.,* 76); Jonathan loves David as himself, *kĕnapšô,* which recalls the oath of the Assyrian vassals to love Assurbanipal as themselves, *kī napšātkunu.*
34. This is already clear from K. Baltzer, *Das Bundesformular* (WMzANT 4; Neukirchen: Neukirchener Verlag, 1960) 40ff. The study of N. Lohfink, *Das Hauptgebot, Eine Untersuchung literarischer Einleitungsfragen zu Dtn 5–11* (Rome: Pontifical Biblical Institute, 1963), offers additional arguments; see also his study on the *Redaktionsgeschichte* of Dt 29–32 in *BZ* NF 6 (1962) 32–56. A. Jepsen, *Verbannung und Heimkehr* (Festschrift Rudolph; Tübingen: J. C. B. Mohr, 1961) 175, rejects any connection with the Hittite vassal treaties, since the Old Testament always speaks of God's covenant (Gottes *berith*) and never of Israel's covenant, and therefore God binds himself, not Israel. The strength of this argument may be judged from passages like "Keep Ḫatti's treaty of peace" (*riksa u šalama ša Ḫatti uṣur,* J. Nougayrol, *Le palais royal d'Ugarit* [Paris: Imprimerie nationale, 1956] IV, 36:19–21) and the many passages in Assyrian literature like "he sinned against my oaths (treaty)" *(ina adêya iḫṭīma),* M. Streck, *Assurbanipal und die letzten assyrischen Könige* (Vorderasiatische Bibliothek VII, Leipzig: J. C. Hinrich, 1916) II, 132:93; cf. *ibid.,* 64:85, 342, Rm II, Nr. 99:87; Waterman, *op. cit.,* 1380:5–12.
35. Many of these have been pointed out in recent literature and need not be noted here. We would call attention only to two. First, the expression, to go after other gods. As N. Lohfink has pointed out to me, Deuteronomy never uses the pejorative *zānâ* (save once, in 31:16, and this in the latest level of the document) but prefers the juridical term, "to go after," that is, to serve; on the legal implications of the term, which is also used of vassal relationships, see P. Koschaker, *art. cit.,* 108, and cf. *EA* 136:11ff., 149:46; 280:20. Second, the expression "with all your heart," which must be considered in the light of the treaty stipulations requiring the vassal to fight with all his

heart (*ina kul libbi,* Weidner, *op. cit.,* 60:17–19, 61:23, 70:11ff.; 9, 132:3; *ina gammurti libbi,* Wiseman, *art. cit.,* 41 iii 169, 51 v. 310, and cf. 33 i 52–53) or to be faithful and fight with all his heart (J. Nougayrol, *op. cit.,* 89:20–21; cf. 1 Macc 8:25).

36. Wiseman, *art. cit.,* 69 col. vii 528–31.
37. Borger, *art. cit.,* 191–92.
38. Streck, *op. cit.,* 79:68–73. The parallel to Deut 29:23ff. is pointed out by Streck, 78, n. 4, with a reference to D. H. Müller's *Ezechielstudien,* 61–62.
39. On the basis of the Assyrian parallel we have slightly modified CCD's translation. Since in the Assyrian text the same ones who ask the question answer it, it is to be assumed that the subjects of *wĕāmĕrû* in vv. 23 and 24 are identical; so also in the parallel passages 1 Kgs 9:8–9; Jer 22:8–9.
40. What remains to be investigated is the *Sitz im Leben* of this form; this we leave to another occasion.
41. The actual parallels may of course be later than the earliest texts in Deuteronomy on the love of God, but they still demonstrate the connection of the deuteronomic tradition with Assyrian treaties.
42. For example, Manasseh may have taken the oath in Assyria to love Assurbanipal; this would be the basis for the tradition preserved in 2 Chr 33:11–13 (cf. Wiseman, *art. cit.,* 4). Since in view of the evidence of the second millennium the oath to love the sovereign hardly arose only in the early seventh century, we may safely assume that kings like Menahem also promised to love their Assyrian lord.
43. MT, "his friends."
44. A. Weiser, *ZAW* 71 (1959) 94–95.
45. Deut 6:19 seems to have been added; cf. 9:4.
46. I proposed this view of Deut 6:10–15 in my lecture notes *Adnotationes in librum Deuteronomii,* 100ff., in 1960, and compared von Rad's study of later levitical preaching (Die levitische Predigt in den Büchern der Chronik, *Gesammelte Studien zum A.T.* [München; Chr. Kaiser, 1958] 248–61). Subsequently and quite independently, as N. Lohfink informs me, H. G. Reventlow proposed a very similar view at the 15th *Orientalistentag.* I should like to express my debt to Lohfink on two accounts: first, following his criticisms, I have here not proposed "him shall you serve and in his name shall you swear" as allusions to 5:9 *(toʿobdēm)* and 5:11, so that the order of the Decalogue is now perfectly preserved in 6:12–15 (5:6,7,10); second, it was the study of his dissertation (cf. n. 34 above) with its invaluable tables on the usage of the terms for law and their observance, as well as his own study of the structure of Deut 6, that allowed me to see the significance of the references to love and keeping the commandments in 6:5, 17. For whatever may be correct therefore in the remarks that follow, a large share of the credit is due to Lohfink.
47. MT, *miṣwōtau,* Ketib, *miṣwātô;* cf. app. crit. in Kittel, *BH*^{3}.
48. Another factor in the omission of *mišpāṭîm* may have been that the Decalogue does not contain *m.*, if *m.* are customary laws (casuistic).

49. We do not consider therefore 1:19; 1:41; 2:37; 10:5; 18:18,20; 31:23; 34:9.
50. Therefore the following passages drop out: 6:20,24,25; 26:13,14.
51. 4:13,23; 5:32,33; 6:17; 9:12,16; 13:6; 17:3; 20:17. The passages of the Decalogue 5:12, 15, 16 constitute a special problem, because the Decalogue is presented as a direct quotation. Whatever their explanation may be, they are not a difficulty for our view on the other passages with the perfect. It may also be noted that the Decalogue in Exodus does not contain these references to the past.
52. 1:3; 4:5,14; 6:1; 28:69.
53. Note the reference in the same verse to the historical prologue of the Decalogue.
54. The immediate reference is to 7:2, but this is a deuteronomic reformulation of an older text (cf. S. R. Driver, *A Critical and Exegetical Commentary on Deuteronomy* [ICC, Edinburgh: T. and T. Clark, 1902] 239–240, who correctly refers to Exod 23:31–33). On the relation of Exod 23:20–33; 34:10–16, and Deut 7:1–5, I again refer to Lohfink's dissertation.
55. C. Steuernagel, *Deuteronomium und Josua* (HK 3. Göttingen: Vandenhoeck u. Ruprecht, 1900) 89, thinks of laws like Lev 13f. and is probably correct in interpreting such a reference as a sign of a late addition.
56. We agree with H. G. Reventlow, *Gebot und Predigt im Dekalog* (Gütersloh: G. Mohn, 1962) 40, that the assumption of a "deuteronomic" redaction of the Decalogue should be buried once and for all. The Decalogue was transmitted and acquired its additions in the cult. It should be remarked that Deuteronomy itself never uses the participle—7:9 cites the Decalogue—but the participle is well attested in the Psalms (5:12; 69:37; 97:10; 145:20; cf. also 31:24).

5

Temple Architecture: What Can Archaeology Tell Us about Solomon's Temple?

Volkmar Fritz

Solomon's Temple presents a double puzzle, one old and the other more recent. The first relates to the fact that the Biblical description of the building is not entirely clear and can be interpreted in several ways. The second puzzle relates to the origin of the architecture: What is the architectural source of the building?

It may seem strange that the Bible's description of Solomon's Temple is so inexact, especially because the Temple furniture and utensils are described so minutely. For example, the bronze laver stands are described in minute detail (1 Kgs 7:27–9); the building description itself lacks all detail except for a brief notice concerning the windows (1 Kgs 6:2–4). No one has ever really explained why the Temple furniture and utensils are so fully described compared to the brief and ambiguous description of the Temple itself.

Certain other aspects of the structure are also given in detail. We are told, for example, that the doors to the Inner Sanctuary *(debir)* were made of olive wood carved in relief with cherubim, palm trees and open flowers, all overlaid with gold (1 Kgs 6:31–32). The side chambers are also described rather extensively (1 Kgs 6:5–10), but this description is probably a later addition and can therefore be ignored for purposes of reconstructing the original plan of that temple.[1]

But the plan of the building itself, as the great Israeli archaeologist

Reprinted by permission from the *Biblical Archaeology Review* 13, no. 4 (July–August 1987):38–49.

Yohanan Aharoni once observed, is "perplexing and complicated," "ambiguous," and at times "even contradictory."[2]

The Temple was the central structure in the Temple compound. Our initial question is whether this central building consisted of one, two or three rooms. Scholars have argued over this question for a very long time. Some interpret the Biblical description as outlining a building of three adjoining rooms, following a so-called tripartite plan, consisting of the entrance hall, the main hall and an inner sanctuary or shrine. Others argue that the building was essentially two rooms, either because, in their view, the entrance hall was simply an open portico or because the shrine was not really a separate room architecturally speaking. Still others say the Temple was really a single room.

I incline to the last view. Actually it is really a matter of definition, whether or not you count the entrance hall and the inner sanctuary or shrine as separate rooms. What is important is that Solomon's Temple was a long-room temple; that is, it was oriented with the entrance on the short side and the shrine at the other end of the building. Viewing the building as a long-room temple, as opposed to a broad-room temple, is the key to understanding its architectural source. Long-room temples vary greatly, but they all belong to one type.

Before pursuing this subject, however, let us return to the Biblical description of Solomon's Temple.

The entire temple building is referred to in the Bible as the House *(bayit)* for Yahweh. It was 60 cubits long, 20 cubits wide and 30 cubits high (1 Kgs 6:2).[3] In the next verse, we are told that there was a portico or porch *(ʾulam)* in front of the Main Hall *(heikhal)* of the House *(bayit)* (1 Kgs 6:3).

In the description of the woodwork, an additional element is mentioned: "Twenty cubits from the rear of the House, he [Solomon] built [a partition] of cedar planks . . . to serve as an Inner Sanctuary *(debir)*, as the Holy of Holies *(Qodesh Ha-Qodashim)*" (1 Kgs 6:16). And again, "In the innermost part of the House *(bayit)*, he [Solomon] fixed an Inner Sanctuary *(debir)* in which to place the 'ark of the Lord's Covenant' " (1 Kgs 6:19).

From this description it is clear that the Temple was built on a long-room plan (like this □), rather than a broad-room plan (like this ▭). This plan, it seems, was something like the drawing in figure 1.

The dimensions of the various parts of the House are a little unclear.

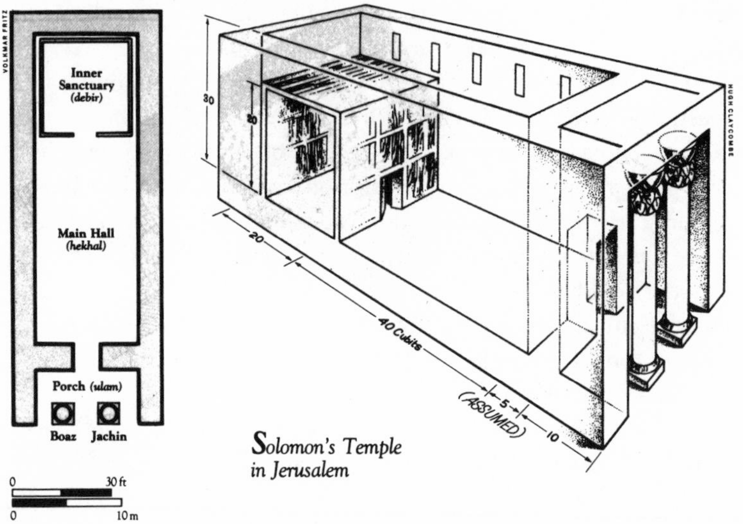

Figure 1

The Portico appears to have been 10 cubits deep (1 Kgs 6:3). The Main Sanctuary was 40 cubits (1 Kgs 6:17). The Inner Sanctuary was 20 cubits (1 Kgs 6:20). This adds up to 70 cubits, not 60 cubits; but 60 cubits is the overall length previously given for the House. Perhaps the Biblical writer did not consider the 10-cubit Portico as part of the House.

The Inner Sanctuary presents its own problems. The Bible tells us it was only 20 cubits *high* (1 Kgs 6:20), but the House itself, however, was 30 cubits high (1 Kgs 6:2). Perhaps the Inner Sanctuary *(debir)* was only a kind of olive wood structure placed within the Main Sanctuary. Above the Inner Sanctuary was probably an empty space 10 cubits high.

Another problem relating to whether the Inner Sanctuary should be considered a separate room involves the nature of the wall separating the Inner Sanctuary from the rest of the Main Sanctuary. The 60-cubit length of the House, consisting of a Main Sanctuary of 40 cubits and an Inner Sanctuary of 20 cubits leaves no room for a wall between the two. Was it simply a thin wooden screen? If so, should the Inner Sanctuary be considered architecturally a part of the Main Sanctuary or should it be considered a separate room? That this Inner Sanctuary was built entirely of wood, rather than stone (the main building material), also

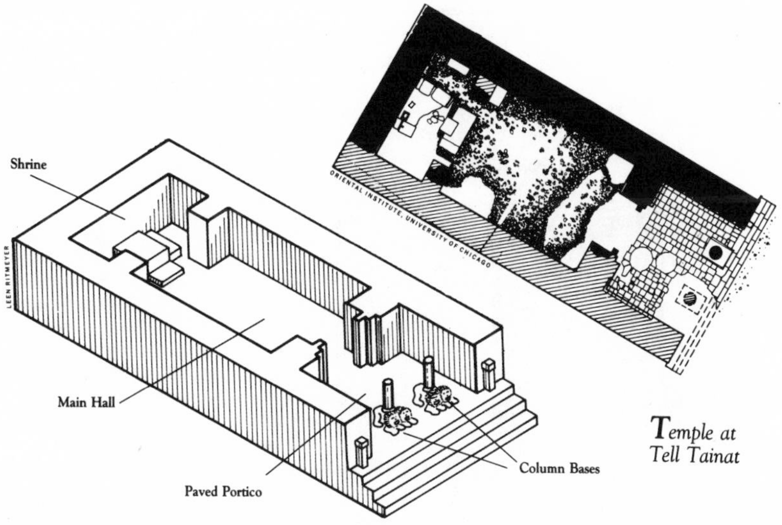

Figure 2

suggests that it should not be considered a separate room, but rather as a kind of shrine.

Another question is whether we should consider the Temple as consisting essentially of the Main Hall; that is, are the House *(bayit)* and the Sanctuary *(heikhal)* synonymous? In this connection, *heikhal* is sometimes used to refer to the entire Temple (2 Kgs 18:16; 23:4; 24:13), although elsewhere it appears to be only one of the parts of the Temple.[4]

As I have already suggested, it really doesn't matter whether we consider Solomon's Temple as one, two or three rooms, as long as we understand it is a long-room temple. Based on the archaeological materials I will discuss, we can conclude that the entrance area was an open hall, consisting of two walls extending like arms from the walls of the building itself. Although this portico was roofed, it was not enclosed on the front. The Inner Sanctuary was basically an internal structure (see figure 1). Whether you consider this one, two or three rooms is important only because scholars have argued about it for so long in their effort to find the architectural source of the structure.

In the past 15 years several new temples have been uncovered in northern Syria which now make clear the source of this architecture.

Temple at Tell Tainat

Figure 3

To understand the significance of these new discoveries, we must first understand the problems that existed prior to their discovery.

In 1930, the University of Chicago's Oriental Institute uncovered a small temple at a site in the Amuq Valley, at the northern Orontes known as Tell Tainat.[5] This temple bore a remarkable resemblance to Solomon's Temple as described in the Bible. It was a long room measuring 82 feet by 39 feet (25 by 12 meters) divided into a portico, a main hall and a shrine (figures 2 and 3). Within the portico stood two columns on lion bases, only one of which was preserved. The shrine was rather small and contained remains of a platform for a statue of the deity. In front of this platform was a square structure that may have served for offerings. This temple stood beside the palace on its southern side.

The temple at Tell Tainat could not have been the source of Solomon's Temple, however, because it was built later than Solomon's Temple, in the eighth century B.C. Moreover, the Tell Tainat temple stood in isolation. It was the only example known from this part of the world. Its own architectural history was unknown.

Since then several temples of the second millennium B.C. have been uncovered in northern Syria which help solve the puzzle. It now appears that the architectural source of the long-room temple is to be found in northern Syria. Moreover, this temple-type itself can now be traced to the *megaron* type of building in Anatolia of the third millennium B.C. In short, we can now trace the development of this architecture with considerable precision. (see figures 4 and 5 comparing Anatolian *megaron* buildings with later temples in Syria and Canaan.)

The *megaron* from the third millennium in Anatolia was a residence consisting of a single long room. The two long walls extended beyond the short front wall like arms, creating an open portico whose roof could be supported by columns. In a variation of this plan, the entrance hall was enclosed; sometimes the main room was subdivided. From the third millennium, variations of this basic house have been found in Troy, Beyʾçesultan, Karataş-Seymayük, Tarsus and Kültepe, all in modern Turkey. The *megaron* disappears in southern Anatolia in the second millennium, but it continues in Greece until about 1200 B.C.[6]

By the second millennium this basic house plan was being used for temple architecture in northern Syria. Strangely enough, in Syria, the plan was not used for residences. Thus, we can say that the long-room temple with projecting arms is a Syrian temple-type.

The famous site of Ebla has produced not only cuneiform tablets, but also much important architecture, including three temples all dated to the first half of the second millennium B.C. Two of them (Temples B1 and N) are simple one-room structures, but the third—Temple D—is a long-room building, with an entrance portico created by the extension of the long walls like arms beyond the front of the building (see figure 4). It also has a niche in the back, presumably for a statue of the deity, which is approached by an elevated step. In addition, between the portico and the main hall is a kind of antechamber from which one goes up three steps into the main sanctuary.[7]

But there are other examples of this basic temple plan from two more sites in northern Syria, both dating to the second half of the second millennium, the period called the Late Bronze Age (1550 B.C.–1200 B.C.). The temples at these two sites—Tell Munbaqa and Emar—reflect a basic long-room plan with an open portico in front (see figure 4).

At each of these two sites, the excavators found two temples near each other. So, in all, we have four temples, each with the same basic plan. Tell Munbaqa on the east bank of the middle Euphrates River was

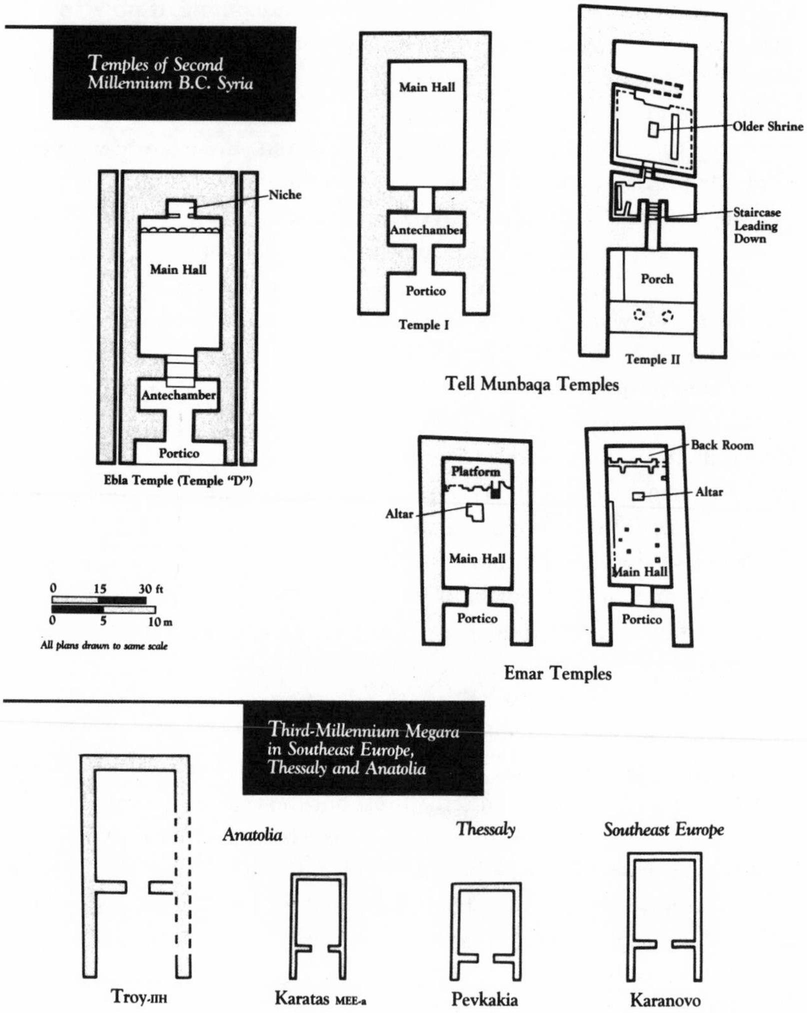

Figure 4

excavated between 1969 and 1974 by the German Oriental Society. As can be seen from the plan on figure 4, Temple I at Munbaqa was quite similar to the Ebla temple; both had an additional room between the portico and the main hall of the temple. About 150 feet from Temple I at Tel Munbaqa was Temple II. The interior of the long room in Temple II at Munbaqa seems to include an older sanctuary, but the basic plan,

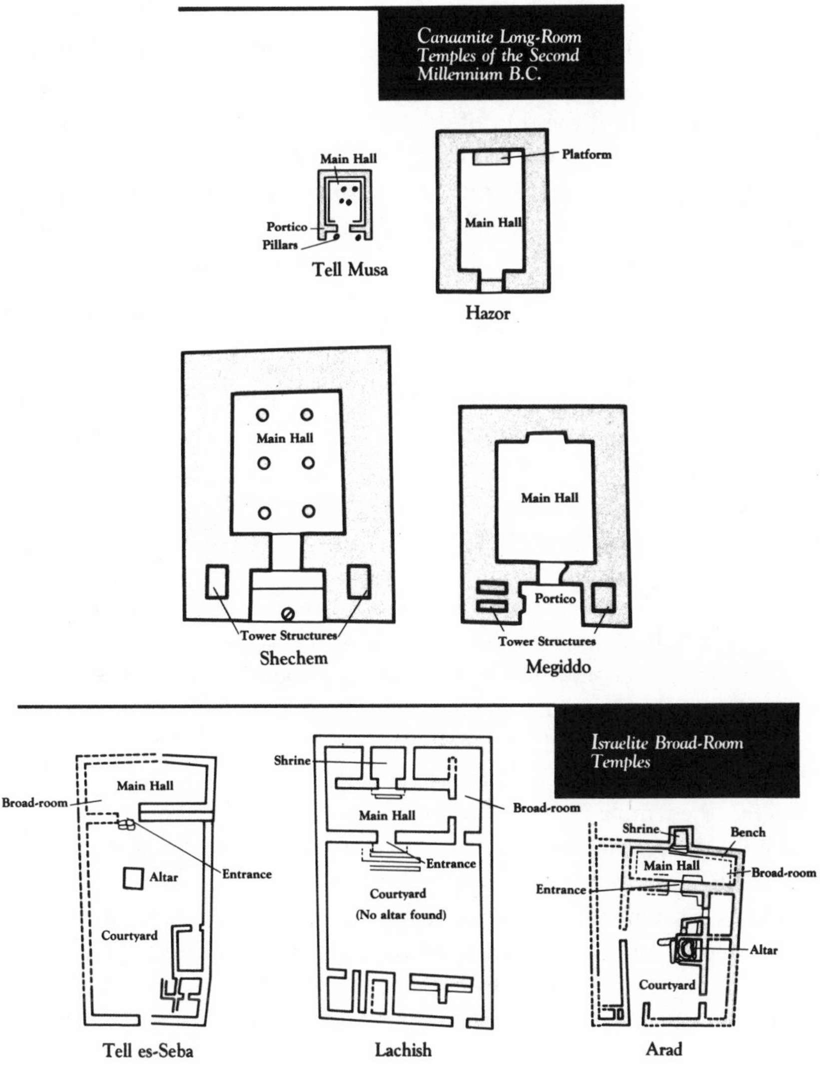

Figure 5

including the portico, is clear. Here the archaeologists even found indications of where the two columns stood that supported the roof of the portico.[8]

Tell Emar is situated on the west bank of the Euphrates. It was excavated between 1972 and 1974 by a French expedition.[9] The two temples there stood side by side on top of the tell and are almost identical. Each consists of a long room and an unenclosed entrance hall formed by the extension of the long walls (plan on figure 4). Incidentally, columns to support the roof of the portico were not found; it is possible that there was no roof. Each of these temples had an altar toward the back of the main room. At the back of one of the temples was a raised platform reached by steps, most probably for a statue of the deity. In the other temple at Emar, a wall at the back of the main room created a separate small room. It is unlikely, however, that this was an inner sanctuary because of the location of the entrance to this room.

Another long-room temple has been found at En Dara in northern Syria. It is a monumental temple, but so poorly preserved that the details of its plan are unclear.[10] However, it is certain that it was a long-room temple dating to the second millennium.

From all these examples, we may conclude that during the second millennium, the long-room temple was widespread in Syria. The details varied. Some may have been just a long room. Others had a portico in front created by projecting walls. Still others had a room between the portico and the main hall. But the basic plan was the same.

During the second millennium, the long-room temple was imported from Syria into Canaan, although only a few examples have been discovered thus far. All of them, however, reflect the same basic plan even though there are also a number of differences. At Hazor, in Upper Galilee, the temple in area A of the upper city consists of only one room, without an entrance porch. Opposite the entrance was a platform[11] (figure 5, upper right).

At Tell Kitan, a small site in the Jordan Valley, we have an example with an open porch formed by two protruding walls. This temple is very small; it only measures 6.9 by 5.5 meters (23 feet by 18 feet); the row of stelae in front of it indicates that it was not a public temple but most probably a private sanctuary.[12]

A special development may be noted at two large temples in Shechem and Megiddo (figure 5). Both were probably erected during Middle Bronze II B (1750–1550 B.C.).[13] In each case, the entrance was flanked by two large towers. The various stages of construction found at the Tower Temple in Megiddo show that these towers were developed out of the enclosed porch.[14] They were probably higher than the building itself and added to the magnificent appearance of the temple.

At Shechem a second temple stood beside the city gate for a brief period during the 16th century B.C. It was a tripartite building: In front of the main hall was an enclosed entrance hall. A small stone platform was built against the back wall, opposite the entrance. A third room in the back of the building could be reached through a small door. This room was by no means an inner sanctuary, because its entrance was located directly beside the outer wall, far off of the central axis of the building.[15]

These temples in northern Syria and Canaan show that the long-room temple was a common type long before Solomon decided to build a temple for Yahweh in Jerusalem.

That is not to say that Solomon's Temple was directly influenced by these earlier temples in northern Syria and Canaan. Basically, King Solomon wanted a palace. He instructed his state officials to build him one—the Temple was to be a part of the palace compound. These state officials turned to craftsmen who were familiar with the necessary planning and building techniques: the Phoenicians. The tradition of this dependence on Phoenician knowledge is preserved in the Biblical account. The cooperation between King Solomon and Hiram of Tyre is indeed described in great detail in 1 Kings 5.

Phoenician temples no longer exist, or at least we have not yet found them. But now with the archaeological evidence I have just recounted, we can be sure that these Phoenician temples, which were the inspiration for Solomon's Temple, were themselves descendants of the long-room type, so well preserved in Syria and Canaan. Thus, the theory about the architectural origin of Solomon's Temple developed by Albrecht Alt long ago[16] has now been confirmed.

The fact that Solomon's Temple relied on exemplars that have not survived should hardly be surprising, but this emphasizes the difficulty of tracing the antecedents of Solomon's Temple. It is as if we were called upon to trace the history of the Gothic cathedral from an example in England, two in France and one in Germany, instead of from the hundreds of Gothic cathedrals that in fact exist. In the case of Solomon's Temple, we are called upon to trace its history from a bare handful of examples spanning a thousand years. In these circumstances, certainty must elude us, although the outlines of this history now seem clear.

This history allows us to draw these conclusions about Solomon's Temple:

1. The Inner Sanctuary *(debir)* should probably be understood as a shrine rather than a separate room. This accords well with the Biblical text, as well as the archaeological evidence.
2. The Portico (*'ulam*) should be understood as an unenclosed porch. The two columns, designated Jachin and Boaz in the Bible (1 Kgs 7:15–22), were within this portico, not outside it, as suggested in many reconstructions. These two columns probably supported the roof of the portico; they also enhanced the appearance of the building, giving it an impressive entranceway.

We cannot conclude this discussion without mentioning the indigenous Israelite temple, which also existed, an example of which was found at Arad. The Arad temple was discovered in 1963 by Israeli archaeologist Yohanan Aharoni.[17] Its discovery came as a great surprise because Arad was a small fortress on the border between the Judean Mountains and the Negev. The fortress was probably established to secure and control the roads leading to the southern deserts and to Egypt. The Bible makes no mention of a sanctuary at Arad, although places of worship are mentioned outside Jerusalem at Shiloh, Bethel, Gilgal, Beer-Sheva and elsewhere.

The Arad temple, like the fortress itself, was apparently founded in Solomon's time. In subsequent generations, however, the temple was rebuilt three times, although with only minor changes. It was finally abolished in the late eighth century during King Hezekiah's reign, probably as part of Hezekiah's religious reform, which centralized worship in Jerusalem and attempted to stamp out cultic centers elsewhere in the country (2 Kgs 18:4).

This temple at Arad is the only Israelite temple discovered so far. It seems clear that the Israelite God Yahweh was worshipped here. The plan of the temple, however, bears no resemblance to Solomon's Temple as described in the Bible. The temple at Arad is a broadroom; that is, the entrance is on the long side and the building is oriented by the long wall.

The main room of the Arad temple is small—approximately 3 by 10 meters, corresponding to 6 by 20 cubits of the Israelite standard measurement in which one cubit equaled 21 inches (52.5 cm). Benches on which bowls with offerings could be placed lined the walls of the main room.

Opposite the entrance a raised niche approached by three steps was added to the room. On the uppermost step two small incense altars were found lying on their sides. Originally they must have flanked the entrance to the niche, in order to separate the Holy of Holies from the main room.

Within the niche two stelae were found. One had fallen over on the floor; the other was built into the rear wall and had probably been covered with plaster. The one on the floor showed signs of red paint and had probably originally been painted.

This stone stela is probably what the Bible refers to as a *maṣṣēbah*. Its use in Yahwistic worship, although condemned, is frequently referred to at Israelite high places and other cult sites. Not a single figurine or other pagan votive offering was found, however. Given the fact that the Arad temple was located entirely within Israelite territory, all these factors point rather clearly to a Yahwistic temple.

In front of the Arad temple was a courtyard with a large altar constructed of field stones. Nearby, under the pavement, the complete skeleton of a sheep was found, together with some juglets.

The plan of the temple of Arad, however, is entirely different from the plan of the temple in Jerusalem built by Solomon. The temple plan of Arad probably goes back to the house architecture of early Israel and must therefore be considered as an authentic Israelite temple form.

Nevertheless, when Solomon wanted to build a house to Israel's God on the Temple Mount in Jerusalem, adjacent to his own palace, he looked not to available Israelite prototypes, but to Phoenician exemplars, which in turn we can now trace back to long-room temples in northern Syria and eventually back to the *megaron* in use in Anatolia, nearly 2,000 years before Solomon built his House of the Lord.

NOTES

1. Konrad Rupprecht, "Nachrichten von Erweiterung und Renovierung des Tempels in 1. Könige 6" *ZDPV* 88 (1972), pp. 38–52.
2. Yohanon Aharoni, "The Solomonic Temple, the Tabernacle and the Arad Sanctuary," in H. A. Hoffner, ed., *Orient and Occident,* The C. H. Gordon Festschrift (Neukirchen-Vluyn, 1973), pp. 1–8.
3. Two cubits were used at this time, the old cubit and the royal cubit. The Bible probably refers here to the royal cubit, measuring 52.5 centimeters. The old cubit is 45 centimeters. See R. B. Y. Scott, "Weights and Measures

of the Bible," *BA* 22 (1959), 22–40, especially pp. 23–27; Gaby Barkay, "Measurements in the Bible—Evidence at St. Étienne for the Length of the Cubit and the Reed," *BAR* 12:2(March/April 1986), p. 37.

4. Ludwig Koehler and Walter Baumgartner, *Lexicon in Veteris Testamenti Libros* (Leiden, 1958), pp. 230–231; T. A. Busink, *Der Tempel von Jerusalem,* I (Leiden, 1970), pp. 180–181. This double usage also occurs in Akkadian. In Akkadian, *ekallu* can mean either an entire building or its "main room" (*Chicago Assyrian Dictionary* E, 60; Wolfram von Soden, *Akkadisches Handwörterbuch I,* 192).
5. Robert C. Haines, *Excavations in the Plain of Antioch, II* (Chicago, 1971), pp. 53–55, plate 103.
6. Rudolph Naumann, *Architektur Kleinasiens* (2nd ed., Tübingen, 1971), pp. 343ff.; J. Warner, "The Megaron and Apsidal House in Early Bronze Age Western Anatolia: New Evidence from Karatas," *American Journal of Archaeology* 83 (1979), 133–147.
7. Paolo Matthiae, *Ebla. An Empire Reconsidered* (Garden City, N.Y., 1981), pp. 112ff.
8. Winfried Orthmann and Hartmut Kühne, "Mumbaqat 1973," *MDOG* 106 (1974), pp. 53–97; Orthmann, "Mumbaqat 1974," *MDOG* 108 (1976), pp. 25–44.
9. Jean Margueron, "Quatre campagnes de fouilles à Emar (1972–1974): un bilan provisoire," *Syria* 52 (1975), p. 62f.
10. F. Seirafi, A. Kirichian and M. Dunand, "Recherches archéologiques à Ayin Dara au nord-ouest d'Alep," *Annales archéologiques arabes de Syrie* XV:2 (1965), pp. 3–20.
11. Yigael Yadin, *Hazor, The Head of All Those Kingdoms, Joshua 11:10* (London, 1972), pp. 102–104.
12. Emmanuel Eisenberg, "The Temples at Tell Kitan," *BA* 40 (1977), pp. 77–81.
13. G. Ernest Wright, *Shechem, The Biography of a Biblical City* (New York and Toronto, 1965), pp. 80–102; G. Loud, *Megiddo II Seasons of 1935–39* (Chicago, 1948), pp. 102–105; Claire Epstein, "An Interpretation of the Megiddo Sacred Area During the Middle Bronze II," *Israel Exploration Journal* 15 (1965), pp. 204–221.
14. Immanuel Dunayevsky and Aharon Kempinski, "The Megiddo Temples." *ZDPV* 89 (1973), pp. 161–187.
15. William G. Dever, "The MB II C Stratification in the Northwest Gate Area at Shechem," *Bulletin of the American Schools of Oriental Research* 216 (1974), pp. 31–52.
16. Albrecht Alt, "Verbreitung und Herkunft des Syrischen Tempeltypus," *Kleine Schriften,* II (Munich, 1953), pp. 100–115.
17. Aharoni, "Arad: Its Inscriptions and Temple," *BA* 31 (1968), pp. 2–32.

6

Egyptian Wisdom and the Old Testament

Ernst Würthwein

The *rediscovery of the ancient Near East* may be considered one of the most interesting events in modern historical research. While our knowledge of the ancient peoples who lived in Mesopotamia and along the Nile, in Syria and Asia Minor had previously been quite meager, that situation altered radically as archaeological research began in those regions in the nineteenth century and a wealth of heretofore unknown materials of the most diverse sorts came to light. Among these, texts—written on papyrus, clay tablets and other material—which had survived the millennia proved to be especially instructive, and were now accessible as authentic records to the first ranks of scientific investigation. New branches of science, egyptology and cuneiform studies arose and made available the new-found documents of historical, religious, juridical, economic and other contents, whose number, already almost incalculable, continues to grow. Thus, direct and extremely vivid insights into every area of the life of these ancient peoples became possible as a result. The limits of our historical understandings, in the broad sense of the word, were pushed back by millennia. The process itself has become familiar to a wide public through popular scientific publications, so that I may content myself here with a brief allusion to it.

The rediscovery of the ancient Near East also served to show the OT

Originally appeared as "Die Weisheit Ägyptens und das Alte Testament: Rede zur Rektoratsübergabe am 29. November 1958," *Schriften der Philips-Universität Marburg* (Marburg: N. G. Elwert Verlag, 1960). Translated by Brian W. Kovacs, in James Crenshaw, ed., *Studies in Ancient Israelite Wisdom* (New York: Ktav, 1976), 113–33. Reprinted here by permission of N. G. Elwert Verlag and Ktav Publishing House.

in a new light. Israel, whose literature handed down through the OT had until then been considered incomparably old, now proved itself in truth to be a newcomer among the peoples of the ancient Near East. That in many respects it stood under the spiritual influence of those cultures could not be denied. Did that mean, however, that it was almost fully devoid of any originality, as a certain school contended in the famous Babel-Bibel controversy? Matters are more complicated and more deeply entangled. Doubtless, Israel opened itself to outside influences, but it equally abruptly rejected and opposed what it perceived to be incompatible with its beliefs. For example, it could take over the god El from the Canaanite pantheon and identify him with its God Yahweh, through which the former acquired new characteristics. The god Baal, however, whose orgiastic cult was seen as abominable, it virulently detested along with his followers and persecuted them cruelly at times. It is part of the essence of OT faith that it "bears a polemical and usurping character, that it does not remain static, but lives in constant dialogue, takes hold of assimilable thoughts, concepts and ideas out of other religions and, transforming them, incorporates them into itself,"[1] but also clearly rejects what would endanger it. This entire living process is more comprehensible to us today than ever before, when the sayings of the OT can be confronted with archaeological material and texts from its surroundings.

I.

The so-called *OT wisdom* portrays a particular kind of segment from this problem area. In that, it concerns a specific literary form with quite definite features of form and content, which is represented in the OT by the books of "Proverbs," "Job," "Qoheleth," and a few Psalms, in the post-canonical literature by "Jesus Sirach" and other literary works; I must limit myself, in this address, to the OT itself.

This literature goes back to a specific class, the so-called wise, who are mentioned between priests and prophets at Jer 18:18 in an enumeration of the authoritative classes in the spiritual life of Israel, which gives clear evidence that they were so acknowledged.

The OT tradition of King Solomon, whose wisdom was famed to be greater than that of all the sons of the orient and than the wisdom of Egypt (1 Kgs 5:10), is considered its most luminous representative, shrouded in legendary fame. This comparison with wisdom outside of Israel is significant. While one perceived the law given to Israel and the word of God mediated through its prophets as incomparable, he also knew: there is wisdom outside of Israel as well. Indeed, it is clear to us today that Israelite-Jewish wisdom forms only a branch of the universal ancient Near Eastern wisdom. In particular, since the 1870's, so many Egyptian wisdom teachings from the period of about 2800 up to 100 B.C. have become known, that we can construct a clear picture of the nature and appearance of Egyptian wisdom.[2] Certainly, there was a wisdom literature in Babylonia and Assyria as well, though the remaining fragments provide no such clear picture as for Egyptian wisdom. As in other areas (e.g., in the organization of the state and the kingship ritual), the influence of Egypt was also more intense that that of other cultures. This was proven decisively in the 1920's, when the Instruction of Amenemope, which originated in the first half of the first millennium B.C., was published and a portion of the Book of Proverbs, viz. 22:17–23:10, was discovered to be dependent upon it. This discovery threw significant light on the entire form.

When Israelite tradition tied wisdom in a special way to King Solomon, to that extent it happened to hit on something right, since in his time for the first time the pre-conditions were given for an influx, particularly, of Egyptian wisdom. His father David had created an empire with which the other nations had to reckon. Political and economic connections with the surrounding world were established, an Egyptian princess moved into Jerusalem as the wife of Solomon. Magnificent structures designed by foreigners rose in Jerusalem; a brilliant court life unfolded according to foreign patterns. At the royal court of Solomon and his successors, foreign or foreign-trained scribes were inevitable as higher officials, diplomats, etc. Thus, even in the cultural realm, there came about a departure from the narrowness and isolation of ancient Israelite life, at least at the royal court and its environs. There, too, wisdom found its first place of cultivation as well as its students among the youths who were destined for official careers; but later, especially in the post-exilic period, it encompassed wider circles. A new, foreign spirituality thus gained a foothold in Israel. Just as what was set in motion under Solomon later led to serious problems in the area of politics, religion and social life, so too the assimilation of wisdom contained the stuff of conflict and possibilities for momentous developments. To my mind, the seed has already been sown here for the teachings of retribution characteristic of late Jewish nomism.

II.

We shall now attempt briefly to characterize wisdom. It concerns a *practical* wisdom, a wisdom which wants to help man to master life successfully. It does that by setting up rules in the form of proverbs:

> Like a city with torn-down walls
> is a man without self-control. (Prov 25:28)

or formulated as admonitions:

> Do not presume to honor before the king
> and do not put yourself in the place of the great;
> for better that one should say to you: come up here,
> than that one should set you down before a noble. (Prov 25:6f.)

How one gets through life successfully is shown in sayings concerning domestic, professional, public life, concerning conduct toward friends and enemies, wife and children, superiors and inferiors, in family and society. The wise do not approach life as either alien or frightening. They are of the opinion that it proceeds according to fixed laws and that one can discern these laws after the fact and organize them into an elegant pattern so that he can master life with their help.

In that connection, there is also no lack of religious sayings. The "fear of God," i.e. piety, is proclaimed the beginning and fundament of wisdom. One could attempt to assemble such and similar kinds of sayings in order to project from them a theology of wisdom. This venture, however, would hardy lead us to the heart of wisdom. There seems to me to be an alternative, more productive question, concerning the understanding of God, world, man, that stands behind wisdom and this is presupposed as the well-established foundation of all endeavors beyond further reflection or discussion. Only when we have managed to grasp that understanding of existence and that feeling of life which guides the wise, will we achieve an adequate understanding of the individual, yet quite diverse, sayings which encompass the height and the depth, the exalted and the trivial. Thus, we shall now turn to the Egyptian wisdom.

III.

Earlier research, whose views are still influential today, generally tended to perceive a kind of secular book of etiquette in the *Egyptian instructions*. Moreover, since hardly any admonition fails to make reference to what excellent success adherence to it will bring along with it, the wisdom books appear to be instructions for ambitious youths who want to establish careers and attain the highest possible level within the Egyptian hierarchy of officialdom. Even when truth and righteousness are recommended, they are to be understood pragmatically. Whoever strives for them finds them to be advantageous to him in his way of life as a means of advancement. No wonder that wisdom literature is considered thoroughly secular and from a religious perspective rather impoverished. One first believes he becomes aware of deeper more pious and moral tones in the late wisdom teaching of Amenemope from the first half of the first pre-Christian millennium. It is significant enough that Oesterley,[3] e.g., would like to trace this uniqueness of Amenemope's back to Israelite influence. So little do people attribute original religious character to an Egyptian wisdom book. This view, however, is not true to the actual content of the Egyptian instructions. More recent studies, among which I call special attention to those of the Egyptologists de Buck and Brunner and of the religious historian Henri Frankfort[4] have shown that a thoroughly religious understanding of life and the world stands behind the often utilitarian-sounding counsels.

One must immediately state that the ancient cultures knew no such distinction between worldliness and religion as is familiar to us. Religion reached into every area and all things have a religious dimension. Thus, it would be notable if the Egyptian wisdom were to bear the secular character which some scholars have attributed to it. Actually, one misses the implication of many sayings if he does not sufficiently attend to their religious presuppositions. And, indeed, it is the concept of *Maat* which has decisive significance for Egyptian wisdom. Here, it is basically a question of a central concept in the Egyptian view of life and the world. We have no word in our modern languages which can adequately render the content of Maat, because Maat is at once a cosmological and ethical idea. It may be translated as "truth," "rightness," "justice," "primordial order."

As a goddess, Maat belonged to the Heliopolitan religious system, where she appeared as the daughter of the sun-god. She came down to men in the beginning as the proper order of all things. Through the evil assaults of Seth and his comrades, this order was upset, but restored through the victory of Horus. As the embodiment of Horus, each new king renews this right order through his coronation: a new state of Maat, i.e. of peace and righteousness, dawns.[5]

Frankfort defines this Maat in the following words: Maat is "the divine order erected at the time of the creation; this order is manifest in nature through the normal course of events; it is manifest in society as righteousness; and it is manifest in the life of the individual as truth."[6]

The goal of the wisdom instructions is nothing less than this Maat, "which derives from god, thus is fully removed in its nature from all human influences . . . thereby paving the way for it to be transmitted on."[7] Therefore, one wants to establish a harmonious situation in state and society and help the individual to the best-possible state of fortune.

How did the Egyptian teachers of wisdom attain knowledge of Maat, the divine order? They were nowhere commissioned, like the OT lawgiver and prophet, through transcendent revelation; they have, "rather, read Maat from the course of this world and . . . dressed it in an attractive style for their sons."[8]

As god-given order, Maat has claim on absolute validity. It is said of her, that she is powerful, she is immense, she endures. Life, fortune, prosperity, each is only possible in that one joins himself to her. Whoever goes in opposition to her is like one who swims against the stream; he cuts himself off from the fountain of life. He will have no success in everyday life, and can expect no mercy from the judges at the judgment of the dead. On the other hand, the normal consequence of Maat is life, prosperity. "Maat is great, and its appropriateness is lasting; it has not been disturbed since the time of him who made it, (whereas) there is punishment for him who passes over its laws. It is the (right) path before him who knows nothing. Wrongdoing has never brought its undertaking into port. (It may be that) it is fraud that gains riches, (but) the strength of Maat is that it lasts."[9] Following that it brings profit, even in the other world: Whoever comes to the judges of the dead without sin "will be like a god in the kingdom of the dead, freely proceeding like the blessed dead."[10]

A fixed order thus lies at the base of life and to observe it is the beginning of wisdom. Once that becomes clear, then some counsels also acquire a deeper significance that might appear to us at first glance as reprehensible opportunism. Hence, e.g., a demeanor toward superiors is commended that one might well term base servility: "Keep your face down until he greets you, and speak only when he has greeted you. One does not know what evil is in his heart. Laugh when he laughs. That will please his heart and what you do will be agreeable."[11] As a result, one may be tempted to find here the speech of a shrewd and crafty courtier. But it would be wrong. The superior in Egypt obviously has a higher, to some extent god-given authority. Hence, it is of great significance that one respect him—not only for the sake of his person; insofar as one honors him, one observes the order. To despise him would mean to disturb the order, the Maat, and whoever disturbs Maat brings about his own cutting-short: it remains, but the rebel perishes because of his opposition to it.

Since the way of Maat undoubtedly leads to life, to success, and since this way is teachable and learnable, it remains within man's power to structure his life toward the good. Whoever patterns himself according to the rules of wisdom will lack for nothing. Thus, the feeling of security which appears to us in this literature. Man lives "in a world that is neither antagonistic nor ultimately problematic."[12] If only man goes the right way, then all external circumstances will also work propitiously for him.

What significance does the deity have for this order? God appears in the Egyptian wisdom first as the one who gave the right order and through it ordered all of life, and second as the one who in omniscience and righteousness saw that this order was kept protected. He punishes whoever violates it; he rewards the followers, the "ones who hear." This applies as much to this life as to life after death. Thus, in the "Instruction for King Merikare," even the king—a god-king!—is admonished to do right so long as he exists on earth with the explanation that the hour can come unforeseen when his deeds will be judged. "And he is a fool who despises the judges of the dead."

God's activity thus takes place entirely in the context of firmly established, unchangeable order. Even the deity cannot step outside of it, because he cannot act against his own laws. When it says in the Instruction of Ptahhotep, "what men prepare for never occurs; what god commands, occurs," it does not mean a sovereign, arbitrary act of god. Rather, if man attempts, in madness, to burst through the barriers of divine commands, he must come to ruin on god's determination to carry out his laws.[13]

The concept of a righteous order which governs life is absolutely basic to the Egyptian teachers of wisdom. Even if an occurrence in this world should raise some questions about righteousness, they can always be allayed by reference to retribution in the next world. Therefore, the problem of the righteousness of god can never be so clearly perceived as in Israelite religion where, as is well known, belief in a survival into the next world only quite late played any role. In sum, the understanding of existence of the Egyptian wisdom instructions can be characterized as follows:

1. Life proceeds according to a fixed order.
2. This order is teachable and learnable.
3. Man is thereby handed an instrument with which to determine and secure his way through life. Because,
4. God himself must pattern himself according to this order, this law.

Hence, the Egyptian wisdom is most closely bound up with the religiously determined understanding of the world and life. Belief in a god-given order is not only ornament, but fundament, upon which the undertaking of the wisdom teacher depends. Even where this order is not expressly mentioned, belief in it is presupposed. Above all, it gives the sayings their deeper sense.

IV.

When wisdom, first within courtly circles, was taken over *into Israel*, people may not have been conscious of its ideological and religious content. But it was there and it proved itself to be effective. What is remarkable in the entire process is not that some individual phrases were taken over from the Egyptian wisdom teachings, but rather that people grew up through them into the implicitly maintained understanding of existence. That people affirmed the possibility of securing human life and worked intensely toward its realization. Thus there developed a type of man who was new to Israel and whose self-confidence must have been offensive to the genuine Israelite faith, which prophetic criticism also confirms (e.g., Isa 5:21; 29:14; Jer 4:22; 8:8). We shall make the special position of wisdom within the OT clear through several points.

a.) Like the Egyptian, Israelite teachers of wisdom speak of a moral *lawfulness* which governs life. Whoever is good and upright, his life proceeds in well-being and security; but the wicked person meets misfortune of every sort:

> No ill befalls the righteous,
> but the wicked are filled with trouble. (Prov 12:21, RSV)
> The house of the wicked will be destroyed,
> but the tent of the upright will flourish. (Prov. 14:11 RSV)
> The righteous has enough to satisfy his appetite
> but the belly of the wicked suffers want. (Prov 13:25 RSV)

This connection between deed and consequence is extraordinarily narrow. It is almost a question of an internal regularity which could best be compared to natural law. The well-known picture of Psalm 1 is especially striking: as a tree that is sufficiently well-watered turns green and bears fruit, so the upright person flourishes. That is a law that obtains in the nature of the matter. Therefore, the older Israelite wisdom also entirely avoided speaking of a retributing Power in this connection. In the preceding examples, which could easily be multiplied, no such entity is mentioned. Nevertheless, that may remind one very much of the Egyptian teaching concerning Maat. One could still assume that the Israelite wisdom teachers saw Yahweh himself as the guarantor who assured that the moral order of life remained intact, just as god is sometimes mentioned in the Egyptian wisdom in just such a context.

If life proceeds according to that internal regularity postulated by wisdom, then particular possibilities result for man. Actually, wisdom has very high regard for a person's power. All of those goods of life, highly treasured in Israel as throughout the ancient Near East, he can attain and secure for himself; long life in good health until he dies old and sated with life, flourishing flocks of children who guarantee continuance of the family, material possessions, honor and reputation. One need only make use of that regularity according to which life proceeds, must prove himself to be upright: then all the rest will not, indeed cannot, fail. Thus, a person has the power to structure his life toward success and good fortune. He can also earn the blessing of God.

In that connection, there is only silence about what otherwise has such central significance in the OT and which we must regard as authentically Israelite. At the focal point of almost every book of the OT stands the covenant people Israel, and what it is and what it should become is a product of its history. It is the nation with whose fathers God made his covenant, to whom he gave promises and on whom he laid responsibilities, whom he led out of Egypt through the wilderness and into Palestine, and in whose history he is continually present with his grace and his mission, his salvation and his judgment. When one reads the wisdom literature, one almost gets the impression that its author knew nothing at all of these matters. It seems to have little meaning for them, at least as we must interpret it, that these things should have anything concrete to do with Israelites. Within the OT that is highly unusual. Only its foreign origins and the resulting entirely different conceptual orientation toward the unhistorical individual person make it conceivable that wisdom for so long a time overlooked the central themes of Israelite religion. What correlates with that—which is of special significance—is the fact that the relation between human act and divine blessing is determined completely differently from that in genuine Israelite Yahwistic faith. In the traditions of the Israelite twelve-tribe coalition, covenant and law are most closely bound up with each other. In fact, the relationship is such that the law is subordinated to covenant. Thus, the Decalogue begins with a reference to the continuing covenant and Yahweh's activity: "I am Yahweh your God who brought you out of Egypt," and only then do the commands follow which Yahweh places on his community. There are commandments of Yahweh to Israel because of the fact that there is a covenant. Not the reverse: commandments do not create covenant. Further, the blessing of Yahweh does not follow from fulfillment of the commands; it precedes instead. And, the law has only *the* intent of insuring the exclusivity of the relationship between God and nation, i.e., to prevent any sort of departure from faith in the *one* God and covenant partner.[14] "Thus, even in the OT laws—and indeed especially in Deuteronomy—the divine blessing is a gift, which was *prior* to the law and its fulfillment, and therefore independent of it also, which is certainly assured through fulfillment of the law but which cannot first be earned."[15]

It was a momentous alteration of this conception when wisdom aroused the impression that a person might be able to strive for and attain the divine blessing in and of himself and outside of the covenant. Perhaps that was Egyptian thinking, but not genuine Israelite.

b.) Now, wisdom's understanding of existence also has important consequences for the *idea of God*. God's working can only unfold within the bounds of that regularity which governs the totality of life. Correspondingly, Yahweh appears in wisdom first and foremost as retributor:

> A bulwark to him who walks in innocence is Yahweh,
> but consternation for the evil-doers. (Prov 10:29)[16]
> A good man obtains favor from the Lord.
> but a man of evil devices he condemns. (Prov 12:2, RSV)

Thus, God is the guarantor of that order which interpenetrates all of life. Through it, however, he himself is bound: even the deity cannot set aside the law which governs all of life. His power is limited to taking care that it retains its validity by means of proper retribution. Hence, Yahweh becomes a calculable God because he is bound to a determinable law in his dealings.

There is no time to show in detail how wisdom's notion of God stands in extreme tension to that of the rest of the OT. It is quite clear that the God of the covenant, whose realm above all is history and before whom nations are like drops in a bucket (Isa 40:15), is entirely different in his entire fundamental conception from the God of wisdom who acts as retributor in the life of the individual. This retributive God, in his activity, is clear, rationally comprehensible, calculable—so to speak, without being a puzzling enigma. However, the God who called forth one people from the circle of nations and dealt with them specially is ultimately incomprehensible in his purposes. Sovereign, he disposes over man who is like clay in the hand of the potter before him (Jer 18:6; Isa 45:9; 64:8); he is also sovereign in his grace: "I am merciful to whomever I wish to be merciful, and I have pity on whomever I wish to have pity." (Exod 33:19)

It is not surprising that in Israel it came to controversy with this wisdom founded upon alien presuppositions. It becomes literarily comprehensible for us in the books of Job and Ecclesiastes, for which the Hebrew term is Qoheleth, which belong to the OT's late period.[17]

V.

As we concern ourselves now with Ecclesiastes (Qoheleth), we must establish that he vehemently contested the understanding of the existence of wisdom in part of his aphorisms, and quite obviously as a man who himself had gone through wisdom and for whom, as a wisdom teacher, the school-tradition of his class had been called into question.

a) As the *ethical order of life* was applied, according to which every earthly event should work out, he observes that it proves itself non-existent in reality:

> There is something empty which happens on earth:
> There are righteous who meet with
> What the wicked deserve.
> And there are wicked who meet with
> What the righteous deserve.
> I say: This too is empty. (8:14)

How offensive these sayings of Qoheleth were perceived to be by a Judaism that had made a wisdom's teaching of retribution its own as an important dogma is seen by the fact that in 8:12f. glosses were added that should correct Qoheleth's heresies.[18]

Even in the fact of *death*, the wise had maintained man's relative power: whoever is upright assures himself of long life, the wicked must die prematurely. Qoheleth had observed, however, that the reality appeared otherwise:

> Both have I seen in the days of my empty life:
> There are righteous who perish in their righteousness,
> And there are godless who live long in their wickedness (7:15)

The wisdom teachers wanted to take the sting out of the difficult problem of death by making a distinction between the death of the righteous and the death of the wicked. To Qoheleth's clear gaze, however, it proved to be an illusion. Death is death—it is the same for all, for righteous and wicked, for pure and impure, for those who sacrifice as for those who do not, for those who take vows as for those who foreswear them;

> That is evil by everything that happens under the sun:
> That all meet *one* fate,
> and indeed: their end is with the dead.[19] (9:3)

b) Whoever so reveals the order of life postulated by wisdom to be a fiction will also re-evaluate *man's possibilities*. Wisdom maintains that all possibilities are open for the person who treads upon the stage of life. It is up to him to determine his own destiny. Qoheleth, however, contests this exalted freedom and power. It has long since been disposed concerning man, his destiny is fixed:

What happens is long since determined,
determined what a man will be.
And he cannot go into court
With him who is stronger than he. (6:10)

Correspondingly, human deeds do not admit of calculation to what result they will lead. Entirely other than human factors decide:

Once again I saw under the sun:
Not the swift win the race,
Nor the heroes the battle,
Nor the wise bread,
Nor the understanding riches,
Nor the knowing favor.
Rather, all meet time and chance. (9:11)

And now the worst is that man does not know his time; he fumbles in the dark, and suddenly it lays hold of him:

For man does not know his time:
Like fish caught in a net,
Like birds caught in the snare,
Thus the children of men will be ensnared
In an evil time,
When it suddenly overtakes them. (9:12)

Thus, while human life appears to the wise comprehensible, clear even, because it proceeds according to fixed laws and is therefore calculable; for Qoheleth, it is obscure, dark, because governed by an alien purpose. When, however, an unknown factor is everywhere determinative, how shall a person know, with regard to the future, what is "good"? Hence, Qoheleth's question:

Yes, who knows what in life is good for a man
As long as the days of his empty life continue,
Which he passes "in the" shadows?
Yes, who can tell a man
What will be after him under the sun? (6:12)

Still another place shows how uncertain, ridiculous, any calculation portrays life for Qoheleth:

Throw your bread into the water,
Still, you can find it after many days.
Give portions to seven or eight.
Still you do not know what evil may come upon the earth. (11:1f.)

If one throws his bread into the water, he thinks it is lost. But it must not be so. If one puts his money in seven or eight different places, then he acts cautiously. According to human reckoning, he will preserve his money in at least a couple of places. However, that must not be so! "Whether one does something completely foolish or entirely thought-out: the former can turn out well, the last can be useless; it does not depend on someone's willing or pursuing, one can never calculate how an event will turn out."[20]

How far removed we are in all these sayings from the secure, spontaneous act, like wisdom's feeling of life that trusts the ordered process of life. Precisely in that antipathy, however, we sense that Qoheleth formulated his views obviously with a glance toward wisdom. They contain an indirect polemic.

c) That also applies, now, to the sayings that he produced concerning *God*. In wisdom, God functioned principally as righteous retributor. "The world is order, cosmos, even God conforms to these laws and does not overstep them. He is the crowning and guarantor of this order, whose inner structure is accessible to the observation of the wise."[21]

Within this order, God and man work together. Wherever man goes the right way, God takes care that he attains the proper success. That Qoheleth, conversely, asserted the determinedness of man, we have already seen. But God, so he continues, is entirely free in whatever he does:

> Because to a man who pleases him
> He gives wisdom, knowledge and happiness.
> To whoever displeases him, he gives the toil
> Of gathering and heaping up,
> And giving it to whoever pleases him.
> That too is empty and straining after wind. (2:26)

Here, God appears entirely sovereign, bound to no consideration of human endeavor or a moral order. Qoheleth, however, does not feel himself driven now to protest against God, whose caprice, or better enigmatic character, he has recognized, as Job did. He only confirms it. This confirmation, though, means a total denial of the image of God in wisdom.

God's conduct, which man cannot reduce to any simple formula therefore, is inalterable:

I recognized: Everything God does,
It is for eternity.
To that there is no adding,
From it there is no taking away.
God has done it that man might fear before him. (3:14)

It is impossible to influence God's actions. Man must accept them as inalterable, conclusive. As a result, he becomes conscious of how powerful and sovereign this God is in his acting and how much man is different from him. The result is that fear of this God overtakes man. He has wished it so. Now, wisdom literature often talks of the fear of God; but it is something well-tempered: reverence, piety. For Qoheleth, though, it has other, more original features. "Fear is a constitutive moment in Qoheleth's portrait of God. As a consequence, the idea of the fear of God has recaptured much of its original freshness, the mysterious awe before an overwhelming force, as opposed to *ḥokmah* (= wisdom)."[22]

Just as God is powerful and sovereign, he is unsearchable in whatever he does:

He has made everything beautiful for its time . . .
Only that man might not comprehend
The work that God does from beginning to end. (3:11)

In every event, God is decisive. But, wisdom's pretentious assertion to have comprehended the internal structure of the world's course, proves as a result to be frivolous. "God does not permit his secrets to be found out. Man can only take what God gives him. But he has not stood in the divine council."[23]

Here, Qoheleth collides with the central claim of the wise and the most important presupposition of their enterprise. Thus, it is entirely understandable that he does not content himself with mere antitheses but crosses over into outright polemic in which he calls the opponent by name:

I saw in every deed of God
That man could not comprehend
The work that occurs under the sun.
Even though man exerts himself
To search it out, he does not find it.
Even when the *wise man* claims to comprehend it,
He can not find it out. (8:17)

In spite of the efforts and the claim of the wise, God shows himself to be unsearchable, veiled. "The God whom Qoheleth faces is the hidden God, only the hidden one."[24]

To summarize, we can say that Qoheleth sought to prove wisdom to be a confusion at decisive points. In opposition to the bright picture they paint of life proceeding in the harmony of act and consequence, he assiduously emphasized the dark sides. He showed man his limitedness: matters have already been disposed concerning him, God has determined his fate, while man himself fumbles in the darkness, not knowing in whatever he does how it will turn out for him. And the end is the same death for all.

Above all, however, Qoheleth conceived God entirely differently from the wise; he saw him in his power and sovereignty and in his wholly-otherness, which makes him completely unintelligible to man. To the extent that Qoheleth diligently emphasized this aspect of God, he showed that he had clearly perceived the weakest point—from the point of view of Israelite faith—in wisdom: the impotence of God. Thus, Qoheleth brought into play in his own sayings significant features of the OT view of God, and one can say on the basis of this observation that he has made himself the advocate of the OT belief in God. On the other hand, something decisive is lacking. Qoheleth removes God so far from man that trust in him is hardly possible any more, and scarcely even prayer. Hence, caution is advised toward God in visiting the Temple, prayer and vows (5:1ff.). Is that conceivable on the basis of the OT? One might well conclude that the developing crisis of wisdom apparent in Qoheleth is not determined by OT faith alone, although this has proven a vital part of it. The way he conducts the debate shows Qoheleth to be a thinker of great individuality whose spiritual attitude one might want to make intelligible by reference to Greek spirituality. But, repeated attempts to prove conclusively a Greek source for Ecclesiastes have not yet succeeded.

VI.

Like Qoheleth, the dialogue and divine speeches of the *Book of Job* must also be understood as a debate with wisdom. The discussions which are conducted between Job and his friends revolve about three themes which are decisive for wisdom: about the law of harmony between deed and consequence, about the possibilities of man and about the governance of God. That the three friends move entirely within the paths of the wisdom teachers in their expositions of these three question areas is readily apparent to anyone who reads at all into their speeches. Because of time considerations, we must forego here any detailed proof. But even for Job himself, it is true that he argues from afar on the basis of a dialogue with the fundamental views of wisdom. It should indeed have been the case that God acts as the righteous retributor in the way wisdom maintains. But because it is not so, one must protest against this God, call him to account. Only the divine speeches move beyond this understanding of God.

According to the self-portrait he gives in chapters 29–31, Job was a man after the wise's own hearts: he led a life of justice and righteousness, and received good fortune and wealth. That seemed to him to be thoroughly in order, and he believed himself to be secure in his life's fortunes. Then, misfortune broke upon his life without any perceptible reason and proved the principles by which he had lived up till then to be illusion. Where his misfortune was concerned, he had to dispute with utter determination that he had merited it: the moral order of the world maintained by the friends, and in which he himself had believed in better days, had broken down. But not only in his case does it happen; as he goes on in chap. 21, there is—what could never be, according to the teachings of the wise—a good fortune of the godless, and life's course is filled with difficult puzzles.

Job can only see the cause for it in God. He does not doubt for a moment that God is the lord of man and his life and that from his hand comes everything that happens to a man. But how does God prove himself to be now toward man? That he is a righteous retributor is a belief that Job must let drop because it seemed impossible to him to interpret his suffering on that basis. He himself has experienced how God, in power and freedom, not to mention arbitrarily, acts toward man:

> He snatches away, who can hinder him?
> Who says to him: What are you doing? (9:12)

God acts irresistibly, in absolute sovereignty. There are no limits to his activity: no external ones, because no one can oppose him, to hinder him. But also no internal one, because he does whatever he wishes without being bound through any ethical principle; and no one can call him to account.

That thought is so contradictory to wisdom that one can only interpret these sayings from the Book of Job as a direct polemic against wisdom whose view of the God-man relationship is thus proven to be internally untrue, unrealistic. In this, Job argues not only from the experience of his own life, but also refers to the irresistible omnipotence of God in nature (9:5–7) and in the life of nations (12:14–25). Here, he assiduously raises the frightening, destructive, enigmatic side of God. With real delight, he confronts the harmless contingent God of his friends, who reigns only within the scheme of the dogma of retribution, over against the dreadful, sinister, threatening God shown him through nature and history. In fact, he does not shrink from attributing to him thoroughly demonic characteristics:

> Thus is everything one! Therefore I declare:
> Innocent or guilty, he destroys.
> If "his" scourge suddenly kills,
> He laughs at the fears of the guiltless.
> The earth "he gave" into the hand of the wicked,
> He veiled the face of its judge. . . . (9:22–24)

Can faith in an ethical world-order which offers man security, this trust in God, be more cruelly shattered than it is here?

In these and similar sayings, Job is concerned with destroying the inoffensive image of God of his friends which is identical with that of wisdom—to expose the vacuity of their naive-optimistic understanding of existence which proclaims man's power. God is overwhelming, and man completely relinquishes his will in good and evil.

On the other hand, admittedly there is no lack of words of trust, in which Job clings to God. Precisely because he alone is powerful, he becomes the ultimate refuge of the suffering and despairing man. Still, one can hardly be permitted to find the solution to Job's problem in such sayings because at the same time he adjudges the divine speeches of chaps. 38–41 to be a later addition.

Taken by itself, the dialogue, i.e. chaps. 3–37, offers no solution at all. What Job says concerning God is too much the antithesis of wisdom's view to be able to touch the reality of God. This last only becomes apparent when God manifests himself in the thunderstorm and answers Job (chaps. 38–41). It is instructive and significant there how the poet worked with the traditional materials of wisdom. The rhetorical questions, with which God makes the questioner Job into the questioned and finally calls him into question, derive their stylistic form from the Egyptian wisdom school.[25] Equally, the content of the divine speeches which take their subject matter from the extensive realm of nature hark back to the "onomastica," name-lists, of Egyptian science which served in the curriculum of the wise's scribal schools. In Job 38ff., however, their intent has been totally changed. "While those (Egyptian) lists arose from and were produced by the intense capacity of human knowledge to gain control over nature, the poet of Job transformed that [literary] form entirely into the spirit of the OT so that it served him as proof of the limits of human knowledge over against the overwhelming divine creative power and wisdom in nature."[26] Hence, even at this point, the disagreement with wisdom is clearly at work.

The divine speeches counterbalance the preceding sayings about the relation of God and man since they place Job before God who is visible in his creation and at the same time incomprehensible. The introductory question:

> Who is this who declares (God's) counsel as darkness? (38:2)

is directed toward making Job conscious of his situation as a man. The excursion through creation, put as questions which are to be interpreted as variations of that basic question, shows him to be limited in time, power, knowledge and ability before that God who is active in all and from the beginning, eternally reflecting, and incomprehensible.

If, however, the relationship of God and man is to be seen in this way, then the claim of the wisdom represented by the friends to comprehend the entire course of life including him who stands over it and to perceive it in its regularity is thereby set aright just as in Job's denial. In the face of this God, there is neither claim nor protest. Therefore, Job surrenders:

> See, I am too small, what can I reply to you? (40:4)

And further:

> I had known that you could do everything;
> Nothing that you intend is impossible for you.
> From hearsay I had heard of you;
> Now, however, have my eyes seen you.
> Therefore, I recant and repent in dust and ashes. (42:2, 5, 6)

The culmination of the OT faith is thus not an order like "Maat" which binds God and man in the same way, but rather a personal God who stands over against the world and the individual person as *Lord.*

VII.

What we have seen is a significant and instructive example of Israel's encounter and controversy with oriental cultures. In some circles, it opens itself to them with a certain joyfulness and gives them room within it. Then, however, some become conscious of the alienness of this spirit and must set themselves off from it on the basis of what is Israel's own: its belief in a sovereign God who cannot be understood nor reckoned according to human criteria but who is and remains wholly other and incomprehensible to human understanding. Thus, the wisdom books—Proverbs, Ecclesiastes, Job—are not only witnesses to an interesting cultural history, but a theological controversy over the profoundest question of human existence, the question of the understanding of God and man, world and life. The question poses itself to every one of us as well. The various answers we sketched are possibilities for us, too. Whether we adopt one of them and if so, which, is a decision that lies beyond our [purely] scientific undertakings.

NOTES

1. J. Hempel, *ZAW* 13 (1936), pp. 293f.
2. A pleasant overview of the surviving instructions is given by H. Brunner, *Handbuch der Orientalistik* I, 2 (1952), pp. 96ff.
3. W. O. E. Oesterley, *ZAW* 4 (1927), pp. 9ff.
4. A. de Buck, "Het religieus karakter der oudste egyptische wijsheid," *Nieuw Theologisch Tijdschrift* 21 (1932), pp. 322ff. Brunner, pp. 90ff. *Idem, Altägyptische Erziehung* (1957), *passim.* H. Frankfort, *Egyptian Religion* (1948), pp. 59ff.
5. Brunner, p. 93.
6. Frankfort, p. 63.
7. Brunner, p. 93.
8. *Ibid.* p. 95.
9. Instruction of Ptahhotep (5th dynasty, about 2400 B.C.), 95ff. Translation according to Wilson in *ANET* (2d ed.: 1955), p. 412. Wilson's translation of Maat is "justice."

10. Instruction for King Merikare (10th dynasty, the end of the 3d millennium B.C.), 57. Translation [German] according to F. W. von Bissing. *Altägyptische Lebensweisheit* (1955), p. 55.
11. Ptahhotep, 120ff.; von Bissing, p. 46.
12. Frankfort, p. 60.
13. Brunner, p. 98. This interpretation of Brunner's is unquestionably preferable to that of those who want to find our "Man proposes but God disposes" in the statement of Ptahhotep.
14. M. Noth, *Die Gesetze im Pentateuch* (1940), p. 42 (*Gesammelte Studien* [1957], p. 70).
15. *Ibid.*, p. 83 (*Ges. St.*, p. 132).
16. Emended text; cf., B. Gemser, *Sprüche Salomos, HzAT* (1937), pp. 42f.
17. Even in Proverbs, some sayings already appear which could be interpreted as a reference to a divine authority independent of any human activity and could be meant as a dispute with wisdom's view of God (e.g. 16:1, 9; 21:30f.; cf. H. Gese, *Lehre und Wirklichkeit in der alten Weisheit* [1958], pp. 46ff.). But, apart from the fact that they partially admit of another interpretation as well, their value should not be exaggerated. They depict marginal phenomena and cannot really rectify the portrait of God which finds its expression in the overwhelming majority of sayings (cf. also W. Zimmerli, *ZAW* 10 [1933], pp. 189ff.)
18. Cf. K. Galling in Haller-Galling, *Die Fünf Megilloth, HzAT* (1940), pp. 80f.
19. On the restoration of this text, see Galling, p. 80.
20. H. W. Hertzberg, *Der Prediger, KAT* (1932), p. 174.
21. W. Zimmerli, *Die Weisheit des Predigers Salomo* (1936), p. 11.
22. H.-J. Blieffert, *Weltanschauung und Gottesglaube im Buch Kohelet* (Rostock Dissertation; 1938), p. 56.
23. Hertzberg, p. 88.
24. Galling, p. 62.
25. G. von Rad, *SVT* 3 (1955), pp. 293ff.
26. A. Weiser, *Das Buch Hiob,* ATD (2d ed.; 1956), p. 243.

III

COMMON THEMES AND MOTIFS

7

A Forerunner of Biblical Prophecy: The Mari Documents

Abraham Malamat

For the previous studies that we have devoted to prophecy at Mari and in the Bible we had at our disposal only ten out of the presently known twenty-eight "prophetic" documents from Mari.[1] In the meantime eighteen documents have been added to the "prophetic" corpus from Mari and several works have appeared that discuss the entire material (save one new document published in 1975; see below).[2] The full body of data now available enables us to advance our understanding of the topic at hand, inviting at the same time certain revisions.

TWO PATTERNS OF PROPHESYING AT MARI

Let us commence our discussion in an unconventional manner. We cite a Mari letter that is not really related to our subject but that may possibly serve as a key for understanding the reality behind the practices of prophesying at Mari. Bahdilim, the palace prefect of Mari under its last king, Zimrilim, advises his lord: "[Verily] you are the king of the Haneans, [but] secondly you are the king of the Akkadians! [My lord] should not ride a horse. Let my [lord] ride in a chariot or on a mule and he will thereby honor his royal head!" (ARM VI, 76:20–25). According to this statement, the two strata making up the population were, on the

Reprinted by permission from Patrick D. Miller, Jr., Paul D. Hanson and S. Dean McBride, eds., *Ancient Israelite Religion* (Philadelphia: Fortress Press, 1987), 33–52. Copyright © 1987 Fortress Press.

one hand, the West Semitic (Haneans, the dominant tribal federation of the kingdom) and, on the other hand, the old-time Akkadian component. The symbiosis between these two elements usually left its imprint on every walk of life, including religion and cult. We therefore witness at Mari, and for the present practically at Mari alone, the coexistence of two patterns of predicting the future and revealing the word of the gods.

On the one hand we find at Mari, as at every Mesopotamian center, the practice typical of Akkadian civilizations, namely, divination and specifically the art of extispicy. This field was served by specially trained experts and above all by the *bārû,* the haruspex. At Mari, we are familiar with a number of such experts, the best known of whom was Asqudum, whose spacious mansion was recently uncovered east of the Mari palace.[3] These professionals usually dealt with the crucial matters of the Mari kingdom, such as seeking omens for the security of the city, the conduct of war, and military enterprises.[4]

Alongside the academic and supposedly "rational" system of predicting the future, we are confronted at Mari, and chronologically for the first time ever, with an atypical phenomenon for Mesopotamia: the remarkable manifestation of intuitive divination or, rather, prophecy, acquiring the word of the god through informal channels. This type of prophesying should properly be seen as a link in a chain of social and religious practices exclusive to Mari and in part similar to what is found in the Bible. These include the covenant-making ceremony, the ban as penalty for transgression, and the more controversial procedure of census-taking accompanied by ritual expiation.[5] This assemblage of procedures, which could be described as a system of interrelationships, is undoubtedly an expression of the other component of the Mari experience—the West Semitic tribal heritage.

Does the above warrant the conclusion, not usually considered,[6] that the message of the diviner-prophets was pronounced originally in West Semitic dialects, conventionally designated as "Amorite"? Should this be the case, then, in the documents before us the words of prophecy have already undergone translation into the chancery language, Akkadian, either by the officials writing to the king or by scribes who are not mentioned at all. Such an assumption may also explain the fact that the "prophetic" texts display a relatively greater number of West Semitic idioms and linguistic forms than the rest of the Mari documents. There is, however, still no basic study of this matter. If these assumptions are in fact correct, they point to a considerably complex process of transmission of the prophetic word—*ipsissima verba*—until it reaches the king's ear.

INTUITIVE PROPHECY

Whatever the case, informal prophesying at Mari places biblical prophecy in a new perspective, for inherent to both is the intuitive element. In neither of them is the prophecy the direct result of a mantic or magic mechanism that requires professional expertise but the product of the experience of divine revelation, namely, a psychic, nonrational phenomenon. The essential nature of prophecy of this type entails certain dominant characteristics, three of which are most significant:[7]

1. The prophetic manifestations are spontaneous and result from inspiration or divine initiative in contrast to the mechanical, inductive divination that is usually initiated by the king's request to acquire signs from the deity. Compare in this connection the utterance of the Israelite prophet: "I was ready to be sought by those who didn't ask for me; I was ready to be found by those who didn't seek me. I said, 'Here am I, here am I' " (Isa 65:1).

2. The prophets are imbued with a consciousness of mission and take their stand before the authorities to present their divinely inspired message.

3. A more problematic characteristic is the ecstatic element in prophecy for the definition of ecstasy is not unambiguous. We would do well to lend this concept a broad and liberal definition, letting it apply to anything from autosuggestion to the divinely infused dream. Only in rare instances does this quality appear in the extreme embodiment of frenzy, and even then it is not clear whether it is accompanied with loss of senses, for the utterances of the prophets are always sober and purposeful and are far from being mere gibberish.

These particular characteristics, which are not necessarily found in conjunction, link the diviner-prophet at Mari to the Israelite prophet more than any other divinatory type known to us from the ancient Near East (except for the *rāgimu* [fem. *rāgintu*], "the pronouncer," "speaker" of the Neo-Assyrian period, addressing Esarhaddon and Ashurbanipal). Nevertheless, in a comparative study of Mari and the Bible we must direct our attention to the great difference in the source material: first-hand documents versus compositions that underwent a lengthy, complex literary process. Furthermore, the documentation concerning prophecy at Mari is restricted to a very short span of time, perhaps the last five to ten years of Zimrilim's reign. In comparison, the activity of the Israelite prophets extended over an expanse of centuries, especially if we include for our present purposes both the early, "primitive," as well as the late, "classical," prophets, which were not so decidedly distinct from each other, as many scholars would have us think.[8] In other words, Mari presents a synchronic picture, from one particular point in time, while the Bible permits a diachronic view that enables us to follow the development of the prophetic phenomenon.

SIMILARITY AND DIFFERENCES IN PROPHECY AT MARI AND IN THE BIBLE

Despite the external, formal similarity between the diviner-prophets at Mari and the Israelite prophets, there is an obvious gap in the content of the divine message and in the function it assumes and apparently also in the position occupied by the prophet within the society and the kingdom. In Israelite society it seems that the prophet usually enjoyed a more or less central position, even though there are kinds of prophets that are peripheral. At Mari, however, the prophets apparently played only a marginal role.[9] Admittedly, this distinction may be merely an illusion deriving from the nature of the sources at our disposal. Judging according to place of origin and activity, in both corpora many prophets are from rural localities—in Mari from the provincial towns of Terqa, Tuttul, and others, and in the Bible Amos from Tekoa, Micah from Moresheth, Jeremiah from Anathoth, and his rival Hananiah from Gibeon—while others reside in the respective capital cities.

As for contents, the prophecies at Mari are limited to material demands on the king, such as constructing a building or a city gate in a provincial town (ARM III, 78; XIII, 112), urging the offering of funerary sacrifices (ARM II, 90; III, 40), demanding the dispatch of valuable objects to various temples (A 4260), or requesting property for the god (A 1121; the reference is certainly to a landed estate granted to a sanctuary and its priestly staff). Furthermore, many of the more recently published prophecies refer to military affairs and, above all, the concern for the welfare of the king and his personal safety. He is warned against conspirators at home and enemies abroad (ARM X, 7; 8; 50; 80), especially Hammurabi, king of Babylon (see below), who was actually about to conquer Mari in a short time. This sort of message is significantly distinct from biblical prophecy, which presents a full-fledged religious ideology, a socioethical manifest, and a national purpose alongside the universal vision. This picture of a glaring contrast may well be considerably distorted. At Mari, nearly all the "prophetic" documents were discovered in the royal-diplomatic archive of the palace (room 115), and this would explain their tendency to concentrate on the king. Prophecies directed toward other people presumably existed, but on account of their nature they were not preserved. In comparison, had only the historiographic books of the Bible—Samuel, Kings, and Chronicles—survived, we would be faced with a picture resembling that at Mari, in which Israelite prophecy as well was oriented primarily toward the king and his political and military enterprises.

On the other hand, a recently published prophetic message from Mari (A 2731) contains a first glimmer of social and moral concern.[10] A diviner-prophet in the name of the god Adad from Aleppo urges Zimrilim: "When a wronged man or woman cries out to you, stand and let his/her case be judged." This command has an exact parallel in Jeremiah's prophecy concerning the kings: "Execute justice in the morning, and deliver from the hand of the oppressor him who has been robbed" (Jer 27:12; cf. Jer 22:3).

A tangible example of imposing obligations on the king of Mari may be found in one letter (ARM X, 100) in which a divinely imbued woman writes to the king directly, with no intervention of a third party (although apparently a scribe was employed). The woman (whose name should be read Yanana) addresses Zimrilim in the name of Dagan concerning a young woman—perhaps her own daughter or perhaps a companion—who was abducted when the two women were on a journey. Dagan appears in the woman's dream and decrees that only Zimrilim is capable of saving and returning the lass to the writer. The gist of the matter is that a woman who was wronged turns to the king seeking justice in the spirit of the prophetic commands adduced above.

All told, it is, for the present, difficult to determine the nature of the analogy between the prophecy at Mari and that in Israel, the two being set apart by a gap of more than six centuries. Furthermore, there are no intermediary links whatsoever. It would be therefore premature to adopt the view that Mari presents the prototype of prophecy in Israel.[11] But one cannot belittle this earliest manifestation of intuitive prophecy among West Semitic tribes at Mari, which is still an enigma. Nonetheless, we can put forward in this regard two reasonable assumptions that are not mutually exclusive:

1. Intuitive prophesying was basically the outcome of a specific social situation—an originally nonurban, seminomadic, tribal society. Urban sophistication, no matter how primitive, naturally engenders institutionalized cultic specialists, such as the *bārû* (haruspex), the foremost of the diviner types in Mesopotamia and part and parcel of the cult personnel of any self-respecting town or ruler.

2. The phenomenon of intuitive prophecy was a characteristic of a particular cultural sphere, which extended across the west, from Palestine and Syria to Anatolia in the northwest and to the east as far as Mari. This assumption is based mainly on the ecstatic element in prophecy, attested throughout this region, albeit rather sporadically. It is found outside the Bible, in such cases as the prophets in Hittite sources, at Byblos mentioned in the Egyptian Tale of Wen-Amon, and in Syria in the Aramatic inscription of Zakkur, king of Hamath, and according to references in classical literature.[12]

After these general observations, let us now present the data at hand concerning prophecy at Mari. Since 1948, twenty-eight letters have been published, all addressed to the king and containing reports on prophecies and divine revelations. The senders of the letters are high-ranking officials and bureaucrats from all over the kingdom. About half are women, mostly ladies of the palace headed by Shibtu, Zimrilim's major queen. Several of the letters contain two separate visions, and thus the total number of prophecies reaches as many as thirty-five—a very respectable quantity. In a few cases the correspondent is the prophet himself (even though we deem the letters to have been written down by a scribe; compare Baruch son of Neriah, Jeremiah's amanuensis). Thus we find correspondents prophesying in the name of Shamash of Sippar (A 4260), the court lady Addu-Duri (ARM X, 50), and a woman named Yanana (mentioned above; ARM X, 100). As we already noted at the outset, the words of the diviner-prophets, whether transmitted through intermediaries or even if dispatched directly to the king, were generally formulated with utmost lucidity, a fact perhaps due to the time elapsed between the actual prophetic experience and committing the vision to writing. How much more so is this the case in connection with biblical prophecy, which underwent continuous editing, even though certain prophecies may have been preserved in their original form.

PROFESSIONAL PROPHETS AT MARI AND THEIR RESEMBLANCE TO ISRAELITE PROPHETS

The diviner-prophets at Mari were of two types: professionals, recognizable by their distinctive titles (as were the biblical *rōʾeh, ḥōzeh, nābîʾ*, and *ʾîš ʾĕlōhîm*), and lay people, with no title whatsoever (see below). We know thus far five different titles at Mari, which may be seen as designating "cultic" prophets, if we may use a term accepted in biblical studies.

1. A priest (*šangûm*) is mentioned once as a prophesier (ARM X, 51). He was imbued with a prophetic dream containing a warning for Zimrilim; in the Bible too the prophet Ezekiel was originally a priest, and so too the priest Pashhur son of Immer prophesied (Jer 20:1–6).

2. There are three references to prophesying *assinnus* (ARM X, 6; 7; 80),[13] a term not yet completely elucidated. On the basis of later sources, he had been considered a eunuch, a male prostitute, or a cultic musician. This functionary served in a temple in Mari and prophesied in the name of the goddess Annunītum, apparently while disguised and acting like a woman, perhaps like a present-day transvestite or coccinell. Therefore, he prophesies in the name of a female deity, who would normally be associated with women rather than men.

3. In one solitary case a prophetess is mentioned bearing the title *qabbatum* (not to be read *qamatu!*) (ARM X, 8), derived undoubtedly from the Akkadian verb *qabû* ("to speak," "to proclaim").[14] It is tempting to link this term to the Hebrew root *qbb,* mentioned frequently in connection with the prophecy of Balaam, who announces *māh ʾeqqōb lōʾ qabbōh ʾel* . . . (Num 23:8; the form *qabbōh* is irregular and possibly it is to be derived from a root *qbh*).

But the best known of the professional prophets at Mari are the *muḫḫûm* and the *āpilum,* whom we have already discussed in the past. Suffice it here to add certain new details and examine problems that have arisen in the meantime.

4. The *muḫḫûm* (fem. *muḫḫūtum*), as the etymology indicates, was some sort of ecstatic or frenetic. The *purrusum* form of the noun is

peculiar to Mari (in other Akkadian sources we find the form *maḫḫûm*). This nominal form designates bodily defects and is functionally like the Hebrew *qittēl* form used in such words as *ʿiwwēr* ("blind"), *pisseăḥ* ("lame"), and *gibbēn* ("hunchback"). Thus this type of prophet, because of his peculiar behavior, was perceived of as a madman, similar to the biblical *mĕšuggāʿ*, a term used occasionally as a synonym of *nābîʾ* (2 Kgs 9:11; Jer 29:26; Hos 9:7). To these conclusions, which we have already reached in our previous studies,[15] we should now add the instances of the verb *immaḫu* (third person preterite) derived from the same root as *muḫḫûm*. The verb is used in the N stem resembling *nibbāʾ* (see also *hitnabbēʾ*) in the Bible and has the ingressive meaning "became insane," "went into a trance" (ARM X, 7:5–7; 8:5–8).

In addition to the five nameless *muḫḫû*s mentioned in the "prophetic" documents, there is now new administrative material available in three recent volumes of the Mari documents.[16] They do not contain the prophetic messages as such but list four *muḫḫû*s by name along with the deities they serve. These prophets figure in lists of personnel who received clothes from the palace, just as in previous lists there was already one reference to an *āpilum* (ARM IX, 22:14 and see below). These data certainly imply that these two prophetic types derived material support from the royal court. But it is surprising that all four *muḫḫû*s have strictly Akkadian and not West Semitic names: Irra-gamil, *muḫḫûm* of Nergal; Ea-maṣi, *muḫḫûm* of Iturmer (ARM XXI, 333:33′/4′; XXIII, 446:9′, 19′); Ea-mudammiq, *muḫḫûm* of Ninhursag; and lastly a prophetess named Anu-tabni, *muḫḫūtum* of the goddess Annunītum (ARM XXII, 168:8′ and 326:8–10), as befitting women who appear in the service of female deities. I have no satisfactory explanation for the nature of the names of the newly attested prophets, for we would generally expect West Semitic names. It is, however, possible that those prophets who were dependent on the court of Mari had already assimilated into Akkadian culture. In any case, the direct contact with the royal court calls to mind the court prophets in Israel, the likes of Nathan, the *nābîʾ*, and Gad, the *ḥōzeh,* who served David and Solomon, or the Baal and Asherah prophets, who functioned in the court of Ahab and Jezebel.

5. Finally, we turn to the *āpilum* (fem. *āpiltum*), a prophetic title exclusive to Mari, meaning "answerer," "respondent" (derived from the verb *apālum,* "to answer").[17] In contrast to the noun, the verb is frequently associated with mantic techniques. Unlike the rest of the proph-

ets, the *āpilum* acts on occasion in concert, in groups similar to the bands of prophets in the Bible *ḥebel/lahăqat nĕbîʾîm*). He is attested over a wider expanse than any of the other prophets, from Aleppo in northern Syria to Sippar near Babylon in the south.

The *āpilum* of Shamash of Sippar addresses the king of Mari directly without any intermediary, demanding a throne for Shamash and one of the king's daughters for service in his temple.[18] He also requests objects for other deities, among them an *assaku* (a consecrated object) for Adad of Aleppo (A 4260). Within these geographical extremities we find an *āpilum* of the Dagan temple in Tuttul (near the confluence of the Balih with the Euphrates) and an *āpiltum* in the Annunītum temple in the city of Mari itself. It is noteworthy that in these very same sanctuaries both the *muḫḫûm* and the *muḫḫūtum* functioned as well, indicating that two essentially different types of diviner-prophets could be found side by side. Furthermore, in the Dagan temple of Terqa even three types of prophets were at work simultaneously: a *muḫḫûm*, a *qabbatum*, and a dreamer of divine dreams.

AFFINITY TO HEBREW TERMINOLOGY AND CONTENT OF BIBLICAL PROPHECY

It seems that the very terms *āpilum* and *muḫḫûm* have counterparts in biblical terminology concerning divine revelations. To the biblical terms *ʿānāh*, *ʿōneh* ("answer," "answerer"), as indications of divine revelation, discussed by us elsewhere,[19] we may now add several pertinent passages.

Most significantly, the verb *ʿānāh* is at times used to describe the prophet's acting as God's mouthpiece, whether actually responding to a query put to the deity or not. This is clearly seen, for instance, in 1 Sam 9:17: "When Samuel saw Saul, the Lord *answered him*, 'Here is the man of whom I spoke to you! He it is who shall rule over my people.' " This is also the case of Jeremiah's words that invalidate the use of the expression *maśśāʾ YHWH* as a legitimate designation for a divine revelation, requiring in its stead the figure of speech: "What has the Lord *answered* and what has the Lord said?" (Jer 23:37). The term *maʿăneh ʾĕlōhîm* (lit. "God's answer") denoting the word of the Lord occurs once in the Bible, in Micah's prophecy (Mic 3:7), which also makes the illuminating use of *ʿnh* in connection with the oracles of Balaam: "Remember now, O my people, remember what Balak king of Moab devised and what

Balaam the son of Beor *answered* him" (Mic 6:5). The verb *ʿānāh* does not indicate here any response to a specific question that Balak put forward to Balaam but rather the prophetic oracle Balaam was compelled to deliver on behalf of Israel. It is not impossible that this foreign diviner, who is never called *nābîʾ*, was a prophet of the *āpilum* ("answerer") type. That is hinted at also by the cultic performances resorted to by Balaam, on the one hand (Num 23:3, 14–15, 29), and by the band of the *āpilu,* on the other (A 1121, esp. lines 24–25), both aimed at acquiring the divine word.[20]

It is of interest that the recently discovered Balaam inscription from Deir ʿAllā, dating to the end of the eighth or early seventh century B.C., and apparently composed in either an Ammonite or an Israelite-Gileadite dialect, enumerates various types of sorcerers, including a woman designated *ʿnyh*. The term most likely means "female respondent," that is, a semantic equivalent of the Mari term *āpiltum.*[21] This interpretation gains cogency by the following words referring to the woman: *rqḥt mr wkhnh* ("a compounderess of myrrh and a priestess"). Even more significant is the Aramaic inscription of Zakkur, king of Hamath, from about 800 B.C. In his hour of peril, the king turns to his gods "and Baalshamayn responded to me (*wyʿnny*) and Baalshamayn [spoke to me] through seers and diviners (*ʿddn*)" (lines 11–12).[22]

The possible intersection between the prophetic activity of the *āpilum* and the *muḫḫûm* is probably indicated in a letter containing the message of a *muḫḫūtum*—a prophetess. She implores the king of Mari not to leave the capital to wage war and declares: "I will *answer* you constantly" (*attanapal;* ARM X, 50:22–26). In other words, there are cases where a *muḫḫûm* would be involved in the act of "answering" *(apālum).*

Before turning to the lay prophets, let us examine two prophecies of similar content and reminiscent of the biblical "oracles against the nations," one of an *āpilum* (spelled here peculiarly *aplûm*) and the other of "the wife of a man," that is, a lay person. Both reports were transmitted to Kibri-Dagan, Zimrilim's governor of Terqa. The *āpilum*/*aplûm* "arose" in the name of Dagan of Tuttul "and so he said as follows: 'O Babylon! Why doest thou ever (evil)? I will gather thee into a net! . . . The house of the seven confederates and all their possessions I shall deliver into Zimrilim's hand!' " (ARM XIII, 23:6–15). The prophecy, which contains several motifs well known from biblical prophecies of doom,[23] reflects the deteriorating relations between Mari and Babylon on account of Hammurabi's expansionist aspirations. The other prophecy explicitly mentions the name of Babylon's king, Hammurabi, as an enemy of Mari (ARM XIII, 114). A divinely inspired woman approaches Kibri-Dagan late one afternoon with the following words of consolation: "The god Dagan sent me. Send to your lord; he shall not worry [. . .], he shall not worry. Hammurabi [king] of Babylon . . ." (continuation broken). The urgency of the matter is indicated by the fact that the letter bearing this encouraging message was dispatched the very day after the utterance.

From these two prophecies, and possibly from most of the visions concerned with the king's safety, it is apparent that they were recorded at a time of political and military distress afflicting Mari. This too would be analogous to Israelite prophecy, which particularly thrived in times of national emergency, such as during the Philistine threat in the days of Samuel and Saul, Sennacherib's campaign to Jerusalem, and especially Nebuchadnezzar's invasion of Judah. The crisis factor was certainly one of the principal forces engendering prophetic manifestations both in Mari and in Israel.[24] However, in contrast to the Bible with its prophecies of doom and words of admonition against the king and the people, the messages at Mari were usually optimistic and sought to please the king rather than rebuke and alert him. Such prophecies of peace and salvation (see ARM X, 4; 9; 10; 51; 80), colored by a touch of nationalism, liken the Mari prophets to the biblical prophets of peace or "false prophets," and surely the corresponding prophecies are greatly similar. Indeed, one of the prominent "false" prophets in the Bible, Hananiah of Gibeon, Jeremiah's rival, rashly proclaims in the name of the Lord (and not in the name of a foreign god) the impending return of the Judean exiles from Babylonia, "for I will break the yoke of the king of Babylon" (Jer 28:4). How reminiscent this is of the *āpilum*'s prediction against Babylon (see above, ARM XIII, 23). In both instances the message is pleasant to the ear and whitewashes the crisis situation, for the prophets of peace serve the establishment and express its interest (compare the four hundred prophets at Ahab's court who prophesy "with one accord"; 1 Kgs 22:13).[25]

In contrast to Mari, the Bible is replete with prophecies unfavorable to the king and to the people. Their heralds, the so-called prophets of doom or "true" prophets, are constantly harassed by the authorities. One well-known case is Amos, who in the royal sanctuary at Bethel foretells King Jeroboam's death and the exile of the people (Amos 7:10–13). In reaction the priest Amaziah, by order of the king, expels the prophet disgracefully to Judah. Jeremiah provokes an even more violent response, in the days of both Jehoiakim and Zedekiah. Pashhur, the priest in charge of the Temple in Jerusalem, when confronted with the prophet's words of wrath, "beat Jeremiah the prophet, and put him in the stocks that were . . . in the house of the Lord" (Jer 20:2).

On the other hand, at certain times we find close cooperation between the king, the priest, and the prophet. A priest occasionally officiated as an intermediary between king and prophet, as when King Hezekiah sent emissaries to Isaiah (2 Kgs 19:20 = Isa 37:2–4) and Zedekiah to Jeremiah (Jer 21:1–2; 37:3). Similarly, Hilkiah, the high priest, headed the royal delegation that Josiah sent to the prophetess Hulda (2 Kgs 22:12–20). The roles are inverted at Mari, where a prophet's report could be conveyed to the king via a priest. According to two documents (ARM VI, 45; X, 8), prophetesses appear before the priest Ahum, who served in the temple of Annunītum located in Mari proper. Once Ahum reports the message to Bahdilim, the palace prefect, to be relayed to the king, and at another time he transmits the prophetic words to Queen Shibtu.[26] In this latter case, a new element appears to which we have only briefly alluded previously—the frenetic here was a mere maidservant, called Ahatu, who had no prophetic title, being simply a lay person. This brings us to the lay prophets.

LAY PROPHETS

More than half of the "prophetic" documents from Mari deal with lay persons not functioning as professionals attached to a sanctuary. Among these so-called lay prophets we find such designations as a "man," a "woman," a "man's wife," a "youth," a "young woman" (or "maidservant"), and certain persons who are mentioned merely by their personal names. In one case, we encounter a prophetic message elicited from a "man and a woman" (lit. "male and female"), who prophesy jointly (ARM X, 4). Because this latter manner of prophecy is uncommon and astounding in Mari, it should be examined briefly.

Queen Shibtu writes to her husband that she has asked a man and a woman to foretell the fortunes of Zimrilim's forthcoming military expedition against Ishme-Dagan, king of Ashur. The mode of predicting the future here is exceptional and has led to different interpretations among scholars.[27] We present here the key sentence at the opening of Shibtu's letter in accordance with a recent collation: "Concerning the report on the military campaign which my lord undertakes, I have asked a man and a woman about the signs *(ittātim)* when I plied (them with drink), and the oracle *(egerrûm)* for my lord is very favorable" (ARM X, 4:3–37). Shibtu immediately inquires about the fate of the enemy Ishme-Dagan and the oracle "was unfavorable." Further on, Shibtu cites in full the prophecy proclaimed by the two persons, which contains several motifs found in biblical prophecies.[28] How are we to perceive this kind of divination? It has been suggested that the man and the woman themselves served as a sign and portent, partly on the basis of the words of Isaiah (Isa 8:18): "Behold, I and the children the Lord has given me are signs and portents in Israel," but this interpretation seems forced. It seems, rather, that the queen turned randomly to select a man and a woman and offered them a drink, perhaps wine, so as to loosen their tongues and acquire an *egerrûm* oracle, which is based on "chance" utterances. It has already been suggested that this type of oracle is reminiscent of the divinatory method referred to as a *bat qôl* (lit. "a trace of a voice," usually translated "echo") in Talmudic sources, where it serves as a substitute for authentic prophecy.[29]

Among the lay prophets, as well as among the transmitters of prophetic reports, there is an unusually large proportion of women, mostly from Zimrilim's entourage. One of the king's daughters turns to her father, stating explicitly: "Now—even though I am (only) a woman—may my father and lord harken unto my words. I will constantly send the word of the gods to my father" (ARM X, 31:7′–10′). Some women, including female dreamers, send their prophecies directly to the king without mediation (ARM X, 50; 100). More than anyone else, Queen Shibtu serves as an intermediary for conveying prophetic messages to her husband, the king. Also among the professional prophets, as we have seen, there are a considerable number of women. This brings to mind the prophetesses in the Bible, the outstanding ones being Deborah wife of Lappidoth (Judg 4:4) and Huldah wife of Shallum (2 Kgs 22:14). In both instances, the Bible specifies in particular that they were married, probably to stress their stable position and reliability; this is the case of the "wife of a man," one of the Mari prophetesses (ARM XIII, 114:8).

Are there any characteristics that separate the professional prophets from the lay? Two prominent distinguishing features have been noticed by scholars: (1) In the case of the professional, and only the professional, the actual message is preceded by the verb "to arise" *(tebû)*—"he/she rose"—which alludes to the stimulation of the prophets in the temple (perhaps getting up from a sitting or crouching position).[30] Synonymous expressions are used as well in connection with the prophets of the Bible (Deut 13:2; 18:15, 18; 34:10; Jer 1:17; etc.), and note in particular Ezekiel: "And set me upon my feet: (Ezek 2:2; cf. 3:22–24; Dan 8:17–18; 10:10–11). (2) Among the lay prophets the dream is prevalent as a prophetic means, while this medium is totally absent among the professionals.

PROPHETIC MESSAGE DREAMS

From a third to a half of all the published prophecies from Mari originated in dreams. Thus, phenomenologically speaking, there are two distinct categories of acquiring the divine word. The professional prophets enjoyed direct revelations while awake; the lay persons, on the other hand, were usually dreamers of dreams. Divine revelations through dreams were a widespread phenomenon throughout the ancient Near East, including Israel.[31] But at Mari, as well as in the Bible, alongside regular revelatory dreams we find a specific subcategory of "message dream," namely, a dream in which the message was not intended for the dreamer himself but rather for a third party (as for the Bible, see Num 12:6; Jer 23:25–32; 29:8; Zech 10:2).

The above two categories of prophesying now illuminate with greater clarity the parallel distinction made in the Bible, especially in the legal corpora: "If a prophet arises among you, or a dreamer of a dream, and gives you a sign or a wonder . . ." (Deut 13:1–5). In an incident involving Saul, the Bible explicitly differentiates between as many as three distinct divinatory methods: "The Lord did not answer him, either by dreams or by Urim or by prophets" (1 Sam 28:6; and see v. 15).[32] Jeremiah still regarded the dreamer as a distinct type of prophet (Jer 27:9). But he already belittles the dream, contrasting it with "the word of God" and associating it with the false prophets: "Let the prophet who has a dream tell the dream, but let him who has my word speak my word faithfully. What has the straw in common with wheat?" (Jer 23:28). This deflated status of the dream as a source of prophetic inspiration finds clear expression in the rabbinic dictum comparing sleep to death just as "a dream is withered prophecy" (*Gen. R.* 44:17).

The letters that report dream revelations are usually structured according to a regular scheme: the writer's presentation of the male or female dreamer; the opening formula of the dreamer: "(I saw) in my dream"—*(ina šuttīja)*, which is an obviously West Semitic form identical with biblical Hebrew *baḥălômî* (Gen 40:9, 16; 41:17);[33] the content of the dream which is based on a visual or, more often, on an auditory experience (hearing the voice of the god); finally, comments of the writer of the letter. In many cases these include a statement that, along with the report of the prophet, a lock of his or her hair and the hem of his or her garment are dispatched to the king.

Let us dwell here upon one illuminating incident at Mari where the same dream recurred twice, night after night. The dreamer was a mere youth *(ṣuḫārum)* to whom a god appeared in a nocturnal vision. The dream was eventually reported to the king by Kibri-Dagan: "Thus he saw (a vision) as follows: 'Build not this house . . . ; if that house will be built I will make it collapse into the river!' On the day he saw that dream he did not tell (it) to anyone. On the second day he saw again the dream as follows: 'It was a god (saying): "Build not this house; if you will build it, I will make it collapse into the river!" ' Now, herewith the hem of his garment and a lock of hair of his head I have sent to my lord . . ." (ARM XIII, 112:1′–15′). The boy, who apparently had no previous prophetic experience, did not at first realize the source of his dream; only when it recurred the next night did he become aware of its divine origin and of the mission imposed upon him. This immediately calls to mind young Samuel's initial experience while reposing in the temple at Shiloh (1 Samuel 3). The Lord informs him in a nocturnal vision of the impending demise of the Elide clan, but in this case it was only after the fourth beckoning (on the very same night) that Samuel became convinced of the divine nature of the vision.[34]

In general, novice and inexperienced prophets were unable to identify revelations when they first encountered them (in the case of Samuel see 1 Sam 3:7); hence the repetition of the manifestation, whether at Mari or in the Bible. As for the latter, most illuminating is the initial call vision of Jeremiah, who is reluctant to accept his prophetic mission, pleading his youthfulness before God (Jer 1:6–7). After having had his confidence bolstered, God tests him by a vision: "And the word of the Lord came to my saying: 'Jeremiah, what do you see?' and I said: 'I see a rod of almond *(šāqēd)*.' Then the Lord said to me, 'You have seen well for I am watching *(šōqēd)* over my word to perform it" (Jer 1:11–12). God in his response confirms the reliability of the prophet's perception, a totally unique event in the realm of prophetic visions in the Bible. It proves that Jeremiah passed the test and is fit to undertake the prophetic mission.[35]

A NEW PROPHECY FROM MARI AND THE QUESTION OF PROPHETIC RELIABILITY

We shall conclude our discussion of prophetic dreams with the last one to be published—one that has not yet been brought to bear upon the issue of prophecy at Mari.[36] In this fragmentary document (A 222) the name of the male or female writer has been lost as has been the name of the recipient, most likely King Zimrilim, as in the rest of the letters. We read:

(The writer): The woman Ayala saw *(iṭṭul)* in her dream as follows:
(The dreamer): "A woman from the place Shehrum (5) (and) a woman from Mari in the gate of (the temple of) Annunītum [line missing] which is at the edge of the city—quarreled among themselves. Thus (said) the woman from Shehrum (10) to the woman from Mari: 'Return to me my position as high priestess *(enūtum)*; either you sit or I myself shall sit.' "
(The writer): By the *Hurru*-bird I have examined this matter and (15) she saw (the dream well—*naṭlat*). Now her hair and the hem of the garment I am sending along (20). May my lord investigate the matter!

The nature of the dispute between these two women is not entirely clear, although it may involve rivalry between two localities and their representatives over the seat of the high priestesshood. But highly illuminating is the concluding passage where the writer reports that he confirmed the validity of the vision by means of augury, referring probably to examination of the behavior and flight patterns of the birds. This divinatory device, well known in the classical world, was performed at a very early period in West Asia.[37] The examination proved that the woman actually did see *(naṭlat)*. On the basis of the synonymous and interchangeable verb for "to see (a dream)" *(amāru)*, the intention could be that the woman was indeed competent and experienced in the art of dream oracles.[38] Thus the meaning is, as the editor of the text translated:

'Elle a bien eu ce songe!" just like the words of God to Jeremiah, "You have seen well" *(hēṭabtā lirʾôt)*! The writer does not stop with his own examination of the dream but sends the woman's personal items—her hair and the hem of her garment—to the king for his own examination. This unique practice, attested in connection with the Mari prophets, is mentioned on nine different occasions, that is, in a third of all the "prophetic" letters. This peculiar procedure has led to several scholarly interpretations, all of which remain in the realm of speculation. Since a lock of hair and a piece of garment were very personal objects—objects that could have served as some sort of ID card, we may assume that this procedure was assigned to determine the identity and even the very existence of the prophet and to confirm the authenticity of his or her message, as we have tried to demonstrate elsewhere.[39]

The credibility of prophetic revelation was obviously a sensitive matter, not to be taken for granted. Thus it was often verified by means of accepted mantic devices, which were considered more reliable and preferable to intuitive prophesying.[40] If we ignore the still obscure practices of sending the hem of the garment and the lock of hair of the prophesier, we encounter the following examples: Queen Shitbu writes Zimrilim that she personally examined a prophet's message prior to sending it to the king and found the report to be trustworthy (ARM X, 6); in another letter, a lady of the royal household reported a vision and then advised the king: "Let my lord have the haruspex look into the matter . . ." (ARM X, 94); in a third letter, another woman implores the king to verify the vision of an *āpiltum* by divinatory means (ARM X, 81); the same woman advises the king following the prophecy of a *qabbatum* (see above) to be alert and not to enter the city without inquiring of omens (ARM X, 80).

In contrast, in Israel the prophetic word, whether accepted or rejected by the king or the people, is never subjected to corroboration by cultic means; it is simply vindicated by the test of fulfillment (cf. Deut 18:22; Jer 28:9; Ezek 33:33).[41]

NOTES

1. A. Malamat, "Prophecy in the Mari Documents," *EI* 4 (1956) 74–84 (Hebrew; English summary, pp. vif.); idem, "History and Prophetic Vision

in a Mari Letter," *EI* 5 (1958) 67–73 (Hebrew; English summary, pp. 86*f.); idem, "Prophetic Revelations in New Documents from Mari and the Bible," VTSup 15 (1966) 207–27; idem, "A Mari Prophecy and Nathan's Dynastic Oracle," *Prophecy: Essays Presented to G. Fohrer,* ed. J. A. Emerton (BZAW 150; Berlin: Walter de Gruyter, 1980) 68–82.

2. We list here only general works on the entire corpus of "prophetic" materials and not studies of individual Mari documents: F. Ellermeier, *Prophetie in Mari und Israel* (Herzberg: Verlag Erwin Jungler, 1968); W. L. Moran, "New Evidence from Mari on the History of Prophecy," *Bib* 50 (1969) 15–56; idem, *ANET*^{3}, 623–25, 629–32; H. B. Huffmon, "Prophecy in the Mari Letters," *BA Reader* 3 199–224; J. F. Craghan, "The ARM X 'Prophetic' Texts: Their Media, Style and Structure," *JANESCU* 6 (1974) 39–57; E. Noort, *Untersuchungen zum Gottesbescheid in Mari* (AOAT 202; Neukirchen-Vluyn: Neukirchener Verlag, 1977); R. R. Wilson, *Prophecy and Society in Ancient Israel* (Philadelphia: Fortress Press, 1980) 98–115; A. Schmitt, *Prophetischer Gottesbescheid in Mari und Israel* (BWANT 6/14; Stuttgart: Kohlhammer Verlag, 1982); I. Nakata, *Acta Sumerologica* 4 (1982) 143–48.

3. See J. Margueron, "Rapport préliminaire sur la campagne de 1979," *M.A.R.I.* 1 (1982) 9–30; ". . . de 1980," ibid., 2 (1983) 9–35; ". . . de 1982," ibid., 3 (1984) 8–14, 197–206. On the archive of Asqudum discovered on the site, see now D. Charpin, "Les archives du devin Asqudum dans la résidence du 'chantier A' " *M.A.R.I.* 4 (1985) 453–62.

4. The texts have recently been collected by S. Parpola, *Letters from Assyrian Scholars to the Kings Esarhaddon and Assurbanipal* (AOAT 5/2; Neukirchen-Vluyn: Neukirchener Verlag, 1983) 2. 486–91. For extispicy in Mesopotamia in general and at Mari in particular, see now I. Starr, *The Ritual of the Diviner* (Bibliotheca Mesopotamica 12; Malibu, Calif.: Undena Publications, 1983), and index s.v. "Mari" (p. 141); and cf. J. Bottéro in *Divination et rationalité* (Paris: Éditions du Seuil, 1974) 7–197.

5. See A. Malamat, "The Ban in Mari and the Bible," *Biblical Essays—Proceedings of the 9th Meeting of Die Ou-Testamentliche Werkgemeenskap in Suid Africa* (1966) 40–49; idem, "Mari," *BA* 34 (1971) 18–21; E. A. Speiser, "Census and Ritual Expiation in Mari and Israel," *JBL* 79 (1960) 157–63; M. Held, "Philological Notes on the Covenant Rituals," *BASOR* 200 (1970) 32–37; and see now H. Tadmor, "Treaty and Oath in the Ancient Near East: A Historian's Approach," *Humanizing America's Iconic Book: SBL Centennial Addresses 1980,* ed. G. M. Tucker and D. A. Knight (SBL Centennial Publications; Chico, Calif.: Scholars Press, 1982) 127–35.

6. An exception is J. M. Sasson's remark in his review of Noort's book (above, n. 2) in *AfO* 27 (1980) 130a.

7. Noort (*Untersuchungen zum Gottesbescheid,* 24ff.) rejects the characteristics mentioned below as typical of prophesying at Mari and accordingly denies any relationship to biblical prophecy. But his approach is too extreme in requiring every single characteristic to appear in each and every "pro-

phetic" text. He has been justifiably criticized by, e.g., I. Nakata, *JAOS* 102 (1982) 166–68.

8. This identification has gained currency ever since the overemphasis on the Canaanite origin of early Israelite prophecy by G. Hölscher, *Die Profeten* (Leipzig: J. C. Hinrichs, 1914), and cf. J. Lindblom, *Prophecy in Ancient Israel* (Oxford: Basil Blackwell, 1962) 47, 105ff. In contrast, subsequent scholars occasionally pointed out the continuity of certain early elements through the period of classical prophecy; see, e.g., M. Haran, "From Early to Classical Prophecy: Continuity and Change," *VT* 27 (1977) 385–97 (with previous literature).
9. The question of center and periphery in the status of the prophets has been raised only in recent years under the influence of sociology. See Wilson, *Prophecy and Society,* which emphasizes the peripheral role of all Mari prophets when compared with the central role of the *bārû*; and see most recently D. L. Petersen, *The Roles of Israel's Prophets* (Sheffield: JSOT Press, 1981). The author considers the *nābîʾ* and the *ḥōzeh* to be "central" in both Israel and Judah, while the *rōʾeh* and the *ʾîš hāʾĕlōhîm,* as well as the *bĕnê nĕbîʾîm* ("sons" of the prophets), are regarded as peripheral.
10. This document has recently been joined to the text A 1121, published long ago; see B. Lafont, *RA* 78 (1984) 7–17. For earlier treatments, see M. Anbar, *UF* 7 (1975) 517ff. and Malamat, "A Mari Prophecy," 73, and n. 6.
11. Here I fully agree with Noort, *Untersuchungen;* see his summary on p. 109; I do reject, however, the remarks such as those of Schmitt, *Prophetischer Gottesbescheid,* 13.
12. The West as a separate sphere of culture from the East (Southern Mesopotamia) with regard to certain basic religious elements has been appreciated by A. L. Oppenheim, *Ancient Mesopotamia: Portrait of a Dead Civilization* (Chicago: University of Chicago Press, 1964) 221ff. For the ecstatic prophesier in Hittite sources, see *ANET*[3], 395a; for the prophet from Byblos, see most recently A. Cody, "The Phoenician Ecstatic in Wenamum," *JEA* 65 (1979) 99–106. The author derives the Egyptian word *ʿdd* from the West Semitic *ʿdd,* which in the Aramaic inscription of Zakkur (see below) designates a type of diviner-prophet, and see Malamat "Prophetic Revelations," 209 and n. 2.
13. For this prophesier, see most recently Wilson, *Prophecy and Society,* 106–7 with bibliography.
14. For this term and additional bibliographical references, see now *CAD* Q, 2b.
15. Malamat, "Prophetic Revelations," 210–11 and n. 4, for additional references and earlier literature. Cf. now J. Renger, *ZA* NF, 25 (1969) 219ff.; *CAD* M/I 90 including Old Babylonian references outside Mari.
16. J. M. Durand, *Textes administratifs des salles 134 et 160 . . . ,* ARM(T) 21 (1983); J. R. Kupper, *Documents administratifs de la salle 135 . . . ,* ARM(T) 22 (1983); G. Bardet et al., *Archives administratives de Mari* 1, ARM 23 (1984).

17. Malamat, "History and Prophetic Vision," 71ff.; idem, "Prophetic Revelations," 212f. and n. 2, for the various spellings *apillû, aplû, āpilum*; see now *CAD* A/II, 170a; idem, "A Mari Prophecy," 68ff.; M. Anbar, *RA* 75 (1981) 91.
18. Interestingly, compliance with this prophetic demand seems to be alluded to in the female correspondence. Further on in our document the name of Zimrilim's "daughter" is given as Erishtī-Aya. Indeed, a woman by this name sends several doleful letters to her royal parents from the temple at Sippar; see ARM X, 37:15; 43:16; etc. Cf. F. R. Kraus, *Königliche Verfügungen in altbabylonischer Zeit* (Leiden: E. J. Brill, 1984) 98 and n. 224.
19. Malamat, "History and Prophetic Vision," 72–73.
20. Balaam was certainly not a prophesier of the *bārû* type, as was long ago suggested by S. Daiches, "Balaam—a Babylonian bārû," *H. V. Hilprecht Anniversary Volume* (Leipzig: J. C. Hinrichs, 1909) 60–70. This claim has often been correctly refuted; see recently A. Rofé, *The Book of Balaam (Numbers 22:2–24:25)* (Jerusalem: Sinor, 1979; Hebrew) 32 n. 53. Offering sacrifices in preparation for deriving the word of the deity as is found in the Balaam pericope is similarly alluded to in the beginning of the Mari texts ARM XIII, 23 and A 1221 (cf. Malamat, "A Mari Prophecy," 69–70); it is explicitly mentioned in a "prophetic" document that has so far been published only in French translation. A 455: ". . . One head of cattle and six sheep I will sacrifice . . .", i.e., seven sacrificial animals. In what follows, a *muḫḫûm* "arises" and prophesies in the name of Dagan. Compare the seven altars, seven bulls, and seven rams that Balaam had Balak prepare before delivering his oracle (Num 23:29–30).
21. See the Deir ʿAllā inscription, first combination, line 11; J. Hoftijzer and G. van der Kooij, *Aramaic Texts from Deir ʿAllā* (Leiden: E. J. Brill, 1976) 180, 212. The editors interpreted *ʿnyh* as female answerer indicating a prophetess, following our conclusion about the title *āpilum* at Mari and its relationship to biblical terminology. This opinion has been accepted by Rofé, *The Book of Balaam,* 67 and n. 33, among others. Indeed, in the dialect of this inscription, verbs with a third weak radical are spelled preserving the *yod* before the final *he,* like Hebrew *bōkiyāh* (courtesy B. A. Levine). This term has nothing to do with "poor woman," despite the Hebrew homograph *ʿnyh,* as various scholars contend; see, e.g., A. Caquot and A. Lemaire, *Syria* 54 (1977) 200; P. K. McCater, *BASOR* 234 (1980) 58; H. and M. Weippert, *ZDPV* 98 (1982) 98; J. A. Hackett, *The Balaam Text from Deir ʿAllā* (HSM 31; Chico, Calif.: Scholars Press, 1984) 133 s.v. "*ʿnyh.*"
22. See J. C. L. Gibson, *Textbook of Syrian Semitic Inscriptions* (Oxford: Clarendon Press, 1975) 2.8ff. The author translates the word *ʿddn* as (prophetic?) "messengers" on the basis of *ʿdd* in Ugaritic (p. 15), and cf. above n. 12. For a possible connection between prophecy at Mari and at Hamath, see J. F. Ross, "Prophecy in Hamath, Israel and Mari," *HTR* 63 (1970) 1–28.

23. Especially the motifs of gathering into a net and delivering into the hand, which are found frequently in both ancient Near Eastern and biblical literature in connection with vanquishing the enemy; see Malamat, "Prophecy in the Mari Documents," 82, and "Prophetic Revelations," 217f.; cf. J. G. Heinz, VTSup 17 (1969) 112–38, who relates these motifs to the "Holy War" in the ancient Near East and the Bible.
24. This has been indicated by, among others, B. Uffenheimer, *Early Israelite Prophecy* (Jerusalem: Magnes Press, 1973; Hebrew) 27, 37; Noort, *Untersuchungen* 93, 109; and recently J. Blenkinsopp, *A History of Prophecy in Israel* (Philadelphia: Westminster Press, 1983) 45. Remarkably, just before the conquest of Mari by Hammurabi there is a noticeable rise in future-telling activities of the *bārû*; see Starr, *Ritual of the Diviner,* 107.
25. For the "false" prophets and their dependence on the Israelite establishment, see among others M. Buber, *Der Glaube der Propheten* (Zurich: Manesse Verlag, 1950) 253ff., F. L. Hossfeld and I. Meyer, *Prophet gegen Prophet* (Fribourg Universitätsverlag, 1973); S. de Vries, *Prophet Against Prophet* (Grand Rapids: Wm. B. Eerdmans Publishing Co., 1978).
26. Moran ("New Evidence from Mari," 20) holds that ARM VI, 45 deals with the same event as ARM X, 50, while Sasson (*AfO* 27 [1980] 131b) associates it with ARM X, 8. Neither suggestion is compelling. ARM X, 50 does not mention a priest by the name of Ahum, while ARM X, 8 mentions a prophetess by name but without title, and ARM VI, 45 speaks of an anonymous *muḫḫūtum*. It may be assumed, therefore, that before Ahum, a priest in Mari, both professional and lay prophesiers would occasionally appear.
27. On ARM X, 4, and the mode of prophesying, see the recent studies: A. Finet, "Un cas de clédonomancie à Mari," *Zikir Šumim* (F. R. Kraus Festschrift; ed. G. van Driel et al.; Leiden: E. J. Brill, 1982) 48–55; J. M. Durand, "In vino veritas," *RA* 76 (1982) 43–50; *M.A.R.I.* 3 (1984) 150ff. C. Wilcke, *RA* 77 (1983) 93.
28. Note, above all, the motif of the gods marching alongside the king in time of war and saving him from his enemies, a motif resembling the intervention of the Lord in the wars of Israel. This involves as well driving the enemy into flight (cf. "Arise, O Lord, and let thy enemies be scattered," Num 10:35; see also Ps 68:2) and eventually decapitating the foe who will be trampled under the foot of the king of Mari. Cf. M. Weinfeld, "Ancient Near Eastern Patterns in Prophetic Literature," *VT* 27 (1977) 183ff.
29. For this type of oracle, see *CAD* E, *egirrû,* 45: ". . . oracular utterances . . . which are either accidental in origin (comp. with Greek *kledon*) or hallucinatory in nature." For the parallel with Hebrew *bat qôl,* see D. Sperling, "Akkadian *egirrû* and Hebrew *bt qwl,*" *JANESCU* 4 (1972) 63–74.
30. See in particular Moran, "New Evidence from Mari," 25–26; Weinfeld, "Ancient Near Eastern Patterns," 181–82.
31. Malamat, "Prophecy in the Mari Documents," 83; idem, "Prophetic Revelations," 221–22 and n. 1 on p. 222, for literature on the dream in the

Bible. For the ancient Near East, see the basic study of A. L. Oppenheim, *The Interpretation of Dreams in the Ancient Near East* (Philadelphia: American Philosophical Society, 1956).

32. An exact parallel to these three alternative means of inquiring of the deity may be found in the Plague Prayers of the Hittite King Murshili II; see *ANET*³, 394b–95a, and S. Herrmann, *Die prophetischen Heilserwartungen im Alten Testament* (Stuttgart: W. Kohlhammer, 1965) 54f.

33. The West Semitic form was pointed out by Held; see *apud* Craghan, "The ARM X 'Prophetic' Texts," 43 n. 32. The standard Akkadian form would be *ina šuttim ša lāmuru/aṭṭulu;* compare a similar West Semitic usage in one of the first prophecies published: *ina panīya* (lit. "in front of me," meaning "on my way"); Malamat, "Prophecy in the Mari Documents," 81.

34. See Malamat, "Prophetic Revelations," 223ff. The phenomenon of an identical dream recurring several times is known especially from the classical world; see J. S. Hanson, "Dreams and Visions in the Graeco-Roman World and Early Christianity," *Aufstieg und Niedergang der Römischen Welt,* II, 23/2 (Berlin: Walter de Gruyter, 1978) 1411, and the passages from Cicero, *De divinatione,* cited there.

35. See A. Malamat, *Jeremiah Chapter One—The Call and the Visions, Iyyunim* 21 (Jerusalem: Jewish Agency 1954; Hebrew) esp. 39–40.

36. The document was published by G. Dossin, "Le songe d'Ayala," *RA* 69 (1975) 28–30 (attributed by him to King Yahdunlim!); and see the comments of J. M. Sasson, *JAOS* 103 (1983) 291. His interpretation of *enūtum* (see below) as "utensils" rather than "priesthood" is unsatisfactory.

37. Divination by bird behavior is a typically Western practice; cf. Oppenheim, *Ancient Mesopotamia,* 209–10. This practice was especially widespread among the Hittites; see A. Kammenhuber, *Orakelpraxis. Träume und Vorzeichenschau bei den Hethitern* (Heidelberg: C. Winter, 1976). The book deals only briefly (p. 11) with the kind of bird mentioned in our document: *MUŠEN HURRI;* see for this bird A. Salonen, *Vögel und Vogelfang im Alten Mesopotamien* (Helsinki: Suomalainen Tiedeakatemia, 1973) 143–46; and cf. J. P. McEwan, *ZA* 70 (1980) 38, 58ff.

38. See *CAD* A/II, *amāru* A 2, p. 13: "to learn by experience (especially stative . . .)." The stative form with the meaning "experienced" or "trained" is especially prevalent in the Mari idiom, and we may therefore assume the same nuance for the stative of *naṭālu: naṭlat* in our document.

39. Malamat, "Prophecy in the Mari Documents," 81, 84; "Prophetic Revelations," 225ff. and notes. For other explanations, see now Uffenheimer, *Early Israelite Prophecy,* 29–33; Ellermeier, *Prophetie,* 97–110; Moran, "New Evidence from Mari," 19–22; Noort, *Untersuchungen;* and Craghan, "The ARM X 'Prophetic' Texts," 53ff. Note in two documents (A 455:25; ARM X, 81:18) the illuminating but problematic addition appearing after the dispatch of the hair and hem; in the latter: "let them declare (me) clean" *(lizakkû);* according to Moran, "New Evidence from Mari," 22–23: ". . . it is the haruspex who 'tries the case' and it is his response that will in effect

declare the prophetesses clean." Cf. now ARM X, 267, ad loc.; Noort, *Untersuchungen,* 85–86; and S. Dalley et al., *The Old Babylonian Tablets from Tell al Rimah* (London: British School of Iraq, 1976) 64 f., no. 65.

40. See Moran, "New Evidence from Mari," 22–23; Craghan, "The ARM X 'Prophetic' Texts," 41–42; and H. W. F. Saggs, *The Encounter with the Divine in Mesopotamia and Israel* (London: Athlone Press, 1978) 141.

41. This study was prepared by a grant from the Fund for Basic Research, administered by the Israel Academy of Sciences and Humanities, and during my term as Fellow of the Institute for Advanced Studies of the Hebrew University.

8

Widow, Orphan, and the Poor in Ancient Near Eastern Legal and Wisdom Literature

F. Charles Fensham

In any civilized modern state the rights of widow, orphan, and the poor are protected. This protection is in many cases seen as a product of religious zeal and regarded as a religious duty. Indeed, the whole idea of Muslim charity, one of the pillars of that religion, is born from a realization of this duty. This religion requires kindness to orphans and widows and charity to the poor.[1] The same idea is present in Christianity. Through the influence of Christianity orphanages were erected for the protection of orphans and special laws were promulgated to protect the weak. It is thus of some interest to trace the roots of this disposition back to history, almost into the dark ages of prehistory.

The protection of widow, orphan, and the poor was the common policy of the ancient Near East. It was not started by the spirit of Israelite propheticism or by the spirit of propheticism as such.[2] From the earliest times on a strong king promulgated stipulations in connection with protection of this group. Such protection was seen as a virtue of gods, kings, and judges. It was a policy of virtue, a policy which proved the piety and virtue of a ruler. Great Mesopotamian kings like Urukagina, Ur-Nammu and Hammurapi boast in their legal inscriptions that they have accomplished this principle. Success was not possible if this principle was not carried through. It is also obvious that this policy was closely connected to social reform or a new legal promulgation. In bad

Reprinted by permission of the author's estate and the University of Chicago Press from the *Journal of Near Eastern Studies* 21 (1962): 129–39.

times, in times of decay, the protection of widow, orphan, and the poor was neglected. Widows, orphans, and the poor were sold as credit-slaves[3] and kept in a state of slavery for a lifetime. To obliterate this abuse, laws and also religious pressure were used as compulsory methods to protect the rights of this group.

The policy of protection of the weak occurs also in the wisdom literature of the ancient Near East. There exists a close link between style and contents of wisdom literature and the ancient legal codes. The wisdom literature was used as didactic material to instruct people how to behave.[4] Legal material, on the other hand, comes with a casuistic stipulation on a transgression of normative conduct prescribed by wisdom literature. The punishment on the transgression is prescribed in the second part of the stipulation. Wisdom literature, optimistic or pessimistic, gives us a policy of conduct. It is noteworthy that this policy bears a close relation to certain parts of the prologue and epilogue of legal codes. To see how close this connection is we may turn to the Old Testament tradition concerning the combination of sound, impartial judgment and wisdom in the person of Solomon.[5] It is therefore not surprising to find the policy of protection of widow, orphan, and the poor present in both legal and wisdom literature. We have narrowed the scope of our study down to these two genres of literature, because to include cultic psalms and prophetic literature would take us too far afield. It will suffice to draw attention to the fact that the plea of prophets for restoration of morality and protection of the weak points to times of absolute decay and negligence of the commonly accepted policy of the gods and strong kings; in case of the Israelite prophets, from the principles of the religion of Yahweh.

MESOPOTAMIA

We turn in the first place to Mesopotamia. The oldest witness to the policy is present in the reformatory measures taken by Urukagina, king of Lagash in the Ur I period, approximately 2400 B.C. We read that mighty people were not allowed to do injustice to the orphan and widow.[6] The stipulations of this reformatory action were regarded as a treaty between the god, Ningirsu, and Urukagina. The mention of Ningirsu is surprising, because in later texts the protection of the weak is connected to the sun-god, Shamash or Sumerian Utu (Babbar).[7] Our knowledge of early Sumerian religion is, however, too fragmentary to make any far-reaching conclusions. All we know is that some connection existed between Ninurta, the weather god, and Ningirsu.[8] In the legal code of Ur-Nammu (*ca.* 2050 B.C.) recently discovered by S. N. Kramer in the Istanbul Museum, the same idea as in the case of Urukagina is present, viz. in the prologue the protection of orphan, widow, and the poor (man of one shekel) is mentioned. The tablet is unfortunately broken and it is impossible to ascertain to which god the execution of justice is ascribed.[9] It is interesting to note that the idea of protection is placed in the prologue where the religious background and general policy of the king is stated. A very important occurrence of this policy is found in the famous Code of Hammurapi (CH) (1728–1686 B.C.). In the prologue there is reference to justice executed by the king and the statement is made that the strong are not allowed to oppress the weak,[10] so that the sun (Utu-Shamash, god of justice) may rise over the people.[11] Almost the same statement is made in the epilogue, but an important addition is present, viz. that justice might be given to the orphan and widow.[12] Lower down in this inscription Shamash is called in to maintain justice in the land. A few observations can be made at this stage. Important is the fact that Shamash is called judge of heaven and earth. This means that religious and social ethics are closely connected here.[13] The protection of the weak is regarded vertically and horizontally. The vertical protection comes from the god Shamash, which therefore falls in the religious sphere, while the horizontal protection comes from the king, the substitute of the sun-god, which thus falls in the social sphere. This was the case with divine and royal policy, but is there any indication that the protection of widow and orphan was carried through in practical life? In his admirable study on Old Babylonian law of inheritance Klíma proves that this question must be answered in the affirmative. When a woman married a husband in Mesopotamia, she had left the house of her father and had no right whatsoever remaining. She had also no right of inheritance of the property of her husband. Yet she was not left without anything. In CH §§ 171–74 it is stipulated that she must receive the *šeriktu* and a gift of her husband *(nudunnû)* and has also the right to stay in her husband's house. A difference is made between a first wife *(ḫi-ir-tum)* and a widow *(almattum)*, but in every case she was left with sufficient protection to ensure a comfortable life.[14] Credit-slavery was a common phenomenon in Mesopotamia. This was usually inflicted on the poor or in certain circumstances on widows and orphans. One of the most humane laws of CH was promulgated to limit the severity of credit-slavery. In §§ 117–18 it is stipulated that credit-slaves must be released after three years, a very narrow limitation of the period of slavery in comparison with e.g., the Hebrew law where the period is six years.[15] This limitation was fixed to discourage credit-slavery and the exploitation of the poor and unprotected.

The idea that the poor man is protected by Shamash and that this is expected as a way of life amongst his people occurs frequently in Babylonian wisdom literature.[16] In the great majority of these texts reference is made to the poor in general but not specifically to the widow and orphan.[17] In the Babylonian Theodicy (± 1000 B.C. according to Lambert), where a discourse takes place between a friend and a sufferer, the sufferer contrasts in ll. 265–75 the greedy life of the strong man with that of the weak whom he oppresses. In a pessimistic mood he shows that the strong man is assisted and enjoys success, while the weak has to suffer.[18] The friend answers the sufferer by pointing out that from the creation of mankind they had been so perverse that the cause of the rich was advanced and the harm of the poor man plotted.[19] Conduct over against the feeble and downtrodden is prescribed in the Babylonian precepts and admonitions, also called the Proverbs of Utnapishtim. Kindness must be shown to the feeble, and sneering at the downtrodden is forbidden. A transgressor of this way of life must expect punishment from Shamash.[20] Another interesting piece of evidence is the bilingual (Sumerian and Akkadian) hymn possibly addressed to Ninurta, in which various forbidden things are mentioned. In l. 11 the matter of oppression of the poor is stated.[21] Interesting is the possibility that this tablet was intended as a hymn to Ninurta. The fact that some connection existed between Ninurta and Ningirsu and that the latter was linked with the reformatory measures of Urukagina points to the probability that these gods were regarded in some places of Mesopotamia as protectors of justice. A very important text is the hymn to the sun-god, Shamash, where assistance to the weak is mentioned as pleasing to Shamash.[22] In another passage the cry of the weak for help and justice is mentioned.[23] It is obvious that the assistance of the poor was regarded as a virtue. Very important is the fact that kings were called on to carry through this policy. Hammurapi is pictured in front of Shamash in a gesture of adoration on the stelas on which the laws are inscribed. Another example can be mentioned, viz. the foundation inscription of Iaḫdun-Lim of Mari, discovered in 1953 by Parrot and published by Dossin. This inscription is dedicated to Shamash, who is called king of heaven and earth, judge *(ša-pi-iṭ)* of gods and men.[24] This discovery proves beyond doubt that a sanctuary of Shamash at Mari existed from the earliest times.[25] Important for our purpose is the fact that Shamash is called "judge" with a pure West Semitic word, viz. *šapîṭu*. Words derived from the same stem were used to connote the judicial activities of a king in favor of widow and orphan, as we shall see further on.

EGYPT

Our material concerning widow, orphan, and the poor is much more restricted in Egyptian literature. This is due to the fact that no legal code has as yet been discovered, while the extant demotic code is still unpublished.[26] The absence of a legal code is attributed by various scholars to the fact that the word or command *(mdw, wḏ)* of the reigning king was regarded as actual law and no written law could have existed beside it.[27] This is, however, a hypothesis which is not yet proved.

If we turn to the existing material, a few interesting things turn up. The protection of the weak was also the ideal of kings and nomarchs (rulers of a district). At the beginning of Dynasty XII there lived a nomarch named Ameny who boasted that he ruled his province with justice, respecting the poor man's daughter and the widow.[28] If we take a glance at the occurrence of this ideal and policy in the wisdom of literature, it is obvious that the ideal of respecting the rights of the weak, widow, and the orphan flourished in times of decay or at the beginning of a new period. We have ample evidence of this policy at the end of the First Intermediate Period and the beginning of the Middle Kingdom (± 2000 B.C.). In the didactic discourses of the Eloquent Peasant, the peasant says to Rensi, the chief steward: "Because thou art the father of the orphan, the husband of the widow. . . ."[29] This statement by the peasant is of the utmost importance, because a married woman had no legal personality after her husband's death, as was also the case with minor orphans. It was, thus, the duty of the king or nomarch to protect their rights in the same way as the father of the family should have done. In the Instructions of Merikare the conduct of a king against his people is prescribed. One of the maxims indicates that, if the king desires long life on earth, he must not oppress the widow and annex the property which someone has inherited from his father.[30] The latter part of the maxim clearly refers to the orphan. Another text which originated not long after this is the Instructions of King Amenemhet. In Pap. Millingen 1:6–7 the great acts of the king are enumerated. One of these is charity to the poor and the elevation of minors.[31] Emphasis on this policy and ideal is quite understandable when we take into consideration the confusion and abuse of the general rights of the people during the First Intermediate Period. The following quotation may suffice: "A man smites his brother, his mother's son. Men sit in the bushes until the benighted traveller comes, in order to plunder his load. . . . He who had no yoke of oxen is now possessor of a herd," etc.[32] In bad times the weak were unprotected and the widow and orphan bereaved of their rights. With the Eleventh and Twelfth Dynasties mighty kings stepped in and widow, orphan, and the poor were not mentioned in wisdom literature until the Twenty-first Dynasty *ca.* 1000 B.C. It is true that during the Second Intermediate or Hyksos Period chaos ensued, but a very important difference is to be noted, because this chaos was not instigated by a social revolution as in the First Intermediate Period, but came mainly from outside. It is true that during the Thirteenth Dynasty and later, numerous petty kings ruled in different parts of Egypt, but this is only a proof of weakness and not of a social upheaval and drastic changes.

Unfortunately the reformatory measures taken by Haremheb after the decay during the Amarna Period, which are inscribed on a defective stela from Karnak, are so difficult to interpret that no evidence can be gleaned from them.[33] The famous Instructions of Amenemope originated *ca.* 1000 B.C. Here again there is concern for the oppressed and disabled. A maxim declares that the oppressed must not be robbed and that no harshness may be inflicted on the disabled.[34]

We have ample evidence that kings and rulers were encouraged to protect the weak. Is there any religious connection between this policy and the Egyptian gods? Surprisingly enough this connection existed and the sun-god, Re, or his supplanter, Amon, was regarded as protector of the weak par excellence.[35] In a Late Egyptian text, Anastasi II, 6:5 ff. Amon-Re is called vizier of the poor. His judgment is impartial.[36] This text has clearly something in common with the above-mentioned material in the Instructions of Merikare. The obligation felt by the king toward the god, to act righteously toward the poor, the widow, and the orphan, is expressed in Papyrus Harris I, where Rameses III boasts to the god Ptaḥ that he has given special protection to widows and orphans.[37] This protection is also reflected in the few legal documents of inheritance at our disposal. It is obvious from certain testaments that the wife of the deceased had also the right of inheritance. Obviously enough each of the children of the deceased obtained his part of his father's property.[38]

In spite of the lack of legal material and the fact that we have mainly used wisdom literature as our source, the parallel trend between Mesopotamian policy of the protection of the weak and that of Egypt is clear. It is regarded as a virtue of kings and rulers and as an important part of the duty of the sun-god. As in Mesopotamia the religious ethics are closely intertwined in Egypt with the social ethics. It is to a certain extent, however, possible to trace the social policy of protection back to its very roots in Egyptian history. The conception of social justice started probably with the First Intermediate Period when almost a reversion of social classes took place.

UGARIT

Unfortunately no legal code or wisdom book is found in the Ugaritic literature which gives us a clear picture of Canaanite culture before the Iron Age. There is, however, in the epic of Aqhat something worthy of mention. While Daniel the king was waiting for the god of crafts, Kothar-waḫasis, to bring a bow for Aqhat, his son, he was busy judging (the stem *ṯpṭ*) the cause of the widow and orphan. Ginsberg translates:

> Straightway Daniel the Rapha-man,
> Forthwith Ghazir the Harnam[iyy]-man,
> Is upright, sitting before the gate,
> Beneath a *mighty tree* on the threshing floor,
> Judging the cause of the widow,
> Adjudicating the case of the fatherless.[39]

Again the judgment in favor of widow and orphan is idealized. Important is the fact that the stem *ṯpṭ* is used to connote the exercising of justice.[40] We have seen above that this West Semitic stem is used to characterize the judicial activity of Shamash over gods and men. The idea of protection and of judging the case of the weak was, thus, not unfamiliar to the Western Semites.

THE OLD TESTAMENT

Now we have to turn to the Hebrew world, where references to the protection of widow, orphan, and the poor are numerous. Professor Böhl protested against the fact that H. Bolkenstein in his book *Weldadigheid en Armenzorg* ("Charity and Care for the Poor") gives a few pages to Egypt and Israel and does not mention anything about Mesopotamia.[41] It is true that other scholars working on social problems in the Old Testament have totally neglected the parallel material from Mesopotamia and Egypt. We cannot agree e.g. with H. Bruppacher that compassion for widow and orphan is something unique in the Old Testament over against other literatures.[42] A welcome new interpretation is presented by C. van Leeuwen with necessary references to extra-biblical material, although the full scope of this material is not used.[43] It is, however, not our purpose to discuss the rich literature of modern scholars which grew around the concept "poor." The more important works are ably discussed in a study of J. van der Ploeg in *Oudetestamentische Studien*.[44]

We desire to start our study with a discussion of certain trends of Psalm 82 which gives us the clue to a better understanding of the position of widow, orphan, and the poor in Israel. The interpretation and date of this psalm offer severe difficulties and are differently interpreted by modern scholars.[45] Various scholars place it in the period between the seventh and fourth centuries B.C.[46] This is not the place to argue on possible dates and interpretation of this psalm, but to my mind it is perfectly clear that it is strongly influenced by Canaanite mythology which is to a certain extent purged to fit in with Israelite conceptions and also to show the absolute domination of Yahweh over the heathen gods.[47] The possibility is not excluded that it was also used shortly after it was purged as a kind of missionary poem to convince the Canaanites that Yahweh is a God of justice and no other is beside him. The important part for our study is vv. 3–4 in which God challenges the gods to give justice (stem *šāpaṭ*) to orphans and the poor and to save the wretched from the power of the evildoers. The gods fail to accomplish this command and the verdict of death is pronounced over them. The last verse of the psalm brings to God the victorious command to give justice to the world. Out of this we may deduce that the only One who can give justice and deliverance to the weak is God. The God of Israel is regarded as the only true judge and protector of the weak. The important difference between this conception and that of Mesopotamia and Egypt is that the exercising of justice is narrowed down to one God and all the others are excluded. In light of this must we proceed to the legal and the wisdom literature.

In the Covenant Code we have two distinct pronouncements on justice to widow, orphan, and the poor. Oppression of widow and orphan is forbidden in Exod 22:21–24 and a severe punishment is pronounced. In 23:6 the command is given not to abuse the rights of the poor. The style of both is apodictic as a direct command from God to his people.[48] The vertical line is drawn and closely linked up with the horizontal responsibility to the poor. There is, furthermore, a special interest in the fate of the widow and orphan in Deuteronomy. In Deut 10:18 the protection of this group is linked with the Supreme Judge, Yahweh, who is not willing to accept bribery, but willing to do justice to widow, orphan, and *ger* (stranger). This text is the basis for all the later stipulations in this group. In Deut 14:28–29 the command is that widow and poor must be allowed to feast on the tithes. In 16:11, 14 the Israelite receives the command to let the widow, orphan, and *ger* partake in his feasts. In 24:17–22 special stipulations concerning this group are made, e.g., the rights of the widow must not be abused, and furthermore, food must be left on the land for them.[49] In 27:19 a person who abused the rights of *ger,* widow, and orphan is cursed. Every time the lead is given, Yahweh gives justice to this group and everybody has to do likewise. Something extraordinary in the Old Testament in contrast to other literatures is the balanced view on this policy. The command is given to execute justice to the weak, but at the same time the warning is given not to favor the poor in spite of their guilt (Exod 23:3, Lev 19:15). In the Covenant Code as in CH a protective measure is taken against the abuse of credit-slavery. In the Covenant Code it is stipulated that a credit-slave must go free after six years.[50] The just execution of this stipulation was neglected in times of decay as is illustrated by Jeremiah in the time of Zedekiah.[51]

An interesting and illuminating discussion of the legal status and the protection of widow and orphan in Bedouin society in comparison with Israelite society is given by Samuel Nyström.[52] He points out that widows and orphans are legally protected, because the widow has the right to go back to the house or family of her father. The same is applicable to the orphans. If the nearest relatives are dead, they have the right to claim protection from remote relatives. Insofar the position in Bedouin society. Do we have the same kind of conception in Israelite and Near Eastern circles? The whole idea of the levirate marriage is important, of which the Book of Ruth is sufficient evidence. The difference between the Bedouin idea and that of Israel is that in Israel (as in Mesopotamia) the widow was assimilated to the family of her husband and not to that of her father. A woman was usually sent back to the house of her father in certain circumstances, e.g., when she was divorced by her husband on legal grounds, and she had the right to reclaim her dowry which she had received from the house of her father. M. David, however, makes the point that a widow in the ancient Near Eastern connotation means that she or her children has no direct family ties. He holds the view that the common practice was that the wife of a deceased man and her children must go back to the house of her father, where they are protected.[53] This view is in accord with the common practice in Bedouin society. The problem, however, is not solved. What about the levirate marriages? Was this marriage only contracted when the widow had no remaining family ties? The position becomes a little more illuminated when we bear in mind that the married wife was brought by her husband from the house of her father (bride's price in Akkadian *tirḫatu* and in Hebrew *mohar*). After her husband's death his family had the right to keep her in the family or else they would suffer damage.[54] This is the basis of levirate marriage, as is also the case with the other kind of levirate in which the husband of a deceased wife has the right to marry one of her sisters.[55] In the case of Naomi and Ruth, the former went back from Moab to her own people for protection, the latter accompanied her and was allowed before her marriage to Boaz to enjoy the favors of a widow as prescribed in Deuteronomy (24:17–22).[56] In other words, Ruth was regarded as a widow according to law until she was assimilated to the family of Boaz.[57] We may argue, however, that Ruth might have had no family ties. We have one case in the Old Testament where the levirate took place in spite of family ties. In the story of Tamar we have evidence that the levirate marriage was contracted; but after the death of Onan, Tamar's second husband, brother of Er, her former husband, Judah had sent her back to the house of her father until the youngest son should reach marriageable age (Gen 38). We have, thus, definite evidence to the fact that a widow was allowed to go back to the house of her father in certain circumstances and with the consent of the head of the family of her deceased husband. I do not think that with all this evidence we can narrow the meaning of widow and orphan down to people without family ties.[58] It is true that the common policy of protection was mainly concerned with the poor widow and orphan, but it may also include those who were temporarily without legal protection as was the case with Ruth.

The prescribed way of life in Old Testament wisdom literature takes care of the weak. It is definitely regarded as the policy of God to protect the widow and poor. God maintains the borderline of a widow's property (Prov 15:25). Anybody who abuses the rights of widow, orphan, and the poor acts contrary to the will of God. The oppressor of the weak reproaches his Maker (Prov 14:31). The oppression of widow, orphan, and the poor is carried out by evildoers and, according to a pessimistic attitude, they are prosperous in spite of their sins (Job 24:1–4). Anyone who assists the weak will receive blessings from the Lord. The man who gives bread to the poor (Prov 22:9), who has compassion with the weak (Prov 19:17) is blessed by God. A command is issued to respect the rights of this group. E.g., one is forbidden to enter the property of the orphan, viz. to claim it as his own (Prov 23:10).[59] Another command, also in the corpus related to Amenemope, is not to rob the poor because of his poverty (Prov 22:22, cf. Amenemope, Chap. 2:IV).[60] Another important fact is that in Old Testament wisdom literature the protection of the poor is described as a virtue of kings (Prov 29:14)

This policy was regarded as the will of God, the virtue of kings, and the duty of the common people. The execution of the policy is embodied in the Old Testament legal literature. Severe punishment is pronounced on those who have transgressed this principle. In the wisdom literature protection of the weak is regarded as the correct way of life.

CONCLUSIONS

We have remarkable similarities and analogies between the conception of protection of the weak in Mesopotamian, Egyptian, and Israelite literature. Still some minor differences occur, as we have pointed out in a few cases.

1. The basic conception in all the literature discussed is that the

protection of the weak is the will of the god. In polytheistic religions this characteristic is ascribed to a special god in the pantheon; in Mesopotamia Shamash, the sun-god, is regarded as the protector of the poor, although in some instances Ningirsu and Ninurta are mentioned. This divine protector is also held as judge of heaven and earth, of gods and men. In Egypt the protection is also ascribed to the sun-god, Re (or Amon-Re). He is also held as judge. In one special text, the Destruction of Mankind, he is shown as the one who exacts punishment on mankind and orders Ḥatḥor to obliterate the human race.[61] In some circles Ptaḥ is regarded in the same role as god of justice. Yahweh is described in Old Testament literature as the protector of the weak par excellence. With direct apodictic style of command and prohibition Yahweh takes the weak under his protection. This is one of the important ethical doctrines of the Old Testament, but definitely not unique in comparison with conceptions in neighboring cultures. The only basic difference is that Yahweh is regarded as the only protector. He is even placed in opposition to the gods of foreign nations and hailed as the only true Supreme Judge of the world (Psalm 82). This fact might have been emphasized annually by a cultic festival. In all the material discussed the vertical line is drawn to emphasize the protection. This was done to sanction the protection of the weak in society.

2. The principle of protection of the weak is regarded in Mesopotamian, Egyptian, and Israelite literature as the virtue of a great king. The king was the direct representative of the god on earth. In some cases he was regarded as a substitute for the god, but still a human being, as in Mesopotamia. In other cases he was regarded as a divine being, as in Egypt, where the king was the son of the sun-god. In Israel he was regarded as the representative of Yahweh with granted powers to rule the nation. The close link between the god and the king is obvious from the above-mentioned examples. Therefore, if protection of the weak is the will of the god, it is the duty of the king to execute it in practical life. In the early Israelite community this was done almost in the way of a Bedouin sheikh who sits down to hear the complaints of his people. Cf. e.g. in 2 Sam 14 in which David listened to the complaints of the woman of Tekoah. In later Israelite times the principle of protection of the weak was abandoned by kings and this was more than anything else responsible for the ethical and moral preaching of the prophets on this point.

The kings had failed in one very old, deep-rooted principle, viz. to protect as representative of God the widow, orphan, and the poor (Isa 1:17).

3. The general conception of protection of the weak is, furthermore, expanded as a common way of life of ordinary people. They have to respect the rights of the poor or else receive punishment, if not through legal means, then through direct punishment of the god. That these rights were abused is true especially of decadent society as in the First Intermediate Period of Egypt and in Israelite society during the times of the prophets. The vertical command and prohibition by the god is to be executed in horizontal relations.

4. The similarities are not restricted to common policy but are also observable in parallel ideas. Thus a clear parallel between the Babylonian Theodicy and Job exists. The Babylonian sufferer complains that the strong man succeeds in oppressing the poor, and the weak has to suffer. This complaint originated out of the pessimistic conception that the evildoer succeeds, but the pious is oppressed without hope of assistance.[62] The same idea occurs in the Book of Job where the sufferer complains about acts of oppression by evildoers exacted on orphan, widow, and the poor. He says: "Yet God layeth not folly to them" (AV). Another parallel is that a long reign of life is promised to the king or man (judge) who protects the weak. This appears in the Maxims of Merikare, the Hymn to Shamash, and in Proverbs.[63] Another similarity occurs in the hymn to Amon-Re in which he is regarded as the vizier of the poor whose judgment is impartial. In the Hymn to Shamash the judge is encouraged to be impartial in his judgment, as this would be pleasing to Shamash. The same idea occurs in Deut 10:18 where the impartial judgment of Yahweh is stressed. An interesting parallel between Egyptian and Israelite material is the following. The Maxims of Merikare forbid one to eject another from the property of his father, referring here to the orphan. The same idea occurs in Prov 23:10 where one is forbidden to enter the property of the orphan.

5. The attitude taken against widow, orphan, and the poor is to be looked at from a legal background. These people had no rights, no legal personalities, or in some cases possibly restricted rights. They were almost outlaws. Anyone could oppress them without danger that legal connections might endanger his position. To restore the balance of society these people must be protected. Therefore, it was necessary to

sanction their protection by direct command of the god and to make it the virtue of kings.

It is, however, surprising at what early stage in the history of the ancient Near East the compulsion was felt to protect these people. I do not think that it is correct to speak of borrowing of ideas concerning our subject. It was a common policy, and the Israelites in later history inherited the concept from their forebears, some of whom had come from Mesopotamia, some had been captive in Egypt, and others had grown up in the Canaanite world. In the Israelite community this policy was extended through the encouragement of the high ethical religion of Yahweh to become a definite part of their religion, later to be inherited by Christians and Muslims.

NOTES

1. Alfred Guillaume, *Islam* (1954), p. 64.
2. Cf. G. Lanczkowski, "Ägyptischer Prophetismus," *ZAW* 70 (1958), 38.
3. Cf. I. Mendelsohn, *Slavery in the Ancient Near East* (1949), pp. 14 ff., 19ff., 23 ff.; cf. also my "A Few Aspects of Legal Practices in Samuel in Comparison with Legal Material from the Ancient Near East," in *Studies in the Book of Samuel* (Die Ou Testamentiese Werkgemeenskap in Suid-Afrika 1960), pp. 19 ff.
4. Cf. H. Gese, *Lehre und Wirklichkeit in der alten Weisheit* (1958), pp. 5–6, for a definition of the *Gattung* of wisdom literature taken over from Van Dijk. E.g. exhortation concerning moral life and a maxim concerning the norm for morals and prudence. Cf. also S. du Toit, *Bybelse en Babilonies-Assiriese Spreuke* (1942), pp. 128ff.
5. For the evaluation of wisdom and Solomon cf. J. Bright, *A History of Israel* (1959), pp. 198–99.
6. A. Deimel, "Die Reformtexte Urukaginas," *Or* 2 (1920). Cf. for a translation by Moortgat Scharff-Moortgat, *Ägypten und Vorderasien im Altertum* (1950), pp. 242–43.
7. Cf. F. M. Theo de Liagre Böhl, *Godsdiensten der Wereld*, I (1948), 119, and his very important article "De Zonnegod als Beschermer der Nooddruftigen," *Opera Minora* (1953), pp. 188–206. I want to think him for drawing my attention to this article.
8. Cf. J. Bottéro, *La religion babylonienne* (1952), p. 45.
9. Cf. S. N. Kramer, "The Oldest Laws,"*Scientific American* (Jan. 1953) pp. 26–28, and *idem, History Begins at Sumer* (1958), pp. 91 ff.
10. Cf. A. Deimel, *Codex Hammurabi*, III (1950) *dan-nu-um, en-sa-am a-na la ḫa-ba-li-im.*

11. CH. §§37–41.
12. Cf. Meek's translation in *ANET* (1955), pp. 164, 178.
13. Cf. Böhl, "De Zonnegod," p. 193.
14. J. Klíma, *Untersuchungen zum altbabylonischen Erbrecht* (1940), pp. 52 ff.
15. For a discussion of these stipulations cf. Driver-Miles, "Code of Hammurabi," §§ 117–19, *SD* (1939), pp. 65–75; W. F. Leemans, *The Old-Babylonian Merchant* (1950), p. 17, note 60; F. R. Kraus, *Ein Edikt des Königs Ammi-Saduqa von Babylon* (1958) pp. 167–72.
16. Cf. the latest works on Sumerian and Babylonian wisdom, van Dijk, *La sagesse suméro-accadienne* (1953); A. M. van Dijk, "Culture sumérienne et bible," in *L'Ancien Testament et l'Orient* (1957) pp. 17 ff.; S. du Toit, *op. cit.;* F. M. Böhl, "De Zonnegod"; and the admirable work of W. G. Lambert, *Babylonian Wisdom Literature* (1960).
17. In *Shurpu,* II, 19, 45, 46 reference is made to a widow, but the position is not clear, cf. du Toit, *op. cit.*, p. 162.
18. Cf. Lambert, *op. cit.*, pp. 86–87, Gese, *op. cit.*, pp. 51 ff.
19. Ll. 276–86. Cf. Lambert, *op. cit.*, pp. 88–89.
20. *Ibid.*, pp. 100–101 and also B. Gemser, *Spreuken II, Prediker, Hooglied van Salomo* (1931), pp. 51 ff.
21. Lambert, *op. cit.*, p. 119.
22. Cf. *ibid.*, pp. 132–33 (ll. 99–100) and Böhl, "De Zonnegod," p. 203.
23. Lambert, *op. cit.*, pp. 134–45 and Böhl, *op. cit.*, p. 204.
24. G. Dossin, "L'inscription de fondation de Iaḫdun-Lim, roi de Mari," *Syria,* 32 (1955), 12.
25. Dossin, *op. cit.*, pp. 1–2.
26. To be published by Girgis Matta, as Professor W. F. Albright has informed me.
27. Cf. J. A. Wilson, *The Culture of Ancient Egypt* (1956), p. 49.
28. Cf. Sir Alan H. Gardiner, *Egypt of the Pharaohs* (1961), p. 129.
29. For the text cf. E. Suys, *Étude sur le conte due fellah plaideur* (1933), pp. 24–25 aand *8; for a translation, J. A. Wilson in *ANET,* p. 408 and cf. Lanczkowski, *op. cit.*, p. 38.
30. Aksel Volten, "Zwei altägyptische politische Schriften," *Analecta Aegyptiaca* 4 (1945), pp. 22–23.
31. *Ibid.*, p. 107.
32. Gardiner's translation in *op. cit.*, p. 109.
33. *Ibid.*, pp. 244–45.
34. Cf. A. E. Wallis Budge, *The Teaching of Amenem-apt* (1924), p. 188, and Wilson in *ANET,* pp. 421–24 for a good translation. The book of Lange was not available.
35. For a discussion cf. J. H. Breasted, *Development of Religion and Thought in Ancient Egypt* (1912), pp. 353 ff.
36. Cf. for the text A. H. Gardiner, *Late-Egyptian Miscellanies,* "Bibliotheca Egyptiaca," 7 (1937), p. 16; a translation by R. A. Caminos, *Late Egyptian Miscellanies* (1954), pp. 9–10.

37. Cf. Günther Roeder, *Die ägyptische Götterwelt* (1959), p. 55.
38. Erwin Seidl, *Einführungin die ägyptische Rechtsgeschichte bis zum Ende des Neuen Reiches* (1951), pp. 57–58.
39. H. Ginsberg in *ANET*, p. 151. Cf. for the text Gordon, *Ugaritic Manual* (1955), p. 179.
40. Cf. my "The Judges and Ancient Israelite Jurisprudence, " in *Die Oud Testamentiese Werkgemeenskap in Suid-Afrika* (1959), pp. 15–17.
41. Böhl, "De Zonnegod," pp. 194–95.
42. H. Bruppacher, *Die Beurteilung der Armut im Alten Testament* (1924), p. 16.
43. C. van Leeuwen, *Le développement du sens social en Israel avant l'ère chrétienne* (1955), e.g. p. 27 where the Code of Hammurapi is used.
44. Cf. J. van der Ploog, "Les pauvres d'Israël et leur piéte," *OTS*, 7 (1950), 237–42.
45. We refer to the "*Thronbesteigung*" theory of Mowinckel, where this psalm is interpreted in light of the battle myth in which Yahweh annually overcomes the rival gods of foreign nations. Cf. S. Mowinckel, *Das Thronbesteigungsfest Jahwäes und der Ursprung der Eschatologie* (1920) and J. Ridderbos, *Die Psalmen,* II (1958), pp. 325–27.
46. Cf. G. Ernest Wright, *The Old Testament Against its Environment* (1950), p. 37, although he admits that there is no certain means to date it.
47. Cf. for the Canaanite background R. T. O'Callaghan, "A Note on the Canaanite Background of Psalm 82," *CBQ,* 15 (1953), 311–14.
48. Cf. for stylistic analysis A. Alt, *Die Ursprünge des israelitischen Rechts* (1934). Alt's view that the apodictic style is typically Israelite is challenged by a few scholars, e.g. Landsberger and Meek; B. Landsberger, "Die babylonische Termini für Gesetz und Recht," *SD* (1939), p. 223, n. 19; T. Meek in *ANET,* p. 183, n. 24. The latest article on the subject is by Stanley Gevirtz, "West-Semitic Curses and the Problem of the Origins of Hebrew Law," *VT* 11 (1961), 137 ff. and p. 138 for a criticism of Alt's view.
49. Robert North, S. J., *Sociology of the Biblical Jubilee* (1954), pp. 118–19.
50. For a discussion cf. my "A Few Aspects," p. 20.
51. Cf. M. David, "The Manumission of Slaves under Zedekiah," *OTS* (1948), pp. 63–79.
52. Samuel Nyström, *Beduinentum und Jahwismus* (1946), pp. 139–47.
53. M. David, *Vorm en Wezen van de Huwelijkssluiting naar Oud-Oostersche Rechtsopvatting* (1934), pp. 7–9.
54. Cf. e.g. P. Koschaker, *Quellenkritische Untersuchungen zu den altassyrischen Gesetzen* (1921), p. 46.
55. *Ibid.*, p. 47.
56. Cf. for the legal position in Ruth, M. David, *Het Huwelijk van Ruth* (1941), *passim.*
57. For stipulations concerning levirate in Israel, cf. Deut 25:5 ff.
58. Also against J. Pedersen, *Israel,* I–II (1926), 44–46.
59. Some scholars conjectured *ʿolām* to *ʾalmānâ*. Cf. C. H. Toy, *Proverbs,* (ICC,

1948), pp. 431–32; but cf. du Toit, *op. cit.*, p. 161. B. Gemser, *Sprüche Salomos,* (HAT, 1937), pp. 66–67 accepts *ʾalmānâ* because of the parallel with Amenemope VII.

60. The whole question of the relation between Prov. 22:17 ff. and Amenemope is very difficult. The majority of scholars hold the view that the author of Prov 22:17 ff. borrowed from Amenemope. Cf. A. Erman, "Das Weisheitbuch des Amenemope," *OLZ* 27 (1924), 241–52; H. Gressmann, "Die neugefundene Lehre des Amenemope und die vorexilische Spruchdichtung Israels," *ZAW* 42 (1924), 272–96. Other scholars hold the opposite view, that Amenemope borrowed from Israelite wisdom. Cf. W. O. E. Oesterley, *The Wisdom of Egypt and the Old Testament* (1927); recently E. Drioton, "Sur la sagesse d'Aménémopé," *Mélanges bibliques rédigés en l'honneur de André Robert* (1957), pp. 254 ff.
61. Cf. J. Vandier, *La religion égyptienne* (1949), pp. 37–38.
62. Cf. Gese, *op. cit.*, pp. 62 ff.
63. Volten, *op. cit.*, pp. 22–23, Lambert, *op. cit.*, pp. 132–33, and Prov 29:14.

9

Noah, Danel, and Job, Touching on Canaanite Relics in the Legends of the Jews

Shalom Spiegel

Toward the end of the book (Job 42:10), the Lord is said to have "turned the fortunes" of Job, or restored him to grace. He similarly revives, it would seem, the theories on Job. When they complete their cycle of mortality, the old doctrines start afresh on a new period of favor or fashion.

Richard Simon[1] was the first to doubt the integrity of the book of Job. Cautiously, almost cursorily, he suggested that chapters 1 and 2, like the superscriptions to the Psalms, were added by the makers of the biblical collection. More than half a century later, Albert Schultens[2] ventured the guess, also rather hurriedly, that the prologue and epilogue, or chapters 1, 2, and 42:7–17, were appended to the book at the time of its admission to the canon. Another half a century was to elapse before the conjecture was elaborated, and the discrepancies between the poem and the framework of Job were set forth in detail.[3] The original dialogue was still believed to date from the days of King Solomon,[4] but the prologue and epilogue were assigned to the age that assembled the literary remains of Hebrew antiquity.

The disagreements between the dialogue and its framework led later, after the abandonment of the Solomonic date for the poem, to the hypothesis of an earlier folk-tale, or even a separate *Volksbuch* of Job.[5] The commentaries of K. Budde[6] and B. Duhm[7] made this view quite

Reprinted by permission from *Louis Ginzberg Jubilee Volume* (New York: American Academy of Jewish Research, 1945), 305–55.

popular in their day. It seems to have been advanced for the first time by J. Wellhausen.[8] He believed that both the prologue and epilogue embodied a genuine folk-saga which survived intact in substance as well as in form, within the present text of Job.

The rebuttal of this thesis, mostly on linguistic grounds,[9] made it necessary to revise the view. It was now commonly held that the poet of Job availed himself of the older folk-story in creative freedom, just as Plato borrowed ancient myths or Goethe reshaped the legend of Faustus to unfold their own insights. So amended, the theory may be said to have gained wide acceptance.[10]

Recent investigations,[11] however, seem to hark back to the first stirrings of critical doubt in the days of Simon and Schultens. Once more the poem is asserted to antedate the framework of the book. The wheel has come full circle, and it now appears as if the cycle of Job were to be reversed and the discarded theories returned to new vogue.

Is the evidence available simply inconclusive? The history of interpretation seems to suggest it. Somehow all attempts at a definite solution end in the ancient sigh of Jerome: "*Obliquus . . . totus liber . . . et lubricus: . . . ut si velis anguilam aut muraenulam strictis tenere manibus, quanto fortius presseris, tanto citius elabitur.*"[12] [The whole book is oblique and slippery, just like an eel or a little moray—the more tightly you squeeze it, the more quickly it slips away.——F.G.]

1. DANIEL OR DANEL?

Gelingt es aber zu ermitteln, wer eigentlich Ezechiels Daniel ist, so werden wir auch weitergeleitet werden auf die Spur Hiobs.

—Ferd. Hitzig, *Das Buch Hiob* (1874) p. xiv.

Ezek 14:14 ff. remains the basal passage with which all inquiry into the pre-literary tale of Job must begin. The curious collocation of the names has baffled centuries of exegesis: What did Noah, Daniel, and Job have in common to be mentioned in one breath?[13] In addition, the chronological sequence appears disturbed with Daniel preceding Job.[14] True, all three were righteous men (vv. 14 and 20), yet one cannot help feeling that they were here linked together for some particular reason,[15] perhaps because a like fate or fable was known to underlie their life-story. The rabbis of old were right in sensing that the ancient worthies were bound by a similar destiny, even though their interpretation of the passage is hardly more than a devout exercise: Noah, Daniel, and Job all survived the wreckage of an old world order, and lived to see a new world reborn.[16]

The exegesis of medieval and modern days was hampered by futile comparison with the biblical story of Daniel.[17] Here and there one finds the correct surmise that "sons and daughters" (vv. 16 and 18), or at least "a son and a daughter" (v. 20) must have played some part in the tale behind Ezek 14:14 ff.[18] However, the biblical Daniel was not known to have had any children,[19] and so the guess leads nowhere. In despair some will always resort to force: if the puzzling passage cannot be explained, it can be expunged.[20]

Closer scrutiny did not fail to notice that whenever the name occurs in the book of Ezekiel, it is spelled consistently Danel,[21] and not Daniel. May not another person be meant?[22] The discovery of the Ugaritic legend of Danel[23] seemed at once to resolve the chronological difficulty, and the identification with the biblical Daniel was dropped with relief. Recent commentaries carry invariably some reference to the epic of Ras Shamra.[24] But even now, neither the passage in Ezekiel, nor the story of Job seems to be understood any better. Moreover, the disagreement in the interpretation of the fragments of Danel, and their want of relation or relevance to the biblical text, soon raised the doubt whether, after all, there is any real connection between the myth of Ugarit and the passage in Ezekiel.[25]

2. THE LAY OF AQHAT

Since its publication in 1936, the legend of Danel has engaged the attention of a number of scholars whose patience and perspicacity has penetrated the mists, so that now the outline of a story is slowly emerging.[26] It is true, several salient passages still elude us, some tablets are broken at painful points of the narrative, and the beginning and the end are missing. Nevertheless, the areas of doubt are narrowing, and little by little the fragments assemble into a coherent account.

If *mlk* (I 2:152) refers to our hero, as seems likely, Danel was a king.[27] He is often called *mt hrnmy* or man of *Hrnm* which 1 Enoch seems to have identified with the region of Mount Hermon.[28] His palace *(hkl)* and court *ḥẓr),* his harness of silver and saddlery of gold *(gpnm dt ksp, dt yrq nqbnm)* comport with his station in life. His garments *(kst* and *ʾall)* are not described, but he, too, must have been arranged in his robes like the kings of Israel and Judah (1 Kgs 22:10=2 Chr 18:9), whenever he sat to perform the duties of his office, as is twice told in the poem (I 1:21–25 and II 5:6–8).

b ap ṯǵr	At the entrance of the gate,
tḥt adrm d b grn	Under mighty trees near the threshing-floor,
ydn du almnt	He judges the case of the widow,
yṯpṭ ṯpṭ ytm	And helps the fatherless to his right.

Lady *Dnty* was a dutiful wife, efficient in her household and quick to accommodate any guest even at short notice (11 5:16 ff.). But she had no son, and that made the couple very sad. When the years passed, and all hope for an heir proved futile, Danel decides in desperation to storm heaven with supplication and sacrifice. It is here that our poem commences, the broken lines narrating how he offers viands and oblations, lodging in the sanctuary for days and nights, even for a whole week. The missing verses in all likelihood described his grief, as in the epic of *Krt:* sobbingly he repeats his prayer, and sheds his tears like quarter-shekels[29] Until Baal is moved to mercy, and takes up Danel's case before the head of the Ugaritic pantheon, the kindly El (II 1:20):

in bn lh km aḫh	He has no son like his brethren,
wšrš km aryh	Nor a root like his kin.

El promises to grant *Dnty* a male issue. Danel proceeds in joy to his home, and bids welcome to the *Kṯrt,* the biblical *kôšārôt,*[30] guardian goddesses of the newborn and givers of all good bounty, like the Greek charities.[31] He lavishly feeds them for fully seven days, until they depart. Thereupon he numbers the moons, eagerly keeping count for the blessed day. Three months pass and four—and here the tablet breaks off.

The narrative seems resumed in II 5:2 ff. One morning, when Danel attends his court-session in the gate, he sees *Kṯr* coming, the craftsman-god or Hephaestus of Ugarit. He brings a gift from his heavenly workshop, a bow for Danel's son, Aqhat. (The *Kṯrt,* as their name implies, stand in some special relation to *Kṯr*—one of the Graces is the wife of Hephaestus[32]—and we may surmise that the generous hospitality shown by Danel to the *Kṯrt* is now being rewarded, perhaps at their request, by *Kṯr*).

The bow of the divine smith did not bring luck to Aqhat. It aroused the envy of the war goddess Anath who resolved to obtain the bow at any price. She offered to pay for it in precious ore, and even promised to make Aqhat immortal.[33] But the lad would not part with his weapon, the grant of a god to his father. Offended by such *hybris* of a mortal, Anath threatens to humble Aqhat on his "path of pride and presumption" (*b ntb pšʿ//bntb gʾan,* II 6:43f.). She sets her face toward the source of the rivers where the father of the gods resides. At the feet of El she bows, and at once denounces Aqhat—but little more is recoverable from the mutilated tablet. One can only guess that the infuriated goddess did not hesitate to slander the youth, or even swear at the godhead himself (if III 6:11f. is properly rendered or related to this point of the narrative): "I will make thy hoar beard flow with blood!",[34] Anath threatens, browbeating the wrinkled El to some sort of compliance.

The story appears to be continued in III 1 where Anath instructs her henchman *Yṭpn* in *Qrt Ablm* or its vicinity. She promises to make *Yṭpn* "like an eagle in her scabbard, like a vulture in her sheath" and set him over Aqhat. *Yṭpn* is then to strike the lad "twice on the head, thrice on the ear." The orders of the goddess are obeyed, and Aqhat is killed: "his soul went out like a wind, his spirit like smoke."

There is no need to trace in detail what follows, or what is legible. Bereaved of his only son, rent with grief and rage, Danel prays to the gods to scorch the land by drought for seven years: "Let there be no dew, nor rain! No surging of the two deeps, nor the goodness of Baal's voice!"[35] Even fiercer are the curses he hurls upon the cities round about his slain son (cf. Deut 21:2): "Woe unto thee, *Qrt Ablm!* If the murderer of Aqhat be in thy midst, may Baal strike thee with blindness, from now on and forevermore, henceforward throughout all generations!"[36]

We do not learn whether the death of Aqhat was avenged, but in the last lines of the lay (I 4:220 f.), we find the assassin *Yṭpn,* drinking heavily, in the company of Danel's daughter *Pǵt.* He brags as his tongue is loosed by liquor:

yd mḫṣt Aqht ǵzr	The hand that smote Aqhat, the Mighty,
tmḫṣ alpm ʾib	Will smite thousands of foes!

He thus betrays himself to *Pǵt* who had not hidden for nought a sword under her raiment, nor asked in vain for her father's blessing (I 4:196 f.):

ʾimḫṣ mḫṣ aḫy	Let me smite him that smote my brother,
a[kl m]kly [ʿ]l umty	S[lay the s]layer of my mother's [l]ad!

However, as has been said, the tablets stop abruptly, leaving the reader haunted by the shades of Jael and Judith. Or is one to think rather of Rizpah the daughter of Aiah, the gods having been entreated for the famished land (2 Sam 21:14) to give it rain after seven years of drought only when the bones of Aqhat had been buried?

Anyway, Danel does sedulously bury whatever remains of Aqhat he is able to retrieve. Such care in collecting and conserving the limbs of the dead seems to be the prerequisite of resurrection. So, too, Anath inhumed Aliyn Baal: "She weeps for him and buries him, she sets him in the hollows of the silent ones of the earth,"[37] acts not only out of piety, but apparently also in preparation for his rebirth. Probably the same idea underlies the ritual of Aqhat's interment. There are indications in the poem that Aqhat will be recalled to life,[38] and Anath seems to be charged with the duty of making him whole again, and breathing into his nostrils the breath of new life.[39] The details escape us, but El in his gentle wisdom must have found a way to calm or compensate the bellicose goddess, perhaps by ordering for her another bow from the smithy of *Kṯr*.[40] There is reason to expect that in the end Danel is not left uncomforted, and his son Aqhat is given back to him.

One is even tempted to conjecture how the minstrel of Ugarit might have completed his lay. If repetition, especially frequent repetition, betrays the point the poet is eager to make or the interest he has at heart, one cannot fail to notice a long passage reproduced in the preserved portions of the epic fully four times.[41] It is an enumeration of the services a dutiful son performs for his father. Indeed, what a son means to a father appears to be the central theme of the tale. It is no accident that the passage each time consists of fourteen hemistichs, or twice the sacred number *seven* which recurs so often as an element of the cult or embellishment of the style in these ancient texts.[42] One suspects, therefore, that the *catalogue of filial duties* was likewise reproduced seven times. Following this clue, one might hazard the guess that the anguish of the bereaved father was brought once more to the attention of El, whereupon there followed, for the fifth time in the poem, the list of kindnesses rendered by a devoted son. El cannot well refuse such a plea, for after all, it was he who awarded a son to the pious parents. He must cheer them again, probably by the annunciation of Aqhat's rebirth.[43] Here, for the sixth time, all the loving deeds of a loyal son are rehearsed. When at last his lad is revived, and Danel sees for himself, and his eyes behold, and not another, Aqhat actually waked from the dust, the love of the heptad and of the happy ending made perhaps the bard of Ugarit wind up his tale with a refrain now sufficiently familiar to his hearers to join in it. Danel breaks sorrow and laughs, resting his foot on a footstool.[44] Now he can leisurely twiddle his thumbs, wet or whet his whistle, and sing away all sad thoughts:

For I have a son in my home,
A root in the midst of my palace.
. . . . .

Who takes me by the hand when I am drunk,
Who carries me when I am sated with wine.
. . . . .

Who plasters my roof when it leaks,
Who washes my clothes when they are dirty![45]

Perhaps the very name of Aqhat, thus far not satisfactorily explained,[46] intends to connote filial piety or obedience,[47] the leitmotif of the lay.

3. EZEKIEL 14:14 ff.

Ezekiel seems independently to confirm, and perhaps even to clarify, the evidence of the Ugaritic legend. For regardless of any attempts at reconstructing the missing sections of the poem, all of which a new find may put to shame, this much may be reasonably inferred on the basis of what is implied or even expressed in the preserved text.[48] Aqhat is delivered in the end and returned to life. Ezekiel would appear to convey that it was the prayer or piety of his father, the righteousness of Danel (verses 14 and 20), which achieved the miracle and redeemed his son.

The concatenation with Noah and Job makes it plain. "Noah was a just man and perfect in his generations" (Gen 6:9), and it was his righteousness that rescued all his house, his wife, his sons, and his daughters or sons' wives (ibid. 6:18; 7:1, 13; 8:16, 18; 9:18). And Job, of course, was a man "perfect and upright" (Job 1:1, 8; 2:3), and can also be said to have regained his children, even though new children. Or does the passage in Ezekiel suggest that in the old tale, Job actually saved his selfsame children, just as Danel saved Aqhat or Noah his own family? Such an interpretation of the story of Job, entirely irrespective of the text in Ezekiel, was advanced long ago, e.g. by Nahmanides.[49] It must be admitted that Ezekiel's choice of the three exemplars of piety would be particularly appropriate, if the mere mention of their names were to bring to mind a parallel feat or fortune, in short, if in common all three were known to have ransomed their children by their righteousness. The clue in Ezek 14:14ff. in itself would be too meager, but fortunately, it is confirmed, as we shall see, by a trace of such a story of Job preserved independently elsewhere.[50]

First, however, we must try to ascertain whether the context of the passage in Ezekiel fits or favors such an interpretation. Why did the prophet disquiet the three shades of the past to bring them up in this particular connection? Is an historical circumstance or situation recognizable? Can the utterance be assigned a date?

The ministry of Ezekiel, despite recent doubts,[51] is datable. The book of Ezekiel spans the years of his captivity, 593–568 B.C., including perhaps a few earlier oracles, spoken while the prophet was still in Palestine, before his departure for or deportation to Babylonia.[52] If *mʿl* is not loosely used in Ezek 14:13, but refers to a definite event, as it does unmistakably in Ezek 17:20, one could venture a closer date for our passage. Rabbinic tradition would see in Ezek 17 the beginning[53] of his prophetic career in Palestine.[54] This may well have been the case,[55] and the prophecy may be understood as a warning against the war-propaganda and the hopes bound up with the accession of Psammetichus II (cf. Ezek 17:15), the real power behind the revolt of the principalities of Canaan against Babylon (cf. Jer 27:3). Chapter 17 in Ezekiel could accordingly be dated in the fourth year of Zedekiah (Jer 28:1) or about 593 B.C. As is known, Judah soon withdrew, or was forced to withdraw, from the anti-Babylonian coalition, and the penalty then exacted from Zedekiah and his people can be inferred only from Jer 51:59. Be that as it may, shortly thereafter we find the prophet Ezekiel among the captives "in the land of the Chaldeans by the river Chebar" (Ezek 1:2 f.).[56]

Ezek 14:12 ff., also, contains a grim warning to the nation about the horrors that a reckless and hopeless rebellion will unleash upon the land: "the sword, and the famine, and the evil beasts, and the pestilence, to cut off from it man and animal" (v. 21). But unlike chapter 17, Ezek 14:12 ff. seems to stress more particularly the peril to "sons and daughters," thrice mentioned in the speech (vv. 16, 18, 20). In 24:21 the prophet plainly told the parents in Babylonia, separated from their children in Palestine: "Your sons and daughters *whom ye have left behind* shall fall by the sword." Ezek 14:12 ff. would seem to presuppose a similar *exilic situation,* and bespeak the anxiety felt among the captives for their children in Judaea. If so, the utterance is to be dated *after 590,*[57] when Zedekiah finally succumbed to the war party and openly broke with Babylon, or perhaps was about to do so.

Ezekiel condemned all attempts at insurrection as a breach of good faith and repudiation of solemn treaties (Ezek 17:19 f. and 14:13) and hence as predictable disaster. He believed it his duty to prepare the exiles for the worst: The Lord abandoned Jerusalem, and will consign to flames even His own shrine. One can easily comprehend the consternation and the resentment of the captivity when it first heard such direful predictions. No wonder that they sought to restrain or even silence altogether such dismal divining (cf. Ezek 3:25). Ezekiel himself is fully aware of the offense he must give and often hesitates to heap more "moaning and woe" upon the sorrow-laden exiles (2:8 ff.). But "the hand of the Lord was strong" upon him, and obey he must "in bitterness" (3:14). There are days in which he simply cannot "open his mouth" (3:15, 26 f.; 24:27; 29:21; 33:22), sick of rubbing salt into the gaping wounds of his people. In the light of subsequent history, one must admit that it was precisely the unrelenting consistency of the prophetic monition that helped the people to survive the political defeat. Forewarned by their seers, the Jews learned to accept deportation, debacle of the kingdom, even desecration of the sanctuary, as the design, and not the defeat of God. The shock was salutary, as it paved the way toward the future reconstitution of Israel on the foundations of the prophetic faith.

But the death of the children left behind in Jerusalem, such personal hurt to the parents, punished enough by banishment and separation, was it not needless and pointless cruelty? Why should the prophet outrage paternal feelings of the exiles and, in advance of the final catastrophe, threaten the youth in distant Judah with wholesale slaughter? He had to correct himself in Ezek 14:22 f., a postscript written after 586, where he candidly concedes that his threat, and the theology behind it, were refuted by the facts of history.[58]

Since the prophecy did not come true, it is a genuine prophecy, spoken undoubtedly before the events, and not thereafter retouched to suit them. Does Ezekiel intend to frighten the captives, and dissuade them from embroilment by the spokesmen of intransigence in Babylonia? Or does he even aim at having the influence of the captivity exerted at home to prevent the rebellion of Zedekiah? They could avert the death of their children by opposing the war party in Judah. The most prominent leaders and trusted elders of the nation were in Babylon and, if consulted, could caution and calm the rebels in Jerusalem. If this be the case and such the purpose of Ezekiel, the utterance precedes the revolt of Zedekiah, and is to be dated before or *about 590*.

But if spoken after the outbreak of the ill-fated war, when the exiles could no longer arrest its course, the words were meant perhaps as an *apology* rather than as an admonition. The primary business of a prophet was to intercede on behalf of the people,[59] and the captives must have asked Ezekiel to pray for their children in the embattled city, indeed to pray for the rescue of Jerusalem. But like Jeremiah,[60] Ezekiel could not do so, convinced that it was too late to "stand in the breach before Him for the land, that He should not destroy it" (Ezek 22:30).[61] All one could do now was to salvage the belief in a just and holy God, hence the particular pains Ezekiel takes to emphasize the doctrine of retribution. The righteous alone will escape, at best, and there is not anyone, alive or dead, whose prayer could stave off disaster. Were Noah now in the land, he could save no one but himself, Danel could not redeem Aqhat, nor would Job's piety avail his children. When such holy men and masters of intercession must fail, how much more helpless must be Ezekiel, the son of Buzi. How can he be asked to try by his feeble prayer to stay divine justice, or exempt therefrom the sons and daughters left in the hapless land.[62]

4. THE PRIMITIVE TALE OF JOB

The legend of Job, as preserved in chapters 1 and 2, revolves about the question: "Doth Job fear God for nought?" (Job 1:9). The same thought underlies the discussion of the rabbis, whether Job served God out of fear or out of love.[63] Translated into modern idiom, the issue may be stated: *Is there such a thing as unselfish virtue?* The legend of Job answers this question in the affirmative. Job stands the test of suffering and proves thereby that disinterested piety does exist.

It has been long observed that the last chapter of the book contains variant versions which in their present location do not jibe with the story and mar its sequence. When Job has been restored and the Lord has doubled all his possessions (ibid. 42:10), the condolence call of his family and friends (42:11) is both belated and pointless. And so is their charity, each presenting him with a coin and an earring, a poor pittance for a man who now possesses twice his original, very handsome, fortune. It is amusing to watch the straits to which exegetes are driven: the verb "to condole" is pressed to yield—here alone and nowhere else—precisely the opposite of its meaning, and so the visit becomes one of congratulation.[64] It has been likewise noticed[65] that the succeeding verses, 42:12–17, while showing ample concern for Job's property and progeny, say nothing about his own recovery. Albrecht Alt,[66] therefore, concluded that 42:12–17 originally followed chapter 1, forming with it an earlier phase of the saga: Job himself was as yet unscathed, he lost his wealth and his children, but "for all this he sinned not" (1:1–22). At this point of the narrative, in 42:11, his immediate family and acquaintances—not the three friends as in 2:11—come to console him and help him to a new start in life, all chipping in with a small gift. The Lord, however, did beyond compare, He "blessed the later end of Job more than his beginning," and our story-teller delights in detailing the bounty of heaven.

There is no gainsaying that such a sequence of events makes smoother sense. The remainder of Alt's reconstruction (1:1–2:13 and 42:7–10 representing the later phase of the saga) seems less convincing, as will be shown.[67]

Whatever the particular distribution of the verses may be, of greater consequence is the fact, observed repeatedly by former and newer students, that the epilogue to the book of Job preserves *older layers of the tale*. Frequent retelling froze the story, crystallizing its salient features, or even the elements of its form.[68] They sank so firmly into the popular mind and memory that taking liberty with the familiar parts or passages seemed almost frivolous or bad taste. Only so do we understand why vestiges of older versions were not obliterated or retouched. To cite an observation often made: 42:11 speaks of "all the evil *the Lord* had brought upon Job." Satan is not yet the author of all the evil in the story.[69] This would seem to tally with 1:13, perhaps another trace of the earlier tale.[70] If the verse followed once closely after 1:5, the subject of the sentence was perfectly clear. In its present position, preceded immediately by the figure of Satan,[71] the reference to "*his* sons and daughters" (1:13) is ambiguous, and needs clarification as in the Septuagint: *Job's* sons and daughters *(hoi huioi Iōb kai hai thygateres autou)*. The failure to smooth over the inconcinnity in both instances (42:11 and 1:13) is not due to negligence, it is deliberate. It bespeaks regard for the earlier source or story (42:11), and respect for what was still remembered as the older tradition (1:13). The ancient poet retains the form, even when he transcends it in spirit, and his audience found particularly enjoyable such recurrence of the familiar in the new.

Awareness of this literary technique makes one wary of emendations which often miss a helpful clue by deleting it. The text in 42:10 is a good instance. The current commentaries complain that the phrase: "*when he prayed in behalf of his friend(s)*" has either come by error from verse 42:9,[72] or is "a gloss to unite the two sections: its present position is almost meaningless."[73] Of course, it is easy to rewrite 42:9 to read: "and the Lord accepted Job, when he prayed for his friend(s)". This is usually accompanied by the alteration of *rēᶜēhû*, which looks very much like a singular, into the more regular and expected plural *rēᶜāyw*.[74] But then, in turn, why does the author—only here and nowhere else in the book—single out for a special rebuke Eliphaz, adding, as if in postcript, his two friends (42:7)? The three friends alike had "not spoken the thing that was right." Indeed, why should the writer of Job have introduced the motif of prayer at all which seems alien and irrelevant in this connection.[75]

These difficulties, observed long ago and often enough, seem to dissolve when the workmanship of the ancients is remembered. *The older tale of Job had all these features,* and the poet wished to retain them. He accommodated his poem to the *familiar end* of the story of Job. In other words, 42:10 is not the result of corruption or carelessness. On the contrary, by design an ancient text is here left intact as the well-known conclusion of a cherished tale.

wyhwh šāb ᵓet šĕbût ᵓiyyôb	And the Lord *healed* Job
bĕhitpalĕlô bĕᶜad reᶜēhû	when *[as soon as]* he *prayed* for his friend [neighbor, *for the other*]

The traditional exegesis of the rabbis[76] was quick to detect the moral burden of the story: for praying for someone other than himself, although one be himself in need of mercy, does attest the selflessness of virtue. Such a conclusion is indeed fitting for the ancient tale centering around the question: is piety calculated or disinterested?

The later legend of Job harks back to this theme. Witness e.g. the unknown midrash, quoted in late medieval commentaries,[77] how Job, smitten with sore boils, would continue his deeds of charity, as he sat among the ashes. Whenever poor people passed by, Job would ask his wife to feed them. On one such occasion, she could refrain no longer and asked in astonishment: "Dost thou still hold fast thine integrity?" (2:9).[78]

In the *Testament of Job* there is a tender story of his wife's devotion: to keep her sick husband from starving, she cut off her hair, and purchased bread with it.[79] It is at this point of the narrative that the Arabic legend of Job[80] makes the patient sufferer break down. Learning of the sacrifice and humiliation of his wife, he bursts into tears and prays for her sake, whereupon he is at once rewarded, God sending Gabriel to "renew Job as fully as the moon on the fourteenth night."[81] Here too the implication seems to be that unselfish prayer is readily granted.

Something similar must have formed the conclusion of the primitive tale of Job. Himself in woe and want, Job continued in his uprightness to "strengthen feeble knees" and "uphold him that was falling" (4:4) or even redeem the sinner "through the cleanness of his hands" (22:30),[82] traits apparently taken over from the old folk-tale. A particularly poignant example of self-abnegation probably served as the climax of the story, when Job, mindless of his own misery, invoked mercy upon some one else, praying *bĕᶜad reᶜēhû,* for a fellow creature in pain. Then or only then, all the world, even Job's adversary in heaven, had to acknowledge with one voice: *ḥinnām yārēᵓ ᵓiyyôb ᵓĕlōhîm* [Does Job fear God for nought?].[83]

In the foregoing 42:10 was rendered: "The Lord *healed* Job," but *šāb šĕbût,* although undoubtedly including the miracle of his cure as well,[84] has a wider range of meaning. *Restitutio in integrum*[85] does not exhaust it, nor does it sound as a term borrowed from the legal sphere[86] or prophetic eschatology.[87] It seems older than both,[88] and to reach back to the world of myth and fable, where time is reversible, and death not beyond remedy as in stubborn reality. In that dream-land a loss can be retrieved, life recalled from the beyond,[89] and the joys of a former day restored by the grace and goodness[90] of a god who can *make bygones come back*.[91]

If such be the signification of *šāb šĕbût*, as the broad scope and varied use would suggest, the old tale concluded in 42:10 not only with Job's recovery, but with the return of his children as well. Selfless prayer achieves the humanly impossible, and Job regains all that life holds dear. Or to quote Ezek 14:14ff. once more, by his righteousness Job delivered both himself and his sons and daughters.[92]

The poet of Job resolved to dismiss his hearers with the household words of the ancient tale. The original conclusion (42:10) was too often quoted and too well-known to permit any modification or deviation. The poet had, therefore, to introduce *the feature of prayer,* extraneous to his own narrative, but forming the climax of the older story. This is achieved by having the Lord command the friends to beg for Job's forgiveness and intercession. The poet had to adapt, also, the plural of his dramatis personae to *the singular* in the conclusion of the tale. True, *bĕᶜad rēᶜēhû* could be made to mean, as the ages in fact have understood it: "as Job prayed for each of his friends"[93] or "as Job prayed for his neighbor," i.e., for people other than himself,[94] which could then refer to the three friends as well.[95] But the ground had to be prepared, and the reader forewarned for the sudden transition from the plural of the dialogue to the singular of the tale. It is, therefore, that the poet *singles out Eliphaz* (42:7), probably as the oldest among the friends (cf. 15:10), again a feature otherwise inexplicable or irrelevant in the poem. In short, the poet's procedure becomes at once obvious, if the finale of the primitive tale, or 42:10, was too familiar to brook the slightest change.

5. THE CONCLUSION OF THE POEM OF JOB

Skillful accommodation to the last line in an ancient tale might elicit some admiration for the art or artifice of the poet. But from the author of Job—"one of the grandest things ever written with the pen" (Carlyle) —we will expect more, a message and meaning worthy of his poem.

Some of the prevailing theories about the conclusion of the dialogue in 42:7–10 betray a want of consideration which a great writer deserves as a matter of course. The assumption that the earlier tale of Job comprised a primitive dialogue of the friends, more lowbrow than the discourse in the poem, and that the author simply retained the words of the old narrative without change and without a meaning of his own,[96] bespeaks merely the embarrassment of the critics. It is incidental to a false exegesis of which the author, or even the editor,[97] are entirely innocent.

Even in its own setting, the supposed older dialogue of Job,[98] and the fictitious restorations which have been attempted[99] seem to fall short of the better insight and art of the folk-story. The friends are alleged to have tempted Job as his wife has done, and hence Job has to make an atoning sacrifice for them.[100] One would expect a similar kindness shown to Job's wife, but no entreaty is made on her behalf. Nor are her words adjudged as mildly as the fancied folly or blasphemy of the friends (contrast 2:10 with 42:7). The folk-tale makes the wife speak bitterly, but out of love and pity for the unbearable agony of her husband.[101] But the ritual in 2:12 would seem to indicate that the friends think of their own safety first.[102] This is outright the complaint of Job in the poem (6:21): "Ye see disaster, and are afraid!"[103]

It seems much likelier, therefore, to see in the three speakers (introduced by their full name,[104] unlike the nameless wife and sons of the tale) the invention of the poet. The folk-tale, as we saw in 42:11, does not know them. The poet created the interlocutors needed for the unfolding of the religious and philosophical problems which he engrafted in the primitive story. Incidentally, the suggestion would rid the poet of an attack of drowsiness which made him copy thoughtlessly words sensible in a conjectured lost setting, but senseless in his own extant creation.

If, therefore, 42:7–9 is the poet's own work and his conclusion to the colloquy on the ways of God with men, it must have a meaning of its own, and not be merely an adaptation to the familiar end of the old tale in 42:10.

The poem of Job does not pursue the issue of the folk-tale: Is piety unselfish? Instead, it concerns itself with the problem of *unmerited suffering*. Born undoubtedly of personal sorrow, the poem boldly assails the dogma of retribution as both untrue and unfair. Everyday experience seems to the poet to proclaim with a thousand tongues that disease has nothing to do with the moral worth of its victim. Moreover, a doctrine which takes sin to be the cause of all suffering, makes men view sickness with suspicion rather than sympathy, and thus heaps malice upon malady. It condemns without evidence, or turns misfortune itself into evidence of misdeed, and is therefore doubly odious: It drives the sufferer to despair, and his fellow men to cruelty.

It is the glory of the poem, and of the faith of which it is a flowering, that this challenge of the prevailing doctrine neither issues, nor results in unbelief. Quite the contrary, it stems from the passionate conviction that although condemned by men, the innocent sufferer does not incur the displeasure of God, nor is he barred from His grace. However afflicted, his is still the nearness and fellowship of a loving God. Since such favor is forever denied to the wicked, the latter's lot, even in prosperity, is pitiable rather than enviable.[105]

The friends in the dialogue uphold the traditional dogma. They fear that its denial would imperil religion (15:4), and hence should never be allowed. They must therefore seek of necessity for some secret sin which will prove to their satisfaction that what failed is not virtue, for virtue cannot fail. The course of the dialogue discloses how a false principle will debase character. For if a doctrine cannot be abandoned, and being false, it must clash with the facts, a zealous adherent will sooner or later do away with the unwelcome facts. He will learn before long to find or invent the facts which invariably favor his theory, and wittingly or unwittingly he will end in mendacity.[106] Admirable is the art, and the restraint of the author who vehemently disagreed with the spokesmen of the orthodoxy of his day, and yet did not suffer ire or irony to creep into his pen and caricature the views of his opponents.

He could safely do so because of one exceedingly effective device: his selection of the folk-tale of Job as the framework for his dialogue. The poet availed himself of this fiction not in order to secure the admission of his book into the inner circle of the Synagogue, although such was the ultimate result. Rather was he prompted by the desire to communicate to the reader something of his own assurance of innocence despite all affliction. Without the setting provided by the tale of Job, the unceasing insistency on being blameless could easily be misunderstood. Where a cornerstone of the creed is at stake, one will always prefer to suspect that the writer was a trifle self-righteous rather than surrender a cherished belief. By the choice of the story of Job the poet succeeded in putting his entire argument upon a rock of certainty: there *is* undeserved suffering.

We can now grasp the full purport of the censure in 42:7 ff: *lō dibbartem ʾēlay nĕkônâ kĕʿabdî ʾiyyôb*. In the immediate context of the narrative, or on the level of fable, the words mean, first, the exoneration of Job. His friends must make amends for their conduct toward him and words about him which, as the outcome proved, were *not proper*.[107] In the sequel to the dialogue, or on the plane of the religious discourse, the words mean, secondly, the disavowal of the doctrine of individual retribution which the friends consistently championed, but which is here said expressly to be *not true*.[108] To have God exhausted in a single formula is, to say the least, humorless. Lastly, at their summit, the words mean the recoil from all that is *not sincere*.[109] In a farewell to the reader, the poet seems to sum up all his probings into the relation between God and man. There is little we may claim to know about God, but this much is certain, one cannot come before Him save in integrity of heart and mind. It would not do to try to feign or fib for the greater glory of God. It cannot be required of man, and surely it can never be made a duty, to plead falsely to the God of truth. For his refusal to do so, Job is blessed in the end, and his friends are rebuked who, in the interest of a doctrine,[110] would have him confess sins he was unaware of committing. The fearless seeker of truth, even the honest blasphemer[111] is nearer to God than the liars for the benefit of religion.

Will you serve God with words of fraud?
For His sake speak deceit?
Him do a favor? Play advocate to God!
What if He searches you through?
You tricking Him, as were He a man to be tricked!
He will, be assured, reprove you,
If you stealthily give Him the advantage.
Shall not His grandeur affright you,
Shall not fall upon you His dread?[112]

ADDITIONAL NOTE 1: DANEL IN THE BOOK OF ENOCH

1 Enoch 6:7 and 69:2 names Daniel among the fallen angels. As long as only the biblical Daniel was known, his inclusion among the chiefs of the rebel angels made little sense, and the text appeared in need of

emendation.[113] With the emergence of the Canaanite epic of Danel, one is struck by two other similarities in name. In 1 Enoch 13:9 the defiled angels gather in a place between Lebanon and Senir called Abilene[114] which is reminiscent of the city of Abilim *(qrt ablm)* in whose environs Aqhat was slain. Moreover, the conspiracy of the angels takes place on Mount Hermon, or rather Hermonim,[115] which recalls the appellation of Danel in the Ugaritic epic as *mt hrnmy.*[116]

Are these agreements mere coincidence, or have we in the pseudepigraph echoes, however distant, of the Canaanitish saga?

In the case of the two localities, obviously a play upon the words is intended: The angels mourn in Abilene *(ʾblyn bʾbylyn)* and bind themselves by an oath and imprecation on Hermon *(ḥrm ḥrmwn).* This may be the nucleus of an old aetiological legend which sought to account for the name of the site *ablm,* and the fierce grandeur of Mount Hermon. Indeed, a fragment of the Book of Noah which Syncellus states was derived from the first book of Enoch *(ek tou prōtou bibliou Enōch)* tells why from the mountain on which the rebel angels conspired "cold shall not depart for ever, nor snow nor hoar-frost, and dew shall not descend on it except it descend on it for a curse."[117]

One wonders whether in the epic of Ugarit which knows of a curse of Danel upon the city of Abilim,[118] or of his prayer that no dew descend upon the land (although only for "seven, even eight years"[119]), the aetiological motive was also at work. The lacunae in the extant texts, and in our present understanding of them, leave us here in the dark. However, it may well be that *qrt ablm* in the ancient epic did not suggest mourning or desolation at all,[120] and only a later popular etymology read into the name such meaning as in Gen 50:11. Similarly *mt hrnmy* may have in common with Mount Hermon but the semblance of sound.[121]

As for Danel, he appears in the Book of Enoch as one of the leaders of the two hundred children of heaven[122] who lusted after the daughters of men, and having married them, taught them the eternal secrets. "Azazel taught men to take swords, and knives, and shields, and breastplates, and made known to them the metals and the art of working them . . . Shemjaza taught enchantments and root-cuttings, . . Shamsiel the signs of the sun, and Sariel[123] the course of the moon" (1 Enoch 8:1–3). What did Danel reveal to men?

The name of Danel seems to have been omitted or obliterated in 1 Enoch 8:3.[124] In the Ugarit epic, Danel received a gift from the heavenly armory, and could therefore appear as the inventor of the composite bow.[125] But since the art of making all kinds of weapons was taught to men by Azazel (1 Enoch 8:1), it seems more likely that as in the case of his companions, Danel's contribution to the knowledge of men is indicated in his very name. Danel is the promulgator of *dīn*[126] or such rudiments of law as make communal life possible. Not by chance is he figured in the Ras Shamra texts as sitting at the gate, judging the fatherless and pleading for the widow.[127]

Traces of such a cycle of legends are still discernible. The Book of Jubilees 4:15 knows of nobler motives for the descent: The angels of the Lord, those who are named the Watchers,[128] were sent by God "to instruct the children of men *to do judgment and uprightness*"[129] The Clementine Homilies portray the angels as grieving at the ingratitude of men, and asking for the permission to come into the life of men and to change into their nature, "in order that living holily, and showing the possibility of so living" *(hina hosiōs politeusamenoi kai to dynaton tou politeuesthai deixantes),* they help to establish on earth a righteous government.[130] Commodianus, also, makes the angels visit the earth at God's behest in order "to beautify the nature of the world" and teach men the dyeing of wool and other skills and crafts.[131] In like manner Lactantius speaks of God's forethought in dispatching the angels "for the protection and improvement of the human race" *(ad tutelam cultumque generis humani).*[132] This view is still preserved in the Chronicles of Jerahmeel[133] where Shemhazai and Azael ask and receive permission to descend among the creatures in order to sanctify the divine name among men.

It would seem, therefore, that originally these legends told how the arts and sciences were revealed to men by emissaries from heaven, benefactors of the human race and founders of civilization. To one of them, Danel, a beloved of the gods[134] and a friend of men, the origins of law and order were attributed.

The later saga is not as cheerful: it stresses the abuses and vices of civilization, and inquires into the genesis of evil among men. It speaks no longer of messengers or servants of the gods, but of insurgents who abused divine favor, and "taught *all unrighteousness* on earth, and revealed the eternal secrets which were preserved in heaven" (1 Enoch 9:6) and thereby wrought harm to men and "filled the earth with blood and *lawless deeds*"[135] (ibid. vv. 9–10). For their indiscretion the rebel angels must suffer punishment: for seventy generations they will remain in chains and darkness,[136] pinned under the hills of the earth,[137] only to be hurled on the day of great judgment into the fiery abyss.[138]

A lingering memory of these "myths of civilization"[139] survives in the inclusion of Danel among the fallen angels. In the Book of Jubilees 4:20, Daniel is made father-in-law of Enoch[140] "who was the first among men who learnt writing and knowledge and who wrote down the signs of heaven and recounted the weeks of the jubilee"[141] (ibid. 4:17). The literature of the Synagogue did not view such heathen tales with favor.[142] It robbed Danel of his glory, and did not hesitate to enter Enoch into the register of the wicked:[143] *wayyithallēk Ḥănôk ʾet-haʾĕlōhîm wĕʾênennû. ʾAmar Rav Ḥamaʾ be-Rav Hoshaʿyaʾ: ʾEino niktav be-tokh ṭomosan shel ṣadiqim ʾelaʾ ṭomosan shel reshaʿim.*

ADDITIONAL NOTE 2: HEYYIN AND HIS BROTHER IN RABBINIC AND MOSLEM LEGEND

In the cycle of legends on the fallen angels there survived a curious story[144] about the first children born from the alliance with the daughters of men. These lusty fellows, we are told, consumed daily a thousand camels, a thousand horses, and a thousand steers.[145] With his sons having such a stake in the livestock of the world, the father was naturally perturbed to learn that God had resolved to destroy all flesh: if a deluge is to come upon the whole earth, where will the two brethren find their daily meat rations? The lads, too, had frightening dreams. One saw lines upon lines of writing obliterated, until but four letters were left intact. The other dreamt of an orchard in which all the trees were cut down, and only a single tree survived with three of its branches. From their father they soon learnt the meaning of their dreams:

A[146]	B[147]	C[148]
ʿAtid ha-Qadosh Barukh Hu le-haviʾ mabbul veloʾ yeshayyer ʾelaʾ Noaḥ u-vanayv. Keivan she-shameʿu kakh hayu ṣoʿaqin u-vokhin. ʾAmar la-hem: "ʾAl tiṣtaʿaru, she-shemoteykhem loʾ yikhlu min ha-beriyyot,	*ʿAtid ha-Barukh huʾ le-haviʾ mabbul le-ʿolam u-le-haḥrivo ve-loʾ yeshayyer bo ʾelaʾ ʾadam ʾeḥad ve-shalosh banayv. Mi-yad ṣaʿaqu u-vakhu ve-ʾameru: "ʿAkhshav mah teheʾ ʿaleinu ʾo ba-mah yizzakher shemenu."*	"God is about to bring a flood upon the world, to destroy it, so that there will remain but one man and his three sons." They (*sc.* the brethren) thereupon cried in anguish, and wept, saying: "What shall become of us, and

she-kol zeman she-gozer gezeirot ʾo maʿalin ʾavanim ʾo sefinot shem-oteikhem hen mazkirin heywwaʾ we-heyyaʾ." *Mi-yad nitqareru daʿatan*	*ʾAmar lahem:* "*ʾAl taḥu-shu ve-ʾal tiṣtaʿaru. She-shemotekem loʾ yikhlu mi-tokh ha-beriyyot le-ʿolam, she-kol zeman she-yigreru ve-yistabelu ʾavanim ve-ʿeṣim ve-khol ṣorkhehem ʾeinam ṣove-ḥim ʾelaʾ ʿal shemey-khem heyhaʾ ve-heyyaʾ. Mi-yad nitqarerah daʿatan.*	how shall our names be perpetuated?" "Do not trouble yourselves about your names. Heyya and Aheyya will never cease from the mouths of creatures, because every time that men raise heavy stones, or ships, or any heavy load or burden, they will sigh and call your names." With this his sons were satisfied.

Light is thrown upon this fancy of the rabbis by a fragment from *The Phoenician History* of Sanchuniathon, as "translated" into Greek by Philo of Byblos and excerpted by Eusebius in his *Preparation for the Gospel.*[149] It deals with the discoverers of the necessaries of life whom grateful posterity revered as gods.[150] Among these benefactors of the race are mentioned Agreus[151] and Halieus, the inventors of hunting and fishing,[152] and then the story of their children is told:[153]

ex hōn genesthai dyo adelphous sidērou heuretas kai tēs toutou ergasias hōn thateron ton Chousōr[154] *logous askēsai kai epōidas kai manteias einai de touton ton Hēphaiston, heurein de kai ankistron kai delear kai hormian kai schedian, prōton de pantōn anthrōpōn pleusai dio kai hōs theon auton meta thanaton esebasthēsan kaleisthai de auton kai Dia meilichion hoi de ton adelphon*[155] *autou toichous phasin epinoēsai ek plinthōn*	From them (*sc.* Agreus and Halieus) were born two brethren, discoverers of iron and of the mode of working it. One of them, *Khousōr,* was skilled (lit. exercised himself) in words, and incantations, and divinations. It is he who was Hephaestus, and invented the hook, and bait, and (fishing) line, and raft, and was the first of all men to navigate: wherefore he too was worshipped after his death as a god, and he was also called Zeus Meilichios. And some say that *his brother* devised (the way of making) walls from *stone blocks.*[156]

Now, the first man to travel by water is the natural choice for a patron of *mallāḥîm* or sailors, and it is Philo of Byblos who equates him with Zeus Meilichios.[157] The first to make walls of stone is of course the patron of the *gōdĕrîm*[158] or the masons. As inventors of iron tools, the two brethren made stonecutting and shipbuilding possible, wherefore their memory may be said to continue among the living:

she-kol zeman she-goderin gedeirot[159] *ʾo maʿalin ʾavanim ʾo sefinot shemotei-khem hen mazkirin*	Whenever men build[160] walls,[161] or haul up stones or ships, they (will) invoke your names.

Obviously the story is meaningful only if mariners and masons could be heard cheering each other at work, and perhaps occasionally even swearing, by something that sounded like Heyya and Aheyya. That this was actually the case with seamen, we learn from *Pesaḥim* 112b: *nizhaʾ de-ʾarbaʾ heyyaʾ heyyaʾ* ("The sailor's cry is 'heyya!' 'heyya!' ")[162] Perhaps Samuel b. Meir[163] was right in interpreting the passage as referring to *clamor helciariorum* or the shout of bargemen towing ships or lighters against the current.[164] From the midrash of the rabbis we may derive that like cries or calls accompanied the lifting of stones and the labor of masons.[165]

It is not hard to guess what *heyyaʾ* implied on the lips of workmen. In the vernacular *heyyaʾ* was an ordinary adverb meaning "quick."[166] In several languages *heyyaʾ*, also, serves as an exclamation to incite to action or greater effort: *on! up!*[167] In either case, the adverb and the interjection tend, in special urgency or impatience, to be repeated[168] *heyyā-ā-heyyā!* Thus the twain brothers were born.

As in our day, but much oftener in antiquity, exclamations were known to be addressed to divinities. In some instances, the shout with which a god was invoked became his very name.[169] The cry *heyya* or "quick" seemed particularly appropriate for the "quick" or deft *Heyyin*, the alternate name for Khousōr or *Kṯr* in the Ugarit religious texts. Seafaring men being mostly god-fearing men,[170] it is quite possible that their *heyyaʾ heyyaʾ* was indeed a minced form of Heyyin or a way to invoke him, and that at least on certain occasions, it was felt or intended to be a plea for aid from the god of shipping and shipmen.[171]

In brief, Heyya and Aheyya in the midrash of the rabbis seem no other but Heyyin, i. e. Khusōr and his brother in the account of Phoenician antiquities by Sanchuniathon. The inventor of the raft is made to be also an expert in speech and spells, for only such power of the word as could command and compel disciplined and united action was believed by the ancients to have made navigation possible.[172]

But who was Khusōr's brother, and what was his name? In the Ugarit records we read of *Kṯr-w-Ḫss*,[173] and the assumption seems reasonable that the hyphenation preserves the memory of what was formerly a pair of gods: *Kṯr* or "cunning" had a brother named *Ḫss* or "clever."[174] It is more difficult to explain how popular fancy (perchance by relating it to *ḥṣṣ* or a kindred root?[175]) read into the name the suggestion of stonework, and thus made *Ḫss* the hero eponymous of the masons.

If this guess be right, the name of Heyyin's brother was not borrowed, but freely invented by the rabbis. Heyya and Aheyya, or the variants,[176] are a pair of pendant names like Eldad and Medad,[177] Ḥilleḳ and Billeḳ,[178] or Jannes and Jambres.[179] The Arabs particularly seem to enjoy putting together such assonant names, and both Muhammad and the post-Ḳur'ānic tradition indulged in this fancy: *Yāǵūǵ* and Māǵūǵ for Gog and Magog,[180] *Hārūn* and *Ḳārūn* for Aaron and Korah,[181] *Hābīl* and *Ḳābīl* for Abel and Kain,[182] or *Ḫillīt* and *Millīt* for the first dwellers of hell.[183]

In the same class belong the two angels in *Bābil, Hārūt* and *Mārūt* who teach people "how to cause division between man and wife" (Sūra 2, 96). The Moslem tales, cited in the commentaries to this passage,[184] echo rabbinic legends[185] about the fallen angels. Having spoken contemptuously of the sins of men, the angels receive permission to send two of their number to earth, and they very soon prove that angels on earth would not do any better than men.[186] *Hārūt* and *Mārūt,* the two[187] disgraced angels, were condemend to be suspended by the feet in a rocky pit at Babylon, where they teach men magic. The name of the pair has been variously explained, but neither the derivation from 1 Enoch 6:7,[188] nor from 2 Enoch 33:11,[189] and least of all, from the Avestan *Haurvatāt* and *Ameratā,*[190] seems well founded.

It would appear that as in the case of Heyya and Aheyya, only one of the names was actually borrowed from earlier tradition, and that the other name grew from Arabic fondness for assonance. Goliath and Saul may serve as an illustration of the freedom and playfulness with which new names were invented. The Jews were often heard to speak of their *gālūt,* sometimes, also, as a crumb of comfort, of their *rēš gālūtā,* until the Philistine chief became *Gālūt,*[191] whereupon his opponent, and paronomastic counterpart, was dubbed *Ṭālūt,* the "tall" king (from the verb *ṭāla*).[192] It has been similarly suggested that the one name which can be traced to pre-Moslem tradition is *Mārūt,* a "quite common Syriac word for power, it possibly contains a remembrance of *Azael,* while its parallel was formed by Muḥammad simply altering the first consonant of the other name.[193]

Here again the Ugarit texts may contain a useful clue. Heyyin is said to be a *ḥrš,* a *craftsman* or master artificer.[194] But *ḥrš,* also, means *magician,*[195] and it may well be that this twofold meaning of *ḥrš* gave rise to the cycle of legends about the discoverers of tools and skills who also revealed to men the black arts.[196] Once *Hārūt* was born, or rather adopted, his companion sprang from a rhyme and reminiscence about *rebellious* angels who *subjugated* the heavenly bodies by means of witchcraft and defied God's *lordship* of the world.[197] Some of these tales or terms may have vaguely haunted his mind, when Muḥammad chose the name of *Mārūt* for the second member of the pair.

The tale of *Hārūt* and *Mārūt,* even though one of the names is newly coined, is thus an offshoot of the Canaanite myth about Heyyin and his brother. Like the story of Heyya and Aheyya, it became interlaced with the legends about the fallen angels who teach sorcery and tempt to adultery.

This sequel to the tale of the twin brethren may perhaps contain a hint that the rabbis were not unaware of the Phoenician provenance of the myth. The *midrash* tells of the penance of Shemhazai who suspended himself between heaven and earth, head downward, for he is too ashamed to open his mouth before God. However, Azael, his fellow rebel, never repented of his mischief, and continues to entice men to sin with his devilish dyes and feminine finery:[198]

ʿAzaʾel loʾ ḥazar bi-teshuvah ve-huʾ memunneh ʿal kol minei ṣivʿonin ve-ʿal kol minei takhshitin shel nashim she-mefattim ʾet benei ʾadam le-hirhor ʿaveirah . . . ve-ʿadayin huʾ ʿomed be-qilqulo le-hasit benei ʿadam le-dabber ʿaveirah be-vigdei ṣivʿonim shel nashim.

Does not this stress on *kol minei ṣivʿonin* and *bigdei ṣivʿonin shel nashim* hide perhaps a taunt and thrust at the purple garment industry which gave Phoenicia its very name: *"land of the purple dye"?*[199]

Moreover, some of the angelic names appear to carry faint vestiges of the ancient sites and sagas of Phoenicia. We are indebted again to Sanchuniathon for having preserved for us the story of a feud between two brethren, Samemrumos and Usoos[200] in whom scholars have recognized the founding fathers of Sidon and Tyre.[201] The rivalry of these two sister-cities, or perhaps the ascendancy of Sidon over Tyre found its mythical expression in the quarrel between Samemrumim and Uzu.[202] Is the angel Uzza[203] none other than Uzu, a residue of Tyrian myths?[204] In another passage of his Phoenician antiquities, Sanchuniathon calls the first intelligent beings *Zophesemin* or seers of heaven.[205] May not a similar signification be concealed in Shemhazai, chief of the archangels (1 Enoch 6:3, 9:7, and 69:2) who sat the first in the kingdom of heaven and hence saw the king's face?[206]

However, it is quite possible that the angelic names in our records are no longer transmitted in their original form. Rabbinic doctrine demanded that the name of God be combined with every angel[207] to indicate beyond a shadow of doubt that all powers, either in the depth or in the height above, are subject and subservient to the sovereign will of God. By making the names of angels theophorous, the Jewish homilists not only disguised many a foreign importation, but also retrieved them from oblivion. Our *midrash* may serve as an example. For this faded fragment of a myth about a pair of Canaanitish divinities, patrons and protectors of mariners and masons, would have hardly reached our day, were it not for the skill with which the *Rabbanan d'Aggadta,* or the teachers of the Haggadah, had adapted it to the biblical setting, and converted it to support the Jewish ritual.[208]

NOTES

1. *Histoire critique du Vieux Testament* (Rotterdam, 1675), p. 30.
2. *Liber Jobi* (Leiden, 1737) Praef., p. 34.
3. Joh. Gottfr. Hasse, "Vermuthungen über das Buch Hiob," in: *Magazin für die biblisch-orientalische Litteratur und gesammte Philologie* 1 (1789) 161–92, esp. 162–71.
4. *ʾIyyov bi-yemei malkat shevaʾ hayah* (*Gen. R.* 57:4; *y. Soṭa* 5:8, 20d; *b. B. Bat.* 15b reads *malkhut sheva*ʾ and argues against *ha-ʾomer malkat shevaʾ ʾishah hayetah*. King Solomon as the author of Job is assumed by Gregory Nazianzen (*Oratio* XIX, *PG* 35, p. 1061) and contemplated by Luther (*Tischreden* [Weimar, 1912] vol. 1, p. 207: "*Possibile est Salomonem ipsum scripsisse eum librum*"). Otherwise the Solomonic age is postulated by Luther (ibid., p. 68: "*Videtur mihi scriptus esse tempore Salomonis.*" See also ibid., p. 375, and vol. 3 [1914], p. 9), a view still upheld by K. Schlottmann, *Das Buch Hiob* (Berlin, 1851) pp. 105ff. and Franz Delitzsch, *Das Buch Job*[2] (Leipzig, 1876) pp. 13ff.
5. T. K. Cheyne, *Job and Solomon* (London, 1887) pp. 66ff., conjectured that the first two chapters originally formed the principal part of a distinct "prose book of Job" which could not be dated "before the Chaldean period."

6. *Das Buch Hiob* (Göttingen, 1896, ²1913).
7. *Das Buch Hiob* (Freiburg im Breisgau, 1897).
8. In his review of Aug. Dillmann, *Das Buch Hiob*³ (Leipzig, 1869) in *Jahrbücher für deutsche Theologie* 16 (1871) 555. See also his *Israelitische und jüdische Geschichte*⁷ (Berlin, 1914) p. 207, n. 2.
9. Karl Kautzsch, *Das sogenannte Volksbuch von Hiob* (Tübingen, 1900).
10. J. Meinhold, *Einführung in das A.T.* (Giessen, 1919), p. 278; Paul Dhorme, *Le livre de Job* (Paris, 1926) p. LXVII; O. Eissfeldt, *Einleitung in das A.T.* (Tübingen, 1934) p. 512; Adolphe Lods, "Reserches récentes sur le livre de Job," in *Revue d'histoire et de Philosophie religieuses* 14 (1934) 501ff.; Gustav Hölscher, *Das Buch Hiob* (Tübingen, 1937) p. 5; and Robert H. Pfeiffer, *Introduction to the Old Testament* (New York, 1941) pp. 670ff. where a full review of the literature will be found.
11. B. D. Eerdmans, *Studies in Job* (Leiden, 1939) pp. 5, 17, 19f.; E. G. Kraeling, *The Book of the Ways of God* (New York, 1939) pp. 189, 206; and N. H. Torczyner, *Sefer ʾIyyov* (Jerusalem, 1941) pp. 17, 534ff.
12. Hieronymus, Praefatio in 1. Job (*PL* 28, pp. 1139–40). Cf. also his Second Preface to Job (ibid., vol. 29, p. 62): "decurtatus et laceratus currosusque liber."
13. *Mi-penei mah hizkir sheloshah ʾeleh mikkol hanevîʾim? (Midrash Ḥadash ʿal ha-Torah,* ed. by Jacob Mann, *The Bible as Read and Preached in the Old Synagogue* [Cincinnati, 1940], Hebrew part, p. 151). Cf. Jerome: "*Cum et Abraham et Isaac et Jacob, Moysesque quoque et caeteri patriarchae justi fuerint, cur horum tantummodo fiat mentio?*" (*PL* vol. 25, p. 120). Similarly Joseph Kaspi (ed. Last, *ʾAdnei Kesef* [London, 1912] p. 32): *ve-loʾ ʾAvraham Yiṣḥaq ve-Yaʿaqov ʾo Mosheh ʾAharon u-Shemuʾel, ve-zeh sod gadol.*
14. Cf. Moses Ḳimḥi (ed. I. Schwartz, *Tikvat ʾEnosh* [Berlin, 1868] p. 126): *samhu ha-katuv ʾaḥaron le-Noaḥ ve-Danîʾel baʿavur ḥesron maʿalato mi-maʿalatam ki hem hayu nevîʾim be-ʾemet.* Similarly the Karaite Jacob b. Reuben, *Sefer ha-ʾOsher* (Eupatoria, 1834): *ve-Danîʾel . . . hiqdim min ʾIyyov ki hayah nikhbad bi-nevuʾah.* See also the attempts of Simon be Zemah Duran, *ʾOhev Mishpaṭ* (Venice, 1589) f. 45b, and of S. D. Luzatto, *Perushei Shadʿal* (Lemberg, 1876) p. 146 to account for *seder zeh she-loʾ ke-seder zemaneihem.*

    The passage bears also on the problem of dating. Contrast the changed critical outlook from the days of E. W. Hengstenberg (*The Prophecies of Ezekiel* [Edinburgh, 1869] p. 123: "Daniel is designedly placed in the middle of the two primeval personages to glorify him, as it were to canonize him") to the days of C. C. Torrey (*Pseudo-Ezekiel and the Original Prophecy* [New Haven, 1930] p. 98: "The widely read and widely quoting author" of Pseudo-Ezekiel, writing about 230 B.C., "was familiar both with our book of Job and with chaps. 1–6 of the book of Daniel").
15. Eliezer of Beaugency (ed. Poznański [Warsaw, 1909] p. 21): *kulam be-ʾereṣ ʾaḥeret she-loʾ be-ʾereṣ Yiśraʾel hayu.* A. D. Lebenson, *Torat ha-ʾAdam*

(Vilna, 1858) p. 60: *tafas li-venei ha-galut ʾet ha-mefursamim lahem mi-ṣad she-qivreihem sham . . . ʾArarat . . . ve-ʿUṣ . . . semukhim ʾel . . . Bavel.*

16. *Sheloshah raʾu sheloshah ʿolamot banuy ve-ḥarev u-vanuy.* So Rashi and David Ḳimḥi *ad loc.* and *Tosafot ha-Roʾsh (Sefer Hadar Zeqenim* [Leghorn, 1840]) f. 3b. So also Jacob b. Hananel Sikli (ed. Mann, *loc. cit.*, p. 282), Isaac Abravanel ad Ezek 14:14 and Isaac b. Solomon Hacohen, *Sefer ʾIyyov ʿim Perush* (Constantinople, 1545) f. 2b. Simon Duran, *loc. cit.* reads: *sheloshah ʿolamot yishuv ve-ḥorban ve-yishuv.*

    The idea is old. Cf. Jerome: *"Alii dicunt quia hi tantum tres viri et prospera et adversa et rursum prospera conspexerunt"; Tanḥuma, Noaḥ* 5 and *Tanḥuma Buber* I, *Noaḥ raʾah ʿolam be-yishuvo . . . be-ḥorbano . . . be-tiqquno . . . ʾIyyov . . . hayah tam ve-nityasser . . . ve-aḥarei khen nitrappeʾ. Midrash Haggadol Genesis,* ed. Schechter, p. 141 (see also *Midrash Bereshit Rabbati,* ed. C. Albek, p. 65): *Noaḥ raʾah yishuv ha-ʿolam ve-ḥorbano ve-yishuvo, ʾIyyov raʾah yishuv beito ve-ḥorbano ve-yishuvo, Daniʾel raʾah yishuv Yerushalayim ve-ḥorbanah ve-yishuvah,* and *Midrash Ḥadash ʿal ha-Torah,* ed. Mann, p. 151: *Noaḥ raʾah ʿolam meshukhlal ve-ḥarev u-meshukhlal, ʾIyyov raʾah beito banuy ve-nifraṣ u-vanuy, Daniʾel raʾah beit ha-miqdash meyussad u-shamem u-meyussad,* and Buber, *Liqquṭim Mim-midrash Abkir,* p. 4, n. 8 = Yalḳ. Shimeoni, Noaḥ 50. See Louis Ginzberg, *The Legends of the Jews* (Philadelphia: Jewish Publication Society of America, 1937), vol. 5, p. 388, n. 35.

17. Cf., e.g., Hugo Grotius, *Annotationes in V.T.*, vol. 2 (Halle, 1776); R. Smend, *Der Prophet Ezechiel* (Leipzig, 1880); G. A. Cooke, *The Book of Ezekiel* (Edinburgh, 1936).

18. A. Bertholet, *Das Buch Hesekiel*[1] (Freiburg i.B., 1897) p. 75: "Nach Ez 14:16 stünde zu erwarten, dass in der Danielsgeschichte auch von Daniels Kindern etwas bekannt gewesen sei." See also A. B. Ehrlich, *Randglossen zur hebr. Bibel,* vol. 5 (Leipzig, 1912) p. 49.

19. Cf. Isaac Abravanel, *ad loc.: Daniʾel loʾ naśaʾ ʾishah ve-loʾ holid banim.* Rabbinic fancy connects Isa 39:7 with Daniel and makes him a eunuch *(b. Sanh.* 93b: *sarisim mamash).* The legend was known to Origines (*Comm. in Matt.* 15:5) and to Jerome (on Isa 39:7), see Louis Ginzberg, "Die Haggada bei den Kirchenvätern VI" in *Jewish Studies in Memory of George A. Kohut* (New York, 1935) p. 309. *Y. Shabb.* 6:9 f. 8d knows of Daniel's recovery *(hayu sarisim ve-nitrappeʾu),* while a figurative interpretation *(she-nistarsah ʿavodah zarah bi-yemeihem, b. Sanh. loc. cit.)* would leave Daniel "without blemish" and "without hurt" (Dan 1:4 and 3:25). See Louis Ginzberg, *The Legends of the Jews,* vol. 6, p. 415, n. 78. Another legend (Ginzberg, ibid., vol. 4, p. 378) identifies Daniel with Memucan who married a wealthy and wayward Persian lady, cf. II Targ. Esth 1:16, cited as *midrash* by Tosafoth *Meg.* 12b s.v. *Memucan.*

20. Georg Heinr. Bernstein, "Über das Alter . . . des Buches Hiob," in Keil and Tzschirner's *Analekten* 1,3 (Leipzig, 1813), p. 11: "Ich möchte die Behaup-

tung wagen: entweder rührt dieses ganze Orakel von einer weit jüngeren Hand der, oder es haben ursprünglich statt Daniel und Hiob zwei andere Namen in dem Texte gestanden"; J. Halévy, *REJ* 14 (1887) 20 reads: *Noaḥ Ḥanokh ve-ʾEnosh;* W. A. Irwin, *The Problem of Ezekiel* (Chicago, 1943) p. 158 retains as genuine one verse only, Ezek 14:13, the rest or Ezek 14:14–23 is "prose and spurious."

21. See David Ḳimḥi to Ezek 14:14 and 28:3: *Daniʾel ḥaser ha-yod,* and N. Krochmal, *Moreh Nevukhei ha-Zeman* (Lemberg, 1851) p. 118 (ed. Rawidowicz, Berlin, 1924, p. 138).

22. See. H. A. Chr. Hävernick, *Commentar über den Propheten Ezechiel* (Erlangen, 1843) p. 207. L. Zunz, *ZDMG* 27 (1873) 676ff. (=*Ges. Schriften* I [Berlin, 1875] p. 228f.) suggests that the three saints were non-Israelites.

23. *Syria* 12 (1931) 21f. 77, 193. See also W. F. Albright, *JBL* 51 (1932) 99ff.; *BASOR* 46 (1932)19; and ibid. 63 (1936) 27.

24. A. Bertholet, *Hesekiel*[2] (Tübingen, 1936) p. 53; G. A. Cooke, *loc. cit.*, p. 153; and W. A. Irwin, *loc. cit.*, p. 158.

25. See A. Bea, "Archäologisches und Religionsgeschichtliches aus Ugarit-Šamra," in *Biblica* 20 (1939) 445.

26. Charles Virolleaud, *La Légende Phénicienne de Danel* (Paris, 1936); James A. Montgomery, "Ras Shamra Notes VI: The Danel Text," *JAOS* 56 (1936) 440–45; Josef Aistleitner, "Zum Verständnis des Ras-Shamra-Textes I D," in *Dissertationes in hon. Dr. E. Mahler* (Budapest, 1937) pp. 37–52; Theodor H. Gaster, "The Story of Aqhat," in *Studi e Materiali di Storia delle Religioni* 12 (1936) 126–42, 13 (1937) 25–56, and 14 (1938) 212–15; A. Herdner, "Quelques remarques sur 'La Légende Phénicienne de Danel,'" in *RES* (1938) 120–27; Umberto Cassuto, "La Leggenda fenicia di Daniel e Aqhat," *Reale Academia Nazionale dei Lincei:* Rendiconti dell Classe di Scienze morali, storiche e filologiche, ser. 6, vol. 14, pp. 264–68; idem, "Daniel e la Pioggia fecondatrice nella tavola I D di Ras Shamra," in *RSO* (August, 1938); idem, "Daniel e le spighe: Un episodio della tavola I D di Ras Shamra," *Or* 8 (1939) 338–43; idem, "Daniel et son fils dans la tablette II D de Ras Shamra, *REJ* 105 (1940) 125–31; George A. Barton, "Danel, a pre-Israelite Hero of Galilee," *JBL* 60 (1941) 213–24; Cyrus H. Gordon, "The Saga of Aqhat, Son of Daniel" in his book *The Loves and Wars of Baal and Anat* (Princeton, 1943) pp. 33–43; E. A. Singer, "*Ha-Mem ha-Sofit be-Śefat Luḥot ʾUgarit,*" *Bull. Jew. Pal. Expl. Soc.* 10 (1943) 61f.; W. F. Albright, *Archaeology and the Religion of Israel* (Baltimore, 1942) p. 106 and p. 203 n. 31; W. F. Albright and G. E. Mendenhall, "The Creation of the Composite Bow in Canaanite Mythology," *JNES* 1 (1942) 227–29; W. F. Albright, "The 'Natural Force' of Moses in the Light of Ugaritic," *BASOR* 94 (1944) 32–35; H. L. Ginsberg, "A Ugaritic Parallel to 2 Sam 1:21," *JBL* 57 (1938) 209–13; idem, "Women Singers and Wailers among the Northern Canaanites," *BASOR* 72 (1938) 13–15; idem, "Two Religious Borrowings in Ugaritic Literature II," *Or* 9 (1940) 40–42; idem, "The Ugaritic Texts and Textual Criticism," *JBL* 62 (1943) 111f.; idem,

"The North-Canaanite Myth of Anath and Aqhat," *BASOR* 97 and 98 (1945).

I take this opportunity to thank Professor Albright for his ever ready helpfulness, and for his kindness in communicating to me his version of II Aq 1:27ff. before it appeared in print. I am indebted also to my friend and colleague Professor H. L. Ginsberg with whom I have frequently discussed various texts of Ras Shamra and who always generously has lent me not only his books and pamphlets on *Ugaritica,* but also his third ear for all matters of Ugaritic language and literature.

27. So also J. Pedersen, "Die Krt Legende," *Berytus* 6 (Kopenhagen, 1941) p. 64.
28. Cf. Additional Note 1.
29. Cf. I 2:82 *ytk dm[ʿth k]m rbʿt ṯqlm.* See Charles Virolleaud, *La Légende de Keret* (Paris, 1936) p. 34 l. 28f.: *tntkn udmʿth km ṯqlm arṣh.*
30. See Ginsberg, *BASOR* 72 (1938) 13 and Cassuto, *Tarbiz* 12 (1940) 11. It seems to me that in Ps 68:7 deliverance in *childbirth* is meant. Compare *môšîb yĕḥîdîm* with Ps 113:9: He helps the solitary to a family and a barren woman to a houseful of children. Contrast Job 3:10ff. and cf. Gen 29:31 or 30:22, and for the verb *yṣʾ*, Gen 38:28, Job 1:21 and Isa 65:9. Cf. *Gen. R.* 71:1.

The craft of the *kōšārôt* combined skill in word and deed, cf. the *mĕyalledet* Gen 35:17 and 38:28f., also *Gen. R.* 82:8, *memasmesin nafshah shel ḥayyah,* cf. *b. Yeb.* 42b: *memasmesaʾ lēh be-veṣim ve-ḥalav.* Cf. also the various etymologies of the name Puʿah (*b. Soṭa* 11b: *she-hayetah poʿah [u-moṣiʾah] le-valad; Eccl. R.* 7:1: *she-hayetah poʿah be-ʾishah veha-valad yoṣeʾ; Exod. R.* 1:13: *she-hayetah mefiʿah ʾet ha-tinoq keshe-hayu ʾomerim met* or *Pu-ʿah she-hayetah nofaʿat be-tinoq ʾaḥar ʾimmah,* which Dr. S. Lieberman (in Rabbi M. M. Kasher's *Torah Shelemah,* vol. 8 [1944] p. 263) connects with *y. Shabb.* 18:3 f. 16c: *ʾei zehu siyyuaʿ? Meviʾ yayin ve-nofeaḥ le-tokh ḥoṭmo.* Knowledge of the proper spells and swaddlings is ancient lore of women (cf. *b. Shabb.* 66b: *ʾamerah li ʾem kol minyanei bi-shemaʾ de-ʾimaʾ ve-khol qiṭrei bi-semoʾlaʾ*), but it is especially the business of the *sage-femme* or *ḥakhemah* (*m. Shabb.* 18:3, *m. Rosh. Hash.* 2:5).

T. Nöldeke, *Neue Beiträge zur semitischen Sprachforschung* (Strassburg, 1910) p. 79 and 88 discussed the meaning of *ḥyh,* Aramaic *ḥytʾ,* Mandaic *hʾytʾ.* But perhaps just as the *Kṯrt* are related to *Kṯr,* so *ḥyh* is related to *Hyn d ḥrš ydm* (II Aq 5:18f. and 24f.) or "Heyyin of the Handicrafts." See Bauer, *OLZ* 37 (1934) 245 and *ZAW* 53 (1935) 57 who compares Arabic *hayyin,* "facile," and Syriac *haunā,* "cleverness." The Targumim understood similarly Exod 1:19, *kî ḥāyôt hēnnâ,* Pal. Targ. I: *zerizin ve-ḥakhimān.* The *ḥyh* must be "quick" and "deft," for bungling or tarrying may cost the life of the child (cf. *Gen. R.* 60:3: *bein ḥayyataʾ le-meḥabaltaʾ ʾazal baraʾdirevitaʾ*).

Perhaps in this connection *mafteaḥ shel ḥayah* may also be mentioned (*b. Taʿan.* 2a bottom and *b. Bekhor.* 45a, also *Yer. Targ.* Deut 28:12

mafteḥaʾ de-ḥayyataʾ). Damascius, *De Primis Principiis* § 125, ed. Jos. Kopp, p. 385, calls *Kṯr* "the Opener" *(anoigeus),* thus identifying him with the Egyptian smith-god Ptaḥ. The authors of the Ugarit religious texts were conscious of this identity, see Ginsberg, *Or* 9 (1940) 42. Besides, the ancients associated fire with fecundity, cf. Varro, *De lingua latina* 5, 61: "mas ignis, quod ibi semen"; J. Lydus, *De mensibus* 4, 54: *Hēphaistos gonimon pyr;* Servius to Virgil's *Aeneid* 8, 389: "Vulcanus maritus fingitur Veneris, quod Venerium officium non nisi calore consistit." See O. Gruppe, *Griech. Mythologie und Religionsgeschichte* (Munich, 1906) pp. 726f, 859f., and 1311ff.

Professor Saul Lieberman was kind to bring to my attention a reading in *Tos. B. Batra* 10:2 (see his *Tosefeth Rishonim* vol. 2 [Jerusalem, 1938] 148): *ha-ʾishah she-hayetah kosheret ve-ʿamedah ve-hishbiḥah ʾet ha-nekhasim,* where *kosheret* means "skilful, adroit, efficient."

Perhaps *kosheret* and *ḥyh* were synonyms for *ḥakhemah?* They were thought alike to be disciples and devotees of the *Kṯrt,* or the patron goddesses of *minstrelsy and midwifery,* twin arts in antiquity. See notes 153 and 172.

31. So rightly T. H. Gaster, "On a Proto-Hebrew Poem from Ras Shamra," *JBL* 57 (1938) 82. R. Dussaud, *Les découvertes de Ras Shamra et l'Ancien Testament* (Paris, 1937) p. 82 compares the *Parcae* of the Romans. See also A. Goetze, "The Nikkal Poem from Ras Shamra," *JBL* 60 (1941) 360f.
32. *Iliad* XVIII 382: "Charis of the gleaming veil" *(Charis liparokrēdemnos),* later identified with Aglaia, youngest of the Charites (Hesiod, *Theog.* 945: *Aglaiēn d'Hēphaistos . . . hoplotatēn Charitōn thalerēn poiēsatʾ akoitin*).
33. II Aq 6:17ff. See Albright, *BASOR* 94 (1944) 32ff. and Ginsberg, *BASOR,* 97 and 98 (1945).
34. III Aq 6:11f. as restored by Singer, *loc. cit.* and now rendered by Ginsberg, *BASOR* 97, p. 5, n. 13.
35. Ginsberg, *JBL* 57 (1938) 209f. and 62, 111f.
36. I Aq 4:167f. On the meaning of *l-ht wʿlmh ʿnt p-drdr,* see Ginsberg, *Or* 7 (1938) 9, n. 4.
37. I AB 1:16f. *(tbkynh wtqbrnh tštnn bḫrt ʾilm arṣ)* and I Aq 3:111f. *(abky w aqbrnh ašt bḫrt ʾilm arṣ).* On *ʾilm*=*ʾillĕmê,* see Ginsberg, *Or* 5 (1936) 167.
38. I first suggested the resurrection of Aqhat, mainly on the basis of Ezek 14:14ff., at the meeting of the Society of Biblical Literature on Dec. 28, 1939 (*JBL* 59 [1940]VIII). The suggestion was adopted by Dr. C. H. Gordon, *The Living Past* (New York, 1941), p. 155 who aptly observes that the story was known in antiquity not as the epic of Danel, but as the epic of Aqhat (cf. the rubric I Aq 1:1 *l Aqhat*).
39. I Aq 1:8f. *hḫrṣ abn ph,* "I will shape (rebuild) his mouth like clay" (in the potter's hand? Jer 18:6 and 19:1, or [molten] glass? See II Aq 6:37 and the remarks of Ginsberg and Albright *BASOR* 98, pp. 22 and 24 f.). The speaker may be Anath, as would seem from I Aq 1:14–17 where the warrior goddess offers her regrets or apology for having slain Aqhat—just to obtain

his bow, but "him will I revive" (*hwt l aḥw,* first rendered correctly by J. A. Montgomery, *JAOS* 56, 441. See C. H. Gordon, *Ugaritic Grammar* [Rome, 1940] pp. 23 and 67). In III Aq 1:13 Yṭpn makes sure before the murder that Anath will keep Aqhat alive: "him wilt thou revive" *(hwt l t[ḥwy],* see Montgomery, ibid., p. 443 and now Ginsberg, *BASOR* 97, p. 7, n. 15). Anath ends her instructions to her partner in crime: *b ap mhrh ank l aḥwy,* "into the nostrils of his *mhr* I will blow life," l. 26f. Lastly, when Aqhat falls dead, Anath weeps (*w tbk,* l. 39) and apparently promises once more to bring him back to life l. 40f.): *abn ank k*(!) *ʿl[qštk mhṣtk mḫṣtk ʿl] qṣʿtk at lḥ[wt],* "I will (re)build thee, for I slew thee (but) for thy bow, I slew thee for thine arc. As for thee, mayest thou live!" See Ginsberg, *loc. cit.*

40. IV Aq is too fragmentary, and the new fragments published by Virolleaud are inaccessible to me. I desist therefore from speculating whether El achieved another compromise by consigning Aqhat for a part of the year to the shades. On the connection with the Adonis myth, see Albright, *BASOR* 94 (1944) 34 and Ginsberg, *BASOR* 97 (1945) 4, n. 8.
41. II Aq 1:26ff. and 43ff. II Aq 2:1ff. and 14ff.
42. Cf. U. Cassuto, *Tarbiz* 13 (1942) 207 and in his new book, *Me-ʾadam ʿad Noaḥ* (Jerusalem, 1944) pp. 4f. See also Robert Gordis, "The Heptad as an Element of Biblical and Rabbinic Style," *JBL* 62 (1943) 17ff.

    Dr. Saul Lieberman suggests as a parallel, *miṣvot she-ha-ben ḥayyav laʿasot le-ʾaviv, y. Ḳidd.* 1:7f. 61a: *ʾei zehu kibbud? Maʾakhil u-mashqeh malbish u-mekhasseh u-manʿil makhnis u-moṣiʾ*. On *mekhasseh,* see Exod 22:26 *(bammeh yiškāb);* Judg 4:18; Jer 3:25. These *seven* services are condensed to *five* in agreement with the five obligations of the father, ibid.: *u-khe-shem she-huʿ* [sc. *ha-ʾav le-ven*] *zakhah lo ba-ḥamishah devarim kakh huʾ* [sc. *ha-ben leʾav*] *ḥayyav lo ba-ḥamisha devarim, ve-ʾeilu hen maʾakhil u-mashqeh malbish manʿil manhig*. See, however, ibid. 61b, where instead of *manhig* we read again *u-makhnis u-moṣiʾ*. To *manhig* cf. Isa 51:18, and *b. Yeb.* 65b *ḥuṭraʾ le-yadah.* On the number *five* in Rabbinic literature cf. Gerhard Kittel, *Rabbinica* (Leipzig, 1920) pp. 39f. and S. Lieberman, *Greek in Jewish Palestine* (New York, 1942) p. 31, n. 18.
43. Cf., e.g., I AB 3:8ff.
44. II Aq 2:10ff. = I AB 3:15ff.
45. Herdner, *loc. cit.;* Cassuto, *REJ* 105, 125ff.; Albright, *BASOR* 94, p. 35.
46. Aistleitner, *loc. cit.*, p. 38 considers—"nur vermutungsweise"—Arabic *ḳahada* "mit kurzen Schritten gehen," wherefrom the *ʾafʿalu* form *ʾaḳhadu* "der Trippelnde."
47. *Yqht [ʾm],* Prov 30:17 and Gen 49:10. Perhaps also the name *Yaqeh,* Prov 30:1. In South-Arabic *qht* means "command," cf. J. H. Mordtmann and E. Mittwoch, *Himyarische Inschriften in den staatl. Museen zu Berlin* (Leipzig, 1932) p. 24, l. 5: *bqht ʾmrʿhmw,* "auf Befehl ihrer Gebieter." Similarly *Corp. Inscr. Himyar.* 332.2. See note 126.
48. See the five passages discussed above n. 39.
49. On Job 42:10: *Ha-saṭan yadaʿ ki reṣon ha-ʾel be-nissayon levad ve-loʾ raṣah*

li-shloaḥ ba-hem yad le-hamitam . . . ha-kol nishbah be-yad ha-saṭan ve-hushav lo ʿatah [sc. *le-ʾIyyov*] *ʿal ken loʾ ʾamar ha-katuv "wayyiwwālĕdû lô šibʿâ bānîm" ka-ʾasher ʾamar bi-teḥillah* (1:2) *[ki ʾim] "wayĕhî-lô šibʿānâ bānîm"* (42:13) *ve-ʾulay ha-nun ha-nosaf be-millat "šibʿānâ" morah ʿal ha-yediʿah,* which Benjamin Szold, *Sefer ʾIyyov* (Baltimore, 1886) p. 495, rightly explains to mean: *u-lefi ha-Ramban . . . "šibʿānâ" morah ʿal ha-yediʿah lomar she-hem hem ha-banim ha-qodemim ʾasher hayu ba-shevi ve-shavu ʿatah li-gevulam.* See also Meir b. Isaac Arama, *Sefer Meʾir ʾIyyov* (Salonica, 1517) on Job 42:10: *ḥazeru lo ʾotam shivʿah ha-banim she-hayu ve-shalosh ha-banot.*

50. See § 4 n. 92.
51. See Robert H. Pfeiffer, *Introduction to the Old Testament,* pp. 528ff. for a judicious summary of present-day research.
52. *JBL* 54 (1935) 169f.
53. Mekhilta, Shirah 7,40b (ed. Lauterbach II, 54): *"Ben-ʾādām ḥûd ḥîdâ" zeh haya teḥillat ha-sefer.*
54. Targ. Ezek 1:3; Mekhilta, Bo 1b (ed. Lauterbach I, 6); Tanḥuma, Bo 5; cf. also the anecdote in *b. Moʿed Ḳaṭ.* 25a. On the symmetrical rather than chronological sequence of chapters see *Tos. Soṭa.* 6:11 and Torrey, *Pseudo-Ezekiel,* p. 60ff.
55. Ezek 17:20 must have been spoken before the events of 2 Kgs 25:6 which disproved it. See *JBL* 56 (1937) 407.
56. See *"Matay Galah Yeḥezqeʾel?"* in *Sefer Ṭurov* (Touroff; Boston, 1938) pp. 206–12.
57. Albrecht Alt, in *Festschrift Procksch* (1934) p. 15.
58. See also Ezek 12:16. Reality played havoc with his theories, hence the theological inconsistencies of Ezekiel which translators and commentators tried to read away, cf. LXX Ezek 21:8 and *b. Ab. Z.* 4a. See also *b. Baba Ḳama* 60a, or the realistic observation in the Mekhilta, ed. Lauterbach I, 85.
59. Jer 27:18; I Sam 12:23; Gen 20:7.
60. Jer 7:16; 11:14; 14:11; 21:2ff.; 37:3ff.
61. Cf. Ps 106:23 and Gen 18:22. See *JBL* 54 (1935) 152.
62. Jer 15:1 is an instructive parallel. Jeremiah himself became later the intercessor par excellence, cf. 2 Macc 14:14. Ezekiel chose three fathers whose probity or prayer saved their children.
63. *M. Soṭa* 5:5: Johanan b. Zakkai infers from *yĕrēʾ ʾĕlōhîm* in Job 1:1 *loʾ ʿavad ʾIyyov ʾet ha-Maqom ʾelaʾ mi-yirʾah.* Joshua b. Hyrcanus cites Job 13:15 and 27:5 as proving *loʾ ʿavad ʾIyyov ʾet ha-Qadosh Barukh Huʾ ʾelaʾ me-ʾahavah.* See also *Tos. Soṭa* 6:1, *y. Soṭa* 5:7f. 20c, and *b. Soṭa* 31a.
64. See A. Schultens, *Liber Jobi,* f. 1227b. Zeraḥiah of Barcelona (ed. I. Schwarz, *Tiqvat ʾEnosh,* p. 293): *"Wayyānudû lô" ʿal mah she-qarah lo mi-teḥillah mi-mitat banayv levad, "wayĕnaḥămû ʾōtô" ki shillem lo ha-Shem ṭovah taḥat ha-raʿah.* P. Volz, *Hiob und Weisheit* (Göttingen, 1921) p. 8: "Die Freunde kommen hinterdrein, denn bis sie das Geschehene gehört haben

und den umständlichen Weg zurücklegen konnten, hat sich alles schon abgespielt." Friedr. Delitzsch, *Das Buch Hiob* (Leipzig, 1902) p. 11 deletes 42:10c since in the following verse Job is "doch noch ein armer Mann." See Tosafoth *b. Baba B.* 116a s.v. *ki: "wayyitĕnû-lô ʾîš qĕśîṭâ"—loʾ mi-penei she-hayah ʿani ʾelaʾ doron hayu meviʾin lo.*

65. L. W. Batten, "The Epilogue to the Book of Job," *Anglican Theol. Review* 15 (1933) 125ff. and B. D. Eerdmans, *Studies in Job,* p. 19.
66. "Zur Vorgeschichte des Buches Hiob," *ZAW* 55 (1937) 265ff.
67. See note 96.
68. Cassuto, *"Shirat ha-ʿAlilah be-Yisraʾel"* in *Knesset* 8 (1944) 142 presupposes the existence of a poetic version of the story of Hiob upon which our Job chs. 1–2 and 42:7–17 is based.
69. A. Heiligenstedt, *Comment. in Jobum* (Leipzig, 1847) p. XVIIff. On earlier similar guesses cf. K. Kautzsch, *Das sog. Volksbuch von Hiob,* p. 7. So also N. Peters, *Das Buch Job* (Münster in Westf., 1928) p. 52* and Louis Finkelstein, *The Pharisees* (Philadelphia, 1938) p. 235.
70. Joh. Hempel, "Das theologische Problem des Hiob," *Zeits. für syst. Theologie* 6 (1929) 643f. First advanced by J. Hooykaas, *Gesch. der beoefening van de wijsheid onder de Hebrën* (Leiden, 1862) p. 191ff. See the summary by A. Kuenen, *Hist.-krit. Einl. in die Bücher des A.T.* (Leipzig, 1894) vol. 3 1, p. 136.
71. Albert Brock-Utne, "Der Feind. Die alt-testamentliche Satansgestalt im Lichte der soz. Verhältnisse des nahen Orients," *Klio* 28 (1935) 219–27; N. H. Torczyner, "How Satan Came into the World," *ExpT* 48 (1937) 563–65 and in the *Bulletin of Hebrew University,* no. 4 (Jan. 1938) 14–20; J. Morgenstern, "The Mythological Background of Psalm 82," *HUCA* 14 (1939) 41ff.; and A. Lods, "Les Origines de la figure de Satan, ses fonctions à la cour céleste," in *Mélanges Syriens offerts a R. Dussaud* (Paris, 1939) vol. 2, pp. 649–60.
72. First suggested, it would seem, by F. Hitzig, *Das Buch Hiob* (Leipzig and Heidelberg, 1874) p. 314 and often adopted, e.g. by G. L. Studer, *Das Buch Hiob* (Bremen, 1881) p. 78; N. Peters, *loc. cit.,* p. 49*; E. J. Kissane, *The Book of Job* (Dublin, 1939) p. 295. Cf. S. R. Driver and G. B. Gray, *The Book of Job,* vol. 1, p. 375.
73. K. Fullerton, "The Original Conclusion of Job," *ZAW* 42 (1924) 127, n. 1. See B. Duhm, *loc. cit.,* p. 204 ("vielleicht von einem Leser hinzugesetzt") or N. Peters, *loc. cit.,* p. 498.
74. I find it first emended by C. Fr. Houbigant, *Notae Criticae in V.T.* (Frankfurt a.M., 1777) vol. 2, p. 217. So also in Kittel-Kahle, *Biblia Hebraica* (Stuttgart, 1937) p. 1154.
75. Cf. J. Lindblom, "Die Vergeltung Gottes im Buch Hiob," in *Abhandl. der Herder Gessellschaft zu Riga* vol. 6, no. 3 (1938) p. 82: "Sehr merkwürdig ist, dass die Wiederaufrichtung Hiobs nicht direkt damit motiviert wird, dass er im Leiden seine Treue behielt, sondern dass er für seine Freunde (bezw. Seinen Nächsten) Fürbitte einlegt."

76. *B. Baba Ḳama* 92a derives from Job 42:1 *kol ha-mevaqqesh raḥamim ʿal ḥavero ve-huʾ ṣarikh le-ʾoto davar huʾ naʿanah teḥillah,* cf. *Tos. Baba Ḳama* 10:29 and *y. Baba Ḳama* 8:10 f. 6c. See also Tanḥ. Buber I 104; Agadath Bereshith, ed. Buber, p. 57 and Pes. Rab. c. 38 f. 165a: *hayetah middat ha-din metuḥah . . . ve-keivan she-nitpallel ʿal ḥaveirayv mi-yad nitraṣṣah lo ha-Qadosh Barukh Huʾ.*
77. Meir Arama, *Sefer Meʾir ʾIyyov* (Salonica, 1517) f. 7a and Isaac b. Solomon Hacohen, *loc. cit.,* f. 11a, reprinted by Wertheimer, *Leqeṭ Midrashim* (Jerusalem, 1904) and *Sefer Midrash ʾIyyov* (Jerusalem, 1926).
78. Ibid., *"ʿōdĕkā maḥăzîq bĕtummātekā"—mah raʾatah lomar lo kakh? ʾElaʾ le-lammedkha she-loʾ hinniaḥ ṣidqo ve-hayu ha-ʿaniyim nikhnesim ʾeṣlo ve-huʾ ʾomer lah: parnesi ʾet ʾelu. Be-ʿotah shaʿah ʾamera: "ʿōdĕkā maḥăzîq bĕtummātekā."*
79. *Test. of Job* 23:7ff. (ed. K. Kohler, V 20ff., p 302 and transl. p. 323, in *Semitic Studies in Memory of Alexander Kohut* [Berlin, 1897]). See the comment of Ginzberg, *Legends of the Jews,* vol. 5, p. 387, n. 29.
80. N. Apt, *Die Hioberzählung in der arabischen Literatur* (Hiedelberg, 1913) pp. 27f.
81. Ibid., p. 65. See also the Moorish version quoted by M. Grünbaum, *Neue Beiträge zur semit. Sagenkunde* (Leiden, 1893) p. 296.
82. The verse was so understood by the rabbis, cf. *b. Taʿan.* 23a: *"yĕmallēṭ ʾî-nāqî"—dor she-loʾ hayah naqi millaṭṭato bi-tefillatkha, "wĕnimlaṭ bĕbōr kappeykā"—milaṭṭato be-maʿaseh yadeykha ha-berurin."* On Job 22:30 see now Robert Gordis, *JNES* 4 (1945) 54f.
83. Cf. *Aboth de R. Nathan,* ed. Schechter, p. 164: *be-ʾotah shaʿah heʾeminu kol baʾei ha-ʿolam she-ʾein kamoto be-khol ha-ʾareṣ.*
84. Cf. Hos 6:11, 7:1, and Jer 33:65f where the parallel verb is *rpʾ*. See also Deut 30:3, LXX *iasetai.* Joseph b. David Ibn Yahya, *Perush Ḥamesh Megillot . . . ʾIyyov* (Bologna, 1538): *"šĕbût ʾiyyōb"—she-nitrappeʾ ve-shav le-ʾeitano ha-rishon bariʾ ʾulam.* Similarly Isaac b. Solomon Hacohen: *veha-kavvanah bo refaʾot ʾIyyov.*
85. Hugo Winckler, *MVAG* 11 (1906) 24ff.: "ein Terminus des Staatsrechts."
86. Eberhard Baumann, *ZAW* 47 (1929) 17ff.: "ethisch-juridische Sphäre: 'die Schuldhaft aufheben.' " The derivation from *šbh* renews the argument of Erwin Preuschen, *ZAW* 15 (1895) 18ff. and is attested by the versions [Theodotion and Symmachus: *apostrephein (epistrephein) tēn aichmalōsian,* Targum: *tuv (ʾativ) galutaʾ*, Syriac: *hafakh (ʾafnei) shevitaʾ*, Jerome: *convertere (avertere, reducere) captivitatem,* also *captivos reverti facere*].
87. Ernst L. Dietrich, *Šub Šĕbût. Die endzeitliche Wiederherstellung bei den Propheten* (Giessen, 1925) p. 60. Similarly H. Gunkel *Die Psalmen* (Göttingen, 1926) pp. 234, 373, 551: "Kunstausdruck der prophetischen Endverkündigung."

J. Barth, *ZDMG* 41 (1887) 618f. connects it with Arabic *ṯâba* and *ṯabā,* "die Sammlung sammeln." A. B. Ehrlich, *Randglossen zur hebr. Bibel* (Leipzig, 1909) vol. 2, p. 337 construes *šābût* as a partic. pass. of the verb *šābat,* translating the entire phrase: "to restore what was (temporarily) *interrupted.*" Nivard Schlögl, *WZKM* 38 (1931) 68–75 vocalized *šabût:* "die Schicksalswende (von Unheil zum Heil) herbeiführen."

88. Job 42:10 is the only occurrence of the phrase with the name of an individual, hence very likely older than the figurative application to a city (Ezek 16:53) or land (Jer 33:11), people (Hos 6:11, Ps 14:7) or nation (Ezek 29:14).
89. Cf. Ps 85:2,5,7 and 71:20f.
90. Accompanied with *rḥm,* Deut 30:3; Jer 30:18 and 33:26. Cf. Pes. Rab. c. 26 f. 132a, *ḥazarti ve-niḥamti ᵓet ᵓIyyov.*
91. The stress on *ta prōta* seems characteristic of the phrase: *kĕbārīᵓšōnâ,* Jer 33:7,11. *ʿAl-mišpāṭô,* Jer 30:18, *lĕqadmātān* (thrice) Ezek 16:(53)55. Job 42:11f. *lĕpānîm* and *mērēᵓšîtŏ,* though an independent version, convey a kindred thought. See also Isa 1:26 and 58:12 (cf. Amos 9:14) and especially Lam 5:21 which may be said to state best the wish which was father to our phrase: *hăšîbēnû yhwh ᵓēleykā wenāšubâ ḥaddēš yāmênu kĕqedem.* "To return the returning" = "to renew the renewal." Cf. also the imagery of Ps 126:4, born in the Palestinian landscape where seasonal rains bring plenitude after dearth.

    The Masorah oscillates not only between *šĕbût* and *šĕbît,* but also the plural: *bĕšûbî ᵓet-šĕbûtêkem.* The plural *-ôt* easily blends with the abstract *-ût: hărisōtāyw* Amos 9:11, *hărisūtēyk* Isa 49:19, cf. also *ᵓalmĕnûtayik* Isa 54:4. The early confusion with the root *šbh* may have caused the variant *šbyt,* although such changes are known also elsewhere, cf. *trmyt* and *trmwt* Jer 14:14 Ket. A similar confusion of all three forms is to be found in Eccl 5:10 *rᵓît, rᵓût, rᵓôt.* See P. Kahle, *Der masoretische Text des A.T. nach der Überlieferung der bab. Juden* (Leipzig, 1902) p. 82 and Alexander Sperber, "Hebrew Based upon Greek and Latin Transliterations," *HUCA* 12–13 (1937–38) p. 129.

    On transitive *šwb* (Ps 85:5) see Abraham Ibn Ezra, *Ṣaḥot,* ed. Lippmann, f. 49a.
92. See §3 n. 50.
93. Rashi, *ad loc.: ʿal kol reaʿ ve-reaʿ.* Zeraḥiah of Barcelona, *loc. cit.: beʿad kol eḥad me-ḥaverayv.* Moses Alshekh, *Sefer Ḥelqat Meḥoqeq* (Venice, 1603): *she-hitpallel ʿal kol ᵓeḥad bifnei ʿaṣmo.* Cf. E. F. C. Rosenmüller, *Scholia in V.T. Jobus* p. 1003: *pro unoquoque ex sociis, singulare partivum pro plurali.*
94. K. Budde, *Das Buch Hiob* (Göttingen, 1896) p. 255: "*rēʿēhû* nicht *rēʿāyw:* für *den* Nächsten, nicht die Freunde." See also Ehrlich, *ad loc.*
95. Moreover *rēʿēhû* = *rēʿêhû* 1 Sam 30:26, 1 Kgs 16:11, and Prov 19:7. Cf. also *šôsēhû* = *šôsêhû* 1 Sam 14:48. See David Ḳimḥi *ve-ḥaserah yod ha-ribbui me-hamikhtav ve-nishᵓarah ba-mivtaᵓ,* repeated by Solomon Ibn Melekh, *Sefer Mikhlol Yofi* (Amsterdam, 1660). Simon Duran, *loc. cit.,* f.

199b: *"rēʿēhû" kemo "rēʿāyw" . . . ki shimmush ha-heʾ meṣaʾnuhu bi-leshon rabbim "ûmaʿălōtēhû"* (Ezek 43:17) *kemo "ûmaʿălôtāyw" ve-khen aḥerim.*

96. See Duhm, *Das Buch Hiob,* p. 16, and also p. 204 where he seems to admit that the verses 42:7ff., borrowed from the old folk-book, do not fit the poem ("aus Quellen, die eigentlich nicht passen"). See the stricture of Budde, *loc. cit.*[2], p. 271. A. Alt, *ZAW* 55 (1937) 265 revives the hypothesis that 42:7–10 is the conclusion of the folk-story which originally contained also an argument among the friends, decided by God in Job's favor. No attempt is made to account for its retention by the poet, probably because the problem does not belong "Zur Vorgeschichte des Buches Hiob" with which alone the paper deals.
97. It is difficult to charge the editor with the wording of 42:7 which appears to be older than its present position in the book. In it God is said to be the last speaker, but what precedes it in our text is spoken by Job (42:2–6).
98. First, and still most attractively, argued by Duncan B. Macdonald, "The Original Form of the Legend of Job," *JBL* 14 (1895) 63–71. See also his "Some External Evidence on the Original Form of the Legend of Job," *AJSL* 14 (1898) 137–64. T. K. Cheyne, *Jewish Religious Life after the Exile* (New York and London, 1898) p. 161 essays to reconstruct the missing portion of the dialogue. He is followed, among others, by J. Lindblom, *Abh. der Herder Gesellschaft zu Riga* 6 (1938) 82.
99. Frants Buhl, "Zur Vorgeschichte des Buches Hiob," in *Festschrift K. Marti* (*BZAW* 41; Giessen, 1925) pp. 52–61, thought to discover in Job 27:5–7 three verses which survived from the older disputation. His guess is endorsed by J. Hempel, *Zeits. f. syst. Theol.* 6 (1929) 642.
100. See Duncan B. Macdonald, *The Hebrew Literary Genius* (Princeton, 1933) p. 31.
101. The rabbis hesitate to consider Job's wife as *diaboli adiutrix,* as Augustine calls her. Theirs is the belief: *ʾein moneaʿ min ha-ṣadiqim nashim kesherot,* Midrash Mishle (ed. Buber) p. 111 top. It is true, his wife used the very words spoken to and by Satan (cf. 2:3,5 and 2:9 and the *Commentary on Job* by Berechiah, ed. W. A. Wright [London, 1906] p. 6: *"ʿōdĕkā maḥăzîq bĕtummātekā" bi-leshon she-ʾamar lo ha-Qadosh Barukh Huʾ ʾel ha-saṭan, "wĕʿōdennû maḥăzîq bĕtummātō," u-vi-leshon birkat ʾeloqim she-ʾamar lo ha-saṭan "ʾim-lōʾ ʾal-pāneyka yĕbārĕkekā"),* but her intentions were altogether worthy: *ʾamar Rav ʾEliezer: Ḥas ve-shalom she-ʾamerah ʾotah kesherah ha-davar ha-pagum ha-zeh . . . ʾefshar she-hayah huʾ kasher ve-ʾishto loʾ hayetah kesherah? Ve-lamah ʾamerah lo khen? ʾElaʾ ʾamerah lo: hitpallel lifnei ha-Maqom she-tamut, kedei she-telekh min ha-ʿolam ha-zeh shalem ve-ṣadiq ʿad she-loʾ tavoʾ li-yedei ḥetʾ. ʾElaʾ "bārēk ʾĕlōhîm wamut" she-ʾein ʾatah yakhol le-qabbel ʾet ha-ṣaʿar u-teheʾ toheʾ*, an unknown midrash preserved by Meir Arama, *loc. cit.,* f. 71 and Isaac b. Solomon Hacohen, *loc. cit.,* f. 10b. See Wertheimer, *Leqeṭ Midrashim* (Jerusalem,

1904) p. 5a (corrected by Ginzberg, *Legends,* vol. 5, p. 386, n. 27) and *Sefer Midrash ʾIyyov,* ibid. (1926) p. 8.

Not that the rabbis did not enjoy a crack at women or Job, see the sermon of R. Meir (*y. Ḥagigah* 2:1 f. 77b) now ingeniously recovered from *Tos. Ḳid.* 5:17 by Saul Lieberman, in *Studies in Memory of Moses Schorr* (New York, 1944) pp. 186f. Abba bar Kahana identifies Job's wife with Dinah on the basis of Gen 24:7 and Job 2:10, *Gen. R.* 57:4 and *b. Baba B.* 15b.

102. The rite of mourning calls for putting dust upon the head (Josh 7:6, Ezek 27:30, Lam 2:10), not for throwing it heavenward (Job 2:12). The latter seems rather like a charm to ward off the danger of *sheḥin* with which Job was smitten (2:7). The similarity with Exod 9:8–10 did not escape Isaac b. Solomon Hacohen, *loc. cit.,* f. 12b: *"wayyizrĕqû ʿāpār"—ʿal derekh "ûzĕrāqô mōšeh haššāmaymâh" ke-ʾilu hayu mevaqqeshim le-haviʾ ʿal-eihem ha-sheḥin . . . kedei she-yiṣtaʿaru haṣaʿar ʿaṣmo she-hayah ʾIyyov miṣṭaʿer.* Morris Jastrow, Jr., "Dust, Earth and Ashes as Symbols of Mourning among the Ancient Hebrews," *JAOS* 20 (1899) 147 and M. Buttenwieser, *The Book of Job* (New York, 1922) *ad loc.,* cite Acts 22:23 where the same tearing of garments and throwing of dust into the air bespeak an act of repudiation.

103. Isaiah di Trani the Elder (ed. Schwarz, *Tiqvat ʾEnosh* p. 40ff.): *"ʾatem roʾim haḥatat sheli ve-ʾattem yereʾim mimmennu u-maḥanifim lo.* Similarly Isaac b. Solomon Hacohen, *loc. cit.: reʾitem ḥatat she-baʾ li vi-yereʾtem le-nafshekhem.* The Septuagint charges the friends with being "without pity: beholding my wound ye are afraid" *(aneleēmonōs, hōste idontes to emon trauma phobēthēte).* Fr. Baumgärtel, *Der Hiobdialog.* (1933) p. 23 unnecessarily seeks behind *trauma* and another reading (*ḥly,* cf. Jer 10:19 LXX).

104. *Eccl. R.* 7:2, *shalosh reʿei ʾIyyov . . . nitpareshu shemotan.*

105. Cf. Job 13:16; 27:8–10.

106. I so interpret Job 22:5–9.

107. *Lōʾ nākôn laʿăśôt kēn,* Exod 8:22.

108. *ʾĔmet nākôn haddābār,* Deut 13:15, 17:4.

109. *ʾÊn bĕpîhû nĕkônâ . . . lĕšônām yaḥălîqûn,* Ps 5:10. Cf. *lēb ṭahôr . . . wĕrûaḥ nākôn,* Ps 51:12. The poet of Job is a subtle craftsman who deliberately plays with several meanings of a Hebrew word. Cf., e.g., Job 7:6 where *tiqwâ* is not only "hope," but in keeping with the metaphor of a weaver's shuttle, also "thread" (Josh 2:18). See Abraham Ibn Ezra, *ad loc.* Job 9:17 *biśʿārâ* conveys the irony: a "hurricane" about a "hair"! (cf. Targ. and Syr. *bĕśaʿărâ* with which the parallel *ḥinnām* does agree. See Ehrlich, Dhorme, and Baumgärtel *ad loc.*). Cf. also the double meaning of *bōr* in Job 9:30 (Targ. and Sept. *bōr* as in Isa 11:25) or of *šaḥat* 9:31. See the note of J. N. Epstein, *Tarbiz* 5 (1933) 16, n. 28a and the other examples, also from the book of Job, collected by David Yellin, ibid. = repr.

Ketavim Nivḥarim (Jerusalem, 1939) vol. 2, pp. 104ff. (*"Mishneh ha-Hora'ah ba-Tanakh"*).

110. Gregory the Great, *Morals on the Book of Job,* part III, book XI: Whilst they set themselves to defend, they only offend God (*"Deum dum defendere nituntur, offendunt."* *PL* 75, p. 959).

111. *Y. Ber.* 7:4 f. 11c and *y. Meg.* 3 end f. 74c: *'amar rabbi Yiṣḥaq ben ʿElazar: yodeʿin hen ha-nevi'im she-'elu-hen 'amiti ve-'einan maḥanifin lo.*

112. Job 13:7–11.

113. G. Kuhn, "Beiträge zur Erklärung des Buches Henoch," *ZAW* 39 (1921) 245 reads: *"Thananiēl = Tanani'el* d. h. Rauchengel." Ginzberg, *Legends* vol. 5 (1925), p. 153: Danel is a scribal error for *Laneiēl = Laleiēl* "angel of the night," as in the Hebrew Book of Enoch: *Layli'el she-memunneh ʿal ha-laylah.* See Hugo Odeberg, *3 Enoch* (Cambridge, 1928) p. 19 = Jellinek, *Bet ha-Midrash* vol. 5, p. 176.

114. The Gizeh Greek verrsion reads: *en Ebelsata* (Eth. *'Abelsjâîl*) *hētis estin ana meson tou Libanou kai Senisēl* (Eth. *Sênêsêr*). See R. H. Charles, *The Book of Enoch*[3] (Oxford, 1912) p. 289 and his note on p. 31.

115. 1 Enoch 6:5, the Greek version pereserved in Syncellus has *Hermonieim* and *Hermōm (sic).* The Gizeh version 13:7 *Hermōnieim.* See Charles, *loc. cit.,* pp. 278 and 289. The plural *ḥermônîm* also Ps 42:7. See Ps 89:13 LXX and M. Abel, *Géographie de la Palestine* (Paris, 1933) p. 357 who distinguishes *Hermōnieim* from *Aermōn,* ibid. pp. 347f.

116. In the manner of *'îš miṣrî,* Exod 2:11, 2 Sam 23:21? See Virolleaud, *La Légende Phén. de Danel,* pp. 87f.

117. Charles, *loc. cit.,* p. 14.

118. I Aq 4:163ff.

119. I Aq 1:42ff.

120. See Ludwig Köhler, "Ein hebräisch-arabischer Brunnen-Terminus," *ZDPV* 60 (1937) 135ff.: Arabic *iblātun,* "Eindeckung eines Brunnenmundes" (to which perhaps the verb in Ezek 31:15 may be related?). Cf. *'ābēl māyim* 2 Chr 16:4 (see 1 Kgs 15:20) and I Aq 3:152 *qr mym.*

121. *Hrnm* occurs in a Ramesside list as a place-name in Syria, see W. F. Albright, *JBL* 58 (1939) 97, and Virolleaud, *Syria* 21 (1940) 271, n. 4 who refers to Pap. Anast. I. (Hugo Gressmann, *Altorient. Texte zum A. T.*[2] [Berlin and Leipzig, 1926] p. 103), and again *Syria* 22 (1941) 7. I owe the reference to Dr. H. L. Ginsberg.

122. See now on Gen. 6:2, U. Cassuto, *"Maʿaseh Benei ha-'Elohim u-Venot ha-'Adam,"* in *Essays presented to J. H. Hertz* (London, 1944) pp. 35–44, and his commentary *Me-'Adam ʿad Noaḥ* pp. 170ff.

123. = *Saharie'el,* "angel of the moon." On the list of angels see Adolphe Lods, *Le Livre d' Hénoch* (Paris, 1892) pp. 106f., and Charles, *loc. cit.,* p. 17.

124. Ginzberg, *Legends,* vol. 5, p. 153: "one name fell out." Cf. ibid. his remark about the two traditions or sources combined in the book of Enoch, one enumerating *twenty* archangels (cf. the list in *3 Enoch,* ed. Odeberg *loc.*

cit. Jellinek, *loc. cit.*, transl. Ginzberg, *Legends*, vol. 1, p. 140), the other *ten* (see Ginzberg, *Eine unbekannte Sekte* [1922] p. 243 where *y.* ʿ*Erubin* 1 f. 19d *maḥaneh* ʾ*elohim* ʿ*aśarah* is so interpreted. Cf. idem, *Legends* vol. 5, p. 23).

125. See W. F. Albright and G. E. Mendenhall, *JNES* 1 (1942) 227ff.

126. Cf. *Gen. R.* 26:5 (ed. Theodor-Albek, p. 247): *"bĕnê hāʾĕlōhîm"—R. Shim*ʿ*on ben Yoḥai qarei le-hon benei dayyanah* and Ginzberg, *Die Haggada bei den Kirchenvätern* (Berlin, 1900) p. 75. Cf. Eusebius, *Evang. Praep.* I 10, 13 on the Phoenician genii Misor and Suduc *(mîšôr* and *ṣedeq),* attributes of a judge (Isa 11:4; Ps 45:7f. and 67:5). It is perhaps not without significance that the name of Danel's son suggests "law-abiding" or "law-enjoining." See note 47.

127. I Aq 1:22ff. and II Aq 5:6ff.

128. Dan 4:10, 14, 20; 1 Enoch 1:5; 14:1; 20:1 etc. Ginzberg, *Eine unbek. Sekte,* p. 243, n. 4 translates: "the Wakeful," those who sleep not (1 Enoch 39:12f.; 40:2; 61:12; and esp. 71:7), for sleep is a sign of mortality, cf. *Legends* vol. 5, p. 80, n. 25.

129. See Charles, *The Book of Jubilees* (London, 1902) p. 36 and Ginzberg, *Legends* vol. 5, p. 154.

130. *Clementis Romani Homiliae* VIII. c. 12 and 13, ed. A. R. M. Dressel (Göttingen, 1853) p. 188f.

131. *Commodiani Carmina* I c. 3, ed. B. Dombart (Vienna, 1887), p. 7:

> Cum Deus omnipotens exornasset mundi naturam,
> Uisitari uoluit terram ab angelis istam . . .
> Ab ipsis in terra artis prolatae fuere,
> Et tingere lanas docuerunt et quaeque geruntur.

132. *Div. Institutiones* II.15, *PL* 6, p. 330. Cf. *Epitome Div. Inst.* c. 27, ibid. p. 1035: "angelos suos misit, ut vitam hominum excolerent, eosque ab omni malo tuerentur."

133. XXV.3, transl. by M. Gaster (London, 1899) p. 53. See also Yalk. Gen 44 (transl. Ginzberg, *Legends* vol. 1, 149): *ten lanu reshut ve-nadur* ʿ*im ha-beriyyot ve-tir*ʾ*eh* ʾ*eikh* ʾ*anu meqaddeshin shemekha.*

134. Minos, lawgiver of Crete, was *Dios megalou oaristēs* (*Odyss.* 19.179) which already Clement of Alexandra, *Stromata* II.5 (*PG* vol. 8, p. 952f.) compares, or rather traces to Exod 33:11. See Ginzberg, *Legends* vol. 5, p. 207, n. 4 on "the beloved of God," and Fr. Dornseiff, *ZAW* 53 (1935) 166 on the lawgiver as *aitas* or *eispnēlas* of the godhead. Cf. Ugaritic: *ǵzr n*ʿ*m* ʾ*ilm wnšm, SS* 17f. and the passages quoted by Virolleaud, *loc. cit.*, p. 89.

135. *Din* may mean also "torture" (see Saul Lieberman, *JQR* 35 [1944] 15, n. 99) or else, in the Arabic sense, "religion." See II Targ. Yer. Gen 10:9 where Nimrod demands of the people to follow an idolatry of his own making: ʾ*idbequ be-dino de-Nimrod.* The "fallen" Danel could be blamed for all manner of cruelty or impiety.

136. Syr. Apoc. of Baruch 56:13 and 1 Enoch 14:5 and 69:28. Cf. also Jude 6 and 2 Peter 2:4.
137. 1 Enoch 10:11ff. and Jub 5:6,10.
138. The interval of their being bound is ten thousand years in 1 Enoch 18:16 and 21:6. *Deut. R.* 11 end: *ʿUzah ve-ʿAzaʾel . . . talita ʿotam bein ha-ʾareṣ la-raqiaʿ* (cf. Yalk. Gen. 44) is embroidered in later legends. The giants are bound with "chains of iron" to "mountains of darkness" and shrink to fingerlings each year and then grow once more to their former size. They teach sorcery to those who consort with them. See introd. *Agadath Bereschith* ed. Buber, p. XXXIX as corrected by Ginzberg, *Hazofeh* 4 (1915) 30 (ibid., *Lebends* vol. 5, p. 171) on the basis of a citation from *Ḥuppat ʾEliyahu* in Jacob Sikli's *Yalquṭ Talmud Torah*. See *Hazofeh* 3 (1914) 9 and now also David S. Sassoon, *ʾOhel David* (Oxford, 1932) II, p. 627b. Cf. the *ṭurei ḥashokhaʾ* and *shalshalʾei de-parzelaʾ* and *ʾulpin ḥarashin u-qesamin li-venei nashaʾ*, a favorite theme of the *Zohar* I 9b; 58a; 126a; III 208a and esp. 212a and *Zohar Ḥadash*, Ruth (ed. Berditchev, 1825, f. 96c). Bizarre items of still later sources are assembled in *Yalkut Rubeni* on Gen 6:2 (ed. Lemberg, 1860, p. 53b) and discussed by M. Grünbaum, *ZDMG* 31 (1877) 235ff. = *Ges. Aufsätze zur Sprach- und Sagenkunde* (Berlin, 1901) pp. 72f.
139. See Ignaz Goldziher, *Mythology among the Hebrews* (London, 1877) pp. 198ff, and appended to it: H. Steinthal, "The Original Form of the Legend of Prometheus," ibid. p. 363ff. Already Josephus, *Ant.* I. 73 observed that the deeds ascribed by tradition to the fallen angels resemble Greek myths.
140. On the angelic names of the patriarchs and their wives in the Book of Jubilees, see C. Kaplan, *AJSL* 50 (1934) 176.
141. In the Ugaritic poem, *Pǵt* or Danel's daughter is repeatedly lauded as "knowing the course of the stars" (*ydʿt hlk kbkbm,* I Aq 2:51f., 56). In Jub 4:20 her name is *Ednî,* but in 1 Enoch 85:3 *Ednā,* like the wife of Methuselah (Jub 4:27).
142. See Ginzberg, *Die Haggada,* p. 72, and *Legends* vol. 5, p. 156: "In the entire Tannaitic literature and in both Talmudim no mention is made of Enoch."
143. *Gen. R.* 25:1, ed. Theodor-Albek, p. 238.
144. Yalkut Gen. 44 = Jellinek, *Beth ha-Midrash* IV, 127f. In later editions (but not in the *ed. pr.,* cf. Ginzberg, *Legends* vol. 5, p. 169, n. 10) the source is given as *Abkir.* On this midrash, see A. Marmorstein, in *Devir* 1 (Berlin, 1923) 141.
145. The new-born babes *Šḥr* and *Šlm,* as soon as they are weaned, stretch "one lip to earth and one to heaven"—or in a parallel passage, "one row of teeth to the ground, and one to the stars" *(špt lʾarṣ špt lšmm, [šn lšdm] šn lkbkbm)* "and into their mouth went the birds of the air and the fish of the sea," *SS* 61f. Hans Bauer, *Die alphab. Keilschrifttexte von Ras Schamra* (Berlin, 1936) p. 32. See H. L. Ginsberg, "Notes on 'The Birth of the

Gracious and Beautiful Gods,' " *JRAS* (Jan. 1935) 45ff. and idem, *Or* 5 (1936) 187.

In 1 Enoch 7:2 the giants have the height of three thousand ells, in Test. 12 Patr., Reuben 5:7 they reach to heaven. See Ginzberg, *Eine unbek. Sekte,* p. 13 and *Legends* vol. 5, p. 181.

146. Yalk. Gen. 44 (ed. princeps, Salonica, 1526).
147. *Midrash Bereshit Rabbati,* ed. Ch. Albek (Jerusalem, 1940) p. 30f.
148. *The Chronicles of Jeraḥmeel,* transl. by M. Gaster (London, 1899) c. 25, p. 54.
149. Sanchuniathon was said by Philo to be *anēr palaitatos kai tōn Trōikōn chronōn, hōs phasi, presbyteros* (Eusebius, *Ev. pr.* I 9) which would place him about 1200 B.C. Before the finds of Ras Shamra, he was dismissed as pure fiction (see Otto Gruppe, *Die griech. Culte und Mythen in ihren Beziehungen zu den orient. Religionen* [Leipzig, 1887] p. 375) or set in the Seleuicid era (so E. Renan, "Mémoire sur l'origine et le caractère véritable de l'histoire phénicienne qui porte le nom de Sanchoniathon," *Mém. de l'Acad. des inscript. et belles-lettres* 23 [1858] part 2, pp. 241–334). Contrast W. F. Albright, *BASOR* 70 (1938) 24 on the name *Sknytn* and the problem of date. O. Eissfeldt, *Ras Schamra und Sanchunjaton* (Halle S., 1939) p. 67ff. infers a date before 700 B.C. or nearly a millennium before Philo of Byblos who lived under Hadrian. Eusebius of Caesarea wrote his *Ev. Pr.* ca. 320 C.E.
150. Such an approach is associated with the name of Euhemeros of Messene (ca. 300 B.C.) and is of course the contribution of the Greek "translator," or Philo. See Eissfeldt *loc. cit.,* pp. 29, 83–88, 122ff. The theory was known to the Jewish schools, cf. Ginzberg, *Legends* vol. 5, p. 150.
151. Among the later descendants of Agreus there appears also Agrotes to which usually Gen 25:27 *ʾîš yōdeaʿ ṣayid ʾîš śādeh* is compared. See Carl Clemen, *Die phönikische Religion nach Philo von Byblos* (Leipzig, 1939) p. 52, and Eissfeldt, *loc. cit.,* p. 147, n. 1. The midrash of R. Abbahu on the same verse: *ṣeidoni sodani* (*Gen. R.* 63:10, ed. Theodor, p. 693) resembles the Greek wordplay *agreutēs agrotēs* (or *agrōtēs*), the latter in the sense of *agrestis* or *ferus,* "uncouth" or "savage." Abbahu liked to play with Greek words, see S. Lieberman, *Greek in Jewish Palestine* (New York, 1942) pp. 21f. Cf. idem, in *Annuaire de l'Institut de Philologie et d'Histoire Orientales* published by the Université Libre de Bruxelles in New York, 1944, vol. 7, p. 397ff. See also *b. Ber.* 44b, *b. Men.* 71a, and *b. Niddah* 12ab where Raba, resident of "The City" or Maḥoza, nicknames Papa, who lived in the townlet of Naresh: *sodani.* It is not exactly a compliment, as gentle Rashi suggests: *talmid ḥakham ʿal shem "sôd yhwh lîrēʾāyw"* (Ps 25:14); *b. Niddah* ibid., differently *b. Ber.* ibid., combined *b. Men.* ibid.), but on the other hand, as the Gaonim assure us: *ʾeino mekhoʿar liqraʾ leven kefar ʿirani ve-sodani.* See *Otzar ha-Gaonim,* ed. B. M. Lewin (Haifa, 1928) vol. 1, pp. 85 and 104.

152. Obviously *ṣîdôn* is derived from *ṣayid,* used of fishing as well as hunting. Comp. Justinus (Trogus Pompeius) 18,3,4: a piscium ubertate, nam piscem Phoenices *sidon* vocant. Cf. Eccl 9:12. The founder of *Ṣidon Yam,* one of the three districts of "Greater Sidon" (Josh 11:8 and 19:28) may be meant. See Clemen, *loc. cit.,* p. 48 and Eissfeldt, *loc. cit.,* p. 66.
153. Eusebius, *Evangelica Praeparatio* I 10,35bc (ed. E. H. Gifford, Oxford, 1903, vol. 1, p. 47f.).
154. *Chrysōr* or *Chonsōr* are corruptions of *Chousōr.*
155. Does the plural *tous adelphous* contain a trace of an original trinity of craftsmen-gods? See notes 174 and 187.
156. Usually translated: "walls of brick" (Gifford, *Preparation for the Gospel* [Oxford, 1903]), "le murs de briques" (M. J. Lagrange, *Études sur les religions sémitiques* [Paris, 1903] p. 375), "Mauern aus Ziegeln" (Clemen, *loc. cit.*). But this is refuted by the sequence, Eusebius I 10,35d, which knows in a later generation two other youths who "devised to mingle straw with the clay of bricks, and to dry them in the sun" *(epenoēsan tōi pēlōi tēs plinthou symmignyein phoryton, kai tōi hēliōi autas tersainein).* Still later men learned how to make "courts, and enclosures, and caves" or cellars, to establish "villages and sheepfolds," until at last Kronos "built a wall round his own dwelling and founded the first city, Byblos." A similar progress is described in shipbuilding: the first raft is but a rude affair, and only after agriculture had made sail and ropes possible, did the Dioscuri or Cabeiri *(kabirim)* construct a real ship. See Gruppe, *Die griech. Culte,* p. 398.

    In Attic building accounts, *plinthos* (or *plinthis*) denotes ordinary blocks of a wall, or stones squared for building. See L. D. Caskey and B. H. Hill, *Amer. Journ. of Archaeol.* 12 (1908) 186. Cf. H. G. Liddell and R. Scott, *Greek-Engl. Lex.* (new ed., Oxford, 1940) p. 1422.
157. H. Ewald, "Abhandlung über die phönikischen Ansichten von der Weltschöpfung und den geschichtlichen Werth Sanchuniathon's," *Abhandl. der Ges. der Wissensch. zu Göttingen* 5 (1851) 17f., first suggested that Meilichios is a Grecised form of the Semitic word for *sailor.* Fr. G. Movers, *Die Phönizier* (Bonn, 1841) I, p. 325 combined Meilichios with Moloch, a view which commended itself to sundry scholars including M. Mayer, in W. H. Roscher, *Lexikon der griech. und röm. Mythologie,* vol. 2 pt. 1, p. 1521, see also Höfer, ibid. vol. 2, pt. 2, p. 2561; H. Lewy, *Die semitischen Fremdwörter im Griechischen* (Berlin, 1895) p. 242f., and W. Prellwitz, *Etymologisches Wörterbuch der griech. Sprache*[2] (Göttingen, 1905) p. 286. More recently, Greek scholars seem resolved to "turn a deaf ear to all Semitic Sirens and seek an explanation nearer home," see A. B. Cook, *Zeus* (Cambridge, 1925) vol. 2, pt. 2, pp. 1091–1160 where the literature on *Zeus Meilichios* is surveyed.
158. 2 Kgs 12:13 and 22:6.
159. This is the reading in the Oxford Ms. of the Yalkut, photostats of which I

was able to consult thanks to the friendship of Professor Saul Lieberman. *Gdyrwt* can easily turn into *gzyrwt,* see Pes. Rab. c. 26f. 131b *gedeirot gedeirot shel ʾavanim* ("heaps" or "ruins," cf. Lieberman, *Yerushalmi ki-Feshuto,* p. 220) and Yalkut Jer. 300 where the parallel version reads *gezeirot shel ʾavanim.* For a translation of the printed text, see Leo Jung, *Fallen Angels in Jewish, Christian and Mohammedan Liberature* (Philadelphia, 1926) p. 105. Cf. Bernard Heller, "La Chute des Anges, Shemhazai, Ouzza et Azaël," *REJ* 60 (1910) 206, n. 1. Bialik and Ravnitzky, *Sefer ha-ʾAggadah,* rev. ed. I, p. 34 read *keshe-gozerim gezarot.*

160. *B. Moed Kat.* 11a *godelin tannur,* "to build a stove," occurs, as I am instructed again by Professor Lieberman, twice in the Palestinian Talmud as *gdr, y. Moed Kat.* 1:9 f. 80d bottom, and *y. Ned.* I end f. 37a.

161. Comp. Ezek 42:7 where *gdr* is a *wall,* not a hedge or fence. See H. Guthe, "Gader, Gadara, Gedor," *Mittheilungen und Nachrichten des deutschen Palästina Vereins* (1896) 8.: "Das Hauptwort *gader* bedeutet eine aus unbehauenen Feldsteinen ohne Mörtel aufgeführte Mauer. . . . Die Merkmale sind: unbehauene, oder doch nur roh behauene Steine, trockene Herstellung, ohne Verwendung von Mörteln."

162. Or *ḥeyyaʾ ḥeyyaʾ*. See R. Rabbinovicz, *Diqduqei Soferim* (Munich, 1874) VI, p. 346.

163. Disagreeing with Rashi *ad loc.: ve-nirʾeh be-ʿeinay she-ʾeino laḥash ʾelaʾ geʿarah . . . kedei she-yaʿaseh melaʾkhah . . . "nizhaʾ de-ʾarbaʾ" kedei le-moshkhah be-ḥevel ule-holikhah le-nahar.* As for *nizheʾ de-toraʾ hen hen* [or *nahum de-toraʾ zeʾ zeʾ] nizhaʾ de-gamlaʾ daʾ daʾ* (see the various readings in *Diqduqei Soferim*) cf. English *gee* or *haw,* in driving oxen or a team of cattle, used also as a verb, *to haw and gee,* or to *hie* horses (turn to the left) or *hup* them (in the opposite direction).

164. Cf. Martial, *Epigrams* IV, 64, 21f., describing the tranquility of a country seat

> Quem nec rumpere nauticum celeuma
> Nec clamor valet helciariorum.

The *celeuma* (or *celeusma*) is the summons or command of the *keleustēs,* the chief oarsman or boatswain, who gives the stroke to the rowers, and the *helciarius* (from *helkō,* "to pull") is one who draws small vessels up the stream.

165. Cf. Aristophanes, *The Peace* 459ff., where men bend down to the labor of pulling out Peace, as if they were to lift stones, or draw a boat up on the beach. The verb is *helkō* (470), or *exelkō* (294), or *aphelkō* (361 *tous lithous,* moving stones), and also *katagō* (458 *katage* = "bring her in," used of boats), or exactly as in our midrash *maʿalin ʾavanim ʾo śefinot.* Of course, the idea of *Peace* being hauled up is the contrivance of the comedian, but the exertions and exclamations of the workers, as they tug and labor at the ropes, are drawn from real life (I quote lines 459–63, 487–89, 517–19, and the transl. by B. B. Rogers [London, 1927] p. 42ff.):

ō eia.	*Hermes:*	Yo ho! pull away.
eia mala.	*Chorus:*	Pull away a little stronger.
ō eia.	*Hermes:*	Yo ho! pull away.
eia eti mala.	*Chorus:*	Keep it up a little longer.
ō eia, ō eia . . .	*Hermes:*	Pull, pull, pull, pull . . .
eia mala.	*Trygaeus:*	Keep it up a little longer.
ō eia.	*Hermes:*	Yo ho! pull away.
eia nē Dia . . .	*Trygaeus:*	Yes, by Zeus! a little stronger.
ō eia nyn, ō eia pas,	*Chorus:*	Pull again, every man, all he can
ō eia, eia, eia, eia, eia, eia		Pull, pull, pull, pull, pull
ō eia, eia, eia, eia, eia, pas		Pull, pull, pull, pull, all together.

The shouts become a song, cf. Apollinaris Sidonius, *Epistulae* II, 10: "chorus helciariorum / responsantibus alleluia ripis."

166. *B. Gittin* 34a, Raba dispatching a letter of divorce: "*ʾashur havu lah hayyaʾ!*" or *b. Shabb.* 119a end, the blind R. Sheshet devising how to speed his students to the Sabbath meal: *Rav Sheshet be-qayṭaʾ motiv leho le-rabbanan heikhaʾ de-maṭyaʾ shimshaʾ, be-sitvaʾ motiv la-hen le-rabbanan heikha de-maṭya ṭullaʾ ki heikhi di-lequmei hayyaʾ.*

167. See A. J. Maclean, *A Dictionary of the Dialects of Vernacular Syriac* (Oxford, 1891) p. 75: *hîyû, héyû, hayû, hayô,* "come!" Cf. Arabic *hy* and Greek *eia* in the dictionaries. The Latin *heja,* "come on!" in gentle persuasion or impatient exhortation, e.g., Virgil, *The Aeneid* IV, 569: *heia age, rumpe moras!* "Up ho! break off delay!" or ibid. IX,38. Horace, *Satires* II,6,23f., illustrating the annoyances of living in the metropolis where at the most inopportune of hours one may be whisked to court:

> . . . Romae sponsorem me rapis: "*heia,*
> ne prior officio quisquam respondeat, urge."

The dictionaries list in this sense also *ḥayyaʾ de-ʾahan sabaʾ de-ʿavdat leih shoshivtaʾ, y. Ab. Z.* 3:1 42c, also *y. Pea* 1:1, 15d, however the passage is still puzzling, see *Gen. R.* 59:4 and the note of Theodor p. 633, and Louis Ginzberg, *Genizah Studies* vol. 2 (New York, 1929) p. 335.

168. R. Abba expediting preparations for Sabbath: *ʾashur hyyʾ! ʾashur hyyʾ!* "hie thee, quick!" *b. Shabb.* 119a and Rashi *ad loc.* Cf. the repeated *eia eia* or *iō iō* or *iou iou.*

169. The god invoked with the cry *iē, iēios,* also *ēios,* epithet of Apollo. *Euios* or *Euhius,* name of Bacchus, from the cry *euai, euoi.*

170. *M. Ḳid.* 4:14 (82a): *ha-sappanim rubban ḥasidim.*

171. In driving oxen one will use the exclamation: *gee!* But on the lips of the driver, *Gee!* may also be an abbreviation of Jesus.

172. See above note 30. One may perhaps recall in this connection also the last item in the argument of the *dikologos* before Hadrian: *ʾein tov min ha-dibbur ba-ʿolam . . . ʾiluleʾ ha-dibbur loʾ hayu ha-sefinot poreshot ba-yam.* Yalk. Numbers 738 and Proverbs 946.

173. E.g. II Aq 5:18f. and 23f.

174. See H. Bauer, *OLZ* (1934) p. 245, and *ZAW* 53 (1935) 57: Akkadian *ḫassu* "astute, discerning"; cf. Maisler, *Tarbiz* 5 (1934) 378f. Perhaps the third name *Hyn* betokens an original triad of gods: *Cunning, Clever,* and *Quick,* a trace of which seems to survive in Rabbinic and Mohammedan legend. See note 187 and note 155.

175. *Ḥāṣāṣ,* "stones" or "gravel," Prov 20:17, Lam 3:17; *ḥoṣeṣ,* "to break up" (Rabbinic Hebrew: "to partition"), perhaps also "to array" (Prov 30:27 LXX *eutaktōs*). Cf. *b. Baba Bat.* 2a, *mai*ʾ *meḥiṣah goda*ʾ *kide-tanya*ʾ *meḥiṣat ha-kerem she-nifreṣah* ʾ*omer lo gedor gādēr haddēḥûyâ,* Targ. Ps 62:4 *guda*ʾ *re*ʿ*i*ʿ*atah.* An angel Gadreel is mentioned in 1 Enoch 69:6, but his is the business of deadly weapons, not stonework.

176. *B. Niddah* 61a: *Siḥon ve-*ʾ*Og benei* ʾ*Aḥiyah bar Shemḥazai havo,* cf. *b. Moed Kat.* 20b: *R. Ḥiyya leḥod R.* ʾ*Aḥiyah lĕḥod.* The gutterals *ḥ* and *h* are easily interchangeable: hence *hyy*ʾ *wḥyyh* (R. Martini, *Pugio Fidei* [Leipzig, 1687] p. 938) or *hyy*ʾ *whyy*ʾ (Jellinek VI, p. XXIV, n. 1). Yalk. Gen 44 = Jellinek IV, 127: *hyww*ʾ *whyy*ʾ. If authentic, perhaps related to the midrashim on *haḥiwwî* (Josh 9:7): *she-*ʿ*asu ma*ʿ*aseh ḥivei;* "cunning as a serpent," *y. Ḳid.* IV, 65c; cf. *b. Shabb.* 85a on Gen 36:2 (and 21), and on *hā*ʿ*awwîm,* Deut 2:23 in *Gen. R.* 26:7, ed. Theodor, p. 254; also the various derivations of the name *ḥawwāh* Gen 3:20 (*Gen. R.* 20:11 cf. Wellhausen, *Die Comp. des Hexateuchs*[3] [Berlin, 1899] p. 305, and Ginzberg, *Legends,* vol. 5, p. 91 and 134). "Charmer," "seducer," even "skilled in words" (verb *ḥwh*) would not be an inappropriate name. However, *waw* may be a scribal error for *yod. Midr. Ber. Rabbati,* ed. Albek p. 31 reads *hyh*ʾ *whyy*ʾ, cf. however ibid. p. 30.

177. Num 11:26f.

178. *B. Sanh.* 98b; *b. Ḥullin* 19a.

179. 2 Timothy 3:8; Targ. Y. Exod 1:15 and 7:11; *b. Men.* 85a. Ginzberg, *Eine Unbek. Sekte,* p. 240, n. 3 and *Legends,* vol. 5, p. 425, points out that the older form of the legend knew only of Jannes.

180. Ḳurʾān S. 21:96 (and 18:93).

181. S. 28:76.

182. S. 5:30. The names of the "two sons of Adam" are not mentioned in the Ḳurʾān, "perhaps long antedating it," so Charles C. Torrey, *The Jewish Foundation of Islam* (New York, 1933) p. 50.

183. See J. Bergmann, *MGWJ* 46 (1902) 531ff. Contrast Josef Horovitz, *Koranische Untersuchungen* (Berlin and Leipzig, 1926) p. 148, n. 1.

184. Especially Ṭabarī, *Tafsīr, ad loc.,* translated and discussed by E. Littmann, "Hārūt and Mārūt," in *Festschrift Friedr. C. Andreas* (Leipzig, 1916) pp. 70–87.

185. Abraham Geiger, *Was hat Mohammed aus dem Judenthume aufgenommen?*[2] (Leipzig, 1902) pp. 104–6.

186. Littmann, *loc. cit.,* p. 87 praises as a particularly fine feature of the saga, "wie sie uns im islamischen Gewande vorliegt, dass die Engel, die sich sündenfrei fühlen und pharisäisch auf die schwache Menschheit hinabse-

hen, für ihren Hochmut bestraft werden dadurch dass sie, mit menschlicher Schwäche behaftet, dieser auch nicht widerstehen können." "Dieser ethische Zug" is precisely the burden of Yalk. Gen 44 or *Gemar[a] Derekh Ereṣ* (Sassoon, *ʾOhel David* vol. 2, p. 626b, cf. ibid., p. 627b) = *Masekhtot Kallah* ed. Michael Higger, p. 231.

187. Some versions speak of *three* angels who were sent to earth (Littmann, *loc. cit.*, p. 81), their names, according to Thaʿlabī, being *Azza, Azabiya,* and *Azriyail* (Heller, *REJ* 60 [1910] 209). Cf. *Seder Eliahu Zuta* c. 25 ed. M. Friedmann, p. 49: *ʿUzah ve-ʿUzi ve-ʿAzaʾel,* and 1 Enoch 69:5 *Asbeêl ʿAzbiʾel.* See above note 155 and note 174, and Ginzberg, *Legends,* vol. 5, p. 170.

188. Armaros is taken to go back to *har marot* = Mārūt, so Jos. Halévy, *JA* 19 (1902) 148ff.

189. In the Slavonic Book of Enoch, the angels Orioch and Marioch are commanded to guard the revelations of Enoch. To this pair W. Bousset, *Religion des Judentums*[2] (Berlin, 1906) p. 560, would trace Hārūt and Mārūt. Similarly Jos. Horovitz, "Jewish Proper Names and Derivatives in the Koran," *HUCA* 2 (1925) 164f., and his *Koran. Untersuchungen,* p. 147f. See however Ginzberg, *Legends, loc. cit.*, p. 160.

190. So Paul de Lagarde, *Gesammelte Abhandlungen* (Leipzig, 1866) p. 15, and Fr. C. Andreas, see Littmann, *loc. cit.*, p. 84. These beneficent genii are female, their names mean "perfection" and "deathlessness," and they represent the reward promised to the blessed after death, all very unlike Hārūt and Mārūt. Furthermore, the hypothesis would make Muḥammad acquainted with the Old Iranian or Avestan form of the names, instead of the Middle Persian or Pahlavi, *Khurdāt* and *Amurdāt,* see Horovitz, *HUCA* 2, p. 64, and *Koran. Untersuchungen,* p. 147.

191. Horovitz, *HUCA* 2, p. 163, and *Koran. Untersuchungen,* p. 106.

192. Geiger, *loc. cit.*, p. 179.

193. A. J. Wensinck, *Enc. of Islam* (London and Leyden, 1927) vol. 2, pp. 272f.

194. E.g., II Aq 5:18f.

195. So probably Isa 3:3 *ḥăkam ḥărāšîm,* as the parallel *nĕbôn lāḥaš* would suggest. Cf. Targ. and Syr. Exod 22:17 *ḥarašaʾ laʾ taḥei.*

196. 1 Enoch 7:1, 8:3, 65:6. See the following note and note 138.

197. Tanh. Bereshit 12, as emended by Ginzberg, *Legends,* vol. 5, p. 152: "*ʾanšê haššēm*" (Gen 6:4) *melammed she-hayu moridin ḥamah u-levanah ve-ʿośin keshafim. ʿAleihem huʾ she-ʾamar "hēmmâ hāyû bĕmōrĕdê-ʾôr"* (Job 24:13)—*hemmah hagibborim* (cf. Gen 6:4) *she-hayu qashin u-moridin u-mekhashfin "wayyōʾmĕrû lāʾēl sûr mimmennû wĕdaʿat dĕrākeykā lōʾ ḥāpāṣnû mahšadday kî-naʿabdennû"* (Job 24:14f). Cf. Midrash Hag-Gadol Gen., ed. Schechter, p. 131: *ʾAmar Rav ʾEliezer: she-hayu moridin ḥamah u-levanah ve-ʿosin bahem keshafim she-neʾemar, "hēmmâ hāyû bĕmōrĕdê-ʾôr." ʾAl tiqraʾ "bĕmōrĕdê-ʾôr" ʾelaʾ "bĕmōrîdê-ʾôr."* Seder Eliahu Zuta c. 25 ed. Friedmann, p. 49: *ʿAzah ve-ʿUzi ve-ʿAzaʾel she-yaredu la-ʾareṣ ve-ḥamedu benot ha-ʾadam ve-heḥetiʾu ʾotam ve-limmedu ʾotam keshafim she-moridin*

ba-hen ḥamah u-levanah maʿaseh yaday u-maseru la-hem. See 3 Enoch, ed. Jellinek, *Bet ha-Midrash,* vol. 5, p. 172f.: *ʾUzaʾ ve-ʿAzaʾel hayu melammedin lahem keshafim she-hayu moridin . . . ḥamah u-levanah kokhavim u-mazzalot la-ʿamod lifneihem mi-yeminam umi-semoʾlam le-shammesh ba-hem ke-derekh she-hayu meshammeshim lifnei ha-Qadosh Barukh Huʾ she-neʾemar "wĕkŏl-ṣĕbāʾ haššāmayim ʿōmēd ʿālāyw mîmînô ûmiśśĕmōʾlô"* (1 Kgs 22:19). Cf. Pirke R. Eliezer c. 22: *ha-moredim she-maredu ba-Maqom,* and Tanh. Buber I, p. 26 on Gen 6:4 *"ʾanšê haššēm" she-hayu qashim u-moredim be-ha-Qadosh Barukh Huʾ,* (cf. also the idioms *b. Ber.* 48a *laʾ meqabbelei marut* or *Gen. R.* 55:7 *marutaʾ de-ʿalmaʾ* which Job 21:14, used in these midrashim, is defying).

Less perceptible are the echoes about the descent in the generation of *Jared* (Jub 4:14; 1 Enoch 6:6 and 106:13) when the very depth of *degradation* was reached: *ve-lamah niqraʾ shemo Yered she-be-yamayv yaredu doro le-madregah ha-taḥtonah,* Agadath Bereshith, p. XXXVII f. See Ginzberg, *Legends,* vol. 5, p. 153.

198. Yalk. Gen. 44; Ber. Rabbati ed. Albek, p. 31; R. Martini, *Pugio Fidei* (Leipzig, 1687) p. 938.

199. E. A. Speiser, "The Name *Phoinikes,*" *Language* 12 (1936) 121–26. (see also W. F. Albright, in the W. G. Leland volume, *Studies in the History of Culture* (Menasha, Wis., 1942) pp. 25f. However, the association of *bigdei ṣivʿonim* with Azael may be also due to their excitatory effects, Prof. S. Lieberman referring me to *m. Zabim* 2:2, *b. Yeb.* 76a, and *b. Ab. Z.* 20ab.

200. Eusebius, *Ev. Pr.* I 10, 34d: *Samēmroumos ho kai Hypsouranios kai Ousōos.* See Clemen, *loc. cit.,* p. 21f.

201. Usoos is a personification of the coastal city of Tyre, Egyptian *ʾU-ṯu,* Amarna *Uzu,* Assyrian *ú-šu-ú,* Greek *Palae-tyrus.* The first to suggest it was T. K. Cheyne, "The Connection of Esau and Usöos," *ZAW* 17 (1897) 189. On the site cf. Eduard Meyer, *Gesch. des Altertums,*[2] vol. 2, pt. 2 (Stuttgart 1931): "der Tyros gegenüberliegende Vorort *Usu* . . . von den Griechen Palaityros genannt, was dann den Irrtum erzeugt hat, ursprünglich habe Tyros hier gelegen." M. Noth, "Die Wege der Pharaonenheere in Palästina und Syrien," *ZDPV* 60 (1937) 219: "das *ušu* der ass. Königsinschriften, das . . . nach Sanherib, Taylorzyl. II 40 zweifelsfrei als die der Inselstadt Tyrus gegenüberliegende Festlandssiedlung zu bestimmen ist, damit das *Palaityros* der Klassischen Autoren." See also on the name W. F. Albright, *The Vocalization of the Egyptian Syllabic Orthography* (New Haven, 1934) p. 35.

Samemrumos must stand in some relation with *šmm rmm,* the one of the three districts of greater Sidon over which Bodashtart, in his temple inscription, describes himself as reigning. See Charles C. Torrey, in his first publication of the "Phoenician Royal Inscription," *JAOS* 23 (1902) 159ff. and again with new observations ibid. 57 (1937) 408, and Eissfeldt, *loc. cit.,* pp. 62–67: "Schamemrumim, Hoher Himmel, ein Stadteil von Gross-Sidon," and Clemen, *loc. cit.,* p. 47.

202. Samemrumos is said to have settled in (continental) Tyre, and to have opposed his brother Usoos *(stasiasai de pros ton adelphon Ousōo)* who, driven into the sea, founded the island-city of Tyre. This is probably the historical kernel of the tale about the tempest which ignited the trees of Tyre, whereupon "Usoos took a tree, and having stripped off the branches, first was so bold as to venture upon it into the sea" *(prōton tolmēsai eis thalattan embēnai)*. See Eusebius, *loc. cit.*, I 10, 35a, and Nonnos of Panopolis, *Dionysiaca* 40, 444–634 who makes Heracles help the Tyrians to build a ship and establish themselves upon the islands near Tyre on the sea *(anchi Tyrou para ponton)*. See Eissfeldt, *loc. cit.*, pp. 65 and 134ff.

On Tyre as the seat of the Sidonian government, and the capital of the Sidonians, and on the latter as a synonym of Phoenicians, see W. F. Albright, in the Leland volume, pp. 33f.

203. *ʿUzaʾ ve-ʿAzaʾel, b. Yoma* 67b; so also 3 Enoch, ed. Jellinek, vol. 5, p. 172 and again p. 173; Agg. Bereschit, p. XXXIX, and ibid. p. XXXVIII *ʿUzaʾ ve-ʿUziʾel; Masekhet Kallah Rabbati* ed. Higger, p. 239 *ʿUzaʾ ve-ʿUziʾel* cf. Targ. Y. Gen 6:4 *ʿUziʾel* and Sed. Eliahu Zuta ed. Friedmann, p. 49 *ʿAzah ve-ʿUzi ve-ʿAziʾel.* Otherwise *ʿAzah ve-ʿAzaʾel* Deut. R. end; or *ʿAzah ve-ʿAzaʾel* Pes. R. c. 34f 159a, so also Jellinek, vol. 1, 129, Jacob Sikli (*Hazofeh* III, p. 9 and Sassoon, *ʾOhel David,* vol. 2, p. 626b and 627b), and so consistently in the Zohar I 9b, 19b, 23a, 25b, 37a, 55a, 58a, 126a. Perhaps the spelling *ʿAzaʾ* aims at a differentiation from *ʿUzaʾ sar shel Miṣrayim?* Jellinek, vol. 1, p. 39.

204. I find Ewald, *loc. cit.*, p. 48, first called attention to Targ. Y. Gen 6:4, although he fully endorsed J. Scalinger's identification of Usoos with Esau. Discussing the names *Shemḥazai ve-ʿUziʾel,* Ewald wonders: "sollte man vermuten, noch in diesem entfernten Gebiete sei ein Andenken an jene . . . phönikischen *Semrum* (sic) und *Usoos* gekommen, und diese beiden Namen seien . . . nur wenig umgebildet."

205. Eusebius, I 10, 33d: *zōa noera, kai eklēthē Sōphasēmin* (rectius *Zōphēsamin*) *tout estin ouranou katoptai.*

206. Esth 1:14; 2 Kgs 25:19 = Jer 52:25. Cf. Gen 32:31 and 33:10; Exod 24:10 and 33:20; Judg 6:22 and 13:22; Isa 6:5. The verb *ḥzh* Exod 24:11; Num 24:4; Ps 17:15; Job 19:26. See also 2 Chr 26:5 *hammēbîn birʾōt hāʾĕlōhîm,* weakened to *yirʾat hāʾĕlōhîm* in LXX, Syr. and Targ., also *y. Soṭa* IX 13 f. 24b. Cf. 1 Enoch 39:12f. and esp. 71:7 on the angels who "guard the throne of His glory," and 40:2ff. on the four presences or *malʾakhei ha-panim* (Isa 63:9). See *Seder Eliahu Rabba,* ed. Friedmann p. 163: *ʾein malʾakhei ha-sharet roʾin ʾoto, she-ʾafilu ḥayyot nośeʾot kisʾo ʾein roʾot ʾet ha-kavod.* Cf. what powers accrued to the *mistakkel be-ziv ha-shekhinah,* 3 Enoch ed. Jellinek, *loc. cit.*, vol. 5, p. 172. Is *ṣapah la-merkavah* (*b. Meg.* 24b) such a quest to be as the angels? Cf. Tanh. Buber I p. 141: *raʾah ʾet ha-Qadosh Barukh Huʾ ve-ʾet ḥadrei ha-merkavah,* cf. also *Seder Eliahu Rabba* p. 161: *roʾin shekhinah mi-bifnim . . . ha-nikhnasin be-kiseʾ kavod shelo.* See Gershom G. Scholem, *Major Trends in Jewish Mysticism* (Jer-

salem, 1941) pp. 45ff. and 355. On the spelling of the name Semjâzâ or Samîazâz (*Semiaza* and *Semiazas*), see Charles, *The Book of Enoch*, p. 17. *Yalkuṭ* ed. princ. reads *škḥzy; b. Niddah* 61a *šmḥzʾy;* R. Martini, *Pugio Fedei* p. 938 *šmḥwzy* and *šmḥzʾ;* Bahya b. Asher, *Beiʾur ʿal ha-Torah* (Fano, 1507; end *Ḥuqqat*) has *šmḥzʾl.*

207. See Ginzberg, *Legends,* vol. 5, p. 152, n. 56.

208. Cf. *b. Yoma* 67b: *Tanaʾ debei R. Yishmaʿʾel ʿAzaʾzel mekhapper ʿal maʿaseh ʿUzaʾ ve-ʿAzaʾel* and Yalk. Gen 44: *Shaʾalu talmidayv ʾet R. Yosef mahu ʿAzaʾel. ʿAmar lahem . . . u-lekhakh hayu Yisraʾel maqrivin qorbanot be-yom ha-kippurim ʾayil* [i.e. *seʿir*] *ʾeḥad le-Yhwh she-yekhapper ʿal Yisraʾel ve-ʾayil [seʿir] ʾeḥad le-ʿAzaʾel she-yisbol ʿavonoteihem shel Yisraʾel ve-huʾ ʿAzaʾzel she-ba-Torah.* The mention of the Palestinian school of R. Ishmael about the middle of the second century C.E., and of Rab Joseph bar Hiyya (d. 333), successor of Rabba b. Nahmani in the Babylonian school of Pumbeditha, may help to indicate the times and the places in which these traditions were current among the Jews.

10

The Biblical Book of Lamentations in the Context of Near Eastern Lament Literature

W. C. Gwaltney, Jr.

I. INTRODUCTION

The biblical book of Lamentations has enjoyed a surprising renewal of interest in recent years. In extensive studies over the past twenty years the text, philology, and theology of Lamentations have received the lion's share of attention.[1] Other questions remain unanswered, however. What are we to make of the five compositions comprising Lamentations in terms of poetic analysis? May we reconstruct these compositions in a metrical pattern as *Biblica Hebraica* did? Is Freedman's syllable-count method[2] to be preferred to the older system of counting stresses? May we even use the concept of meter in regard to Hebrew and Near Eastern poetry? What are the characteristics of Near Eastern poetry anyway? The question of poetry, metrics, and the use of acrostics is far from settled.

Another matter of serious note has been treated in the commentaries in a somewhat cavalier manner. What are the Near Eastern antecedents of the kind of literature we find in the biblical book of Lamentations? To date only one serious attempt (that of McDaniel[3]) has appeared in print to explore the claim of Kramer:

> There is little doubt that it was the Sumerian poets who originated and developed the "lamentation" genre—there are Sumerian examples dating possibly from as early as the Third Dynasty of Ur . . . and as late as the Parthian period

Reprinted by permission from William W. Hallo, James C. Moyer, and Leo G. Perdue, eds., *Scripture in Context II* (Winona Lake, Ind.: Eisenbrauns, 1983), 191–211.

. . . and that the Biblical Book of Lamentations, as well as the "burden" laments of the prophets, represent a profoundly moving transformation of the more formal and conventional Mesopotamian prototypes.[4]

Ten years later Kramer wrote:

But there is little doubt that the biblical *Book of Lamentations* owes no little of its form and content to its Mesopotamian forerunners, and that the modern orthodox Jew who utters his mournful lament at the "western wall" of "Solomon's" long-destroyed Temple, is carrying on a tradition begun in Sumer some 4,000 years ago, where "By its (Ur's) walls as far as they extended in circumference, laments were uttered."[5]

Because of advances in the realm of Sumerian and Akkadian literary analysis during the 1970s, a reappraisal of Thomas F. McDaniel's pioneer critique is imperative to investigate this question of possible Sumerian antecedents. This paper will argue that McDaniel's conclusions can no longer be maintained and that Kramer's views are more defensible now than when he made them in 1959 and 1969.

McDaniel begins by pitting Kramer,[6] Gadd,[7] and Kraus[8] against Rudolph[9] and Eissfeldt[10] to demonstrate that scholarly opinion is divided on the question of Sumerian influence on the biblical Lamentations (pp. 199f.). He then proceeds to "present and evaluate the parallel motifs appearing in both the Hebrew and Sumerian works . . ." (p. 200). These "parallel motifs" number fourteen and represent terms, concepts, and choices in wording. McDaniel then judges, "All of the motifs cited from Lamentations are either attested otherwise in biblical literature or have a prototype in the literary motifs current in Syria-Palestine."[11] Furthermore McDaniel affirms that

certain dominant themes of the Sumerian lamentations find no parallel at all in this Hebrew lament. For example, one would expect to find the motif of the "evil storm" . . . somewhere in the biblical lamentation if there were any real literary dependency.[12]

Next McDaniel questions how a second millennium Mesopotamian genre could have influenced a first millennium Palestinian work. He argues that evidence is lacking to demonstrate the survival of an eastern cuneiform tradition in Iron-age Syro-Palestine. The only possible means he sees to bridge this spatial and temporal chasm is the intervening Canaanite, Hurrian, and Hittite literature whose remains have failed to provide us with exemplars of the lament genre. He also disagrees with Gadd's contention that exiled Judeans adopted this genre in Babylon. He reasons that exiled Israelites would not have been in any mood to adopt a literary form of their captors, especially since they had "their own rich local literary traditions" (p. 209). "At most the indebtedness would be the *idea* of a lamentation over a beloved city."[13] Of his arguments, the most crippling to Kramer's, Gadd's, and Kraus's position is the spatial and temporal gap separating Lamentations from the Sumerian city-laments. This chapter will summarize the history of the Mesopotamian lament genre, give a brief analysis of the later evolved lament form, and show that there no longer exists a significant spatial and temporal gap between the Mesopotamian congregational lament form and the biblical book.

II. MESOPOTAMIAN LAMENTS

Early Mesopotamian Lamentations

Following the pioneering publications of Kramer[14] and Jacobsen[15] in the 1940s and 1950s a younger group of scholars (W. W. Hallo,[16] Mark E. Cohen,[17] Raphael Kutscher,[18] Joachim Krecher,[19] and Margaret Green[20]) has delineated and analyzed the Sumero-Akkadian genre of laments in dissertations, articles, and monographs. Although it is still premature to attempt a definitive treatment of the genre, the broad outline of the development of laments in Mesopotamian culture can be shown to span nearly two millennia.

Kramer remarked as early as 1969 that the "incipient germ [of the lament genre] may be traced as far back as the days of Urukagina, in the 24th century B.C."[21] He cited a list of temples and shrines of Lagash which had been burned, looted, or otherwise defiled by Lugalzagessi as being the first step in the creation of the lament genre. No laments are extant for the Akkadian, Gutian, or Ur III eras. Laments were invented as a literary response to the calamity suffered throughout Sumer about 2000 B.C.E. immediately after the sack of Ur in the days of Ibbi-Sin, the last of the Third Dynasty rulers of Ur.

At present five Old Babylonian Sumerian city-laments form the earliest stage of the lament genre. They are the "Lamentation over the Destruction of Ur"[22] which has received the greatest amount of attention, the "Lamentation over the Destruction of Sumer and Ur,"[23] the

"Nippur Lament" to be published by Å. Sjöberg,[24] the "Uruk Lament," edition in preparation by M. Civil and M. W. Green,[25] and the "Eridu Lament," critical edition by M. W. Green.[26] The so-called "Second Lamentation for Ur," the "Ibbi-Sin Lamentation," and the "Lamentation over the Destruction of Sumer and Akkad" have all turned out to be parts of the "Lamentation over the Destruction of Sumer and Ur."[27] Nor are we including here the so-called "Curse of Agade" even though it employs lament or complaint language.[28] The usually accepted *terminus ante quem* for the five major city-laments is 1925 B.C.E.[29]

The city-laments describe one event,[30] were written largely in the Emesal dialect of Sumerian[31] by *gala*-priests, and were composed to be recited in ceremonies for razing Ur and Nippur sanctuaries in preparation for proper restoration.[32] They were not reused in later rituals and did not become a part of the priests' ritual stock of available religious poetry for liturgical use. In the Old Babylonian scribal schools they became a part of the scribal curriculum but ceased to be copied during the first millennium. Kutscher, remarking about the literary merit of these city-laments, writes, "From a literary point of view these laments display a masterful use of the classical Sumerian language, freshness of style and a sincere creative effort."[33]

The Old Babylonian *Eršemma*

The second stage in the history of the Mesopotamian lament genre occurred in the Old Babylonian era with the nearly simultaneous creation of the *eršemma*-composition and the *balag*-lament. Cohen suspects that the *eršemma*, a liturgical composition of the *gala*-priests in Emesal dialect, may have preceded the *balag* slightly on the grounds that the *eršemma* had a more compact form while the *balag* appears to have had a more composite nature.[34] Unfortunately, clear textual evidence is lacking for us to fix priority within the Old Babylonian period.

Although the term *eršemma* means "wail of the *šèm*-([Akkadian] *ḫalḫallatu*-) drum," not all *eršemma*s are completely mournful since at points the subject matter served to praise a god.[35] However, a large percentage of *eršemma*-subject matter centered on catastrophes or the dying-rising myth of Inanna, Dumuzi, or Geshtinanna.[36] Kramer as recently as 1975 published two Old Babylonian *eršemma*-incipit catalogs from the British Museum from which he isolated no less than 109 *eršemmas*.[37] Of these, about 100 are unknown to us at this time. Cohen has demonstrated that in general the Old Babylonian *eršemmas* are characterized as being a single, compact unit addressed to a single deity.[38] Cohen has also contended that the *gala*-priests, when called upon repeatedly to provide more liturgical compositions to be chanted on the occasion of rebuilding cities and temples, borrowed *eršemma* material to create new *eršemmas* and appropriated hymnic Emegir material for insertion into new *eršemmas*.[39] Also Old Babylonian *eršemmas* and *balags* occasionally shared lines of text.[40] Cohen was not able to determine the direction of this borrowing.[41] The exact Old Babylonian cultic use of the *eršemma* remains a mystery, although we may speculate that they were intoned in a liturgical context similar to that of the *balag*-laments.[42]

The Old Babylonian *Balag*

The *balag* was created as a lamentation form about 1900 B.C.E. as a literary outgrowth of the older city-lament. In support of this thesis Cohen has established a "high probability of direct relationship between the city-laments and the *balag*-lamentations"[43] by examining four factors: (1) the structure and form of city-laments and Old Babylonian *balags*,[44] (2) their content,[45] (3) their ritual use,[46] and (4) whether there was sufficient opportunity for development to occur.[47] Even though we may conclude there was a close association between the *balag*-lament and its older city-lament predecessor, we must note several differences between the two. City-laments were composed for one specific "performance" to be retired afterwards to the scribal academy as a classical work;[48] *balags* were adopted for further liturgical use and were copied over and over down into the Seleucid era. City-lament subject matter concentrated on one specific disaster in detailed description; *balags* were more general in their description of disaster and could be borrowed from city to city. City-laments were use in a narrow setting of temple demolition and reconstruction; *balags* were recited in broader contexts apparently as "congregational laments."

Although most compositions of this genre were not called by the title "*balag*" in the Old Babylonian era, five examples in which such was the case have been recovered.[49] One of these five, a *balag* to Dumuzi (CT 42, 15), was composed in the Larsa period about 1870 B.C.E.[50] Kutscher has explained this low number of labeled examples as arising from the fact that the term "*balag*" in Babylonian times designated function, not generic title. The composition was to be intoned to the accompaniment of the *balag*-instrument,[51] in all likelihood a drum.[52] Cohen observed that the unusual length of the *balag*s caused them to be written on large tablets or in a series of smaller tablets, so that the final lines with their colophons were lost in many cases, with the result that the designation "*balag*" is missing.[53] The form of the general all-purpose lament had already emerged in the Old Babylonian era even though the label "*balag*" was not always attached to the extant Old Babylonian recensions.

Kutcher's publication of YBC 4659[54] which preserves stanzas IV–XIII of the *balag, a-ab-ba ḫu-luḫ-ḫa* (Oh Angry Sea), makes clear that even in its Old Babylonian form this particular *balag* may be roughly divided in half.[55] The first half was devoted to lamentation presumably to be chanted during ceremonies at the demolition of an old temple. The second half (a hymn and prayer to Enlil) was probably "recited during the ceremonies marking the laying of the foundation to the new temple."[56] Cohen points to the concluding line in some Old Babylonian *balag*s, "This supplication . . . return the 'x-temple' to place," as indicating the use of the *balag* in temple-restoration ceremonies.[57] The Old Babylonian *balag*s also appear to have been included in liturgies for various festivals and for certain days of the month.[58]

The First Millennium *Balag* and *Eršemma*

The Middle Babylonian period marked an advance in the lament genre although documentary evidence for it is meager. In fact, none of the main Emesal hymnic types of the first millennium—the *balag,* the *eršemma,* the *šuilla,* and the *eršaḫunga*—are attested in Middle Babylonian times.[59] Several *eršemma*s were possibly composed during Kassite times, however. Cohen somewhat tentatively suggests that the joining of *balag*-laments with *eršemma*-compositions to form a new composite genre occurred at some point during the Kassite era (ca. 1600–1160 B.C.E.).

> During the Middle Babylonian period the two genres [*balag* and *eršemma*] had apparently been so closely identified with each other, presumably on the basis of ritual function, that each *balag* was assigned one *eršemma* as its new conclusion. The *eršemma* was then reworked, adopting a second concluding unit which

contained the plea to the heart of the god and the concommitant *[sic]* list of deities, although this list was drastically reduced in size from the final *kirugu* of the Old Babylonian lamentation.[60]

Interestingly, Kutscher was able to amass exemplars of the Old Babylonian *balag* titled *a-ab-ba ḫu-luḫ-ḫa* (Oh Angry Sea) for the Old Babylonian, Neo-Assyrian, Neo-Babylonian, and Seleucid periods but could not locate even a one-line scrap of Kassite origin.[61] Even the Middle Assyrian era provided two scraps consisting of eight lines of text.[62] A Middle Babylonian catalog may, however, list Kutscher's *balag* under the title *a-ab-ba ḫu-luḫ-ḫa* ^{d}*en-líl-lá*.[63]

Precisely how the text of earlier *balag*s and *eršemma*s passed into the first millennium from their Old Babylonian point of origin is not totally clear. We may postulate, however, that these compositions had become essential ingredients in liturgies and were, therefore, preserved by the clergy. At any rate, from the Neo-Assyrian period through the Seleucid, *balag-eršemma* laments are exceptionally well documented from three major sources: (1) incipit catalogs, (2) ritual calendar tablets, and (3) copies of the laments themselves together with their colophons indicating *inter alia* the nature of the genre.

During the first millennium older lament material from both *balag*s and *eršemma*s became somewhat interchangeable. Cohen was able to produce two *eršemma*s of this era which had been created from earlier *balag* material with some modification.[64] The more general term *ér* = "lament," came to be used for the wide range of lamentations in keeping with the broadening of both the form and its function.

The ritual use of the *balag-eršemma* in the first millennium was even broader than in the Old Babylonian era. Numerous texts detailing the cultic performance of *gala*-(Akkadian *kalû*-) priests reveal how the *balag-eršemma* laments were integrated into complex rituals for a variety of situations.[65] Furthermore, the *balag-eršemma*s provided the ritual wording for ceremonies conducted on certain days of the month as noted in numerous calendar texts.[66] Often on such occasions a lament was recited while offerings and libations were being presented to a deity. The *balag-eršemma* continued to be sung on the occasion of razing an old building.[67] Caplice has given us a case of a lament's being chanted as a part of a *namburbi*-ritual for warding off a portended evil.[68] Cohen has also presented other examples when an evil portent prompted a *namburbi*-ritual which included a god-appeasing lament.[69] Thus the lament served the purpose of tranquilizing the potentially destructive god so that catastrophe could be prevented. The ritual for covering the sacred kettledrum involved the singing of a *balag* with its *eršemma* accompanied by the newly covered kettledrum later on in the rite.[70] Libations and offerings were not presented on this occasion. Cohen interpreted the occasion as a formal testing of the drum.

III. ANALYSIS OF LAMENTATION FORM

City-Laments

On its most superficial level of organization the city-laments were divided into "songs" called *kirugu,* usually equated with Akkadian *šēru* = Hebrew *šîr.*[71] The number and length of these stanzas were seemingly at the composers' discretion. Each stanza, except the last, was followed by a one- or two-line unit called *gišgigal,* usually interpreted as "antiphon."[72] The *gišgigal* summarized the content of its *kirugu* or repeated a key line or two from the *kirugu.* Beyond these divisions the city-laments seem not to have had further formal external structure.[73]

Margaret Green in an unpublished Chicago dissertation[74] has discussed the poetic devices used in the city-laments.[75] Significant among these devices are: (1) the use of couplets, triplets, and even longer units of lines in which only one element is changed from line to line, (2) parallelism, (3) repeating units of a part of a line or a whole line or several lines, (4) complex interweaving of two or more refrains, and (5) use of lists. All these devices appear in Sumerian poetry of various genres and are not restricted to laments. Beyond these structural techniques two other characteristics appear to a greater or lesser extent in all five city-laments. For one thing, the composition alternates between first, second, and third persons. Such change in speaker possibly reflects the dramatic function of the city-laments. Furthermore, the dialect alternates between Emesal and standard Emegir Sumerian. This alternation has provoked a minor debate over whether the city-laments were "Emesal compositions" or "Emegir compositions."[76] Without entering the technicalities of this question, we may observe that whenever a goddess speaks the Emesal dialect is used. In spite of Green's argument, however,[77] we are not yet entitled to judge that every occurrence of Emesal implies a female speaker.

Gala-priests intoned a wide range of liturgies in the Emesal dialect even when a female speaker is not implied.[78]

Although the five preserved city-laments are quite individualized in theme and theme development as well as in style and structure, they have certain underlying themes in common.[79] The most prominent theme is destruction of the total city: walls, gates, temples, citizens, royalty, nobility, army, clergy, commoners, food, crops, herds, flocks, villages, canals, roads, customs, and rites. Life has ceased. A second common theme lies in the concept that the end has come upon Sumer by virtue of a conscious decision of the gods in assembly. The invading hordes, whether Subarians, Elamites, Amorites, or Gutians, "storm" the land by the "word" of the gods. A third theme centers around the necessary abandonment of the city by the suzerain-god, his consort, and their entourage. The lament may scold the god for his callous abandonment. The goddess in longer or shorter monologues pleads with either her divine spouse or Enlil or the council of gods to show mercy and relent. In the fourth place, the city-laments either specifically mention, or at least presume, restoration of the city or sanctuary. As a fifth common element, the chief god eventually returns to his city with his entire company. The five laments do not all handle this theme in identical fashion, but in every case the god's return is indispensable to the plot. The final common thematic element is a concluding prayer to the concerned god involving either praise, plea, imprecation against the enemy, self-abasement, or a combination of these elements.

The exact cultic circumstances for the recitation of the city-laments are not totally agreed upon. Jacobsen proposed that their "Sitz im Kultus" was the demolition of the ruins of a temple and its rebuilding.[80] Hallo[81] and Cohen[82] have followed this line of thinking. Green, however, offers the alternative that the lament was performed by the king in his priestly function at the installation ceremony when the god's statue returned to its refurbished shrine.[83] The god's leaving may not always have been caused by foreign devastation but may have been forced by needed renovations of the temple in peacetime.[84] That the five major city-laments arose from something more serious than a renovation in peacetime appears evident from the extreme violence they depict. Perhaps Green's suggestion has merit in explaining the function of Old Babylonian *balag*s and *eršemma*s. As for the king's reciting the lament before the cult image, we may question the king's acumen and literacy to read and recite both Emesal and Emegir dialects in complex poetry.

First Millennium *Balag-Eršemma*s

The first millennium composite lament form, the *balag-eršemma,* has been clarified by Kutscher in his study of the history of the long-lived *balag* called *a-ab-ba ḫu-luḫ-ḫa* (Oh Angry Sea). He shows that this *balag* originated in Old Babylonian times but was expanded for public ritual use during Neo-Assyrian, Neo-Babylonian, and Seleucid times in at least nine recensions.[85]

In terms of poetic devices this *balag* in Emesal makes use of the usual techniques: repetition, refrain, parallelism, listing, division into stanzas (unlabeled in some recensions), use of divine epithets, and apparent antiphonal performance. The *gišgigal*-unit (antiphon) is absent.

The later form of this lament may be outlined as follows:[86]

A. "Prayerful Lament," lines 1–152 (stanzas II–X)
  1. Enlil's epithets, lines 1–12 (stanza II)
  2. Nippur's and Babylon's ruin, lines 13–27 (stanza II)
  3. "How long?" plea to Enlil, lines 28–40 (stanza (III)
  4. Wailing and mourning, lines 41–48 (stanza IV)
  5. Enlil's power, lines 49–72 (stanza V)
  6. Enlil's dignity, lines 73–98 (stanzas VI–VII)
  7. "How long?" plea with "return to the land!", lines 99–118 (stanza VIII)
  8. Enlil's dignity, lines 119–25 (stanza IX)
  9. Plea to Enlil to "restore (your) heart," lines 126–52 (stanza X)

B. Hymn to Enlil, lines 153–236 (stanzas XI–XVII)
  1. Enlil sleeps, lines 153–59 (stanza XI)
  2. List of devastated areas of the city, lines 160–71 (stanza XI)
  3. Let Enlil arise!, lines 172–84 (stanza XII)
  4. Enlil sees the devastation, lines 185–91 (stanzas XIII)
  5. Enlil caused the destruction, lines 192–212 (stanzas XIV–XV)
  6. The exalted Enlil, lines 213–24 (stanza XVI)
  7. Lines 225–36 (stanza XVII) broken

C. *Eršemma,* lines 237–96
  1. Plea for Enlil to "turn around and look at your city!", lines 237–53

2. Plea for Enlil to "turn around and look at your city!" from various locations, lines 254–72
3. The flooded cities in couplets, lines 273–80
4. The gluttonous man starves, lines 281–82
5. The fractured family, lines 283–87
6. The population rages, lines 288–91
7. Death in the city streets, lines 292–96

We may observe that section A (stanzas II–X) calls attention to Enlil's destructive power as evidenced by the devastation. Section B (stanzas XI–XVII) concentrates on awakening Enlil in hopes of encouraging his return so that the city may regain its lost glory. The *eršemma* seeks to inspire some spark of pity within Enlil.

Cohen demonstrates that the *balag* exhibited a certain development within its history.[87] In its Old Babylonian form the *balag* like the city-lament had a rather formal external structure of *kirugu*-divisions in which each stanza was followed by "first, second, etc. *kirugu*."[88] In some cases there followed a one-line *gišgigal* (antiphon) as in the city-lament. Many scribes set the *kirugu* and *gišgigal* off by horizontal lines across the text both above and below these labels. As time passed, the labels tended to drop out leaving only the horizontal lines to mark stanzas. Another Old Babylonian convention of *balag* construction was the "heart pacification-unit" in the concluding stanza of older Enlil-*balag*s.[89] *Balag*s to other divinities omit this plea that the wrathful god's heart and liver might be pacified. Following this unit comes the formula expressing the wish that x-temple should return to its place, then the rubric *kišubim* which means something like "coda."

Modification in *balag* structural organization became necessary, however, following the later joining of *balag* and *eršemma*. Each first millennium *balag*-lament had an *eršemma* attached to its end. In its new function as last stanza the *eršemma* had to be redesigned.[90] For one thing, even though their first millennium counterparts always were one-unit compositions, the first millennium *eršemma*s often consist of two or three units each.[91] In these cases the last unit either begins with or contains a "heart pacification-unit" which seems to have originated in Old Babylonian Enlil *balag*s. The "heart pacification" is followed by a list of gods who were to add their pleas to those of the priests and worshipers. In this composite form the *balag-eršemma* continued to serve as liturgical material during hundreds of years through the Seleucid era.

When comparing these later laments with their ancient ancestors, the city-laments, the modern literary critic may think of them as grossly inferior. Kutscher,[92] for example, uses such descriptions as "repetitive," "unimaginative," "composed to a large extent of clichés, and devoid of poetic rhythm," "stereotyped," and we may add boring. Their longevity and broad range of use suggest to us, however, that the ancients found great merit in them.

IV. THE FIRST MILLENNIUM MESOPOTAMIAN LAMENT AND BIBLICAL LAMENTATIONS

In order to draw meaningful comparisons between the book of Lamentations and Mesopotamian laments we will create a typology in summary form for the first millennium Mesopotamian lament genre under four major headings: Ritual Occasions, Form/Structure, Poetic Techniques, and Theology. Then we will compare the book of Lamentations with this typology to formulate a hypothesis regarding the relationships of the two.

In the present state of cuneiform scholarship[93] we find four categories of religious circumstances when lamentations were employed in the cults of Mesopotamia. They are: (1) before, during, or after daily sacrifices and libations to a wide range of deities, (2) special services, feasts, or rituals like the Akitu festival or the ritual for covering the sacral kettle-drum, (3) *namburbi* incantation rites to forestall impending doom, and (4) especially those circumstances of pulling down sacred buildings to prepare the site for rebuilding.

The structure of first millennium laments was flexible but usually followed a broad pattern as follows:

1. praise to the god of destruction, usually Enlil
2. description of the destruction
3. lamenting the destruction ("How long?")
4. plea to the destructive god to be pacified
5. plea to the god to gaze upon the destruction

6. plea to other deities (often a goddess) to intercede
7. further description of the ruin.

Those poetic techniques employed by lament composers may be outlined under the following captions:

1. interchange of speaker (third, second, first person) involving description (third person), direct address (second person), monologue (first person), dialogue (first, second, and third persons)
2. use of woe-cries and various interjections
3. use of Emesal dialect apparently to simulate high-pitched cries of distress and pleading
4. heavy use of couplets, repeating lines with one word changed from line to line, and other devices of parallelism
5. antiphonal responses
6. tendency to list or catalog (gods, cities, temples, epithets, victims, etc.)
7. use of theme word or phrase which serves as a cord to tie lines together, or whole stanzas.

We may outline the underlying ideas under three major captions: divinity, humanity, and causality.

A. Divinity
   1. The god of wrathful destruction, usually Enlil, abandons the city, a signal for devastation, often called a "storm," to begin.
   2. This chief god may bring the havoc himself or may order another deity to attack the city or sanctuary.
   3. In any case, Enlil's will is irresistible; he has the backing of the council of gods.
   4. Enlil is described and addressed in anthropomorphic terms:
      (a) a warrior
      (b) the shepherd of the people
      (c) his word destroys
      (d) his "heart" and "liver" must be soothed
      (e) he must be roused from sleep
      (f) he must inspect the ruins to see what has occurred
      (g) he must be cajoled to change his mind.

5. Yet there is an unknowable quality to Enlil; he is unreachable.
6. Lesser deities must intercede with the chief god to bring an end to the ruin.

B. Humanity

Surprisingly, humans are of little significance in the laments. The gods occupy the limelight. The following ideas about the place of human beings do emerge, however:

1. Human tragedy is described in terms of
   (a) death
   (b) exile
   (c) madness
   (d) disruption of families
   (e) demolishing the buildings associated with the general population.
2. Mesopotamian society placed great emphasis on job definition; it is a tragedy when people cannot fulfill their jobs.
3. The citizens were seen as Enlil's flock but were "trampled" by Enlil.
4. The only response the population can make to the disaster is to mourn and offer sacrifices and libations. There seems to be a pervading sense of helplessness before the gods' power.
5. A gap separates the citizens and the gods. People must keep their distance. A sign of the tragedy is that the temple is demolished and people can see into the holy sanctuary.

C. Causality

In Mesopotamian experience ultimate causation lies in the largely unseen world of the gods. Storms of barbarians may crash upon the city, but they were called upon the scene by a decision of Enlil in consultation with the council of the gods. The emphasis of the laments is upon the power of the divine, not upon the rightness of the decision. There appears no resort to the justness of the gods. The humans have committed no particular crime or sin which moves the gods to their decision. The devastation is not judgment on evil humans. In fact the Eridu lament says, "The storm, which possesses neither kindness nor malice, does not distinguish between good and evil."[94] There does not appear to be a primitive magical use made of the laments, however. To recount the havoc and recite the appeasement of the god is the same as experiencing the disaster physically. The lament becomes a means of avoidance of ruin, in other words, a means of controlling the causality which resides with the gods.

When we look at the biblical Lamentations in the light of this typology, we are impressed with both similarities and differences. In order to move from the clearest to the least clear category, we begin with some observations relative to the theology of Lamentations. Those points of similarity and difference are:

1. God's majesty and irresistible power, 5:19 (but Lamentations goes beyond Mesopotamian laments by insisting on God's righteousness in 1:18, 3:22, 26, 32)
2. God was the cause of the city's fall, 1:5, 12–15, 17; 2:1–8, 17; 3:1–16 (God brings misery on the "man"), 32–38, 43–45; 4:11, 16; 5:22
3. God abandoned his city, 2:1 (refused to remember), 6 (spurned), 7 (spurned and rejected), 8 (thought to destroy); 5:20–22
4. God as a mighty warrior, 2:2–8, 20–22; 3:4–13, 16, 34; 4:11
5. God's wrath, 2:1–4, 6, 21, 22; 3:1, 43, 65–66; 4:11
6. God caused the destruction by his word, 2:17; 3:37, 38
7. God called upon to look at the havoc, 1:9, 11;2:20; 3:61 (God is to hear the enemy's plots), 63; 4:16 (God refuses to look); 5:1 (God is to remember)
8. A goddess wanders about the destroyed city and bemoans its sad plight (Of course, Israelite theology could not tolerate such an idea, but the city Jerusalem fulfills this role especially in 1:12–17)
9. God to be aroused from sleep is totally lacking in biblical Lamentations
10. God's heart to be soothed and his liver pacified is likewise missing
11. God called upon to return to his abandoned city is missing
12. The theme of lesser gods called upon to intercede with the destroyer god is obviously lacking.

More space is devoted to humans and their plight in biblical Lamentations than in Mesopotamian laments. In both, the personified city occupies much of the description. Social grouping appears in rather general terms: king, princes, and elders; priests, prophets, and Nazirites;

army men, pilgrims, and citizens; old men, mothers, young men, virgins, children, and infants; orphans and widows. Skilled craftsmen are not enumerated. The description of the horrors of war suffered by the population is in some ways a bit more gruesome in the biblical Lamentations. For example, young and old dying in the streets of thirst and hunger, the lethargic march of the priests, mothers eating their children, cruel enslavement of one-time nobles, the shame of ridicule and exposure —all are expressed in poignant detail.

As in the Mesopotamian laments the biblical Lamentations clearly placed ultimate causation with God, but God is justified in the decision since the citizenry of Jerusalem was guilty of numerous crimes (1:5, 8, 18, 20; 4:6). The prophets (2:14; 4:13), priests (4:13), and fathers (5:7) must bear a large portion of the guilt for their failure to correct the evils which prompted God to take his angry action. God's extreme action in warring against Jerusalem has produced repentance on the part of the survivors, however. Now the mercy and love of God are being sought to change the fortunes of the people and, especially, the city.

In comparing poetic techniques, we find the interchange of speaker involving first, second, and third persons with accompanying change in perspective reminiscent of dramatic or liturgical performance. Likewise woe-cries and interjections occur to intensify dramatic effect. Parallelism of various orders runs throughout the five Lamentations poems. Only the Mesopotamian predilection for cataloging is lacking in biblical Lamentations.

In addition, other strategies utilized by Mesopotamian laments appear in biblical Lamentations either directly or with modification. Among these devices are: the poet addresses God (1:10 and the whole of chapter 5), but God never answers; the poet addresses or questions Jerusalem who seems to function in Lamentations much as the goddess functions in Mesopotamian laments (2:13–16, 18–19; 4:21, 22); invective against the enemy (1:21, 22; 3:55–66; 4:21, 22), the city which weeps or speaks (1:1–3, 8, 9, 11–15, 16, 18–20, 22; 2:11, 20–22; 3:48–51, 55–66; 5:17), the city ridiculed or embarrassed (1:7, 8, 17, 19, 21; 2:15–17; 3:14 [the "man"], 30 [the "man"], 45 [the citizens], 46, 63; 4:12, 15), detailed description of the carnage (1:4, 5, 18–20; 2:2, 5–12, 20–22; 3:4–16 [the "man" is a prisoner]; 4:1–10, 14–15, 17–19; 5:1–18). The stock-in-trade woe-cry "How long?" does not occur in biblical Lamentations. Neither is restoration stated though we may infer that the total work envisions Jerusalem's rebuilding as do several statements which recall God's mercy (3:22–27, 31–33; 4:21, 22; 5:20–22).[95]

When we come to a comparison of structure and organization, we find a decided lack of similarity. God is not honored by reciting a long list of epithets. The simple order of movement perceivable in Mesopotamian laments does not occur (abandonment, invasion by the "storm," plea to the god to awake, rouse himself, and gaze upon the ruins, lesser gods involved to add weight to the pleas, further recalling the ruination). Each of the five poems does show "poetic development" especially discernible in change of speaker, but not a plot type of movement.

We come finally to the question of cultic context. On this question we are without documentation to inform us. Of the four cultic occasions when first millennium Mesopotamian laments were recited, the most likely candidate for the biblical is that of temple restoration.

Jer 41:5 informs us that some 80 mourners of Shechem, Shiloh, and Samaria brought offerings and incense to the "House of Yahweh" during the Gedaliah days following the temple's destruction at the hands of the Babylonians. The signs of their mourning were shaved off beards, ripped clothing, and gashed skin. Zech 7:3–5 refers to mournful fasts at Jerusalem in the fifth and seventh months which have been observed "these 70 years." Apparently a commemoration of the sack of Jerusalem and the burning of the Temple occurred in the fifth month and a memorial to the slain Gedaliah in the seventh month. Zech 8:19 adds to the fifth- and seventh-month fasts by citing fasts in the fourth month (the breaching of the walls) and in the tenth month (the onset of Nebuchadnezzar's final siege). We may assume from the statement in Jer 41:5 that some form of religious practice continued on the site of the largely demolished Temple. The other fasts likewise focused on the ruined city, walls, and Temple. Finally the time came for rebuilding the Temple immediately following the Persian conquest of Babylon and Cyrus's edict of toleration in 539. Exiles, including priests from Babylonia familiar with long-practiced Mesopotamian liturgies for rebuilding demolished shrines, joined with their brothers who had been left behind "these 70 years" to live within sight of the ruins and to fast and mourn among the Temple's ruins. Together they bewailed the fallen sanctuary as clearing the site began in preparation for reconstruction. Such an occasion would provide a fit setting for the recitation of Lamentations and could have provided the impetus for writing or editing these five lament-poems for the performance.

V. CONCLUSION

McDaniel rejected direct Sumerian influence on the biblical Lamentations on the grounds that there was too great a gap between them in terms of both time and space.[96] Furthermore he argued that there were no distinctively Mesopotamian elements in the biblical book.[97] On the basis of the discoveries of the 1970s we can now fill the gap in time between the city-laments and biblical Lamentations with the lineal liturgical descendants of the city-laments, the *balag-eršemma*s. Gadd's suggestion[98] that the Babylonian Exile provided the opportunity for the Jewish clergy to encounter the laments has proved correct. We may add that the exiles of the Northern Kingdom also had similar opportunities in the cities of Assyria to observe or participate in these rituals. Thus the spatial gap has been closed also. Beyond these considerations, we have demonstrated strong analogies between the Mesopotamian lament typology and that of the biblical book of Lamentations though there were dissimilarities also. Because of the polytheistic theology underlying the Mesopotamian laments and their ritual observance, they could not be taken over without thorough modification in theology and language. Still the biblical book of Lamentations was more closely associated with the Near Eastern lament genre than simply borrowing the "idea" of a lament over the destruction of a city as McDaniel conceded.[99]

NOTES

1. Several studies must be highlighted as bringing scholarly criticism up to date on Lamentations. Delbert Hillers' volume, *Lamentations,* in the Anchor Bible series (Garden City: Doubleday, 1972) is a good starting point because of its clear statement of the critical problems relating to Lamentations, its selective bibliography, and its informative and balanced notes. Hillers made good use of several noteworthy studies from the 1960s which applied the best of available scholarship to questions of text, philology, higher criticism, theology, and form analysis. Those leading commentaries were A. Weiser's *Klagelieder* (ATD 16; Göttingen: Vandenhoeck and Ruprecht, 1962) pp.

297–370, W. Rudolph's *Das Buch Ruth—Das Hohe Lied—Die Klagelieder* (KAT 17/1–3; Gütersloh: Gütersloher Verlagshaus Gerd Mohn, 1962), and Hans-Joachim Kraus's *Klagelieder* (BKAT 20; 3d ed.; Neukirchen-Vluyn: Neukirchener Verlag, 1968). These three German commentaries provide exhaustive bibliographies as well. Norman Gottwald's chief contribution, *Studies in the Book of Lamentations* (SBT 1/14, 2d ed.; London: SCM, 1962), lies in his perceptive treatment of Lamentations' theology. Specific texts within Lamentations have been elucidated by numerous detailed studies. Bertil Albrektson (*Studies in the Text and Theology of the Book of Lamentations* [Lund: CWK Gleerup, 1963]) has communicated an extremely valuable tool, a critical Syriac text of Lamentations, and has made a detailed study of the MT in the light of LXX, Peshitta, and Latin versions. Gottlieb's shorter study (*Å Study on the Text of Lamentations* [Århus: Det Laerde Selskab, 1978]=Acta Jutlandica 48, Theology Series 12) discusses textual matters either not treated by Albrektson or those where Gottlieb wishes to take issue with Albrektson or others. The essay of Lanahan, ("Speaking Voice in the Book of Lamentations," *JBL* 93 [1974] 41–49) draws attention to the literary and dramatic effect of the change of speaker in Lamentations.

2. D. N. Freedman, "Acrostics and Metrics in Hebrew Poetry," *HTR* 65 (1972) 367–92.
3. Thomas F. McDaniel, "The Alleged Sumerian Influence upon Lamentations," *VT* 18 (1968) 198–209.
4. S. N. Kramer, "Sumerian Literature and the Bible," AnBib 12 (Studia Biblica et Orientalia 3 [1959]) 201, n. 1.
5. S. N. Kramer, "Lamentation over the Destruction of Nippur: A Preliminary Report," *Eretz Israel* 9 (1969) 90.
6. McDaniel draws from Kramer's published work as of 1968 including "The Oldest Literary Catalogue: A Sumerian List of Literary Compositions Compiled about 2000 B.C.," *BASOR* 88 (1942) 10–19; "New Literary Catalogue from Ur," *RA* 55 (1961) 169–76; *Sumerian Literary Texts from Nippur in the Museum of the Ancient Orient at Istanbul* (AASOR 23; New Haven: American Schools of Oriental Research, 1943–44) 32–35; *Lamentation over the Destruction of Ur* (Assyriological Studies 12; Chicago: University of Chicago, 1940); "Lamentation over the Destruction of Ur," *ANET*[2] 455–63; "Sumerian Literature, A General Survey," *The Bible and the Ancient Near East* (Albright Anniversary Volume; Garden City: Doubleday, 1961) 249–66.
7. McDaniel cites C. J. Gadd, "The Second Lamentation for Ur," *Hebrew and Semitic Studies Presented to Godfrey Rolles Driver* (ed. D. W. Thomas and W. D. McHardy; Oxford: Oxford University, 1963) 59–71.
8. McDaniel cites Hans-Joachim Kraus, *Klagelieder* (*Threni*) (BKAT 20; 2d ed.; Neukirchen-Vluyn: Neukirchener Verlag, 1960) 10.
9. McDaniel cites Wilhelm Rudolph, *Das Buch Ruth—Das Hohe Lied—Die Klagelieder*, p. 9.

10. McDaniel cites Otto Eissfeldt, *Einleitung in das Alte Testament* (3d ed.; Tübingen: Mohr, 1964) 683.
11. McDaniel, "Sumerian Influence," 207.
12. Ibid.
13. Ibid., 209.
14. See above, n. 6. Add to the Kramer bibliography: "Literary Texts from Ur VI, Part II," *Iraq* 25 (1963) 171–76; "Lamentation over the Destruction of Sumer and Ur," *ANET*³ 611–19; and "Two British Museum iršemma 'Catalogues,' " *StudOr* 46 (1975) 141–66.
15. See T. Jacobsen in his review of Kramer, *Lamentation over the Destruction of Ur* in *AJSL* 58 (1941) 219–24; *Proceedings of the American Philosophical Society* 107 (1963) 479–82.
16. See especially W. W. Hallo, "Individual Prayer in Sumerian: The Continuity of a Tradition," *JAOS* 88 (Speiser Anniversary Volume, 1968) 71–89, where he traced the development of the individual lament from the older letter-prayer genre. Other articles of W. W. Hallo relating to Sumerian literary genre history include: "The Cornation of Ur-Nammu," *JCS* 20 (1966) 133–41; "The Cultic Setting of Sumerian Poetry," *Actes de la XVII*ᵉ *Rencontre assyriologique internationale* (Ham-sur-Heure: Universite Libre de Bruxelles, 1970) 116–34; "Another Sumerian Literary Catalogue?" *StudOr* 46 (1975) 77–80 with additions in *StudOr* 48:3; and "Toward a History of Sumerian Literature," *Sumerological Studies in Honor of Thorkild Jacobsen on His Seventh Birthday* (AS 20; Chicago: University of Chicago, 1975) 181–203.
17. Mark E. Cohen, *Balag-compositions: Sumerian Lamentation Liturgies of the Second and First Millennium* B.C. (Sources from the Ancient Near East, vol. 1, fasc. 2; Malibu: Undena, 1974) and *The eršemma in the Second and First Millennia* B.C. (Unpublished doctoral dissertation at the University of Pennsylvania, n.d.).

    His significant study, *Sumerian Hymnology: The Eršemma* (*HUCA Supplement* 2 [Cincinnati: Hebrew Union College-Jewish Institute of Religion, 1981]), appeared while this study was in press, and consequently, could not be incorporated into the body of this essay. Although most of Cohen's later conclusions were anticipated in the earlier form of his dissertation, one major refinement requires a modification in the discussion of the first millennium *eršemma* offered above.

    On pages 27, 41, and 42 Cohen calls attention to *eršemma*s labeled *kidudû* which appear in incipit lists unrelated to any *balag*. These independent *eršemma*s were recited in various ceremonies such as those relating to the covering of the sacred building. Thus the *eršemma* enjoyed two forms of usage in the first millennium, that is, as a separate work and as the last section of the composite *balag-eršemma*. The recognition of this independent status of the *eršemma* does not alter the conclusions drawn concerning the composite *balag-eršemma,* however.
18. Raphael Kutscher, *Oh Angry Sea (a-ab-ba ḫu-luḫ-ḫa): The History of a*

Sumerian Congregational Lament (YNER 6; New Haven: Yale University, 1975).

19. Joachim Krecher, *Sumerische Kultyrik* (Wiesbaden: Otto Harrassowitz, 1966).
20. Margaret W. Green, *Eridu in Sumerian Literature* (Unpublished doctoral dissertation at the University of Chicago, 1975), chap. 9: "Sumerian Lamentations" and chap. 10: "The Eridu Lament." See also M. W. Green, "The Eridu Lament," *JCS* 30 (1978) 127–67.
21. Kramer, *Eretz Israel* 9 (1969) 89.
22. See Kramer's treatments cited in n. 4.
23. See Kramer, "Lamentation over the Destruction of Sumer and Ur," *ANET*[3] 611–19.
24. Green, *Eridu,* 279. See also D. O. Edzard, *Die "Zweite Zwischenzeit" Babyloniens* (Wiesbaden: Otto Harrassowitz, 1957) 86–90.
25. Ibid.
26. Green, *Eridu,* chap. 10, 326–74 and Green, "Eridu Lament," 127–67.
27. See Kramer, *ANET*[3] 612 and n. 9 as well as C. J. Gadd and S. N. Kramer, *Literary and Religious Texts, Ur Excavation Texts, 6, Part* 2 (London: British Museum, 1966) 1 for the joins of tablets to show the unity of these fragments.
28. See Kramer's comments in "The Curse of Agade: The Ekur Avenged," *ANET*[3] 646f. See also M. W. Green's remarks in Green, *Eridu,* 279f. and Kutscher's in *Oh Angry Sea,* 1.
29. Cohen, *balag,* 9. M. W. Green ("Eridu Lament," 129f.) raises the possibility of finding the origin of the Eridu lament in the reign of Nur-Adad of Larsa (1865–50 B.C.E.) but prefers an earlier date in the reign of Išme-Dagan of Isin (1953–35).
30. Cohen, *balag,* 11.
31. Kutscher *(Oh Angry Sea,* 3) claims that city-laments were written in the standard Emegir dialect, while Cohen (*balag,* 11 and 32) claims they were Emesal compositions.
32. See Cohen, *balag,* 11.
33. Kutscher, *Oh Angry Sea,* 3.
34. Cohen, *eršemma,* 24.
35. Ibid., 9.
36. Ibid.
37. Kramer, "Two British Museum iršemma 'Catalogues,' " 141–66.
38. Cohen, *eršemma,* 9f., 12.
39. Ibid., 22–24.
40. Ibid., 24.
41. Ibid.
42. Ibid., 27f.
43. Cohen, *balag,* 11.
44. Ibid., 9f.
45. Ibid., 10f.
46. Ibid., 11.

47. Ibid.
48. Ibid.
49. Ibid., 6.
50. Ibid., 12.
51. Kutscher, *Oh Angry Sea,* 3.
52. Cohen, *balag,* 31 (Excursus on the *balag*-instrument).
53. Ibid., 6.
54. Kutscher, *Oh Angry Sea,* 25–27 (history of YBC 4659), 52–54 (transliteration of YBC 4659), 143–53 (translation of the composite text), plates 6 and 7 (copies of YBC 4659 [*sic!* Captions inadvertently interchanged with those of Plates 1 and 2.]).
55. See ibid., 6f., for this interpretation.
56. Ibid., 7.
57. Cohen, *balag,* 11.
58. Ibid., 13, 15.
59. See E. Sollberger's remarks in his review of J. Krecher, *Kultlyrik,* which was published in *BO* 25 (1968) 47a.

    This hiatus in documentation is probably caused by the fact that following the fall of Babylon about 1600 B.C.E. the scribal schools of Nippur and Babylon closed, and their scholars, taking their texts with them, fled southward to the Sealand. Under the Kassites, however, new scribal schools were established to perpetuate the classical literary tradition. In this corpus, which Hallo calls "Post-Sumerian" and "Bilingual," cultic texts and especially laments dominated. In fact, this bilingual collection survived as the canon for the remainder of the history of classical Mesopotamian literature through the Seleucid era into the Arsacid period. See W. W. Hallo, "Problems in Sumerian Hermeneutics," *Perspectives in Jewish Learning* 5 (1973) 6f. and "Toward a History of Sumerian Literature," 189–91, 198, 201, on bilinguals in the history of the canons.
60. Cohen, *balag,* 9
61. See Kutscher, *Oh Angry Sea,* 9f., for a chart of the texts he was able to combine to reconstruct this *balag.*
62. Ibid., 11. Kutscher's Ca (=VAT 8243, ll.32–37) and Db (=VAT 8243, ll. 143 and 143).
63. Ibid., 17 (TMH NF 53:21).
64. Cohen, *eršemma,* 25f.
65. See, for example, Kutscher, *Oh Angry Sea,* 5; Cohen, *balag,* 13–15.
66. Cohen, *balag,* 13–15.
67. Ibid., 13.
68. R. Caplice, "Namburbi Texts in the British Museum, IV," *Or* 39 (1970) 118f.
69. Cohen, *balag,* 14f.
70. Ibid.
71. On *kirugu* see A. Falkenstein, "Sumerische religiöse Texte," *ZA* 49 (1950) 104f. where he interpreted the term as meaning "to bow to the ground."

Šēru is probably related to Sumerian *šìr,* a generic title for poetry and/or song; see *AHw* 1219a. See also Green, *Eridu,* 283–85.

72. On *gišgigal* see Falkenstein, "Sumerische religiöse Texte," 92, 93, 97f., 101. Falkenstein interpreted the term simply as "antiphon." See also Green, *Eridu,* 285f. See *AHw* 641a, sub *me/iḫru,* 3) where *giš-gál* = *mi-ḫir za-ma-ri* = antiphonal song and *giš-gi₄-gál* = *me-eḫ-ru/rù.*
73. See Cohen, *balag,* 8 and Green, *Eridu,* 283–86 on structural matters.
74. See n. 20 above.
75. See Green, *Eridu,* 286–89. For a fuller analysis of Sumerian poetic form, see C. Wilcke, "Formale Gesichtspunkte in der sumerischen Literatur," *Assyriological Studies* 20 (Chicago: University of Chicago, 1975) 205–316.
76. See n. 31 above.
77. Green, *Eridu,* 288f.
78. Kutscher (*Oh Angry Sea,* 5) takes the position that *gala*-priests "specialized in Emesal" and that when they composed or recited compositions in worship settings, they employed the Emesal dialect. Krecher (*Kultlyrik* 27f.), however, maintains that other cult personnel, namely the *nārū*-singer, also sang the Emesal compositions. Krecher, however, admits that the Emesal songs were almost exclusively sung by the *kalû*-(=*gala)*priests. Cohen (*balag,* 11) attributes the composition of the city-laments, as well as *balag*s and *eršemma*s, to the *kalû*=priests. See also Cohen, *balag,* 13, 15, and 32 as well as Cohen, *eršemma,* 9, 11, 17, and 24. Hallo ("Individual Prayer in Sumerian," 81b) shows that "the later penitent commissioned the gala-singer to recite his prayer orally." Such *eršaḫunga*-prayers were also composed in Emesal (see Krecher, *Kultlyrik,* 25 and Hallo, "Individual Prayer," 80–82) and were recited, at least on occasions, to the accompaniment of the *halhallatu*-drum (Cohen, *eršemma,* 27). For a discussion of the *gala*-priests as Old Babylonian cult personnel, see J. Renger, "Untersuchungen zum Priestertum der altbabylonischen Zeit," *ZA* 59 (1969) 189–95.
79. In outlining these six common themes I am following Green, *Eridu,* 295–310.
80. Jacobsen, *AJSL* 58 (1941) 219–24.
81. Hallo, "Cultic Setting," 119.
82. Cohen, *balag,* 11.
83. Green, *Eridu,* 309f.
84. Green, *Eridu,* 311f.
85. Kutscher, *Oh Angry Sea,* 21.
86. Translation in ibid., 143–53.
87. Cohen, *balag,* 8, 11f.
88. Ibid., 8.
89. Cohen, *eršemma,* 17.
90. Ibid., 28.
91. Ibid., 12.
92. Kutscher, *Oh Angry Sea,* 4.

93. Cohen, *eršemma,* 9f., 27f.; Cohen, *balag,* 11, 13–15; Kutscher, *Oh Angry Sea,* 6f.; Krecher, *Kultlyrik,* 18–25, 34.
94. Green, *Eridu,* 342, l. 1:20.
95. See Gottwald's discussion of the interplay of doom and hope in Lamentations in his chap. 3 ("The Key to the Theology of Lamentations"), chap. 4 ("The Theology of Doom") and chap. 5 ("The Theology of Hope") in *Studies in the Book of Lamentations.*
96. McDaniel, "Sumerian Influence," 207f.
97. Ibid., 207.
98. Gadd, "Second Lamentation," 61, cited in ibid., 209.
99. McDaniel, "Sumerian Influence," 209.

IV

"FOREIGN" ELEMENTS IN ANCIENT ISRAEL

11

The Hebrews

Henri Cazelles

It is important, in historical studies, to distinguish between Hebrews and Israelites. We are used to identifying them and, nowadays, one speaks of the Hebrew language,[1] not of the Israelite language. But this identification is late. A similar identification is that of the Jews with the Israelites, which only took place after the fall of Samaria; even at the time of the New Testament the Jews, or Judeans, are often distinguished from the Samaritans and the Galileans. In the same way the careful study of the Bible and archaeological discoveries has made it necessary to distinguish between Hebrews and Israelites.

The identification of the two terms seems to have come from the famous story of Joseph in Genesis, where the word Hebrew *(ʿibrî)* is very often applied to the Israelites (Gen 39:14–Exod 10:3). At first sight these texts seem to oppose Israelite and Egyptian nations. But further attention shows that the opposition does not lie precisely there. In the tradition represented by Exodus the Israelites did not depart alone, but with a large mixed group of non-Israelites (Exod 12:38; Num 11:4). It is the contrast between masters and servants that is here underlined, whether they are the servants of Potiphar or the servants of pharaoh; the texts concern the period when Egypt controlled Canaan, which contemporary scribes called Hurru, and where they made prisoners or recruited their personnel. In these texts "Hebrew" is a very general term, which is used by the Egyptians or when someone is talking to Egyptians. The

Reprinted by permission of Oxford University Press from D. J. Wiseman, ed., *Peoples of Old Testament Times* (Oxford: Clarendon Press, 1973), 1–28. © Oxford University Press 1973.

"land of the Hebrews" (Gen 40:15)[2] is the land without political unity, "the place of the Canaanites, the Hittites, the Amorites, the Perizzites, the Hivites and the Jebusites" (Exod 3:8). The God of the Hebrews (Exod 3:18; 5:3; 7:16; 9:1, 13; 10:3) is an expression used in the dialogue with pharaoh to distinguish him from the gods of pharaoh and from pharaoh himself. The same expression is found in cuneiform texts, and the Bible itself states that Israelites and Midianites together honoured him (Exodus 18). Finally the statement that "the Egyptians might not eat bread with the Hebrews" (Gen 43:32) concerns a social rather than a national distinction, for Genesis 46:34 says that "every shepherd is an abomination to the Egyptians," the shepherds here being Jacob and his household. Koch does not accept "Hebrew" as a sociological category. For him it designates a "wider circle" of population than the Israelites.[3] A similar conclusion is reached later in this chapter. Koch believes that before the J redaction a "Hebrew" story of the Exodus had already been written, and this was used by J for his "Israelite" history.[4] As the term "Hebrew" disappears before the Exodus (after Exodus 10:3), reappears only in Numbers 24:24 (as *ʿeber*), and is related to the Kittim, this postulated Exodus source for J is very doubtful. The term "Hebrew" does not seem to have entered the biblical vocabulary from the Hebrew population itself, but from its use by Egyptians and their Philistine successors when alluding to Asiatic foreigners. The workers and prisoners called *ʿprw* in Egypt, as will be shown, do not seem to be identical with the *ʿbr* peoples of Genesis 10:25–30. The latter include the Arabian tribe of Yoktan and South Arabian tribes including Hadramaut and Ophir. The notion of a *ʿbr* population wider than Israel does not seem to belong to the old Israelite traditions, but comes from an international concept by which Abraham, the father of nations (Gen 17; P) or father of the Keturah tribes (Gen. 25; J), could include among his descendants more than Israel.

Indeed, those who speak of "Hebrews" in the Bible, after the references by Egyptians, are the Philistines, who, traditionally, came from Câphtor (Crete) and are allied to other Sea Peoples. The Philistines were, for a time, the heirs of the pharaohs on the "Palestinian" coast land. These city dwellers considered the Hebrews as a motley crew from the hinterland, to be treated with contempt (1 Sam. 4:6, 9; 13:3, 7; 14:11; 29:3). The Israelites are included, but other elements are meant as well. This is proved by three texts which have often been studied, most recently by Weingreen, Weippert, and Koch, and which can only be fully understood if a distinction is made between Israelites and Hebrews. 1 Samuel 14:21[5] concerns the Hebrews "who had been with the Philistines before that time" and the Israelites who were fighting with Saul and Jonathan; the Hebrews change sides and join the Israelites. In the previous chapter (13:6 and 7) Hebrews and Israelites had taken different attitudes towards the Philistine army; the Israelites stayed where they were, even though they had to hide themselves in caves and among bushes and rocks, while the Hebrews crossed the Jordan to the land of Gad and Gilead. Finally there is 1 Samuel 13:3, where the distinction is less clear. The text as we have it has perhaps been edited under the influence of the identification between Israelites and Hebrews, but the Greek text can be useful here. Saul wishes to let all the "Hebrews" know of the victory of Jonathan over the Philistines; he also tries to attract to the side of the Israelites, who had become odious to the Philistines, a more numerous following.

After Saul the term "Hebrew" practically disappears from the spoken language. Deuteronomy (15:12) and Jeremiah (34:9, 14) employ the term, but only in reference to an older text, the law concerning the "Hebrew" slave in Exodus 21:2. It is really only a quotation. As for Jonah 1:9, it is an isolated text from a period which tends to use archaic expressions; the hero, speaking with foreign sailors, is more or less in the same situation as Joseph speaking with the Egyptians, even if, with Koch, it is noted that Jonah's ship left Joppa on the Philistinian coast. But Joppa was never one of the five Philistine cities. According to the Eshmunazar inscription (l. 19), certainly by the fourth century B.C., it was a Phoenician city. One can say that after the reign of David, who built up the state by means of a policy of assimilation, and that of Solomon, who set up administrative districts[6] in areas where the Israelites constituted a minority of the population, the distinction between the various elements of the population fades, and the word "Hebrew" is only used in texts which reproduce a more ancient tradition. Whatever their tribe, the Israelites consider themselves as "sons of Israel." The kingdom of Saul and David is the kingdom of Israel the ancestor (1 Sam 24:20), although they also considered themselves as connected with Abram the Hebrew (Gen 14:13), father of a multitude of nations, including the Midianites, the Dedanites, and many others (Gen 25:1–4).

I. THE DISCOVERY OF THE *'APIRU/ḪAPIRU*

The distinction between Hebrews and Israelites is important because Egyptian texts discovered in the nineteenth century A.D. mention on the one hand Israel and on the other people whom the hieroglyphs indicate as *ʿprw,* the *w* being the sign of the plural. These texts do not all come from the same period. Merenptah, successor of Ramesses II, in the fifth year of his reign (*c.* 1230 B.C.), when he was campaigning between Canaan and Hurru, came across Israel near Yanoam, Ascalon, and Gezer. Israel was not sedentary at the time, since the text uses the determinative of the tribe and not that of the city. Neither Ramesses II nor Sety I, at the beginning of the same thirteenth century B.C., had come across Israel in their Asiatic campaigns. But they had met the *ʿprw,* or at least Sety I had, for he mentions their "revolt" on one of the two stelas which he erected in Palestine itself, at Beth-Shan.

At least nine Egyptian texts clearly mentioning the *ʿprw* are now known. These texts range from the first quarter of the fifteenth century B.C. to the eleventh century B.C. They are therefore both earlier and later than the stela of Merenptah. The fifteenth-century texts mention either warriors in Canaan or captives employed as servants to "strain wine." In the twelfth century under Ramesses III they were prisoners given to the temples. Then, under Ramesses IV, *ʿprw* are found in the quarries of the Wadi Hammamat. In the eleventh century they disappear from Egyptian sources, just as they disappear from the living language of Israel in the tenth century.

The identification of the *ʿprw* of the Egyptian texts with the *ʿbrm* of the Bible seemed to imply no problems from the linguistic point of view since, after Müller and Burchardt, there was evidence for the correspondence of Egyptian *p* and Semitic *b*. The vowels were to prove more troublesome, however. The Egyptian texts do not record the vowels, but the fourteenth-century cuneiform texts found in Egypt do (Tell el Amarna letters). In the area where the pharaohs were fighting the *ʿprw,* and taking them prisoners, the diplomatic correspondence of the court of Amenophis III and Amenophis IV mentions rebels called *ḫabiru* or *ḫapiru* (the same syllable can be read *bi* or *pi*). Their name is written out in full in the letters sent to pharaoh by the King of Jerusalem (Amarna letters 286–90). It is clearly the same elements, or similar groups, who are called in other letters (Amarna 88, 34) SA.GAZ in ideographic

(Sumerian) writing. These Ḫapiru were active in Canaan and also further north in Phoenicia. Later on evidence was discovered showing that these SA.GAZ/Ḫapiru were present in a much wider area, as far as Mesopotamia, beyond the Tigris and in Asia Minor. They are mentioned in texts which range from the third to the first millennium B.C. The later texts in fact reproduce ancient traditions and speak of these people and of their gods in the past.

Should one identify the Egyptian *ʿprw,* the cuneiform Ḫab/piru and the biblical *ʿbrm?* Scholars were divided on this question and they remain so. Many considered the vocalic elements in *ʿibrî* (pl. *ʿibrîm,* rarely *ʿibriyyîm* [Exodus 3:18] and fem. *ʿibrīyah*) as incompatible with *Ḫabiru.* But, as Bruce has emphasized,[7] what mattered most in the discussion was the parallel which scholars tried to draw between the actions of the *Ḫabiru* and the conquest of Joshua. It was a false starting-point, and it soon became clear that it is impossible to reconcile the account of the conquest of Canaan in the book of Joshua with the movements of the *Ḫabiru* so far as they can be deduced from the Amarna letters.

However, the discovery of other texts from the fourteenth and thirteenth centuries B.C. has allowed some progress to take place, and has put an end to certain controversies. These texts, discovered at Ras-Shamra (Ugarit), are written in different languages and writings, one of these being close to the cuneiform of Amarna and the other close to Hebrew. One city called Halbi (like Aleppo) is given four names, which are perhaps the four quarters of the city. One of these names was written *Ḫal-bi* SA.GAZ in syllabic cuneiform and *ḫlb ʿprm* in West Semitic.[8] This provided the equation *Ḫapiru* = SA.GAZ = *ʿprm* (plural). There was no further objection to the identification of the *Ḫab/piru* of Amarna with the Egyptian *ʿprw.*

But to all appearances the gap had widened between these *Ḫapiru* and the biblical *ʿibr(iyy)îm.* However, the gap proved to be less than was at one time thought, at least as far as the consonants were concerned. The correspondence of the Hebrew ʿ to the *ḫ* was no problem, since the *ʿain* cannot be directly rendered in cuneiform. As for *b/p,* the passage from the unvoiced to the voiced consonant is frequent in Semitic dialects; moreover, certain late Babylonian texts (end of the second millennium B.C.) have a rare rendering *Ḫa-bir-a* (which could not have been pronounced *Ḫapira*), and this makes it more probable that the pronunciation may have evolved towards the end of the second millennium B.C., the biblical texts having been composed, at the earliest, at the end of the same second millennium.

Biblical criticism has made progress too. It has not only established the distinction between Hebrews and Israelites; it has also discerned how the basic data have been edited differently during the centuries. It came to recognize as late Genesis 14, where Abram the Hebrew is mentioned at Hebron, and Genesis 23, where the same Abraham buys a cave at Hebron *ḫbrn)* from Ephron *(ʿprn)* the Hittite. Nevertheless, the conclusions to be drawn from these observations are still under discussion. They prepare the solution to the problem, but one cannot yet say that they have given a solution. Before working out the relation of the Hebrews (and of the Israelites to the *Ḫapiru* it is necessary to inquire who the *Ḫapiru* were.

II. EXPANSION, ACTIVITY AND STATUS OF THE *ḪAPIRU/ʿPRW*

This inquiry is greatly helped by the publication of two collections bringing together and classifying the texts which concern the *Ḫapiru:* that of J. Bottéro (of which the numbering has been reproduced here as B.), and that of M. Greenberg (G.).[9] A few rare texts, already known, are missing from one or other of these collections. Others have since been published; they come from the Sumerian (Falkenstein),[10] from the ancient Hittite empire (Otten),[11] from Nuzi to the east of the Tigris (E. Cassin),[12] from Ugarit (Nougayrol[13] from Virolleaud),[14] Amarna (Edzard),[15] and Egypt.

The first question arising is this: It is certain that *ḫapiru* in certain places and at certain periods have been considered as being SA.GAZ. But it does not follow that we can read *ḫapiru* for every occurrence of the term SA.GAZ. Indeed the Mesopotamian and West Semitic lexicographers have never given in their list of equivalents the equation SA.GAZ (or its variants SAG.GAZ, SA.GAZ.ZA, SA.GA.AZ, GAZ) = *ḫapiru*. The Akkadian equivalent for the Sumerian SA.GAZ is always *ḫabbatu,* which means "brigand, highway robber." SA.GAZ does not mean anything in Sumerian; SAG.GAZ would mean something ("head-breaker"?) but it is an exceptional way of writing and is a late interpretation. B. Landsberger and A. Falkenstein therefore consider SA.GAZ to be a Sumerian adaptation of the Akkadian *šaggašu,* which means "aggressor"; this interpretation is helped by the fact that GAZ can be read GAS.

It seems to be confirmed by the description of the SA.GAZ in the text studied by Kramer and considered anew by Falkenstein: "The SA.GAZ, these people without clothes who travel in dead silence, who destroy everything, whose menfolk go where they will, whose womenfolk have spindles . . . they established their tents and their camps . . . they spend their time in the countryside without observing the decrees of my king Shulgi." At the end of the third millennium B.C. the SA.GAZ are therefore marauders on the edge of the ordered society dominated by the Third Dynasty of Ur. But the name can be applied to any nonsedentary population which is scarcely subordinate to authority.

The term SA.GAZ is thus a generic term which is wider in application than the *Ḫapiru;* we are not entitled to consider every SA.GAZ automatically as a *ḫapiru.* We must await the appearance of the word written out syllabically in full before we can treat of the *ḫapiru* and try to see why they were considered as SA.GAZ. Great caution is needed when dealing with the texts of Ur III and of the period of Agade. However, on a tablet from Tell Brak, which Gadd dated from the period of Agade, one finds the personal name *ḫa-b/pi-ra-am* (B.6); this takes us to the Upper Habur, west of Nineveh. A little further north, in a text of Alishar from the Assyrian colony in Cappadocia, we meet with the *Ḫapiru;* this is from the latest period of Kultepe, probably under Warad-Sin, and these *Ḫapiru* are prisoners. They are described as *awīlu,* which is not necessarily an honorific title at that period, but they have sufficient wealth to buy themselves out of captivity (B.5).

At about the same time (Larsa period, nineteenth century B.C.) the *Ḫapiru* appear in Southern Mesopotamia in administrative texts. They are generally referred to as SA.GAZ, but one text, identical in form to the others, spells out clearly *ḫa-pi-ri.* Whereas in the Laws of Lipit-Ishtar (*c.* 1934–1924 B.C.) one can still be doubtful as to the nature of the SA.GAZ, here it is clear that the SA.GAZ are *Ḫapiru.* They are soldiers (B. 16) with a chief (B. 17), and they receive supplies of food. In a similar text found at Susa in Elam, sheep are recorded as supplied to them (B. 35) and to certain other groups as well; all these groups are called "soldiers of the West," which is interesting.

At the same period one meets them in numerous texts from Mari on the Euphrates, to the west of Babylonia. These *Ḫapiru* (never written SA.GAZ) are also soldiers (B. 18, B. 20) with their chiefs, and one of their groups is recorded as having reached the number of 2,000 (B. 18).

They pass from the service of one chief to another (B. 29) "in the district of Shubat-Shamash." As a result of this mobility they are identified by geographical element; they are "from the (flat) country" (Bottéro), or "from the country" (Kupper; *ša mâtim*) (B. 18), from Yamutbal (B. 19), from Suḫu (south of Mari) (B. 33), and one of them flees from Eshnunna (B. 30). They own donkeys (G. 15). They carry out raids in Idamaraz, and they capture towns like Iahmumum, Suruzum, Ashushik, and Luhaia, though they do not keep them. In order to stir up trouble they join other groups like the inhabitants of Talhaia and of Aslakka (B. 27). Disagreeable as they are to the king of Mari, they are sometimes even more so to the king of Assyria.

In a slightly later text (eighteenth century B.C.) found further west, at Alalakh in Syria, the *Ḫapiru* make peace with the king of the land, Irkabtum, under the leadership of a certain Šemuba. A treaty accompanied by oaths is also made between *Ḫapiri* and Hittite troops in two texts from the old Hittite empire, i.e. contemporary with or slightly later than the Mari period (Otten). Other texts from the old Hittite empire show the *Ḫapiri* as organized troops whom the Hittite king can employ. He is able to group as many as 3,000 of them, whom he employs on garrison duty. It is important to note that in the same chronicle, in archaic Hittite, a text which is unfortunately badly damaged mentions together a leader of the Hurrian army and 3,000 *Ḫapiru* soldiers. In no other text of this period are the *Ḫapiru* either the foes or the allies of the Hurrians: one is justified in asking whether the *Ḫapiru* do not constitute a Hurrian element (B. 72′).

We shall find the *Ḫapiru* again at the end of sixteenth century B.C. and at the beginning of the fifteenth in the region of Alalakh, which was pervaded by Hurrian elements, so that Garelli can say that they constituted "the overwhelming majority of the population." The *Ḫapiru* have Hurrian names (B. 41, B. 44, B. 45, G. 50). When the word is written out in full it ends with the vowel *-i,* but the scribes usually employ the ideogram SA.GAZ. They are soldiers (B. 40, B. 41), or even quarrymen, under the orders of SA.GAZ leaders. One SA.GAZ from Tapduwa has fifteen soldiers under him; the SA.GAZ chief from Šarkuhe has twenty-nine; another has 1,436. They can form separate groupings, such as the one with which king Idrimi took refuge (B. 37); but they constitute an important social class, since in a list giving the names of offices (B. 39) the *Ḫapiru* come between a "royal son" and an officer of the palace. We shall find the same situation in Canaan. They can own houses and, as in the Mari period, we can see them spread in different regions and places (B. 44). They are people who must be reckoned with.

During the course of the fifteenth century also the *Ḫapiru* appear in large numbers, but in different conditions, to the east of the Tigris in another Hurrian city, Nuzi. The documents, already numerous, have been increased by the work of Bottéro and Greenberg (E. Cassin). In certain respects the status of the *Ḫapiru* at Nuzi is similar to that at Mari or Alalakh, but in other ways it is different. At Nuzi *Ḫapiru* is always written out in full and never with the ideogram SA.GAZ, which was rather pejorative in Mesopotamian eyes. They can receive food rations, as do horses (HSS XV. 237), and clothing (HSS XIII. 123, 152) but they are capable of owning horses (HSS XIV. 53; XV. 239). They can be stone-carvers (*nurpiannuḫlu,* B. 64);[16] they can be "decurions" (*emantuḫlu,* HSS XV. 62), an office which can refer to soldiers or to workers; they have a status which in the ration lists associates them with fishermen (HSS XIV. 102), carpenters (HSS XV. 237), and indeed with horses.

This status appertains to men and to women (B. 60, 61, 63, 65, 66). It is not always the same in all respects for men and women. Woman is more restricted than man, and it is in the case of women breaking a contract (*nabalkutu,* lit. "transgress, turn away") that it is said: "her eyes will be plucked out and she shall be sold." It is not certain that the expression is to be taken literally. A man can go away as long as there is compensation, either in the form of a substitute (B. 60) or a tenfold substitute (B. 56), or else on payment of a rather large sum, one gold and one silver mina (B. 66 c). Neither men nor women were independent. They could be put at the disposal of the palace (B. 64) or of personages like Tehiptilla: Sukri-Teshup is able to take a *Ḫapiru* to the land of Arrapha, which was, however, not far away (B. 64). But their condition could become worse. In the case of theft or misbehaviour the *Ḫapiru* sank to the level of *wardu,* "slave" (B. 54).

The *Ḫapiru* are not slaves, therefore, although their masters exercise "lordship" *(ewurutu)* over them. There was, however, a difficulty of terminology at Nuzi on this point, for normally they enter "*ana warduti,*" which should be translated "into service" (B. 59). There is one case of a *Ḫapiru* entering into adoption *(ana martūti),* but this seems to be a case involving two contracts; the woman Watija enters the household of Paitae as adopted daughter and introduces her own son, who had been up till then *wardu* of Tehiptilla and who now becomes a *Ḫapiru* like his mother (able to depart as long as there is compensation). The important thing is that the *Ḫapiru* enters into this condition freely, "of his own accord" *(ana ramānišu)* or "from his mouth and from his lips"; he can keep it during his lifetime, but he can also leave it, under the conditions mentioned above. Sometimes the master has to pay a price to acquire the right of "lordship" over them. The status of *Ḫapiru* is often acquired by people coming from another town (Lupti, HSS XVI. 396; Zarimena, HSS XIII. 152; Patwa, HSS XVI. 438), or from a foreign land like Assyria (B. 49, B. 50) or Akkad, i.e. Babylonia (B. 56, B. 63). In some cases they only enter into this status after a certain time (B. 56, in the year after arrival from Akkad).

Finally, it must be noted that the condition of the *Ḫapiru* at Nuzi can vary. We have seen that they could be stone-carvers or "decurions." They may also be *ubbutu* (HSS XV. 237, line 12). This term is associated with the *taḫlulu* (HSS XIV. 166) and with the *bīt kīli,* and has been studied by E. Cassin. It concerns "men who are the object of bodily restraint and who perform thereby forced labour for the profit of a creditor."[17] They were capable therefore, not only of buying themselves out, but also of contracting debts and of putting themselves into the legal situation known from Israelite institutions, the *ʿbṭ* (Deut 15:6; 24:10; Joel 2:7; Hab 2:6). This comparison is as important from the philological as from the historical point of view.

The *Ḫapiru* of Nuzi thus have obvious connections with the Hurrian population of the place, and one must ask whether it was not because of these connections that a better status than that of the slave was conferred on these refugees from Assyria, Babylonia, and elsewhere. Another connection must be noted. It can happen that a *Ḫapiru* provides as substitute a "man of the Nullu," i.e. Lullu. Now other texts from the fifteenth century B.C., Hittite texts, provide at least thirteen examples where the parallel expressions are Lullu and *Ḫapiri,* the gods of the *Ḫapiri*[18] and the gods of the *Lulaḫḫi* (Hurrian ending *he/i?*). These gods are witnesses in treaties contracted between the Hittite kings and various other populations, not only those of the Middle Euphrates. The *Lulaḫḫu* were a people who lived to the east of the Hittites and not very far from Nuzi. It is tempting but perhaps erroneous to identify Lulaḫḫu with the land of Elaḫut; A. Goetze considers Elaḫut to be the same as the Luhaia which is mentioned in a Mari text as having been laid waste by the *Ḫapiru* and the people of the Talhaia.

However, another fifteenth-century Hittite text represents the *Lulaḫḫu* and the *Ḫapiru* as of an inferior social condition: this is a witchcraft text, which places the 'tongue' of the *Ḫapiri* and the *Lulaḫḫi* after that of the nobles, priests, and Awisili(?) men, but before that of the dead, the living, and the magicians. A Luwite text which lists related pairs has *Ḫapiru-Lulaḫḫi* after father-mother, brother-sister, slave-slave girl. Whereas the *Ḫapiru* had a status superior to that of the slave at Nuzi, we can see that in non-Hurrian Asia Minor they had an inferior status.

Historical texts are rare. One of them is probably a list of booty made up of prisoners: 600 SA.GAZ are given to the "god of the temple" *(ili bîti)*, just as we shall find them given to the Egyptian temples of the Delta by Ramesses III. An unfavourable Babylonian omen which did not mention *Ḫapiru* was translated into Hittite (B. 87), and the translation shows that the Hittites considered the *Ḫapiru* as dangerous foes who would "enter the land" if the omen were to be fulfilled. Finally, a century later Mursilis II (*c.* 1334– 1306 B.C.), in an arbitration treaty between Duppi-Teshub of Amurru and Tudhaliya of Carchemish,[19] recalls that the town of Jaruwatta in the land of Barga (probably south of Aleppo and west of the Orontes) had been captured by the king of the Hurrian country and given to the "grandfather of Tette, the SA.GAZ." We thus find once more a Hurrian-SA.GAZ (or *Ḫapiru*) connection among the enemies of the Hittites. Mursilis I returns the town to Abiradda, whom the SA.GAZ had dispossessed.

These Hittite texts have taken us down to the fourteenth century B.C., and even later than the period of the Amarna letters. These letters reveal the activity of the SA.GAZ-*Ḫapiru* not only in Syria, but also in Phoenicia, near Sumur, Batrun and Byblos, in Upe near Damascus, and further south as far as Jerusalem. This is not surprising, since the Egyptians had met with *ʿprw* since Amenophis II in the fifteenth century B.C. In a campaign dating from the year 9 of his reign, which does not seem to have gone beyond North Palestine, he had taken prisoner "127 kings, 179 brothers of kings, 3,600 *ʿprw* 15,200 Shasu alive, 36,300 Hurrians, 15,070 *ngś* alive, and 30,652 of their *ʿḏt(?)*."[20] This last element is a puzzle, and it is possible that the possessive pronoun refers to the people of Syria *(ngś=Nuḫasse)*, previously mentioned. In any case, the sociological position of the *ʿprw* is clear. Both in numbers and in position they are between the kings and brothers of kings, on the one hand, and, on the other, the mass of the Shasu (nomads or semi-nomads) and of the Hurrians. They are thus the exact equivalent of the groups of military aristocracy that we have found at Mari, at Alalakh, and in the Hittite texts.

A similar sequence is found in an Amarna letter written about seventy years later by Biriawaza, governor of Upe, near Damascus, to Amenophis IV (B. 132). It gives Biriawaza, then his brothers, then the SA.GAZ, then the Sutu, who in the cuneiform texts are more or less the equivalent of the Egyptian Shasu. Once they are associated with the *ḫabbati,* highway robbers (Bottéro on B. 148), and are called "wandering dogs" *(ḫalqu)* (B. 93). They can be bribed (B. 115). The name of any of their chiefs is never mentioned.

They are, however, a powerful military factor (ERIM, B. 93, B. 97, etc.). They are capable of winning over towns (Sumur, B. 99,), mayors (*ḫazanu,* B. 96) and kings like the King of Hazor (B. 127). They were particularly hostile towards Rib-Addi, governor of Byblos, and made an alliance against him with Abd'Ashirta of Amurru, and later with Aziru his son. Sumur, Batrun, Shigata, and Ambi were taken and occupied (B. 99, 106). Byblos and Ibirta suffered the same fate (B. 111), and so did the towns of Taḫši and Upe later on (B. 131). Labaya of Shechem grants them a territory (B. 145).

From the letters recently published by Edzard[21] we know that some groups could come under the jurisdiction of the Egyptian king and be sent to "the towns of Kašu to dwell there." Is Kašu Nubia? This is not necessarily so here, since in the Posener Execration texts (E. 50-1) a country *Kwšw* is mentioned which is certainly in Asia and not in Nubia. Some biblical texts connect this Cush or Cushan with Midian and Judah (Hab 3:7; Judg, 3:8);[22] the Kushite wife of Moses seems to have been the same as the Midianite Zipporah (Exod 2:21; Num 12:1). In the Amarna letters originating from Jerusalem *Kaša/u* does not appear to refer to a place so far off as Nubia. It is also said that the SA.GAZ *a-pu-ar-ra* will dwell in it *(ina libbišu, (ki)?-mu-ú ša aḫ-ta-bat-šu-nu-t(i),* "an (St)elle derer, die ich weggeführt habe," Edzard). It is noteworthy that the pharaoh uses the root *ḫabātu,* the equivalent of SA.GAZ in the Akkadian syllabaries. It is to be noted too that this transfer of population is similar to another transfer alluded to by Harmhab.[23]

They are in league with other "lords" *(awīlū)*. Thus one of them who has an Egyptian name, Amenhatpi, lord of Tushulti, takes them in after each more or less successful engagement against Mahzibi, Giluni, and Magdali (Migdol). He is compelled to hand over forty of them who have made their escape after their defeat before Hazi. He himself becomes suspect, however, and has to flee to some other SA.GAZ (B. 130). In the south the king of Jerusalem was hostile to them, although he is the only one to write their name out in full and not with the pejorative form SA.GAZ; perhaps this is because he himself has a Hurrian name, which Thureau-Dangin read as Abdi-Hebat.[24] Harabu, Suwardata of Kelle (the Keilah of the Bible), and Iapahi fight against them. But Iapahi's youngest brother goes to Muhhazi in order to come to terms with them (B. 147); it is likely that he is the Milki-ilu who, in league with Labaya of Shechem and his sons, will deliver his territory over to the SA.GAZ, preferring to come to terms with them rather than with pharaoh's commissioners. This gives the SA.GAZ more facility for taking action against Aialuna (Ayyalon) and Ṣarḫa (Samson's Zorah). However, it is not clear whether they kept the towns they captured any longer than did the *Ḫapiru* at Mari, or the sons of Jacob at Shechem (Gen 34).

We know that about 1300 B..C Sety I was obliged to cope with what he considered a revolt on the part of the SA.GAZ. They came from the mountain of Iarimuta and from Tjr, which are difficult to identify, and the pharaoh was compelled to afford protection against them to the Asiatics of *Rhm(?)*. In the tale of the capture of Joppa, which was composed about this time by an Egyptian scribe, they constitute once again an element hostile to Egyptian power; there is the danger that they will insinuate themselves in liaison with the *maryannu*[25] who are asking for fodder for their animals (the *maryannu* are an Indo-European element, and are often linked with the Hurrians; they are mentioned after the *'prw* in a list of Ramesses III, B. 189); however, the relation between the two is not clear and the text is damaged.

Posener has recently found a mention of the *'prw* in the first line of an ostracon in the Strasbourg Library.[26] These men are connected with the handling of stones. As the script seems to be that of Ramessid times (Nineteenth Dynasty), such an activity fits well with the *'prw* workers under Ramesses III and IV.

In the thirteenth century B.C. the *Ḫapiru* are known to us mainly by the texts from Ugarit in Syria. They are still foreign and untrustworthy elements, capable of destroying a castle (*dimtu,* B. 162), and in a text which reproduces an older tradition (B. 157) the SA.GAZ is placed between the thief and the evildoer. It was a privilege in a royal grant to receive the assurance that a SA.GAZ would not enter the house, and that the service of the royal messengers would not be required (i.e., probably, that they would not have to be given lodgings, B. 159).

The SA.GAZ, however, show a tendency towards settlement. We have already seen that in the territory of Ugarit there was a town or a district called Halbi of the *'prw.* A treaty between Hattusilis III the Hittite (1275–1250 B.C.) and the king of Ugarit mentions the territory of the SA.GAZ in the Hittite land, where fugitives from Ugarit could take refuge; the Hittite king undertakes to extradite them. A Hittite text mentions a town of the *Ḫapiru* (G. 137). A certain *Ḫapiru* is party to a lawsuit before the king of Carchemish and the king sends him elsewhere as he does not reside there (B. 158), but it would have been possible for him to do so. We learn from the personal names of Ugarit that nearly half of the population was Hurrian.[27] A note concerning a debt of oil has the name of a *Ḫapiru,* son of Kuiaba (B. 160), which reminds one of the Nuzi name, ARDU-Kubi; this should perhaps be read "Abdu-Kubi," as Thureau-Dangin does for the name of the king of Jerusalem. Elsewhere, next to a certain Ari-Teshub who bears a characteristically Hurrian name, a *Ḫapiru* is mentioned (B. 163).

Other personal names of this type will occur; but they will disappear as a group. As J. Bottéro has noted, SA.GAZ in divination texts and lexicographical collections need not be rendered *Ḫap/biru;* it stands for *ḫabbatu,* "dangerous brigands." Certain isolated personal names occur with the epithet "Habirean," and reading with *b* becomes more and more likely;[28] this is especially so in the case of *Ḫa-bir-a-a,* who is the beneficiary of a gift of real estate from Marduk-aḫḫē-eriba (*c.* 1060 B.C., B. 166); also in the case of *Ḫarbi-si-*ḪU, who is called the Habirean in a letter of Ninurta-nādin-šumati of Babylon (*c.* 1150 B.C., B. 165), putting him at the disposal of the king of Assyria. It had been surmised that a neo-Assyrian text describing Nineveh mentions a god Ḫabiru, next to Kube, which would have paralleled the *Ḫapiri* gods of the Hittite texts. But there is now agreement that this refers to the gods *of the Ḫapiri;* W. von Soden prefers to see a reference to a deity *ḫa-wi-ru,* adored in the same temple. Just as there is no reference to contemporary Hebrews in texts of the first millennium from Israel, so, too, cuneiform and Egyptian texts of the same period do not know of any *ḫapiru/'prw* groups.

III. ORIGIN AND NATURE OF THE *ḪAPIRU/'PRW*

Having thus brought together the historical and geographical evidence, scholars have tried to discover the etymology of the name and the origins of the group.

Most of them have favoured a Semitic etymology. Since the form with *p* has proved to be older than the form with *b*, the root which is usually put forward at present is *eperu (epru, ḫaparu* at Amarna) in cuneiform texts, *'eper* in Massoretic Hebrew, which means "dust." E. Dhorme first put this forward, and the suggestion was taken up again forcefully by Borger. W. F. Albright supports it, and quotes in its favour the text of Falkenstein on the SA.GAZ who haunt the steppe and live in camps and tents.

However, this description is very like the accounts by the Babylonians of the Asiatics from the West, the Amorites and their god,[29] those whom the Egyptian wisdom text of Merikare[30] calls the "miserable Asiatics." This description hardly fits the *Ḫapiru* as such. It is strange, moreover, that the Egyptian scribes never used before *'prw* the determinative of the legs, of the land, or the desert countries; not even that of the boomerang of the nomads. They used a determinative difficult to interpret (Gardiner Aa 20, "doubtful"), used also for the verb *'pr,* meaning "to equip, to provide" (an ideogram which is hard to explain).[31] This does not correspond to the Semitic "dust" but to the Akkadian *epēru.* This was the etymology which W. F. Albright used to support; A. Goetze still seems to be in favour of it and adduces in support *ḫabatu,* meaning "to receive subsidies from another," which is a homonym of *ḫabatu,* = SA.GAZ. However, the existence of this *ḫabatu* has been called in question, and the homonyms given in B. 157 for AMA (Ugarit) require as equivalent to SA.GAZ not *ḫabatu* "provide" but *ḫabbatu* "brigand." As for the verb *ḫapārum* (B.5′), the relevance of which has been underlined by Landsberger, it is hardly mentioned in the current dictionaries. The Chicago Assyrian Dictionary (Ḫ, 217b, *sub ḫubullu*) proposes the translation "went over"; this relates it to the Hebrew *'ābar,* but does not fit in with the original *p* of the root, which is now well established.

It therefore seems established that there was an attempt on the part of the Akkadian scribes, or the scribes in their tradition, to link this term to a Semitic root. But they never knew exactly whether to see in it *ebēru*, *ḫabru* or *epēru*. They passed from one to another and they influenced the Egyptian scribes in the direction of *epēru*, "provide." It seems to me that B. Landsberger was right in seeing objections only where a Semitic etymology is concerned, and R. Dussaud was of the same opinion.

G. Dossin therefore considered the possibility of the Sumerian GABIRI meaning "desert." The *Ḫapiru* would have been warrior bands in the desert, the beduins of those times. For a long time I considered this opinion as valid, for want of a better.[32] But the Sumerian texts only know of SA.GAZ, and they describe them rather as MAR.TU, people of the West, than as *Ḫapiru*. The milieu where we find *Ḫapiru* is not a Sumerian one. The Susa tablet specifies that the *Ḫapiru* are soldiers from the West.

The milieu where we do find *Ḫapiru* is in fact a Hurrian one. They appear in Cappadocia as neighbours of the Hittites and of the Assyrian colonists; and it is now in the region north-east of the Tigris that scholars are looking for the first habitat of the Hurrians:

> The heaviest concentrations can be observed to the east of the Tigris, but there are also Hurrians in Upper Mesopotamia, where they control several small states, and they have gained a foothold on the western bank of the Euphrates. It looks as if, coming from a generally north-eastern direction, the Hurrians moved down in ever-increasing numbers from the mountainous border of the Fertile Crescent and advanced to meet the Amorites . . . (Kupper).[33]

The Hurrians appear in history as early as 2300 B.C., and it is in a region which is to become Hurrian-dominated, the region of the Upper Khabur, that the personal name *Ḫapiram* appears (Tell Brak). The language of the area from Urarṭu to the Caucasus will be related to theirs. Later we find Hurrians at Mari. Kupper estimates that nearly a third of the population of Chagar Bazar was Hurrian. Although for a time the Hurrian element was thought to have been minimal at Mari, round which *Ḫapiru* groups gravitated, Kupper has counted four or five princes with Hurrian names, like Arishenni of Nahur and Shukru-Teshub of Elahut.

We have to ask whether it is by chance that numerous *Ḫapiru* are found in the regions of Alalakh and Nuzi, which were extensively settled by Hurrians. Is it by chance that in Hittite texts the *Ḫapiri* are treated as strangers and intruders in the same way as the Hurrians? At the same period, the fifteenth century B.C., Egyptian texts reveal their presence in Canaan at a time when Egyptian scribes call the area "Hurru." In the Amarna period, it is the Hurrian king of Jerusalem who writes their name out in full and avoids using the pejorative ideogram SA.GAZ, even though he is their enemy. They then fade away and disappear, just as in the Bible the Hurrian wave of invasion is only a memory from the patriarchal age which has left hardly any trace, apart from "the Horites, the sons of Seir in the land of Edom" (Gen 36:21).

The connection between the *Ḫapiru* and the Hurrians can therefore be considered as proven. But the texts do not permit the identification of the Hurrians with the *Ḫapiru,* well distinguished as they are from each other on the stela of Amenophis II. One can but follow the painstaking studies of Bottéro and Greenberg, for whom the *Ḫapiru* appear to be not an ethnic entity but a social category. It should therefore be asked whether the *Ḫapiru* are not the Indo-European aristocracy who, like Artatama, Suttarna, Biriawaza, and others,[34] lived alongside (or among) the Hurian population both in Mitanni and in the Canaan of the Amarna letters. Unless this were the case, the Amenophis II list of prisoners would have ignored them. We know that Biriawaza of Upe speaks of his brothers and of his SA.GAZ in a list which resembles that of Amenophis II; Biriawaza himself has an Indo-European name. It is precisely "to the man of Damascus" at Upe that pharaoh writes concerning the transfer of *Ḫapiru* in Kush "in the place of people whom the pharaoh has removed from there" (*EA* 53, 63); these letters were studied by Edzard at the 1970 Congress at Munich. It remains to be seen whether the Kush mentioned there is to be identified with Kasi, hostile to the king of Jerusalem, as were the *Ḫapiru.* Finally, we may be able to find an Indo-European etymology, since the Hittite root *ḫapparija*[35] implies "transfer," "abandon," "sale," "market." This root can explain *iḫpiar* in the Cappadocian text B.5′, since it concerns a fugitive for debts.

Against this are the following considerations. The Egyptian scribes had a name for Indo-European warriors; they called them *maryannu,* even if one admits with Helck that in the minds of the scribes at the end of the second millennium B.C. *maryannu* meant mainly the cavalry and *ʿprw* was used for the infantry. Moreover, the Indo-European Šuwardata of the Amarna letters was an enemy of the *Ḫapiru.* Finally, what *Ḫapiru* names we know are not Indo-European but Hurrian names. J. Bottéro tells us that "few" Alalakh names could be Semitic, "most of the names are Hurrian" (p. 185), as are Akiptilla, Giddudu, and Hutanapu from Nuzi (E. Cassin). As E. Speiser had already pointed out: "Hurrians and Hapiru were thus coextensive to a remarkable degree; apart from this their paths diverge sharply."[36] The latest studies show us, however, that it is mainly from the sociological point of view that they differ from each other. Ipri-beli (B. 42; Alalakh p. 185) is particularly interesting in its Semitic form: "Ipri is my lord." The *ipri* or *ḫapiru* would be the Hurrian warrior aristocracy, capable of discussion with Hittite kings and of treating with them as with equals, capable of dominating Syria and penetrating Canaan as far as Jerusalem. Elements of this group, dispersed in the great Mitanni upheaval of the fifteenth century B.C., are scattered in Assyria and Babylon (Akkad), but receive a special status when they take refuge in the Hurrian area of Nuzi.

In view of this, one is compelled to look for a Hurrian etymology; since "lord" is written in cuneiform Hurrian *ewri, epri* or *ibri,*[37] this hypothesis must be examined. But there is straightaway a tremendous difficulty. *ipri* is written with an *'aleph* and not with an *'ain* in the cuneiform alphabet of Ugarit, whereas the equivalent of *Ḫapiru* is *'pr* with the *'ain.* There is a second difficulty which is scarcely less serious, namely that certain ways of writing *ḫapiru* make it practically certain that the Akkadian and Hittite scribes intended to indicate a long *î* in the second syllable. Thus personal names are written *ḫa-pi-i-ri* on several occasions. For a long time these two objections seemed to me insuperable; I now think them less so, for three reasons.

Firstly, as Speiser[38] and Laroche[39] in particular have observed, Hurrian does not have an *'ain.* It appears at Ugarit in Hurrian texts only for words of foreign composition. This is so for *'prm*=SA.GAZ. When the Ugarit scribes had to write down a Hurrian word used by the numerous Hurrian population, like *ewir* or *ipri,* they noted it with an aleph, e.g. *ewr-šr.* When they had to deal with *'prm,* who had been called *ḫapiri* for a long time in the scribal schools, they put in an *'ain.*

Secondly, the resemblance between the *ubaru* or *ubru* and the *ḫapiru* has been noted. They are two distinct groups at Nuzi and at Ugarit. But there are strange analogies in their situation. They are strangers from outside the country but who can be guests; in his grants, the king can confer the exemption from having to lodge either group. The *ubaru* of the Hittite texts studied by von Schüler[40] is a protected person who has access to the king; he is a vassal of the Hittite empire and can take part in the cult. Any Semitic etymology is unlikely, since the Arabic word *wabara* means "to halt" and, especially, "to be hairy." This hardly suggests the idea of a "guest." But the connection with the West Semitic *ʿpr* has become more likely since E. Cassin has found at Nuzi *ḫapiri ubbutu,* where the *ubbutu* corresponds to the Hebrew *ʿbṭ;* this increases the likelihood of an *ubru* or *upru* corresponding to *ʿiwri* or *ʿipri.*

Thirdly, concerning the long *î* in *ḫapiri,* this could come from the tendency of the scribes to create a *qâtîl* or *qattîl* form, just as they tended to attach the word to a Semitic root. It is striking that the Akkadian *i* of the second syllable disappears in Hebrew West Semitic. Abiram becomes Abram, Ahiab becomes Achab. Forms like ʻAmram, Elnathan, etc. would be transcribed by cuneiform scribe with an *i* in second position.

It is therefore not impossible that all these groups may have a common origin, as long as one admits that they evolved separately, so that they appear as distinct groups after five centuries of *Ḫapiru* wanderings. This common origin would be a military[41] Hurrian aristocracy, which was already without a stable habitat in the Mari period. They are fringe groups in relation to the major states, and even the minor states, of the second millennium B.C. Idrimi takes refuge with one of the groups for seven years as a fugitive. Kings make use of them, fight against them, and make treaties with them. They no longer belong to an organized ethnic group, and their status as foreigners or refugees becomes more marked before they tend to become assimilated.

IV. *'APIRU* AND HEBREWS

Weippert took up again the problem of the *ʻapiru* when he became aware of Mendenhall's theory on the establishment of the Israelites in Canaan. Mendenhall identified Israelites and *ʿapiru,* and he defined a member of the latter as a person who "has renounced any obligation to the society in which he formerly had some standing and has in turn deprived himself of its protection".[42] We have seen why this definition does not fit. Weippert was able to prove that the Israelites were not *ʿapiru,* and that one could not see in the Israelite conquest a sort of Peasants' Revolt against the Canaanite cities.

Weippert rightly underlined the importance of the law of *ʿibrī* (pronounced *ʿivrī* or *ʿiwrī*) slave in Exodus 21:1–11. As others had done before him, he showed the similarity of status between the *ḫapiru* at Nuzi and the *'ebed 'ibrî;* the latter also enters into an obligation for a limited period only, and is able to recover the status of *ḥopši* (cf. the *ḫupšu* of Alalakh and Amarna) after a seven-year period. This period is the same as the time that Idrimi spent as a refugee with the *'apiru;* Weippert suggests that he may have become an *'apiru* himself.

Weippert has studied the phonetic problem more closely. He thinks that *'apiru* is a form of the *faʿîl* type which developed into a segolated form *faʿl* or *fiʿl;*[43] Brockelmann's *Grundriss* gives cases of the juxtaposition *malku/milku.* If one maintains that the original form is a Hurrian *ipri, iwri* or *ibri* (all of which are found in the texts) the problem is a little different. The Bible would then be nearer to the original form than the Akkadian scribes; these would appear to have wanted to take the term as the participle of a verb *ḫāpar* "to pass," and have sometimes made it evolve into a verbal adjective of *parîs* form. One can admit with Weippert that the length of the vowels depends on the cases of *scriptio plena* given by von Soden.[44] Moreover, Weippert gives about fifteen examples of words written with either *b* or *p* without alteration of the meaning. There is no insurmountable obstacle, therefore, in the way of maintaining that when the Israelites penetrated into Canaan they found there the remnants of the Hurrian military aristocracy, in a state of decay certainly, but having nevertheless afforded to the Egyptians and the Philistines the occasion of using their name as a generic term for the population of the hinterland. The Israelites even went so far as to adopt the old law of the *'ibrî* servant for the cases when they might acquire servants and incorporate them into their families by the special rite carried out at the door of the house.

It is more difficult to determine how the Israelites defined their relations with these *'ibrîm.*

Genesis 10:21ff. gives a table of peoples which considers *'eber* as a descendant of Shem through Arpachshad; the South Semitic tribes are linked to Eber through his son Joktan. Since Shem's eldest son is Elam, it is clear that this is a geographical rather than ethnic list. Arpachshad has long been compared with Arrapḫa, which is precisely where the Hurrians of Nuzi were to be found, as well as the *Ḫapiru* who took refuge at Nuzi. Joktan is linked to Eber through his brother Peleg, whose name is explained by the division of the earth, if that is really the meaning of the verb. It is anyway a sociological consideration, and we have seen how important these are in the question of the *Ḫapiru*/*ʿprm*.

There is a gap in the J tradition on the relation between Abram and Eber in chapters 10 and 11 of Genesis. But the P tradition in Genesis 10:10–29 is clear; this leaves open the question whether it is the simplification of more complex relations.

In Genesis 14:13 Abraham is called *ʿibrî*. Weippert is right in drawing attention to the fact that the same text makes Mamre into an Amorite, whereas it was a geographical sacred place which was still in use as a market in the fourth century A.D. This episode presents a warrior Abram, with a rather different character from that in the other Genesis episodes, in which Abram is never a warrior. We have here what is really a typical *ḫapiru* of the Amarna type. The battle takes place at Hobah near Damascus, which is where we find the *Ḫapiru* of Amarna. The tradition reproduced in the episode is very ancient; but it appears to have been combined with another one, which refers to Jerusalem and Hebron where Abram buys from Ephron *(ʿprn!)* the cave of Machpelah (Gen 23). All these elements are valuable, but it is impossible to disentangle all the historical and sociological elements which have been preserved in these chapters. I admit with Astour[45] that there has been a Deuteronomic edition of chapter 14, but it is not clear to me whether the epithet *ʿibrî*, given to Abram, is an editorial element to be connected with the P genealogy of Genesis 10. It does seem possible that the epithet *ʿibrî* given to Abram belongs to one or other of the two traditional elements which seem to me to underlie the story as we have it; that is, either the great coalition which ends in a battle north of Damascus, or the episode of Melchizedek further south. This is not the place for a discussion of the difficulties involved in an exegesis of Genesis 14; it is sufficient to remember that the editor gives as allies of Abram two geographical names, Mamre the sacred tree and Eshcol the valley. His intention is to evoke a pre-Israelite period, and he considers that Abram, the father of a multitude of nations and the descendant of Eber, according to P, was the sign of assembly for populations more numerous than the *bĕnê Yisraʾel*; this is a confirmation of the genealogy in Genesis 25:1–6, which gives the descendants of Abraham by Keturah. All the names of his descendants are of good Semitic formation, as is the name "Abram" itself. But the population of Hebron was not necessarily Semitic, and the name of Ephron the Hittite evokes the *'prm* once more. It could be that the tradition or the documents employed by Genesis 14 underlined the geographical connections and not the ethnic ones, just as Genesis 10:22 counts the non-Semitic Elam among the descendants of Shem.[46]

V. CONCLUSIONS

In view of the present state of the information and of research, any conclusions must be extremely tentative.

The Hebrews of the Bible, *'ibr(iyy)îm,* can be identified with the *Ḫapiru* of cuneiform texts, the *'prw* of Egypt and the *'prm* of Ugarit. They are not so much an ethnic group as a sociological phenomenon. This "class" seems to be linked with the Hurrians, following their movements without being identified with them. They appear in Upper Mesopotamia at the end of the third millennium B.C. as a military aristocracy. These groups are a menace for their non-Hurrian neighbours, who call them SA.GAZ, "brigands," even when they make contracts with them or make use of their services, either individually or collectively. They go down into Canaan at the time when Egyptian scribes call the country "Hurru," but they are not thereby identified with the Hurrians. They disappear as distinct groups at the same time as the Hurrians disappear, at the end of the second millennium B.C. The Israelites are conscious of a certain common condition with them, especially in relation to the Philistines and the Egyptians, but this is a geographical rather than an ethnic link. However, the Israelites do not identify themselves with them, and, at the time of the monarchy, they cease to see in them a living population, even though they inherit certain of their customs dating from the patriarchal period.[47]

NOTES

1. On this point cf. M. Gray, "The Habirû-Hebrew Problem in the Light of the Source Material Available at Present," *HUCA* 29 (1958) 35–202.
2. D. B. Redford, "The Land of the Hebrews in Genesis 40:15," *VT* 15 (1965), 529–32.
3. K. Koch, "Die Hebräer vom Auszug aus Aegypten bis zum Grossreich Davids," *VT* 19 (1969), 37–81, esp. 46–49.
4. Ibid., 62.

5. The translation proposed by Meredith Kline ("The Ha-BI-ru, Kin or Foe of Israel?" *The Westminister Theological Journal* 20 [1957] 50) are not convincing ("both" is not in the text and the "selected troops" are presented as being the Israelite army), but the author's observations underline effectively the fact that for the biblical editor there was a common destiny between Israel and the Hebrews.
6. A. Caquot ("Préfets," *Supplément du Dictionnaire de la Bible,* 7, fasc. 43 [Paris, 1968], p. 284) prefers to attribute this "integration" to David.
7. *AOTS,* p. 13.
8. C. Virolleaud, *CRAIBL* (1939), 329; *RES* (1940), 74ff.
9. The correspondence between the numbers in J. Bottéro, *Le problème des Habiru* (IVe Rencontre Assyriologique internationale, Paris, 1954) and M. Greenberg, *The Hab/piru* (New Haven, Conn., 1955) will be found in *BiOr* 13, nos. 3,4 (1956), 149f.
10. *ZA* 19 (1959) 286, n. 32. See also S. Kramer, *JAOS* 60 (1940), 253, and F. R. Kraus, *BiOr* 15 (1958), 77–78.
11. "Zwei althethitische Belege zu den Ḫapiru (SA.GAZ)," *ZA* 18 (1957), 216–23. On B. 72 see *RHA* 75 (1965), 35.
12. "Quelques remarques à propos des archives administratives de Nuzi," *RA* 52 (1958), 16–28; "Nouveax documents sur les Habiru," *JA* 246 (1958), 225–36.
13. PRU iv (1956), 17.238 (pp. 107ff); 17.341 (pp. 161–63); 17.232 (p. 239).
14. PRU v. (1965), 18.148 (no. 62, pp. 88–89).
15. At the Rencontre Assyriologique, Munich, July 1970, published in *Beiträge zur Altertumskunde* v (Bonn, 1970), pp. 52–62.
16. Cf. E. Cassin, *JA* 246 (1958), 236. On the equivalence: alphabetic ʿ= syllabic *ú* see A. Jirku, "Die Umschrift ugaritischer Laryngale durch den akkadischen Buchstaben ú," *ArOr* 38 (1970), 129f.
17. E. Cassin, *JA* 246 (1958), 231–32.
18. This is the correct translation, with A. Gustavs, "Der Gott Hapiru," *ZAW* 40 (1922), 314; "Was heisst *ilâni Hapiri?*" *ZAW* 44 (1926), 25–36, and the note by M. Wieppert, *Die Landnahme der israelitischen Stämme in der neueren wissenschaftlichen Diskussion* (Göttingen, 1967), p. 73, n. 3.
19. See H. Klengel, "Der Schiedespruch des Mursilis II hinsichtlich Barga," *Or* 32 (1963), 32–55.
20. On this text and the related bibliography see R. Giveon, *Les bédouins Shosu des documents égyptiens* (Leiden, 1971), pp. 12–15.
21. D. O. Edzard, "Die Tontafeln vom Kamid el-Loz," *Beiträge zur Altertumsurkunde* (Bonn, 1970), pp. 52–62, 12–14.
22. Cf. W. F. Albright, *BASOR* 83 (1941), 34, n. 8; not disproved in *BASOR* 95 (1944), 33, n. 19; B. Maisler (= Mazar), *Revue de l'histoire juive en Égypte* 1 (1957), p. 37f.
23. Cf. W. Helck, "Die Bedrohung Palastinas durch einwandende Gruppen am Ende der 18. und Anfang der 19. Dynastie," *VT* 18 (1968), 476.
24. "Le nom du prince de Jérusalem au temps d'El Amarna," *Memorial La-*

grange (Paris, 1940), pp. 27–28. However the first sign is read, the goddess Heba or Hebat is a Hurrian deity.

25. For Helck (p. 530) the *ʿprw* are the infantry and the *mryn* are the cavalry.
26. In line 3 of this ostracon the *rmṯ mšʿ n jmnty* expression is quite close to the *ṣabē* (ERIM) of cuneiform texts. The men are Egyptian workers and are not the same *ʿprw* as in I. 1 even if they do similar work.
27. C. Schaeffer, *Ugaritica* iv (Paris, 1962), p. 87.
28. This is confirmed by *A Vienna Demotic Papyrus on Eclipse- and Lunar Omina,* edited by R. A. Parker (Brown University Press, 1959), which dates probably from the first Persian domination. It mentions four countries, Amurru, Egypt, Syria and *ʿybr* (or *ybr* A II 18–24), no longer *ʿpr*. As in the case of the biblical texts, the root *ʿbr* may have exerted an influence. R. J. Williams (*JNES* 25 [1966] 69) considers it to be the province of Eber-nâri, the *ʿabar-Nahara* of Ezra 4:10.
29. See J. R. Kupper, *Les Nomades en Mésopotamie au temps des rois de Mari* (Paris, 1957), p. 160.
30. See J. A. Wilson in *ANET,* p. 416.
31. Posener (*apud* Bottéro, p. 166) compares this with *ʿprw,* meaning "the crew" (of a ship, but also of workmen, *JEA* 13, 75); Helck translates "Abteilung." Gunn and Gardiner translate "gangs." This administrative letter (Sixth Dynasty) is interesting, since the *ʿprw* receive clothing (cf. B. 16, Larsa period) and the writer of the letter is a military leader.
32. There was an unfortunate trace of this in my article, "Hébreux, Ubru et Hapiru" (*Syria* 35 [1958] 198–207), and M. Liverani deduced from the article an interpretation which differs from what the article was trying to say (*Storia di Ugarit nell' eta' degli archivi politici* [Studi Semitici 6; Rome, 1962], p. 87).
33. "Northern Mesopotamia and Syria," *CAH,* rev. edn., ii, fasc. 14, p. 26.
34. See the study by P. E. Dumont in R. O'Callaghan's *Aram Naharaim* (Rome, 1948); M. Mayerhofer, *Die Indo-Arier im alten Vorderasien* (Wiesbaden, 1966), pp. 140–147.
35. See J. Friedrich, *Hethitisches Wörterbuch* (Heidelberg, 1952), p. 54. I. M. Diakonoff (*MIO* [1967] 364) has noted in the different versions of the Hittite Code, §48, *ḫipparas* = A.SI.RUM ("prisoner"); he compares with this the Hattusil III-Ugarit Treaty (B. 161). One wonders if *ḫipparas* is a Hittite adaptation of the word which is transcribed elsewhere *ḫapiru.*
36. "Ethnic Movements in the Near East in the Second Millennium B.C.," *AASOR* 13 (1933), 34.
37. Cf. the *ḫipparas* in the Hittite Code, §48.
38. "Introduction to Hurrian," *AASOR* 20 (1941), 44–49.
39. *Ugaritica* v, p. 527.
40. "Hethitische Kultbräuche in dem Brief eines ugaritischen Gesandten," *RHA* 72 (1963), 45. On the analogies and differences between *ḫapiru* and *ubaru* cf. *Syria* (1958), 207–11.
41. ERIM, *ṣābe,* can be applied to non-military groups, but there is so much

evidence of the military activity of the *ḫapiru* that it is best to leave these terms with their usual signification.

42. *BA* 25 (1962), 71.
43. Ibid., p. 84.
44. W. von Soden, *Grundriss der akkadischen Grammatik* (Rome, 1952), §7e.
45. "Political and Cosmic Symbolism in Genesis 14 and in its Babylonian Sources," *Biblical Motifs*, edited by A. Altmann (Harvard University Press, 1966), pp. 65–112.
46. The Kittim, *ʾšr* and *ʿbr* are mentioned together in the last Balaam oracle (J). In this I see a relation with the Sea Peoples and the Philistine settlement on the coast, together with the *Aššurim* of Gen 25:3 and of the Egyptian topographical list (*jsr;* Sety I and Ramesses II, in Simon's lists XVII.4 and XXV.8, with a spelling different from Assur), perhaps 2 Sam 2:9 and the word written *gšr* in Josh 13:2, on the border of Egypt. The Minean *ʾʾšr* in *Répertoire Epigraph. Sem.* (Paris, 1900–) 2771, 3–4, and 3022, 1, parallel to *mṣr* ("Egypt") raises other problems. K. Koch rightly stresses the relation between *Shosu* and *ʿprw* in the two Sety stelae (Karnak and Beth-Shan, op. cit., 60). But for a necessary distinction between these two see R. Giveon, *Les bédouins Shosu des documents égyptiens* (Leiden, 1971), pp. 4, 14.
47. It has not been possible to consult the article on "Habiru" by J. Bottéro since published in *RLA* iv, i (1972), 14–27.

12

"And Dan, Why Did He Remain in Ships?" (Judges 5:17)[1]

Yigael Yadin

FOREWORD

Most scholars who have made a study of the tribe of Dan as depicted in Biblical sources admit that much of the information supplied about it is strange and puzzling. This applies not only to the status of the tribe and the character of the tales of Samson, but also to its areas of tribal settlement and the course of its northward wanderings. These difficulties, which the scholars usually make no attempt to conceal, derive largely from their common starting-point. On the one hand they set out to clarify the contradictions between the various Bible sources in accordance with the rigid approach of the Bible as finally redacted, while at the same time they tend to disregard the happenings in Philistia reflected and recorded in external sources. In order to bring the difficulties into relief it is fitting to give a brief account of each of the Biblical texts that are connected with the matter under consideration.

THE TRIBE OF THE DANITES

The Status of the Tribe of Dan

The most interesting verse in this connection is undoubtedly Genesis 49:16; translated in the Authorised Version as: "Dan shall judge his

Reprinted by permission from the *Australian Journal of Biblical Archaeology* 1 (1968): 9–23.

people as one of the tribes of Israel." The difficulties of the scholars reach their height when they try to give this a significance that runs counter to the apparent meaning: ". . . It seems to me"—one of them remarks, for example, "that here the text implies that Dan stands *at the head* [my italics, Y.Y.] of the tribes of Israel."[2] And yet the straightforward meaning of this verse appears rather to signify some kind of amphictyonic council admitting the tribe of Dan into the covenant of the tribes of Israel.[3] Until that time Dan would appear to have been *outside* the covenant. Henceforward he would judge his people *as one* (i.e., as any other one) of the tribes of Israel.

This conclusion would appear to be quite significant. As we shall see, it is well suited to the remaining information about the tribe of Dan, which seems very remarkable if it is interpreted in light of the view that attributes a supremacy over the tribes of Israel as a whole to Dan.

The Problem of the Portion of the Tribe of Dan

The difference between the tribe of Dan and the tribes of Israel as a whole finds its clearest expression in the Biblical description of its portion, found in Judges 18:1: "In those days there was no king in Israel; and in those days the tribe of the Danites sought them an inheritance to dwell in, *for unto that day their inheritance had not fallen unto them among the tribes of Israel.*"

Here as well the *prima facie* meaning of the text clearly indicates that at this stage the tribe of the Danites had no inheritance *among or within* the tribes of Israel. This would also seem to be indicated by the text in Joshua, 19:47: "And the border of the children of Dan went out from them" (in the AV "*was too little for them*"). The problem of the inheritance of Dan appears particularly acute in light of the verses preceding the one quoted above, which includes within the list of the inheritances of the tribes of Israel not only Zorah, Eshtaol *et al.,* in the inheritance of Dan, but also "Gath-rimmon and Mei-jarkôn and Rakkon with the border over against Joppa." The same applies to the list of the cities of the Levites found within the inheritance of Dan according to Joshua 21:24: "Gath-rimmon with her suburb."[4]

These lists give rise to a serious difficulty. For according to the now generally accepted view the tribe of Dan never dwelt along the coasts of the Mediterranean at all (see below). If we accept the version or opinion that the lists date back to the days of Solomon, it is hard to understand why those cities should have been attributed to the heritage of Dan, which is assumed never to have dwelt in them at all. The only explanation would seem to be that such passages derive from a far more ancient tradition, which echoes the possession of these places by this particular tribe. The difficulties of the scholars are evidenced *inter alia* by the view which rejects the assumption "that Dan ever held so extensive an area. It seems reasonable to assume that when the term 'Dan' is applied to this extensive area, it is only the historical name of a relatively small district which was expanded over a far larger one when it came to be included within the borders of Israel."[5] In other words, it is assumed here that there was an attempt at a historical *reconstruction*. But one must ask: "Reconstruction" of what?

It may be inferred that the two sources quoted involve a very striking contradiction at first sight. For according to one of them Dan has no heritage at all among the tribes of Israel, while according to the other its boundaries contain many cities, some of them very definitely "Philistine."

In addition, the Bible provides information about the semi-nomadic character of the tribe of Dan at a certain period. In part it is a nomadic group, and in part is casually settled at the "Mahaneh (camp of) Dan." (This is stated to have shifted from time to time, being found on one occasion between Zorah and Eshtaol—Judg 13:25—and subsequently near Kiryath-Jearim—Judg 18:12. Some of the tribal families, or clans, move (in connection with the tale of the northern migration, and see below) in armed troops with their women and children.

No less interesting is the verse which indicates that there was a certain stage at which the main pressure came not from the Philistines but, specifically, from the Amorites: "And the Amorites forced the children of Dan into the hill country for they would not suffer them to come down to the valley," etc. (Judg 1:34–35). Yet there can be no doubt that one of the most instructive passages regarding the tribe of Dan, a passage directly connected with the subject-matter of our problem is that which deals with the migration of the Danites northward. The facts are known, and therefore we shall restrict ourselves to stressing those details which are directly connected with our subject.

During the period when the Danites dwelt in the region of Zorah and Eshtaol, they once again sought a place to settle down, on account of the pressure from east and west. Following a survey far to the north,

Laish "was revealed" to them and they conquered it. The essence of this narrative is that the people who lived in Laish before them were closely connected with the Sidonians, who for some reason could not come to their aid (Judg 18:2ff., 28ff.). And the Danites changed the name of the city and called it Dan, after their forefather.

At this stage Dan, as remarked, was semi-nomadic, as is shown by the passage in Judges 18:21ff.: "So they turned and departed and put the little ones and the cattle and the goods before them . . . angry fellows." This process of wandering and conquering Laish is also connected, according to Biblical tradition, with the steps taken by Dan to adopt for themselves a priest descended from Gershom, the son of M(N)ShH.[6] This story also contains something that seems "peculiar," unless we assume that here as well as there is some hint of a certain change that came about in the religion and worship of the tribe of Dan.

In any case it is clear that the verse found in Deuteronomy 33:22 ("Dan is a lion's whelp, that leapeth forth from Bashan") refers to the northern portion of the tribe.

"And Dan, Why Did He Remain in Ships?"

As though to complicate the in-any-case complicated problem of the tribe of Dan still further, we have the verse from the Song of Deborah which serves as the title to the present study. This verse, possibly more than any others connected with the subject, has enjoyed countless interpretations which derive from two difficulties.[7] First, it is not clear whether the passage refers to the period when Dan dwelt in the north or in the south; and second, the reference to the ships is vague.

Those who argue that the words refer to the northern area must avail themselves of the forced explanation that these ships are the boats that were used in the Hula Lake, or similar interpretations. The ancient and medieaval commentators already found difficulties in interpreting the word given here as "remain," the original Hebrew of which is *yagur*. This word *per se* may equally well derive from a homonymous root meaning "fear" or "dread"; and early commentators were hesitant as to which meaning they should select. The Targum Jonathan, for instance, is followed by Rashi when he exclaims: "Dan put his money in ships so that he could rise and flee."[8] Rabbi David Kimhi similarly remarks: "He does not refer to sea ships since his portion was not by the sea, for that was where the portion of Zebulun was . . . And although Joshua states, regarding Dan's portion (19:46), 'against Jaffa,' nevertheless, Jaffa was not in his portion; so this means the ships were on the Jordan. As much as to say that he crossed the Jordan and fled for fear of the Gentiles, and bore his belongings away to the other side of the Jordan" and so on and so forth.

Undoubtedly, this verse is particularly hard to comprehend according to the "northern" view, as several scholars have already pointed out at length.[9] Yet even those who claim that it is the Dan of the south that is referred to, immediately meet with another difficulty, which derives from the approach referred to above, namely: What did the southern Dan have to do with ships? They therefore had to give meanings such as: He fears the ships of the enemy that are upon the Great Sea;[10] he dwells as a slave in the ships of the Sidonians; and more of the same.

None of these offer any solution to the essential problem. The "northern" view involves many difficulties, but the "southern" opinion, in the sense mentioned above, does not clarify the connection between the words and the content of the Song of Deborah either. Is the fact that Dan fears the ships of the foe on the Great Sea sufficient to deter him from entering into battle?

Comparison with the other verses regarding those tribes which did not join in the war seems to indicate that there is a hint here *of Dan being engaged with ships,* for which reason the tribe did not gird itself for war, like Reuben staying amid the sheepfolds or Asher which dwells on the sea-coast. Yet if the reference is to Dan and its occupation in the south—we again meet the same original difficulty that Dan does not seem to have dwelt by the shore, and therefore, what can be the connection between them and ships in general? In order to overcome these difficulties one must inevitably reach the conclusion that this verse, as it stands, refers to a stage at which Dan dwelt by the shores of the Great Sea and engaged in ships, of which more will be said below.

Absence of Genealogical Lists of the Tribe of Dan and Description of the Conquest of Cities in His Heritage

No less astonishing is the fact, already remarked on by commentators, that Scripture contains no genealogical lists of the tribe of Dan, nor details of the conquest of the cities in the southern heritage. Genesis is restricted to the fragmentary sentence "And the sons of Dan, Hushim" (46:23). Nor can any evidence in this respect be found in the genealogical lists of Chronicles. Indeed, the point has justly been stressed by various scholars,[11] but the colourful explanations offered do not afford any direct answer to the question before us.[12] The account of the conquest, likewise, does not indicate the cities mentioned in the heritage of Dan, nor are they in the list of the thirty-one kings found in Joshua 12.

Our surprise at all these anomalies (in respect of the tribes of Israel as a whole) in reference connected with the tribe of Dan leads us to an additional problem: the problem of Samson.

Samson

Samson, the outstanding hero of the tribe of Dan, has a special status among all the judges. For that matter, he can scarcely be regarded as a judge in the usual sense. The account in Scripture gives the clear impression that his heroic deeds are not the result of any external pressure on the tribe nor the fruit of an aspiration to aid Israel, but are a response to *personal* injury. In all that is told regarding Samson there is no evidence of any close link whatever between his family, or the tribe of Dan as such, and the other tribes of Israel.[13] On the contrary, all the contacts preceding his acts of vengeance against the Philistines indicate that there were *normal and family relations* between the Danites and the Philistines.[14] The fact is that Samson and his family maintain close ties with the Philistines alone. His first wife is Philistine (Judg 14:1), a daughter of the uncircumcised who dwelt in Timnah. He has ties with a harlot in Gaza (ibid. 16:1); and his second wife, Delilah, dwells in the Valley of Sorek and is the confidante of the chiefs of the Philistines. Samson's main physical strength is connected with the braided hair of his head, while his "spiritual" strength finds expression in his gift for *asking riddles;* and he participates in riddle contests that have dangerous results.

His deeds of valour include the slaying of the lion; the slaying with the jawbone of an ass; the roguery with the foxes; and finally a brave deed in Gaza, and a daring incursion into Ashkelon (ibid. 14:19). He finds himself in difficult and peculiar situations, and certain places appear to have been named on account of events that befell him there; such as the hollow at Lehi which opened so wondrously when Samson was almost dead of thirst. Indeed, it is not surprising that in consideration of the similarity between his feats on the one hand, and his name and that of the cities of his vicinity (Har Heres, ʿIr Shemesh, etc.) on the other, various scholars have compared Samson to some mythological sun-hero and particularly to Hercules, Perseus, etc. All this is familiar.

Interim Summary

At a certain stage the tribe of Dan was not a member of the amphictyonic league of the tribes of Israel, nor does it have any genealogical lists. Although its most ancient heritage clearly had some connection with the Mediterranean coast between Philistia and northern Sharon, the Bible does not know of any conquests among those of the tribes of Israel. The relations between this tribe and the Philistines at certain specific periods are exceedingly close and even find expression in ties of marriage.

In consideration of all that has been said above there is room to examine what was happening along the Philistine coast at about that period in the light of extra-Biblical surces as well.

THE PEOPLES OF THE SEA

Of all the "Peoples of the Sea" who invaded the land of Canaan and settled along the coast, the Bible actually knows only the Philistines and not only because they constituted the most considerable element in this group of nations, but chiefly because they were the principal foe of the tribe of Judah. Yet, after all, the Bible is not a history of Palestine, but a work dealing with events and national or tribal groups, only in so far as these were directly connected with Israel. It is therefore natural that if we had only the Scripture to rely on, we would have known nothing at all about the existence of the "Peoples of the Sea" and the fact that several of them, in addition to the Philistines, settled in Palestine. The Philistine penetration of the country is connected with the battles of the group of "Peoples of the Sea" with Rameses III, which are commemorated so magnificently on his reliefs in the temple at Medinet Habu.[15] From his reliefs and inscriptions we learn of two main battles, one on land and one at sea. The Peoples of the Sea are depicted and described here as shipmen *par excellence,* and as semi-nomads moving in wagons with their wives and children, accompanied by armed warriors. The group of Peoples of the Sea is composed chiefly of five tribes or peoples including the Philistines, who differ from one another in their costumes and hair-dress and some of whom are also circumcised.[16]

The Tjeker

Among the Peoples of the Sea there is a group called Tjeker.[17] If we had to rely on the Bible alone, we would never have known that this group or part of them settled on the coast of Palestine at the same time as the Philistines established themselves there. Happily we have at our disposal an Egyptian document of primary significance which sheds light on the situation along the eastern coast of the Mediterranean in the eleventh century, B.C. This is the now familiar Wen-Amon Story.[18]

Let us briefly report all it relates regarding the Tjeker. Wen-Amon served as a priest at the Temple of Amon in Karnak and was sent to Byblos on the Phoenician coast to obtain cedars with which to build the ceremonial barge of the god. The adventurers of Wen-Amon are instructive in themselves, and *inter alia* show the decline of Egypt at that period. But we are particularly interested in what happened to Wen-Amon when he reached Dor on the Sharon coast, where his money was stolen from him. At this time, according to the document, the ruler in Dor was Beder of the Tjeker.

These Tjeker, whose centre was at Dor, were outstanding seamen, owning a powerful navy, and later Beder was capable of sending eleven warships to Byblos in order to arrest Wen-Amon. From this document we learn that parallel with the occupation of the south by the Philistines, a sea-going group of the Peoples of the Sea, the Tjeker settled along an important section of the coast, namely northern Sharon.

The Dny(n)

As already remarked, five "Peoples of the Sea" are represented on the Egyptian reliefs in separate groups, each in its own costume. Among these groups, one of three peoples stands out in particular. These three resemble one another in their costume and appearance, although slight differences in details can be observed. The group was studied not long ago by Wainwright.[19] They all wear the familiar feather helmets, and all have thickly plaited hair, which is carefully settled under their helmets.

Attention should be drawn to an interesting fact: The group consists of Philistines, Tjeker and a third tribe of whom more will be said below. Since the Philistines settled in the south of the country and the Tjeker along the coast of northern Sharon, we have a special interest in ascertaining the identity of the third people.

In the battle document dating from the days of Rameses III, this people is called DENE or DNE. Their name is also given in an additional form on account of which it is the practice to refer to them in contemporary literature as the DANUNA. Gardiner has proved in his basic study[20] that DNE is the original form, at least in respect of the final form which is some kind of ethnic suffix.[21]

We have no document of the period of the Judges analogous to that of Wen-Amon, describing the history of the Danuna or their place of settlement after the defeat. But their close ties with the Philistines and the Tjeker may well give rise to the assumption that when they settled on the shores of Palestine they did so in the presumably vacant area, between the Tjeker and the Philistines, i.e., between Dor and northern Philistia.

In order to trace the Danuna of the Egyptian records we have to turn to the Greek "Danai" who claimed descent from their forefather Danaus who settled Argolis. The assumption of identity between the "Egyptian" Danuna and the Greek Danai was strengthened in 1946 with the discovery at Karatepe by the expedition headed by Bossert, of the bilingual (Phoenician and Hittite) inscription[22] of Azitawadda, King of the Danunites. Azitawadda (Adorer of Wandash, the sun-god) declares that he is a descendant of the House of MPSh, which Alt and Barnett at once identified with the Mopsus of Greek mythology.[23]

This discovery led scholars to recognise an absolute identity between the Greek Danai and those referred to in the Egyptian records, and also between them and the Danunites who settled in Asia Minor. Indeed, Barnett has justly remarked that it should not be concluded from this that the Greek Danai invaded Asia Minor and Egypt; on the contrary the Danai arrived in Greece from the east, as is attested by Greek tradition.

In view of all this, it is proper to survey what is known from Greek sources about Danaus, the forefather of the Danai, Mopsus and other heroes connected with this tribe; and their relations with the eastern shores of the Mediterranean.[24]

Danaus

Danaus originates from the east. His "father" is Belus (Baʿal or Bel) while his "brother" is Aegyptos. Danaus is a shipman and according to one tradition he invented the "fifty-oar" ships and the art of navigation. Most of the tales about Danaus in Greek sources are connected with his daughters and his dispute with Aegyptos. The sons of Aegyptos wished to wed the daughters of Danaus, but the latter refused and he fled with them to Argos in Greece. Aegyptos and his sons pursued them and in the absence of any alternative Danaus agreed to the marriages. The main point of this story is Danaus' advice to his daughters to slay their husbands; that is, the participation of women in order to obtain the murder of husbands.

Perseus, Hero of the Sun

Another and far better-known Danaian hero whose "history" is closely connected with our subject, is Perseus, who founded Tiryns (according to another tradition, Mycenae) whose principal hero was Hercules. Most of the legends about Perseus deal with his adventure near Jaffa[25] and the familiar story of Andromeda, daughter of the King of the Ethiopians, who was bound to a rock in the sea at Jaffa. On his return from slaying the Medusa, Perseus rescues her from a sea monster. This connection between the Jaffa coast and Perseus has always been regarded by scholars as a proof of some connection between the Greek Danai and this stretch of the Mediterranean coast. Among the many tales told of Perseus, mention should be made of the remark by Pausanius that Mycenae obtained its name on account of the mushroom *(mykes)* from which water burst miraculously when Perseus was thirsty.

Mopsus

We also find much to interest us in the story of Mopsus, who was undoubtedly a historical individual in the more modern sense of the word. As can be learnt from the Karatepe inscription he was a Danaian. The following are his principal characteristics and main events of his life, according to Greek sources.

He is the son of Apollo, god of the sun, and a priestess. His life story is more particularly connected with wanderings in Asia Minor, Phoenicia and Palestine, immediately after the Trojan War (twelfth century B.C.). At various places he found cities which bear his name, and builds altars to Apollo. He is best known for his outstanding use of riddles. One of the stories connected with him records a riddle contest between him and the sooth-sayer, Calchas, in which Mopsus is victorious and causes the death of his rival. As remarked, Mopsus was wandering across the Middle East during the twelfth century at the head of a band of warriors. According to one source (Athenaeus)[26] he invaded Ashkelon which he conquered. According to Strabo, the tribes of Mopsus invaded the eastern part of the Mediterranean and settled sections along the coasts of Cilicia, Syria and Phoenicia.[27] According to one of the sources he died as a result of snakebite.

The Danai and the Coast of Jaffa

The close ties between the coast of Palestine and the Danai or their heroes according to Greek tradition, as well as the fact that the Danai constitute the third element among the groups of the Peoples of the Sea who fought against Rameses III (the other two being the Philistines and the Tjeker) would appear to provide a basis for the assumption that part of the Danai also settled along the shores of Palestine. Since the Philistines settled from Jaffa southwards, while the Tjeker made their home in the vicinity of Dor, the only area which comes into consideration for the Danai is that which stretched between Dor and Jaffa. And here arises a problem which is also of archaeological interest, for one of the cities within this region of coast is Tel Qasila. Unlike the specifically port cities, such as Dor and those along the Philistine coast which were inhabited before they were settled by the Tjeker and the Philistines—from the Late Bronze Age at least—Tel Qasila was founded about the middle of the twelfth century B.C.[28] Furthermore, the material and ceramic remains of the first city (Stratum XII) is "Philistine"; that is, pottery of the type characteristic of the dwelling-places of the Peoples of the Sea, including the Tjeker at Dor. If the Danai or part of them settled along this stretch of coast, it would seem that the foundation of the Stratum XII city should be attributed to them, for neither the Tjeker in the north, nor the Philistines in the south needed to build new port cities, since good harbours and ports were at their disposal. The city of Stratum

XII was destroyed in a great fire, but the city above it, namely Stratum XI, is also "Philistine" archaeologically speaking.

From this it may be concluded that after the Stratum XII city (which goes back to the days of the Peoples of the Sea) was destroyed a new city was built and was also settled by the Peoples of the Sea. In this connection it may be proper to mention the Onomasticon of Amenope in the eleventh century B.C. which refers to the following peoples in the following order:[29] Shardans 268; Tjeker 269; Philistines 270; The Shardani are also one of the Peoples of the Sea, and for a long time—even before the contest with Rameses III—they were among the mercenaries of the Egyptian army. Yet they differ entirely in their costume from the group of the Philistines, the Tjeker and the Danuna.

If we assume that the list marks these peoples according to the order of their settlement, it would follow that in the eleventh century a relatively large group of Shardans lived north of the Tjeker. On the other hand, Alt[30] has suggested that at this period the Shardans lived along the stretch of coast between the Tjeker and the Philistines.[31] In any case it does seem permissible to assume that the residents of Stratum XII (if indeed they were Danuna) were driven from Tel Qasila and their place was taken by other Peoples of the Sea (according to the evidence of the pottery) who may have been Shardans. The wandering of the inhabitants of Stratum XII took place round about the year 1100, as this stratum belongs to the latter part of the twelfth century and the first half of the eleventh century B.C.

The Time When the Tribe of Dan Wandered North

Quite independent of these considerations, there is room to ask: When was it that the Tribe of Dan wandered north to Laish? From the Biblical account it is clear that the conquest of Laish took place at a time when Sidon, which should have helped the inhabitants of Laish, had been completely weakened and did not have the strength to do its duty. This situation could only have been round about the end of the twelfth century (near the year 1100), both following the victory of Ashkelon over Sidon and as a result of the campaigns of Tiglath-Pileser I.[32] That geopolitical situation would appear to provide a solution of this important problem, for it seems impossible to imagine that the tribe of the Danites settled themselves by force in a territory which had been under the influence of the kingdom of Sidon until that time. Whether by chance or otherwise, this date accords precisely, as we have already seen, with the date of the destruction of Stratum XII at Tel Qasila.

SUMMARY

The Tribe of Dan

The Biblical data discussed at the beginning of this study seems to show that at a certain stage of its settlement the tribe of Dan was very close indeed to the Peoples of the Sea. When this tribe first settled, there would appear to have been no formal link between it and the convenant of the Tribes of Israel. Its principal occupation was with ships, and its men were very specifically seamen. There is reason to think that its hero and his activities are linked with sun-worship. The tribal area of settlement was along the coast near Jaffa to begin with, i.e., in the district lying between the settlement areas of the Philistines and Tjeker. At a certain stage it was forced into the interior, and was finally compelled to wander away from the entire area and proceed northward to the vicinity of Laish.

The Danai

From the information available in both historical and historico-mythological sources, it is possible to ascertain the following facts: The tribe of the Danai originates in the east, and the introduction of the alphabet to Greece is attributed to it. Its members were outstanding seamen who had some special connection with sun-worship. Its heroes had a special capacity for asking riddles. Sections of this tribe wandered as warrior bands, invaded various places and established cities which they named for the fathers of the tribe. Sections of the tribe of the Danai are particularly associated with the eastern Mediterranean littoral in general, and the vicinity of Jaffa in particular.

Conclusions

From all that has been said above it would prove that only one of two conclusions can be drawn: either there were two different tribes (the

Danites and the Danai) with an identical name and similar characteristics which operated in the identical geographical region and period, or that there is a link between the tribe of Dan and the tribe of the Danai, and possibly even a certain measure of identity. The former case would constitute an exceedingly peculiar and remarkable concatenation of circumstances; whereas the second case, which appears more realistic, enables us to explain various phenomena linked with the Danai themselves, and particularly, all that affects the tribe of the Danites. From this we may feel entitled to conclude that Dan was an ancient tribe which spread throughout the east, and that at the most ancient period it already had some link with the tribes of Jacob. Certain sections settled in Palestine and at the beginning of the twelfth century drew near to the tribes of Israel (again?) and were admitted to the amphictyonic covenant and given the status of one of the tribes of Israel. At an early stage of their settlement (that is, at the time of the Song of Deborah) they dwelt on the seashore—between the Tjeker and the Philistines[33]—and were engaged with shipping as of old; but after they were forced inland from the coast (by the other Peoples of the Sea) apparently about the end of the twelfth century, when the kingdom of Sidon began to weaken, they wandered northwards. In any case the second alternative permits a re-examination of several facts connected with the tribe of Dan which it has hitherto been impossible to account for in any other way. It is only fitting to close with the words of Hecataeus of Abdera as summarised by the late Professor Yehoshua Gutmann, together with the latter's doubts and conjectures,[34] which may serve to strengthen our approach in this study.

> Hecataeus commences his essay on the Jews with the Exodus. Once a pestilence broke out in Egypt, which the local inhabitants attributed to the wrath of the gods. . . . The Egyptians therefore resolved to expel the strangers. The best and most courageous of the strangers united together and went forth to Greece and other countries; and their most famous leaders were Danaus and Kadmos. But most of the people went to Judaea, which was entirely desolate in those days.
>
> The link which Hecataeus establishes here between the Exodus from Egypt and the arrival of Danaus in Argos may possibly be the first case in which Greek mythology has been combined with the narrative in the Torah. . . . It is hard to know what the sources of Hecataeus can have been. . . . It is hard to understand why he saw fit to associate the people of Israel and the Danai in the story of the Exodus. The only possibility which comes into consideration here is that, pre-

cisely as in the details of his essay on the Jews, wherein he used information he received from Jews here and there, so he may have heard of the Exodus from Jews. The question is: Did he hear about the Exodus only from Jews, himself combining this with the departure of the Danai? Or were there some Jews who linked the Jews and the Danaians together?

NOTES

1. I have done my best to preserve the following presentation in its original form as a lecture to the Nineteenth Meeting of the Israel Exploration Society, and not to transform it into an essay bristling with references and footnotes. There were two reasons for this: First, because I desire the reader to consider a certain suggestion I have to offer, without being too definite in formulating it; and second, the essential material about the tribe of Dan may be assumed to be familiar to the reader and has already been discussed in numerous publications. I am, therefore, restricting myself to references which are easily available and which are directly connected with the subject-matter of the lecture. During my London visit in 1962, I outlined the essential idea to Professor Cyrus H. Gordon, who agreed with me about one of the problems to be discussed below (VTSuppl. 9 [1963] 21). After my lecture Mr. E. Margalit gave me a copy of his essay entitled "The Parallels between the Legend of Samson and the Legends of the Peoples of the Aegaean Sea" (*Beth Mikra* 11 [1966] 122–30–F.G.). Although his main subject is the problem of Samson, as shown by the title of his essay, Mr. Margalit reaches a number of conclusions resembling my own.
2. H. Gevaryahu, in the discussion of B. Z. Luria's lecture on "The Settlement of the Tribe of Dan," which was delivered to the Bible Circle at the home of Mr. D. Ben-Gurion. And see: *Studies in the Book of Joshua,* ed. Chaim Rabin *et al.* Jerusalem, 1960, p. 263 (Hebrew).
3. The word-play in the verse in question is based on the shorter form of the name. See also: S. E. Loewenstamm, *Biblical Encyclopaedia* (Jerusalem, 1954, Hebrew) on this subject. See also: "And Rachel said, God hath judged me (in Hebrew *danani*) and hath also heard my voice and hath given me a son; therefore called she his name Dan" (Gen 30:6).
4. On the proposed identification of Gath-Rimmon with Tel-Jerisha see: B. Mazar, *Biblical Encyclopaedia* (Hebrew) s.v.
5. Z. Kallai. *The Northern Boundaries of Judah* (Jerusalem, 1960), pp. 27–28 (Hebrew).
6. Although the text indicates only the general family origin of the priest, there are some who view it specifically as a hint of the early period of the wandering of the Danites not long after the period of Moses. See, e.g., B. Mazar, *Studies in the Book of Joshua* (*supra* n. 2) p. 272.
7. On the various opinions of this verse see, e.g., B. Z. Luria's lecture (*supra* n.

2) p. 250 ff. Also the essay of the late I. Ben-Zvi in *Oz Ledavid* (Jerusalem, 1964), pp. 117 ff (Hebrew).

8. On these views see the lecture of B. Z. Luria (*supra* nn. 2 and 7).
9. See particularly Luria and Ben-Zvi (*supra* nn. 2 and 7).
10. E.g., M. Haran, *Studies in the Book of Joshua* (Heb.) (*supra* n. 2) p. 262; also Ben-Zvi (*supra* n. 7).
11. See: B. Z. Luria (*supra* n. 2) p. 254. In the discussion on the lecture, Mr. Z. Shazar also repeatedly called on the lecturer to find an answer to "the main question: why have no genealogical lists of the Sons of Dan survived?" (idem. p. 269). Furthermore, members of the tribe of Dan are referred to here and there as children of mixed marriages. And cf. Leviticus 24:10 *et seq.*).
12. See, e.g., S. Yeivin, *Biblical Encyclopaedia* (Heb.) II. col. 679 on Dan: ". . . it is suggested that in essence this tribe (Dan) was nothing more than a group of families which emerged from the miscegenation of the followers of the sons of Jacob with Hivite elements in the vicinity of Shechem".
13. Even after Samson fled to the "parting of the Etam Rock" in Judah the men of Judah did not object to his activities against the Philistines but to the fact that he sought a *refuge* within the boundaries of Judah: "Surely you know that over us (over Judah!) rule the Philistines, so what is this that you have done to us? Why have you fled to our confines?" Indeed, it was their intention to surrender him to the Philistines, who had made demands to them in this connection.
14. The commentators have noted this without attempting to draw any conclusions from it. See, for example, the following passage: "Between them [the Philistines—Y. Y.] and the Danites there is no state of war but unrestricted intercourse, *connubium* and *commercium*—nay, the whole life of the Danites seems to gravitate towards the Philistine cities" (K. Budde, *apud:* Hastings, *Dictionary of the Bible* [New York, 1911], s.v. *Samson*, p. 379a.).
15. On these reliefs and the relevant literature see, e.g., Y. Y. *The Art of Warfare in Biblical Lands* (New York, 1963), pp. 247–253; plates 333–338.
16. See also: A. H. Gardiner, *Ancient Egyptian Onomastica, I* (Oxford, 1947), p. 196*.
17. See also: *ANET,* p. 262b (Tjeker).
18. *Ibid.*, p. 25 ff. Also see now: B. Mazar, "The Philistines and the Foundation of the Kingdoms of Israel and Tyre" (Heb.), *Publications of the Israel Academy for Sciences and Humanities, I,* 7, p. 2.
19. G. A. Wainwright, "Some Sea Peoples," *JEA* 47 (1961), pp. 71 ff.
20. Gardiner (*supra* n. 16), p. 124* ff.
21. On this see also: R. D. Barnett, *Journal of Hellenic Studies* 73 (1953) p. 142, n. 1: "The form Daniuna recorded on the Egyptian monuments is to be derived from **Daniya-wana*. The ending *wana(s)* is the regular ethnic suffix in the Hittite hieroglyphic language." See more particularly the essay by O'Callaghan in *Orientalia* 18 (1949) pp. 199 ff.

22. See *apud* Pritchard (*supra* n. 17), p. 499 ff. and literature there.
23. See Barnett's article (*supra* n. 21), note 4.
24. On this see *The Oxford Classical Dictionary,* ed. M. Cary *et al.* (Oxford, 1949), under "Danaus," "Mopsus," and "Perseus"; the articles by Wainwright and Barnett mentioned above (nn. 19 and 21); also below.
25. See particularly: S. Tolkowsky, *The Gateway of Palestine: A History of Jaffa* (London, 1924) pp. 27 ff.
26. Athenaeus VIII, 37: C. & T. Mueller, *Fragmenta Historicorum, I,* 38, Fig. 11. See in particular Wainwright's study (*supra* n. 19), p. 80, n. 1, and the literature there.
27. Strabo, XIV, IV, 3.
28. B. Maisler (Mazar) *IEJ 1* (1950), pp. 73 ff; also his article (*supra* n. 18, p. 7).
29. For a detailed discussion see Gardiner (*supra* n. 16), p. 194* ff.
30. A. Alt, "Syrien und Palaestina in Onomastikon des Amenope," *Kleine Schriften I* (Munich, 1959), p. 244, n. 1.
31. *Ibid:* ". . . das Gebiet zwischen den Tkr und den Philistern insbesondere an die Gegend von Japho und Aphek denken."
32. On this problem see *in extenso* the study of B. Mazar (*supra* n. 18).
33. Also cf: *Antiquities*, V, 87, where Josephus defines the area of the Danites on the coast between Ashdod and Dor.
34. Yehosha Gutmann, *The Beginnings of Jewish-Hellinistic Literature* (Jerusalem, 1958) pp. 50–51 (Hebrew).

V

BIBLICAL DIFFERENCES FROM THE ANCIENT NEAR EAST

13

New Moons and Sabbaths: A Case-Study in the Contrastive Approach

William W. Hallo

Since Dr. Glueck's untimely death, the particular combination of archaeological and theological interests which he championed, indeed the entire comparative approach to Biblical Studies, has been subjected to ever more serious challenges. The comparative method has been attacked as a form of "pseudorthodoxy" by Morton Smith,[1] and more recently some of its most cherished results have been demolished, point by point, in the works of John van Seters[2] and Thomas L. Thompson,[3] particularly in respect of the patriarchal narratives and their possible historicity. Even those of us who have heeded Benno Landsberger's strictures on the "conceptual autonomy" of each of the principal ancient Near Eastern cultures,[4] and Samuel Sandmel's valid warnings against "parallelomania,"[5] have nevertheless been suspected of reactionary tendencies—as if we wanted to reduce Assyriology once more to the role of handmaiden to Biblical Studies—or vice versa.

Nothing could be further from the mark, at least as far as my own intentions are concerned. I have defended and applied the comparative method in numerous studies, some literary and others historical, in which it seemed to me that cuneiform sources and biblical texts could fruitfully illuminate each other. But for me the method requires only the commensurability of the two terms, not a prejudgement as to their equation. If A is the biblical text, or phenomenon, and B the Babylonian one, I am quite prepared to test the evidence for a whole spectrum of

Reprinted by permission from the *Hebrew Union College Annual* 43 (1977): 1–13.

relationships, expressed "mathematically" not only by $A=B$ but also by $A\sim B$ or $A<B$ or $A>B$ and even $A\neq B$. The last possibility needs stressing, because a comparative approach that is truly objective must be broad enough to embrace the possibility of a negative comparison, i.e., a contrast. And contrast can be every bit as illuminating as (positive) comparison. It can silhouette the distinctiveness of a biblical institution or formulation against its ancient Near Eastern matrix. It is perhaps unfortunate that scholarly usage has tended to slight this notational breadth implied in true comparison, that is has the well-worn symbol cf. (confer) for positive comparison but none for negative ones. Perhaps one may suggest cs. for contrasta.

Be that as it may, I would propose the "contrastive method" as a particularly valid one within the overall comparative approach to biblical studies.[6] Apart from numerous contrasts in detail, consider only what is perhaps the single most pervasive contrast of all: the role of the king in the ancient Near East. Over and over again it contrasts with the bearers of that role in the biblical ethos. As source, warrant and enforcer of law, the Mesopotamian king is replaced by the biblical deity, as chief ministrant by the high priest, as responsible for both cultic and ethical observance initially by Israel as a whole and later by each individual Israelite. But it is not my intention to pursue this illustration here. Rather, I wish to test my method against a subject less transcendent and more immanent, and one where ancient Israel's unique contribution to the social order of all subsequent ages has too often been obscured by facile abuse of the comparative approach. I refer to the calendar of ancient Israel or rather that part of its cultic calendar which, in the form of the week, has become a virtually universal legacy to posterity.

It is perhaps not unfitting that I address this theme here, for Hebrew Union College and the *Hebrew Union College Annual* have long played a role in the debate. In the very first volume of the *Annual,* Julian Morgenstern published "The Three Calendars of Ancient Israel"—and in the next forty-five years, when he contributed a major article to each of the next forty volumes (a record not likely to be ever broken) he returned four more times to the same subject. Hans Lichtenstein edited the *Megillat Taʿanit* in volumes 8–9, while Julius and Hildegard Lewy investigated "The Origin of the Week and the Oldest West Asiatic Calendar" in volume 17. More recently, Drs. Weisberg and Wacholder have given us a comparative study on cuneiform and rabbinic sources for observations of the new moon (volume 42), and Dr. Wacholder has written extensively on the sabbatical cycles (volumes 44 and 46). My own approach to the subject will, of necessity, be different from all these models while adhering, I hope, to the high scholarly standards that they set. Much of my argument has, I will admit, been anticipated by G. H. Meesters in a study that appeared in 1966. But this study has been largely neglected,[7] perhaps because it is in Dutch—it is entitled *Op Zoek naar de Oorsprong van de Sabbat*[8]—and also I have a good deal of new cuneiform evidence for lunar festivals in neo-Sumerian and neo-Babylonian times.

My thesis in brief is this: the cultic calendar of ancient Mesopotamia, like its civil calendar, was largely tied to the phases of the moon, and not at all to the week (or: a week); in Israel, the cultic calendar was only minimally connected to lunar phases, whereas the sabbatical cycle was all-important. Certain conclusions will be deduced from this contrast. To begin my case, I must ask you to indulge me in a somewhat technical run-down of the Mesopotamian evidence for "lunar festivals." It is abundant, but I will present it in all possible brevity.

Our first detailed records of cultic practices in Mesopotamia date from the end of the Early Dynastic Period in the 24th century B.C. These records already include reference to the "house (or chapel or station) of the crescent" called u4-s a k a r in Sumerian and later borrowed into Akkadian as *uskaru* or *askaru*.[9] The general sense of this term can be fixed as crescent[10] by three lines of evidence which may be mentioned here to illustrate some of the lexicographic techniques available to the Sumerologist.

1. The Sumerian logogram(?) is written with elements whose separate meaning is "day" or "light"[11] etc. and "growing"—the latter a nice etymological parallel to "crescent."
2. The various contexts of the Sumerian word and its Akkadian derivative show, in addition to the basic sense of lunar crescent, such derived meanings as an ornamental or votive moon-disc, a part of the wheel, a part of the door, a crescent-shaped area in a mathematical problem-text,[12] and a crescent-shaped formation in the liver of a sacrificial sheep.[13]

3. The lexical texts equate the Sumerian word with Akkadian *arḫu, ūm arḫim* and possibly *ṣīt arḫim,* i.e. day of the moon, that is "new moon."[14]

Special offerings for this new moon festival are attested at pre-Sargonic Lagash (both at Sirara[15] and at Uruku[16]) but there is not enough evidence to demonstrate a monthly observance of the rites. The same is true of the Sargonic period. From Nippur, we have a number of offerings for the new moon festival dating from the early part of the great Sargonic dynasty,[17] and one even specifies that the offerings were made by Sargon himself.[18] In these texts, the new moon festival is called "head of the crescent."[19] Under his grandson, Naram-Sin the Great, the expression "head of the month (by name)" was introduced.[20]

It is, however, only with the end of the Sargonic period in the 22nd century and the beginning of the neo-Sumerian period in the 21st that we find evidence of a regularized lunar festival. In the celebrated cylinders of Gudea of Lagash, we are introduced to the generalized Sumerian term for lunar festival è š - è š, literally perhaps "all sanctuaries," in the form of the compound verb è š - è š . . . a k, "make, do, perform the *eššeššu*-festival."[21] This compound recurs in one of the most popular royal hymns of the succeeding Ur III period, the hymn known today as Šulgi A. Šulgi, greatest of the Ur III kings, boasts there of having run from Ur to Nippur (and back) in one day, so that, as he says "verily I celebrated the *eššeššu*-festivals of (both) Nippur (and) Ur on one and the same day." We can actually date this improbable achievement to the 6th year of Šulgi's long reign (*ca.* 2089 B.C.),[22] for the following year was named after it,[23] in an interesting and early instance of what I take to have been the institutionalized commemoration of events in hymns, royal inscriptions and date formulas at the beginning of every year or every other year in the Classical phase of Mesopotamian civilization.[24] But the new *terminus technicus* was not restricted to literary contexts. Among the Ur III economic texts at Leiden (Netherlands) which I had the privilege of publishing while still at Hebrew Union College is one otherwise undistinguished little tablet which records the assignment of nine assorted sheep and goats to the high priestess (n i n-d i n g i r) at Lagash on two separate occasions in the first year of Šulgi's son and successor Amar-Sin.[25] One of these occasions involved five of the principal deities of Lagash and their sanctuaries and is labeled "lunar festival of the high priestess performed on the (day of the) chariot."

This laconic entry is a precious clue to the numerous references in other Ur III accounts which allude to offerings for the è š - è š in general, or specifically for the rites of the new moon (u 4 - s a k a r g u - l a), the first crescent (literally the "chariot of the 7th day") or the full moon (literally the "crescent of the 15th day"). These references have been collected and analyzed in two studies, one published by Limet in 1970[26] and one, as yet unpublished, by my student Marcel Sigrist, now of the École Biblique in Jerusalem,[27] and I am happy to acknowledge my indebtedness to both. A third study, which attempted to refine the evidence by elaborate calendric and astronomical calculations,[28] rests on too shaky a foundation to be utilized here.[29]

It may be noted at the outset that only three lunar phases were observed in this period, i.e., no special account was taken of the 3rd crescent. Secondly, the archives of the various cities used a variety of different terms to identify the specific phases and their celebration. The new moon was variously called "great crescent at (or of) the head of the month" (u 4 - s a k a r s a g - i t i - g u - l a), "great crescent" (u 4 - s a k a r g u - l a), "head of the crescent" (s a g - u 4 - s a k a r [a]) or simply "(the) crescent" (u 4 - s a k a r). The first crescent was called the "station (é) of the 7th (or 6th) day" and, more rarely, "the chariot of the 7th (or 6th) day." The full moon occurs as "crescent of the station of the 15th day" or simply "station of the 15th day."[30] The explanation for the introduction of the term "chariot" appears to rest on the symbolic identification of the half-moon with the two semi-circular blocks of wood which were joined to make up the solid chariot wheels typical of this period.[31]

The cultic dispositions for these festivals are abundantly attested. Numerous comestibles are provided for, including cakes, oil, beer, etc.; large and small cattle are sacrificed; there are ritual ablutions, and special garments including sandals are issued for the occasion. The specific allotments differ again as between the different cult-centers, but only one of them can be highlighted here, and that is the capital of the Ur III empire, the city of Ur itself. Here we find a peculiar historical situation revealed by the terse economic texts which, though their intent is simply to record cultic expenditures against a future audit of temple stocks, nevertheless provide us with a kind of after-the-fact or descriptive ritual record comparable in some ways to certain biblical passages like Numbers 7 which preserve for all time the pious offerings dedicated to the sanctuary.[32] At the end of the 21st century, the Ur III empire suffered a series of reverses and lost one after another of its outlying provinces. Its last king, Ibbi-Sin, retreated to Ur together with the deposed governors of the lost provinces. But in spite of these straitened circumstances, the cult was maintained, together with the meticulous bookkeeping that characterized it. Particular attention was paid to that peculiar neo-Sumerian institution, the amphictyony. In its heyday, this institution provided for the temples of the religious capital at Nippur by monthly liturgies levied on all the central provinces through their governors.[33] Now, however, the deposed governors simply offered pitifully small numbers of sacrificial animals to the two principal sanctuaries at Ur in the context of the "royal lunar festivals"—but were still dignified with the designation "governor of the amphictyonic obligation" when they did so.

From the hapless Ibbi-Sin, Ur passed into the successive rule of the kings of Isin, Larsa, Babylon, and the Sealand. From the middle of this lengthy period, two texts may be cited here to illustrate both the continuity and the evolution of the lunar festivals. Both texts were edited by Baruch Levine and myself in the *HUC Annual* for 1967 and plotted on elaborate charts which taxed the ingenuity of the printer and, no doubt, the budget of the *Annual*.[34] But the charts do help to make it graphically clear that the three lunar festivals of the Sumerian tradition survived intact, and that, in the interval, they had been augmented by a fourth festival falling on the 25th day of the lunar month. The 25th day cannot be readily correlated with a phase of the moon, however, and the way was thus opened for detaching the *eššeššu*-festival from its original lunar association. In the subsequent evolution, this detachment was carried further. Hemerologies and other literary texts of the late second and early first millennium changed the *eššeššu*-festivals to the fourth, eighth, and seventeenth days of the month, and by the second half of the first millennium, there were as many as eight *eššeššu*-festivals per month.[35]

It might be thought that we have pursued the topic into a cul-de-sac. But as is often the case when tracking down a millennial institution, we must allow for the survival of an old institution under a new name. In the first place, the terms for the individual lunar phases were translated into Akkadian and appear together in the Old Babylonian Atrahasis epic as *arḫu sebūtu u šapattu* "first, seventh, and fifteenth day of the month."[36] In the second place, the concept of lunar festivals in general did not simply die out when the original Sumerian term changed its meaning. Rather, I submit that it reemerged in Akkadian guise in the form of the *ḫitpu*-offerings. The root *ḥtp* is familiar in Arabic, Hebrew and Aramaic in connection with slaughtering or hunting and occurs already in a Ugaritic text in the specific context of sacrifice.[37] We read, in a prayer to Baᶜal, "A bull, oh Baᶜal, we consecrate (to you), a votive offering, oh Baᶜal, we dedicate (to you), the first fruits, oh Baᶜal, we consecrate (to you), the booty, oh Baᶜal, we offer (to you), a tithe, oh Baᶜal, we tithe (to you)." The word translated "booty" here is *ḥtp*, comparable to the *ḥetep* ("prey") of Proverbs 23:28. Given the context, however, the word may already foreshadow the connotation of a kind of sacrifice. That is surely the meaning of Akkadian *ḫitpu* which occurs in monthly sacrificial lists of the late first millennium.[38] This neo-Babylonian *ḫitpu* offering typically fell on the 7th, 14th, 21st, and 28th day of the month in the Achaemenid texts from Uruk; sometimes they are entered one (or even two) days earlier. Albert T. Clay published a sizeable number of such lists from the Yale Babylonian Collection; additional examples remain to be published from there or have appeared meanwhile in other collections. Clay himself edited the texts under the provocative title of "The Babylonian Sabbath."[39] The debate which he thus inaugurated was carried forward, not without some acrimony, by A. L. Oppenheim and J. Lewy on the basis of a rather different line of evidence, namely the lexical lists, which need not concern us here, for it is now clear that this adds nothing to the case.[40]

Let me rather turn now to the biblical side of the equation by asking you to consider what evidence there may be, first of all, for festivals based on lunar phases in ancient Israel. I think you will agree that it is fairly minimal. There is, of course, the observance of the new moon: "Sound the horn on the new moon" we are told in Ps 81:4—but whether *kese* in the continuation of the verse means that the full moon is also to be celebrated may be and has been doubted.[41] The ritual calendar of Numbers 28:11–15 prescribes the monthly offerings of the new moon, and other aspects of its observance are alluded to elsewhere in the Bible as when Hosea or Isaiah condemn the hypocritical observance of "new moon and sabbath" in one and the same breath.[42] But only the first day of Tishri had the character of a special holiday, and even here the biblical text, as is well known, avoids the term *rōš haššānā*, head of the year. In passing, it may be noted that the Babylonian month Tashrîtu was similarly singled out for special treatment in the Akkadian hemerologies.[43]

No special treatment was accorded to the first crescent[44] (or the last) in the biblical calendar; indeed we do not even know a special term for these days—and certainly that is not for want of words to describe the lunar crescent or its iconographic representations.[45] As for the full moon, the two principal "seasonal festivals" were gradually related to it in some way.[46] To this day, the approaching full moon signals the coming of Pesach in Nisan and Sukkoth in Tishri and comes as close as a luni-solar calendar can to marking the vernal and autumnal equinox, respectively. But there are ample hints to suggest that this is the terminal stage of a long evolution, and that at an earlier stage, the spring festival was celebrated on the new moon of the month of Nisan or Aviv,[47] or throughout its first quarter,[48] and the fall festival may similarly have fallen on the new moon of the seventh month before some of its functions were assumed by the New Year's festival. Thus, there is little in the ritual calendar of the Bible to compare with the persistent importance of moon-worship and the celebration of the various lunar phases that we encounter in Mesopotamia.

Now contrast, if you will, the case for the sabbatical conception in the Bible. Nothing could be more persistent. As early as the time of Solomon, we are entitled to detect a seven-day cycle in the festivities marking the dedication of his temple.[49] The double injunction to work for six days and to rest every seventh is the most fundamental piece of social legislation written into the Decalogue—though it is a moot point which of its two provisions is more often violated. The cultic counterpart of this legislation permeates every one of the many ritual calendars in the Pentateuch. Creation itself is retroactively cast into the mold of the seven-day week, as also of the Exodus typology, and thus secondarily turned into the justification for the earthly ordinance.[50] Every Sabbath the Kiddush reminds us of the connection, evening and morning each in its own way. The Sabbath is a "memorial to the week of creation" and "a reminder of the exodus from Egypt." It is "a sign forever that the Lord made the heavens and the earth in six days, and rested and refreshed on the seventh."[51] There is nothing in the biblical evidence to suggest that the sabbatical conception depended in any way on the luni-solar calendar; on the contrary, that calendar was progressively adjusted to the sabbatical conception and its final post-biblical determination manages to avoid such conflicts as Yom Kippur falling on Friday or Sunday.

Already in biblical times, moreover, the sabbatical conception was extended beyond its ritual application to the week. We see this first in the feast of weeks, originally a seasonal festival without fixed date, to be celebrated fifty days after the offering of the first sheaf of the barley harvest which in its turn was prescribed for the "morrow after the Sabbath" (Lev 23:15)—a date that gave rise to much debate. Beyond even this concept of a week of weeks, the Bible decreed a "week of years" as the foundation of the system of *šĕmiṭṭā*, or Sabbatical year, and "seven weeks of years" as the basis for *yōbēl*, or jubilee year.[52] The apocryphal Book of Jubilees made the sabbatical cycle the basis for both chronology and cultic legislation.

I would not enter into the details of all these institutions even if I could, but cite them only as evidence for the extraordinary extent to which the sabbatical idea permeated all biblical legislation. The week was fundamental to the biblical calendar and immune to violation by any other consideration, least of all the phases of the moon. Even though these consist of *ca.* 7⅜ days each, the biblical week is wholly independent of them.[53] I must, however, ask you to return with me for a moment to Mesopotamia in order to drive home this point.

Scholars have never tired of looking for Mesopotamian antecedents to the biblical week. The seven-day festival celebrating Gudea's dedication of the great temple at Lagash has been studied in detail by Sauren[54] and compared by some scholars to Solomon's aforementioned one, as has "A seven-day ritual in the Old Babylonian cult at Larsa" which was published in the *Annual* by my own HUC student, Edwin Kingsbury. But these festivals were, to all appearances, one-time occurrences and owe their particular seven-day duration at most to the widespread popularity or sanctity of the number seven, to which whole monographs have been devoted.[55] They tell us nothing about the institutionalization of a seven-day week on a regular basis. On the contrary, when we look at non-cultic cuneiform texts, we see again that Mesopotamia, in its classical phase, organized its days of labor and rest by the month, not the week. For the Ur III period, for example, we have long tallies of hired or conscripted labor, and these indicate clearly that as many as six days per month were set aside as rest-days (u 4 - d u 8 - a).[56] Thus, for example, the records of the great textile establishments at Umma specify that for 3,000 man-hours (or rather women-days, since slave girls were involved and the input was counted in days), 500 had to be set aside as free time.[57] Another text from Umma calls for slave girls to work for 23 days in each of eleven successive months, presumably when they were hollow (i.e. 29 days in length) and perhaps 24 when they were full (i.e. 30 days in length).[58] Just how these six rest-days were arrived at is clear from an essay describing the life of the Sumerian school which specifies, in Kramer's translation,[59] "Here is the monthly record of my attendance in school, my vacation days (u 4 -d u 8 - a - m u) each month are three, my recurrent(?) monthly holidays (e z e n - a š - a š - b i)[60] are three, (that leaves) twenty-four days each month that I must stay in school—(and) long days they are." This must surely mean that in a month of 30 days, three days were set aside for the lunar festivals and three for other reasons. By Old Babylonian times, these generous schedules were even exceeded if we are to believe royal claims that corvée duty was reduced to 10 or even four days per month.[61]

Briefly we must also cast our eyes northward to Assyria, for there the Lewys and others were convinced they had found "The origin of the week and the oldest West Asiatic calendar," to quote the title of their celebrated article in the *HUC Annual* for 1943. But subsequent research has not borne out their estimate of the length of the so-called *ḫamuštum*, either as a fifth of a year or else as 50 days, or even as seven days, or indeed the whole complex theory of pentacontad cycles which Morgenstern took over from them. According to the latest synthesis of the evidence,[62] the *ḫamuštum* represented a time-span much closer to the biblical week—perhaps one-fifth of a month (i.e. six days), or a week of five days. In any event, the system of this Old Assyrian week, in use in different forms both at Assur and in the Anatolian colonies, was not demonstrably independent of the lunar calendar: what few indications there are suggest that the first day of such a week coincided with the beginning of the month in eight months of the luni-solar calendar, and with the full moon in the other four.[63]

An institution shared by Assyria and Babylonia in this, the "patriarchal" period, was the periodic remission of debts, and liberation of distrainees, or debt-slaves. Both of these prerogatives have hoary Sumerian antecedents, n i g - s i - s á . . . gar being attested at least as early as the laws of Ur-Nammu of Ur, and a m a r - g i 4 already under Entemena of Lagash.[64] Their Akkadian equivalents, *mīšaru* and *andurāru*, are cognate to Hebrew *mēšār (mīšōr)* and *dĕrōr* respectively. The latter term is used in Leviticus 25 in the injunction to "proclaim *dĕrōr* throughout the land, to all the inhabitants thereof," as well as in prophetic allusions to the jubilee. It has naturally been compared to the Akkadian *andurāru* or *durāru*, most convincingly in Julius Lewy's study on "The Biblical institution of '*derôr*' in the light of Akkadian documents."[65] Recent research has permitted refinements of our understanding of the Akkadian concepts[66] but what is crucial in the present connection is whether the underlying institution already displayed the periodic or cyclical character of the biblical jubilee. I can only cite here J. J. Finkelstein's conclusion for the Old Babylonian *mīšarum*-enactments. Although it is not yet possible to establish any fixed interval of recurrence for them, he concludes that probably, "apart from the period of the royal accession, (they) took place also at fairly regular intervals thereafter."[67] These intervals vary from six to eleven or even 21 years, but in any case they were dependent on the accident of the royal succession. They thus provide a remote model of sorts for the biblical instituion, but hardly for its integration into the sabbatical cycle.

I forebear to pursue yet other and weaker proposals to find Mesopotamian antecedents to the biblical week or the sabbatical cycle. And it is hardly necessary to pursue even more improbable antecedents in the literature of Canaan[68] or the calendars of Egypt or Greece, as illustrated by the so-called "planetary week."

In ancient astronomy, sun, moon, and the five planets then known formed a heptad whose order, however, differed in the Babylonian and Greek tradition. The Greeks arranged the "seven planets" in the order, Sun—Venus—Mercury—Moon—Saturn—Jupiter—Mars. When these seven planets are each assigned every seventh hour of the 24-hour day, it will be noted that, after every 24 hours, a new planet begins the next day until, after seven 24-hour days, the cycle begins again. This is the basis of our own 7-day week, and of the names assigned to them. But the 24-hour day is a Hellenistic scheme derived ultimately from Egyptian models, and owes nothing to Babylonian (or Jewish) sources. There is simply no evidence for the planetary week before Hellenistic times. The Christian week, then, may well be a wedding of the Hellenistic planetary week with the Israelite week, but there are no grounds for finding in the biblical sources the astronomical speculations involved in the planetary week.

The attempt, for all that, has been made often enough, notably by appeal to the enigmatic passage in Amos 5:26 which in the Revised Standard Version

The Planetary Week

HOURS	SUNDAY DIMANCHE	MO(O)NDAY LUNDI	TUESDAY MARDI	WEDNESDAY MERCREDI	THURSDAY JEUDI	FRIDAY VENDREDI	SATURDAY SAMEDI
1	SUN	Moon	Mars	Mercury	Jupiter	Venus	Saturn
2	Venus	Saturn	SUN	Moon	Mars	Mercury	Jupiter
3	Mercury	Jupiter	Venus	Saturn	SUN	Moon	Mars
4	Moon	Mars	Mercury	Jupiter	Venus	Saturn	SUN
5	Saturn	SUN	Moon	Mars	Mercury	Jupiter	Venus
6	Jupiter	Venus	Saturn	SUN	Moon	Mars	Mercury
7	Mars	Mercury	Jupiter	Venus	Saturn	SUN	Moon
8	SUN	Moon	Mars	Mercury	Jupiter	Venus	Saturn
9	Venus	Saturn	SUN	Moon	Mars	Mercury	Jupiter
10	Mercury	Jupiter	Venus	Saturn	SUN	Moon	Mars
11	Moon	Mars	Mercury	Jupiter	Venus	Saturn	SUN
12	Saturn	SUN	Moon	Mars	Mercury	Jupiter	Venus
13	Jupiter	Venus	Saturn	SUN	Moon	Mars	Mercury
14	Mars	Mercury	Jupiter	Venus	Saturn	SUN	Moon
15	SUN	Moon	Mars	Mercury	Jupiter	Venus	Saturn
16	Venus	Saturn	SUN	Moon	Mars	Mercury	Jupiter
17	Mercury	Jupiter	Venus	Saturn	SUN	Moon	Mars
18	Moon	Mars	Mercury	Jupiter	Venus	Saturn	SUN
19	Saturn	SUN	Moon	Mars	Mercury	Jupiter	Venus
20	Jupiter	Venus	Saturn	SUN	Moon	Mars	Mercury
21	Mars	Mercury	Jupiter	Venus	Saturn	SUN	Moon
22	SUN	Moon	Mars	Mercury	Jupiter	Venus	Saturn
23	Venus	Saturn	SUN	Moon	Mars	Mercury	Jupiter
24	Mercury	Jupiter	Venus	Saturn	SUN	Moon	Mars

(1962) was still rendered "You shall take up Sakkuth your king, and Kaiwan your star-god, your images, which you made for yourselves." Sikkūt and Kiyyūn were thus explained as the Babylonian name and epithet respectively of Saturn (Sakkud[69] and *kajamānu*[70]) and from this alleged testimony for the worship of Saturn it was only a small step to deduce the Israelite observance of a planetary week culminating or even beginning with Saturn's day. But a more reasonable interpretation of the Amos passage was offered by Stanley Gevirtz in 1968:[71] "But you carry (these things) to the shrine of your (god) MLK, and to the abode of your images—the host of your gods that you have made for yourself!" and I am glad to say that this rendering has in most of its essentials found its way into the New English Bible of which the Study Edition was recently edited by Samuel Sandmel.[72]

Personally I would agree that Sikkut and Kiyyun are common nouns in the Amos passage, but not necessarily with the translations of Gevirtz and NEB, i.e.

	Gevirtz	NEB	Hallo
Sikkūt	shrine	shrine	image
Kiyyūn	abode	pedestal	sacrificial cake

With *sikkūt,* I would compare *sukkōt bĕnôt* in 2 Kgs 17:30a, recently explained as "image."[73] With *kiyyūn,* I would compare *kawwān,* the sacrificial cake (in shape of vagina)[74] in Jer 44:19[75] which in turn has been compared to Akkadian *kamānu.*[76]

In sum, the uniquely biblical conception of the week and the sabbatical cycle stands out equally by virtue of its pervasiveness in biblical laws and letters, as by its absence from the surrounding Near East. What conclusions are we entitled to draw from these somewhat tedious observations? Time permits only an apodictic formulation. The sabbatical concept in its biblical form is fundamentally an expression of social or socio-economic justice and natural (I would almost say: ecological) equity. The inviolate recurrence of a day of rest is ordained in the context of the commandment to work the other six; the sabbatical year is part and parcel of a planned agricultural economy; the jubilee definitely serves to preserve the independence of the small farmer in the face of an emerging urban-royal society;[77] even if its actual application fell into early disuse,[78] the same effect continued to be achieved by the cancellation of debts in the sabbatical year.[79]

Equally unique in all the ancient Near East, however, is the manner in which these essentially socio-economic provisions were woven into the cult. The intermingling of ethical and cultic prescriptions is, of course, a well-known characteristic of biblical legislation, and one that clearly distinguishes it from the legal corpora of Babylonia, Assyria, and Asia Minor, where civil or criminal law and ritual prescriptions are kept carefully apart. But the intermingling is particularly profound in the case under discussion, beginning with its very motivation. The Sabbath is motivated by the divine work of creation; land-redemption is a guaranteed right "because (God says) *mine* is the land" (Lev 25:23); and the release of the debt-slaves in the jubilee is justified on the grounds that "to *me* the children of Israel are slaves, they are *my* slaves" (Lev 25:42, 55). Beyond motivation, the Sabbath and the sabbatical cycle are woven deeply into all Pentateuchal legislation, not only both versions of the decalogue but also the codes assigned by the documentary hypothesis to each of the separate strands making up the final redaction.[80]

Finally, the importance of the Sabbath must be seen in the context of the continuing deemphasis of the lunar festivals. Moon worship flourished wherever Mesopotamian culture spread, and even after its demise it survived at places like Harran.[81] But in Israel it failed to gain a foothold; the full moon was not worshipped, the quarters were not specially observed, and even the new moon was ultimately relegated to the status of a half holiday.[82] We may sum up the contrast as follows: the ancient Mesopotamian year was based on the month, and the worship of the moon went hand in hand with it. The Israelite year was based on the week, and remained independent of the month even when the luni-solar calendar was adopted from Babylonia. The Mesopotamian jubilee was based on the royal succession and on royal whim; the Israelite jubilee was (at least ideally) ordained by God in inviolate successions of sabbatical cycles. Here, then, two of the great contrasts between biblical Israel and its Near Eastern matrix meet: sabbatical cycles versus lunar calendars, and divine versus royal authority. The legacy of these contrasts is with us to this day. I hope that their enduring character will justify my lengthy peregrinations through the evidence.[83]

NOTES

1. "The Present State of Old Testament Studies," *JBL* 88 (1969) 19–35.
2. *Abraham in History and Tradition* (Yale University Press, 1975).
3. "The Historicity of the Patriarchal Narratives" (=*BZAW* 133, 1974).
4. "The Conceptual Autonomy of the Babylonian World," *Monographs on the Ancient Near East* 1 (1976) 57–71.
5. "Parallelomania," *JBL* 81 (1962) 1–13.
6. The contrastive method likewise has its dangers; see J. J. M. Roberts, "Myth vs. History: Relaying the Comparative Foundations," *CBQ* 38 (1976) 1–13.
7. See the review by Hubertus Vogt, *BiOr* 26 (1969) 101. I have not noted others. For a recent treatment of the subject which utilizes Meesters, see Niels-Erik A. Andreasen, *The Old Testament Sabbath: A Tradition-Historical Investigation*" (=SBL Dissertation Series 7, 1972).
8. *Studia Semitica Neerlandica* 7, 1966.
9. F. R. Kraus, *RA* 68 (1974) 2 f., reads *uzkaru* and adds the interesting suggestion that the near homophony with *iškaru*, "(literary) series" (i.e., book) accounts for the (mis)use of the logogram U_4SAKAR in the sense of *iškaru* in the Verse Account of Nabonidus, for which see Hallo, *JAOS* 83 (1963) 176. [For a similar confusion, cf. ^{d}TIR.AN.NA=*qîštu* (forest) of heaven for ^{d}BAN.AN.NA=*qaštu* (bow) of heaven, rainbow as in NBC 7799; see Hallo, *JCS* 17 (1963) 53 and n. 22.]. Kraus questions the connection I drew between Adapa and the astrological omen series in Rm 618 (lines 2 f.!), but the connection between this series and Nabonidus now

appears confirmed by CT 46:48 iii(!) 2–5 as republished and edited by W. G. Lambert, "A New Source for the Reign of Nabonidus," *AfO* 22 (1968–69) 1–8. In passing it may be noted that one of Nabonidus' own Harran inscriptions refers to the name of the new moon as "crescent(!) of Anu" comparable to the astrological name applied to the new moon (or the first quarter) elsewhere: see W. Röllig, "Erwägungen zu neuen Stelen König Nabonids," *ZA* 56 (1964) 231; cf. *CAD* Z 115a; differently: *ANET*[3] 563a.

10. For u_4-sakar in the sense simply of "moon" see A. Sachs and O. Neugebauer, *JCS* 10 (1956) 133 (only in late astronomical texts).
11. Cf. UD = *ṣētu* in *CAD s.v.*: "light, shining appearance of the sun, moon, and stars" etc. For the etymology, see Landsberger *ZA* 42 (1934) 161 f.
12. For all these meanings, see A. Goetze, *JCS* 2 (1948) 35; Hallo, *BiOr* 20 (1963) 140.
13. Bezold, *Glossar, s.v.*
14. MSL 13 (1971) 257:231; 258:244 (Ká-gal = *abullu* G).
15. *DP* 47 and 166; cf. Y. Rosengarten, *Le Concept sumérien de consummation* (1960) 217, 281.
16. *DP* 44; 200; Nik. 29; 149.
17. TMH 5:82 and 85, edited by A. Westenholz, *Early Cuneiform Texts in Jena* (1975) pp. 52 f. For the dates see *idem, JCS* 26 (1974) 154–56.
18. TMH 5:84, edited by Westenholz, *Jena* p. 52.
19. Written sag-ITI.SAR, for which cf. Westenholz, *Jena* p. 52 and *OSP* 1 (1975) p. 4.
20. TMH 5:92, edited by Westenholz, *Jena*, pp. 55 f.
21. Cylinder A ii 23.
22. A. Falkenstein, *ZA* 50 (1952) 82 f.
23. E. Sollberger *AfO* 17 (1954–55) 15 prefers to assign the date to Šulgi 2 not 7, but he misconstrues the sense of the formula to arrive at this conclusion.
24. See for now Hallo, *RAI* 17 (1970) 118 f.
25. TLB 3:8.
26. "L'organisation de quelques fêtes mensuelles à l'époque néo-sumérienne," *RAI* 17 (1970) 59–74.
27. "Les èš-èš durant l'époque néo-sumérienne" [see *RB* 84 (1977) 355-92—F.G.].
28. H. Sauren, "Les fêtes néo-sumériennes et leur péroidicité," *RAI* 17 (1970) 11–29. Sauren even questions the strictly lunar character of the month in Ur III times on the basis of texts from Ibbi-Sin's 9th year; *ibid.* 22 f.
29. See the critique by H. Hunger, "Zur Periodizität neusumerischer Feste," *WZKM* 65–66 (1973–74) 69–75. But note that some of Hunger's premises are also shaky, notably his assumption of a 49-year reign for Šulgi.
30. Limet, *RAI* 17 (1970) 64 f.; M. deJ. Ellis, "A note on the 'Chariot's Crescent'," *JAOS* 90 (1970) 266–69. Cf. e.g. Holma-Salonen No. 20: sá-dug_4 of Šulgi and Amar-Sin for u_4-sakar-gu-la, ^{giš}gigir-u_4-6, ^{giš}gigir-u_4-7 and u_4-sakar-u_4-15.

31. M. Civil, "Išme-Dagan and Enlil's chariot," *JAOS* 88 (Speiser Memorial Volume, AOS 53, 1968) 3, note 13.
32. B. A. Levine, "The Descriptive Tabernacle Texts of the Pentateuch," *JAOS* 85 (1965) 307–18; cf. *idem,* "Ugaritic Descriptive Rituals," *JCS* 17 (1963) 105–11. For a partly dissenting view, see A. F. Rainey, *Biblica* 51 (1970) 485–98.
33. Hallo, "A Sumerian Amphictyony, *JCS* 14 (1960) 88–114. For the Ibbi-Sin texts, see *ibid.,* 96 with notes 66–68.
34. Levine and Hallo, "Offerings to the Temple Gates at Ur," *HUCA* 38 (1967) 17–58.
35. *CAD E s.v. eššešu.* On the alleged Middle Assyrian personal name Ward-eššešu (*ib.*) see Hallo, *Symbolae . . . Böhl* (1973) 182, note 7.
36. W. G. Lambert and A. R. Millard, *Atra-ḫasīs: the Babylonian Story of the Flood* (1969) 56 f. (I 206). Cf. *CAD* A s.*v. arḫu* where there are also similar references from an Old Babylonian letter (TCL 1:50:28 f.) For a Sumerian parallel see H. G. Güterbock, *ZA* 42 (1934) 45 III 7′ (Lugalannemundu). Both cited by K. Balkan, "The Old Assyrian Week," *Studies . . . Landsberger* (AS 16, 1965) 160.
37. A. Herdner, "Une prière à Baal des Ugaritains en danger," *CRAIBL* 1972: 694 (RS 24:266 Rev. 15); BKR BᶜL NŠQDŠ, ḤTP BᶜL NML ᶜU. The Ugaritic prayer to Baʾal, intended to accompany a ritual of desperation for a city under siege, has been restudied by A. Spalinger, "A Canaanite Ritual Found in Egyptian reliefs," *Society for the Study of Egyptian Antiquities* 8 (1978) 47–60, esp. p. 55 and notes 40–45. Spalinger suggests an Egyptian cognate for *ḥtp* in the sense of offering, food offering and the like.
38. It occurs almost never outside these lists, which makes the exact interpretation difficult. Dr. Weisberg kindly refers me to the fragmentary YBC 16299, to be published in his forthcoming volume of Nebuchadnezzar texts from Yale as No. 117.
39. YOS 1 (1915) pp. 75–81.
40. A. L. Oppenheim, "Assyriological Gleanings II," *BASOR* 93 (1944) 16 f.; J. Lewy, "Neo-Babylonian Names of the Days of the Week," *ibid.* 95 (1944) 34–36; Oppenheim, "The Neo-Babylonian Week Again," *ibid.* 97 (1945) 27–29.
41. André Caquot, "Remarques sur la fête de la 'néoménie' dans l'ancien Israel," *RHR* 158 (1960) 1–18. As Caquot notes, Mowinckel took this verse to refer to the New Year and Tabernacles respectively, while Snaith, *Jewish New Year Festival* (1947) even thinks both halves of the text refer to the preexilic festival of the 15th of Etanim which combined both New Year and Tabernacles. Cf. also below, n. 47 and F. Wilke, "Das Neumondfest im israelitisch-jüdischen Altertum," *Jahrbuch der Gesellschaft für die Geschichte des Protestantismus in Österreich* 67 (1951) 1–15 (cited Fohrer, below note 51, p. 116, note 32).
42. Hosea 2:13; Isaiah 1:13; cf. R. de Vaux, *Ancient Israel: Its Life and Institutions* (1961) 469 f.

43. Especially its first eight or nine days. See Peter Hulin, "A Hemerological Text from Nimrud," *Iraq* 21 (1959) 42–53.
44. Cf. however Ezekiel 45:18–20 for special offerings on the first and seventh days of the first month (Nisan); Ezek 46:1 is sometimes regarded as the earliest reference to the Sabbath.
45. Isa 3:18; cf. Hallo, *BiOr* 20 (1963) 141 with notes 82 f. Cf. *šĕbîšîm* for sun discs in the same passage and *šimšot* in Isaiah 54:11 f., with which J. C. Greenfield, *JAOS* 89 (1969) 134 compares Qumran *špš*.
46. The Book of Jubilees even dates Shavuoth to the 15th of Sivan. For Purim, cf. Esth 9:18.
47. H. L. Ginsberg in a forthcoming study on the northern ("Ephraimite") origins of Deuteronomy (lecture of 11-19-75) points out that in the oldest biblical legislation, Pesach is ordained for the new moon of Aviv (Exod 13:4, cf. Exod 23:15; 34:18; Deut 16:1). Only P and H date Passover to mid-month. Caquot, on the contrary, concludes that *ḥōdeš* in these passages indicates the full moon and that this marked the beginning of the month in an earlier calendar (above, note 41)!
48. I.e., seven days starting with the new moon.
49. Cf. E. C. Kingsbury, *HUCA* 34 (1963) 27 and n. 130. Differently H. and J. Lewy, *HUCA* 17 (1943) 127 f. Note that the "bridal week" too lasted seven days (Gen 29:27 f.; Judges 14:12; later fourteen: Tobit 8:20; 10:7), But the seven days of mourning in later Judaism have no biblical basis to my knowledge.
50. W. G. Lambert seems to dispute this derivation. Instead he argues for an original seven-day creation tradition in which the creation of man on the sixth day and God's rest on the seventh are counterparts to the creation of man so that the gods might rest from their labor in the Babylonian Atra-ḫasis epic; see "A New Look at the Babylonian Background of Genesis," *JTS* 16 (1965) 297 f. Dussaud makes a similar suggestion on the basis of the Ugaritic myths; below, note 68.
51. Cf. the role of these liturgical motifs in Franz Rosenzweig, *The Star of Redemption* (tr. W. W. Hallo, 1971) 315–17. On one view, the connection to the Exodus is Deuteronomic (Deut 5:15), that to Creation Priestly in inspiration (Exod 20:11; 31:17): G. Fohrer, *History of Israelite Religion* (1972) 117.
52. For the vast literature on this subject, see R. North, "Sociology of the Biblical Jubilee" (=*Analecta Biblica* 4, 1954) and E. Neufeld, "Socio-economic background of yōbēl and šemiṭṭa," *RSO* 33 (1958) 53–124, each with extensive bibliographies.
53. See most recently and emphatically M. Tsevat, "The Basic Meaning of the Biblical Sabbath," *ZAW* 84 (1972) 447–59 and *idem, Yeivin Jubilee Volume* (1969–70) 283–288 (in Hebrew). Tsevat advances the interesting thesis that the, or a more, original intention of the Sabbath was to express God's sovereignty over time; the strikingly parallel legislation for the Sabbatical year correspondingly acknowledged his sovereignty over space.

54. "Die Einweihung des Eninnu," *RAI* 20 (1975) 95–103.
55. Notably Johannes Hehn, *Siebenzahl und Sabbat bei den Babyloniern und im Alten Testament* (LSS 2/5, 1907). For extensive references to seven-day cycles in biblical and Near Eastern literature, see Andreasen, *op. cit.* (above, n. 7) 113 f., note 4.
56. J. P. Gregoire, *Archives Administratives Sumériennes* (1970) p. 175.
57. T. B. Jones and J. W. Snyder, *Sumerian Economic Texts* (1961) 274:323–25; for a detailed analysis of this text see Hallo, "Obiter dicta ad SET," in *Studies in Honor Tom B. Jones,* ed. Marvin A. Powell, Jr. and Ronald H. Sack (AOAT 203; Kevelaer: Butzon & Bercker, Neukirchen-Vluyn: Neukirchener Verlag, 1979) pp. 1–14.
58. TLB 3:70, to be edited by me in SLB3.
59. *RAI* 18 (1972) 119. For an earlier rendering cf. *idem, Iraq* 25 (1963) 174. Cf. perhaps also TLB 1:163 where women work 24 days a month under Hammurabi; differently: Leemans, SLB 1/3 (1960)94 and *CAD* E, p. 220c.
60. Phonetic spelling for ezen-èš-èš-bi?
61. D. O. Edzard, *Die "Zweite Zwischenzeit" Babyloniens* (1957) 96 f.
62. M. Trolle Larsen, "The Old Assyrian City-State and its Colonies" (*Mesopotamia* 4, 1976) 354–65 and 383–85. Previously Balkan, *loc. cit.* (above, n. 36) 159–74.
63. N. B. Jankowska, "A System of Rotation of Eponyms of the Commercial Association at Kaniš (Asia Minor XIX B.C.)," *ArOr* 35 (1967) 524–48, esp. pp. 531 f. Cf. *eadem, Klinopisnye Teksty iz Kjul'-Tepe* (1968), pp. 254–59. The schedule of the week-eponymy was fixed by the lunar year, their ordinal number, so far as known, being from No. 1 to No. 50. (Discrepancies are levelled by assuming intercalary days.). For the rotation within the *ḫamuštum*-committee, cf. the system reconstructed for the Old Babylonian village of Ṣupur-Šubula by Landsberger, "Remarks on the Archive of the Soldier Ubarum," *JCS* 9 (1955) 121–31, esp. pp. 125 f. For a partial critique of Jankowska's solution see Trolle Larsen, *loc. cit.* (above, note 62).
64. See most recently D. O. Edzard, " 'Soziale Reformen' im Zweistromland . . . bis ca. 1600 v. Chr: Realität oder literarischer Topos?," *apud* J. Harmatta and G. Komoróczy, eds., *Wirtschaft und Gesellschaft im alten Vorderasien* (1976) 145–56, esp. n. 7.
65. *Eretz-Israel* 5 (1958) 21*–31*.
66. For *andurāru* (in Ilušuma's case essentially a grant of trading privileges to Babylonians in Assur!) see especially Trolle Larsen, *op. cit.* (above, note 62); for *mišaru* see J. J. Finkelstein, "Some New *misharum* Material and its Implications," *Studies . . . Landsberger* (AS 16, 1965) 233–46; cf. F. R. Krauss, "*Ein Edikt des königs Samsu-iluna von Babylon,*" in *ibid.*, 225–31; Finkelstein, *RA* 63 (1969) 45–61.
67. Finkelstein, *AS* 16 (1965) 245. These public proclamations of generalized debt-remission may have survived in the *šudūtu*-proclamations of the Nuzi

texts (for which see B. Eichler, *YNER* 5 [1973], 32–34; A. Shaffer, *Or* 34 [1965], 32–34), but must be distinguished from the distrainee's release after three years provided in § 117 of the Laws of Hammurabi; cf. Kraus, "Ein Edikt des Königs Ammi-ṣaduqa von Babylon" (=*SD* 5, 1958) 167–72.

68. The seven-day cycles of the Ugaritic epics such as I Baʿal III 14–19 and 2 Aqhat I 6–12 may for the time being be regarded as literary conventions; see René Dussaud, *Syria* 34 (1957) 241 f.; S. E. Loewenstamm, "The Seven-day Unit in Ugaritic Epic Literature," *IEJ* 15 (1965) 121–33.
69. The reading seems assured by KAV 46 obv. 12 *(sa-ak-ku-ud)* which corresponds to line 44 of the "Weidner God List" as most recently edited by Jean Nougayrol, *Ugaritica* 5 (1968) 210–30 in spite of Weidner's own reservations in *AfK* 2 (1924–25) 16, where he reads Madan. But Madānu is the reading or translation of [d]SA.KUD ([d]Di-kud) according to R. Frankena, *Tākultu* (1953) 102:134.
70. Written MUL.SAG.UŠ or (MUL). GENNA (=TUR+DIŠ); see *SL* 4/2 *s.vv.*
71. "A New Look at an Old Crux: Amos 5:26," *JBL* 87 (1968) 267–76.
72. "No but now you shall take up the shrine of your idol king and the pedestals of your images (Heb. adds: the star of your gods), which you have made for yourselves."
73. Of Banītu. E. Lipiński, "*SKNT*, 'aspect, image'," *UF* 5 (1973) 202–4. For Banitu in Transjordan, see J. R. Tournay, *RB* 74 (1967) 248–54 and A. Haldar, *BiOr* 31 (1974) 34 f. *ad. loc.*
74. So H. Hirschberg, *VT* 11 (1961) 376; cf. CIS II 199 for Nabataean KWNʾ.
75. Joseph Reider, "A New Ishtar Epithet in the Bible," *JNES* 8 (1949) 104–7.
76. H. Hoffner, "Alimenta Hethaeorum" (AOS 55, 1974) 174. *CAD* K *s.v.* derives *kamānu* from *kamû/kawû,* "to bake, roast." For the equivalent Sumerian g i d e š t a (NINDA ⅔ SÌLA etc.) cf. just possibly TLB 3:8, for which see above, note 25.
77. Edward, Neufeld, "The Emergence of a Royal-Urban Society in Ancient Israel." *HUCA* 31 (1960) 31–53.
78. Ben Zion Wacholder, "The Calendar of Sabbatical Cycles during the Second Temple and the Early Rabbinic period," *HUCA* 44 (1973) 153 f.
79. Although the Sabbatical year provided technically only for the cancellation of debts, this necessarily involved the freeing of debt-slaves as well, according to Nahum Sarna, "Zedekiah's Emancipation of Slaves and the Sabbatical Year," *Orient and Occident* (Essays . . . Cyrus H. Gordon, AOAT 22, 1973) 143–49 (ad Jeremiah 34).
80. DeVaux, *Ancient Israel* (1961) 479.
81. H. Lewy, "Points of Comparison between Zoroastrianism and the Moon-Cult of Harrân," *A Locust's Leg* (=Studies . . . Taqizadeh, 1962), 139–61.
82. For relics of observance (including by women), see Hayyim Schauss, *The Jewish Festivals* (1938) 273–76; for the biblical evidence, cf. above, note 41.
83. An interesting new example of a seven-day ritual (in the context of a sacred

marriage?) has now been found in the Middle Babylonian level of Emar (Meskene) on the Euphrates; see provisionally Daniel Arnaud, *Annuaire de l'École Pratique des Hautes Études* (Ve Section) 84 (1975–76) 223f. For the latest views on Amos 5:26 (above, notes 69–76) in light of LXX, NT (Acts 7:42 f.) and the Damascus Covenant (7:14 ff.), see C. W. Isbell *JBL* 97 (1978) 97–99 and J. Murphy-O'Connor *BA* 40 (1977) 105.

14

Some Postulates of Biblical Criminal Law

Moshe Greenberg

I.

The study of biblical law has been a stepchild of the historical-critical approach to the Bible. While the law had been a major preoccupation of ancient and medieval scholars, in modern times it has largely been replaced by, or made to serve, other interests. No longer studied for itself, it is now investigated for the reflexes it harbors of stages in Israel's social development, or it is analyzed by literary-historical criticism into strata, each synchronized with a given stage in the evolution of Hebrew religion and culture. The main interest is no longer in the law as an autonomous discipline, but in what the laws can yield the social or religious historian. It is a remarkable fact that the last comprehensive juristic treatment of biblical law was made over a century ago.[1]

The sociological and literary-historical approaches have, of course, yielded permanent insights, yet it cannot be said that they have exhausted all the laws have to tell about the life and thought of Israel. Too often they have been characterized by theorizing which ignores the realities of early law and society as we know them at first hand from the written records of the ancient Near East. Severities in biblical law are alleged to reflect archaic notions that have no echo in either ancient civilized, or modern Bedouin law. Humane features are declared the product of urbanization, though they have no parallels in the urban codes of Mesopotamia. Inconsistencies have been discovered and ar-

Reprinted by permission from Menahem Haran, ed., *Studies in Bible and Jewish Religion: Yehezkel Kaufmann Jubilee Volume* (Jerusalem: Magnes Press, 1960), 5–28.

ranged in patterns of historic evolution where a proper discrimination would have revealed that the laws in question dealt with altogether separate realms.

The corrective to these errors lies ready to hand. It is that considerable body of cuneiform law—especially the law collections[2]—which lends itself admirably to elucidate the meaning and background of the biblical law corpora. The detailed studies of these cuneiform collections, made chiefly by European scholars, furnish the student of the Bible with models of legal analysis, conducted without the prejudgments which frequently mar discussions of biblical law.

No clearer demonstration of the limits of literary-historical criticism can be found, for example, than that afforded by the studies made upon the laws of Hammurapi. Inconsistencies no less glaring than those which serve as the basis of analyzing strata in the Bible are found in this greatest corpus of Mesopotamian law. In this case, however, we know when, where, and by whom the laws were promulgated. We know, as we do not in the case of the Bible, that the code as we now have it was published as a whole, and intended—at the very least—as a statement of guiding legal principles for the realm of the king. When like discrepancies were pointed out in biblical laws, it had been possible to defend stopping short with a literary-historical analysis by arguing that the discrepancies and inconsistencies of the present text were not found in the original documents that went into it. Attempts to interpret the biblical laws as a coherent whole were regarded as naïve and unscholarly. It was not possible to argue this way in the case of Hammurapi's laws. The discrepancies were there from the beginning, and though, to be sure, they may well have originated in earlier collections, the fact remained that there they were, incorporated side by side in one law.

Two attitudes have been taken toward this problem in the code of Hammurapi. One, represented best by Paul Koschaker, is historical-critical. It aims at reconstructing the original laws which have gone into the present text and have caused the discrepancy; having attained this aim, its work is done. The other, represented by Sir John Miles, is that of the commentator, whose purpose is to attempt "to imagine how this section as it stands can have been interpreted by a Babylonian court."[3] The commentator is compelled in the interest of coherence to look for distinctions of a finer degree than those made by the literary historian.

Such distinctions are not merely the recourse of a modern harmonist to escape the contradictions of the text; they are, it would seem, necessary for understanding how an ancient jurist, how the draftsman himself, understood the law.[4] It must be assumed that the laws of Hammurapi were intended as a consistent guide to judges, and had to be interpreted as they stand in as consistent a manner as possible.

The realization that careful discrimination between apparently contradictory laws is needed for this most carefully drafted ancient law corpus is highly pertinent for an understanding of biblical law. The literary-historical aim leads all too readily to a disregard of distinctions in favor of establishing a pattern of development. Only by endeavoring to interpret the laws as they now stand does one guard himself against excessive zeal in finding discrepancies which involve totally different subjects rather than a historical development. Adopting the method of the commentator, then, we are thrown back much more directly upon the laws themselves. Recourse to literary-critical surgery is resisted until all efforts at making distinctions have failed.

Another virtue of the commentator is his insistence on understanding a given body of law in its own terms before leaping into comparisons with other law systems. To do so, however, means to go beyond the individual rules; for it is not possible to comprehend the law of any culture without an awareness of its key concepts, its value judgments.[5] Yet much of the comparative work done in Israelite-Near Eastern law has been content with comparing individual laws rather than law systems or law ideologies. But until the values that the law embodies are understood, it is questionable whether any individual law can be properly appreciated, let alone profitably compared with another in a foreign system.

In the sequence I shall attempt to indicate some instances of the gain accruing to the study of biblical law from the application of these two considerations: the insistence, first, upon proper discriminations, and second, upon viewing the law as an expression of underlying postulates or values of culture. The limitations of the sociological and literary-historical approaches will emerge from the discussion. My remarks are confined to the criminal law, an area which lends itself well to comparative treatment, and in which the values of a civilization come into expression with unmatched clarity.

II.

Underlying the differing conceptions of certain crimes in biblical and cuneiform law is a divergence, subtle though crucial, in the ideas concerning the origin and sanction of the law.

In Mesopotamia the law was conceived of as the embodiment of cosmic truths *(kīnātum,* sing. *kittum).* Not the originator, but the divine custodian of justice was Shamash, "the magistrate of gods and men, whose lot is justice and to whom truths have been granted for dispensation."[6] The Mesopotamian king was called by the gods to establish justice in his realm; to enable him to do so Shamash inspired him with "truths."[7] In theory, then, the final source of the law, the ideal with which the law had to conform, was above the gods as well as men; in this sense "the Mesopotamian king . . . was not the source of the law but only its agent."[8]

However, the actual authorship of the laws, the embodying of the cosmic ideal in statutes of the realm, is claimed by the king. Hammurapi repeatedly refers to his laws as "my words which I have inscribed on my monument"; they are his "precious" or "choice" words, "the judgment . . . that I have judged (and) the decisions . . . which I have decided."[9] This claim is established by the name inscribed on the stele, and Hammurapi invokes curses upon the man who should presume to erase his name.[10] Similarly in the case of the laws of Lipit-Ishtar: Lipit-Ishtar has been called by the gods to establish justice in the land. The laws are his, the stele on which they are inscribed is called by his name. The epilogue curses him "who will damage my handiwork . . . who will erase its inscription, who will write his own name upon it."[11] While the ideal is cosmic and impersonal, and the gods manifest great concern for the establishment and enforcement of justice, the immediate sanction of the laws is by the authority of the king. Their formulation is his, and his too, as we shall presently see, is the final decision as to their applicability.

In accord with the royal origin of these laws is their purpose: "to establish justice," "that the strong might not oppress the weak," "to give good government," "stable government," "to prosper the people," "abolish enmity and rebellion"[12]—in sum, those political benefits which the constitution of the United States epitomizes in the phrases, "to establish justice, ensure domestic tranquillity, promote the general welfare."

In the biblical theory the idea of the transcendence of the law receives a more thoroughgoing expression. Here God is not merely the custodian of justice or the dispenser of "truths" to man, he is the fountainhead of the law, the law is a statement of his will. The very formulation is God's; frequently laws are couched in the first person, and they are always referred to as "words of God," never of man. Not only is Moses denied any part in the formulation of the Pentateuchal laws, no Israelite king is said to have authored a law code, nor is any king censured for so doing.[13] The only legislator the Bible knows of is God; the only legislation is that mediated by a prophet (Moses and Ezekiel). This conception accounts for the commingling in the law corpora of religious and civil law, and—even more distinctively biblical—of legal enactments and moral exhortations. The entire normative realm, whether in law or morality, pertains to God alone. So far as the law corpora are concerned there is no source of norm-fixing outside of him. Conformably, the purpose of the laws is stated in somewhat different terms in the Bible than in Babylonia. To be sure, observance is a guarantee of well-being and prosperity (Exod 23:20 ff.; Lev 26; Deut 11:13 ff., etc.), but it is more: it sanctifies (Exod 19:5; Lev 19) and is accounted as righteousness (Deut 6:25). There is a distinctively religious tone here, fundamentally different in quality from the political benefits guaranteed in the cuneiform law collections.

In the sphere of the criminal law, the effect of this divine authorship of all law is to make crimes sins, a violation of the will of God. "He who acts wilfully (against the law) whether he belongs to the native-born or the aliens, is reviling the Lord" (Num 15:30). God is directly involved as legislator and sovereign; the offense does not flout a humanly authored safeguard of cosmic truth but an explicit utterance of the divine will. The way is thus prepared to regard offenses as absolute wrongs, transcending the power of men to pardon or expunge. This would seem to underlie the refusal of biblical law to admit of pardon or mitigation of punishment in certain cases where cuneiform law allows it. The laws of adultery and murder are cases in point. Among the Babylonians, Assyrians, and Hittites the procedure in the case of adultery is basically the same. It is left to the discretion of the husband to punish his wife or pardon her. If he punishes his wife, her paramour also is punished; if he pardons her, the paramour goes free too. The purpose of the law is to defend the right of the husband and provide him with redress for the wrong done to him. If the husband, however, is willing to forego his right, and chooses to overlook the wrong done to him, there is no need for redress. The pardon of the husband wipes out the crime.[14]

In biblical law it is otherwise: "If a man commits adultery with the wife of another man, both the adulterer and the adulteress must be put to death" (Lev 20:10; cf. Deut 22:22, 23)—in all events. There is no question of permitting the husband to mitigate or cancel the punishment. For adultery is not merely a wrong against the husband, it is a sin against God, an absolute wrong. To what extent this view prevailed may be seen in few extra-legal passages: Abimelech is providentially kept from violating Abraham's wife, Sarah, and thereby "sinning against God"—not a word is said about wronging Abraham (Gen 20:6). Joseph repels the advances of Potiphar's wife with the argument that such a breach of faith with his master would be a "sin against God" (39:8 f.). The author of the ascription of Psalm 51—"A psalm of David, when Nathan the prophet came to him after he had gone in to Bath-sheba"—finds it no difficulty that verse 4 says, "Against thee only have I sinned." To be sure the law also recognizes that adultery is a breach of faith with the husband (Num 5:12), yet the offense as such is absolute, against God. Punishment is not designed to redress an injured husband for violation of his rights; the offended party is God, whose injury no man can pardon or mitigate.

The right of pardon in capital cases which Near Eastern law gives to the king[15] is unknown to biblical law (the right of the king to grant asylum to homicides in extraordinary cases [cf. 2 Sam 14] is not the same). Here would seem to be another indication of the literalness with which the doctrine of the divine authorship of the law was held in Israel. Only the author of the law has the power to waive it; in Mesopotamia he is the king, in Israel, no man.

III.

Divergent underlying principles alone can account for the differences between Israelite and Near Eastern laws of homicide. The unexampled severity of biblical law on the subject has been considered primitive, archaic, or a reflex of Bedouin vendetta customs. But precisely the law of homicide cannot be accounted for on any such grounds.

In the earliest law collection, the Covenant Code of Exodus, it is laid down that murder is punishable by death (Exod 21:12 ff.). If homicide is committed by a beast—a goring ox is spoken of—the beast must be stoned, and its flesh may not be eaten. If it was known to be vicious and its owner was criminally negligent in failing to keep it in, the owner is subject to death as well as the ox, though here the law allows the owner to ransom himself with a sum fixed by the slain person's family (vv. 28 ff.). This is the sole degree of culpability in which the early law allows a ransom. It is thus fully in accord with a later law of Numbers (35:31) which states, "You shall not take a ransom for the life of a murderer who is guilty of death, but he shall be surely put to death." A ransom may be accepted only for a homicide not committed personally and with intent to harm. For murder, however, there is only the death penalty.

These provisions contrast sharply with the other Near Eastern laws on homicide. Outside of the Bible, there is no parallel to the absolute ban on composition between the murderer and the next of kin. All Near Eastern law recognizes the right of the slain person's family to agree to accept a settlement in lieu of the death of the slayer, Hittite law going so far as to regulate this settlement minutely in terms of the number of souls that must be surrendered as compensation.[16] Bedouin law is no different: among the Bedouin of Sinai murder is compensated for by a tariff reckoned in camels for any life destroyed.[17] The Qurʾan is equally tolerant of composition: "Believers", it reads (2:178), "retaliation is decreed for you in bloodshed: a free man for a free man, a slave for a slave, and a female for a female. He who is pardoned by his aggrieved brother shall be prosecuted according to usage and shall pay him a liberal fine."

In the Babylonian law of the goring ox, otherwise closely paralleling that of the Bible, no punishment is prescribed for the ox.[18]

On both of these counts biblical law has been regarded as exhibiting archaic features.[19] To speak in terms of legal lag and progress, however, is to assume that the biblical and non-biblical laws are stages in a single line of historical development, a line in which acceptance of composition is the stage after strict talion. This is not only incapable of being demonstrated, the actual history of the biblical law of homicide shows that it followed an altogether different principle of development from that governing Near Eastern law.

A precise and adequate formulation of the jural postulate underlying the biblical law of homicide is found in Genesis 9:5f.: "For your life-blood I shall require a reckoning; of every beast shall I require it. . . . Whoever sheds the blood of a man, by man shall his blood be shed; for in the image of God was man made." To be sure, this passage belongs to a stratum assigned to late times by current critical opinion; however that may be, the operation of the postulate is visible in the very earliest laws, as will be seen immediately. The meaning of the passage is clear enough: that man was made in the image of God—the exact significance of the words is not necessary to decide here—is expressive of the peculiar and supreme worth of man. Of all creatures, Genesis 1 relates, he alone possesses this attribute, bringing him into closer relation to God than all the rest and conferring upon him highest value. The first practical consequence of this supremacy is set forth in 9:3f.: man may eat beasts. The establishment of a value hierarchy of man over beast means that man may kill them—for food and sacrifice only (cf. Lev 17:4)—but they may not kill him. A beast that kills a man destroys the image of God and must give a reckoning for it. Now this is the law of the goring ox in Exodus: it must be stoned to death. The religious evaluation inherent in this law is further evidenced by the prohibition of eating the flesh of the stoned ox. The beast is laden with guilt and is therefore an object of horror.[20]

Babylonian law on the subject reflects no such theory as to the guilt the peculiar value of human life imposes on all who take it. Babylonian law is concerned with safeguarding rights in property and making losses good. It therefore deals only with the liability of the owner of the ox to pay for damages caused by his ox. The ox is of no concern to the law since no liabilities attach to it. Indeed, one could reasonably argue that from the viewpoint of property rights the biblical law is unjust: is it not unduly hard on the ox owner to destroy his ox for its first offense? Ought he to suffer for an accident he could in no way have foreseen and for which he therefore cannot be held responsible?

This view of the uniqueness and supremacy of human life has yet another consequence. It places life beyond the reach of other values. The idea that life may be measured in terms of money or other property, and *a fortiori* the idea that persons may be evaluated as equivalences of other persons, is excluded. Compensation of any kind is ruled out. The guilt of the murderer is infinite because the murdered life is invaluable; the kinsmen of the slain man are not competent to say when he has been paid for. An absolute wrong has been committed, a sin against God which is not subject to human discussion. The effect of this view is, to be sure, paradoxical: because human life is invaluable, to take it entails the death penalty.[21] Yet the paradox must not blind us to the judgment of value that the law sought to embody.

The sense of the invaluableness of human life underlies the divergence of the biblical treatment of the homicide from that of the other law systems of the Near East. There the law allows and at times fixes a value on lives, and leaves it to the kinsmen of the slain to decide whether they will have revenge or receive compensation for their loss in money or property. Perhaps the baldest expression of the economic valuation of life occurs in those cases where punishment of a murderer takes the form of the surrender of other persons—a slave, a son, a wife, a brother—"instead of blood," or, "to wash out the blood," or to "make good" the dead person, as the Assyrian phrases put it.[22] Equally expressive are the Hittite laws which prescribe that the killer has to "make amends" for the dead persons by "giving" persons in accord with the status of the slain and the degree of the homicide. The underlying motive in such forms of composition is the desire to make good the deficiency in the fighting or working strength of the community which has lost one of its members.[23] This seems to be the meaning of Hittite Law 43: "If a man customarily fords a river with his ox, another man pushes him aside, seizes the tail of the ox and crosses the river, but the river carries the owner of the ox away, they [i.e. the authorities of the respective village or town] shall receive that very man." The view of life as a replaceable economic value here reaches its ultimate expression. The moral guilt of the homicide is so far subordinated to the need of restoring the strength of the community that the culprit is not punished but incorporated;[24] this is the polar opposite of the biblical law which requires that not even the flesh of the stoned homicidal ox may be eaten.

That the divergence in law reflects a basic difference in judgments of value, rather than stages in a single line of evolution, would seem to be borne out by examining the reverse of the coin: the treatment of offenses against property. Both Assyrian and Babylonian law know of offenses against property that entail the death penalty. In Babylonia, breaking and entering, looting at a fire, night trespass—presumably for theft—and theft from another's possession are punished by death; Assyrian law punishes theft committed by a wife against her husband with death.[25] In view of this, the leniency of biblical law in dealing with all types of property offenses is astonishing. No property offense is punishable with death. Breaking and entering, for which Babylonian law prescribes summary execution and hanging of the culprit at the breach, is punished in biblical law with double damages. If the housebreaking occurred at night the householder is privileged to slay the culprit caught in the act, though this is not prescribed as a punishment (Exod 22:1 f.).[26]

This unparalleled leniency of biblical law in dealing with property offenses must be combined with its severity in the case of homicide, just as the leniency of non-biblical law in dealing with homicide must be taken in conjunction with its severity in dealing with property offenses. The significance of the laws then emerges with full clarity: in biblical law life and property are incommensurable; taking of life cannot be made up for by any amount of property, nor can any property offense be considered as amounting to the value of life. Elsewhere the two are commensurable: a given amount of property can make up for life, and a grave enough offense against property can necessitate forfeiting life. Not the archaicness of the biblical law of homicide relative to that of the cuneiform codes, nor the progressiveness of the biblical law of theft relative to that of Assyria and Babylonia, but a basic difference in the evaluation of life and property separates the one from the others. In the biblical law a religious evaluation; in non-biblical, an economic and political evaluation, predominates.

Now it is true that in terms of each viewpoint one can speak of a more or a less thoroughgoing application of principle, and, in that sense, of advanced or archaic conceptions. Thus the Hittite laws would appear to represent a more consistent adherence to the economic-political yardstick than the law of Babylonia and Assyria. Here the principle of maintaining the political-economic equilibrium is applied in such a way that even homicides (not to speak of property offenses) are punished exclusively in terms of replacement. It is of interest, therefore, to note that within the Hittite system there are traces of an evolution from earlier to later conceptions. The Old Kingdom edict of Telepinus still permits the kinsman of a slain man to choose between retaliation or composition, while the later law of the code seems to recognize only replacement or composition.[27] And a law of theft in the code (parag. 23) records that an earlier capital punishment has been replaced by a pecuniary one.

In the same way it is legitimate to speak of the law of the Bible as archaic in comparison with postbiblical Jewish law. Here again the jural postulate of the biblical law of homicide reached its fullest expression only later: the invaluableness of life led to the virtual abolition of the death penalty. But what distinguishes this abolition from that just described in the Hittite laws, what shows it to be truly in accord with the peculiar inner reason of biblical law, is the fact that it was not accompanied by the institution of any sort of pecuniary compensation. The conditions that had to be met before the death penalty could be inflicted were made so numerous, that is to say, the concern for the life of the accused became so exaggerated, that in effect it was impossible to inflict capital punishment.[28] Nowhere in the account of this process, however, is there a hint that it was ever contemplated to substitute a pecuniary for capital punishment. The same reverence for human life that led to the virtual abolition of the death penalty also forbade setting a value on the life of the slain man. (This reluctance either to execute the culprit or to commute his penalty created a dilemma which Jewish law cannot be said to have coped with successfully.)[29]

Thus the divergences between the biblical and Near Eastern laws of homicide appear not as varying stages of progress or lag along a single line of evolution, but as reflections of differing underlying principles. Nor does the social-political explanation of the divergence seem to be adequate in view of the persistence of the peculiarities of biblical law throughout the monarchial, urbanized age of Israel on the one hand, and the survival of the ancient non-biblical viewpoint in later Bedouin and Arab law on the other.

IV.

Another divergence in principle between biblical law and the non-biblical law of the ancient Near East is in the matter of vicarious punishment —the infliction of a penalty on the person of one other than the actual culprit. The principle of talion is carried out in cuneiform law to a degree which at times involves vicarious punishment. A creditor who has so maltreated the distrained son of his debtor that he dies, must lose his own son.[30] If a man struck the pregnant daughter of another so that she miscarried and died, his own daughter must be put to death.[31] If through faulty construction a house collapses killing the householder's son, the son of the builder who built the house must be put to death.[32] A seducer must deliver his wife to the seduced girl's father for prostitution.[33] In another class are penalties which involve the substitution of a dependent for the offender—the Hittite laws compelling a slayer to deliver so many persons to the kinsmen of the slain, or prescribing that a man who has pushed another into a fire must give over his son; the Assyrian penalties substituting a son, brother, wife, or slave of the murderer "instead of blood."[34] Crime and punishment are here defined from the standpoint of the paterfamilias: causing the death of a child is punished by the death of a child. At the same time the members of the family have no separate individuality vis-à-vis the head of the family. They are extensions of him and may be disposed of at his discretion. The person of the dependent has no independent footing.

As is well known, the biblical law of Deuteronomy 24:16 explicitly excludes this sort of vicarious punishment: "Parents shall not be put to death for children, nor children for parents; each shall be put to death for his own crime." The proper understanding of this requires, first, that it be recognized as a judicial provision, not a theological dictum. It deals with an entirely different realm than Deuteronomy 5:9 and Exodus 20:5, which depict God as "holding children to account to the third and fourth generations for the sins of their parents."[35] This is clear from the verb *yûmāt*, "shall be put to death," referring always to judicial execution and not to death at the hand of God.[36] To be sure. Jeremiah and Ezekiel transfer this judicial provision to the theological realm, the first promising that in the future, the second insisting that in the present, each man *die* for his own sin—but both change *yûmat* to *yāmût* (Jer 31:29; Ezek 18:4 and passim).

This law is almost universally considered late. On the one hand, it is supposed to reflect in law the theological dictum of Ezekiel; on the other, the dissolution of the family and the "weakening of the old patriarchal position of the house father" that attended the urbanization of Israel during the monarchy.[37] This latter reasoning, at any rate, receives no support from the law of the other highly urbanized cultures of the ancient Near East. Babylonian, Assyrian, and Hittite civilization was surely no less urbanized than that of monarchial Israel, yet the notion of family cohesiveness and the subjection of dependents to the family head was not abated by this fact.

A late dating of the Deuteronomic provision is shown to be altogether unnecessary from the simple fact that the principle of individual culpability in precisely the form taken in Deuteronomy 24:16 is operative in the earliest law collection of the Bible. What appears as a general principle in Deuteronomy is applied to a case in the Covenant Code law of the goring ox: after detailing the law of an ox who has slain a man or a woman, the last clause of the law goes on to say that if the victims are a son or a daughter the same law applies (Exod 21:31). This clause, a long-standing puzzle for exegetes, has only recently been understood for what it is: a specific repudiation of vicarious punishment in the manner familiar from cuneiform law. There a builder who, through negligence, caused the death of a householder's son must deliver up his own son; here the negligent owner of a vicious ox who has caused the death of another's son or daughter must be dealt with in the same way as when he caused the death of a man or woman, to wit: the owner is to be punished, not his son or daughter.[38] This principle of individual culpability in fact governs all of biblical law. Nowhere does the criminal law of the Bible, in contrast to that of the rest of the Near East, punish secular offenses collectively or vicariously. Murder, negligent homicide, seduction, and so forth, are punished solely on the person of the actual culprit.

What heightens the significance of this departure is the fact that the Bible is not at all ignorant of collective or vicarious punishment. The narratives tell of the case of Achan who appropriated objects devoted to God from the booty of Jericho and buried them under his tent. The anger of God manifested itself in a defeat of Israel's army before Ai. When Achan was discovered, he and his entire household were put to death (Josh 7). Again, the case of Saul's sons, who were put to death for their father's massacre of the Gibeonites in violation of an oath by YHWH (2 Sam 21). Now these instances are not a matter of ordinary criminal law but touch the realm of the deity directly.[39] The misappropriation of a devoted object—*ḥērem*—infects the culprit and all who come into contact with him with the taboo status of the *ḥērem* (Deut 7:26; 13:16; cf. Josh 6:18). This wholly analogous to the contagiousness of the state of impurity, and a provision of the law of the impurity of a corpse is really the best commentary on the story of Achan's crime: "This is the law: when a man dies in a tent every one that comes into that tent, and every thing that is in the tent, shall be unclean" (Num 19:14). Achan's misappropriated objects—the story tells us four times in three verses (Josh 7:21, 22, 23)—were hidden in the ground under his tent. Therefore he, his family, his domestic animals, and his tent, had to be destroyed, since all incurred the *ḥērem* status. This is not a case, then, of vicarious or collective punishment pure and simple, but a case of collective contagion of a taboo status. Each of the inhabitants of Achan's tent incurred the *ḥērem* status for which he was put to death, though, to be sure, the actual guilt of the misappropriation was Achan's alone.

The execution of Saul's sons is a genuine case of vicarious punishment, though it too is altogether extraordinary. A national oath made in the name of God has been violated by a king. A drought interpreted as the wrath of God has struck at the whole nation. The injured party, the Gibeonites, demand life for life and expressly refuse to hear of composition. Since the offending king is dead, his children are delivered up.

These two cases—with Judges 21:10 f. the only ones in which legitimate collective and vicarious punishments are recorded in the Bible[40]—show clearly in what area notions of family solidarity and collective guilt are still operative: the area of direct affronts to the majesty of God. Crimes committed against the property, the exclusive rights, or the name of God may be held against the whole family, indeed the whole community of the offender. A principle which is rejected in the case of judicial punishment is yet recognized as operative in the divine realm. The same book of Deuteronomy that clears parents and children of each other's guilt still incorporates the dictum that God holds children to account for their parents' apostasy to the third and fourth generation (5:9). Moreover, it is Deuteronomy 13:16 that relates the law of the *ḥērem* of the apostate city, ordaining that every inhabitant be destroyed, including the cattle. For the final evidence of the concurrent validity of these divergent standards of judgment the law of the Molech worshiper may be adduced (Lev 20:1–5): a man who worships Molech is to be stoned by the people —he alone; but if the people overlook his sin, "Then I", says God, "will set my face against that man, and against his family . . .".[41]

The belief in a dual standard of judgment persisted into latest times. Not only Deuteronomy itself, but the literature composed after it continues to exhibit belief in God's dooming children and children's children for the sins of the parents. The prophetess Huldah, who confirms the warnings of Deuteronomy, promises that punishment for the sins of Judah will be deferred until after the time of the righteous king Josiah (2 Kgs 22:19f.). Jeremiah, who is imbued with the ideology of Deuteronomy, and who is himself acutely aware of the imperfection of the standard of divine justice (31:28f.), yet announces to his personal enemies a doom that involves them and their children (Jer 11:22; 29:32). And both Jeremiah and the Deuteronomistic compiler of the Book of Kings ascribe the fall of Judah to the sins of Manasseh's age (Jer 15:4; 2 Kgs 23:26 f.; 34:3 f.). Even Job complains that God lets the children of the wicked live happy (21:7 ff.). Thus there can be no question of an evolution during the biblical age from early to late concepts, from "holding children to account for the sins of parents" to "parents shall not be put to death for children, etc." There is rather a remarkable divergence between the way God may judge men and the way men must judge each other. The divergence goes back to the earliest legal and narrative texts and persists through the latest.

How anomalous the biblical position is can be appreciated when set against its Near Eastern background. A telling expression of the parallel between human and divine conduct toward wrongdoing is the following Hittite soliloquy:

> Is the disposition of men and of the gods at all different? No! Even in this matter somewhat different? No! But their disposition is quite the same. When a servant stands before his master . . . [and serves him] . . . his master . . . is relaxed in spirit and is favorably inclined (?) to him. If, however, he (the servant) is ever dilatory (?) or is not observant (?), there is a different disposition towards him. And if ever a servant vexes his master, either they kill him, or [mutilate him]; or he (the master) calls him to account (and also) his wife, his sons, his brothers, his sisters, his relatives by marriage, and his family. . . . And if ever he dies, he does not die alone, but his family is included with him. If then anyone vexes the feeling of a god, does the god punish him alone for it? Does he not punish his wife, his children, his descendants, his family, his slaves male and female, his cattle, his sheep, and his harvest for it, and remove him utterly?[42]

To this striking statement it need only be added that not alone between master and servant was the principle of vicarious punishment applied in Hittite and Near Eastern law, but, as we have seen, between parents and children and husbands and wives as well.

In contrast, the biblical view asserts a difference between the power of God, and that of man, over man. Biblical criminal law forgoes entirely the right to punish any but the actual culprit in all civil cases; so far as man is concerned all persons are individual, morally autonomous entities. In this too there is doubtless to be seen the effect of the heightened stress on the unique worth of each life that the religious-legal postulate of man's being the image of God brought about. "All persons are mine, says the Lord the person of the father as well as that of the son; the person that sins, he shall die" (Ezek 18:4). By this assertion Ezekiel wished to make valid in the theological realm the individual autonomy that the law had acknowledged in the criminal realm centuries before. That God may impute responsibility and guilt to the whole circle of a man's family and descendants was a notion that biblical Israel shared with its neighbors. What was unique to Israel was its belief that this was exclusively the way of God; it was unlawful arrogation for man to exercise this divine prerogative.

The study of biblical law, then, with careful attention to its own inner postulates, has as much to reveal about the values of Israelite culture as the study of Psalms and Prophets. For the appreciation of this vital aspect of the biblical world, the riches of cuneiform law offer a key that was unavailable to the two millennia of exegesis that preceded our time. The key is now available and the treasury yields a bountiful reward to those who use it.

NOTES

1. J. L. Saalschütz, *Das Mosaische Recht, mit Berücksichtigung des spätern Jüdischen,* 2 vols. (Berlin, 1848).
2. The following law collections are pertinent to the discussion of the criminal law of the Bible: the laws of Eshnunna (LE), from the first half of the 19th century B.C.; the code of Hammurapi (CH), from the beginning of the 18th century; the Middle Assyrian laws (MAL), 14th–11th centuries; and the Hittite laws (HL), latter half of the 2nd millennium. All are translated in *ANET*, pp. 159 ff.
3. *BL* (Oxford, 1952, 1955) I, p. 99; cf. also p. 275, where Koschaker's approach is characterized and Miles' approach contrasted.
4. Contrast, e.g., the historical explanation of the discrepancies in the laws of theft given by Meek in *ANET,* p. 166, note 45, with Miles' suggestions in BL I, 80 ff. The historical explanation does not help us understand how the draftsman of the laws of Hammurapi conceived of the law of theft.
5. The point is made and expertly illustrated in E. A. Hoebel, *The Law of Primitive Man* (Harvard, 1954); cf. especially chap. 1.
6. Inscription of Yaḫdun-lim of Mari, *Syria* 32 (1955), p. 4, lines 1 ff. I owe this reference and its interpretation to Professor E. A. Speiser, whose critique of this part of my discussion has done much to clarify the matter in my

mind; cf. his contribution to *Authority and Law in the Ancient Orient* (Supplement to the *JAOS*, No. 17 [1954]), especially pp. 11 ff.

7. Cf. CH xxvb 95 ff.: "I am Hammurapi, the just king, to whom Shamash has granted truths." We are to understand the laws of Hammurapi as an attempt to embody this cosmic ideal in laws and statutes. (After writing the above I received a communication from Professor J. J. Finkelstein interpreting this passage as follows: "What the god 'gives' the king is not 'laws' but the gift of the perception of *kittum,* by virtue of which the king, in distinction from any other individual, becomes capable of promulgating laws that are in accord or harmony with the cosmic principle of *kittum.")*
8. Speiser, *op. cit.,* p. 12; this Mesopotamian conception of cosmic truth is a noteworthy illustration of Professor Kaufmann's thesis that "Paganism conceives of morality not as an expression of the supreme, free will of the deity, but as one of the forces of the transcendent, primordial realm which governs the deity as well" *Toledot ha-ʾEmunah ha-Yiśraʾelit,* I/2, p. 345.
9. CH xxivb 76f., 81; xxvb 12 f., 64 ff., 78 ff., 99; xxvib 3 f., 19 ff.
10. Ibid. xxvib 33 f. It is not clear, in the face of this plain evidence, how it can still be maintained that the relief at the top of the law stele depicts Shamash dictating or giving the code to Hammurapi (E. Dhorme, *Les religions de Babylone et d'Assyrie* [Paris, 1949], p. 62; S. H. Hooke, *Babylonian and Assyrian Religion* [London, 1953], p. 29). The picture is nothing more than a traditional presentation scene in which a worshiper in an attitude of adoration stands before, or is led by another deity into, the presence of a god; it may be inferred from the context (i.e. the position of the picture above the code) that the figures of this highly conventionalized scene represent Hammurapi and Shamash. See the discussion in H. Frankfort, *The Art and Architecture of the Ancient Orient* (Harmondsworth, 1954), p. 59 (note that Frankfort does not even go so far as Meek who sees in the scene "Hammurabi in the act of receiving the commission to write the law-book from . . . Shamash" [*ANET,* p. 163]). For this and similar representations see J. B. Pritchard, *The Ancient Near East in Pictures* (Princeton, 1954), nos. 514, 515, 529, 533, 535, 702. Miles aptly sums up the matter of the authorship of the laws thus (BL I, 39): "Although [Shamash and Marduk] . . . are mentioned a number of times, they are not said to be the authors of the Laws; Hammurabi himself claims to have written them. Their general character, too, is completely secular, and in this respect they are strongly to be contrasted with the Hebrew laws; they are not a divine pronouncement nor in any sense a religious document."
11. Epilogue to the laws of Lipit-Ishtar, *ANET,* p. 161.
12. See the prologue and epilogue of the laws of Lipit-Ishtar and Hammurapi.
13. The point is made in Kaufmann, *op. cit.,* I/1, p. 67.
14. CH 129; MAL 14–16; HL 198; cf. W. Kornfeld, "L'adultère dans l'orient antique," *RB* 57 (1950), pp. 92 ff.; E. Neufeld, *Ancient Hebrew Marriage Laws* (London, 1944), pp. 172 ff.
15. HL 187, 188, 198, 199; cf. LE 48.

16. HL 1–4.
17. A. Kennett, *Bedouin Justice* (Cambridge, 1925), pp. 49 ff.
18. LE 54; CH 250, 251.
19. Strict retaliation of life for life is "primitive," a "desert principle"; cf. T. J. Meek, *Hebrew Origins* (New York, 1936), pp. 66, 68; A. Alt, *Die Ursprünge des israelitischen Rechts,* in *Kleine Schriften zur Geschichte des Volkes Israel* (München, 1953), pp. 305 ff.; A. Kennett, *op. cit.,* p. 49; on the goring ox, cf. BL I, 444; M. Weber, *Ancient Judaism* (Glencoe, 1952), p. 62. For the widely held theory of the development of punishment which underlies this view, see BL I, 500.
20. The peculiarities that distinguish this biblical law from the Babylonian are set forth fully by A. van Selms, "The Goring Ox in Babylonian and Biblical Law," *ArOr* 18 (1950), 321 ff., though he has strangely missed the true motive for stoning the ox and tabooing its flesh.
21. From the comment of Sifre to Deut. 19:13a it is clear that this paradox was already felt in antiquity.
22. G. R. Driver and J. C. Miles, *The Assyrian Laws* (Oxford, 1935), p. 35.
23. *Ibid.,* p. 36; Kennet, *op. cit.,* pp. 26 f., 54 f.
24. This interpretation follows Goetze's translation (*ANET,* p. 191, cf. especially note 9). Since no specific punishment is mentioned, and in view of the recognition by Hittite law of the principle of replacing life by life (cf. HL 44) there does not seem to be any ground for assuming that any further punishment beyond forced incorporation into the injured community was contemplated (E. Neufeld, *The Hittite Laws* [London, 1951], p. 158).
25. CH 21, 25; LE 13 (cf. A. Goetze, *The Laws of Eshnunna,* AASOR 31 [New Haven, 1956], p. 53); CH 6–10; MAL 3. Inasmuch as our present interest is in the theoretical postulates of the law systems under consideration, the widely held opinion that these penalties were not enforced in practice, while interesting in itself, is not relevant to our discussion.
26. The action of v. 1 occurs at night; cf. v. 2 and Job 24:16. V. 2 is to be rendered: "If it occurred after dawn, there is bloodguilt for (killing) him; he must make payment only (and is not subject to death); if he can not, then he is to be sold for his theft" (but he is still not subject to death—contrast CH 8). For the correct interpretation see Rashi and U. Cassuto *Commentary on Exodus* (Jerusalem, 1951), *ad loc.* (Hebrew); Cassuto points out *(ibid.,* p. 196) that this law is an amendment to the custom reflected in CH's laws of theft—a fact which is entirely obscured by the transposition of verses in the Chicago Bible and the Revised Standard Version. Later jurists doubtless correctly interpreted the householder's privilege as the result of a presumption against the burglar that he would not shrink from murder; the privilege, then, is subsumed under the right of self-defense (Mechilta, *ad loc.*).
27. O. Gurney, *The Hittites* (London, 1952), p. 98.
28. *M. Sanh.* 5.1 ff., *b. Sanh.* 40b bottom; cf *m. Makkot* 1.10.
29. To deal with practical exigencies it became necessary to invest the court with extraordinary powers which permitted suspension of all the elaborate

safeguards that the law provided the accused; cf. J. Ginzberg, *Mishpatim Le-Israel, A Study in Jewish Criminal Law* (Jerusalem, 1956), part I, chap. 2; part II, chap. 4.

30. CH 116
31. CH 209–210; cf. MAL 50.
32. CH 230.
33. MAL 55.
34. HL 1–4,44; see also note 22 above.
35. Ibn Ezra in his commentary to Deut 24:16 already inveighs against the erroneous combination of the two dicta; the error has persisted through the centuries (cf. e.g. B. D. Eerdmans, *The Religion of Israel* [Leiden, 1947], p. 94).
36. Later jurists differed with regard to but one case *wĕhazzār haqqārēb yûmāt* (Num 1:51; 3:10; 18:7) according to *b. Sanh.* 84a (cf. *m. Sanh.* 9:6); but the scholar to whom the Gemara ascribes the opinion that *yûmāt* here means by an act of God (R. Ishmael) is quoted in the Sifre to Num 18:7 as of the opinion that a judicial execution is intended (so Ibn Ezra at Num 1:51). The unanimous opinion of the rabbis that Exod 21:29 refers to death by an act of God (Mechilta) is a liberalizing exegesis; see the ground given in *b. Sanh.* 15b.
37. J. M. Powis Smith, *The Origin and History of Hebrew Law* (Chicago, 1931), p. 66; Weber, *op. cit.*, p. 66.
38. Cassuto, commentary *ad loc.;* P. J. Verdam, "On ne fera point mourir les enfants pour les pères en droit biblique," *Revue internationale des droits de l'antiquité* 2/3 (1949), p. 393 ff. Professor I. L. Seeligmann calls my attention to the fact that this interpretation was earlier advanced by D. H. Müller, *Die Gesetze Hammurabis* (Wien, 1903), pp. 166 ff. A. B. Ehrlich's interpretation (in his *Randglossen zur hebr. Bibel* [Leipzig, 1912] *ad loc.)* taking *bēn* and *bat* to mean "free man" and "free woman" in contrast with *ʿebed, ʾāmâ* of v. 32 may now be set aside, ingenious as it is (though forced as well: the suggested parallels John 8:35 and Prov 17:2 [Seeligmann] deal with matters of inheritance and ownership where son [not "free man"!] and slave are apt contrasts; not so here. Note also the particle *ʾô* in Exod 21:31, indicating the verse to be an appendix to the foregoing, rather than connecting it with the new clause, v. 32, beginning with *ʾim.*
39. Recognized by Verdam, *op. cit.*, p. 408, and already by S. R. Driver in his commentary to Deuteronomy (ICC, 1909), p. 277.
40. The massacre of the priestly clan at Nob (1 Sam 22:19) and the execution of Naboth's sons (2 Kgs 9:26) are not represented as lawful. Both cases involve treason, for which it appears to have been customary to execute the whole family of the offender. This custom, by no means confined to ancient Israel (Cf. Jos. *Antiq.* 13.14.2), is not to be assumed to have had legal sanction, though it was so common that Amaziah's departure from it deserved to be singled out for praise (2 Kgs 14:6).
41. This interpretation of Lev 20:5, understanding the guilt of the family before

God as due merely to their association with the Molech-worshiper, is open to question. The intent of the text may rather be to ascribe the people's failure to prosecute the culprit to his family's covering up for him; see Rashi and Ibn Ezra. In that case "his family" of 5a is taken up again in "all who go astray after him" of 5b, and the family is guilty on its own.

42. Gurney, *op. cit.*, pp. 70f.

VI

THE IMPORTANCE OF CONTEXT

15

Bible and Babel: A Comparative Study of the Hebrew and Babylonian Religious Spirit

Jacob J. Finkelstein

I.

One of the most absorbing aspects of the study of the civilizations of the ancient Near East, and especially of Mesopotamia, since the decipherment of cuneiform writing about a century ago, has been the continuous illumination it has thrown on the history, society, and religion of ancient Israel. These civilizations have, of course, a fascination in their own right, and the Assyriologists of today are not primarily concerned with the impact of implications of their work on the understanding of the Old Testament. But to the Western mind the Near East still represents the "Bible Lands" despite the current turmoil in the area occasioned by other interests; Egypt is still the land where the Israelites were in bondage, the land whence they emerged under Moses as a nation dedicated to a new religious idea, and Mesopotamia is traditionally the land of Abraham's birth, the land with which, by the testimony of the Bible itself, the Israelites continued to have important political and cultural contact throughout their history.

For the religiously oriented Westerner, Christian and Jew alike, it is naturally that part of the Babylonian record which has a direct bearing on the religious thought and literature of the Bible that attracts his most serious attention. Most of the West is committed in some degree to the belief that the monotheism of the Old Testament represents the highest

Reprinted by permission from *Commentary* 26 (November 1958): 431–44. Copyright © 1958, American Jewish Committee.

level of theological perception yet attained by man, and that the religion of ancient Israel—or at least the religious thought of the prophetic age—embodies the most exalted spiritual conceptions ever attained by any ancient nation. When Babylonian religious and literary works were discovered, showing unmistakable relations with Biblical counterparts, such as the Creation and Flood stories in Genesis, it was therefore inevitable that they should be very carefully scrutinized for the contrasts as well as for the parallels they displayed with the Biblical versions. Given the cultural background of the investigating scholars—many of them had in fact had a theological training and were committed to accepting the Biblical word as divine inspiration—it was also inevitable that they would find the Biblical stories superior in religious, ethical, and other qualities to their Babylonian counterparts. It may even be charged that this conclusion was a prior assumption, and that the investigation was undertaken with the implicit purpose of demonstrating the truth of this assumption.

On the surface the Biblical versions of these stories do seem to exhibit a greater awareness of ethical values while lacking all the mythology of the Babylonian versions. Such considerations, when viewed against the larger background of the Babylonian religious system with its thoroughgoing polytheism, magic, astrology, and related religious institutions, served only to confirm Biblical scholars and theologians late in the nineteenth century in their conviction that the monotheism of Israel was the superior theological concept, in that it provided the basis for an ethical rule of life unavailable to the polytheistic system of the Babylonians. In their zeal to uphold the superiority of the religion of the Old Testament these scholars ignored a body of substantial evidence which might have cast a more favorable light on Babylonian religious thought. Numerous Babylonian religious texts such as hymns and prayers had already been published which reflected a high moral and ethical consciousness and a deep awareness of sin and retribution. There were indeed many Babylonian compositions that for moral and spiritual elevation could hold their own with some of the noblest passages in the Bible. The conclusions of these scholars, in brief, accorded scant justice to the Babylonian record, and little, as we shall see, to the Biblical one.

It was therefore not surprising when the leading Assyriologist at the turn of the century, Professor Friedrich Delitzsch of the University of Berlin, in a series of three public lectures beginning in 1902, entitled

"Babel and Bible," undertook to champion Babylonian religion and culture against the Biblical scholars and theologians.[1] Although the declared purpose of the lectures was to synthesize the results of Mesopotamian archaeology and Assyriological study for the general public, the theme turned out to be nothing less than an all-out defense of the spiritual, ethical, and moral qualities of Babylonian culture and religion despite its obvious polytheism. It was at the same time an almost unrestrained attack on the claims made for the superiority of the religion of the Old Testament in these very same qualities.

Delitzsch epitomized his belief in the overall ethical superiority of Babylonian to Israelite civilization, apart from its obvious chronological priority, by giving Babel (Babylon) deliberate precedence over Bible in the title of his lectures. He compared the very same stories, including the Creation and Flood tales, which the Biblical scholars had appealed to in support of their claim for the ethical superiority of the Bible, and purported to show that the Babylonian versions were superior in this respect. He went so far as to deprive the Israelites of the glory of having conceived of that unrivaled boon to Western living, the Sabbath, claiming instead that "there can therefore be scarcely the shadow of a doubt that in the last resort we are indebted to this ancient nation on the banks of the Euphrates and Tigris for the plenitude of blessings that flows from our day of Sabbath or Sunday rest." He even cast doubt upon the ultimate glory of Israelite religion by producing alleged evidence that the worship of Yahweh as the sole god was already known to "Canaanite" tribes who migrated to Mesopotamia before 2000 B.C.E. He also cited other texts which seemed to indicate that the Babylonians ultimately developed a monotheism centered on the god Marduk, the patron deity of the city of Babylon. Israelite religion was thus shorn of virtually all credit for the major contributions to religious and ethical thought which Judaism and Christianity had claimed for it.

Even a cursory reading of Delitzsch's lectures will reveal that, together with a deep passion for his subject and a justifiable resentment against the high-handed manner with which Biblical scholars often used it, he harbored a deep antipathy to the religion of the Old Testament. This last failing led him into errors of overstatement, and even ignoring such parts of the records on both sides as were prejudicial to his thesis. These were, to be sure, common scholarly weaknesses to which the Biblical scholars had themselves succumbed. Such weaknesses, however, might escape notice in the work of defenders of the Bible, but they were likely to stand out when displayed by someone on the other side. Delitzsch himself provided his opponents with the main weapons for their attack which followed on the heels of his very first lecture.

The authorities of the Lutheran Church, and conservative theologians and Biblical scholars of most Christian denominations, voiced violent objection to the thesis of the lectures on purely doctrinal grounds. They rightly regarded it as a direct assault on the fundamental Christian doctrine of the divine election of Israel, and thus, by implication, on Christian teaching about the ministry of Jesus. Delitzsch freely admitted that he did not himself hold these beliefs, and in a private interview with the Kaiser he admitted further that he did not believe in the divinity of Jesus, nor that any passage in the Old Testament foretold his coming. Wilhelm II thereupon issued a lengthy statement dissociating himself and the German Lutheran Church (of which he was the nominal head) from Delitzsch's views, pronouncing them a menace to public faith and morality. To quote the famous theologian Harnack in approval of the Kaiser's decision, it became "the talk of the streets that 'the Old Testament no longer amounts to much!' " Royal sponsorship was withdrawn from the last lecture, and the public was exhorted not to take on faith any of Delitzsch's opinions as they affected the orthodox view of the Old Testament.

Such attacks from organized and conservative Christian quarters were to be expected, but scholars and liberal theologians equally failed to come to grips with the essence of Delitzsch's thesis. They contented themselves with pointing out Delitzsch's excesses and even his misrepresentations; none was apparently moved to reconsider the entire basis of the common belief in the superiority of Israelite theology and ethics in the light of the cogent evidence which Delitzsch adduced to show that the Babylonians, despite their polytheism, similarly reached high levels of ethical and spiritual thought.

The scholars were thus easily able to expose the baselessness of Delitzsch's claim for the Babylonian origin of the Sabbath. The basic facts are as follows: the seventh, fourteenth, nineteenth, twenty-first, and twenty-eighth days of every month were known as "evil days" to the Babylonians, and of these days the nineteenth (which Delitzsch ignored for the obvious reason that it did not fit into the Sabbath pattern) was considered the most baneful. These days were considered dangerous for many kinds of activities, and for some of them lamentation was prescribed. The Babylonian term *shapattu*—possibly connected etymologically with Hebrew *shabbat* (Sabbath)—was never applied to these days as Delitzsch claimed, but only to the fifteenth day of each month, which was never counted as one of the "dangerous" days. The term *shapattu* did have a connotation of "ending" or "termination," but this did not refer to any ceasing of work, but to the ending of the first half of the month, or the time of the full moon. Although it is still possible that the Hebrew term for Sabbath is derived ultimately from the Babylonian term, the character of the days to which the Israelites applied it bears only the remotest relation to comparable Babylonian days.

Delitzsch's alleged evidence for the worship of Yahweh among certain "Canaanites" dwelling in Mesopotamia is more readily disposed of. It was not easily refuted at the turn of the century because of the imprecise knowledge of dialectal Akkadian grammar current in Delitzsch's day. The word which had been interpreted as referring to Yahweh we now know to be nothing more than the first person possessive pronoun. At all events, it is now commonly recognized that the name Yahweh is excluded in all the cited occurrences. We shall refer later to the texts which allegedly indicate a tendency toward monotheism on the part of the Babylonians.

II.

Many other details of evidence cited by Delitzsch in support of his thesis were refuted in his day, and even more can be discounted in light of our present knowledge. But the crux of Delitzsch's thesis raised a dilemma which his critics virtually ignored. If it is true that many Babylonian religious texts—not to mention the implications of the great collection of the laws of Hammurabi discovered at the very time that Delitzsch's lectures were in progress—reflected a deep consciousness of ethical and moral principles, wherein then lay the reputed superiority of the monotheistic system of Israel to the polytheistic system of Babylonia? Could we not speak as appropriately of "ethical polytheism" as we are wont to speak of "ethical monotheism"? It certainly cannot be argued that monotheism per se represents a higher understanding of cosmological truth than polytheism does, especially if both conceptions are predicated on an ethical and moral order of the universe. The Chinese, after all, seem to have arrived at a moral and ethical conception of the universe without a theistic system at all.

But if the Biblical scholars did not actually come to grips with this problem, they revealed an awareness of it. The superiority of the religion of Israel, they claimed, is manifested by the greater concern with ethical and moral considerations in the Biblical record than in comparable Babylonian compositions. In other words, they grudgingly admitted the existence of ethical and moral motivation in Babylonian thinking, but claimed what might be described as a *quantitative* superiority for the ethical thought of the Old Testament. But this was precisely the level on which Delitzsch chose to fight. The debate was reduced to a sort of ethics contest, in which each side sought to prove the higher ethical content of its favorite. It might be instructive to follow the lines of the debate as it centered around the Babylonian and Biblical Flood stories, whose interrelation is acknowledged on all sides, with the chronological priority of the Mesopotamian account being similarly unchallengeable.

There are, in point of fact, various Mesopotamian versions of the Flood episode, in the early Sumerian language as well as in the Semitic dialect of Akkadian, and there appears to be some organic connection among all of them. The best-known version is the latest and the most completely preserved one, the story of the Flood comprising the entire eleventh tablet of the most famous Babylonian literary work, the Epic of Gilgamesh. It is set in the form of a recounting by Utanapishtim—the Babylonian counterpart of Noah—of the circumstances of the great Flood, the means of his escape and the subsequent unique gift of immortality which the great god Enlil had bestowed upon him. The story is told to Gilgamesh who had finally sought out Utanapishtim at the end of a long series of journeys in search of the secret of immortality. By means of the recitation Utanapishtim seeks to convince his listener that this boon was granted only once to a mortal under unique circumstances and can never again be achieved by a mortal being. Here are the essential features of the episode as set out in this version:[2]

The great gods were prompted to produce a flood. The god Ea, lord of wisdom and the god most favorably disposed toward mankind, secretly warns Utanapishtim of the gods' plans and advises him to tear down his house and build a ship, to "Give up possessions, seek life; Despise property and keep the soul alive."

He is to take aboard the boat "the seed of all living things." The god also gives him the design of the boat, which is apparently to be in the form of an exact cube. When Utanapishtim wonders what to tell his fellow citizens when they see him at work on his strange project, Ea advises him to explain that he has to leave the city because Enlil, the chief of the gods, has taken a dislike to him, and that he is therefore going to live with Ea in the Apsu (the subterranean waters in Mesopotamian cosmology, which are the domain of Ea); a reply which was technically true, but purposely deceitful, for Enlil's dislike was of course directed against all of mankind. This deceit is underscored by the double meaning of the words of reassurance which Ea tells Utanapishtim to relay to his fellow citizens. He is to tell them that the gods will send down upon them a "rain of wheat"; but the word for wheat in Akkadian may also be understood as "woe." The context clearly indicates that the populace is expected to construe the message as a favorable one while Utanapishtim understands its true meaning. This subterfuge is apparently dictated by the desire to avoid having Utanapishtim tell an outright lie, especially on the advice of a god. The deceit clearly worked, the populace was touched by his explanation, and all apparently pitched in to help him get his ark ready by contributing equipment and supplies and aiding in the construction. He then loaded aboard all possessions, family, relatives, "the seed of all living things" and—in a characteristic Mesopotamian touch—a representative of each known craft.

The description of the ensuing storm is presented in mythological terms. Adad, the god of storm and rain, sends the flood-storm, preceded by twin destructive deities representing perhaps atmospheric disturbances such as the tornado; the major underworld god Negral opens the dam on the subterranean waters; the war and irrigation god Ninurta breaches the dikes. The constant flash of lightning is described as the action of the host of earthly gods who "raised their torches to the sky, lighting up the land with their brightness." But the fierceness of the storm was such that even the gods became terrified, and they fled to the safety of the old sky-god Anu where they huddled crouching in fear "like dogs" beneath a wall. From this safe vantage point they observed the flood waters filled with the corpses of man and beast and were overcome with remorse for having consented to such destruction. Ishtar, the great mother goddess, gave loud voice to this grief with the words:

How could I have ordered evil in the divine assembly,
Have ordered war to destroy my people,
When it is I myself who give birth to my people!

All the gods—with the apparent exception of Enlil, the chief of the pantheon—thereupon plunge into mourning. After raging for seven days, the flood subsided. In the words of Utanapishtim:

I then opened a vent [or: hatch] and light struck my face.
I looked about the sea; all was silence,
And all mankind had returned to clay.
The landscape was level as a flat roof.
I bent low and sat down weeping,
Tears running down my face.
I looked about in all directions for the ends of the sea;
At a distance of twelve [double hours] a mountain range emerged.
At Mount Nisir the ship came to a halt.

On the seventh day after this landing:

I sent forth the dove, setting her free.
The dove went forth and returned;
No resting-place appeared for her, so she returned.
I sent forth the swallow, setting her free.
No resting-place appeared for her, so she returned.
I then sent forth the raven, setting it free.
The raven went forth and saw the subsidence of the waters.
It eats, circles, caws, and does not return.
I let everything free to the four winds, and offered a sacrifice.
I poured out a libation on the top of the mountain.
Seven and seven vessels I set out.
Beneath them I heaped up cane, cedar, and myrtle.
The gods smelled the savor,
The gods smelled the sweet savor;
The gods gathered like flies around the sacrificer.

The goddess Ishtar arrives at the scene, vowing that she will never forget the Deluge, and attempts to prevent Enlil from sharing in the sacrifice, as it was he who brought on the Deluge "without reflection." When Enlil arrives, he sees the ship, and, realizing that some mortals had escaped destruction, he turns in anger on the rest of the gods. They then reveal to him that it was Ea who was responsible. Ea then addresses Enlil most eloquently:

O Valiant one, thou art the wisest of the gods.
How couldst thou without reflection bring on the Deluge?

> On the sinner impose his sin; on the transgressor impose his transgression.
> But be lenient lest he be cut off; be patient lest he [perish].

Ea continues by telling Enlil that (if it was his intention to punish mankind) instead of the Deluge he could have smitten mankind with attacks of wild beasts, famine, or pestilence, which would have served to "diminish" mankind, but not destroy it completely. Enlil is apparently overcome by this speech, and as a form of atonement blesses Utanapishtim, granting him and his wife the unprecedented gift of immortal life.

III.

The parallels between this story and the Biblical Flood episode are fairly obvious. God decides to send down the Deluge because mankind has become evil and has corrupted the entire earth. Noah is to be spared because he is the only righteous person on earth. The dimensions of the ark which God commands Noah to build differ from those in the Babylonian account, but they are described in detail by God himself. He is to take aboard a male and female of each living species. In both versions the Deluge is the result of heavy rains and the simultaneous rising of subterranean waters. The traditional resting place of Noah's ark, Mount Ararat in Armenia, is a notable variation from the Mount Nisir of the Babylonian story, which is in Southern Kurdistan. The most striking resemblances between the two stories occur at the end of the Flood, when Noah opens the window of the ark, and sends forth the dove three times before it stays away for good; the Biblical text at this point parallels the Babylonian almost word for word. Noah, like Utanapishtim, then offers sacrifices, and in a striking parallel to the Babylonian text we read: "God smelled the sweet savor" (Genesis 8:21), which prompts his decision never again to unleash such total destruction against the earth, "for the schemes of man's heart are evil from his youth, and I shall never again destroy all living things as I have done."

The dependence of the Biblical story upon the Babylonian to some degree is granted by virtually all schools of thought. There can be no question about priority in time; the essential details of the Mesopotamian Flood story were already current by at least 2000 B.C.E. In evaluating the two versions, the Babylonian story is generally conceded the prize for its ingenuous human charm, which is enhanced by its being couched in poetic form. On the other hand, it has invariably come off a bad second in the test for moral and ethical content. John Skinner, for example, in his commentary on Genesis (1910) states: "The ethical motive, which is but feebly developed in the Babylonian account, obtains clear recognition in the hands of the Hebrew writers; the Flood is a divine judgment on human corruption; etc." There follows the expected invidious comparison between the "vindictive, capricious" and deceitful gods of the Babylonians and the one "almighty and righteous God—a Being capable of anger and pity, and even change or purpose, but holy and just in His dealings with men." A similar verdict, but in even more severe terms, is pronounced by the modern Assyriologist A. Heidel, in his book *The Gilgamesh Epic and Old Testament Parallels* (1949). He even quotes with approval an earlier contemptuous opinion of the Babylonian Flood story as "steeped in the silliest polytheism." It was just this kind of refusal to appreciate the merits of Babylonian religious thought and literature on their own terms by Biblical scholars that contributed to the violence of Delitzsch's reaction.

Granting for the moment the assumption made by virtually all Western theologians—which, say, an educated Chinese or Indian might conceivably not find so axiomatic—that monotheism is inherently a more advanced, elevated, and ethically superior form of religious conception than polytheism, what logical process dictates the further inference that the religious literature of a polytheistic society must of necessity be baser, cruder, or less moral in outlook than the literature of a monotheistic society? There is no doubt that the entire literature of the Old Testament, regardless of the age, character, or original function of its component elements, is made to conform with its overall theme: the one God and his purposes, especially as they apply to man. But is it necessary to expect that the vision of ethical monotheism will transform every Biblical episode in equal degree or be reflected in it? This is precisely what Biblical scholarship implied by its uniform finding in favor of the Biblical material whenever confronted with Mesopotamian parallels. It is doubtful, however, that an impartial observer would easily discern the higher ethical motivation inherent in the Biblical Flood episode, for example, as opposed to the Babylonian account. It is often pointed out in this connection that in the Babylonian story the gods decide to send down the Deluge without any apparent motivation, while in the Biblical story the Flood is unleashed explicitly as a punishment for man's wicked behavior. The speech of Ea, however, after the Flood is over, is an indication that, to the mind of the Babylonians, the decision was in the first place prompted by man's evil behavior. The reason for its not being stated explicitly is not necessarily due to the weak conception on the part of the Babylonian thinkers of the gods' concern for ethical conduct, to which it is often attributed. It must be remembered that the Babylonian story is presented as a recital by Utanapishtim of the significant events for the purpose of convincing Gilgamesh that his quest for immortality is vain; that his own immortal status was due to the unique circumstances of that ancient event, which can never again be repeated. It was not germane to this purpose to emphasize the causes of the Flood, nor would it have been appropriate for Utanapishtim himself to pass judgment on the alleged depravity of the whole race of his fellow men. The Biblical narrative, on the other hand, is impersonal and its purpose is precisely to set forth God's actions and motives.

There exists, however, a much older version of the Babylonian Flood story than the one incorporated in the Gilgamesh Epic. Here the episode is part of a long impersonal narrative which was conceived as nothing less than a kind of history of mankind. This version of the Flood story is not often quoted in comparisons with the Biblical story—although in numerous details it appears to be closer to the Biblical version than the account in Gilgamesh—due to the fact that the text is still very fragmentary. But the vital point for us is that in this version the cause of the Flood is explicitly given:

> The land became wide, the people became numerous.
> The land hummed like a lyre [or: bellowed like wild oxen].[3]
> The god was depressed by their uproar,
> Enlil heard their clamour
> And said to the great gods:
>
> "The clamour of mankind has become oppressive,
> Because of their uproar I want sleep."

There can be little doubt that the noise of mankind which disturbs Enlil's repose is only the metaphoric or mythological guise for what is clearly meant to be the wicked behavior of man. Biblical scholars will not be in a position to dispute such an interpretation, for these are precisely the terms in which the sinfulness of those most wicked of cities, Sodom and Gomorrah, is described in Genesis 18:20f. and 19:13. It is the noise and clamor of these cities which, having reached an intolerable pitch, impel

God to send down a rain of "brimstone and fire." If the Biblical "noise and clamor" can be interpreted as metaphor, the same consideration may be granted to the Babylonian use of the same terms. It is true that in the Biblical Flood story it is made explicit that Noah is to be spared because he was a "righteous man" while the rest of his generation was corrupt. Again it must be noted that we cannot fairly expect Utanapishtim to say this of himself in his narration to Gilgamesh. In the older text (usually referred to as the Atrahasis Epic, for this is the name of the Babylonian "Noah" in that version of the Flood episode) the section where such a statement might have been expected is missing. There is clear evidence, which we shall soon discuss, that Atrahasis is, in fact, thought to be righteous.

Returning to the reasons for the Deluge, neither the Biblical version nor the Babylonian goes beyond generalizations in describing the alleged wickedness of man. From the Biblical text alone it would appear that the behavior of mankind was no worse before the Flood than after it. It is only that later God becomes reconciled to the fundamentally evil "devisings of man's heart" (Gen 8:21) and decides never again to resort to such extreme forms of punishment for it. Later Jewish rabbis, obviously not satisfied with this kind of motivation for the Flood, had recourse to midrash in order to supply appropriate grounds for such an extreme measure. They speculated on the nature of the wickedness, and imagined that it must have included various forms of sexual depravity, widespread homicide and robbery, or even all three. The ancient rabbis, as well as some modern scholars, were apparently also troubled by the lack of any indication in the Biblical text that God had given mankind any warning of their impending doom, so as to allow them a chance for repentance.

Another disturbing feature was the apparently callous indifference of Noah to the doom of his fellow men. The proper task of a really righteous man (a *tzaddik*) would have been to warn them of the coming catastrophe and to exhort them to repentance. The rabbis proceeded to fill both these deficiencies by means of midrash. Thus God's decision to reduce the normal human life-span from the high hundreds of the prediluvian generations to one hundred and twenty—plainly an etiological tale meant to explain the still proverbial "one hundred and twenty years"—is interpreted by the rabbis as the period of grace during which mankind was given an opportunity to repent and reform its ways. Noah (together with Methuselah) exhorted his fellow men to repentance during this period, warning them of the divine punishment for their wickedness. In the same vein, the rabbis visualized the situation of Noah vis-à-vis his contemporaries when he began building his large and strange craft on dry land—a situation which, as we have seen, presented itself also to the mind of the Babylonian writer—and they appropriately imagined Noah telling them the plain truth: God had decided to destroy all earthly life by means of a flood. The response of the populace, as imagined by the rabbis, was, as to be exprected, derisive laughter. Now there is of course not the slightest warrant in the Biblical text for any of these interpretations. Heidel, nevertheless, chooses to accept the midrashic period of grace as the literal meaning of the life-span episode together with the conception of Noah as preaching to his fellow men during this period. The moral justification for the Flood in the Biblical text was evidently just as deficient to the sensibilities of modern scholars as it was to the ancient Jewish rabbis.

But if midrashic fancy may be exploited as a means of bolstering the moral basis of the Biblical Flood story, how much more justified is Delitzsch who, in championing the Babylonian version, points to the weeping of Utanapishtim when he beheld the aftermath of the Flood, a touch of human compassion absent in the Biblical account. And on these grounds the case for Babylonia is even stronger than Delitzsch himself realized. For in the fragmentary late Assyrian revision of the Atrahasis Epic, in which the final Deluge is only the culmination of a series of lesser punishments, we find Atrahasis interceding with the gods in behalf of his fellow men in the two instances which are still preserved, a feature which is strongly reminiscent of Abraham's intercession with God on behalf of the people of Sodom. In other words, where the Biblical story characterizes Noah as a *tzaddik,* but fails to illustrate it by deed, the Babylonian Flood tradition proves its hero's righteousness much more convincingly precisely by describing his deeds; what had to be supplied for the Biblical account by rabbinic imagination is explicit in the Babylonian accounts.

The foregoing exposition is not, of course, designed as a defense of Delitzsch's thesis. It is meant rather to illustrate the hazardousness of attempting to prove the superiority of Israelite religion and ethics to the Babylonian on the basis of what are essentially trivial details. Parallel traditions, such as the treatment of the Flood legend in Babylonia and

Israel, can be profitably compared only in the light of a full appreciation of the cultural and religious contexts of the respective civilizations. Such understanding is particularly vital when it is clear—as it is in our case—that the theme itself was an object of cultural borrowing. For it is obvious that the cultural context will determine to a great degree the treatment of the theme under observation. In civilizations with such greatly dissimilar religious orientations as Babylonia and Israel, the emphases and treatment of a common theme are bound to differ sharply. But once such differences are taken into account, value judgments based on comparisons will appear all the more meaningless.

IV.

Now monotheism and polytheism—the most fundamental of the contrasts between Babylonian and Israelite theology—bear within themselves a series of cosmological implications which will channel the religious and philosophical responses of the followers of each approach along certain limited and inevitable lines. We cannot, of course, enter here into a lengthy discussion of all these implications, but we shall have to review, however sketchily, those that are basic to our present theme.

What is the essence of polytheism as a theological system? It implies the existence of a plurality of superhuman wills. This very condition precludes the absolute omnipotence of any one of these wills. Even if in the mind of a worshiper one or another of these wills, or deities, is thought to be the head of the pantheon, he must at all times be mindful of the purposes of the other deities which are potentially vitiating to his own designs. As in the case of Ea upsetting Enlil's plan for the destruction of all life by forewarning Utanapishtim of the coming Flood, even the chief deity may sometimes be tricked or deceived. The free expression of the will and personality of any one god is thus under constant threat of a clash with the will and personality of another god. In other words, the gods in a polytheistic system, though operating in an exclusive sphere, face much the same stresses and strains in their efforts at self-realization as man does on earth.

This has the further corollary that the gods cannot *consistently* act in accordance with a humanly conceived moral or ethical ideal. If the first thought of the gods, as that of man, must be "to look out for himself" vis-à-vis his fellow gods, moral and ethical considerations necessarily become secondary. From the point of view of mankind, therefore, the actions of the gods, especially as they affect man, may take on the appearance of caprice or willfulness. But this does not mean, as has sometimes been stated, that gods act purposefully and wantonly to the detriment of man. On the contrary, to the mind of the Mesopotamian, the gods stand in great need of and actually are dependent on the service of man. It is only that in the last resort the needs and welfare of man are of secondary importance in the gods' considerations; it may well happen that a course of action decided upon by the gods for good and sufficient reason to themselves may at the same time be catastrophic for man without his having done anything to incur such treatment. The people, such as the Babylonians, always viewed such misfortune as evidence of the gods' wrath and their own guilt. The profound sense of sin and retribution of the Babylonians is amply attested by their penitential prayers, which give moving expression to this feeling. But the crucial point is not that they possessed an awareness of sin, but that they had no assurance or hope that right conduct would insure their well-being. Sin and misconduct were sure to arouse the gods' anger, but there was no formula that could guarantee divine favor. No god was in a position to offer such assurance; he might at any time be compelled, for private reasons, to ignore such an agreement. For this reason even the concept of such an agreement is completely foreign to a polytheistic system. The gods, for their part, appreciated and even demanded moral and ethical conduct on the part of mankind, but they could offer no guarantees in return. Thus the Babylonian gods are often termed by modern writers (but rarely if ever by the Babylonians themselves) capricious, crafty, and treacherous. They are, to be sure, (for the most part) immortal, but in their needs, desires, and motivations, endowed with all of man's spiritual frailties; they are, in a word, only supermen. Mythology, which, in classical usage, involves the treatment of divine figures in human terms, is an inherent feature of any polytheistic system.

A monotheistic religion by virtue of its inherent characteristics tends, on the other hand, to become an ethical religion. There is no other being who is of the same essence as the single god; the possibility of a *real* rival is beyond conception. The will of this god is therefore incontestable. Though this god must always be conceived of in essentially human terms, man is conscious that this deity is in no way limited by any external forces which could restrict the full expression of his own personality; he has no peers to contend with, no rival wills to counteract. This feature alone renders him as fundamentally different from the gods of a polytheistic system, as from the condition of humanity itself. This god may then be conceived of as being motivated in his decisions by the highest ideals and never by the baser or selfish impulses which inhibit the realization of these ideals by man and polytheistic deities alike. He is therefore completely free to give his complete and unselfish attention to all that goes on in the universe.

By the same token he is in a position to lay down a mandate for man's behavior on earth in accordance with these ideals, and to guarantee man's well-being if his will is complied with, an advantage which, as we have seen, no polytheistic god could possibly enjoy. Man alone is capable of disregarding the divine will, but he does so only in full knowledge of the "Law" and of the inevitable consequences of his actions. The blueprint given by Yahweh to the Israelites for them to follow—the Torah—was conveyed with an unconditional guarantee of success if followed faithfully. Deuteronomy 30:11ff. states the situation with classic simplicity: "For this commandment which I command you this day is not too abstruse for you, nor is it too distant. Nor is it in heaven, that you might say 'Who will ascend for us to heaven to fetch it for us, to let us hear it, that we might observe it?' Nor is it across the sea that you might say 'Who shall go across the sea for us to fetch it for us, to let us hear it, that we might observe it?' For the thing is very near to you; it is in your mouth and in your heart to carry it out." The same text continues with the explicit guarantee of life and prosperity if the commands are faithfully obeyed and an unequivocal warning of extinction if they are disregarded. What is involved here is, in a word, a contract, or "covenant," the essence of which is the freedom of both parties to bind themselves to its terms. This condition could not obtain in a polytheistic system, in which the gods were not absolutely free; the concept of a "covenant" in a polytheistic society is inherently impossible.

The emphasis often placed on the "ethical" character of Israelite monotheism would in this light, therefore, appear to border on the tautologous. The god of Israel is "ethical" precisely because he is the sole deity. It is this uniqueness of Yahweh that carries with it the implication of absolute freedom which is basic to an organized and systematized ethic. Against this background there is little justification for the contempt in which Babylonian religious and ethical thought is often held, *given the polytheistic system under which they had to be conceived.* Nor is this polytheism itself a justifiable object of derision. The theological system of the ancient Greeks was in all essential features similar to that of the Mesopotamians, yet the Greeks have not suffered the abuse and scorn on this account which has traditionally been the lot of the Babylonians. The Babylonians, did, after all, develop a practical system of ethics for human conduct, despite its ineffectiveness as a formula for ultimate salvation. But the wonder is not that their understanding of ethics, sin, and retribution was not as all-embracing or cosmologically anchored as it was in Israelite thought, but that they conceived of such values at all. Indeed, the record of the Babylonians may be of relevance to one of the great issues of our time, whether or not man can be committed firmly to an ethical rule of life that is not rooted in theology. The Babylonians deserve our sympathy perhaps, for their religious system denied them the possibility of coming to satisfactory terms with their universe, but even such an attitude must be tempered with admiration, for the three-thousand-year record of Mesopotamian civilization testifies at least to a remarkable human adaptation to a cosmos in which the future of man was viewed as hopeless.

The seeming preoccupation of Biblical literature with the issue of sin and punishment is similarly a corollary of Israelite monotheism, and deserves no special praise on its own account. By their very possession of the "blueprint," the ideal norms of human behavior, the Israelites experienced a much more profound sense of human inadequacy and weakness than the Babylonians could. The latter had no standard on which they might pattern their lives. Their sense of guilt has a hopeless, almost amoral, character about it; there was always an awareness that their fate in the last resort did not necessarily depend on their guilt or innocence, but on the gods' private purposes. But the possession by the Israelites of such a standard afforded them not only a real perspective on their achievements, but a profound optimism as well; the goal or ideal is always in view, and is approachable if not easily attainable. To achieve salvation nothing more was required than to live up to an ideal that was always believed to have been revealed in the past by God and in force for all time to come. The Babylonians enjoyed no similar advantage. Only occasionally was a particularly favored individual—usually in legend—told what to do by a god, and even then it concerned only the immediate present. On the whole, however, the purposes of the gods were concealed, and were in any event usually prompted by immediate circumstances that could not be predicted far in advance.

The only recourse open to the Babylonians for determining the will of the gods was the process of divination, a procedure which could yield a "message" or "directive" only in the context of the moment, and which had to be instituted on every occasion when knowledge of the god's disposition—his motives were not of human concern—was vital for the undertaking at hand. It is of significance that the message or directive which the divinatory procedure was designed to disclose was called by the Babylonians *tertu,* a word cognate with Hebrew *torah*. The "torah" of the Babylonians, in a real sense, was something that had to be repeatedly elicited from the gods—virtually against their will—as the occasion arose, by the varied and devious means which constituted the elaborate pseudo-science of divination, of which astrology was only the latest and best-known form. Pathetic and barren as all this activity might appear to us today, there was no other method available to the Mesopotamians for ascertaining the will of the gods. The security offered by the monotheistic God of Israel, through a revelation valid for all times, was unavailable to the Babylonians, for their gods, as we have seen, were themselves in no position to grant it.

V.

It will be clear then from the foregoing that most of the features of Babylonian religion which appear base or primitive to modern Western thought are only the inherent characteristics of a polytheistic theology. Western theology feels itself properly indebted to Israelite monotheism for having provided a rationalized basis for a coherent system of ethics offering a hopeful view of man's fate. Such a cosmic view could not have developed within Babylonian polytheism. Yet to hold Babylonian religious thought and ethics in contempt because of this is as legitimate as despising the elephant because he cannot outrace the horse.

In the contrast between a polytheistic system and all its implications and a monotheistic theology and all that it implies, lies the fundamental difference between Babylonia and Israel. But it must constantly be remembered that despite their gloomy view of man's condition, the Mesopotamians were compelled as a matter of practical necessity to organize their society in accordance with at least a *pragmatic* ethic. Men have always demanded ethical behavior on the part of their fellow men, failing at the same time to apply similar standards to their own conduct. The Babylonian gods too, although not themselves *bound* by moral or ethical principles, nevertheless appreciated them and expected man to live by them. The Babylonians, it would seem, fashioned their gods in their own image more faithfully than the Israelites did theirs. The appreciation by the Babylonians of morality and ethical conduct was as intense as that of any nation of the ancient world, and perhaps of the modern as well; their hymns, prayers, and wisdom literature, not to mention the vast and direct evidence of their law promulgations and untold thousands of surviving legal documents, imply precisely this unending concern for justice and morality.

Bearing in mind the fundamental contrast in the theologies and worldviews of the Babylonians and the Israelites, we may return to the comparison of their respective treatments of material common to both of them, such as the Flood episode which we have used as the example in this essay. It will in the first place have to be recognized that the ethical motivations explicit in both versions do not do great credit to the highest concepts of either civilization. We should be in a particularly unfortunate position if we were compelled to deduce all the ethical implications of the Israelite cosmic view from the Flood episode, or, for that matter, from all the narratives in the book of Genesis. But once we are aware of these implications—from other Biblical sources—we may detect their influence even in these portions.

We are struck, then, by the virtually complete absence in the Biblical Flood story of all the mythological byplay which permeates the Babylonian account. Where the Biblical story, for instance, describes the action of the storm as extreme but natural meteorological manifestations, the Babylonian account portrays it in terms of actions by various gods. The Biblical scholars have, of course, appealed also to this as evidence for the more "primitive" character of the Babylonian account. Yet if we recall that mythology, as we defined it earlier, is a corollary of a polytheistic theology and is excluded, by the same token, from a monotheistic one, we may view each version as self-consistent. Nor is there any need to imagine the early Israelite storytellers consciously editing the story they received from Mesopotamia by excising all the "offensive" mythological and polytheistic elements before it might be fit for "local consumption." The Israelite authors, rather, never really "heard" the story in its Babylonian form, for it would have been totally incomprehensible to them. If the notions of edition and excision are at all applicable, these processes must be thought of as unconscious; as the basic elements of the original tale were assimilated by Israelite tradition they were naturally and spontaneously harmonized with the Israelite cosmic view. Elements which were incompatible with this view disappeared of their own accord.

On the other hand, some elements which to modern theological sensibilities appear offensive, but are not intrinsically incompatible with monotheism, are found in the Biblical as well as the Babylonian account. Thus we read in the Biblical story that God locks the boat after Noah and his company are safely aboard, which contrasts with the Babylonian version in which Utanapishtim locks the door himself. Or again, at the end of the Flood we read that "God smelled the sweet savor," a clear echo of the Babylonian scene in which "the gods crowded like flies around the sacrificer." Neither scene in the one version can be said to be "more elevated" in conception than its counterpart in the other version. Yet both versions are internally consistent with their respective theological approach. The Biblical scenes are not mythological, they are only extremely personal or anthropomorphized. What seems to be embarrassing to modern theological conceptions is at bottom only a matter of taste and degree. It can hardly be argued that personalization of the deity is incompatible with even the most exalted brand of monotheism. The God of Reinhold Niebuhr is, after all, identical in all essential respects with "De Lawd" of *The Green Pastures*. Numerous scenes of this type are found throughout the narrative and even the prophetical portions of the Old Testament. Such scenes are no more to be construed as vestiges of "crude" polytheism—as they often have been by Biblical theologians—than are allusions to God's sight, hearing, or love. They are the natural consequence of the conception of a personal god, and are common to polytheism and monotheism alike.

When Delitzsch appealed to certain scenes in the Babylonian Flood story to support his contention that Utanapishtim is presented as a far nobler character than Noah—an argument for which we were able to cite even stronger evidence—it was apparent that he, as well as his critics, was not aware of the essential difference in approach between the two versions. In the Babylonian story the central character and focus of attention is Utanapishtim and the circumstances which enabled him to achieve immortality. It is the story of a human experience in which the role of the gods is secondary. The climax is the bestowal of immortality on the hero. Although the Biblical tale opens with the statement "This is the story of Noah," it is really not the story of Noah; he is just the subject of the moment. The Flood episode, regardless of its original character, had already been recast to fit into a conscious progression of history in which the central theme is God and his dealings with mankind. The points of emphasis in the story are the wickedness of mankind, the contrasting righteousness of Noah, and his consequent exemption by God from the ensuing punishment. But the climax of the story is the covenant made by God never again to send a deluge against mankind, and in this climax—which is in fact the point of the entire story—Noah plays a small role indeed. The covenant made by God is not with Noah alone but with all earthly life. Having received his reward from God for his righteousness, Noah resumes his more modest role in the scheme of Biblical genealogy.

The failure of the Biblical narrative to demonstrate by detail the kindliness and saintliness of Noah is therefore neither an unfortunate omission nor a blemish on the ethical character of the narrative. Such details might have enhanced the artistry of the story, but their essential irrelevance to the theme would have obscured the focal point of the episode. The story thereby retains an austere and unadorned character by comparison with the Babylonian tale. It is significant, in this connection, that the rabbis felt these omissions as deficiencies, and proceeded to add just such midrashic embellishments as were explicit in the Babylonian account. But these are testimony only to the touching human qualities of the rabbis themselves, and serve to explain why the Babylonian Flood story is so much more appealing to our senses than is the Biblical version. And this contrast in focus between the two versions is again only the reflection of the contrasting theological approaches of the two civilizations. The gods of the Babylonians, though more human in attributes and qualities than Yahweh of the Israelites, are yet more remote from human approach and understanding; they do not normally reveal to man their wishes and their plans. What occurs on earth, though attributed to the will of the gods, cannot be described in terms of divine commands and compliance with them. Earthly events and institutions can only be described as the work of men. The famous laws of Hammurabi are, in the words of the prologue and epilogue to the laws, the work of the king himself. They are *not* received from Shamash, the god of justice. This god is conceived of as approving and demanding just action on earth, but he does not "reveal the Law" itself, as the Law of Israel is revealed by Yahweh himself. In the Flood episode, too, this difference is apparent. In the Babylonian account, although the flood is sent by the gods, the events are described from the human point of view; it is a tale of the experiences of human beings. The Biblical story is but a chapter in a larger work, in which every episode is construed as a revelation by Yahweh of his will together with its earthly consequences. The perspective of the Biblical Flood tale is from the vantage point of the divine, and not that of man.

VI.

Having set forth the view that most of the differences between Babylonian and Biblical literature and thought can be attributed directly or indirectly to the contrast between polytheism and monotheism, we must deal at last with the alleged evidence that the Babylonians themselves ultimately approached the monotheistic conception. The text to which Delitzsch appealed in support of this proposition is a late one, in which the various gods are correlated with Marduk, the god of Babylon, in their several spheres of activity thus: Ninurta—Marduk of cultivation; Nergal—Marduk of war; Enlil—Marduk of dominion and counsel; Nabu—Marduk of fortune; Sin—Marduk as illuminator of the night; Shamash—Marduk of truth; Adad—Marduk of rain.

Since Delitzsch's time, similar texts have become known, one of which identifies the gods with the various parts of the body of the god Ninurta; another Assyrian text correlates the activities of the other gods with aspects of Ashur, the chief god of the Assyrians, and still another equates all the female deities with Ishtar, the great goddess of love and war. No serious student of the history of religion today would consider speculations of this kind as evidence for monotheism. They do indicate a common tendency towards syncretism, the identification of the different and independent personalities of the various deities as aspects of a single god. This god is thereby perhaps magnified, but he is not basically transformed in any qualitative way. Such speculations are not monotheistic, for these other personalities continue to have their independent existence in the minds of the very same speculators, as was the case with the worship of Amon-Re during the Empire period in ancient Egypt. The worship of one god is itself not evidence of monotheism. It is best characterized as henotheism or monolatry, a system in which the existence *and effectiveness* of a plurality of deities is recognized within any one civilization although the attention of the worshiper for varying lengths of time and in different localities may be focused on a single one of these deities to the virtual exclusion of the others.

The tendency on the part of certain schools of thought to see in such manifestations tentative gropings toward monotheism is to be attributed in the first place to the tenacious hold which the evolutionary theories of the late ninteenth century still have on the religiously oriented Western mind. Anthropologists have long since discarded the theory of Tylor which postulated the progression of the religious development of the human race from animism to the belief in a supreme deity. And despite the patent absurdities in the "devolutionary" theory of Pater W. Schmidt and his school, the existence of true monotheistic beliefs in primitive cultures cannot be denied. The second reason for the tenacity of the evolutionary theory is the understandable desire of the educated layman to find a rational explanation for the development of monotheism in Israel in the midst of polytheistic surroundings. The evolutionary theory satisfied this desire by supplying the "missing link" of monolatry or henotheism. The fallacy inherent in the entire structure, which has been supported by the egocentricity of Western civilization, has been laid bare by Paul Radin, and need not be elaborated here.[4] Suffice it to say that factual anthropological data have demonstrated that the monotheistic conception of the cosmos can be, and, in fact, has been noted at all stages of social development side by side with the polytheistic conception. And although both views may be found concurrently in the same society, neither is prior to the other; they are in fact mutually exclusive and one cannot develop out of the other.

Monotheism, as Y. Kaufmann recently said,[5] cannot be reached by the gradual reduction of the number of gods to one. Such a process has not been demonstrated in any society, present or past. At some time during the formative period of the Israelite nation, some individual *thinkers,* exactly as has been the case with individuals in primitive societies, viewed the cosmos in a way totally at variance with their co-nationals and contemporaries elsewhere in the civilized world. Following Radin, we may concede the possibility—perhaps the probability—that individuals in ancient Mesopotamia saw the universe in the same light. What is historically significant, however, is not the original conception, which can be found independently in various cultures, but that somehow in ancient Israel alone, this conception—as Radin has shown, usually a minority view—ultimately predominated over the other. The factors which contributed to the establishment of monotheism as the dominant theological view of the Israelites cannot have been inherent in the view itself. This is proved by its failure to take hold in other cultures. The success of monotheism in Israel must therefore be rooted in other conditions, which may be subsumed under the term environmental. To attempt to trace them would be outside the purpose of the present essay.

At all events, Delitzsch was justified, in the light of the prevailing view of the history of religion in his day, in appealing to such "monotheistic" Babylonian texts in support of his thesis. It was in fact an extremely telling point to which there could be no rejoinder. The orthodox theological approach of his critics had itself enthusiastically adopted the evolutionary view of the religious development of mankind, for it provided for the first time a scientific support for Christian apologetic. But if this evolution was possible within the religion of Israel, on what scientific grounds could it be excluded elsewhere? The text adduced by Delitzsch was meant to demonstrate that this "natural" process was not the exclusive property of the Israelites, but took place in Babylonia too, although it did not reach the level it ultimately attained among the Israelites. Against this kind of onslaught there was only one place of refuge, that of dogma; under the comfortable shelter of the belief in the divine election of Israel, all shades of opinion critical of Delitzsch took cover.

The syncretistic tendency manifested in the Babylonian texts alluded to above cannot properly, therefore, be considered even as a "stage on the road towards monotheism." When modern scholars evaluate such speculations as genuinely monotheistic, it is a manifestation only of the attraction that the evolutionary theory still holds for Christian theology. The Babylonian evidence indicates, in the first place, that the other gods did not cease to exist as a result of these speculations. The same thinkers, at other moments, could and did conceive of the separate aspects of the syncretistic deity in their original form, as individual wills and personalities. Secondly, far from approaching the attributes and conception of a true monotheistic god in all his transcendence and omnipotence, this deity remained in every essential characteristic the restricted deity of a polytheistic theology. Nothing has happened to him except that he has been aggrandized.

In summary, then, it may be said that no comparisons between Babylonian and Biblical traditions can be undertaken without constant awareness of the polarity of the Babylonian and Israelite cosmic views, and of the profound effect this contrast had in the religious and cultural development within each civilization. Each system, to be sure, did experience an evolution, but these were internal evolutions; there was never a convergence of the two views towards each other, or, more exactly, a convergence of the polytheistic view towards the monotheistic one. Western man, as the heir of the Israelite tradition, feels that the monotheistic approach affords a firmer basis for his spiritual integration and reconciliation with the universe than was possible within the polytheistic cosmic view of the Babylonians. But this is hardly sufficient warrant for the abuse that the Babylonian experience has suffered at the hands of Western religious scholarship, whether in the form of unconscious condescension or as outright contempt. When Israel was born, civilization in Mesopotamia, based on a social order conceived in terms of high moral and ethical ideals, was already two thousand years old, and the material and intellectual products of this civilization had been diffused all over western Asia. Despite the profound difference of their cosmic orientation from that of the nations around them, the Israelites could and did assimilate with profit such social institutions, literary creations, and even religious usages which served as the practical basis of their own civilization, and which afforded them the institutional framework for the worship of their unique God.

NOTES

1. The English translation of these lectures was published in this country in 1906 by the Open Court Publishing Co. in Chicago.
2. The most felicitous English rendering of the entire epic is by E. A. Speiser in *ANET* (Princeton, 1954). It forms the basis of the translations here.
3. The ambiguity of the original Akkadian phrase presents this rather strangely

contrasting pair of alternative renderings, but the sense of the simile is clear; humanity was setting up a constant din.

4. For a concise summary and evaluation of the entire question see Paul Radin, *Primitive Man as a Philosopher* (rev. ed. New York, 1957) chapter 18.
5. *Great Ages and Ideas of the Jewish People,* edited by Leo W. Schwarz (New York, 1957).

16

The "Comparative Method" in Biblical Interpretation—Principles and Problems[1]

Shemaryahu Talmon

I.

Modern Old Testament studies, from the inception of the historico-literary or *literarhistorische* approach, constitute an illuminating example of interdisciplinary contacts and of the transfer of methods applied in one field of research to another. Thus, the principles underlying the analysis to which the ancient Hebrew literature has been subjected by modern scholarship, especially since the beginning of the nineteenth century—the days of de Wette, Ewald, Kuenen, Graf and Wellhausen, to mention only a few outstanding names—in essence were those formulated by students of classical Greek literature, which were then adopted and adapted by biblical scholars to meet the requirements posed by the particular character of the writings of the Old, and, for that matter, the New Testament.[2] A further illustration of the fructification of biblical studies by other disciplines is the overall complex of "oral tradition" and the "traditio-historical" method, which has freely emulated analytical and interpretative techniques and procedures developed by students of ancient Scandinavian lore and of the epic literature of Eastern European peoples.[3] Similarly, *Werkinterpretation* or "close reading" and the like schools which crystallized in general literary criticism influenced and still influence heavily the contemporary study of Old Testament litera-

Reprinted by permission of E. J. Brill from *Supplements to Vetus Testamentum* 29 (1977):320–56.

ture *qua* literature with concomitant repercussions on other areas of biblical research.[4]

The restating of these well-known facts may be likened to carrying coals to Newcastle, since the dependence of biblical scholarship on other humanistic disciplines and even on the natural sciences with respect to fundamental outlooks as well as tools of the trade is generally admitted and recognized. The perusal of any "History of Modern Biblical Study" or "Introduction to Biblical Literature" will prove the point. However, two considerations induce me to preface my paper with these cursory remarks of a very general nature. Firstly, the fact that a fully detailed, up-to-date analysis of this interdependence still remains a desideratum. And secondly, to remind us that the "comparative method," on which I wish to focus attention, did not emerge independently within the restricted frame of our discipline, but rather was devised and developed in other areas of historical and phenomenological research which gave comparative biblical studies their impetus. Again, this fact will be readily acknowledged by all, and likewise the legitimacy of applying to the biblical literature techniques worked out in quite disparate fields of scholarly endeavour.

Alas, there seems to be a decisive difference between these other disciplines and our own. Sociologists, anthropologists, ethnographers and historians bestow constant attention on the evaluation and re-examination of the conceptual modes by which they guide their comparative investigations; it would appear that in the realm of the Old Testament, however, comparative studies concerning the ancient Hebrew society, its literature and world of ideas, deal preponderantly with particular cases of parallels found or assumed to be present in other cultural complexes. Scholars seem to be less concerned about scrutinizing their methods in the light of the experience gathered from their "field work" and seldom apply themselves to such basic questions as whether the comparative method intrinsically operates under the "assumption of uniformity," as one school advocates, or if the aim should be "a comparison of contrasts rather than a comparison of similarities," as another school would have it.[5]

The even more fundamental dichotomy between comparativists and non-comparativists which is very much in the foreground of contemporary anthropology has barely found an echo in biblical scholarship.[6] Specifically, it may be said that so far as biblical studies have been affected at all by the vigorous forays of the structuralists against the comparativists, the impact came from social scientists like Mary Douglas and E. R. Leach (following C. Lévi-Strauss) who applied to biblical literature the structuralist concepts fashioned in the science of anthropology.[7]

Analogous to what was, and to a degree still is, the practice in other areas of comparative research—history, sociology, ethnography, anthropology, folklore, etc.—so too in biblical studies two main approaches can be discerned. On the one hand we encounter what Marc Bloch defines as "the comparative method on the grand scale . . . the basic postulate of this method, as well as the conclusion to which it constantly returns, is the fundamental unity of the human spirit or, if you wish, the monotony and astonishing poverty of human intellectual resources during the course of history."[8] This generalizing trend, which catalogues rather than explains the phenomena under review, entails a "loss of uniqueness and variegation," and suggests a uniformity which does not really exist in social behaviour.[9] By fastening its attention on what is or appears to be identical or similar in diverse, even widely removed societies—historically and geographically—it lumps these features together, thus providing proof for the axiomatic basic likeness of men and their societies which serves as a philosophical launching pad for the comparative method on the grand scale. At the same time, and in full consciousness, it completely loses sight of what makes cultures, societies and men ready objects for comparison, namely the peculiar and sometimes particularistic traits which one developed independently of and in distinction from others.

In the frame of Old Testament studies, this approach is represented by J. G. Frazer's classical multi-volume work *Folklore in the Old Testament* (1918) which may be considered an offspring of his even more comprehensive opus *The Golden Bough,* first published in 1890 and subsequently republished in constantly expanding editions. These works constituted the summation of scholarly endeavours in the second half of the nineteenth century and concomitantly provided the momentum for numerous less ambitious studies which issued forth from the school of social scientists whose foundations were laid by that eminent British scholar. The comparative approach "on the grand scale" in Old Testament research, as still practised by researchers who like to find resemblances between biblical stories and narrative motifs in other cultures, and in doing so lean heavily on Frazer's work, therefore received its major impetus from the outside. It echoes the emphasis laid on the method in a wide range of general disciplines, primarily but not exclusively in the social sciences, including the study of religion and literature. It tallies with the evolutionist theory which had had a pronounced impact on the sciences generally up to the first half of this century and, nearer home, on modern critical Old Testament research as well. Scholars of various disciplines who adopt this approach in their comparative endeavours meet therefore on shared philosophical premises, in spite of the diversity of their pursuits.

The comparative method on the grand scale will concede that the fundamental equality in thought processes, social organization and societal progress is more decidedly an outstanding characteristic of the "primitive" stages of human development than of the structures and the philosophical horizons of "higher" societies. However, it presumes that the intrinsic unity of mankind yet manifests itself in relics from those early phases which can be identified, and then compared, in societal and conceptual moulds of more developed historical peoples, even unto modernity. Comparisons can be drawn, therefore, between any two (or more) cultures and social organisms which exhibit some similar features, though they be far-removed from one another in time and space. Given this underlying persuasion of the intrinsic equality of men and their societal structures, any extensive investigation of diverse cultures will bring to light parallels in social customs, ritual and lore in as distinct and disparate settings as those of the South American Indians and the kings of France, the Teutons and ancient Egypt, Tiv law and British law, biblical Israel and Arab nomads. Accords and agreements of this kind are the more readily detected the more atomistic the approach, i.e., the more pronounced the discussion of the compared phenomena in isolation from their overall cultural and civilizational context. For example, if we should consider modern by-laws against spitting on the floor in vehicles of public transport or other public places without reference to the pertinent context of contemporary *mores* and attitudes toward hygiene, they could be compared with the prohibition of spitting in the solemn assemblies of the Judean Covenanters for which a parallel can be found in Essene customary law. But to derive from this comparison a similarity in meaning in such diverse cultural contexts produces staggering and indeed nonsensical results. Bronislaw Malinowski's classic stricture, namely that "in the science of culture to tear out a custom which belongs to a certain context leads nowhere," can be enlarged to include clusters of customs or groups of phenomena which may turn up in different cultures.[10]

This criticism which in the main is aimed at the Frazer school is well taken; as will yet be made explicit, random comparison without reference to the general structure and profile of the overall scale of values and beliefs of the societies involved can only mar and distort. Seemingly identical phenomena which may occur in different cultures are often quite differently weighted in the one in comparison with the other. When dealing comparatively with separate features of social and religious life, or with single concepts, motifs and idioms, it is imperative to view them in relation to the total phenomena of the groups involved. As Emile Durkheim observed, "Social facts [in the widest sense of the term, S.T.] are functions of the social system of which they are a part; therefore they cannot be understood when they are detached. For this reason, two facts which come from two different societies, cannot be fruitfully compared merely because they seem to resemble one another."[11]

Of a different scope and character is another type of comparative procedure that has become prominent in Old Testament research since the thirties of the present century in the wake of momentous developments in ancient Near Eastern archaeology which have significantly broadened the outlook of scholars with regard to those social and religious phenomena, modes of thought, literary achievements and linguistic habits distinguishing biblical culture. This comparative method has carved itself a secure niche in contemporary biblical research. Again we observe a parallelism between developments in comparative study generally and in the domain of the Old Testament. Marc Bloch defines this method as one "in which the units of comparison are societies that are geographical neighbours and historical contemporaries, constantly influenced by one another. During the historical development of such societies, they are subject to the same over-all causes, just because they are so close together in time and space. Moreover, they have, in part at least, a common origin" (loc. cit.). While the comparative method in the grand manner may be likened to general linguistics which deal with all human languages, the historically and geographically circumscribed method is closer to comparative philology which is concerned with "language groups within which signs of a common historical origin can be detected,"[12] for instance the Indo-Germanic or the Semitic language families.

It would be difficult to grade the importance of geographic proximity, historical propinquity and other factors for the application of comparative analysis. However, we would tend to accept as a basic rule, *mutatis mutandis,* the scale proffered by James Barr with reference to comparative philology: sources closer to the Old Testament in time take pride of place over considerations of geographic proximity; because of the latter, though, even features observed in relatively late sources may retain traces of earlier common cultural conditions. Thus *date* appears to be more important than *place.* Within this framework, a general closer *affinity* should decide on the actual investigative procedure, i.e. the decision as to which two out of an available selection of compared features, culled from different cultural settings, are most likely to represent a common basic phenomenon. It appears that in dealing not only with linguistic issues but with a wider array of cultural traits which are to be compared, the maxim to be followed is M. J. Herskovits's characterization of the comparative method as pertaining to "the analysis of cultures *lying within a given historic stream,*" since it takes adequately into consideration the aspects of historical and geographical proximity as well as those of cultural affinity.[13]

The historically and geographically defined method of comparison successfully removed biblical Israel from the cultural and conceptual seclusion imposed upon it by the isolationist ideology which characterizes generally the biblical, and particularly the prophetic, outlook. Careful observation, classification and interpretation of the new information which excavators made available to the historian and the sociologist, to the student of literature and of religion, disclosed an elaborate network of channels which had linked ancient Israel with the nations—and the cults and cultures of those nations—in whose proximity, indeed midst, she dwelt: from Egypt in the south, through the Canaanite expanse on both sides of the Jordan, and on to Mesopotamia in the north-east. A synoptic view of the ever-increasing information brought to light from the archives of Ugarit, Nuzu, Mari and the Hittite lands made it exceedingly clear that in the two millennia before the common era the peoples of the ancient Near East indeed lived within a "historic stream" created and maintained by the geographic-historical continuity which made possible a steady transfer and mutual emulation of civilizational and cultural achievements. The existence of propitious physical means such as a well-developed network of roads which opened up the area and furthered communication in times of war and peace and the availability of a *lingua franca,* in addition to the basic linguistic affinities between the languages spoken in the region, made that part of the ancient Near East a veritable market place for the exchange of ideas in the realm of cult, culture and their literary concretizations.

Propelled by these internal developments, even more than by the momentum provided from without the discipline, Old Testament scholars proceeded to assemble a veritable host of facts which witnessed to the interweaving of Israel in that fabric of concepts, customs and social structures in which other peoples of the area were enmeshed. The rapidly growing efforts along the lines of the historico-geographical comparative method brought on a wave of publications demonstrating parallels between Israelite culture and the cultures of her neighbours, drawn from a multiplicity of aspects—language, literary conventions, articles of belief and of ritual, social and political organization. The sheer bulk and compass of these materials wrenched biblical Israel from the position which Old Testament ideology had ascribed to her, that of "a people dwelling alone and not reckoning itself among the (other) nations" (Num 13:9).

With specific regard to the cult, this vigorous scholarly endeavour reached its peak in the "myth and ritual" school. While the question of the origin and identity of the sources of this approach in biblical studies is still under discussion, J. W. Rogerson is most probably correct in presuming that three factors played a decisive role in its evolution: "the emergence of the ritual theory of myth, the publication of certain Babylonian and Assyrian texts about the New Year Festival, and the diffusionist anthropology which apparently dominated England in the 1920's" (p. 67). S. H. Hooke and his followers who initiated the myth and ritual position construed it to prove the existence of a common Canaanite and Mesopotamian cultic pattern (also containing Babylonian elements) to which biblical Israel was a partner. In fact, they did not stop short at the discernment of a general cultic pattern, but rather widened the scope of the comparative inquiry so as to give it a more comprehensive range and to include within its frame of reference conceptual and societal phenomena which cannot be accommodated under the rubric "cult" in the restricted sense of the term. Thus it is presumed, on the basis of comparison, that the specific configurations of the myth and ritual pattern were affected by general societal phenomena and developments: the originally *agricultural* Canaanite version of the shared basic cult supposedly turns up in Israel in a typically *urban* variant, possibly influenced by the Babylonian pattern which also was urban in character.

Again, there is no need on this occasion to go into the intricacies of the issue under discussion as they have been adequately dealt with in recent publications, most extensively and profoundly by Rogerson. What is of present concern is the emergence of a "pattern of culture" school that operated under the premises worked out by the "myth and ritual" position. The method adopted by the "pattern" school for the analysis of myth—namely "to break it down into small units and to find out where these units occur and what combinations they build up"—a method whose legitimacy was defended recently by H. Ringgren, was in fact not only applied to the science of mythology whence it originated, but became the part taken as well by scholars who analysed phenomena of a completely different nature.[14] For this reason, and not simply for the application of such analysis to myths, the school came under heavy criticism from quarters that insisted on the existence of individual patterns of culture among the diverse peoples of the ancient Near East. It is somewhat difficult to concur with Ringgren in the argument that "both parties are right," because they employed the term "pattern" in different ways. While it is true that a synoptic view of the discussion discloses a discrepancy in the use of the term "pattern," the division between these schools of thought remains much more fundamental: it derives from the unbridgeable dichotomy between an "atomistic" and a "holistic" approach.

The "myth and ritual" as well as "pattern of culture" schools, which received their initial impetus from the "historical-geographical stream" method of comparison, proceeded to disclose their Frazerian philosophical underpinnings. The fundamentally non-functionalist position in fact represents a cloaked, and more scientifically acceptable, return to the comparative approach "on the grand scale." While the pattern school in the Hooke tradition is not satisfied with comparing elements alone, it views more comprehensive configurations *sub specie* "combinations," i.e. not as original self-contained units, but rather as secondary cultural constructions. In contrast, the holistic method tries first to understand a cultural configuration in its entirety. Without disregarding resemblances between constitutive elements in two different civilizations from the same "historic stream," it emphasizes the individuality and dissimilarity conferred upon these identified components by their very existence within specific organic cultural totalities. Scholars like T. Jacobsen and H. Frankfort are much more interested in what B. Landsberger defined as the *Eigenbegrifflichkeit* of the diverse cultures, predominantly based on a religio-political circumscription, than in their presumed similarity or similarities. Coming from scholars whose expertise is the study of ancient Near Eastern cultures—archaeologically, historically, sociologically, linguistically and phenomenologically—this insistence on the particularity of the Hebrew culture and its dissimilarity from neighbouring cultures should serve students of the Old Testament as a guideline in their comparative studies.

The diversity and the comprehensiveness of biblical phenomena that invite a comparison with their likenesses in other ancient Eastern cultures will not allow for a full presentation of the problems involved. Nor will it be possible to cover all the different aspects of the material which can be and indeed are submitted to comparative study and which in practice constitute separate subdisciplines in Old Testament research. One could argue in favour of a synoptic view which conceives of these diverse aspects as one continuum and thus would submit complex rather than simple structures to comparative analysis. In the present context, however, it appears advisable to approach the matter in accord with the stratified treatment it is given in contemporary research. Again, selection is imperative. Therefore, we shall illustrate some shortcomings of the procedures often followed by comparativists, and what appear to be necessary rectifications, by examples drawn from essentially two domains of Old Testament study: 1. socio-political institutions, with some reference to matters pertaining to cult and myth; and 2. issues of a philological or literary nature—textual emendations based on external parallels; literary imagery which signifies concepts and modes of thought; literary forms or *Gattungen.*[15] The order of presentation chosen is meant to place increasingly in relief the prevalent atomizing or isolationist approach in comparative research, in contrast to the required investigation of total phenomena, i.e. of single features in relation to their cultural context and their function in more comprehensive organic structures or, with Rowton, "organic processes."[16]

II. SOCIO-POLITICAL INSTITUTIONS

A) Nomadic Survivals

In introducing this necessarily sketchy discussion of what I tend to view as an unqualified application of the comparative method to socio-historical aspects of biblical Israel, I wish to dwell shortly on the presumed presence of a "nomadic ideal" in the ancient Hebrew world of ideas.[17] The issue hinges on the basic assumption of the comparative approach in the evolutionist tradition that early stages in human, and especially in societal development will reveal themselves in vestigial form in higher and later phases of the societies under review. Adopting this line of thought, K. Budde, P. Humbert and their followers discerned in the social web of Israel in the settlement period, and even in the phase of advanced urbanization under the monarchy, residues of nomadic *mores* which decisively affected Hebrew society throughout Old Testament times. Furthermore, primitive nomadic life with its simplicity and direct trust in God, unencumbered by cultic paraphernalia, showed to advantage against the background of the corrupted city society which progressively crystallized in Israel after the establishment of the monarchy. Not urban comfort and civilization, not even the agriculturist's life polluted by his unavoidable attachment to pagan fertility cults, are the ideal to which the spiritual leaders of Israel—*lege* the prophets—aspired; but rather the ascetic life style to which the Rechabites adhered, shunning all forms of settlement, whom Jeremiah assumedly extolled and held up as a socio-economic and religious paradigm for all Israel to emulate (Jeremiah 35). The Rechabites are represented, without sufficient material evidence, as the best-known group to organize a return to the desert and to the nomadic ideal. This ideal supposedly transcends the confines of the Old Testament. It still appears, we are told, in the ideology of some constituent groups of postbiblical Judaism, such as the Qumran Covenanters and the Essenes with whom one tends to identify them. In fact, there are scholars who perceive the Qumran community as a late offshoot of the early, possibly pre-monarchic clan of the Rechabites, again on the basis of "similarity" and without being able to produce any evidence for the presumed historic continuity.

It must be put on record that some scholars indeed sounded a warning note. In his discussion of the "nomadic ideal," R. de Vaux exhorts us to beware of hasty comparisons "which may overlook essential differences." But having said this, he nevertheless concurs with the opinion that after having first lived as nomads or semi-nomads, when the ancient Israelites came to settle down as a nation, they still retained some characteristics of that earlier way of life.[18] When investigated in detail, this statement does not stand up to scrutiny. We could regard this as simply referring to an assumed internal development of the Israelite society, somewhat along the lines which determine the development of most societies in the ancient Near East, and assumedly also in other parts of the world and in other historical settings. At this juncture, however, the comparative approach on the grand scale comes into play, and the issue at hand assumes much wider proportions: since Arabs of pre-Islamic times and even of today either are full-fledged nomads or at least exhibit nomadic habits and traits, reasons de Vaux, "what we know of pre-Islamic, modern and contemporary Arab life can help us to understand more clearly the primitive organization of Israel" (p. 3; French, p. 15).

This comparability of ancient Israel and Arab society, according to some, applies not alone to social organization but also to the constitutive characteristics of the Yahwistic faith. In his *Beduinentum und Jahwismus* (Lund, 1946), S. Nystroem summarized and systematized features and parallels which some of his predecessors (e.g. J. Wellhausen, A. Causse, and M. Buber) already had pointed out. How tenuous the comparison of ancient Israelite with Arab culture is, on how slim a foundation it rests, is illustrated by the contrasting statement of I. Engnell with reference to issues of a literary character: "comparing Israelite material with relatively far-distant lands and cultures—India and Iran, for instance—actually can be more fruitful than comparing it with closer regions, such as Arabia. As a matter of fact, the latter even can be characterized as distinctly dangerous."[19] One wonders on what proved or provable evidence one view bases itself, and on what opposing evidence the other is founded. Is it not perhaps that both derive from intuitive insights and personal predilections, rather than from inquiries and investigations carried out according to appreciably objective criteria?

The issue is further complicated if one brings into account the view first expressed by W. F. Albright and C. H. Gordon that the patriarchal society exhibits characteristics of *tamkaru* life and that the forefathers of

Israel could be more readily likened to "merchant princes" than to Bedouin sheikhs. One realizes that even in the traditions about the historically hazy "Desert Period," Israel is not actually depicted as a typical desert people; so too the Bedouin characteristics discovered in the traditions pertaining to her settled life as a nation are questionable. In short, the exceeding shakiness of the "nomadic theory" and of the comparison with pre-Islamic or Islamic Arabic society is set in full relief.

Even more disturbing than the over-eager search for "similarities" to nomadic societies (with which biblical Israel is assumed to lie in the same historic stream) is the disregard for internal analysis as a means to elicit from the biblical literature itself the ancient Hebrews' concept of the ideal life. Even a cursory survey of the sources shows that nomads and desert-dwellers are abhorred, and that the wilderness is conceived of as the abode of ghoulish spirits, wild beasts of prey and roaming marauders. The vast expanses of parched earth are shunned as the embodiment of all that is dangerous and evil. In contrast to this haunted world, Israel's societal ideal is portrayed in the visions of "the latter days" which are modelled in a restorative fashion on the idealized *Urzeit,* the days of the kingdom of David and Solomon when "Judah and Israel dwelt in safety, from Dan even to Beersheba, every man under his vine and under his fig tree" (1 Kgs 5:5).[20] A comparison of the essential features of the hoped for *Endzeit,* even of the vocabulary and imagery employed in its portrayal, with the above summary of Solomon's reign makes manifest the distortion which inheres in the attribution of a "nomadic desert ideal" to ancient Israel and to the biblical prophets. Thus Micah conceives of that blissful age: then all the nations "shall beat their swords into mattocks and their spears into pruning-knives; nation shall not lift sword against nation nor ever again be trained for war, and each man shall dwell under his vine, under his fig-tree, and no one shall frighten (them)". (Mic 4:3–4; cf. 1 Kgs 5:5). The internal analysis of the Israelite conception of the ideal life produces results which are indeed different from those which ensue from the comparison with desert cultures and societies, be it on the "grand scale" or geared to the "historic stream" approach.

B) Democratic Institutions

Scholarly endeavours to interpret the term *ʿam haʾareṣ* and to arrive by way of an analysis of the extant references at a satisfactory characterization of the social group or groups so designated are severely hampered by the apparent inconsistency in the employment of the term in biblical literature. The problem is compounded by the absence of any inner-biblical attempt to define the conceptual framework within which the term should be understood, beyond the mere recording of some events in history in which the *ʿam haʾareṣ* had been actively involved. This silence on principles and the lack of systematization is the rule rather than the exception and possibly reflects some basic attitudes and ancient Hebrew modes of thought, which seem to have been more empirical, fastening on concrete facts, than analytical and tending towards abstract syntheses. It is for these reasons that the suggestions offered in explanation of the term *ʿam haʾareṣ* and its content differ widely. We should go too far afield if we tried to survey the discussion of the issue in detail; such a review is not required for our present purposes and is moreover easily accessible in recent publications, of which I wish to mention three, since they seem to represent views which differ on principles of analysis and method. E. W. Nicholson, who bases himself almost exclusively on the biblical material, concludes his study of the *ʿam haʾareṣ* with the statement that "the term has no fixed and rigid meaning but is used rather in a purely general and fluid manner and varies in meaning from context to context."[21] This appears to be a counsel of despair which helps in elucidating neither the etymological meaning of the term nor, what is more important, its societal content.

In contrast, H. Tadmor and the present writer have proposed solutions to explain the entire range of usages of the term, though assuming synchronic differences and diachronic developments in its employment. However, despite accord with regard to the circumscribed diversity of meanings inherent in the term *ʿam haʾareṣ* and their diachronic variance, Tadmor and I arrive at different characterizations of the group or groups thus designated within the framework of the biblical polity. This difference arises from the diverse paths taken in the attempt to offer a solution. Tadmor addresses the issue within the wider context of the relation between " 'The People' and the Kingship in Ancient Israel," comparing what he considers to be parallel phenomena in Ephraim and Judah.[22] He further broadens the scope of his investigation in order to compare the Hebrew term and its signification with parallel expressions in other historical and societal contexts, such as *ʿam haʾareṣ* in Byblos, and *niše māti* in Assyria. Adopting a much more restricted approach, I dealt with the Judean *ʿam haʾareṣ* exclusively in historical perspective, leaving aside, at least for the time being, any comparative considerations.[23]

The differing procedures result in quite disparate conclusions. Tadmor subtitles his essay "The Role of Political Institutions in the Biblical Period," thus revealing his intent to present the *ʿam haʾareṣ* and similar phenomena as constituted representatives of the populace *vis-à-vis* the king, i.e. institutions whose intervention in matters of the body politic apparently was regulated by mutually aknowledged rules. The references to institutions which acted on behalf of "the people" both in Ephraim and in Judah, albeit with different degrees of frequency, recur in the summarizing paragraph of the essay, culminating in the statement: ". . . when powerful social groups, such as army commanders, decided upon questions of state, they derived their authority from 'the people,' and drew their power from the people's traditional institutions" (p. 66).

What appears to be implied in this presentation—especially by the choice of such terms as "decided upon questions of state," "derived authority," "the people," and "the people's traditional institutions"—is a situation in which the ascription of roles and the division of power between the monarchy and "the people" in ancient Israel was formally and legally regulated by what amounts to a constitution. Contrast with this view my conclusion that "Contrary to the insitutionalizing tendencies which haunt biblical research, the *ʿam haʾareṣ* of Judah can not be viewed as a democratic or otherwise constitutionally circumscribed institution. Rather is it a body of Judeans in Jerusalem that rose to some power and importance which was ultimately derived from their loyalty to the Davidic dynasty. The *ʿam haʾareṣ* in fact constitutes a sociological phenomenon that belongs to and illustrates a power structure which appears to be typical of a hereditary monarchy without clearly defined constitutional foundations. The readily given support of a group like the *ʿam haʾareṣ* helps in maintaining the political equilibrium by counteracting the possible eroding impact of an ascending class of courtiers and ministers. Unwavering loyalty arising from kin ties balances a pragmatic allegiance rooted in vested interests" (p. 76). Again, while both authors draw attention to the sporadic nature of the intervention of the *ʿam haʾareṣ* (and other such groups, according to Tadmor), the manner of its going into action is differently conceived. According to Tadmor, "the people's institutions convened and acted only sporadically—when the dynastic continuity was disturbed" etc. (p. 68). Against this, I maintain that "The *ʿam haʾareṣ* never was formally convened or called upon by the king or some other agent," because "this body was not an institution at all, but a fairly loosely constituted power group," etc. (p. 75).

What concerns us in the present context is the divergence on principles: on the one hand there is the tendency to identify "institutions," of a more or less "democratic" character, which played an important role in the Israelite body politic. In the case of the *ʿam haʾareṣ* this was done most succinctly at the beginning of the century by M. Sulzberger in his book *The Am ha-aretz—The Ancient Hebrew Parliament* (Philadelphia, 1909) and was repeated some decades later by E. Auerbach who defined it as the "great national council," the democratic representation of the nation *vis-à-vis* the king. At the other end of the spectrum is the "non-institutional" explanation of the term with its application to ever-widening circles: *Landadel,* landed gentry or "lords of the land" (M. Weber, R. Kittel, A. G. Barrois, R. Gordis, S. Daiches, et al.) or even *Die Gesamtheit der Judäischen Vollbürger—l'ensemble des nationaux* (M. Noth and R. de Vaux).

I have presented this controversy in some detail not in order to prove, what does not really require proof, that the same biblical evidence can be interpreted quite differently by different scholars and lead to disparate conclusions. The crux of the matter lies in the method applied. The institutionalist who buttresses his arguments by comparable or assumedly comparable material from extra-biblical sources and non-Israelite political organisms never asks the fundamental question, viz. whether or not ancient Israel at all was inclined to solidify political institutions within the framework of the monarchy or before its inception. Phrased differently: does what we know from the sources at our disposal concerning the intrinsic structure of biblical society and biblical social thought recommend the suggestion that public opinion ever expressed itself in "institutionalized" forms and bodies, even of the variety found in "primitive democracies"? To answer this question adequately a deep and comprehensive analysis of biblical society is required. However, I would venture the suggestion that such an analysis will produce a negative answer. It will prove that with the exception of the institutionalized kingship and priesthood the social components of the ancient Israelite society expressed themselves and their preferences in a form of power play in which pragmatically, sometimes *ad hoc,* consolidated groups were the prime actors.

When we look at the wider sociological context, we are concerned with the correspondence that exists between diverse types of political structures and the forms in which divergent or dissenting opinions assert themselves against the established leadership. In every instance, this or the other particular element will have to be judged and defined not in isolation, but with a view to its functional relation to the totality of the social phenomena, and especially against the background of the "deep" principles of the societal structure. Old Testament scholars will be well advised to pay heed to the criticism levelled by E. Leach against ethnographers and anthropologists who approached their own materials in a similarly "atomistic" fashion: "The classical comparative method, the diffusionist reconstructions of the cultural historians, and the various styles in cross-cultural statistical analysis all rested on the proposition that 'a culture' ('a society,' etc.) is to be conceived of as an assemblage of traits which can be separately compared. Functionalist social anthropology rejects this view. Societies are systems which can be compared only as wholes" (p. 343).

The same considerations apply to another controversy of the "institution versus non-institution" category. In discussing the internal historical events which occurred in Israel after the death of Solomon, A. Malamat attempted to show that, when challenged by the people to reduce the burden of taxes that Solomon had imposed upon them, Solomon's son and successor to the throne, Rehoboam, put the matter to a council which represented the people opposite the king. Rehoboam, in fact, took counsel with two bodies. One, constituted of the "elders" *(zĕqēnîm),* is often referred to in biblical literature, and therefore well known. The other, that of the "young men" *(yĕlādîm),* is never mentioned apart from the events described in 1 Kgs 12:1–17. Discarding other possibilities with regard to the composition and nature of this group, the author arrives at the conclusion "that the assemblies of elders and 'young men' of Rehoboam are not mere spontaneous gatherings of the populace; but they constitute rather formal bodies of official standing in the kingdom" (p. 250).[24] He then goes on to compare this official "bicameral" Israelite assembly with a parallel institution which emerges from the Sumerian "Gilgamesh and Agga" epic, equating the Hebrew *zĕqēnîm* with the Sumerian *abba uru,* "elders of the city," and the *yĕlādîm* with their assumed Sumerian counterpart *guruš,* "council of men." Both bicameral bodies are evidence of a "political system which has been aptly named "primitive democracy" by Thorkild Jacobsen. This form of government rested on *representative institutions* [my italics, S. T.] which functioned alongside of the central powers" (p. 250). Without overlooking "the different circumstances in Sumer and Israel and the individual character of each of the sources," Malamat nevertheless insists that "both of the examples are similar from a typological point of view" and therefore it is of minor importance whether the Sumerian assembly of *guruš* and the Israelite council of the *yĕlādîm* "differed in their very essence and subsequently in their respective functions" (p. 252).

In his criticism of Malamat's thesis, D. G. Evans draws attention to "the difficulties which confront us in discussing political bodies (and indeed others) in the ancient Near East. Not only does the slenderness of the evidence oblige us to make the most of it to a dangerous extent, but it increases the risk, which is always present in studies of the remote past, of importing into our sources modern constitutional ideas and practices which have no place in them."[25] He then analyses the biblical tradition in detail, as Malamat had done. However, his reading of the sources leads to the statement that "To conclude that the *zĕqēnîm* and *yĕlādîm* at Shechem were political bodies of official standing in the kingdom seems to me more than the evidence will support," since neither of the councils at Shechem, if indeed there were two and not one, enjoyed sovereignty but at most acted in an advisory fashion. Decisions were taken and put into practice by the people's assembly or the king. Although in the biblical tradition the term *zĕqēnîm* often indicates a group of men that has a specific standing in the body politic, in the instance under review it would appear that the word is not to be understood in this technical sense. The opposition to *yĕlādîm,* which is never employed as a socio-political term, rather suggests a contrast which is purely internal to the story; the reasons for Rehoboam's preference of one group over the other should be sought in the "generation gap" which existed between men who belonged to the father's generation, on the one hand, and to the son's, on the other.

It appears that in this case too the comparison of two literary units with some, albeit quite disparate, socio-political import, discussed in isolation from the intrinsic structures of the two societies involved, results in an identification of formal political institutions in Israel of the monarchic period which lacks proper foundation. The present writer would certainly opt for a non-institutional explanation.

C) Divine Kingship

Our final example pertaining to the socio-political dimension concerns the position of the king in the Israelite body politic. There is a widespread tendency among students of the Old Testament and the ancient Near East to discern in the biblical literature a concept of monarchy which invests the king with the status of divinity or at least accords him aspects of sanctity which elevate him above the position of a mere human being. This idea seems to derive from an over-simplified literary interpretation of idioms and expressions which extol the greatness of kings in terms culled from the realm of the divine. The comparison of such terminology, as well as the conceptual modes to which these idioms supposedly give expression, with parallels found in ancient Near Eastern literatures, leads scholars to perceive an identical notion of divine kingship in the biblical world of ideas. The impact of the "pattern" school comes into full relief in the "divine kingship" theory, precisely because the phenomenon combines fundamental features of "myth and ritual" with wider aspects of a "pattern of culture." The "divine kingship" theory demonstrates a fusion between two quite diverse aspects of Israelite culture: the world of myth and cult as an expression of ancient Near Eastern religiosity coalesces here with the political and social dimension in which tangible history expresses itself. It is most likely this facet of comparative biblical studies that led to the application of structural analysis, which was initially applied exclusively to non-historical phenomena, also to the interpretation of biblical historical events and situations. In the biblical studies mentioned above, the anthropologist Edmund Leach took his departure from the Genesis stories considered as myth.[26] This attempt was regarded by professional Bible scholars with tolerance, equanimity or a mild lack of interest. Subsequently, though, Leach transferred his attention to the historical books of Samuel and Kings in the endeavour to lay bare "Some Structural Aspects of Old Testament History" in the traditions about Solomon's succession to the throne of David.[27] He claims to discern in these historical traditions structural patterns of a general character which usually are applicable to mythical lore. While acknowledging the challenge which issues forth from Leach's studies for a reconsideration of the traditional work on biblical materials, professional Bible scholars have been very reluctant to endorse the indiscriminate application of myth-oriented structural analysis to reports of actual historical events.[28]

Let me turn now to a critical review of the established "divine kingship" theory, and its inherent "patternism," through an examination of the meaning which adheres to the act of "anointing" the king.[29] The practice of anointing the ruler was well established in ancient Near Eastern societies but in Israel obviously was an innovation of the monarchic regime. It is never mentioned in the preceding period of the Judges or "Saviours," nor in the days of Joshua, Moses or the Patriarchs. Anointing, however, was known to the Hebrews from the context of the cult. Not only were cultic implements anointed, thus to confer upon them a degree of sacredness (Gen. 31:13; Exod 30:26, 40:9–11; Num 7:1, 10, 84, 88), but also the special standing of certain cultic functionaries and other persons of renown was symbolized by the pouring of oil on their heads. There is one biblical report about anointing a prophet, as Elisha is thus appointed by Elijah to become his successor (1 Kgs 19:16). It is of interest to observe that this act is juxtaposed with Elijah's being commanded concurrently to anoint Jehu ben Nimshi king over Israel. This very conjunction of prophet and king with reference to anointing can also be found in Ps 105:15: *ʾl tgʿw bmšyḥy wlnbyʾy ʾl trʿw* (Do not touch My anointed ones; do not harm My prophets), and in 1 Chr 29:22 with reference to Solomon and Zadok the priest.

Anointing was especially practised with regard to the High Priest Exod 28:41, 29:7, 36, 40:13–15; Lev 8:10, 12; Num 3:3, 30:25, et al.), who therefore could be designated *hkhn hmšyḥ* (Lev 4:3, 5, 16, 6:15).

Explicit references to the anointing of kings are found in the Bible only in certain instances: David (1 Sam 2:4, 5:3; Ps 89:21), Solomon (1 Kgs 1:39), Jehu (2 Kgs 9:1ff.), Joash (2 Kgs 11:12). Accordingly opinions are divided as to whether anointing was an indispensable feature of the rites of enthronement or was applied only when special circumstances, such as an interruption of normal dynastic succession, required a renewed affirmation of the king's supposedly sacral status. Without attempting here to arrive at a definite conclusion it may nevertheless be said that the familiar term *mšḥ lmlk* (lit. "anointed [as] king") in the meaning of "to enthrone" (Judg 9:8, 15; 2 Sam 2:4; 1 Kgs 19:15, et al.) and the recurring designation of kings as *mšyḥ yhwh* (1 Sam 24:6, 16, 26:9, 11, 16, 23, et al.) seem to suggest that every king (in Judah and in Ephraim) was anointed, even when our sources are silent about the fact. The dimension of sacredness which adheres to the act of "anointing" with "holy oil" *(šmn hqdš),* which was kept at first in the Tabernacle (Exod 25:6, 37:29; Lev 8:2) and subsequently in the Temple (1 Kgs 1:39), makes it natural that the rite was performed by a priest (1 Kgs 1:39) or by prophet (1 Sam 10:1ff., cf. 9:16; 16:12–13; 2 Kgs 9:6ff., cf. 1 Kgs 19:15–16) on divine command. What calls for some explanation, however, is the fact that the rite of anointing the king is sometimes reported to have been executed by the "people" or possibly by the people's representative(s). According to 1 Chr 29:20–22 "they (i.e. the assembly of all Israel) . . . appointed Solomon, David's son . . . and *anointed him* as the Lord's prince, and Zadok as priest."

In a similar instance concerning the coronation of Joash the son of Ahaziah, king of Judah, 2 Kings reports that "they (either the people or the temple-guards) made him king, and *anointed him,* and they (LXX + the people) clapped their hands, and shouted 'Long live the King' " (2 Kgs 11:12), whereas the parallel version in 2 Chr 23:11 reads "Jehoiada (the priest) and his sons anointed him." Again we are told in 2 Kgs 23:30 that "the *ʿam haʾareṣ* took Jehoahaz the son of Josiah, and they anointed him, and made him king in his father's stead." Lastly, in 2 Sam 19:11, the people propose to rally around David after Absalom's death had brought an end to his rebellion, since "Absalom whom *we anointed over us* died in war." These references seem to imply that while "anointing" indeed was considered a sacral ritual act, which by definition must be carried out by a prophet or a priest, it more decisively bore socio-political significance. Even though conceptually the act of anointing conferred the immunity of sanctification upon the king, in actuality the rite gave concrete expression to the king's dependence on the people (and/or the priest and the prophet as the representatives of the divine sphere). In historical reality, the ritual of anointing was a ceremonial manifestation of the checks and balances which inhered in the Israelite monarchy. Through the granting or withholding of anointing, either of the above-mentioned agents—people or prophet/priest—could effect an important measure of control over the ruler.

When Israelite kingship is viewed in the context of biblical social institutions, and against the background of preceding forms of government, instead of being defined predominantly by means of assumed similarities which comparative research discovers in other ancient Near Eastern societies, the basic singularity of the biblical concept of the monarchy is accentuated. Contrary to widespread scholarly opinion, the presumedly sacral-ritual act of anointing did not enhance the Israelite king's status and power but rather circumscribed it. He was, in fact, more vulnerable than the earlier non-monarchical rulers. Before the establishment of the monarchy, a leader of the people—like the Judge, who was divinely inspired but not anointed—was never deposed once he had been established in office, even if he was found to be failing. Neither the mission of Samson, who angered his parents by marrying a Philistine woman (Judg 14:3; cf. Gen 26:34–35, 27:46), nor that of Gideon, who by erecting the Ephod in Ophra sinned and caused others to transgress (Judg 8:27), was terminated before it had run its course. As the first king, however, Saul is also the first appointed leader of Israel to be dethroned by the prophet who had anointed him (1 Sam 13:13–14, 15:26–28). Because Solomon sinned by marrying foreign wives (like Samson), and set up objectionable cultic places (like Gideon), the rule over ten tribes was divested from his dynasty (1 Kgs 11:1–13) and assigned to Jeroboam ben Nebat (vv. 29–39). Ahab's transgressions caused his son to be deprived of the throne, and Jehu ben Nimshi was made king over Ephraim (2 Kgs 9). The very possibility that the rule of a king could be terminated *de iure,* and not only *de facto* in the wake of rebellions, strongly suggests that kingship was not considered sacrosanct and that the king himself was not believed to have acquired such status. The very possibility that a king's mission could be revoked—whether by God's emissary, a prophet (as in the case of Saul, Solomon and Ahab) or by the people (as in the case of Rehoboam)—evidences a concept according to which kingship was firmly confined within the human sphere.

A functional analysis of biblical traditions about the monarchic period, undertaken in cognizance of the traditions which portray the premonarchic times, proves that biblical idioms, imagery and motifs which appear to disclose an underlying conception of the Israelite king as being imbued with "divinity" are mere figures of speech, a *façon à parler,* which were adopted into the Hebrew vocabulary after having lost their original mytho-cultic significance. The apparent similarity with ancient

Near Eastern royal terminology is external and should not be construed to indicate the existence of a shared cultural pattern of cultic "divine kingship." In his discussion of the supposed divinity of the Israelite kings, H. Frankfort succinctly makes the point:

> Much is made nowadays of Canaanite and other Near Eastern elements in Hebrew culture, and a phenomenon like Solomon's kingship conforms indeed to the type of glorified native chieftainship which we have characterized. . . . But it should be plain that the borrowed features in Hebrew culture, and those which have foreign analogies, *are least significant.* In the case of kingship they are externalities, the less important since they did not affect the *basic oddness* of the Hebrew institution. (My italics, S.T.)[30]

In concluding this part of the discussion, I wish to stress again that my present interest does not lie in the assessment of the accuracy of this or another specific theory, but rather in illustrating the assertion that in dealing with fundamental issues concerning the social and religious history of biblical Israel, scholars often revert to a comparison with external "parallels" without the prerequisite definition of a methodology of procedure and before examining the phenomena under consideration in their inner-biblical context.

One cannot but concur with the strictures Ringgren has voiced concerning this approach:

> Comparative research in the Biblical field has often become a kind of "parallel hunting." Once it has been established that a certain biblical expression or custom has a parallel outside the Bible, the whole problem is regarded as solved. It is not asked, whether or not the extra-Biblical element has the same place in life, the same function in the context of its own culture. The first question that should be asked in comparative research is that of the *Sitz im Leben* and the meaning of the extra-Biblical parallel adduced. It is not until this has been established that the parallel can be utilized to elucidate a Biblical fact. (p. 1)

III. PHILOLOGICAL AND LITERARY ASPECTS

A) Comparative Philology and Textual Emendation

Probably the most spectacular development in comparative biblical studies can be observed in the domain of "language" in the widest sense of the term. One takes note that in linguistics the endeavour to define exact rules for scholarly investigation has borne more fruit than in other areas.

According to J. Barr, comparative linguistics concern "the comparative study of language groups within which signs of a common historical origin can be detected" and which can be fitted into "an historical common scheme" (loc. cit.). In the explanation of linguistic facts, the historical analysis is supplemented by a synchronic or structural examination of the material at hand from a "holistic" point of view, rather than in the "atomistic" fashion.[31] While in actual practice these guidelines are not always followed, it nevertheless can be said that linguistic scholarship has been placed on firmer theoretical ground than other fields of biblical research. The closer the affinity of one language to another, in structure and other basic features which point to a common historic origin, the wider the scope for the comparison of their respective vocabularies. Comparative philology can help in the explanation of *hapax legomena* or rare words and idioms in one language, which in a sister language are more widely used and better understood. Comparativists can point to impressive achievements in the interpretation of some difficult biblical texts, predominantly, though not exclusively, through the utilization of Ugaritic material. However, alongside the salutary effect it has exercised, the Ugaritic-biblical comparative research increasingly has laid itself open to severe criticism.

The more scholars engage in the search for parallels, the more "atomistic" the approach; personal inspiration often takes the place of systematic investigation, and impressionistic *déja vu* insights substitute for the required procedural principles. The results are a mixed blessing. Together with many "good figs," to use Jeremiah's simile, scholars, and more critically, students are fed from an ever-growing bag of "bad figs." Handled with care and the necessary restraint, the collecting of Ras Shamra Parallels[32] can be, and indeed often is, illuminating. But when imagination is given free reign, the resulting "parallelomania" gives Old Testament studies a bad name and puts in question the reliability of biblical lexicography and comparative research generally. To be sure, it would be futile and counterproductive to advocate a radical purism which would abstain altogether from the application of the comparative method to biblical literature, as a result of some doubtful hypotheses and questionable textual emendations. What is to be demanded is that attention be paid to a given set of rules of which one shall be mentioned at this juncture: the solution of a crux in the biblical text should be attempted first and foremost by reverting to the immediate context and to synonymous expressions in similar contexts, with direct and "distant parallelism" holding out special promise for the elucidation of opaque or obscure expressions. Comparison with extra-biblical material should be brought into play only when a properly executed inner-biblical analysis does not produce satisfactory results. Even then it would be wise to pay heed to the warning sounded by Y. Muffs, namely that "only after new meanings emerge naturally from the context of one language should comparative material be brought into the picture."[33]

The comparison of biblical literature with Ugaritic writings presents a particular problem. The similarity of the two languages and the obvious contacts Hebrew cultures had with Ugaritic/Canaanite culture—both lying within a single "historic stream"—have caused scholars to consider the two literatures to be of one cloth. Thus H. L. Ginsberg opined that "from the philological point of view . . . the Hebrew Bible and the Ugarit texts are to be regarded as one literature, and consequently a reading in either may be emended with the aid of a parallel passage in the other."[34] However, one wonders whether this sweeping statement can pass unchallenged. Methodological considerations and some comparative techniques which resulted from this dictum would have one judge the situation less sanguinely. Two literatures, such as the biblical and the Ugaritic, which emanated from different cultures, akin as they may be, can never be identified so unreservedly lest we be prone to consider the Semitic cultures to exhibit "the monotony and astonishing poverty of human intellectual resources" which the old-style comparative method on the grand scale took as a fundamental postulate. Paraphrasing a statement by A. L. Kroeber,[35] I would say that in comparative studies generally our concern is and should be with differences as much as with likenesses. The particularity of Hebrew literature on the one hand, and of Ugaritic writings on the other, must not be blurred so as to facilitate and legitimize their being judged as one cultural whole. In his aforementioned essay, Y. Muffs quotes one instance, the explanation of the common word *ʿōz* in Eccl 8:1, for which H. L. Ginsberg proposed a novel interpretation, namely "anger," by working out the meaning inner-biblically and relating it subsequently to Akkadian *ezzu*, "anger, wrath." Here Ginsberg followed the recommended procedure. However, in other cases, predominantly where assumed Ugaritic parallels are involved, because of the posited "identity" of Hebrew and Ugaritic literature, one sometimes observes a significant departure from this rule.

Occasionally Ginsberg will emend a difficult biblical text on the ground of a Ugaritic parallel, without attempting first to solve the problem inner-biblically.[36] Unfortunately, lesser luminaries in the field of comparative Semitic philology are prone to emulate his technique with less than satisfactory results. A case in point is Ginsberg's famous and widely acclaimed emendation of the puzzling ending of one line in David's lament over Saul and Jonathan: *hry bglbʿ ʾl ṭl wʾl mṭr ʿlykm wśdy trwmt* ("O hills of Gilboa, let there be no dew or rain or *śdy trwmt*"; 2 Sam 1:21).

Numerous proposals had been put forward for the restoration of the assumed original reading underlying the awkward expression *wśdy trwmt* which does not make sense in the context, some utilizing the ancient versions, others resorting to conjectures. None was convincing enough to gain general support. By contrast, there was an almost immediate acceptance of Ginsberg's suggestion to read *šrʿ thmt*—"waters of the abyss"—derived from a line in the Danʾel epic which appeared to be the exact equivalent of the above Hebrew phrase, being set in a functionally identical context: *bl ṭl bl rbb bl šrʿ thmtm* (lit. "no dew, nor rain, nor waters of the abyss"; CTA 19 = 1 Aq. 1.44). Despite reservations subsequently entertained by critics, this emendation of a biblical crux by means of a Ugaritic parallel is still recognized as a classic.

However, the rare attestation of *šrʿ* in the Ugaritic vocabulary where it may well be a *hapax legomenon,* which moreover has no counterpart in the Hebrew Bible, detracts from the appeal of the proposed emendation. There also arose some doubts concerning the correct reading of the passage in the Danʾel epic.

The "waters of the abyss" hardly constitute a proper parallel to "dew" and "rain." In biblical, as in Ugaritic imagery, the "abysmal floods" always carry a negative not a positive connotation, such as is required in the context under review. For all these reasons it seems preferable to conceive of *śdy trwmt* as a parallel to *hry bglbʿ,* both referring to "heights" or mountains on which men are killed in battle. This is a *Leitmotif* in David's elegy which is often employed in other biblical descriptions of wars. A similar idiom is present in the Song of Deborah which exhibits striking affinities with David's lament with respect to genre, function and setting. There, the tribes of Zebulun and Naftali are extolled by the singer for having "risked their very lives . . . on the heights of the battlefield" (Judg 5:18; NEB). The crucial Hebrew expression is *ʿl mrwmy śdh.* On the strength of this phrase, it seems plausible to suggest that *wśdy trwmt* (lit. "fields of offerings") in 2 Sam 1:21 is a synonymous idiom in which the sequence of components has been inverted. It should be understood as *(w)trwmt śdh,* with *trwmh-trwmt* being derived from *rwm-rmh* as a byform of *mrwm-mrwmym,* denoting here "height," and not "offering" or "contribution" which is its prevalent connotation in biblical Hebrew. *Śdh,* probably identical with Akk. *šadu,* here as in many other biblical passages, is equivalent to *hr*—mountain.

Another variant of *mrwm-trwmh* in combination with *śdh/hr* turns up in Lam 4:9 in a literary and situational context which is almost identical with that in which David's lament is set. There we encounter the expression *mtnwbt śdy* in relation to Jerusalemites or Judahites slain in battle. Translations of the crucial passage—*šhm yzwbw mdqrym mtnwbt śdy*—such as "for these pine away, stricken through, for want of the fruits of the field" (RSV), or "these wasted away, deprived of the produce of the field" (NEB) make no sense in the context. The meaning of the stich must be determined by the parallel in the first half of the verse which has been correctly rendered: "They that be slain with the sword are better than they that be slain with hunger" (RSV), or "Those who died by the sword were more fortunate than those who died of hunger" (NEB). It appears obvious to translate the second line accordingly: "for they shed their (blood), speared on the height of the mountains." I suggest that *mtnwbt* resulted from a misreading of *mtrwmt,* still extant in 2 Sam 1:21. Therefore, the latter verse is not to be translated "Ye mountains of Gilboa, let there be no dew or rain upon you, neither fields of offering" (RSV); nor, following Ginsberg's emendation, "Hills of Gilboa, let no dew or rain fall on you, no showers on the uplands" (NEB); but rather, assuming an elliptic-chiastic parallelism, "Hills of Gilboa, no dew and no rain upon you, mountain heights."

I wish again to emphasize that the analysis presented here is not intended merely to prove or disprove the validity of an emendation suggested on the ground of a presumed external parallel. Rather, it is meant to illustrate the need for a definition of the proper procedure to be followed in the comparative philological study of biblical texts and to adduce proof for the maxim that the inner-biblical analysis always should precede the comparison with extra-biblical texts.

B) Literary Imagery

As has already been stated, biblical thinking seldom if ever expresses itself in a conceptual system. The Hebrews' ideas and concepts rather can be gauged from events narrated and from the narrators' attitudes which can be elicited, to a degree, from an analysis of the text. Recurring idioms, phrases and imagery are of considerable help in the discernment of matters and reflections with which the writers' minds were preoccupied; they constitute a form of capsule descriptions which substitute for the detailed presentation of intricate thought processes. On the cognitive level literary images can be employed as concretizations of abstract notions and thus facilitate the transmission of ideas, e.g. in the realm of myth and religious thought. In view of these remarks, it can cause no surprise that literary imagery is a ready object for comparative research (both on the grand scale, and in the "historic stream" manner) often in detachment from the immediate literary or cultural context. In some instances, such research comes into contact with comparative linguistics or philology; indeed the method has special appeal when treating texts or expressions whose connotation cannot be established with the help of the biblical lexicon or through etymology.

A case in point is the speculation about cosmogony and the conception of the world which hinges on the mythic-existential notion of the center of the world, as captured in the idea and the image of the *omphalos*.[37] Essentially the term and the imagery which it signifies point to a representation of the world in the form of a human body. Its centre is marked by a tall mountain representing its navel from which issues forth an imaginary umbilical cord, the *vinculum*, which links our world with the higher spheres, the world of the gods, just as the embryo is bound to his mother's body by the navel cord. W. Roscher, the innovator of modern *omphalos* research, proved the widespread existence of this idea in the classical world and showed that the principal sanctuaries of ancient Greece—Delos, Epidaurus, Paphos, Branchides, Miletus and Delphi—were each considered by their respective adherents to be at the centre of the earth, i.e. to constitute its navel. Roscher further demonstrated that the image of an imposing mountain as the center of the earth was already current among the nations of the ancient Near East. His hypothesis was developed by Wensinck who assembled impressive evidence that the *omphalos* idea persisted in post-classical Greek thought as well as in Jewish-Hellenistic and rabbinic sources.

The term *omphalos* twice appears in the Septuagint as the translation of the Hebrew term *ṭabbûr hāʾāreṣ*. One of these occurs in Judg 9:37 in the Abimelech story and is there connected, in one way or another, with the area of Shechem; the other mention is set in Ezekiel's vision of the onslaught of Gog on the People of Israel who have been gathered into their land Ezek 33:10–12). *Ṭabbûr* thus far has evaded precise etymological determination, nor can its biblical connotation be definitively established. That the LXX and the Vulgate *(umbilicus terrae)* reflect an understanding of *ṭabbûr* as "navel," in perfect accord with its meaning in mishnaic Hebrew, is beyond doubt. However, it remains open to discussion whether the existence of the pre- or extra-biblical "navel of the earth" mythic concept in the ancient Near East as well as the post-biblical notion of a "centre of the world" designated *ṭabbûr-ṭibbûr* or *omphalos* indeed are decisive proof for the presence of that very same concept in the biblical world-view. The paucity of the evidence for the assumed existence of a biblical *omphalos* concept—two solitary mentions of the unexplained term *ṭabbûr hāʾāreṣ,*—appears to neutralize its import, when compared with the prevalence of the concept in other, both earlier and later, cultures. Furthermore, the absence in the above-mentioned biblical passages of any reference to a sanctuary, a feature which is integral to the classical Greek as well as the most significant ancient Near Eastern examples of the "navel of the earth" myth, surely constitutes negative evidence. This deficiency, however, is "remedied" by postulating that since the events related in the Judges passage take place in the vicinity of Shechem and reference is made to "the tops of the mountains" (Judg 9:36), the mention of *ṭabbûr hāʾāreṣ* certainly must pertain to holy Mount Gerizim on the top of which the Samaritan temple stood during later periods. Likewise, one construes the recurrent mention of *hārê yiśrāʾēl* in Ezekiel's Gog of Magog vision (Ezek 38–39) as synonymous with Jerusalem. Thus *ṭabbûr hāʾāreṣ* in that context is understood as an attribute of the holy city and her sanctuary.

Despite the frailty of this argumentation, Old Testament scholars have endorsed the identification of biblical *ṭabbûr hāʾāreṣ* as "navel of the earth" on the basis of the above parallels. In this they were joined by phenomenologists, who now could add ancient Israelite culture to the group of cultures in which the *omphalos* myth was present, thus buttressing the proposition that the idea of a cosmic center was a universal component of the human conception of the world. Furthermore, some patternists attempted to elicit from the biblical sources evidence for the former existence of an Israelite *omphalos* myth. By infusing an abundance of imagination into the comparative procedures, the *omphalos* myth was placed at the very center of Israelite religion, nay was made the "navel" of her conceptual world. S. Terrien's paper "The Omphalos Myth and Hebrew Religion," *VT* 20 (1970), pp. 315–38, serves as an example of the snowballing effect of this search for similarities by which distinct civilizations can be forced into one "pattern of cult" and "culture."

The contemplation of the *ṭabbûr hāʾāreṣ* issue in the context of and in relation to the bases of the ancient Hebrew religion, instead of or even concomitant with its review in the comparative manner, should have convinced scholars of the improbability that the Mesopotamian, Jebusite or Canaanite mythic principle of the *omphalos* could have served as a pillar of ancient Israel's spiritual world. While vestiges of pagan beliefs certainly filtered into the popular cult and religion, it is far-fetched to assume that they were emulated by authoritative biblical authors, like the prophet Ezekiel. Terrien's insistence that "In all probability, the myth of the navel of the earth, far from being an incidental aspect of worship at the temple of Jerusalem, constitutes in effect the determining factor which links together a number of its cultic practices and beliefs that otherwise appear to be unrelated" (p. 317) appears baseless if one bears in mind the fragility and questionability of the evidence on which this claim rests. Indeed the treatment of the issue by the comparativists fully bears out the critical description and evaluation of their procedures by E. Leach: "The practitioners displayed a prodigious range of erudition in that they were familiar with an extraordinary variety of ethnographic facts . . . the ethnographic evidence was always used to exemplify general propositions with the implication that such propositions are validated by an accumulation of positive evidence. Neutral or negative evidence was never considered" ("The Comparative Method," p. 342).

From this discussion emerges a very simple, but fundamental rule which should be observed in the study of biblical texts and their conceptual import: when linguistic aspects provide but unclear and difficult hints toward the explanation of textual cruxes one should not depend on the forced testimony of assumed external parallels, ferreted out by the comparative method. Rather, the elucidation of difficult terms and ideas must be achieved from the biblical books themselves, since they are the only reliable first-hand evidence which mirrors, albeit fragmentarily, the conceptual horizon of ancient Israel and the linguistic and literary modes in which it found its expression. For this reason, internal parallels are of greater help than external ones; their identification can be achieved in a more systematic fashion than the pinpointing of similarities in extra-biblical sources. It appears to be quite appropriate at this juncture to bring forward the exegetical principle formulated by E. J. Kissane which has lost nothing of its force but, alas, often is lost sight of by Old Testament exegetes: "The context is the guide to interpretation, and disregard to the context leads to chaos"(Engnell, "Traditio-Historical Method," p. 5).

In the case under review, the significance of the rare expression *ṭabbûr hāʾāreṣ,* the application of this procedure produces results which are quite different from the thesis put forward by the comparativists. A contextual analysis of the Ezekiel passage, and to a lesser degree of obviousness of the relevant passage in the Book of Judges, makes it evident that in both occurrences the term *ṭabbûr hāʾāreṣ* has no mythic implications whatsoever, but rather describes an open place of settlement—*ʾereṣ perāzôt*—where people live peacefully, assured of their safety without the need of fortifications and ramparts. This idea is clearly the tenor of Ezekiel's oracle about Gog. It sounds a warning to the enemy of his imminent fall and gives assurance to the people of Israel who have returned to their homeland to live there in tranquility. The *Leitmotif* of the oracle is "dwell in security," reiterated in a series of expressions one of which is "dwell on the *ṭabbûr hāʾāreṣ.*" The equation of *ṭabbūr hāʾāreṣ* with "secure place," as the most tangible historico-geographical meaning which can be elicited from a close reading of the Ezekiel passage, is applicable also to the reference in the Abimelech tradition. It can be buttressed by a comparison of the situation described in the Gog oracle with similar descriptions of inimical onslaughts on a peaceful population. The most noteworthy example is found in Judg 18:7, 27–28 which depicts the attack of the Danites on the people of Laish. There phrases are employed which are synonymous with those used in the Gog oracle:

they dwell in security . . . quiet and safe . . . and quarrel with no one . . . (living) in a wide open land . . . in the valley next to (the city of) Bet Rehob. (cf. further 1 Chr 4:40; Jer 39:31–32; et al).

In summary, the elucidation of the twice-used term *ṭabbûr hāʾāreṣ* by means of contextual analysis and an inner-biblical comparison with synonymous expressions in functionally similar settings suggests that no mythic element whatsoever adheres to the term. There is no need or justification to saddle it with a mystic import by means of eisegesis based on the comparative method in the "pattern of cult" tradition.

C) Literary *Gattungen*

I turn now to the problem of the comparability of biblical literary forms or *Gattungen*. Once more our interest will focus on Ugaritic literature because of the proven similarity of its structures, imagery and phraseology with those found in biblical writings. Before presenting a specific example, it may be useful to make a preliminary remark: *per definitionem*, a literary *Gattung* has a specific *Sitz im Leben*, i.e. a well-circumscribed anchorage in the cultic and cultural structure of the society which produced it; it is the formalized literary expression of ideas, social concepts and cultic values which that society fostered. Therefore, the identification of a *Gattung* evidenced in the literature of one society also in the creative writings of another requires the additional proof that in both it had the same *Sitz im Leben*. This means that a comparative study of *Gattungen* must take into account the social context in which specific literary types and forms arise. What must be shown is that this *Gattung* and what it expresses indeed finds its place in the cultic and conceptual framework of both societies. A *Gattung* cannot be contemplated in isolation from the overall socio-cultural web of a society.

Our present concern will be with the application of these thoughts to the question whether there ever existed an Israelite national epic.[38] There can be no doubt that we have no evidence of an epos in biblical literature. U. Cassuto, to whose discussion of the question we shall return, states quite unequivocally that neither the epic nor the epic song proper is found in the biblical books. This statement will achieve common consent, unless one were to maintain that the Hebrew Bible in its entirety constitutes the national epic of the ancient Hebrews. There remains, though, the consideration of the *Vorgeschichte* of the present canon of biblical writings. It is correctly assumed that, in the stages before its crystallization in the form of books, Hebrew literature was current as only loosely connected, preponderantly oral traditions. It is within these earlier, no longer extant stages of this literature that the search for lost epic cycles has been conducted. Scholars concentrated their attention on the supposedly tangible remnants of and references to epic songs submerged in the present prose texts, especially the obscure *spr mlḥmt yhwh* (lit. "Book of the Wars of the LORD," Num 21:14, with a barely intelligible quotation from that work), and the twice-mentioned *spr hyšr* (lit. "Book of Yashar," Josh 10:13; 2 Sam 1:18, again with quotations).[39] With the exception of Tur-Sinai who took *spr* to mean "oral transmission" or "recitation" of God's mighty deeds,[40] it is unanimously held that what the sources refer to indeed are epics which were yet known at the time of the historiographers who quote from them.

With S. Mowinckel the hypothesis achieved its fullest form.[41] According to him, the surmised *Israelitische Nationalepos* had successfully fused heroic epic tales, portraying the historical exploits of the Israelites and their God in the post-Davidic period, with an epic of cosmogony which rightfully belongs in the category of myth. Central to our present concern is the closing section of Mowinckel's essay which widens the scope of the inquiry—until then based altogether on biblical material *sensu strictu*—as the author turned to ancient Near Eastern epic literature in order to support the postulated existence of a Hebrew national-religious epic.

The employment of the comparative method in search of the lost biblical epic reached a new height in the writings of Umberto Cassuto, at whose disposal lay the newly discovered Ugaritic literature.[42] Cassuto collected a good number of isolated expressions and word combinations scattered in biblical prose texts which bear the stamp of poetry, or even are reminiscent of specific literary turns in Ugaritic epics. The evidence which he assembled certainly strengthens the case for the generally accepted notion that biblical Israel had been imbued with vestiges of Ugaritic/Canaanite culture, including elements borrowed from epics of which the Hebrew authors must have known sizeable portions. Yet to jump from the collation of such obviously borrowed materials to the supposition that they help to prove the existence at one time of an originally Hebrew epic (or epics) is a far cry indeed. It is interesting to observe that Cassuto was almost compelled to make this assumption by this correct insight that biblical Israel hardly would have taken over lock-stock-and-barrel the polytheistic literature of the Canaanites. The antagonistic attitude towards the pagan cult and ritual with which the Ugaritic epics are intimately connected simply ruled out such a transfer. Therefore, he maintains that as far as remnants of epic literature are recognizable in the biblical writings, they perforce must derive from original Hebrew epic songs.

It is at this stage of our survey that we encounter once more the issue of method. The combined evidence marshalled by scholars from their survey of biblical literature cannot provide a sound basis for positing the existence of full-fledged Hebrew epics in the biblical period. The evidence as a whole is circumstantial. It is based on inference from observations about the assumed developmental process of national literatures generally, and ancient Near Eastern and foremost Ugaritic literature especially. In addition, the presumed ancient Hebrew epic is discussed in complete isolation from other forms or *Gattungen* extant in the biblical writings. There can be no doubt that in the historiographies, the narratives, Psalms and even in the prophetic books we do encounter features which are characteristic of the epic genre: poetic rhythm, parallelistic structure and formulaic language. However, these features are found also in literature to which the designation "epic" cannot be applied. We still have to ask ourselves the fundamental question "what makes an epic an epic," and in what way can it be clearly distinguished from other forms of narrative "epic-type" literature. Not one of the scholars who engaged in the study of the issue attempted to provide a clear definition of the "epic" as a special *Gattung,* nor was a satisfactory definition offered by students of the history of general literature and of literary criticism.

Of even greater import is the following fact: the outstanding predominance in the Bible of straightforward prose narration which fulfils the functions for which other literatures revert to the epic genre: heroic tales, historiography, even myth and cosmogony. The phenomenon is too striking to be coincidental. I would propose that the ancient Hebrew writers purposefully nurtured and developed prose narration to take the place of the epic genre which by its content was intimately bound up with the world of paganism and appears to have had a special standing in the polytheistic cults. The recitation of the epics was tantamount to a re-enactment of cosmic events in the manner of sympathetic magic. In the process of total rejection of the polytheistic religions and their ritual expressions in the cult, epic songs and also the epic genre were purged from the literary repertoire of the Hebrew authors. Together with the content, its foremost literary concretization fell into disrepute and was banished from the Israelite culture. The epic elements which did survive —preponderantly in the literature of the monarchic period, i.e. from a time when the prophets were active—were permitted to infiltrate as building blocks of other forms of biblical literature, because they had lost their pagan import and had been neutralized. These survivals constitute examples of figurative language whose original connotations had been so diluted that they no longer evoked objection. However, the initial rejection of the epics and the epic genre seems to have been so thorough that they could never be reintegrated into the technical apparatus of the Hebrew *literati.* It can be surmised that the closure of biblical literature against the epic was helped along by the progressive falling into desuetude of this genre in the Semitic world from about the second quarter of the first millennium B.C. The following observation may be added: it would appear that in the framework of the cult, the Hebrew writers developed the historiographical psalm as a substitute for the epic. The great acts of God in the creation of the world and in history thus were related and possibly recited in a specifically and originally Israelite genre.

In summing up this discussion it can be said that the epic is not simply a *Gattung* which can be identified by a given number of literary techniques such as were specified, for example, by W. Whallon.[43] It is rather the expression of a specific societal *Gestalt.* Its presence can be empirically established in those societies which did produce epics and in which it has a special *Sitz im Leben.*[44] It cannot be reconstructed where it does not exist. With reference to the epic as a specific literary genre, Israel presents a deep societal structure which is quite different from those of her neighbours. The cosmological epic requires a rich background of myth for its development; Israel was lacking that background, having rejected myth from the outset. The historical epic has been shown by D. F. Rauber to have flourished in societies in the heroic stages of their development.[45] It is therefore striking that biblical literature did not record even Israel's heroic age—the days of the Judges and the early kings—in the form of epics. Comparativists generally, and in the field of biblical studies especially, would do well to pay heed to differences between cultures and not only to likenesses. Adequate attention must be given to the interpretation of the dissimilarities from other cultures of the ancient Near East which made biblical civilization the peculiar and particular phenomenon it was. These considerations lead us to answer in the negative the question posed by Mowinckel and echoed by Cassuto —"Hat es ein israelitisches Nationalepos gegeben?" Biblical Israel did not produce epics nor did it foster the epic genre.

IV.

In closing this presentation, I wish to return to the issue of procedure to which reference was made in the introductory part and to stress once more the need for the definition of a set of rules which should serve biblical scholars as guidelines in their pursuit of comparative studies. It must be emphasized that the formulation of a methodology of comparative research in matters pertaining to ancient Israelite culture and the Old Testament literature, because of the comprehensiveness and the variety of issues to which this research applies itself, is a task which transcends the framework of this paper and which cannot be carried out single-handed. It demands an interdisciplinary and synoptic grasp, thus requiring the co-operation of experts in diverse areas: philology, literature, folk-lore, theology, sociology, history, and the history of ideas. All that could be attempted here was the delineation of some basic—not always necessarily new—principles which should be followed in the intercultural comparative study of biblical phenomena. These can be summarized as follows:

The interpretation of biblical features—whether of a socio-political, cultic, general-cultural or literary nature—with the help of inner-biblical parallels should always precede the comparison with extra-biblical materials. In the evaluation of a societal phenomenon, attention should be paid to its function in the developing structure of the Israelite body politic before one engages in the comparison with parallel phenomena in other societies. Such comparisons can be applied to societies which lie in the same "historic stream" as biblical Israel. Comparisons on the "grand scale" are better avoided. In this respect, the methodological concerns expressed by Walter Goldschmidt are most pertinent: "Because each culture defines its own institutions there is always an element of falsification when we engage in institutional comparisons among distinct cultures."[46]

In any such study the full range of the available evidence must be taken into consideration: the "holistic" approach always should be given preference over the "atomistic." The abstraction of a concept, an aspect of society, cult or literature from its wider framework, and its contemplation in isolation, more often than not will result in distortion; its intrinsic meaning ultimately is decided by the context, and therefore may vary from one setting to another.

NOTES

1. I wish to thank my assistant, Mr. David Satran, for his help in the preparation of this article.
2. For the history and survey of the literature, see H. F. Hahn, *Old Testament in Modern Research* (Philadelphia, 1954; 1956); H. J. Kraus, *Geschichte der Historisch-Kritiscben Erforschung des Alten Testaments* (Neukirchen, 1956; 1969); R. Smend, *Wilhelm Martin Leberecht de Wettes Arbeit am Alten und Neuen Testament* (Basel, 1958).
3. E. Nielsen, *Oral Tradition* (London, 1954); I. Engnell, "Methodological Aspects of Old Testament Study," *SVT* 7 (1959), pp. 13–30; *id.*, "The Traditio-Historical Method in Old Testament Research," *A Rigid Scrutiny, Critical Essays on the Old Testament,* tr. J. T. Willis (London, 1970), pp. 3–11, to mention only a few relevant items.
4. M. Weiss, "Die Methode der 'Total-Interpretation,' " *SVT* 22 (1971), pp. 88–112, provides a survey and bibliography.
5. Cf. K. E. Bock, "The Comparative Method of Anthropology," *Comparative Studies in Society and History* 8 (1965/66), pp. 269–80; and E. R. Leach, "The Comparative Method in Anthropology," *International Encyclopedia of the Social Sciences* 1 (New York, 1968), pp. 339–45.
6. A thorough discussion of the problem is presented by A. J. F. Köbben, "Comparativists and Non-Comparativists in Anthropology," in R. Naroll and R. Cohen (eds.), *A Handbook of Method in Cultural Anthropology* (New York, 1970), pp. 581–96. Köbben notes (p. 583) that the two trends —one following the principle of "specificity" and "specification," the other that of "homogeneity"—had already been differentiated by Kant in his *Critique of Pure Reason:* "This distinction shows itself in the different manner of thought among students of nature [and of culture, S.T.], some . . . being almost averse to heterogeneousness, and always intent on the unity of genera; while others . . . are constantly driving to divide nature [or

society, S.T.] into so much variety that one might lose almost all hope of being able to distribute its phenomena according to general principles."

7. A notable exception is J. W. Rogerson, *Myth in Old Testament Interpretation* (BZAW 134, Berlin, 1974), especially his analysis of "The Structural Study of Myth" (pp. 101–27). A critical survey and full bibliography of Mary Douglas's research is provided by S. R. Isenberg and D. E. Owen, "Bodies, Natural and Contrived: The Work of Mary Douglas," *Religious Studies Review* 3 (Jan. 1977), pp. 1–17. For Edmund Leach, and his critics, see p. 418, n. 28.
8. "Two Strategies of Comparison," in A. Etzioni and F. L. Dubow (eds.), *Comparative Perspectives: Theories and Methods* (Boston, 1970), p. 41.
9. Köbben, p. 582.
10. As quoted by Köbben, p. 584.
11. *Apud* Köbben, p. 590.
12. J. Barr, *Comparative Philology and the Text of the Old Testament* (Oxford, 1968), p. 77.
13. *Apud* S. C. Thrupp, "Editorial," *Comparative Studies in Society and History* 1 (1958/59) p. 3.
14. "Israel's Place among the Religions of the Ancient Near East," *SVT* 23 (1972), p. 6.
15. The ensuing presentation aims at viewing concisely, and in a more comprehensive framework, several issues which I have discussed elsewhere in greater detail. For this reason, I absolve myself from adducing here full documentation either for opinions approvingly offered or for those critically assessed.
16. The structural approach is well-employed by M. B. Rowton in an interesting series of articles (in process) on "the role of dimorphic structure and topology in the history of Western Asia"; for a full listing see *Oriens Antiquus* 15 (1976), p. 17, n. 4.
17. Cf. S. Talmon, "The 'Desert Motif' in the Bible and in Qumran Literature," in A. Altmann (ed.), *Biblical Motifs—Origins and Transformations* (Cambridge, Mass., 1966), pp. 31–63; *id.*, "Wilderness," *The Interpreter's Dictionary of the Bible—Supplementary Volume* (Nashville, 1976), pp. 946–49.
18. R. de Vaux, *Ancient Israel—Its Life and Institutions*, tr. by J. McHugh, (London, 1961), p. 12ff. = *Les Institutions de l'Ancien Testament* 1 (Paris, 1958), pp. 28ff.
19. "Traditio-Historical Method," p. 8.
20. See S. Talmon, "Typen der Messiaserwartung um die Zeitwende," in H. W. Wolff (ed.), *Probleme Biblischer Theologie, Gerhard von Rad zum 70. Geburtstag* (München, 1971), pp. 571–88.
21. "The Meaning of the Expression *ʿam haʾareṣ* in the Old Testament," *JSS* 10 (1965), pp. 59–66.
22. *Journal of World History* 11 (1968–69), pp. 46–68.

23. *Fourth World Congress of Jewish Studies—Papers* 1 (Jerusalem, 1967), pp. 71–76.
24. "Kingship and Council in Israel and Sumer: A Parallel," *JNES* 22 (1963), pp. 247–53.
25. "Rehoboam's Advisers at Schechem, and Political Institutions in Israel and Sumer," *JNES* 25 (1966), pp. 273–79.
26. *Genesis as Myth and Other Essays* (London, 1969), pp. 7–23.
27. Pp. 25–83.
28. See especially the aforementioned discussion by Rogerson, (n. 7); critical studies by A. Malamat, M. Pamment, and R. C. Culley are reviewed in J. A. Emerton's treatment of the issue in "An Examination of a Recent Structuralist Interpretation of Genesis XXXVIII," *VT* 26 (1976), pp. 79–98.
29. See S. Talmon, "Kingship and the Ideology of the State," *The World History of the Jewish People—The Age of the Monarchies* (Jerusalem, 1977), part 2, pp. 3–26. For a comprehensive survey of the issue, cf. E. Kutsch, *Salbung als Rechtsakt* (BZAW 87, 1963).
30. *Kingship and the Gods* (Chicago, 1948), p. 339.
31. See M. H. Goshen-Gottstein, "Linguistic Structure and Tradition in the Qumran Documents," *Scripta Hierosolymitana* 4 (Jerusalem, 1958), pp. 101–37.
32. L. R. Fisher (ed.), *Ras Shamra Parallels,* 1–2 (Rome, 1972–77).
33. "Two Comparative Lexical Studies," *JANES* 5 *(The Gaster Festschrift 1973),* p. 296.
34. "The Ugaritic Texts and Textual Criticism," *JBL* 62 (1943), pp. 109ff.
35. *Apud* Köbben, p. 590.
36. See S. Talmon, "On the Emendation of Biblical Texts on the Basis of Ugaritic Parallels," *Eretz-Israel* 12 (Ginsberg Volume, Jerusalem, 1978), pp. 117–24 (Hebrew).
37. See S. Talmon, "The 'Navel of the Earth' and the Comparative Method," *Scripture in History and Theology, J. Coert Rylaarsdam Jubilee Volume* (Twin Cities, 1977), pp. 243–68.
38. See S. Talmon, "Did There Exist a Biblical National Epic?" *Proceedings of the Seventh World Congress of Jewish Studies* (Jerusalem, 1981), vol. 2, pp. 41–61.
39. The proposed retroversion of *en bibliōi tēs ōdiēs* mentioned in a Greek addition to 1 Kgs 8:53 (13) and also found in one witness of the Vetus Latina into *spr hšyr,* and the latter's identification with *spr hyšr* (by inversion), is rather questionable in view of the apparent dissimilar content of these two compilations.
40. N. H. Tur-Sinai, "Was there an Ancient 'Book of the Wars of the Lord'?" *BIES* 24 (1960), pp. 146–48 (Hebrew).
41. "Hat es ein israelitisches Nationalepos gegeben?" *ZAW* 35 (1935), pp. 130–52.
42. "The Israelite Epic," *Biblical and Oriental Studies* 2, tr. I. Abrahams (Jerusalem, 1975), pp. 69–109.

43. *Formula, Character, and Context—Studies in Homeric, Old English, and Old Testament Poetry* (Cambridge, Mass., 1969).
44. Cf. the interesting observations on the position of the epic poet in Homeric society in S. C. Humphreys, " 'Transcendence' and Intellectual Roles: The Ancient Greek Case," *Daedalus* 104 (1975), pp. 91–118.
45. "Observations on Biblical Epic," *Genre* 3 (1970), pp. 318–38.
46. *Comparative Functionalism* (Berkeley, 1966), p. 131.

17

The Question of Distinctiveness in Ancient Israel

Peter Machinist

I.

The most remarkable fact about the study of the Hebrew Bible in the last century and a half has been the gradual recovery, through archaeological exploration and decipherment of the ancient texts thus unearthed, of the world in whose midst the Bible was composed and disseminated. The recovery, of course, is still underway; but enough has been done so that when we now speak of the neighbors of ancient Israel—Canaanites, Egyptians, Assyrians, Babylonians, etc.—we can do so mainly from their own writings and material remains. No longer are we confined to the indirect testimony of the Bible, Classical authors, and Jewish, Christian, and Muslim traditions.

At the same time, this increased awareness of the surrounding world has had a profound impact on the way we read the Hebrew Bible itself. Simply put, the Bible now steps forward not merely as a set of theological statements or a group of entertaining and edifying tales, and certainly not at all as a text so peculiar, so *sui generis,* as to be without any normal human reality. Increasingly, it is seen first as an historical artifact: the product of and reaction to a concrete historical environment, which we may describe as the ancient Near East largely, though

Reprinted by permission from I. Eph'al and M. Cogan, eds, *A Highway from Egypt to Assyria: Studies in Ancient Near Eastern History and Historiography Presented to Hayim Tadmor* (Jerusalem: Magnes Press, 1990).

not exclusively, before the invasion of Alexander the Great toward the end of the fourth century B.C.E.

The contacts involved here, as specific analysis reveals, operated on a variety of levels. From the plan of Solomon's temple in I Kings/II Chronicles, with its background in the tripartite sanctuaries of the Bronze and Iron Age Levant, through the laws in Exodus and their Mesopotamian antecedents, to the Canaanite traditions reflected in the word pairs and "climactic parallelism" of Biblical poetry—these and many other examples demonstrate, with ever greater clarity, that ancient Israel and its Bible belonged very much with the other cultures of the ancient Near East. But they raise just as insistently the question: how much? How close was the kinship? Were there also ways in which Israel was distinctive?

II.

Now this question did not originate with the beginning of modern archaeological work in the Near East. It was asked already much earlier, normally in the anxious tones of religious apologetic; and the apologetic has by no means been left behind even now. Consider, for example, a modern British "Bibelist," Norman H. Snaith, who writes:

> We are therefore of the firm opinion that it is high time for us to awake out of our semi-hypnosis, induced by the desire for comprehensiveness and broadmindedness, and by the attractiveness of these studies in . . . comparative religion and native custom. . . . If the Old Testament has, for Jews and Christian, a value which no other book has, then it is essential for us to know and to be very sure what that value is, where it is different from other sacred books, and particularly where it is incomparable. . . . No institution, be it religious or secular, has any right to continue to exist unless it has, and can show in all the market-places of the world, a special and distinct reason for its separate existence. If it cannot do this, then it is encumbering the ground.[1]

Now it is by no means clear that for an institution to be useful or needed, it has to be unique. In any case, the purpose of this essay is not to bury or to praise the faith, but to try to examine, as we can and must do, the question of Israel's distinctiveness unprejudiced by notions of how the results will affect whatever beliefs—religious or otherwise—we may have.

To trace the history of the distinctiveness discussion, however, would take us too far afield. Suffice it to note that the discussion has moved, whether apologetic or not, in two different directions. On the one hand, there has been a determined search for clear concepts and behaviors which would neatly separate Israel from the cultures being compared with it, which in our present instance means the rest of the ancient Near East.[2] The goal here has been a kind of "trait list"—to adapt a term made popular in anthropological studies of a generation or more ago—in which "x" could be marked as present in Israel but absent elsewhere in the ancient Near East, or vice-versa. But establishing such traits is an elusive business, to say the least, the more so when the cultures under study developed in the same region and time frame. Indeed, as the increasing volume of archaeological discoveries makes clear, some correspondence always seems to be waiting to be found somewhere in the ancient Near East, not to mention in other regions of the world, for what is proposed as a distinctive concept or behavior in ancient Israel.

Monotheism is a case in point—perhaps the case one thinks of most readily in the present discussion.[3] No one would contest that, by any of several possible definitions, it played a role in ancient Israel.[4] What is problematic, however, is the assertion that by these same definitions it appeared nowhere else in the ancient Near East. Thus, if monotheism is understood strictly as the view that the divine is conceivable only as a single entity, Biblical passages like (II) Isa 43:10–11 may be adduced:

> "You are my witness," says Yahweh, "and my servant whom I have chosen that you may know and believe in me, and understand that I am he: before me no god was created, nor shall there be any after me. I, I am Yahweh, and there is no savior besides me."

But on the same ground it is not easy to ignore the reform of the Egyptian Pharoah Akhenaton, for here too, as Jan Assmann and Erik Hornung have seen with particular clarity, is an intolerance of other gods in terms both of literary assertions of the unitary existence of the Aton and of practical prohibitions: the defacement of the inscribed names of other deities, and the establishment of essentially an aniconic cult to the Aton.[5]

Alternatively, we can choose to define monotheism more loosely and "practically," as the integration of all power or the investiture of the highest power in one being, especially in the interest of human allegiance and worship. For this definition also—which is usually labelled monolatry or even henotheism, to distinguish it from the first[6]—Biblical evidence is available, indeed much more of it; but so is evidence from other ancient Near Eastern cultures. Compare the Biblical "You (=Israel) shall have no other gods beside me" (Exod 20:3/Deut 5:7) and "Who is like you, Yahweh, among the gods?" (Exod 15:11) with the following extracts from Mesopotamian hymns:

> *dSin ed-diš-šu-ú mu-nam- [mir] -[ru . . .]*
> Sin, unique one, who makes bright. . . .[7]

> an-na a-ba maḫ-me-en za-e ušu-zu maḫ-àm // *ina* AN-*e man-nu ṣi-i-ru at-ta e-diš-ši-ka ṣi-rat*
> ki-a a-ba maḫ-me-en za-e ušu-zu maḫ-àm // *ina* KI-*ti man-nu ṣi-i-ru at-ta e-diš-ši-ka ṣi-rat*
> In heaven, who is exalted? You (=Sin)! You alone are exalted. On earth who is exalted? You! You alone are exalted.[8]

> za-e-na dìm-me-er si-sá nu-tuk-àm // *e-la ka-a-ti i-li muš-te-še-ru ul i-ši*
> Apart from you (=Ištar) I have no god who guides rightly.[9]

To be sure, it has often been objected[10] that despite the formal similarities of these Mesopotamian statements with the Biblical, there is a fundamental difference of semantics, in that the Mesopotamian (and other non-Biblical texts which might be added) are essentially mere flattery of some god by the worshipper, while the Biblical statements go beyond to an ontological assertion about Yahweh's uniqueness. But this supposed difference becomes clear only when the statements are interpreted against what is perceived as the larger polytheistic background of Mesopotamia and the monotheistic of Israel. Considered in themselves, the statements are not so easy to distinguish semantically. In fact, they all appear to serve, really, the same "practical monotheism" of worship, in which the worshipper, at the moment of communication with the divine, sharpens his focus, to augment the efficacy and depth of his involvement, on the particular divinity whose response he hopes for.[11]

As a final approach to monotheism, we could argue that the point is not simply unique existence or the integration of power; it is that the deity transcends—stands outside of and dominates—the phenomenon or phenomena he represents instead of being their mere personification.[12] Or, in the theophany given to the prophet Elijah (I Kings 19:11–12):

And look, Yahweh passed by, and a great and strong wind tore apart the mountains, and shattered the rocks before Yahweh, but Yahweh was not in the wind. After the wind was an earthquake, but Yahweh was not in the earthquake; and after the earthquake, a fire, but Yahweh was not in the fire; and after the fire, a still small voice.

This Elijah theophany, it is clear, establishes that Israel knew of transcendent divinity. Yet once more, it was not the only ancient Near Eastern culture that did. One does not have to search too far among the "great gods" or "sky gods" of, say, Mesopotamia to find a deity like Enki/Ea, who, as the extant tests make clear, is no mere "genius" of the "sweet waters,"[13] but has a cosmic range as god of wisdom and creation.[14]

The correspondences we have been discussing could easily be extended to other areas besides monotheism.[15] But what we have seen, hopefully, has made the point: how difficult the perception of distinctiveness becomes—in the case of Israel as, indeed, for any culture—if we try to encapsulate it in single, pure concepts or behaviors.[16]

With this difficulty in mind, a second approach to distinctiveness has been tried. Here the possibility is allowed that Israel and her Near Eastern neighbors may have shared much the same pool of ideas and behaviors. What, then, is distinctive about each community are the ways in which the ideas were patterned and emphasized. Not individual, pure traits, in short, but configurations of traits become the focus of the modern historian, if he wants to understand the distinctiveness of ancient Israel—or of any culture.[17]

The argument will become clear if we return to the concept of monotheism.[18] Gone now is a fixation on whether it was present or absent in the ancient Near East. Rather, we are asked to observe that whereas other Near Eastern gods could be imagined as inside as well as outside of the phenomena they represented, the Israelite god, at least as described in the Hebrew Bible, was almost always outside. Similarly, the drive toward investiture of exclusive power and eventually exclusive divinity in Yahweh was, as pictured in the Bible, a majority thrust, as against, for example, Mesopotamia or Egypt, where such drives were never as persistently dominant. One need only recall the fate of the Pharaoh Akhenaton and his Atonist "heresy" to see the point.

There is much in this search for distinctive configurations which makes sense, especially when set against the simplistic oppositions that characterize the other search, the one for pure, distinctive traits. Plainly, however, there are problems here as well. For how can we be sure that the configurations we have discerned in the data are actually there? And even if they are there, how representative of the given culture are the data we are using? These problems are serious enough in the study of living cultures, where data are, relatively speaking, available for the asking and native informants exist, even if their perceptions of how things configure may often vary among themselves and with those of outside observers. Matters obviously become worse once we focus on extinct cultures, the data for which are not only much slimmer and harder to generate, but also much harder to appreciate in terms of bias and *Sitz im Leben*—there being no native informants around to help us in the task. And what of an extinct culture like Israel? Here we may be in a still more difficult situation, for the bulk of the data about it are preserved only in a late, highly selective and refractive compendium, the Hebrew Bible. If we want to argue, therefore, that monotheism held a dominant, persistent place in ancient Israel, we must not forget that this proposition has to rest primarily on the Biblical corpus,[19] and cannot easily be confirmed by other evidence. Indeed, other evidence has sometimes been used to modify, if not to reject, it, in the process giving the non-monotheistic elements in the Bible greater historical importance than a reading of the Bible alone might have suggested.[20]

III.

The history of the discussion about Israel's distinctiveness is, in sum, a cautionary tale. For whether we search for cultural configurations or, worse, for individual cultural traits, we must recognize that we are operating in obscure and elusive terrain. Why, then, focus on the issue at all, or, if one feels compelled to do that, on the issue as it affects ancient Israel? One could have chosen any of a number of communities, since all, by definition, have something distinctive about them.

The focus on Israel, clearly, cannot be separated from the apologetic tradition noted earlier, which has imbued practically all of those who have touched the subject, secularists and believers alike, with the sense of being lineal Israelite descendants. But the apologetic is not simply one that these descendants have invented. It was already central to the principal monument and source for ancient Israel, the Hebrew Bible. As a moment's reflection will make plain, the very process of selection and refraction that produced the Bible—which we otherwise label the process of editing and canonization—was an effort at discerning cultural traits and configurations, at putting together an integrated Israelite world-view, or what turns out, really, to be a series of overlapping world-views. This effort, moreover, was no mere antiquarian enterprise. It was part, rather, of a wider struggle to articulate and propagate national-cultural identity during a period when such identity was threatened with major change and even extinction. We should not be surprised, therefore, that the traits and configurations presented in the Bible often appear in polemical, not neutral formulations. Indeed, it is not unusual to find them joined to an explicit preoccupation with the question: how are we different, yes, unique among all groups we know.

The history of the discussion about Israel's distinctiveness, thus, begins with Israel itself, as evidenced in its Bible. Perhaps, then, instead of prolonging our efforts as outside observers to discover some trait or configuration which Israel *actually* held uniquely in the ancient Near East, we should turn to this logically prior issue and ask: how did Israel, in its Biblical canon, pose and answer the distinctiveness question for itself?

To reorient the discussion in this way is not to indulge in any semantic sleight of hand. That is, there is no intent here secretly to continue the search for what actually distinguished Israel by suggesting that it was Israel alone which raised the distinctiveness question. Clearly, such a suggestion would be false. All cultures, like individuals, have to wrestle with the other as part of determining the boundaries and potentialities of the self. And as we shall see, Israel's neighbors in the Near East did indeed ask about their own distinctiveness.

Similarly, there will be no plea here that one or more of the features claimed by Israel itself as unique were, in fact, so. For in this also are problems. On the one hand, many of Israel's claims, like the assertion that Yahweh alone is God, all other deities being idols, are not historically demonstrable. On the other hand, with most, if not all of these claims we have the same difficulty we encountered earlier: that some parallel claim can or will be found somewhere in the steadily ballooning evidence relating to other Near Eastern cultures.

The issue, then, is not the *actual* uniqueness of Israel's questioning. It is, instead: how can the ways in which the questioning was framed and answered in the Bible help us, as outsiders, to understand the shape of Israelite culture as a whole. We may find, in fact, that certain facets do look different by comparison with other cultures; but the goal here is not so much to seek out the differences as to understand, whether different or not, what the culture of Israel was.

There is one more consideration before we begin. Our evidence for Israel's questioning comes, as already noted, from the Hebrew Bible, but what of Israelite society and culture is reflected in this text? No final answer is possible. Still, critical scholarship has taught us to look in two directions. More accessibly, the Bible reflects the canonical organizers who put it together: socially important individuals and groups, spread roughly over the sixth century B.C.E. through the first century C.E., who were, thus, far from homogeneous, although they seem to have built on one another's work. The organizers, however, were hardly the inventors of all they worked on. Behind them stood oral traditions and written texts, representing, it seems, a range of different social, chronological, and geographical groups in ancient Israel. But their presence and exact demarcation in the final Biblical text—with certain exceptions, essentially the sole text that has survived—is still a matter of only partial agreement among modern scholars. In what follows, therefore, we shall consider the Biblical statements first as elements of the canonical organizers' views of what should be normative in Israelite society. Where possible, however, earlier, more localized *Sitze im Leben* for particular statements will be noted.

IV.

We turn now to the Biblical passages themselves. What holds them together is a common content: they all speak of Israel or one of its representative groups or individuals, including its God, as distinct from outsiders, whether humans or gods. They, thus, all involve, though with varying degrees of explicitness, a comparison; and the comparison often, but not always, turns on a specific feature that the one side possesses and the other does not. Except for this rather general notion of structure, however, the passages do not exhibit any fixed form or forms. We encounter, instead, a variety of forms—(rhetorical) questions, declarative statements, commands—chosen, it seems, to fit the specific contexts in which they are embedded. Similarly, while the passages can employ particular words signifying "distinctive,"[21] they do so irregularly, and thus no stereotyped phraseology seems to be at work. The characteristics just mentioned allow us to isolate—though not without a number of ambiguities—approximately 433 distinctiveness passages in the Hebrew Bible.[22] It is impossible to review them all in the present compass, and probably unnecessary as well. We will consider, rather, the principal thematic categories they reflect, with representative examples from each.

We begin with a rather enigmatic remark of the diviner Balaam about Israel, in Num 23:9—"Look, a people (who) is encamped alone *(hen-ʿām lĕbādād yiškōn),* and does not reckon itself among the nations" *(ûbaggôyim lōʾ yitḥaššāb).* The remark appears as part of a praise and blessing Balaam pronounces over Israel, instead of the curse he had been hired and expected to utter. On the face of it, Balaam is exclaiming that Israel is in a class apart from other nations, but the question is what he means by this. Recently, Abraham Malamat has argued, on the basis of a diplomatic letter from Old Babylonian Mari, that the meaning is basically political: unlike other states and polities, Israel is one that exists and can flourish without human allies.[23] This makes good sense from the Biblical context as well, if we understand that Balaam uses the encampment of the Israelite tribes which he sees before him (v. 9a–b), powerful in its vastness (cf. the following v. 10) and physically separated from contact with any other group, as a metaphor reflecting on Israel's isolated, and thus unique, status among nations (v. 9c).[24] The implication, of course, is that Israel can exist "alone" and unallied because it has the only ally it needs, Yahweh, its God (cf. 23:21).

If in the above passage, a foreigner is pictured, and thus commended, for recognizing the distinctiveness of Israel, there are passages by contrast that curse foreigners for denying this status. So against Moab: "Thus says Lord Yahweh, 'Because Moab[25] said, "Behold the house of Judah is like all the other nations," therefore, I will lay open the flank/slope of Moab . . . and upon Moab I will execute judgment,' " (Ezek 25:8–9, 11). Similarly, foreigners who advance their own claims to distinctiveness are denounced, as the Second Isaiah makes clear with regard to Babylon: "You felt secure in your wickedness; you said, 'No one sees me.' Your wisdom and your knowledge led you astray, and you said in your heart, 'I am, and there is no one besides me.'[26] But evil shall come upon you, and you shall not know how to repel(?) it *(šaḥrāh)*[27] . . ." (Isa 47:10–11).[28]

The core of Israel's claim to distinctiveness is her special relationship to her God; so it is not surprising that a large category of distinctiveness passages is to be found here. For example, in Exod 33:16, Moses queries God: "For how shall it be known therefore that I have found favor in your sight, I and your people? Is it not in your going with us that we are distinct *(niplênû),* I and your people, from all the people that are upon the face of the earth?" To Yahweh, thus, Israel is the "treasured possession *(sĕgullâ)* of all the peoples" (Exod 19:15),[29] the nation chosen by him for personal supervision, while to other nations he assigns other divine beings in his retinue (Deut 4:19–20; 32:8–9[30]). And the crucial proof of this special relationship is what the Biblical writers perceive as the unique historical activities of Yahweh in regard to Israel, especially in the Exodus from Egypt. So in Deut 4:34, "Or has any god ever attempted to go and take a nation for himself from the midst of (another) nation by trials . . . according to all that Yahweh your God did for you in Egypt before your eyes?" Interestingly, the prophet Amos, speaking, it seems, before a public gathering of Israelites,[31] has God rejecting the uniqueness of the Exodus—a rejection that serves, however, to indicate the popular fervor with which the uniqueness was affirmed: " 'Are you not like the Ethiopians to me, O Israelites,' says Yahweh. '(If) I brought Israel up from the land of Egypt, did I not (also) the Philistines from Caphtor, and Aram from Qir?' " (Amos 9:7). One additional facet of this whole issue should be noted: the Bible has no real answer as to why Yahweh singled out Israel in the first place. The special relationship is, in short, a mystery, and the mystery itself becomes part of Israel's distinctiveness. Compare perhaps the most explicit meditation on the matter, in Deut 7:7–8: "It was not because you were the most numerous of all the peoples that Yahweh set his love upon you *(ḥašaq bākem)* and chose you, for you were the fewest of all the peoples; but it was because Yahweh loved you and kept the oath which He swore to your fathers that Yahweh brought you out with a strong hand and redeemed you from the house of slaves, from the hand of Pharaoh, king of Egypt."[32]

The unique relationship between Israel and Yahweh only underscores the uniqueness of Yahweh himself—a conviction which likewise, in various forms, pervades the Biblical text. As Exod 15:11 puts it, "Who is like you, Yahweh, among the gods?" The Second Isaiah, as we have seen, goes even farther, by having Yahweh reject the gods altogether:

"Before me no god was formed, nor shall there be any after me" (Isa 43:10). Significantly, on this issue, as on the distinctiveness of Israel itself, foreigners can be singled out positively as they affirm it (so Jethro in Exod 18; cf. v. 11) or for curse as they deny it (the Assyrian *rab shaqeh* in 2 Kings 18:32–35; 19:17–19 / Isa 36:18–20; 37:18–20; 2 Chron 32:13–23).

In all the passages we have been considering, the concern is with what we might call theoretical principles. Other Biblical passages, in turn, seek to draw out the behavioral consequences which are to set Israel apart. Thus, in Lev 18, a whole series of sexual practices is prohibited to Israel, the point of which becomes clear in v. 24: "Do not defile yourselves by any of these things, for by all these the nations which I am expelling before you defiled themselves." It is interesting to note in the post-exilic book of Esther how such prohibitions—as well as other, positive injunctions—came to be seen as a code of laws which no other group possessed: "a certain people, scattered abroad and dispersed among the peoples in all the provinces of your kingdom—their laws are different from those of every other people. . . ." (Esth 3:8). The same point, it may be added, can be made in a converse way, by criticizing Israel when it acts, or wants to act, like other nations. So Ezekiel has God assert: "What you have in mind shall not occur, when you say, 'Let us be like the nations, like the families of the lands, and worship wood and stone' " (Ezek 20:32).[33]

Finally, the success of Israel in exhibiting the behavior required can be viewed as bringing on a unique status from God. Thus, Deut 28:1—"If you obey God's voice and undertake to do all his commandments, which I am commanding you today, then Yahweh your God will set you high above all the nations of the earth." On the other hand, failure to meet the requirements is seen as distinctive in its perversity or else as leading to punishment from God which is distinctive. So in Jer 2:10–11—"For cross to the islands of the Kittim and see; send to Qedar and examine with care. See if there has been such a thing. Has a nation changed its gods, even though they are no gods? But my people has changed its Glory for that which does not profit." Or in Dan 9:12—"He (God) has confirmed his words, which he spoke against us and against our rulers who ruled us, by bringing upon us a great calamity. For under the whole heaven there has not been done the like of what has been done against Jerusalem."[34]

V.

Our survey of the Biblical passages on the distinctiveness of Israel has not attempted completeness. But we have enough now to speculate on the wider implications of these texts for the character of the ancient Israelite community that lies behind them. Several points are worth comment.

First, while the passages obviously belong in the world-view of the canonical organizers of the Hebrew Bible, the diversity of their placement in the Biblical corpus—they are found almost everywhere in it[35] —suggests a diversity of origin in Israel as a whole. More specifically, as various examples allow, we can see that the issue was one of long standing. So at least two of our texts—Balaam's remark in Num 23:9 about "a people (who) is encamped alone" and Exod 15:11 affirming "Who is like you, Yahweh"—seem quite early in date, premonarchic/pre-tenth century B.C.E., if we follow the influential linguistic analysis of them worked out especially by the Albright school.[36] Somewhat later is Amos' rhetorical question denying his public's view of the uniqueness of the Exodus (9:7). How much later, to be sure, is debated, but there is nothing in the question which could not belong in the mid-eighth century B.C.E., when the prophet was active. Indeed, it fits well with a basic emphasis in Amos' book on the parody of well rooted popular beliefs and expectations.[37] Finally, in Deutoronomy we meet what is perhaps the largest and most varied collection of distinctiveness statements in any Biblical source—about fifty passages, covering almost all the themes discussed above[38]—which testifies to the importance of the issue for the originally northern group of literati responsible for this book, whose work on it climaxed in the disasters and persecutions of the first half of the seventh century B.C.E. Distinctiveness, in sum, seems to have been an established and not unpopular preoccupation in Israel well before the advent of the canonical organizers in the sixth century B.C.E. The latter, if we could go farther, were particularly influenced by the Deuteronomists' concern with this issue, as they were by the Deuteronomist anticipation of the very notion of canon itself.[39]

There is a second point, which has to do with focus. Almost all the distinctiveness passages center either on the God or on the "people" (*ʿam* [e.g., Num 23:9]; less frequently, "nation" [*gôy;* e.g., Deut 4:34]) of Israel. Only a very few concern individual Israelites, such as Moses, described as the "humblest *(ʿānāw)* of all men who were on the face of the earth" (Num 12:3), or Solomon, who "was the wisest of all men" (1 Kings 5:11), or, negatively, Manasseh, king of Judah, who "made them stray to do more evil than the nations which Yahweh had destroyed before the Israelites" (2 Kings 21:9). This emphasis on peoplehood or on the god Yahweh—the latter really the same thing, sociologically, since Yahweh is the emblem of Israel, with which his distinctiveness is bound up—should not surprise us. It has been observed by virtually every interpreter of the Hebrew Bible, because so many other features of the text touch on it.

If, then, the distinctiveness passages focus above all on the people Israel, they presume that this people has a beginning *within* already known time: the Exodus from a long established Egypt. Cosmogony where it occurs in the Biblical text is *not* identical with national history.[40] Similarly, there is no notion of autochthonous origins—of a primordial connection between the people and a particular territory.[41] What is distinctive is that God "*goes* with us" (Exod 33:16) "*to take*" us "from the midst of another nation" (Deut 4:34). The land which becomes known as *ʾereṣ yiśrāʾēl* is, of course, important, central, in fact, to the bond between Israel and its God. But it is a land which has to *become* "Israel," when Israel enters it as an outsider, already with its organization essentially fixed; and the assumption is that, however difficult, Israel can exist apart from the land, as the experience in Egypt and later Babylonia demonstrate. This point about outside origins, like that concerning origins in time, has many other echoes in the Bible. Lev 25:23 is one example: "The land will not be sold irretrievably, for the land is mine (=God's), (and) you (=Israel) are aliens and sojourners *(gērîm wĕtôšābîm)* with me." Indeed, even Israel's God is pictured, especially in the older literature (Deut 33:2; Judg 5:4; Ps 68:8–9, 18), as an outsider to the land, only later "domesticated" by being attached to the place of Zion/Jerusalem.[42]

Given that these convictions about outside origins and origins in time are fundamental to the Biblical views of distinctiveness, they stand at some distance from the views which appear in two of the great high cultures of the ancient Near East, Egypt and Mesopotamia. In Egypt, we find no such assertions; the history of nation and the cities within was understood as coterminous with cosmogony.[43] Moreover, except for a rather brief period of openness in the New Kingdom (fourteenth-thirteenth centuries B.C.E.), the issue of inside versus outside was put very sharply: only inside, i.e., in Egypt, were order, harmony, life itself; outside, chaos and deformity reigned supreme.[44] Consequently, only the Egyptians, at least in some texts, deserved the label "people" *(rmṯ)*; and they had constantly to be on guard to prevent an invasion of outside chaos. When such occurred—and periods of internal disorder were normally blamed on outside forces—it was a measure of the severity of the situation that a text like the Admonitions of Ipuwer could remark, "foreigners *(ḫ3styw)* have become people *(rmṯ)* everywhere."[45] Similar, though not identical, are the distinctiveness assertions in Mesopotamia. Here, likewise, the tendency was to equate national history, or even more in this instance, the origins of particular cities or urban regions, with cosmogony.[46] And here, too, the tendency was to see in the home environment the setting for civilized, orderly life—although Mesopotamia did not view the matter as exclusively as Egypt, recognizing that urban civilization could and did exist elsewhere.[47]

Now we know, in fact, that in Mesopotamia as in Egypt cultural continuity, despite periodic influxes, can be traced back into prehistoric periods. Thus, for all practical purposes, we may agree with the substance of the native assertions about autochthonous origins. But Israel, we know just as well, was one of the new societies in the Near East, born, so to speak, in the collapse of the Late Bronze Age condominium of powers and the emergence of the Iron Age. Admittedly, not all of Israel's components were from the outside, as the Bible itself allows (e.g., Josh 2, 9, 24). Nor was Israel the only new society or state of the period that came as an outsider into a land, again as the Bible acknowledges (e.g., Deut 2:20–23; Amos 9:7). But even in the most radical of modern theories about Israelite state formation in Palestine, the outside component is conceded a crucial role.[48] And of all the new political entities, only Israel—why cannot be answered in the present state of historical knowledge—has left us a record, and an extensive literary one at that, of its origins.

It is the fact and problematic of Israel's newness, I would like to suggest, that lie at the heart of the Biblical distinctiveness passages, even as they were an important motivation in the canonization process in general. The problematic was simply, and yet most formidably, this: how to forge an identity for a people that began on the margins of history and thereafter was faced constantly with a return to marginality

—whether cultural, political, military, or a combination of all these—as against older societies like Egypt and Mesopotamia on its outside, and Canaanites and others within its midst. Paradoxically, it is this very status as newcomer and marginal, which at first sight looks so negative and culturally unstable, that is taken by our Biblical passages as the basis for a positive picture. In other words, if newcomer and marginal had meant, say, for the Egyptians, barbarian, immoral, and chaotic, in the Bible they become proof of the choice of the "almighty God"—of new freedom, purity, and power. Recall how Deut 7:7–8 puts it: "It was not because you were the most numerous of all the peoples that Yahweh set His love upon you and chose you, for you were the fewest of all the peoples; but it was because Yahweh loved you and kept the oath which He swore to your fathers that Yahweh brought you out with a strong hand and redeemed you from the house of slaves, from the hand of Pharaoh, king of Egypt."[49] Significantly, the closest one comes to this inversion of images in the older societies of the ancient Near East is in occasional texts justifying *individuals,* especially a new ruler whose ascent to power was not by conventional, "legal" means.[50] In our Biblical texts, however, consistent with what we have discussed, the inversion is pre-eminently used—although it can appear with individuals, too[51]—to justify the *people Israel* as a whole.[52]

If the Biblical distinctiveness passages are, thus, any clue, we may observe in ancient Israel the making of what could be called a "counter-identity." The relevance of this term I owe to a brilliant essay of Amos Funkenstein, who chose, however, to apply it to the post-Biblical Hellenistic and Roman periods of Jewish history.[53] Here the problem becomes easier to see, because we can actually read what non-Jews were writing about Jews, and watch how they reinvert the inversion discussed above. Thus, for the Roman historian Tacitus, "Moses . . . introduced new religious customs contrary to those of the rest of mankind. All that are sacred to us are profane to them; on the other hand, what are permitted by them are for us polluted." And for the Hellenistic Egyptian priest Manetho, the Exodus was the expulsion of Egyptian lepers, led by a renegade Egyptian priest who changed his name from Osarsiph to Moses, and who gave the lepers a "constitution" that was an inverted image of Egyptian practices.[54]

I should like to propose that what Tacitus and Manetho were doing was no innovation of their times, but a continuation, *mutatis mutandis,* of the kinds of pressures which Biblical Israel had to face. Admittedly, we have no evidence of a Mesopotamian or Canaanite Tacitus or an earlier Egyptian Manetho, though we may hear an echo in the Assyrian *rab shaqeh's* speeches to the officials of Jerusalem, which do sound like parodies of Israelite distinctiveness thinking (2 Kings 18:19–35, 19:9–13/Isa 36:4–20, 37:9–13; cf. 2 Chron 32:9–19).[55] In any case, the Bible's very preoccupation with distinctiveness, which we have here explored, is enough to suggest that outside critics, or at least the challenges they represented, were already real to Israel from its earliest period.

NOTES

1. N. H. Snaith, *The Distinctive Ideas of the Old Testament* (New York 1964), 13, 14, 17. Cf. also the frequent use in modern studies of a rubric like "the Bible and the Ancient Near East," which is an historical absurdity in its implication that somehow the Bible is not a product or part of the ancient Near East, and thus can only be made sense of as a (covert) theological statement about the uniqueness of Scripture.
2. See, e.g., *ibid.*, especially chapter I, although despite the author's announced concern to deal "with those elements of Old Testament religion which distinguish it from other religions" (p. 11), he really does not offer any comparison. Other examples of this approach include various works of the so-called "Biblical Theology" movement, prominent in the United States in the last generation, like G. E. Wright, *The Old Testament Against Its Environment* (London 1950).
3. For recent orientation to the discussion as it concerns ancient Israel and the Hebrew Bible, see, e.g., O. Keel (ed.), *Monotheismus im Alten Israel und seiner Umwelt* (Fribourg 1980); E. Haag (ed.), *Gott, der einzige, Zur Entstehung des Monotheismus in Israel* (Freiburg 1985); B. Lang (ed.), *Der einzige Gott, Die Geburt des biblischen Monotheismus* (München 1981). It should be noted that in the above volumes, with the partial exception of the last (including as it does a translation of the English language essay of Morton Smith), a certain amount of non-German Biblical scholarship is left unattended. Particularly noticeable by its absence is Y. Kaufmann's *Toledot Ha-Emunah Ha-Yisraelit* (Tel Aviv/Jerusalem 1937–1956), 8 vols. in 4, accessible for some time in the abridged translation of M. Greenberg, *The Religion of Israel from Its Beginnings to the Babylonian Exile* (Chicago 1960).
4. Though how much and what kind of role are still debated: see note 19 ahead.
5. J. Assmann, *Saeculum* 23 (1972), 109–126; idem, *Ägypten—Theologie und*

Frömmigkeit einer frühen Hochkultur (Stuttgart 1984), especially 232–257; and, attending to the broader New Kingdom context, idem, *Re und Amun, Die Krise des polytheistischen Weltbilds im Ägypten der 18.–20. Dynastie*, (Göttingen 1983). E. Hornung, *Conceptions of God in Ancient Egypt, The One and the Many* (Ithaca 1982), 244–250; idem, in Keel (above note 3), 84–97. See also D. B. Redford, *Akhenaten, The Heretic King* (Princeton 1984), 169–181.

6. The exact distinction, if any, between monolatry and henotheism is difficult to discern, because the definitions of the two terms, especially henotheism, vary so widely. For those who would maintain a distinction, it appears to turn on whether the power and allegiance that an individual or group invests in a single god is something it maintains for a longer (monolatry) or shorter (henotheism) time: see, e.g., B. Hartmann, in Keel (above note 3), 72, 78, who borrows from the work of A. Bertholet.
7. L. W. King, *Babylonian Magic and Sorcery*, London: Luzac, 1986, Pl.1: No.1, obv. 2 = F. J. Stephens, in *ANET*[3], 386a.
8. T. G. Pinches, *IV R*[2], Pl.9: obv. 53–56 = A. Sjöberg, *Der Mondgott Nana-Suen in der sumerischen Überlieferung* (Stockholm: 1960) I, 168–170: 24–25 = F. J. Stephens, in *ANET*[3], 386a.
9. T. G. Pinches, *IV R*[2], Pl.29: No.5, rev 1–2 = S. H. Langdon, *Oxford Editions of Cuneiform Texts* (London: Oxford University Press, 1923–) VI, 81.
10. E.g., by T. J. Meek, *Hebrew Origins* (New York 1960), 195–196.
11. For other kinds of examples from Mesopotamia that have been brought into this discussion of monolatry/henotheism, see, e.g., B. Hartmann, in Keel (above note 3), 50–81, supplemented by the remark of Keel, *ibid.*, 29.
12. Cf., e.g., Kaufmann, *Toledot* 1/2, 417–419 = *Religion of Israel* (trans. Greenberg), 60 (above note 3).
13. As presumed, at least in origin, by Th. Jacobsen, e.g., in *The Treasures of Darkness* (New Haven 1976), 110ff.
14. Cf., e.g., the text "Enki and the World Order": latest edition by Carlos A. Benito, *"Enki and Ninmah" and "Enki and the World Order"* (University of Pennsylvania Ph.D. dissertation, 1969).
15. One such area has been the realm of history, where the claims of Israelite distinctiveness propounded by G. E. Wright (above note 2) and others have been decisively refuted by scholars like J. J. M. Roberts, *CBQ* 38(1976), 1–13 (with reference to the earlier critiques of J. Barr and B. Albrektson).
16. Cf. the trenchant remarks of Jon D. Levenson, and his gracious acknowledgement of our mutual discussions on this point, *JR* 64 (1984) 280–81 and note 21.
17. See H. W. F. Saggs, *The Encounter with the Divine in Mesopotamia and Israel* (London 1978), especially 182. H. Frankfort also employs it in his study of the "forms" of Egyptian and Mesopotamian civilization, *The Birth of Civilization in the Near East* (Bloomington 1951); note especially chap.

I, where he reveals his indebtedness on the matter to Oswald Spengler and anthropologists like Ruth Benedict.

18. Cf. J. J. Finkelstein, *Commentary* 26 (1958), 443b (chapter 15 of this volume); also Saggs (previous note), 185–88.
19. And even on this basis, the proposition is contested. Some, like Kaufmann (above note 3) and, in a different way, W. F. Albright (*From the Stone Age to Christianity* [Garden City 1957], 257–272), assert the original Mosaic character of monotheism. Others, with whom I am in agreement, argue that monotheism, at least in the strict sense defined in the body of this paper, is attested only late in Israel, i.e., the late pre-Exilic or, better, Exilic period: see, e.g., V. Nikiprowetzky, *Daedalus* (Spring 1975), 69–89.
20. Perhaps the major example in this regard has been the question of goddesses in ancient Israel. Here the existence of hundreds of so-called "Astarte" figurines from Israelite sites and the inscriptions from Kuntillet ʿAjrud and Khirbet el-Qôm mentioning Yahweh and Asherah have been used to give prominence to the sporadic mention of goddess worship in the Bible: e.g., W. G. Dever. *BASOR* 255 (1984), 21–37; and D. N. Freedman, *BA* 50 (1987), 241–49. For a recent review of the whole issue, which downplays the affection of Yahwistic religion for goddesses, see U. Winter, *Frau und Göttin* (Göttingen 1983).
21. E.g., *lbdd* (Num 23:9); *nplh* (Exod 33:16); *hplh* (Exod 9:4); *hbdyl* (Lev 20:24); *šnh* (Esth 3:8).
22. The following list, it must be emphasized, is not final, because of the number of passages where the distinctive comparison is not always explicit or even clearly implied. I have erred on the side of including more than fewer passages.

    Gen 12:3; 13:16; 15:5; 17:7–8; 18:18–19; 20:7; 22:17–18; 23:4; 24:3,37–38; 26:4,28; 27:29,46; 28:1,13–14; 32:9, 12; 34:14–17, 30; 35:11–12; 43:32; 45:7; 46:3; 47:29; 49:10.

    Exod 1:9, 19; 3:13, 15; 6:7, 24; 7:16; 8:13–14, 18; 9:4, 14–16; 11:5–7; 12:12–13, 27, 43–49; 14:4; 15:11, 13, 16; 18:11; 19:5–6; 20:2–5; 22:20; 23:9, 13, 32–33; 29:45–46; 33:13, 16; 34:10, 12–17.

    Lev 12:44–45; 18:3–4, 24–30; 19:4, 33–34; 20:7–8, 20–26; 24:22; 25:44–46.

    Num 8:14–19; 13:31; 14:9; 15:14–16, 29; 22:5–6; 23:9, 21–24; 24:7–9.

    Deut 2:25; 3:24; 4:7–8, 19–20, 23–24, 33–39; 5:6–9, 15, 26; 6:4, 14–15; 7:1–8, 14–15, 16, 17–24, 25–26; 10:14–15, 17–18, 19; 11:10–12, 23, 25, 26–28; 12:2–3, 29–31; 13:2–5, 7–12, 13–19; 14:1–2; 17:14; 18:9–15; 20:16–18; 23:3–6, 7–8; 24:17–18, 20–22; 26:18; 28:1, 9–10; 29:9–14, 15–19, 24–25; 30:17–18; 32:8–9, 12, 15–17, 21, 39; 33:26.

    Josh 2:10–11; 5:1; 7:8–9; 9:9–10; 23:4–13; 24:2, 14–24.

    Judg 2:2–3, 7, 11–19; 5:8; 6:10; 8:33–34; 10:6, 10–16; 11:24; 14:3; 15:18; 16:23–24; 19:27–30.

    1 Sam 2:2; 4:8; 5:7–12; 6:2–9; 7:3; 8:5–8, 19–20; 10:19; 12:12, 17, 19, 22; 26:19.

2 Sam 7:9, 10, 13–16, 22–24; 22:32, 50.
1 Kings 8:23, 27, 41–43, 53; 9:6–9; 14:24; 18:21, 39; 20:23–28.
2 Kings 5:15–17; 17:33; 18:32–35; 19:15–17; 21:9; 23:25.
Isa 2:2–3; 26:13–15; 33:19; 36:18–20; 37:16–20; 40:12–14, 18–19, 25–26; 41:2–4, 8–9, 26–29; 42:1, 8, 19; 43:8–13, 19–21; 44:1, 6–8, 21; 45:4, 5–7, 14, 16, 18–19, 20–25; 46:5–6, 9–10; 47:8–11; 48:11, 12–13, 14–15, 20; 49:3, 5; 51:16; 62:12; 63:8, 19; 64:4; 66:7–9, 18–23.
Jer 2:6, 10–11; 7:23; 10:2, 6–8, 10, 11–16; 11:4–5; 13:11; 14:22; 16:19–21; 18:13–17; 19:8; 30:22; 31:1; 32:38; 51:17–19.
Ezek 11:20; 14:11; 16:14–15, 31–34; 20:9–12, 14, 22, 32; 22:4–5; 23:10–11; 25:8–11; 27:3, 32, 35–36; 28:2–10, 12–19, 25–26; 29:15–16; 31:8–9; 32:19; 34:30; 36:3–7, 15, 20; 37:23, 27; 38:16, 23; 39:7, 21, 27; 44:9.
Hos 1:9; 2:1, 3, 15, 18–19, 21–22, 25; 9:1; 11:1; 12:10; 13:4.
Joel 2:17–19, 27; 4:2, 16–17.
Amos 3:2; 6:2; 9:7.
Obad vv. 2, 16–17.
Jonah 1:8–9.
Mic 4:1–2, 5; 5:3; 6:16; 7:15–18.
Nah 1:6; 3:8–9.
Hab 1:5 ff.
Zeph 2:11, 15; 3:9, 19–20.
Hag 1:12, 23; 2:6–7.
Zech 2:8, 11–12; 8:13, 22–23; 9:16: 10:3; 12:3–5; 13:9; 14:9, 16–17.
Mal 1:2–5, 11–12, 14; 3:12, 17.
Ps 2:1–3, 8; 7:8; 8:2, 10; 9:20–21; 10:16; 18:32, 50; 22:28–29; 24:1–2; 33:8–12; 40:6; 44:2–4; 46:11; 47:3–5, 7–9; 48:11; 57:6, 10–12; 65:6–9; 66:3–5; 67:4–6; 68:33–36; 69:35–37; 73:25; 76:8; 79:6; 81:10–11, 12–14; 82:8; 83:19; 86:8–10; 89:27–28; 95:3; 96:4–5; 97:9; 99:2; 105:12–15; 106:2, 34–39; 111:6; 113:4–5; 115:2–9; 132:13–16; 135:5, 15–18; 136:2–4; 138:2, 4–5.
Job 9:8; 25:4–6; 36:22–23, 26.
Ruth 1:16.
Lam 1:1, 12; 2:1, 13, 15; 3:1–3; 4:1–2, 7–8, 11–12.
Qoh 1:16; 2:7, 9.
Esth 3:8; 8:9.
Dan 2:47; 3:12, 14–18, 29; 4:35; 6:5; 9:12, 15.
Ezra 1:2–3; 6:12; 8:22; 9:1–2, 11–14; 10:2–3, 10 ff.
Neh 3:36–37; 9:2, 6–7, 10; 10:31; 13:1–3, 23–28, 30.
1 Chron 16:19–23, 24–26; 17:7–8, 9, 11–14, 20–22; 29:11.
2 Chron 2:5–6; 6:14, 18, 32–33; 7:19–22; 14:10; 15:3–4; 17:10; 20:6; 29:8; 32:7–8, 13–15, 17, 19, 23.

23. A. Malamat, *JQR* 76 (1985), 47–50. On p. 50, note 11, he credits Baruch Levine with drawing his attention to the Balaam verse in the light of the Mari text.

24. *Lĕbādād,* thus, seems to have two senses in this verse: the physical "separation" of the Israelite encampment and, in conjunction with *lōʾ yitḥaššab,* the "isolated" and "unique" status of Israel among nations.
25. So following LXX and Vetus Latina. MT adds *wĕśēʿîr,* which appears to be secondary, with most commentators: see W. Zimmerli, *Ezekiel* 2 (Hermeneia; Philadelphia: Fortress Press, 1983), 8 s.v. 8b.
26. See also Isa 47:8. The statement *ʾănî wĕʾapsî ʿôd* is obviously meant as a deliberate echo, and thus blasphemy.
27. This difficult word appears to refer to some kind of conjuration in conjunction with the parallel *kappĕrāh* of the following v. 11b. The Arabic root *saḥara* has often been compared, as proposed by G. R. Driver, *JTS* 36 (1935), 400. Isaiah is, thus, parodying Babylon's vaunted expertise in magic, which for him is useless against Yahweh's coming punishment.
28. For a similar claim, by Nineveh, see Zeph 2:15.
29. Also Deut 7:6, 14:2, 26:18; Mal 3:17; Ps 135:4. On the meaning of *sĕgullâ,* see M. Greenberg, *JAOS* 71 (1951), 172–174, and M. Held, *JCS* 15 (1961), 11–12. Another Biblical term belonging to the same semantic field is, of course, *naḥălâ.* (Deut. 4:20; etc.).
30. Reading Deut 32:8b *bĕnê ʾēl/ʾēlîm/ʾĕlōhîm* with a fragment from cave 4 at Qumran and, by implication, the LXX, Vetus Latina, and Symmachus, instead of MT *bĕnê yiśrāʾēl.* For a bibliography of the discussion, see P. C. Craigie, *The Book of Deuteronomy* (New International Commentary on the Old Testament; Grand Rapids: W. B. Eerdmans, 1976), 378, n. 18.
31. Who comprised the gathering is not specified, but comparable passages in other parts of Amos (especially 6:1–3) suggest that it was in the first instance the ruling elites of the northern kingdom of Israel.
32. Cf. Deut 9:6.
33. Cf. also 1 Sam 8:5, 20; Isa 63:19.
34. Cf. also Jer 18:13–17.
35. The exceptions include the Song of Songs and the wisdom book of Proverbs, which is not surprising, since each book, in its own way, chooses not to focus on Israel and its particular historical traditions and vicissitudes. One should consider here as well the two other major wisdom compositions, Qohelet and Job, for while they do talk about distinctiveness (Qoh 1:16; 2:7, 9; Job 9:8; 25:4–6; 36:22–23, 26), their statements do not highlight the distinctiveness of Israel *per se.*
36. On the Oracles of Balaam, to which Num 23:9 belongs, see W. F. Albright's groundbreaking article in *JBL* 63 (1944), 207–233, with later remarks by him in his *Yahweh and the Gods of Canaan* (London 1968), 13–14 and note 38, *passim.* Exodus 15 has been treated extensively by Albright's pupils, starting with the joint dissertation of F. M. Cross and D. N. Freedman, *Studies in Ancient Yahwistic Poetry* (Ph.D. Dissertation, Johns Hopkins University, 1950; reprinted with appendix in Missoula, 1975), chap. II. Recently, Freedman has attempted to describe what can be learned about early Israelite religion from these and other "archaic" Biblical poems in

" 'Who is Like Thee Among the Gods?' The Religion of Early Israel," in P. D. Miller, Jr., P. D. Hanson, and S. D. McBride (eds.), *Ancient Israelite Religion. Essays in Honor of Frank Moore Cross* (Philadelphia 1987), 315–335.

37. Cf. Amos 3:2, 4:4–5; 5:4–5, 18–20, 21–24, 25–27; and especially, 6:2. O. Eissfeldt (*The Old Testament: An Introduction* [New York 1965], 398, 400) is among those who ascribe 9:7 to Amos. Of those who do not, R. Coote (*Amos Among the Prophets: Composition and Theology* [Philadelphia 1981], 117–121) is one of the most radical, proposing that 9:7 belongs to a late, Exilic edition (his "C" stage) of the Amos traditions. His subtle argument rests finally on the supposition that 9:7 has a positive meaning, referring not to the original Exodus from Egypt, but to the latter used as a symbol for the return of the Judaean exiles from Babylonia. This symbolic use, of course, is well known elsewhere in Biblical literature, but it normally is marked as such, in a way that it is not here. Further, if 9:7 is read with the following 9:8a, 9–10—9:8b seems, with a large number of commentators, a clear interpolation—then this yields a negative, not positive meaning, not unconnected with 6:2 in the sequence 6:1–3. The point would be, as many interpreters have understood, that Israel's belief in the uniqueness of the Exodus from Egypt is part of her smug confidence in God's favor toward her no matter what she might do—an attitude that God rejects (9:7) and will punish (9:8a, 9–10).

38. See note 22.

39. On this latter issue, remarked on by a variety of scholars, see the discussion in J. Blenkinsopp, *Prophecy and Canon. A Contribution to the Study of Jewish Origins* (Notre Dame 1977), chap. 2.

40. Thus while the first humans are ultimately tied to Israel, the creation stories in Genesis make it quite definite that they are not exclusively so, being the ancestors of all the world's peoples and nations (e.g., Gen 10); Israel's beginnings are at a qualitatively different genealogical stage.

41. Note that in Gen 2–3 the first humans are emphatically not in the land of Israel, but in "a garden in Eden eastward" (2:8).

42. See J. Ebach, "Babel und Bibel oder: Das 'Heidnische' im Alten Testament," in R. Faber and R. Schlesier (eds.), *Die Restauration der Götter, Antike Religion und Neo-Paganismus* (Würzburg 1986), 37–38; and J. D. Levenson, *Sinai and Zion, An Entry into the Jewish Bible* (Minneapolis 1985), 91–92, 19–20.

43. E.g., the Turin Canon and Manetho's Aegyptiaca trace the dynastic history of Egypt from the primeval gods, then the divine spirits/demigods, on through the dynasties of pharaohs beginning with Menes: cf. the recent study of D. B. Redford, *Pharaonic King-Lists, Annals and Day-books, A Contribution to the Study of the Egyptian Sense of History* (Mississauga, Ont. 1986), 1–18, 231–239. Note also the texts from such major religious centers as Heliopolis and Thebes, arguing the claim that each was the site of primeval creation (J. A. Wilson, in *ANET*[3], 1, 8).

44. See W. Helck, *Saeculum* 15 (1964), 103–114 and photographs 1–4.
45. A. H. Gardiner, *The Admonitions of an Egyptian Sage from a Hieratic Papyrus in Leiden (Pap. Leiden 344 recto)* (Leipzig 1909), 20–21:1, 9 = J. A. Wilson, *ANET*^{3}, 441a. On "chaos descriptions" in Egyptian texts, see J. Assmann, in D. Hellholm (ed.), *Apocalypticism in the Mediterranean World and the Near East* (Tübingen 1983), 345–377.
46. E.g., the traditions embodied in the Sumerian flood story (M. Civil, in W. G. Lambert and A. R. Millard, *Atraḫasis* [Oxford 1969], 140–145) and the Sumerian King List (Th. Jacobsen. *The Sumerian King List* [Chicago 1939]), which speak of the gods creating "the black-headed people" (sag-ge_6 = "Sumerians"; cf. the Egyptian *rmṯ* = "people" = "Egyptians"), and then "lowering" for them "kingship from heaven," which migrates over the region of Sumer from one city to another. Not unlike in Egypt, particular cities in Mesopotamia can also claim to be the sites of primeval creation by the gods: thus, Nippur, with the place, Uzumua, in the sanctuary of Duranki (G. Pettinato, *Das altorientalische Menschenbild und die sumerischen und akkadischen Schöpfungsmythen* [Heidelberg 1971]. 67, 31–32, 75, 78, 82–83), and Babylon in the myth of *Enūma eliš*.

    One possible exception to this notion of autochthonous origins may be a brief remark, brought to my attention by Prof. H. Tadmor, in the Cyprus Stela of the Neo-Assyrian king, Sargon II. Talking about the rulers of a district on Cyprus, the king observes that "none of my royal forefathers [had ever he]ard of the name of their land [since] the distant days of the 'taking' of the land of Assyria" ([*ša ul-tu*] *ūmē rūqūte ṣi-bit māt A ⌜š & šur⌝*) (Winckler. *Sar.* I, 180–181, 32–35; L. Messerschmidt and A. Ungnad, *VAS* 1, 71: linke Seite, 32–35; A. L. Oppenheim, in *ANET*^{3}, 284b). It is not at all clear, however, that this latter phrase refers (so J. Lewy, *HUCA* 19 [1945–46], 466–467) to the Assyrians coming from the outside to conquer the land of Assyria for themselves. For, as M. Weippert notes to me, *ṣibtu‹ ṣabātu* in this locution may mean organizing a territory politically and administratively, not conquering it from the outside (cf. *CAD* Ṣ, 16b–17a: f). In any case, the focus is probably not so much on a people taking or organizing a land, as in the Biblical passages, as on the ruler and his god who undertake the task (which Lewy, *op. cit.*, appears to recognize).
47. Thus, the issue for Mesopotamia was more a matter of urban vs. non-urban as the equivalent of civilized vs. uncivilized, than of Mesopotamia vs. the outside. This correlates with the fact that the notion of a Mesopotamia was never as tightly defined with Mesopotamian culture as the notion of an Egypt was within Egyptian. See further P. Machinist, in S. N. Eisenstadt (ed.), *The Origins and Diversity of Axial Age Civilizations* (Albany 1986), 184–191, with notice of other discussions.
48. See G. Mendenhall, e.g., in E. F. Campbell, Jr. and D. N. Freedman (eds.), *The Biblical Archaeologist Reader,* III (Garden City 1970), 107–110, 113; and N. Gottwald, e.g., *The Tribes of Yahweh* (Maryknoll 1979), 493–497 and *passim.*

49. Cf. also Ps 105:12–15/1 Chron 16:19–22; 1 Chron 29:14–15.

50. E.g., the Apology of Hattušiliš III (latest edition by H . Otten, *Die Apologie Hattusilis III, Das Bild der Überlieferung* [Wiesbaden 1981]); and the basalt stela recording "Nabonidus' Rise to Power" (A. L. Oppenheim, in *ANET*[3], 308–311). On these and other "autobiographical apologies," see now H. Tadmor, in H. Tadmor and M. Weinfeld (eds.), *History, Historiography and Interpretation, Studies in Biblical and Cuneiform Literatures* (Jerusalem 1983), 36–57.

51. If the Exodus from Egypt is the primary event by which Israel's marginality is legitimated as new status and power, it also serves that same function for Yahweh himself, as W. W. Hallo and J. J. van Dijk have seen (*Exaltation*, 67–68; elaborated by Th. W. Mann, *Divine Presence and Guidance in Israelite Traditions: The Typology of Exaltation* [Baltimore 1977]). In other words, Yahweh, as the unknown outsider, defeats the Pharaoh, the king-god of the mightiest of nations and so redefines the cosmos in his own terms. That Israel could extend marginality to its own god in this way only proves how central and productive the notion was for its self-image.

53. *The Jerusalem Quarterly* 19 (Spring, 1981), 57–60, especially 59. As Funkenstein notes, the term belongs to the vocabulary of the sociology of knowledge.

54. These two examples are taken from Funkenstein (above note), 59, though that from Tacitus has been partially retranslated. For the texts themselves, and others like them, see the major collection of M. Stern, *Greek and Latin Authors on Jews and Judaism*, 1–3 (Jerusalem 1974–1984), I.78–86 (Manetho); II:18, 25 (Tacitus, *Histories* V:4:1).

55. Note Prof. Tadmor's fascinating suggestion that the *rab shaqeh* was a former Israelite captive, *Encyclopedia Miqra'it*, 7 (Jerusalem 1976), 323–325; M. Cogan and H. Tadmor, *II Kings* (Garden City 1988), 230. This would explain admirably the virtuoso knowledge of Israelite/Judaean thinking demonstrated in the speeches—granting, as seems likely, that the speeches are not simply a literary construct of the Biblical authors, but reflect an underlying historical reality.

General Index

Index of Biblical Passages

About the Editor

Frederick E. Greenspahn is Associate Professor of Judaic Studies at the University of Denver and author of *Hapax Legomena in Biblical Hebrew* and a variety of articles on biblical studies. He has also edited several books exploring contemporary interfaith relations.